The Philosophy of Information

The Philosophy of Information

Luciano Floridi

OXFORD
UNIVERSITY PRESS

OXFORD
UNIVERSITY PRESS

Great Clarendon Street, Oxford OX2 6DP

Oxford University Press is a department of the University of Oxford.
It furthers the University's objective of excellence in research, scholarship,
and education by publishing worldwide in

Oxford New York

Auckland Cape Town Dar es Salaam Hong Kong Karachi
Kuala Lumpur Madrid Melbourne Mexico City Nairobi
New Delhi Shanghai Taipei Toronto

With offices in

Argentina Austria Brazil Chile Czech Republic France Greece
Guatemala Hungary Italy Japan Poland Portugal Singapore
South Korea Switzerland Thailand Turkey Ukraine Vietnam

Oxford is a registered trade mark of Oxford University Press
in the UK and in certain other countries

Published in the United States
by Oxford University Press Inc., New York

© Luciano Floridi 2011

The moral rights of the authors have been asserted
Database right Oxford University Press (maker)

First published 2011

British Library Cataloguing in Publication Data
Data available

Library of Congress Cataloging in Publication Data
Library of Congress Control Number: 2010940315

Typeset by SPI Publisher Services, Pondichery, India
Printed in Great Britain
on acid-free paper by
MPG Biddles Group, Bodmin and King's Lynn

ISBN 978-0-19-923238-3

3 5 7 9 10 8 6 4

Contents

Preface

This book brings together the outcome of ten years of research. It is based on a simple project, which I began to pursue towards the end of the 1990s, following the results reached in a previous work (Floridi (1996)): information is a crucial concept, which deserves a thorough philosophical investigation. So the book lays down what I consider the conceptual foundations of a new area of research: the philosophy of information. It does so systematically, by pursuing three goals. The first is metatheoretical. The book describes what the philosophy of information is, its problems, and its method of levels of abstraction. These are the topics of the first part, which comprises chapters one, two and three. The second goal is introductory. In chapters four and five, the book explores the complex and diverse nature of several informational concepts and phenomena. The third goal is constructive. In the remaining ten chapters, the book answers some classic philosophical questions in information-theoretical terms. The fifteen chapters are strictly related, so I have added internal references whenever it might be useful.

The genesis of the book may be rapidly recounted. In the late nineties, I was searching for an approach to some key philosophical questions (the nature of knowledge, the structure of reality, the uniqueness of human consciousness, the ethical role of artificial agents and so forth) that could be rigorous, rational, and conversant with our scientific knowledge, in the best sense of the analytic tradition; non-psychologistic, in a Fregean sense; capable of dealing with contemporary and lively issues; and less prone to metaphysical armchair speculations and idiosyncratic intuitions. I was looking for a constructive philosophy, which could be free from the self-indulgent, anthropocentric obsession with the knowing subject, and from commonsensical introspections. One day, I realized that what I had in mind was a philosophy grounded on the concept of information. I was in Oxford, at Wolfson College, sitting on the bank of the river Cherwell, when I discovered that the spectacles I was looking for were on my nose. It was the summer of 1998. Six months later, I gave a talk in London, at King's College, entitled 'Should there be a Philosophy of Information?'. The question was rhetorical, and I soon started working on this book. Once I saw the peak of the mountain, all that remained to do was to plan the expedition meticulously, and then execute it carefully. I have been sluggishly climbing ever since. For what I did not realize at the time was how much effort and determination it would require to complete even the first stage of the project.

The essential message of the book is quite simple. Semantic information is well-formed, meaningful, and truthful data; knowledge is relevant semantic information properly accounted for; humans are the only known semantic engines and conscious inforgs (informational organisms) in the universe who can develop a growing knowledge of reality; and reality is the totality of information (notice the crucial absence of 'semantic'). To anyone who wishes to warm up before tackling these themes, I might suggest a much easier and shorter introduction, which I provided in Floridi (2010). Philosophers used to have the good habit of writing different texts, depending on whether they were addressing the scientific community or the educated public. In modern times, Descartes might have started this tradition, Hume certainly followed it, and so did Kant, but Russell was probably the last to pay homage to it. It is a pity, because an exoteric philosophy is still a good idea, and it should not have been survived only by its esoteric sister.

Regarding its style, I am painfully aware that this is not an easy book to read, to put it mildly, despite my attempts to make it as reader-friendly as possible. It will require patience and time, two scarce resources. So one feature that I thought might help the reader to access its contents are the summaries and conclusions at the beginning and the end of each chapter. I know it is slightly unorthodox, but the solution of starting each chapter with a 'Previously in chapter x . . .' should enable the reader to browse the text, or skip entire sections of it, without losing the essential plot. After all, I am telling a rather long story, and some redundancy might be helpful. Science-fiction fans will recognize the reference to Battlestar Galactica.

It might also be useful to clarify at the outset what this book is not. This is not an introductory book for the general reader, nor is it meant to be an exhaustive presentation of a field, the philosophy of information, which is still in its infancy: 'systematic' qualifies the relation between the chapters, not the extent of their coverage. It is also not a book on contributions by computer science to philosophical topics, although, whenever necessary, I will use such contributions to help do the philosophical work. The interested reader might find more on such topics in Floridi (1999b).

Two final comments now on the past and the future of this book. In 1996, I published *Scepticism and the Foundation of Epistemology*. I now understand what an author means when he acknowledges that he would no longer write his book in the same way. There is too much self-consciousness in that text that betrays youth. It has a tart taste. However, I have to admit that I still subscribe to its main theses, which actually led me, rather slowly and more obliquely than I would have wished, to this book. As I wrote then:

The metaepistemological problem of the foundation of knowledge leads to a reconstruction of the encyclopaedia [the totality of semantic information as defined in chapter four and five], whose genesis requires a vindication. The vindication of the genesis of the encyclopaedia can be provided by an interpretation of the demand for knowledge which, in order to avoid resorting to any element of the encyclopaedia already challenged by the sceptical reflection, needs to refer to whatever conceptual space is still occupied by the sceptical reflection itself. Thus, the indirect manoeuvre [to solve the sceptical problem of the foundation of an epistemology] consists in eliminating—i.e. putting under the pressure of sceptical doubt—even the limited extension of knowledge covertly presupposed by the sceptical challenge, and represented by the anthropological assumption that the demand for knowledge [as defined in chapter twelve] is in fact due to a mere desire for knowledge for its own sake, a demand that the sceptic then interprets, to his own advantage, as ephemeral and superfluous. The eradication of the intellectualist interpretation of the desire for knowledge finally clears the ground of all assumptions, leaving us, now that the sceptical challenge has been shown to be just a component of the process of investigation, to seek the most economical interpretation of the demand for knowledge such that, being in itself sufficiently sceptical i.e. anti-intellectualist, satisfies a requirement recognised by the sceptical reflection itself, namely the need for an explanation of the occurrence of a phenomenon such as the search for knowledge and the construction of the encyclopaedia. The analysis of the demand for knowledge as primary and 'compulsory' has provided the approach that now makes a sound vindication of the construction of the encyclopaedia attainable. The occurrence of the encyclopaedia can in principle be vindicated (explained-supported) [accounted for, in the terminology of chapter twelve] by interpreting its genesis as being required by a demand for knowledge whose bearer—i.e. the mind responsible for the production, improvement and study of the encyclopaedia—can persist and flourish exclusively on the basis of the occurrence of the encyclopaedia itself. The problem of the relation of the moderately-coherentist reconstruction of the system of knowledges with an external reference is approached not in terms of isomorphism (Aristotelian-scholastic epistemology) or representative correspondence (post-Cartesian epistemology), but in terms of a reaction. (p. 259).

The mind does not wish to acquire information for its own sake. It needs information to defend itself from reality and survive. So information is not about representing the world: it is rather a means to model it in such a way as to make sense of it and withstand its impact. This was the general conclusion about a negative anthropology that I reached in 1996. It is the way in which Locke's quotation, at the beginning of chapter one, should be read, as a bridge towards that past book. And this leads me to the second comment, about the future.

Authors can hardly resist the temptation of recommending to their readers how they ought to interpret their books. Not only do they wish to be read, they also entreat to be read in a specific way. Hermeneutic instructions are a small sin, and I shall not be a virtuous exception. Without transforming the ear-whispering into a neck-breathing, here is my last piece of advice. This is the first volume of a trilogy; it is self-contained, but all the topics belonging to information ethics (second volume) and some theoretical topics (such as causality and scepticism) have been left to future investigations. It is also a German book, written from a post-analytic-continental divide perspective, more Kantian than I ever expected it to be. But then, ideas have their own way of growing, and sometimes you feel that you can only water, prune, and offer them as a present.

Acknowledgements

I could not have worked on such a long-term project without dividing it into some feasible and much smaller tasks. I must also confess that I was surprised by the fact that they still fitted together in the end. I hope this is not the symptom of a stubbornly closed mind. All the chapters were planned as conference papers first, and then published as journal articles. The bibliographic details are in the list of references below. This way of working was inevitably laborious, but it also seemed inevitable, given the innovative nature of the field. It did require a perseverance and commitment which I hope were not ill-exercised. I wished to test the ideas presented in this volume as thoroughly as possible, and publishing the articles gave me the opportunity and privilege to enjoy a vast amount of feedback, from a very large number of colleagues and anonymous referees. If I do not thank all of them here, this is not for lack of manners or mere reason of space, but because the appropriate acknowledgments can be found in the corresponding, published articles.

There are, however, some people who played a significant role throughout the project and during the revisions of the final text. Kia and I have been married for as long as I have been writing this book. Without her, I would have never had the confidence to undertake such a task, and the spiritual energy to complete it. She has made our life blissful, and I am very grateful to her for the endless hours we spent talking about the topics of this book, for all her sharp suggestions, and for her lovely patience with an utterly obsessed husband. I owe to a former colleague in Oxford, Jeff Sanders, a much better understanding of the more technical aspects of the method of abstraction in computer science. Some of the ideas presented in chapter three were developed and formulated in close collaboration with him, and he should really be considered a co-author of it (see Floridi and Sanders (2004a)), although not someone co-responsible for any potential shortcomings. Mariarosaria Taddeo and I co-authored the two articles of which chapters six and seven are revised versions. I learnt much from our collaboration, and I am very grateful to her for the permission to reproduce our work here. I often relied on Matteo Turilli for philosophical conversations and technical expertise on computational and IT-related issues. Hilmi Demir and Brendan Larvor kindly sent me some embarrassment-saving feedback on the final manuscript. Peter Momtchiloff was pivotal for the realization of the book, both because of his timely invitation to publish it with OUP, and because of his support and firm patience, when it seemed that I would have never completed it. Members of the IEG, the interdepartmental research group on the philosophy of information at Oxford, were very generous with their time and provided numerous opportunities for further reflection on virtually any topic discussed in this book, and a special thanks goes to Patrick Allo and Sebastian Sequoiah-Grayson.

A personal thanks also goes to three members of my family. To my father, for having taught me the 'three wise men' theorem as a social game, when I was a child (see chapter thirteen). To my mother, for having taught me, again as a child, to stop looking at the closed door and concentrate on the open one.[1] And to my brother, who showed me, much later in life, how to break away even the hardest stone at the proper angle and in the right place, by drilling a line of holes, and then systematically pounding the iron wedges inserted in the holes, until a crack forms between them. The pounding makes a particular sound, whose pitch guides the mason in choosing which wedge to hit and how much force to exercise. It is the pitch that I tried to hear when writing the following chapters. Some thoughts can be hard to shape.

Finally, I would like to thank the Universities of Bari, Hertfordshire, and Oxford for having provided me with the time to pursue my research at different stages during the past ten years. The final writing effort was made possible thanks to the Akademie der Wissenschaften in Göttingen, which kindly elected me Gauss Professor during the academic year 2008–9. Penny Driscoll very kindly proof-read the final version of the manuscript, making it much more readable.

References

The fifteen chapters constituting the book are based on the following articles:

Chapter one: Floridi (2002)
Chapter two: Floridi (2003e), (2004c), Greco et al. (2005)
Chapter three: Floridi (2008d); Floridi and Sanders (2004a)
Chapter four: Floridi (2003a), (2005c), Floridi (2008b), Floridi (2009c)
Chapter five: Floridi (2004d)
Chapter six: Taddeo and Floridi (2005)
Chapter seven: Taddeo and Floridi (2007)
Chapter eight: Floridi (forthcoming-c)
Chapter nine: Floridi (2004b)
Chapter ten: Floridi (2006)
Chapter eleven: Floridi (2008e)
Chapter twelve: Floridi (forthcoming-b).
Chapter thirteen: Floridi (2005a)
Chapter fourteen: Floridi (2009a)
Chapter fifteen: Floridi (2004a), Floridi (2008c)

List of Figures

List of Tables

List of Most Common Acronyms

AA   Artificial Agent
AI   Artificial Intelligence
ALife   Artificial Life
BCP   Bar-Hillel–Carnap semantic Paradox
CMC   Computer-Mediated Communication
CTT   Correctness Theory of Truth
GoA   Gradient of Abstraction
HCI   Human-Computer Interaction
ICS   Information and Computational Sciences
ICT   Information and Communication Technologies
LoA   Level of Abstraction
PI   Philosophy of Information
SGP   Symbol Grounding Problem
TSSI   Theory of Strongly Semantic Information
TWSI   Theory of Weakly Semantic Information

1

What is the philosophy of information?

> The only fence against the world is a thorough knowledge of it.
> Locke, *Some Thoughts Concerning Education*

SUMMARY

This is the first of the three metatheoretical chapters introducing the philosophy of information (PI). In the following pages, I shall begin by sketching the emergence of PI through the history of philosophy. I then define PI as the new philosophical field concerned with (a) the critical investigation of the conceptual nature and basic principles of information, including its dynamics, utilization and sciences; and (b) the elaboration and application of information-theoretic and computational methodologies to philosophical problems. I shall argue that PI is a mature discipline for three reasons. First, it represents an autonomous field of research. Second, it provides an innovative approach to both traditional and new philosophical topics. Third, it can stand beside other branches of philosophy, offering a systematic treatment of the conceptual foundations of the world of information and the information society. I describe two ways in which PI may be approached: one analytical and the other metaphysical. The chapter ends with the suggestion that PI might be considered a new kind of first philosophy.

1.1 Introduction

Computational and information-theoretic research in philosophy has become increasingly fertile and pervasive. It revitalizes old philosophical questions, poses new problems, contributes to re-conceptualization of our world-views, and it has already produced a wealth of interesting and important results.[1] Researchers have suggested various labels for this new field. Some follow fashionable terminology (e.g. 'cyberphilosophy', 'digital philosophy', 'computational philosophy'); the majority expresses specific theoretical orientations (e.g. 'formal epistemology', 'philosophy of computer

---

[1] See Bynum and Moor (1998), Colburn (2000b), Floridi (1999b), Floridi (2003f), and Mitcham and Huning (1986) for references.

science', 'philosophy of computing/computation', 'philosophy of AI', 'computers and philosophy', 'computing and philosophy', 'philosophy of the artificial', 'artificial epistemology'). In this chapter, I shall argue that the name *philosophy of information* (PI) is the most satisfactory, for reasons that are fully discussed in section 1.5. Sections 1.2, 1.3 and 1.4 analyse the historical and conceptual process that has led to the emergence of PI. They support the following two conclusions. First, philosophy of AI (Artificial Intelligence) was a premature paradigm, which nevertheless paved the way for the emergence of PI. Second, PI has evolved as the most recent stage in the dialectic between conceptual innovation and what I shall call 'scholasticism'. A definition of PI is then introduced and discussed in section 1.5. Section 1.6 summarizes the main results of the chapter and indicates how PI could be interpreted as a new *philosophia prima*, or *first philosophy*, although not from a *philosophia perennis* perspective. The view defended is that PI is a mature discipline because (a) it represents an autonomous field (*unique topics*); (b) it provides an innovative approach to both traditional and new philosophical topics (*original methodologies*); and (c) it can stand beside other branches of philosophy, offering the systematic treatment of the conceptual foundations of the world of information and of the information society (*new theories*).

1.2 Philosophy of artificial intelligence as a premature paradigm of PI

André Gide once wrote that one does not discover new lands without consenting to lose sight of the shore for a very long time. Looking for new lands, in 1978 Aaron Sloman heralded the advent of a new AI-based paradigm in philosophy. In a book appropriately entitled *The Computer Revolution in Philosophy*, he conjectured

(i) that within a few years, if there remain any philosophers who are not familiar with some of the main developments in artificial intelligence, it will be fair to accuse them of professional incompetence, and

(ii) that to teach courses in philosophy of mind, epistemology, aesthetics, philosophy of science, philosophy of language, ethics, metaphysics and other main areas of philosophy, without discussing the relevant aspects of artificial intelligence will be as irresponsible as giving a degree course in physics which includes no quantum theory. (Sloman (1978), p. 5, numbered structure added)

Unfortunately, the prediction turned out to be inaccurate and over-optimistic. However, it was far from being unjustified.[2] Moreover, Sloman was not alone. Other researchers[3] had correctly perceived that the practical and conceptual transformations caused by ICS (Information and Computational Sciences) and ICT (Information and

---

[2] See also Sloman (1995) and McCarthy (1995).
[3] See for example Simon (1962), McCarthy and Hayes (1969), Pagels (1988), who argue in favour of a complexity theory paradigm, and Burkholder (1992), who speaks of a 'computational turn'.

Communication Technologies) were bringing about a macroscopic change, not only in science, but in philosophy too. It was the so-called 'computer revolution' or 'information turn', what I have defined as the fourth revolution in our self-understanding, after the Copernican, the Darwinian, and the Freudian ones (Floridi (2008a)). Like Sloman, however, they seemed to have been misguided about the specific nature of this evolution and have underestimated the unrelenting difficulties that the acceptance of a new PI paradigm would encounter. Turing began publishing his seminal papers in the 1930s. During the following fifty years, cybernetics, information theory, AI, system theory, computer science, complexity theory, and ICT succeeded in attracting some significant, if sporadic, interest from the philosophical community, especially in terms of philosophy of AI.[4] They thus prepared the ground for the emergence of an independent field of investigation and a new computational and information-theoretic approach in philosophy. Until the 1980s, however, they failed to give rise to a mature, innovative, and influential programme of research, let alone a revolutionary change of the magnitude and importance envisaged by researchers like Sloman in the 1970s. This was unfortunate, but perhaps inevitable. With hindsight, it is easy to see how AI could be perceived as an exciting new field of research and the source of a radically innovative approach to traditional problems in philosophy.

Ever since Alan Turing's influential paper 'Computing machinery and intelligence' [...] and the birth of the research field of Artificial Intelligence (AI) in the mid-1950s, there has been considerable interest among computer scientists in theorising about the mind. At the same time there has been a growing feeling amongst philosophers that the advent of computing has decisively modified philosophical debates, by proposing new theoretical positions to consider, or at least to rebut. (Torrance (1984), p. 11)

Thus, AI acted as a Trojan horse, introducing a more encompassing computational/informational paradigm into the philosophical citadel.[5] Until the mid-1980s, however, PI was still premature and perceived as transdisciplinary rather than interdisciplinary; the philosophical and scientific communities were, in any case, not yet ready for its development; and the cultural and social contexts were equally unprepared. Each factor deserves a brief clarification.

Like other intellectual enterprises, PI deals with three types of domain: *topics* (facts, data, problems, phenomena, observations, etc.); *methods* (techniques, approaches, etc.); and *theories* (hypotheses, explanations, etc.). A discipline is *premature* if it attempts to innovate in more than one of these domains simultaneously, thus detaching itself too

---

[4] In 1964, introducing his influential anthology, Anderson wrote that the field of philosophy of AI had already produced more than a thousand articles (Anderson (1964), p. 1). No wonder that (sometimes overlapping) editorial projects have flourished. Among the available titles, the reader of this chapter may wish to keep in mind Ringle (1979) and Boden (1990), which provide two further good collections of essays, and Haugeland (1981), which was expressly meant to be a sequel to Anderson (1964) and was further revised in Haugeland (1997).

[5] Earlier statements of this view can be found in Simon (1962) and (1996), Pylyshyn and Bannon (1970), and Boden (1984); more recently see McCarthy (1995) and Sloman (1995).

abruptly from the normal and continuous thread of evolution of its general field (Stent (1972)). A quick look at the two points made by Sloman in his prediction shows that this was exactly what happened to PI in its earlier appearance as the philosophy of AI.

The inescapable interdisciplinarity of PI further hindered the prospects for a timely recognition of its significance. Even now, many philosophers regard topics discussed in PI to be worth the attention only of researchers in English, mass media, cultural studies, computer science or sociology departments, to mention a few examples. PI needed philosophers used to conversing with cultural and scientific issues across the boundaries, and these were not to be found easily. Too often, everyone's concern is nobody's business and, until the recent development of the information society, PI was perceived to be at too much of a crossroads of technical matters, theoretical issues, applied problems, and conceptual analyses to be anyone's own area of specialization. PI was perceived to be transdisciplinary like cybernetics or semiotics, rather than interdisciplinary like biochemistry or cognitive science. I shall return to this problem later.

Even if PI had not been too premature or allegedly so transdisciplinary, the philosophical and scientific communities at large were not yet ready to appreciate its importance. There were strong programmes of research, especially in (logico-positivist, analytic, commonsensical, postmodernist, deconstructionist, hermeneutical, pragmatist, etc.) philosophies of language, which attracted most of the intellectual and financial resources, kept a fairly rigid agenda, and hardly enhanced the evolution of alternative paradigms. Mainstream philosophy cannot help but be conservative, not only because values and standards are usually less firm and clear in philosophy than in science, and hence more difficult to challenge, but also because, as we shall see better in section 1.4, this is the context where a culturally dominant position is often achieved at the expense of innovative or unconventional approaches. As a result, thinkers like Church, Shannon, Simon, Turing, Von Neumann, or Wiener were essentially left on the periphery of the traditional canon. Admittedly, the computational turn affected science much more rapidly. This explains why some philosophically minded scientists were among the first to perceive the emergence of a new paradigm. Nevertheless, Sloman's 'computer revolution' still had to wait until the 1980s to become a more widespread and mass phenomenon across the various sciences and social contexts, thus creating the right environment for the evolution of PI.

More than half a century after the construction of the first mainframes, the development of human society has now reached a stage in which issues concerning the creation, dynamics, management and utilization of information and computational resources are absolutely vital. Nonetheless, advanced societies and Western culture had to undergo a digital communications revolution before being able to appreciate in full the radical novelty of the new paradigm. The information society has been brought about by the fastest growing technology in history. No previous generation has ever been exposed to such an extraordinary acceleration of technological power over reality, with the corresponding social changes and ethical responsibilities. Total pervasiveness, flexibility, and high power have raised ICT to the status of the characteristic technology of our time, factually, rhetorically, and even iconographically. The computer presents itself as a culturally defining technology and has become a symbol of the new millennium, playing a cultural role far more influential than that of mills in the Middle Ages, mechanical clocks in the seventeenth century, and the loom or the steam engine in the age of the Industrial Revolution (Bolter (1984)). ICS and ICT applications are nowadays among the most strategic factors governing science, the life of society and its future. The most developed post-industrial societies literally live by information, and ICS–ICT keep them constantly oxygenated. And yet, all these profound and very significant transformations were barely in view two decades ago, when most philosophy departments would have considered topics in PI unsuitable areas of specialization for a graduate student.

Too far ahead of its time, and dauntingly innovative for the majority of professional philosophers, PI wavered for some time between two alternatives. It created a number of interesting but limited research niches, like philosophy of AI or computer ethics, often tearing itself away from its intellectual background. Otherwise, it was absorbed within other areas as a methodology, when PI was perceived as a computational or information-theoretic approach to otherwise traditional topics, in classic areas like epistemology, logic, ontology, philosophy of language, philosophy of science, or philosophy of mind. Both trends further contributed to the emergence of PI as an independent field of investigation.

1.3 The historical emergence of PI

Ideas, as it is said, are 'in the air'. The true explanation is presumably that, at a certain stage in the history of any subject, ideas become visible, though only to those with keen mental eyesight, that not even those with the sharpest vision could have perceived at an earlier stage. (Dummett (1993b), p. 3)

Visionaries have a hard life. If nobody else follows, one does not discover new lands but merely gets lost, at least in the eyes of those who stayed behind in the cave. It has required a third computer-related revolution (the Internet), a whole new generation of computer-literate students, teachers, and researchers, a substantial change in the fabric of society, a radical transformation in cultural and intellectual sensibility, and a widespread sense of crisis in philosophical circles of various orientations, for the new informational paradigm to emerge. By the late 1980s, PI had finally begun to be acknowledged as a fundamentally innovative area of philosophical research, rather than a premature revolution. Perhaps it is useful to recall a few dates. In 1982, *Time Magazine* named the computer 'Man of the Year'. In 1985, the American Philosophical Association created the Committee on Philosophy and Computers (PAC).[6] In the same year, Terrell Ward Bynum,

---

[6] The 'computer revolution' had affected philosophers as 'professional knowledge-workers' even before attracting their attention as interpreters. The charge of the APA Committee was, and still is, mainly practical.

editor of *Metaphilosophy*, published a special issue of the journal entitled *Computers and Ethics* (Bynum (1985)) that 'quickly became the widest-selling issue in the journal's history.' (Bynum (2000), see also Bynum (1998)). The first conference sponsored by the *Computing and Philosophy* (CAP) association was held at Cleveland State University in 1986.

Its program was mostly devoted to technical issues in logic software. Over time, the annual CAP conferences expanded to cover all aspects of the convergence of computing and philosophy. In 1993, Carnegie Mellon became a host site. (from CAP website, www.ia-cap.org).

By the mid-1980s, the philosophical community had become fully aware and appreciative of the importance of the topics investigated by PI, and of the value of its methodologies and theories.[7] PI was no longer seen as weird, esoteric, transdisciplinary, or philosophically irrelevant. Concepts or processes like algorithm, automatic control, complexity, computation, distributed network, dynamic system, implementation, information, feedback or symbolic representation; phenomena like HCI (human–computer interaction), CMC (computer-mediated communication), computer crimes, electronic communities, or digital art; disciplines like AI or information theory; issues like the nature of artificial agents, the definition of personal identity in a disembodied environment, and the nature of virtual realities; models like those provided by Turing machines, artificial neural networks, and artificial life systems. These are just some examples of a growing number of topics that were more and more commonly perceived as being new, of pressing philosophical interest, and academically respectable. Informational and computational concepts, methods, techniques, and theories had become powerful tools and metaphors acting as 'hermeneutic devices' through which to interpret the world. They had established a metadisciplinary, unified language that had become common currency in all academic subjects, including philosophy.

In 1998, introducing *The Digital Phoenix*—a collection of essays this time significantly subtitled *How Computers are Changing Philosophy*—Terrell Ward Bynum and James H. Moor acknowledged the emergence of PI as a new force in the philosophical scenario:

From time to time, major movements occur in philosophy. These movements begin with a few simple, but very fertile, ideas—ideas that provide philosophers with a new prism through which to view philosophical issues. Gradually, philosophical methods and problems are refined and

---

The Committee 'collects and disseminates information on the use of computers in the profession, including their use in instruction, research, writing, and publication, and makes recommendations for appropriate actions of the Board or programs of the Association'. Note that the computer is often described as the laboratory tool for the scientific study and empirical simulation, exploration and manipulation of information structures. But then, 'Philosophy and Computers' is like saying 'Philosophy and Information Laboratories'. PI without computers is like biology without microscopes, or astronomy without telescopes, but what really matters are information structures, (microscopic entities, planets) not the machines used to study them.

[7] See for example Burkholder (1992), a collection of sixteen essays by twenty-eight authors presented at the first six CAP conferences; most of the papers are from the fourth.

understood in terms of these new notions. As novel and interesting philosophical results are obtained, the movement grows into an intellectual wave that travels throughout the discipline. A new philosophical paradigm emerges. [. . .] Computing provides philosophy with such a set of simple, but incredibly fertile notions—new and evolving *subject matters*, *methods*, and *models* for philosophical inquiry. Computing brings new opportunities and challenges to traditional philosophical activities. [. . .] computing is changing the way philosophers understand foundational concepts in philosophy, such as mind, consciousness, experience, reasoning, knowledge, truth, ethics and creativity. This trend in philosophical inquiry that incorporates computing in terms of a subject matter, a method, or a model has been gaining momentum steadily. (Bynum and Moor (1998), p. 1)

At the distance set by a textbook, philosophy often strikes the student as a discipline of endless diatribes and extraordinary claims, in a state of chronic crisis. *Sub specie aeternitatis*, the diatribes unfold in the forceful dynamics of ideas, claims acquire the necessary depth, the proper level of justification and their full significance, while the alleged crisis proves to be a fruitful and inevitable dialectic between innovation and conservatism (which I shall define as scholasticism).[8] This dialectic of reflection, highlighted by Bynum and Moor, has played a major role in establishing PI as a mature area of philosophical investigation. We have seen its historical side. This is how it can be interpreted conceptually.

1.4 The dialectic of reflection and the emergence of PI

In order to emerge and flourish, the mind needs to make sense of its environment by continuously investing data (understood as constraining affordances, see chapters three and four) with meaning. Mental life is thus the result of a successful reaction to a primary *horror vacui semantici*: meaningless (in the non-existentialist sense of 'not-yet-meaningful') chaos threatens to tear the Self asunder, to drown it in an alienating otherness perceived by the Self as nothingness, and this primordial dread of annihilation urges the Self to go on filling any semantically empty space with whatever meaning the Self can muster, as successfully as the cluster of contextual constraints, affordances, and the development of culture permit. This giving meaning to, and making sense of reality (semanticization of Being), or reaction of the Self to the non-Self (to phrase it in Fichtean terms), consists in the inheritance and further elaboration, maintenance, and refinement of factual narratives: personal identity, ordinary experience, community ethos, family values, scientific theories, common-sense-constituting beliefs, and so forth. These are logically and contextually, and hence sometimes fully, constrained and constantly challenged both by the data that they need to accommodate and explain and by the reasons why they are developed. Ideally, the evolution of this process tends

---

[8] For an interesting attempt to look at the history of philosophy from a computational perspective see Glymour (1992).

towards an ever-changing, richer, and robust framing of the world. Schematically, it seems the result of four conceptual thrusts.

1 A metasemanticization of narratives. The result of any reaction to Being solidifies into an external reality facing the new individual Self, who needs to appropriate narratives as well, now perceived as further data-affordances that the Self is forced to semanticize. Reflection turns to reflection and recognizes itself as part of the reality it needs to explain and understand.

2 A de-limitation of culture. This is the process of externalization and sharing of the conceptual narratives designed by the Self. The world of meaningful experience moves from being a private, infra-subjective, and anthropocentric construction to being an increasingly inter-subjective and de-anthropocentrified reality. A community of speakers shares the precious semantic resources needed to make sense of the world by maintaining, improving, and transmitting a language—with its conceptual and cultural implications—which a child learns as quickly as a shipwrecked person desperately grabs a floating plank. Narratives then become increasingly *friendly* because shared with other non-challenging Selves not far from one Self, rather than *reassuring* because inherited from some unknown deity. As 'produmers' (producers and consumers) of specific narratives no longer bounded by space or time, members of a community constitute a group only apparently trans-physical, in fact functionally defined by the semantic space they all wish, and opt, to inhabit. The phenomenon of globalization is rather a phenomenon of erasure of old limits and creation of new ones, and hence a phenomenon of de-limitation of culture.

3 A de-physicalization of nature and physical reality. The physical world of watches and cutlery, of stones and trees, of cars and rain, of the I as ID (the socially identifiable Self, with a gender, a job, a driving license, a marital status etc.) undergoes a process of virtualization and distancing, in which even the most essential tools, the most dramatic experiences or the most touching feelings, from war to love, from death to sex, can be framed within virtual mediation, and hence acquire an informational aura. Art, goods, entertainment, news, work, and other Selves are placed and experienced behind a glass. On the other side of the virtual frame, objects and individuals can become fully replaceable and often absolutely indistinguishable tokens of ideal types: a watch is really a Swatch, a pen is a present only insofar as it is a branded object, a place is perceived as a holiday resort, a temple turns into a historical monument, someone is a police officer, and a friend may be just a written voice on the screen of a laptop. Individual entities are used as disposable instantiations of universals. The here-and-now is transformed and expanded. By speedily multitasking, the individual Self can inhabit ever more *loci*, in ways that are perceived synchronically even by the Self, and thus swiftly weave different lives, which do not necessarily merge. Past, present, and future are reshaped in discrete and variable intervals of current time. Projections and indiscernible repetitions of present events expand them into the future; future events are

predicted and pre-experienced in anticipatory presents; while past events are registered and re-experienced in re-playing presents. The non-human world of inimitable things and unrepeatable events is increasingly windowed and humanity window-shops within it.

4 A hypostatization (embodiment) of the conceptual environment designed and inhabited by the mind. Narratives, including values, ideas, fashions, emotions and that intentionally privileged macro-narrative that is the I, can be shaped and reified into 'semantic objects' or 'information entities', now coming closer to the interacting Selves, quietly acquiring an ontological status comparable to that of ordinary things likes clothes, cars, and buildings.

By de-physicalizing nature and embodying narratives, the physical and the cultural are re-aligned on the line of the virtual. In the light of this dialectic, the information society is the most recent, although not definitive, stage in a wider semantic process that makes the mental world increasingly part of, if not *the* environment in which more and more people tend to live. It brings history and culture, and hence time, to the fore as the result of human deeds, while pushing nature, as the unhuman, and hence physical space, into the background. In the course of its evolution, the process of semanticiza-tion gradually leads to a temporary fixation of the constructive conceptualization of reality into a world view, which then generates a conservative closure, scholasticism.[9]

Scholasticism, understood as an intellectual typology rather than a scholarly catego-ry, represents a conceptual system's inborn inertia, when not its rampant resistance to innovation. It is *institutionalized philosophy* at its worst, i.e. a degeneration of what socio-linguists call, more broadly, the internal 'discourse' (Gee (1998), esp. pp. 52–53) of a community or group of philosophers. It manifests itself as a pedantic and often intolerant adherence to some discourse (teachings, methods, values, viewpoints, canons of authors, positions, theories, or selections of problems etc.), set by a particular group (a philosopher, a school of thought, a movement, a trend, a fashion), at the expense of other alternatives, which are ignored or opposed. It fixes, as permanently and objec-tively as possible, a toolbox of philosophical concepts and vocabulary suitable for standardizing its discourse (its special *isms*) and the research agenda of the community. In this way, scholasticism favours the professionalization of philosophy: scholastics are 'lovers' who detest the idea of being *amateurs* and wish to become professional. Followers, exegetes, and imitators of some mythicized founding fathers, scholastics find in their hands more substantial answers than new interesting questions and thus gradually become involved with the application of some doctrine to its own internal puzzles, readjusting, systematizing, and tidying up a once-dynamic area of research. Scholasticism is metatheoretically acritical and hence reassuring: fundamental criticism and self-scrutiny are not part of the scholastic discourse, which, on the contrary, helps a

[9] For an enlightening discussion of contemporary scholasticism, see Rorty (1982), chs. 2, 4, and especially 12.

community to maintain a strong sense of intellectual identity and a clear direction in the efficient planning and implementation of its research and teaching activities. It is a closed context: scholastics tend to interpret, criticize, and defend only views of other identifiable members of the community, thus mutually reinforcing a sense of identity and purpose, instead of addressing directly new conceptual issues that may still lack an academically respectable pedigree and hence be more challenging. This is the road to anachronism: a progressively wider gap opens up between philosophers' problems and philosophical problems. Scholastic philosophers become busy with narrow and marginal *disputationes* of detail that only they are keen to ponder, while failing to interact with other disciplines, new discoveries, or contemporary problems that are of lively interest outside the specialized discourse. In the end, once scholasticism is closed in upon itself, its main purpose becomes quite naturally the perpetuation of its own discourse, transforming itself into academic strategy.

What has been said so far should not be confused with the naïve question as to whether philosophy has lost, and hence should regain, contact with people (Adler (1979), Quine (1979)). People may be curious about philosophy, but only a philosopher can fancy they might be interested in it. Scholasticism, if properly trivialized, can be pop and even trendy, while innovative philosophy can bear to be esoteric. Perhaps a metaphor can help to clarify the point. Conceptual areas are like mines. Some of them are so vast and rich that they will keep philosophers happily busy for generations. Others may seem exhausted, until new and powerful methods or theories allow further and deeper explorations, or lead to the discovery of problems and ideas previously overlooked. Scholastic philosophers are like wretched workers digging an almost exhausted but not yet abandoned mine. They belong to a late generation, technically trained to work only in the narrow field in which they happen to find themselves. They work hard to gain little, and the more they invest in their meagre explorations, the more they stubbornly bury themselves in their own mine, refusing to leave their place to explore new sites. Tragically, only time will tell whether the mine is truly exhausted. Scholasticism is a censure that can be applied only post-mortem.

Innovation is always possible, but scholasticism is historically inevitable. Any stage in the semanticization of Being is destined to be initially innovative if not disruptive, to establish itself as a specific dominant paradigm, and hence to become fixed and increasingly rigid, further reinforcing itself, until it finally acquires an intolerant stance towards alternative conceptual innovations, and so becomes incapable of dealing with the ever-changing intellectual environment that it helped to create and mould. In this sense, every intellectual movement generates the conditions of its own senescence and replacement.

Conceptual transformations should not be too radical, lest they become premature. We have seen that old paradigms are challenged and finally replaced by further, innovative reflection only when the latter is sufficiently robust to be acknowledged as a better and more viable alternative to the previous stage in the semanticization of Being. Here is how Moritz Schlick clarified this dialectic at the beginning of a paradigm shift:

Philosophy belongs to the centuries, not to the day. There is no uptodateness about it. For anyone who loves the subject, it is painful to hear talk of 'modern' or 'non-modern' philosophy. The so-called fashionable movements in philosophy—whether diffused in journalistic form among the general public, or taught in a scientific style at the universities—stand to the calm and powerful evolution of philosophy proper much as philosophy professors do to philosophers: the former are learned, the latter wise; the former write about philosophy and contend on the doctrinal battlefield, the latter philosophise. The fashionable philosophic movements have no worse enemy than true philosophy, and none that they fear more. When it rises in a new dawn and sheds its pitiless light, the adherents of every kind of ephemeral movement tremble and unite against it, crying out that philosophy is in danger, for they truly believe that the destruction of their own little system signifies the ruin of philosophy itself. (Schlick (1979), vol. II, p. 491)

Three types of forces therefore need to interact to compel a conceptual system to innovate. Scholasticism is the internal, negative force. It gradually fossilizes thought, reinforcing its fundamental character of immobility and, by making a philosophical school increasingly rigid, less responsive to the world and more brittle, it weakens its capacity for reaction to scientific, cultural, and historical inputs, divorces it from reality and thus prepares the ground for a solution of the crisis. Scholasticism, however, can perform one progressive task: it can indicate that philosophical research has reached a stage when it needs to address new topics and problems, adopt innovative methodologies, or develop alternative explanations. It cannot specify which direction the innovation should take. Historically, this is the task of two other positive forces for innovation, external to any philosophical system: the substantial novelties in the environment of the conceptual system, occurring also as a result of the semantic work done by the old paradigm itself; and the appearance of an innovative paradigm, capable of dealing with them more success-fully, and thus of disentangling the conceptual system from its stagnation.

In the past, philosophers had to take care of the whole chain of knowledge produc-tion, from raw data to scientific theories, as it were. Throughout its history, philosophy has progressively identified classes of empirical and logico-mathematical problems and outsourced their investigations to new disciplines. It has then returned to these dis-ciplines and their findings for controls, clarifications, constraints, methods, tools, and insights but, *pace* Carnap (1935) (see especially the chapter entitled 'The Rejection of Metaphysics') and Reichenbach (1951), philosophy itself consists of conceptual investigations whose essential nature is neither empirical nor logico-mathematical. In philosophy, one neither tests nor calculates. To mis-paraphrase Hume: 'if we take in our hand any volume, let us ask: Does it contain any abstract reasoning concerning quantity or number? Does it contain any experimental reasoning concerning matter of fact and existence?' If the answer is yes, then search elsewhere, because that is science, not yet philosophy. Philosophy is not a conceptual aspirin, a super-science, or the manicure of language, but *conceptual engineering*, that is, the art of identifying conceptual problems and of designing, proposing, and evaluating explanatory solutions. It is, after all, the last stage of reflection, where the semanticization of Being is pursued and kept open (Russell (1912), ch. 15). Its critical and creative investigations identify, formulate, evaluate, clarify, interpret, and explain problems that are intrinsically capable of different and possibly irreconcilable solutions, problems that are genuinely open to informed debate and honest, reasonable disagreement, even in principle. These investigations are often entwined with empirical and logico-mathematical issues, and so scientifically constrained but, in themselves, they are neither. They constitute a space of inquiry broadly definable as *normative*. It is an open space: anyone can step into it, no matter what the starting point is, and disagreement is always possible. It is also a dynamic space, for when its cultural environment changes, philosophy follows suit and evolves.

This normative space should not be confused with Sellars' famous 'space of reasons':

in characterizing an episode or a state as that of knowing, we are not giving an empirical description of that episode or state; we are placing it in the logical space of reasons of justifying and being able to justify what one says (Sellars (1963), p. 169).

Our normative space is a space of *design*, where rational and empirical affordances, constraints, requirements, and standards of evaluation as well as epistemic and pragmatic goals all play an essential role in the proper construction and critical assessment of knowledge. It only partly overlaps with Sellars' space of reasons in that the latter includes more (e.g. mathematical deduction counts as justification, and in Sellars' space we find intrinsically decidable problems) and less, since in the space of design we find issues connected with creativity and freedom, not clearly included in Sellars' space.[10]

Thus, in Bynum and Moor's felicitous metaphor, philosophy is indeed like a phoenix: it can flourish only by constantly re-engineering itself. A philosophy that is not timely but timeless is not a *philosophia perennis*, which unreasonably claims unbounded validity over past and future intellectual positions, but a stagnant philosophy, unable to contribute, keep track of, and interact with, the cultural evolution that philosophical reflection itself has helped to bring about, and hence to flourish.

Having outsourced various forms of knowledge, philosophy's pulling force of innovation has become necessarily external. It has been made so by philosophical reflection itself. This is the full sense in which Hegel's metaphor of the Owl of Minerva is to be interpreted. In the past, the external force has been represented by factors such as Christian theology, the discovery of other civilizations, the scientific revolution, the foundational crisis in mathematics and the rise of mathematical logic, evolutionary theory, the emergence of new social and economic phenomena, and the theory of relativity, just to mention a few of the most obvious examples. Nowadays, the pulling force of innovation is represented by the complex world of information and communication phenomena, their corresponding sciences and technologies and the new environments, social life, existential and cultural issues that they have brought about. This is why PI can present itself as an innovative paradigm.

[10] For a discussion of Sellars' 'space of reasons' see McDowell (1996), especially the new introduction. I have analysed it in Floridi (1996), ch. 4.

1.5 The definition of PI

Once a new area of philosophical research is brought into being by the interaction between scholasticism and some external force, it evolves into a well-defined field, possibly interdisciplinary but still autonomous, only if

i. it is able to appropriate an explicit, clear and precise interpretation not of a scholastic *Fach* (Rorty (1982), ch. 2) but of the classic 'ti esti', thus presenting itself as a specific 'philosophy of';

ii. the appropriated interpretation becomes an attractor towards which investigations in the new field can usefully converge;

iii. the attractor proves sufficiently influential to withstand centrifugal forces that may attempt to reduce the new field to other fields of research already well-established; and

iv. the new field is rich enough to be organized into clear sub-fields and hence allow for specialization.

Questions like 'what is the nature of Being?', 'what is the nature of knowledge?', 'what is the nature of right and wrong?', 'what is the nature of meaning?' are such field-questions. They satisfy the previous conditions, and so they have guaranteed the stable existence of their corresponding disciplines. Other questions such as 'what is the nature of the mind?', 'what is the nature of beauty and taste?', or 'what is the nature of a logically valid inference?' have been subject to fundamental reinterpretations, which have led to profound transformations in the definition of philosophy of mind, aesthetics, and logic. Still other questions, like 'what is the nature of complexity?', 'what is the nature of life?', 'what is the nature of signs?', 'what is the nature of control systems?' have turned out to be trans- rather than interdisciplinary. Failing to satisfy at least one of the previous four conditions, they have struggled to establish their own autonomous fields. The question is now whether PI itself satisfies (i)–(iv). A first step towards a positive answer requires a further clarification.

Philosophy appropriates the 'ti esti' question essentially in two ways, *phenomenologically* or *metatheoretically*. Philosophy of language and epistemology are two examples of 'phenomenologies', in the literal sense of being philosophies of a phenomenon. Their subjects are meaning and knowledge, not linguistic theories or cognitive sciences. The philosophy of physics and the philosophy of social sciences, on the other hand, are plain instances of 'metatheories'. They investigate problems arising from organized systems of knowledge, which only in their turn investigate natural or human phenomena. Some other philosophical branches, however, show only a *tension* towards the two poles, often combining phenomenological and metatheoretical interests. This is the case with philosophy of mathematics and philosophy of logic, for example. Like PI, their subjects are old, but they have acquired their salient features, and become autonomous fields of investigation, only very late in the history of thought. These philosophies show a tendency to work on specific classes of first-order phenomena, but they also examine these phenomena working their way through methods and theories, by starting from a metatheoretical interest in specific classes of second-order theoretical statements concerning those very same classes of phenomena. The tension pulls each specific branch of philosophy towards one or the other pole. Philosophy of logic, to rely on the previous example, is metatheoretically biased. It shows a constant tendency to concentrate primarily on conceptual problems arising from logic understood as a specific mathematical theory of formally valid inferences, whereas it pays much less attention to problems concerning logic as a natural phenomenon, what one may call, for want of a better description, rationality. Vice versa, PI, like philosophy of mathematics, is phenomenologically biased. It is primarily concerned with the whole domain of first-order phenomena represented by the world of information, computation and the information society, although it addresses its problems by starting from the vantage point represented by the methodologies and theories offered by ICS, and can be seen to incline towards a metatheoretical approach in so far as it is methodologically critical towards its own sources.

The following definition attempts to capture the clarifications introduced so far:

PI The philosophy of information (PI) is the philosophical field concerned with (a) the critical investigation of the conceptual nature and basic principles of information, including its dynamics, utilization, and sciences; and (b) the elaboration and application of information-theoretic and computational methodologies to philosophical problems.

Some clarifications are in order. The first half of the definition concerns philosophy of information as a new field. PI appropriates an explicit, clear, and precise interpretation of the 'ti esti' question, namely 'What is the nature of information?'. This is the clearest hallmark of a new field. Of course, as with any other field-question, this too only serves to demarcate an area of research, not to map its specific problems in detail. These will be discussed in the next chapter. PI provides critical investigations that are not to be confused with a quantitative theory of data communication or statistical analysis (information theory). On the whole, its task is to develop not a unified theory of information, but rather an integrated family of theories that analyse, evaluate, and explain the various principles and concepts of information, their dynamics and utilization, with special attention to systemic issues arising from different contexts of application and the interconnections with other key concepts in philosophy, such as Being, knowledge, truth, life, or meaning.

By 'dynamics of information' the definition refers to: (i) *the constitution and modelling of information environments*, including their systemic properties, forms of interaction, internal developments etc.; (ii) *information life cycles*, i.e. the series of various stages in form and functional activity through which information can pass, from its initial occurrence to its final utilization and possible disappearance;[11] and (iii) *computation*,

---

[11] A typical life cycle includes the following phases: *occurring* (discovering, designing, authoring, etc.), *processing and managing* (collecting, validating, modifying, organizing, indexing, classifying, filtering, updating,

both in the Turing-machine sense of *algorithmic processing*, and in the wider sense of *information processing*. This is a crucial specification. Although a very old concept, information has finally acquired the nature of a primary phenomenon only thanks to the sciences and technologies of computation and ICT. Computation has therefore attracted much philosophical attention in recent years. Nevertheless, PI privileges 'information' over 'computation' as the pivotal topic of the new field because it analyses the latter as presupposing the former. PI treats 'computation' as only one (although perhaps the most important) of the processes in which information can be involved. Thus, the field should be interpreted as a philosophy of information rather than just of computation, in the same sense in which epistemology is the philosophy of knowledge, not just of perception.

From an environmental perspective, PI is prescriptive about, and legislates on, what may count as information, and how information should be adequately created, processed, managed, and used. However, PI's phenomenological bias does not mean that it fails to provide critical feedback. On the contrary, methodological and theoretical choices in ICS are also profoundly influenced by the kind of PI a researcher adopts more or less consciously. It is therefore essential to stress that PI critically evaluates, shapes and sharpens the conceptual, methodological, and theoretical basis of ICS, in short that it also provides a *philosophy of ICS*, as has been plain since early work in the area of philosophy of AI (Colburn (2000b)).

It is worth stressing here that an excessive concern with the metatheoretical aspects of PI may obscure the important fact that it is perfectly legitimate to speak of PI even in authors who lived centuries before the information revolution. It will be fruitful to develop a historical approach and trace PI's diachronic evolution, as long as the technical and conceptual frameworks of ICS are not anachronistically applied, but are used to provide the conceptual method and privileged perspective to evaluate in full reflections that were developed on the nature, dynamics, and utilization of information before the digital revolution. Consider for example Plato's *Phaedrus*, Descartes's *Meditations*, Nietzsche's *On the Use and Disadvantage of History for Life*, or Popper's conception of a third world. This is significantly comparable with the development undergone by other philosophical fields like the philosophy of language, the philosophy of biology, or the philosophy of mathematics.

The second half of the definition indicates that PI is not only a new field, but provides an innovative methodology as well. Research into the conceptual nature of information, its dynamics and utilization is carried out from the vantage point represented by the methodologies and theories offered by ICS and ICT (see for example Grim et al. (1998)). This perspective affects other philosophical topics as well. Information-theoretic and

sorting, storing, networking, distributing, accessing, retrieving, transmitting etc.) and *using* (monitoring, modelling, analysing, explaining, planning, forecasting, decision-making, instructing, educating, learning, etc.).

computational methods, concepts, tools, and techniques have already been developed and applied in many philosophical areas

1. to extend our understanding of the cognitive and linguistic abilities of humans and animals and the possibility of artificial forms of intelligence (e.g. in the philosophy of AI; in information-theoretic semantics; in information-theoretic epistemology, and in dynamic semantics);
2. to analyse inferential and computational processes (e.g. in the philosophy of computing; in the philosophy of computer science; in information-flow logic; in situation logic; in dynamic logic, and in various modal logics);
3. to explain the organizational principles of life and agency (e.g. in the philosophy of artificial life; in cybernetics and in the philosophy of automata; in decision and game theory);
4. to devise new approaches to modelling physical and conceptual systems (e.g. in formal ontology; in the theory of information systems; in the philosophy of virtual reality);
5. to formulate the methodology of scientific knowledge (e.g. in model-based philosophy of science; in computational methodologies in philosophy of science);
6. to investigate ethical problems (in computer and information ethics and in artificial ethics), aesthetic issues (in digital multimedia/hypermedia theory, in hypertext theory, and in literary criticism) and psychological, anthropological, and social phenomena characterizing the information society and human behaviour in digital environments(cyberphilosophy).

Indeed, the presence of these branches shows that PI satisfies criterion (4). As a new field, it provides a unified and cohesive, theoretical framework that allows further specialization.

PI possesses one of the most powerful conceptual vocabularies ever devised in philosophy. This is because we can still rely on informational concepts whenever a complete understanding of some series of events is unavailable or unnecessary for providing an explanation. In philosophy, this means that virtually any issue can be rephrased in informational terms. This semantic power is a great advantage of PI, understood as a methodology (see the second half of the definition). It shows that we are dealing with an influential paradigm, describable in terms of an informational philosophy. But it may also be a problem, because a metaphorically pan-informational approach can lead to a dangerous equivocation, namely, thinking that since any x can be described in (more or less metaphorically) informational terms, then the nature of any x is genuinely informational. We shall re-encounter this problem in all its vividness in chapter fourteen. The equivocation makes PI lose its specific identity as a philosophical field with its own subject. A key that opens every lock only shows that there is something wrong with the locks. PI runs the risk of becoming synonymous with philosophy. The best way of avoiding this loss of identity is to concentrate on the first half of the definition. PI as a philosophical discipline is defined by what a problem is (or can be reduced to be) *about*, not by *how* the latter is formulated. Although many philosophical issues seem to benefit greatly from an informational analysis, in PI the latter provides a literal foundation not just a metaphorical superstructure. PI presupposes that a problem or an explanation can be legitimately and genuinely reduced to an informational problem or explanation.

So, the criterion for testing the soundness of the informational analysis of a problem *p* is not to check whether *p* can be formulated in informational terms—for this is easily achievable, at least metaphorically, in almost any case—but to ask what it would be like for *p* not to be an informational problem at all. With this criterion in mind, I shall provide in chapter two a review of some of the most fundamental and interesting open problems in PI.

1.6 The analytic approach to PI

Among our mundane and technical concepts, information is currently one of the most important, widely used yet least understood. So far, philosophers have done comparatively little work about it and its cognate concepts and this paradoxical situation counts as one more 'scandal of philosophy'. I am not using the expression here in its original Kantian sense. This referred to the tension between the irrefutability and the untenability of scepticism about the external world. The expression was later adopted by Broad to describe the Humean problem of induction, and then by Hintikka to refer to the problem of the informational nature of deductions (see chapter five). Nor am I using it in the way in which Heidegger modified it to describe the recurring attempts to resolve the tension highlighted by Kant. I am using it to refer to the phenomenon of scholastic (see below) canonization of problems, which, by rigidly fixing the scope of issues that are supposed to be philosophically relevant, fails to keep the philosophical discourse open to new problems, thus preparing the ground for its own overcoming.

Luckily, the problems are fairly recent, half a century or less, and work is already in progress, so we might still be in time to do a good job, before being accused of arriving too late. Philosophy, understood as conceptual engineering, needs to turn its attention to the new world of information. This is a quick and dirty way of introducing the philosophy of information. I believe it to be reasonably convincing. It definitely has the appearance of a reassuring déjà vu, and I have seen it becoming increasingly acceptable even among sceptical minds in the past ten years or so. However, if this is the whole story, then I must admit I am not entirely satisfied. Before explaining why, let me briefly elaborate.

The story is familiar, so I shall merely sketch it. It goes roughly like this. Somehow, somewhere, new conceptual problems, confusions, and *vacua* arise. As these issues are neither easily predictable nor often preventable, I agree with Hegel that philosophers tend to arrive at the crime-scene after things have gone badly wrong, or at least wrong enough to impose themselves upon their attention. They then usually concur to join forces against conceptual vandalism, pollution, or mere slackness, but they soon start differing on the best strategy for taking care of the hard problems, those that are genuinely open to informed debate and honest, reasonable disagreement, even in principle. Inevitably, competing methodologies, analyses, and solutions emerge, until new difficulties call for further work elsewhere and philosophy moves ahead. The optimistic view is that every drop of conceptual clarification helps. Pouring water on the same fire from different corners is the positive outcome of a pluralistic approach, rather than evidence of irrecoverable disagreement and mutual undoing. Two interesting implications are that the source of philosophical activities is fully externalized—philosophers will be in business for as long as humanity generates conceptual muddles and novelties (read: forever)—and that there is a sense in which philosophy does develop, for it can be more or less timely, depending on how successfully it interacts with the culture within which it flourishes.

According to this story, the computer revolution, the informational turn, ICT and the information society have recently generated plenty of conceptual problems, confusions, and *vacua*; many new ideas and unprecedented issues; several new ways to revisit old theories and issues; and so forth. This new combination of informational confusion and virgin territory constitutes the sort of 'reclaimable land' that philosophy is typically called upon to explore, clear, and map. So, the argument goes, today we need a PI understood simply as a (Kuhnianly) normal development in the history of philosophy, an important expansion of the philosophical frontier, whose time has quite clearly come, but that certainly will not be the last.

There is a more cynical version of the story, usually associated with the early Wittgenstein. Nowadays it seems increasingly less popular, but it can be found between the lines in many philosophers, from Descartes to members of the Vienna Circle. Let me introduce it by using an analogy.

Anti-virus companies do not write the viruses that they help to fight, but they do flourish because of them, so urban legends insist on the opposite view: they actually create and disseminate the malware that keeps them in business. It is the simplistic logic of the *cui prodest* (the perpetrator of a crime is whoever profits by it), spiced up by some classic conspiracy theory. Now Wittgenstein, but not only Wittgenstein, had a similar complaint to make about philosophy. Philosophers generate the very mess they appoint themselves to clean, and make a living in between. And just in case you thought this to be some sort of postmodern *maladie*, let me quote Berkeley, who phrased the complaint very incisively:

Upon the whole, I am inclined to think that the far greater part, if not all, of those difficulties which have hitherto amused philosophers and blocked up the way to knowledge, are entirely owing to ourselves—that we have first raised a dust and then complain that we cannot see. Berkeley (1710–1734), Introduction, § 3

Two interesting implications of this view are that now philosophy does not so much interact with the culture within which it develops as with its own intellectual tradition, and that, since the source of philosophical activities is internal, philosophers may put themselves out of business by eradicating their own conceptual problems once and for all (read: never). Admittedly, the cynical view loses in external timeliness, but there is still a sense of philosophical development, gained in terms of internal eschatology. It seems that Heidegger shares at least this much with Wittgenstein.

I am not sure the cynical view may be quite so nonchalantly dismissed as merely another urban legend, but I certainly disagree with its extremism and its lack of hermeneutic charity. Of course, there is much philosophical work that can be explained in its light. If we restrict our attention to PI, we may consider, for example, the trust placed by many philosophers of mind in computational and informational approaches, or Quine's 'cognitivization' of epistemology. In cases such as these, PI can work as a powerful methodology to debug past philosophical mistakes, including those caused by PI itself. The analysis of the misuse of the Church–Turing thesis and of the concept of Universal Turing Machine provides an instructive example (Copeland (2003)). Nevertheless, 'upon the whole', as Berkeley says, we should not confuse the mixture of responsibility, enthusiasm, and relief—naïvely felt by the philosophical community in finding a new conceptual muddle, which will keep it in business for a while—with the wicked desire to see things go badly just for the sake of philosophical exercise, or with a childish incapacity not to generate a messy confusion while playing Berkeley, and hence Wittgenstein, were wrong. For the truth is that philosophy has no external space of reason in which to dump its waste, so philosophers are sometime forced to clean the mess inadvertently left behind by previous generations in the course of their more constructive work. Berkeley simply mistook sawdust for dust.

So far, we have the familiar story and its two well-known interpretations. Both agree on describing philosophy's positive mission as a process of semantic exploration and policing. Both allow, indeed both seem to require, the development of PI as the next step to be taken within the analytical tradition. The line of reasoning is simple. The information revolution has been changing the world profoundly, irreversibly and problematically for some time now, at a breathtaking pace and with an unprecedented scope. It has thus created entirely new realities, made possible unprecedented phenomena and experiences, provided a wealth of extremely powerful tools and methodologies, raised a wide range of unique problems and conceptual issues, and opened up endless possibilities hitherto unimaginable. All this calls for conceptual analysis and explorations, and hence for the development of PI.

1.7 The metaphysical approach to PI

With a picture, one could say that our previous narrative opens, like *Hamlet*, with the philosopher-sentinels on the wall of history, patrolling the foggy unknown and struggling with the appearance of conceptual ghosts. Now, this is a very promising *incipit*, but I find the introduction of PI as an upgraded version of philosophical semantics—one more guard on the wall who, like Barnardo, 'comes most carefully upon its hour' (Shakespeare, *Hamlet*, I.i.vi)—only partly satisfactory. Explaining why is not too hard but it is somewhat embarrassing. For it requires recalling another story that academic manners and intellectual sensitivity may rather leave untold. Here it is.

There is a 'metaphysical crime' at the roots of contemporary philosophy. To remind ourselves about it is to touch one of the most sensitive nerves in the philosophical body. And since talking of the death of God may be in bad taste, let us consider instead the gradual vanishing of that metaphysical principle that, in Descartes, creates *res extensa* and *res cogitans*, keeps them from falling apart, makes sure that knowledge and reality communicate noiselessly and undisturbed by malicious inferences, and holds all eternal truths immutable and fully accessible. Let us call this powerful but brittle principle god. Descartes's god is not Kierkegaard's God (as the latter vociferously lamented) but rather a metaphysical guarantee of an objective, universal semantics that eventually harmonizes and gives sense to nature and history, culture and science, minds and bodies. It may be nothing holy, sacred or transcendent, and this was Kierkegaard's charge against Descartes. Nevertheless, because it is supposed to be the ontic and rational foundation of any reality, it is also the ultimate source of semanticization needed by the Cartesian Ego to escape its solipsism and to make sense of the world and its life in it, as something intrinsically meaningful and fully intelligible.

From Descartes to Kant, epistemology can be seen as a branch of information theory. Ultimately, its task is decrypting and deciphering the world, god's message. From Galileo to Newton, the scientific task is made easier by a theological background against which the message is guaranteed to make sense, at least in principle. So, whatever made Descartes's god increasingly frail and ultimately killed it—and it may well be that very Ego that soon considers itself sufficient for the epistemological foundation of a fully rational and human metaphysics—Nietzsche was right to mourn its disappearance. Contemporary philosophy is founded on that loss, and on the ensuing sense of irreplaceable absence of the great programmer of the game of Being. Already in Hume, and very clearly in Kant, making sense of the world is a heavy burden left entirely on the shoulders of the I. It is indicative, for example, that Husserl revisited the *Meditations* from an Ego-centric perspective that had no more space or role for the Cartesian god. The solitude of the I in a silent universe becomes entirely evident in German Idealism, which can be read as a series of titanic attempts to re-construct an absolute semantics by relying on very streamlined resources: the mind and its dialectics. The grand project is a naturalization of the I and an I-dealization of nature. The natural ally is Greek philosophy, as the pre-theological stage of thought. However, in the end, German Idealism is unable to overcome Kant's dualism by re-acquiring the Greek virginity concerning the unbroken place of the mental within nature. The gap between mind and Being is not erasable by travelling back in time, *pace* Heidegger and his metaphysical nostalgia.

An information-theoretical understanding of ontology and hence a constructionist approach to the conceptualization of reality, an 'object-oriented' treatment of information, and an insightful understanding of the centrality of the dynamic (hence historical) processes of information: the vocabulary has changed, yet these seem to me to be some of the most important and still vital contributions of German Idealism to PI. From Kant to Hegel, the mind is recognized to be essentially *poietic* (that is, constructive), and its ontologization of Being is accepted as the praxis-related condition of possibility of its (the mind's) flourishing. Dualism is beautiful, whether dialectically reconciled (Hegel) or not (Kant), whereas a-theistic monism can only be alienating, as a Being-ization of the I. For there is no openness to Being without annihilation of the opened: witness animal intelligence, which is turned to stone by the world, and hence is absorbed into the world as part of the world. This is something that Heidegger seems to have missed in the history of ontology.

After the failure of the Idealistic effort to synthesize meaning through a theology of the I, the shattered components of the Cartesian picture, subjectivism and naturalism, start floating apart. Dualism is antedated to Descartes himself, rightly in terms of genesis, wrongly in terms of advocacy, since in Descartes mind and Being are still two branches of the same metaphysical tree. The linguistic turn represents the full acknowledgement of the untenability of the modern project of an epistemology that Cartesianly reads a world-message whose original meaningfulness can no longer be taken for granted. The informee is left without informer. Whether there is any meaningful message, instead of a chaotic world of data that underdetermine their models, depends now on whether it is possible to construct a semantics based entirely on the informee, or at most on the environment in which the informee operates, being this society and history, as in Marx,[12] or nature. The debate on scientific realism and the need for a theory of meaning—a direct consequence of the disappearance of Descartes's god—are rightly recognized as two of the most pressing issues in contemporary philosophy. But analytic philosophy initially reacts to the failure of the various Idealisms and the successes of the various sciences by retreating behind the trench of dissection and reconstruction. It is the reaction of a disappointed lover, as Moore, Russell, and Wittgenstein (but also, in a different context, Dewey, Peirce, and C. I. Lewis) testify.[13]

The construction of a fully meaningful view of the world—which can stand on its feet without the help of an external, metaphysical source of creation and semanticization—is postponed. Kant's negative lesson—protecting the frontiers of philosophy from bad metaphysics and plain nonsense—continues to be appreciated as the only good lesson, and dominates the metatheoretical agenda. Philosophers are dispatched to guard frontiers more and more distant from the capital of human interests. In search of a

---

[12] For an interpretation of Marx from an explicitly 'demiurgic' perspective see Kolakowski (1968).

[13] Rockmore (2001) provides an interesting reconstruction of the neo-Hegelian turn in contemporary American philosophy. And although I am not sure I would agree on his interpretation of what are the central and most fundamental aspects of Hegel's philosophy, I find his overview very convincing. As he writes: 'This paper has discussed the massive analytic turning away from Hegel almost a century ago and the recent, more modest, incipient turn, or return as an offshoot of the turn to pragmatism in the wake of the analytic critique of classical empiricism. I have argued that analytic philosophy has misunderstood Hegel on both occasions' (p. 368). In Floridi (2003d) I have tried to show the Idealistic roots of the renaissance of epistemology between the two wars.

theory of meaning from where to begin the re-semanticization of reality, analytic philosophy traverses a syntactic, a semantic and then, more recently, a pragmatic season.[14] The I is first the speaker and then also the agent. The Cartesian Ego is re-embodied and then re-embedded, first within the community of speakers, then in an environment of interacting agents situated in the world. It is naturalized as a cognizer rather than a knower, it is turned into a distributed agent or a society of interacting agents, rather than an individual. Naturalism begins outsourcing epistemic and semantic responsibility. But while searching for a way to fill the semantic gap left by the death of god, the philosophical task remains the same: invigilating over whatever semantics is left in a godless universe. The consequence is a paradoxical abdication of responsibility on the part of philosophy itself, which fails to replace god after having killed it, while allowing (when not programmatically delegating) other narratives to compete for the role of ultimate source of meaning, from political and economic doctrines to religious fundamentalisms. The incomplete deicide generates a sense of semantic suspense: what meaning will the world take, once the gods have been completely excluded from the game of giving sense to it?

The metanarrative that sees philosophy as conceptual analysis was very popular until recently (Dummett (2001)). In more sweetened versions, it is still with us, I suspect mainly for lack of serious competition. To be true, it should not be taken too rigidly. A lot of analytic philosophy has always been far more constructionist that it ever wished to admit without blushing. For many years, the conceptual analysis metanarrative was, politically, the official reply given to sceptical visitors of philosophical departments or funding agencies inquiring about the philosophical trade and its social value. Intellectually, it was also the outcome of the death of god and the following metaphysical crisis, and the trademark that kept philosophy in business during the twentieth century. We should be grateful to past generations for its formulation, for it was a great achievement at a time when philosophy was in danger of extinction, irrational fragmentation, or nostalgic metaphysization. We have also seen that, as a metatheoretical frame, it has aged well, for it can still account, quite convincingly, for the emergence of such a new field as PI. But it also seems to have become increasingly constraining and less satisfactory (see the dialectic of reflection). For, while philosophy was fighting a rearguard action against its own disappearance, the post-Cartesian Ego, whose semantic activities analytic philosophy was supposed to protect, was evolving dramatically. Slowly but surely, it morphed from an agent subject to nature and orphan of its god into a *demiurge*, progressively more accountable for its epistemic and ontic activities, with moral duties and responsibilities to oversee the preservation and evolution of present and future realities, both natural and artificial.

The technical term *demiurge* should be understood here partly in its Platonic sense and partly in its original meaning. Plato's *Demiurge* is not an omnipotent God, who

The larger project of PI is to renew analytic philosophy for a constructionism. This has to be appreciated

---

[14] For an insightful reconstruction see Sandbothe (2003).

God and God for remaining did not die; they were where!

produces the universe out of nothing, but a smaller god, who moulds a pre-existing reality according to reason. On the other hand, *demiourgos*, which literally means 'public worker', was originally used in Greek to refer to any artisan practising his craft or trade for the use of the public. So by *demiurge* I mean here an artisan whose extended, but not unlimited, ontic powers can be variously exercised (in terms of control, creation, modelling, design, shaping, etc.) over itself (e.g. ethically, genetically, physiologically, neurologically, narratively), over society (e.g. legally, culturally, politically, economically, religiously) and over natural or artificial environments (e.g. physically and informationally) for the use of humanity. This demiurge is like a gardener who builds her environment and takes care of it. *Poiesis* emerges as being more primordial than *care*.

The history of contemporary philosophy may be written in terms of the emergence of humanity as the demiurgic Ego, which overcomes the death of god by gradually accepting its metaphysical destiny of fully replacing god as the creator and steward of reality, and hence as the ultimate source of meaning and responsibility. This demiurgic turn is the real watershed between our time and the past. It explains the cultural gap and indeed incommensurability between lay and religious societies and the impossible communication between those who believe themselves to be subject to a greater power and those who cannot even conceive how anyone else but humanity might be in charge and hence responsible for its own future.

After the demiurgic turn, constructing, conceptualizing and semanticizing reality has become as crucial as analysing, reconstructing and vindicating its descriptions. Of course, both tasks have a normative nature and both belong to philosophy. What past philosophy missed was that the new demiurge needs a *constructionist* as well as an analytic philosophy. And here is where an alternative way of interpreting the emergence of PI has its roots. For one of the forces that lie behind the demiurgic turn is the Baconian–Galilean project of grasping and manipulating the alphabet of the universe. And this ambitious project has begun to find its fulfilment in the computational revolution and the resulting informational turn that have affected so profoundly our knowledge of reality and the way we conceptualize it and ourselves within it. Informational narratives possess an ontic power, not as magical confabulations, expressions of theological logos or mystical formulae, but immanently, as building tools that can describe, modify, and implement our environment and ourselves.

Seen from a demiurgic perspective, PI can then be presented as the study of the informational activities that make possible the construction, conceptualization, semanticization and finally the moral stewardship of reality, both natural and artificial, both physical and anthropological. Indeed, we can look at PI as a complete *demiurgology*, to use a fancy word. According to this alternative standpoint, PI has a constructionist vocation. Its elaboration may close that chapter in the history of philosophy that opens with the death of the Engineer. To paraphrase Kant, according to this interpretation PI is humanity's emergence from its wishful state of demiurgic irresponsibility, in which humanity entered with its theological impoverishment, the death of god.

To recapitulate, PI can be seen as the continuation of conceptual analysis by other means, to say it à la von Clausewitz, or as a constructionist project. The analytic approach is metaphorically horizontal and more ('the new frontier') or less ('patrolling the territory') optimistic. The metaphysical approach is metaphorically vertical, for it is clearly foundationalist. It presents PI as the converging point of several modern threads: the death of god, the demiurgic transformation of the I; the scientific revolution; the increasing moral responsibility, shared by humanity, towards the way reality is and should be and what role we should play in it; and the informational turn. Personally, I have privileged the more 'analytic' interpretation when presenting PI metatheoretically, hoping to capture in this way the minimal common ground shared by many different philosophers working in this new area. However, I have opted for the 'metaphysical' interpretation when doing PI the way I understand it, that is, as a constructionist enterprise.[15] Both approaches are normative and perfectly compatible. Indeed, they seem to me to complement each other. Both will play a role in the following chapters. Like the helpers in Plato's *Republic*, the philosopher-sentinels enforce a necessary semantic policing, but they are not sufficient. They need to be joined by the philosopher-rulers, that is, by semantic policy-makers in charge of the present and future realities that are under construction. Horatio and Marcellus need to be joined by Hamlet, to use the previous image.

1.8 PI as *philosophia prima*

As I remarked above, philosophers have begun to address the new intellectual challenges arising from the world of information and the information society. PI attempts to expand the frontier of philosophical research, not by putting together pre-existing topics, and thus reordering the philosophical scenario, but by enclosing new areas of philosophical inquiry—which have been struggling to be recognized and have not yet found room in the traditional philosophical syllabus—and by providing innovative methodologies to address traditional problems from new perspectives. Is the time ripe for the establishment of PI as a mature field? We have seen that the answer might be affirmative because our culture and society, the history of philosophy and the dynamic forces regulating the development of the philosophical system have been moving towards it. But then, what kind of PI can be expected to develop? An answer to this question presupposes a much clearer view of PI's position in the history of thought, a view probably obtainable only a *posteriori*. Here, it might be sketched by way of guesswork.

Samuel Beckett once said that he began to write in French in order to 'impoverish myself still further' ('m'appauvrir encore d'avantage'). This is exactly the way in which philosophy grows, by impoverishing itself. It is only an apparent paradox: the more complex the world and its scientific descriptions turn out to be, the more essential the

---

[15] On philosophy as conceptual constructionism see Deleuze and Guattari (1994).

level of the philosophical discourse understood as *philosophia prima* must become, ridding itself of unwarranted assumptions and misguided investigations that do not properly belong to the normative activity of conceptual modelling. The strength of the dialectic of reflection, and hence the crucial importance of one's historical awareness of it, lies in this transcendental regress in search of increasingly abstract and more streamlined conditions of possibility of the available narratives, in view not only of their explanation, but also of their modification and innovation. How has the regress developed? The scientific revolution made seventeenth-century philosophers redirect their attention from the nature of the knowable object to the epistemic relation between it and the knowing subject, and hence from metaphysics to epistemology. The subsequent growth of the information society and the appearance of the info-sphere, as the environment in which millions of people spend their time nowadays, have led contemporary philosophy to privilege critical reflection first on the domain represented by the memory and languages of organized knowledge, the instruments whereby the infosphere is managed—thus moving from epistemology to philosophy of language and logic (Dummett (1993a))—and then on the nature of its very fabric and essence, information itself. Information has thus arisen as a concept as fundamental and important as Being, knowledge, life, intelligence, meaning, or good and evil—all pivotal concepts with which it is interdependent—and so equally worthy of autonomous investigation. It is also a more impoverished concept, in terms of which the others can be expressed and interrelated, when not defined. This is why PI may be introduced as a *philosophia prima*, both in the Aristotelian sense of the primacy of its object, information, which PI claims to be a fundamental component in any environment, and in the Cartesian–Kantian sense of the primacy of its methodology and problems, since PI aspires to provide a most valuable, comprehensive approach to philosophical investigations.

CONCLUSION

We have now seen what PI is and how it evolved. Understood as a foundational philosophy of information-design and conceptual engineering, PI can explain and guide the purposeful construction of our intellectual environment, and provide the systematic treatment of the conceptual foundations of contemporary society. It enables humanity to make sense of the world and construct it responsibly, a new stage in the semanticization of Being. PI promises to be one of the most exciting and fruitful areas of philosophical research of our time. If what has been argued in this chapter is correct, its current development may be delayed but it is inevitable. It will affect the overall way in which we address new and old philosophical problems, bringing about a substantial innovation in philosophy. This will represent the *information turn* in philosophy. We also saw that PI addresses the question 'what is information?'. Yet this is just an indication of the direction in which research in PI moves. What are the new, and old, philosophical problems tackled by PI, more specifically? Answering this question is the task of the next chapter.

2

Open problems in the philosophy of information

Technology expands our ways of thinking about things, expands our ways of doing things. [. . .] knowing a lot about the world and how it works. That's a major place where computers come in. They can help us to think.

Herbert Simon, quoted in Spice (2000)

SUMMARY
Previously, in chapter one, the philosophy of information (PI) was presented as a new area of research, with its own field of investigation and methodology. Two approaches to PI were also outlined. The rest of this book will seek to combine them. The chapter ended with a request for a more specific investigation of the main open problems discussed in PI. That request is addressed in this chapter. Section 2.1 introduces their analysis. Section 2.2 discusses some methodological considerations about what counts as a good philosophical problem. The discussion centres on Hilbert's famous analysis of the central problems in mathematics. The rest of the chapter is devoted to the presentation of eighteen main problems. These are organized into five areas: problems in the analysis of the concept of *information*, in *semantics*, in the study of *intelligence*, in the relation between information and *nature*, and in the investigation of *values*. Each area is discussed in a specific section.

2.1 Introduction

Technology unveils, transforms, and controls the world, often designing and creating new realities in the process. It tends to prompt original ideas, to shape new concepts, and to cause unprecedented problems. It usually embeds, but also challenges, ethical values and perspectives. In short, technology can be a very powerful force for intellectual innovation, exercising a profound influence on the way in which we conceptualize, interpret, and transform the world and ourselves. Add to that the fact that the more ontologically powerful and pervasive a technology is, the more profound and lasting its intellectual influence is going to be. If we recall that technology has had an escalating importance in human affairs, at least since the invention of printing and the scientific revolution, it then becomes obvious why the conceptual interactions between philosophy and technology have constantly grown in scope and magnitude, at least since Galileo's use of the telescope.

The modern alliance between *sophia* and *techne* has reached a new level of synergy with the computer revolution. We saw in the previous chapter that the latter is not a rigid *post quem* but rather the threshold after which PI started to coalesce as a new way of doing philosophy. We also saw that a genuine new discipline in philosophy is easily identifiable, for it must be able to appropriate an explicit, clear, and precise interpretation of the classic 'ti esti' question, thus presenting itself as a specific 'philosophy of'. 'What is information?' achieves precisely this. However, as with any other field-questions (consider for example 'what is knowledge?'), 'what is information?' is like a sign-post, which only points in the direction in which research could develop, it does not yet provide a map of the problems with which it needs to engage. Now, a new discipline without specific problems to address is like a car in neutral: it might have enormous potentialities, but there is no progress without friction. As Hilbert put it (this and all the following quotations are from Hilbert (1900)):

As long as a branch of science offers an abundance of problems, so long is it alive; a lack of problems foreshadows extinction or the cessation of independent development. [. . .] It is by the solution of problems that the investigator tests the temper of his steel; he finds new methods and new outlooks, and gains a wider and freer horizon.

So the question that needs to be addressed is this: what are the principal problems in PI that deserve our attention? Or, to paraphrase Simon's words, quoted at the beginning of this chapter, how will ICT expand our philosophical ways of thinking?

Trying to review future problems for a newborn discipline invites trouble. Complete failure is one. Poor evidence, lack of insight, inadequate grasp of the philosophical situation, human fallibility, and many other unpredictable obstacles of all sorts, can make a specific analysis as useful as a corrupted file for an old-fashioned program. Another problem is partial failure. The basic idea might be good, the direction even correct, and yet, the choice of problems could still turn out to be embarrassingly wide of the mark, with egregious non-starters appointed to top positions and vital issues not even short-listed. And as if all this were not enough, partial failure may already be sufficient to undermine confidence in the whole programme of research, thus compromising its future development. After all, I argued in chapter one that philosophy is a conservative discipline, with controversial standards but the highest expectations, especially of newcomers. Added to this, there is the Planck effect (Harris 1998). Max Planck once remarked that:

An important scientific innovation rarely makes its way by gradually winning over and converting its opponents: it rarely happens that Saul becomes Paul. What does happen is that its opponents gradually die out, and that the growing generation is familiarized with the ideas from the beginning: another instance of the fact that the future lies with youth. (Plank (1950), p. 97)

If the Max Planck effect can be common in physics imagine in philosophy.

Given these risks, is the visionary exercise undertaken in this chapter really a game worth the candle? Arguably, it is. A reliable review of interesting problems needs to be neither definitive nor exhaustive. Following the Max Planck effect, it does not have to be addressed to one's colleagues as long as it can attract their graduate students. And it fulfils a necessary role in the development of the field, by reinforcing the identity of a scientific community (the Wittgenstein effect),[1] while boosting enthusiasm for the new approach. Obviously, all this does not mean that one should not tiptoe around in this minefield. Looking for some guidance is also another good idea. And since nobody has performed better than Hilbert in predicting what were going to be the key problems in a field, I suggest we first turn to him for a last piece of advice, before embarking on our enterprise.

2.2 David Hilbert's view

In 1900, Hilbert delivered his famous and influential lecture, in which he reviewed twenty-three open mathematical problems

drawn from various branches of mathematics, from the discussion of which an advancement of science may be expected. (Hilbert (1900))

He introduced his review by a series of methodological remarks. Many of them can be adapted to the analysis of philosophical problems.

Hilbert thought that mathematical research has a historical nature and that mathematical problems often have their initial roots in historical circumstances, in the 'ever-recurring interplay between thought and experience'. Philosophical problems are no exception. Like mathematical problems, they are not *contingent* but *timely*. In Bynum and Moor's felicitous metaphor (see chapter one), philosophy is indeed like a phoenix: it can flourish only by constantly re-engineering itself and hence its own questions. A philosophy that is not timely but timeless is likely to be a stagnant philosophy, unable to contribute to, keep track of, and interact with cultural evolution, and hence to grow.

Good problems are the driving force of any intellectual pursuit. Being able to do valuable research hugely depends on having good taste in choosing them. Now, for Hilbert, a good problem is a problem rich in consequences, clearly defined, easy to understand and difficult to solve, but still accessible. Again, it is worth learning the lesson, with a further qualification. We saw in chapter one that genuine philosophical problems should also be *intrinsically open*, that is, they should allow for genuine, reasonable, informed differences of opinion. Open problems call for explicit solutions,

---

which facilitate a critical approach and hence empower the interlocutor. In philosophy we *cannot* ask

that it shall be possible to establish the correctness of the solution by means of a finite number of steps based upon a finite number of hypotheses which are implied in the statement of the problem and which must always be exactly formulated

but we must insist on clarity, lucidity, explicit reasoning, and rigour:

Indeed the requirement of rigour, which has become proverbial in mathematics, corresponds to a universal philosophical necessity of our understanding; and, on the other hand, only by satisfying this requirement do the thought content and the suggestiveness of the problem attain their full effect. A new problem, especially when it comes from the world of outer experience, is like a young twig, which thrives and bears fruit only when it is grafted carefully and in accordance with strict horticultural rules upon the old stem.

The more explicit and rigorous a solution is, the more easily it is criticizable. Logic is only apparently brusque. Its advice is as blunt as that of a good friend. The real trap is the false friendliness of sloppy thinking and obscure oracles. Their alluring rhetoric undermines the very possibility of disagreement, lulling the readers' reason to sleep.

At this point, we should follow Hilbert's advice about the difficulties that philosophical problems may offer, and the means of surmounting them. First, if we do not succeed in solving a problem, the reason may consist in our failure to recognize its complexity. The accessibility of a problem is a function of its size. Philosophy, like cooking, is not a matter of attempting all at once, but of careful and gradual preparation. The best results are always a matter of thoughtful choice and precise dosing of the conceptual ingredients involved, of gradual, orderly, and timely preparation and exact mixture. The Cartesian method of breaking problems into smaller components remains one of the safest approaches. Second, it is important to remember that negative solutions, that is

showing the impossibility of the solution under the given hypotheses, or in the sense contemplated

are as satisfactory and useful as positive solutions. They help to clear the ground of pointless debates (see chapters six, nine, and fourteen).

So far Hilbert; a word now on the kind of problems that are addressed in the following review. To concentrate the reader's attention, I have resolved to leave out most metatheoretical problems. This is not because they are uninteresting, but because they are open problems *about* PI rather than *in* PI, and deserve a specific analysis of their own. Chapter one has dealt with 'what is PI?', and chapter three will deal with 'what is the methodology fostered by PI?'. The only exception is the eighteenth problem, which concerns the foundation of computer ethics.

I have also focused on philosophical problems that have an explicit and distinctive informational nature, or that can be informationally normalized without any conceptual loss, instead of problems that might benefit from a translation into an informational language. In general, we can still rely on informational concepts even if a complete understanding of some series of events is unavailable or unnecessary for providing an explanation (this point is well analysed in Barwise and Seligman (1997)). In philosophy, this means that virtually any question and answer of some substantial interest can be re-phrased in terms of informational and computational ideas. As I argued in chapter one, this metaphorical approach may be dangerous and in the end counterproductive.

For reasons of space, even the problems selected in this chapter are only briefly introduced and not represented with adequate depth, sophistication, and significance. These macroproblems are the hardest to tackle but also the ones that have the greatest influence on clusters of microproblems, to which they can be related as theorems to lemmas. I have listed some microproblems whenever they seemed interesting enough to deserve being mentioned explicitly but, especially in this case, the list is far from exhaustive. Some problems are new, others are developments of old problems, and in some cases they have already been addressed. I have avoided listing old problems that have already received their due philosophical attention. I have not tried to keep a uniform level of scope. Some problems are very general, others more specific. All of them have been chosen because they well indicate how vital and useful the new paradigm is, in a variety of philosophical areas.

I have organized the problems into five groups. The analysis of *information* and its dynamics is central to any research to be done in the field, so the review starts from there. After that, problems are listed under four headings: *semantics*, *intelligence*, *nature*, and *values*. This is not a taxonomy of families, let alone of classes. I see them more like four points of our compass. They can help us to get some orientation and make explicit connections. I would not mind reconsidering which problem belongs to which area or further problems that need to be addressed. After all, the innovative character of PI may force us to change more than a few details in our philosophical map. What I do hope is that the following map, limited as it is, will be better than no map at all. And now, to work.

2.3 Analysis

Let us start by taking the bull by the horns:

P1   THE ELEMENTARY PROBLEM: WHAT IS INFORMATION?
This is the hardest and most central problem in PI and this book could be read as a long answer to it. Information is still an elusive concept. This is a scandal not by itself, but because so much basic theoretical work relies on a clear analysis and explanation of information and of its cognate concepts.

Information can be viewed from three perspectives: information *as* reality (e.g. as patterns of physical signals, which are neither true nor false), also known as *environmental* information; information *about* reality (semantic information, alethically qualifiable); and information *for* reality (instructions, like genetic information, algorithms, orders, or recipes).

Many extensionalist approaches to the definition of information *as* reality or *about* reality provide different starting points for answering P1. The following list contains only some of the most philosophically interesting or influential. They are not to be taken as necessarily alternative, let alone incompatible. I shall discuss them more in detail in chapters four and five, but here is a quick overview:

1. the information theory approach (mathematical theory of codification and communication of data/signals, Shannon and Weaver (1949 rep. 1998) defines information in terms of probability space distribution;

2. the algorithmic approach (also known as Kolmogorov complexity, Li and Vitanyi (1997)) defines the information content of x as the size in bits of the smallest computer program for calculating x (Chaitin (2003));

3. the probabilistic approach (Bar-Hillel and Carnap (1953), Bar-Hillel (1964), Dretske (1981)) defines semantic information in terms of probability space and the inverse relation between information in p and probability of p;

4. the modal approach defines information in terms of modal space and in/consistency: the information conveyed by p is the set of possible worlds excluded by p;

5. the systemic approach (situation logic, Barwise and Perry (1983), Israel and Perry (1990a), Devlin (1991)) defines information in terms of states space and consistency: information tracks possible transitions in the states space of a system;

6. the inferential approach defines information in terms of inferences space: information depends on valid inference relative to a person's theory or epistemic state;

7. the semantic approach (defended in this book) defines information in terms of data space: semantic information is well-formed, meaningful, and truthful data.

Each extentionalist approach can be given an intentionalist reading, by interpreting the relevant space as a doxastic space, in which information is seen as a reduction in the degree of uncertainty or level of surprise in an informee, given the state of information of that informee.

Information theory in (1) approaches information as a physical phenomenon, syntactically. It is not interested in the usefulness, relevance, meaning, interpretation, or aboutness of data, but in the level of detail and frequency in the uninterpreted data (signals or messages). It provides a successful mathematical theory because its central problem is whether and how much data, not what information is conveyed. The algorithmic approach in (2) is equally quantitative and solidly based on probability theory. It interprets information and its quantities in terms of the computational resources needed to specify it. The remaining approaches address the question 'what is *semantic* information?'. They seek to give an account of information as semantic content, usually adopting a propositional orientation (they analyse examples like 'The beer is in the fridge'). Do information or algorithmic theories in (1) and (2) provide the necessary conditions for any theory of semantic information? Are all the remaining semantic approaches mutually compatible? Is there a logical hierarchy? Do any of the previous approaches provide a clarification of the notion of data as well? Most of the problems in PI acquire a different meaning depending on how we answer this cluster of questions. Indeed, positions might be more compatible than they initially appear owing to different interpretations of the concept(s) of information involved.

Once the concept of information is clarified, each of the previous approaches needs to address the following problem:

P2 THE INPUT/OUTPUT PROBLEM: WHAT ARE THE DYNAMICS OF INFORMATION?

The problem does not concern the nature of management processes (information seeking, data acquisition and mining, information harvesting and gathering, storage, retrieval, editing, formatting, aggregation, extrapolation, distribution, verification, quality control, evaluation, etc.) but, rather, information processes themselves, whatever goes on between the input and the output phase. Information theory, as the mathematical theory of data encoding and transmission, provides the necessary conditions for any physical communication of information, but is otherwise of only marginal help. The information flow—understood as the carriage and transmission of information by some data about a referent, made possible by regularities in a distributed system—has been at the centre of philosophical and logical studies for some time (at least since Barwise and Seligman (1997); see also van Benthem (2003)), but still needs to be fully explored. How is it possible for something to carry information about something else? The problem here is not yet represented by the 'aboutness' relation, which needs to be discussed in terms of meaning, reference, and truth (see P4 and P5 below). The problem here concerns the nature of data as vehicles of information. In this version, the problem plays a central role in semiotics, hermeneutics and situation logic. It is closely related to the problem of the naturalization of information. Various other logics, from classic first order calculus to epistemic and erotetic logic, provide useful tools with which to analyse the logic of information (the logic of 'S is informed that p'), but there is still much work to be done (van Benthem and van Rooy (2003); Allo (2005)). For example, epistemic logic (as the logic of 'S knows that p') relies on a doxastic analysis of knowledge ('S believes that p'), and an open question is whether epistemic logic might encompass information logic and the latter encompass doxastic logic. This problem will be addressed in chapter ten. Likewise, recent approaches to the foundation of mathematics as a science of patterns (Resnik (2000)) may turn out to provide enlightening insights into the dynamics of information, as well as benefiting from an approach in terms of information *design* (design is a useful middle-ground concept between *discovery* and *invention*). Information processing, in the general sense of information states transitions, includes at the moment effective computation (*computationalism*, Fodor (1975), Newell (1980), Pylyshyn (1984), Fodor (1987), Dietrich (1990), and Fodor (2008)), distributed processing (*connectionism*, Smolensky (1988), Churchland and Sejnowski (1992)), and dynamical-system processing (*dynamism*, van Gelder (1995), Port and van Gelder (1995), Eliasmith (1996)). The relations between the current paradigms remain to be clarified. Minsky (1990), for example, argues in favour of a combination of computationalism and connectionism in AI, as does Harnad (1990) in cognitive science. Equally in need of further analysis are the specific advantages and disadvantages of each, and the question as to whether they provide complete coverage of all possible *internalist* information processing methods. I shall return to this point when discussing problems in chapters six, seven, and thirteen.

The two previous problems are closely related to a third, more general problem:

P3 THE UTI CHALLENGE:
IS A GRAND UNIFIED THEORY OF INFORMATION POSSIBLE?
The reductionist approach holds that we can extract what is essential to understanding the concept of information and its dynamics from the wide variety of models, theories, and explanations proposed. The non-reductionist argues that we are probably facing a network of logically interdependent, but mutually irreducible, concepts. The plausibility of each approach needs to be investigated in detail. I personally side with Shannon and the non-reductionist (Copeland (2003), Floridi (2010)). The reader interested in a positive answer to the question may wish to read the essays collected in Hofkirchner (1998). Both approaches, as well as any other solution in between, are confronted by the difficulty of clarifying how the various kinds of information are related, and whether some concepts of information are more central or fundamental than others, and should therefore be privileged. Waving a Wittgensteinian suggestion of family resemblance means merely acknowledging the problem, not solving it.

2.4 Semantics

We have seen that many theories concentrate on the analysis of semantic information. Since much of contemporary philosophy is essentially philosophical semantics (a sort of theology without god, see chapter one), it is useful to carry on our review of problem areas by addressing now the cluster of issues arising in informational semantics. Their discussion is bound to be deeply influential in several areas of philosophical research. But first, a warning. It is hard to formulate problems clearly and in some detail in a completely theory-neutral way. So in what follows, I have relied on the semantic frame, namely the view that semantic information can be satisfactorily analysed in terms of well-formed, meaningful, and truthful data. This semantic approach, which will be fully defended in chapters four and five, is simple and powerful enough for the task at hand. If the problems selected are sufficiently robust, it is reasonable to expect that their general nature and significance are not relative to the theoretical vocabulary in which they are cast, but will be exportable across conceptual platforms.

In P1, we have already encountered the issue of the nature of data. Suppose data are intuitively described as uninterpreted differences (symbols or signals, more on this in chapter four). How do they become meaningful? This is the next problem.

P4 DGP or the data grounding problem:

How can data acquire their meaning?

Searle (1990) refers to a specific version of the data grounding problem as the problem of intrinsic meaning or 'intentionality'. Harnad (1990) defines it as the symbols grounding problem and unpacks it thus:

How can the semantic interpretation of a formal symbol system be made intrinsic to the system, rather than just parasitic on the meanings in our heads? How can the meanings of the meaningless symbol tokens, manipulated solely on the basis of their (arbitrary) shapes, be grounded in anything but other meaningless symbols? (Harnad (1990), p. 335)

Arguably, the frame problem (how a situated agent can represent, and interact with, a changing world satisfactorily) and its sub-problems are a consequence of the data grounding problem (Harnad (1993a)). We shall see (P8–P10) that the data grounding problem acquires a crucial importance in the Artificial vs. Natural Intelligence debate. In more metaphysical terms, this is the problem of the semanticization of Being, and it is further connected with the problem of whether information can be naturalized (P16). Can PI explain how the mind conceptualizes reality? (Mingers (1997)). I shall say nothing else here because chapters six and seven are devoted to a full review of the attempts that have been made to solve the problem and to a proposal for a new approach to it, respectively.

Once grounded, well-formed and meaningful data can acquire different truth-values, the problem is how:

P5 The problem of alethization:

How can meaningful data acquire their truth value?

P4 and P5 gain a new dimension when asked within epistemology and the philosophy of science, as we shall see in P13 and P14. They also interact substantially with the way in which we approach both a theory of truth and a theory of meaning, especially a truth-functional one. Are truth and meaning understandable on the basis of an informational approach, or is it information that needs to be analysed in terms of non-informational theories of meaning and truth? To call attention to this important set of issues it is worth formulating two more place-holder problems:

P6 Informational truth theory: Can information explain truth?

In this, as in the following question, we are not asking whether a specific theory could be couched, more or less metaphorically, in some informational vocabulary. This would be a pointless exercise. What is in question is not even the mere possibility of an informational approach. Rather, we are asking (a) whether an informational theory could explain truth more satisfactorily than other current approaches (Kirkham 1992), and (b) should (a) be answered in the negative, whether an informational approach could at least help to clarify the theoretical constraints to be satisfied by other approaches. Note that P6 is connected with the information circle (P12) and the possibility of an informational view of science (P14). I shall return to the problem of truth in chapter eight, where I shall propose a correctness theory of truth.

The next problem is:

P7 INFORMATIONAL SEMANTICS: CAN INFORMATION EXPLAIN MEANING?
Several informational approaches to semantics have been investigated in epistemology (Dretske (1981) and (1988)), situation semantics (Seligman and S. (1997)), discourse representation theory (Kamp (1984)), and dynamic semantics (Muskens (1997)). Is it possible to analyse meaning not truth-functionally, but as the potential to change the informational context? Can semantic phenomena be explained as aspects of the empirical world? Since P7 asks whether meaning can at least partly be grounded in an objective, mind- and language-independent notion of information (naturalization of intentionality), it is strictly connected with P16, the problem of the naturalization of information.

2.5 Intelligence

As McCarthy and Hayes (1969) have remarked:

A computer program capable of acting intelligently in the world must have a general representation of the world in terms of which its inputs are interpreted. Designing such a program requires commitments about what knowledge is and how it is obtained. Thus, some of the major traditional problems of philosophy arise in artificial intelligence. (p. 463)

Thus, information and its dynamics are central to the foundations of AI, to cognitive science, epistemology, and philosophy of science. Let us concentrate on the former two first.

AI and cognitive science study agents as informational systems that receive, store, retrieve, transform, generate and transmit information. This is the *information processing view*. Before the development of connectionist and dynamic-system models of information processing, it was also known as the *computational view*. The latter expression was acceptable when a Turing machine (Turing (1936)) and the machine involved in the Turing test (Turing (1950)) were inevitably the same. The equation *information processing view = computational view* has become misleading, however, because computation, when used as a technical term (effective computation), refers only to the specific class of algorithmic symbolic processes that can be performed by a Turing machine, that is recursive functions (Turing (1936), Minsky (1967), Floridi (1999b), Boolos et al. (2002)).

The information processing view of cognition, intelligence and mind provides the oldest and best-known cluster of significant problems in PI. Hobbes, as it is well known, provides an early presentation of it. Some of their formulations, however, have long been regarded as uninteresting. Turing (1950) considered 'can machines think?' a meaningless way of posing the otherwise interesting problem of the functional differences between AI and NI (natural intelligence). Searle (1990) has equally dismissed 'is the brain a digital computer?' as ill-defined. The same holds true of the unqualified question 'are naturally intelligent systems information processing systems?' Such questions are vacuous. Informational concepts are so powerful that, given the right *level of abstraction* (henceforth also LoA, see chapter three), anything can be presented as an information system, from a building to a volcano, from a forest to a dinner, from a brain to a company. Likewise, any process can be simulated informationally: heating, flying, and knitting. So pancomputationalists have the hard task of providing credible answers to the following two questions:

1. how can one avoid blurring all differences among systems, thus transforming pancomputationalism into a night in which all cows are black, to paraphrase Hegel? And
2. what would it mean for the system under investigation not to be an informational system (or a compultational system, if computation is used to mean information processing, as in Chalmers (1996))?

Pancomputationalism does not seem vulnerable to a refutation (to put it in Popperian terms), in the form of a possible token counterexample in a world nomically identical to the one to which pancomputationalism is applied. Chalmers, for example, seems to believe (see Chalmers (online)) that pancomputationalism is empirically falsifiable, but what he offers is not

a. a specification of what would count as an instance of x that would show how x is not to be qualified computationally (or information-theoretically, in the language of this chapter) given the nomic characterization N of the universe,

but rather

b. just a re-wording of the idea that pancomputationalism might be false, i.e. a negation of the nomic characterization N of the universe in question:

To be sure, there are some ways that empirical science might prove it to be false: if it turns out that the fundamental laws of physics are noncomputable and if this noncomputability reflects itself in cognitive functioning, for instance, or if it turns out that our cognitive capacities depend essentially on infinite precision in certain analog quantities, or indeed if it turns out that cognition is mediated by some non-physical substance whose workings are not computable.

To put it simply, we would like to be told something along the lines that a white raven would falsify the statement that all ravens are black, but instead we are told that the absence of blackness or of ravens altogether would, which it does not.

To return to original problem, a good way of posing it is not: 'is "x is y" adequate?', but rather 'if "x is y" at LoA z, is z adequate?'. In what follows, I have distinguished between problems concerning cognition and problems concerning intelligence.

A central problem in cognitive science is:

P8 DESCARTES'S PROBLEM: CAN (FORMS OF) COGNITION C BE FULLY AND
SATISFACTORILY ANALYSED IN TERMS OF (FORMS OF) INFORMATION PROCESSING IP AT
SOME LEVEL OF ABSTRACTION LoA? HOW IS THE TRIAD <C, IP, LoA> TO BE
INTERPRETED?

The stress is usually on the types of C and IP involved and their mutual relations, but
the LoA adopted and its degree of adequacy with respect to the explanatory goal to
be fulfilled play a crucial role (Marr (1982), Dennett (1994), McClamrock (1991)).
A specific LoA is adequate in terms of constraints and requirements. We need to ask
first whether the analysis respects the constraints embedded in the selected observables
we wish to model (for example: C is a dynamic process, but we have developed a static
model). We then need to make sure that the analysis satisfies the requirements
orienting the modelling process. Requirements can be of four general types:

- *explanation* of x, from the merely metaphorical to the fully scientific level;
- *control*, understood in terms of monitoring, simulating, or managing x's behaviour;
- *modification*, that is, purposeful change of x's behaviour itself, not of its model; and
- *construction*, as implementation or reproduction of x itself.

We usually assume that LoAs come in a scale of granularity or detail, from higher
(coarser-grained) to lower (finer-grained) levels, but we shall see in chapter three that
this is *not* necessarily true, nor is it the most interesting case, especially if we concentrate
on the requirements that LoA satisfy. Consider a building. One LoA may describe it in
terms of architectural design, say as a Victorian house, another may describe it in terms
of property market valuation, and a third may describe it as Mary's house. A given LoA
might be sufficient to provide an explanatory model of x without providing the means
to implement x and vice versa.

Answers to P8 determine our orientation towards other specific questions: is
information processing sufficient for cognition? If it is, what is the precise relation
between information processing and cognition? What is the relation between different
sorts and theories of information processing such as computationalism, connectionism
and dynamicism for the interpretation of <C, IP, LoA>? What are the sufficient
conditions under which a physical system implements some given information processing? For example, externalist or anti-representationist positions stress the importance
of 'environmental', 'situated', or 'embodied' cognition (Gibson (1979), Varela et al.
(1991), Clancey (1997)). Note that asking whether cognition is computable is not yet
asking whether cognition is computation: x might be computable without necessarily
being carried out computationally (Rapaport (1998)).

The next two open problems concern intelligence in general, rather than cognition
in particular, and are central in AI:

P9 THE RE-ENGINEERING PROBLEM (DENNETT (1994)): CAN
(FORMS OF) NATURAL INTELLIGENCE NI BE FULLY AND SATISFACTORILY ANALYSED
IN TERMS OF (FORMS OF) INFORMATION PROCESSING IP AT SOME LEVEL OF
ABSTRACTION LoA? HOW IS THE TRIAD <NI, IP, LoA> TO BE INTERPRETED?

P9 asks what kind or form of intelligence is being analysed, what notion(s) of information is (are) at work here, which model of information dynamics correctly describes natural intelligence, what the level of abstraction adopted is and whether it is adequate. For example, one could try an impoverished Turing test, in which situated intelligent behaviour, rather than purely dialogical interaction, is being analysed by observing two agents, one natural and the other artificial, interacting with a problem-environment modifiable by the observer (Harnad (2000)). Imagine a robot and a mouse searching for food in a maze: would the observer placed in a different room be able to discriminate between the natural and the artificial agent? All this is not yet asking:

P10 TURING'S PROBLEM: CAN (FORMS OF) NATURAL
INTELLIGENCE BE FULLY AND SATISFACTORILY IMPLEMENTED NON-BIOLOGICALLY?

The problem leaves open the possibility that NI might be a IP *sui generis* (Searle (1980)) or just so complex as to elude forever any engineering attempt to duplicate it (Lucas (1961), Penrose (1989), Penrose (1990), Dreyfus (1992), Penrose (1994) and Lucas (1996)). Suppose, on the other hand, that NI is not, or only incompletely, implementable non-biologically, what is missing? Consciousness? Creativity? Freedom? Embodiment? All, or perhaps some of these factors, and even more? Alternatively, is it just a matter of the size, detail and complexity of the problem? Even if NI is not implementable non-biologically, is NI behavioural output still (at least partly) reproducible in terms of delivered effects by some implementable forms of information processing? In chapter thirteen, I will return to this general problem in order to provide a way of discriminating between different types of agents.

The previous questions lead to a reformulation of 'the father of all problems' (its paternity usually being attributed to Descartes) in the study of intelligence and the philosophy of mind:

P11 THE MIB (MIND–INFORMATION–BODY) PROBLEM:
CAN AN INFORMATIONAL APPROACH SOLVE THE MIND–BODY PROBLEM?

As usual, the problem is not about conceptual vocabulary or the mere possibility of an informational approach. Rather, we are asking whether an informational theory can help us to solve the difficulties faced by monist and dualist approaches. In this context, one could ask whether personal identity, for example, might be properly understood not in physical or mental terms, but in terms of information space.

We can now move on to a different set of issues, concerning intelligence as the source of knowledge in epistemology and philosophy of science. The next cluster of problems requires a brief premise.

One of the major dissimilarities between current generation artificial intelligence systems (AIs) and human natural intelligences (NIs) is that AIs can identify and process only data (uninterpreted patterns of differences and invariances), whereas NIs can identify and process mainly informational contents (in the weak sense of well-formed patterns of meaningful data). In saying that AIs are data systems whereas NIs are information systems, one should carefully avoid denying five things:

1. young NIs, for example the young Augustine, seem to go through a formative process in which, at some stage, they experience only data, not information. Infants are information virgins;
2. adult NIs, for example the adult John Searle or a medieval copyist, could behave or be used, as if they were perceiving only data, not information. One could behave like a child—or an Intel processor—if one is placed in a Chinese Room or, more realistically, copying a Greek manuscript without knowing even the alphabet of the language, but just the physical shape of the letters;
3. cognitively, psychologically, or mentally impaired NIs, including the old Nietzsche, might also act like children, and fail to experience information (like 'this is a horse') when exposed to data;
4. there is certainly a neurochemical level at which NIs process data, not yet information;
5. NIs' semantic constraints might be comparable to, or even causally connected with, AIs' syntactic constraints, at some adequate LoA.

Fully and normally developed NIs seem entrapped in a semantic stance. Strictly speaking, we do not consciously cognize pure meaningless data. What goes under the name of 'raw data' are data that might lack a specific and relevant interpretation, not any interpretation. This is true even for John Searle and the medieval copyist: one sees Chinese characters, the other Greek letters, although they do not know that this is what the characters are. The genuine perception of completely uninterpreted data might be possible under very special circumstances, but it is not the norm, and cannot be part of a continuously sustainable, conscious experience, at least because we never perceive data in isolation, but always in a semantic context that attributes some meaning to them, even if it does not have to be the right meaning, as John Searle and the medieval copyist show. On the one hand, when human NIs seem to perceive data, this is only because they are used to dealing with such rich semantic contents that they mistake dramatically impoverished, or variously interpretable, information for something completely devoid of any semantic content. On the other hand, computers are often and rightly described as purely syntactic machines, yet 'purely syntactic' is a comparative abstraction, like 'virtually fat free'. It means that the level of semantics is negligible, not that it is completely non-existent. Computers are capable of (responding to) elementary discrimination: the detection of an identity as an identity and of a difference not in terms of perception of the peculiar and rich features of the entities involved, but as a simple registration of an invariant lack of identity constituting the *relata* as *relata*. And this is a proto-semantic act, after all. Unfortunately, this level of detection and discrimination is also far too poor to generate anything resembling semantics. It suffices only to guarantee an efficient manipulation of discrimination-friendly data. It is also the only vaguely proto-semantic act that present and foreseeable computers are able to perform as 'cognitive systems', the rest being extrinsic semantics, only simulated through syntax, pre-recorded memory, layers of interfaces and HCI (human–computer interaction). Thus, at the moment, data as interpretable but unin-terpreted, detectable and discriminable differences represent the semantic upper-limit of AIs but the semantic lower-limit of NIs, which normally deal with information. Ingenious layers of interfaces exploit this threshold and make possible HCI. As far as we know, we are the only semantic engines in the universe (Floridi (2009d)). The specification indicates that current AI achievements are constrained by syntactical resources, whereas NI achievements are constrained by semantic ones. To understand the informational/semantic framework as a constraint, one only needs to consider any non-naïve epistemology. Kant's dichotomy between *noumena* and *phenomena*, for example, could be interpreted as a dichotomy between data and information, with the *Umwelt* of experience as the threshold where the flow of uninterpreted data regularly and continuously collapses into information flow. Note that conceding some minimal proto-semantic capacity to a computer works in favour of an exten-sionalist conception of information as being 'in the world', rather than just in the mind of the informee. I shall return to this issue when discussing P16.

We are now ready to appreciate a new series of problems.

P12 THE INFORMATIONAL CIRCLE: HOW CAN INFORMATION

BE ASSESSED? IF INFORMATION CANNOT BE TRANSCENDED BUT CAN ONLY BE CHECKED

AGAINST FURTHER INFORMATION—IF IT IS INFORMATION ALL THE WAY UP AND ALL

THE WAY DOWN—WHAT DOES THIS TELL US ABOUT OUR KNOWLEDGE OF THE WORLD?
The informational circle is reminiscent of the hermeneutical circle. It underpins the modern debate on the foundation of epistemology and the acceptability of some form of realism in the philosophy of science, according to which our information about the world captures something of the way the world is (Floridi (1996)). It is closely related both to P6 and to the next two problems.

P13 THE CONTINUUM HYPOTHESIS:

COULD EPISTEMOLOGY BE BASED ON A THEORY OF INFORMATION?
In the following chapter, I will defend a 'continuum hypothesis': knowledge encapsu-lates truth because it encapsulates semantic information (see P5). Compared to informa-tion, knowledge is a rare phenomenon indeed. Even in a world without Gettier-like or sceptical tricks, we must confess to being merely informed about most of what we think we know, if knowing demands being able to provide a convincing account of what one is informed about. Before answering P13, however, one should also consider that some theories of information, e.g. internalist or intentionalist approaches, interpret informa-tion as depending upon knowledge, not vice versa. If knowledge does presuppose

information, could this help to solve Gettier-type problems? In chapter nine, I will argue that it does, by showing that the Gettier problem cannot be solved. Can there be information states without epistemic states (see P15, P16)? In chapter ten, I will support a positive answer. What is knowledge from an information-based approach? In chapter twelve, I will try to explain it. Is it possible that (1) *S* has the true belief that *p* and yet (2) *S* is not informed that *p*? Barwise and Seligman (1997) seem to hold it is, I shall argue that it is not. These questions have been addressed by information-theoretic epistemologists for some time now, but they still need to be fully investigated.

When it comes to scientific knowledge, it seems that the value of an informational turn can be stressed by investigating the following problem:

P14 THE SEMANTIC VIEW OF SCIENCE:

IS SCIENCE REDUCIBLE TO INFORMATION MODELLING?

In some contexts (probability or modal states, and inferential spaces), we adopt a conditional, laboratory view. We analyse what happens in '*a*'s being (of type, or in state) *F* is correlated to *b* being (of type, or in state) *G*, thus carrying for the observer of *a* the information that *b* is *G*' (Dretske (1981), Barwise and Seligman (1997)) by assuming that *F(a)* and *G(b)*. In other words, we assume a given model. The question asked here is: how do we build the original model? Many approaches seem to be ontologically over-committed. Instead of assuming a world of empirical affordances and constraints to be designed, they assume a world already well-modelled, ready to be discovered. The semantic approach to scientific theories (Suppes (1960) and Suppes (1962), Van Fraassen (1980), Giere (1988), Suppe (1989)), on the other hand, argues that

scientific reasoning is to a large extent model-based reasoning. It is models almost all the way up and models almost all the way down. (Giere (1999), p. 56).

Theories do not make contact with phenomena directly, but rather higher models are brought into contact with other, lower models (see chapter nine). These are themselves theoretical conceptualizations of empirical systems, which constitute an object being modelled as an object of scientific research. Giere (1988) takes most scientific models of interest to be non-linguistic abstract objects. Models, however, are the medium, not the message. Is information the (possibly non-linguistic) content of these models? How are informational models (semantically, cognitively, and instrumentally) related to the conceptualizations that constitute their empirical references? What is their semiotic status, e.g. structurally homomorphic or isomorphic representations or data-driven and data-constrained informational constructs? What levels of abstraction are involved? Is science a social (multi-agents), information-designing activity? Is it possible to import, in (the philosophy of) science, modelling methodologies devised in information system theory? Can an informational view help to bridge the gap between science and cognition? Answers to these questions are closely connected with the discussion of the problem of an informational theory of truth (P6) and of meaning (P7). I shall return to these issues in chapters twelve and fifteen, respectively.

The possibility of a more or less informationally constructionist epistemology and philosophy of science leads to our next cluster of problems, concerning the relation between information and the natural world.

2.6 Nature

If the world were a completely chaotic, unpredictable affair, there would be no information to process. Still, the place of information in the natural world of biological and physical systems is far from clear. (Barwise and Seligman (1997), p. xi)

The lack of clarity stressed by Barwise and Seligman prompts three families of problems.

P15 WIENER'S PROBLEM: WHAT IS THE ONTOLOGICAL STATUS OF INFORMATION? Most people agree that there is no information without (data) representation. This principle is often interpreted materialistically, as advocating the impossibility of physically disembodied information, through the equation 'representation = physical implementation'. However, we shall see in chapter four (section seven) that the issue is metaphysically more complicated than that. Here, let me stress that the problem is whether the informational might be an independent ontological category, different from the physical/material and the mental, assuming one could draw this Cartesian distinction. Wiener, for example, thought that

Information is information, not matter or energy. No materialism which does not admit this can survive at the present day. (Wiener (1948), p. 132)

If the informational is *not* an independent ontological category, to which category is it reducible? If it is an independent ontological category, how is it related to the physical/material and to the mental? I have addressed these issues in chapters fourteen and fifteen. Whatever the answers to these questions are, they determine the orientation a theory takes with respect to the following problem:

P16 THE PROBLEM OF LOCALIZATION: CAN INFORMATION BE NATURALIZED? The problem is connected with P4, namely the semanticization of data. It seems hard to deny that information is a natural phenomenon, so this is probably not what one should be asking here. Even elementary forms of life, such as sunflowers, survive only because they are capable of some chemical data processing at some LoA. The problem here is whether there is information in the world independently of forms of life capable to extract it and, if so, what kind of information is in question. An informational version of the teleological argument for the existence of God, for example, argues both that information is a natural phenomenon and that the occurrence of environmental information requires an intelligent source. If the world is sufficiently information-rich, perhaps an agent may interact successfully with it by using 'environmental information' directly, without being forced to go through a representation stage in which the world is first analysed informationally. 'Environmental information' still presupposes (or perhaps is identical with) some physical support, but it does not require any higher-level cognitive representation or computational processing to be immediately usable. This is argued, for example, by researchers in AI working on animats (artificial animals, either computer simulated or robotic). Animats are simple reactive agents, stimulus-driven. They are capable of elementary, 'intelligent' behaviour, despite the fact that their design excludes in principle the possibility of internal representations of the environment and any effective computation (see Mandik (2002) for an overview, the case for non-representational intelligence is famously made by Brooks (1991)). So, are cognitive processes continuous with processes in the environment? Is semantic content (at least partly) external (Putnam)? Does 'natural' or 'environmental' information pivot on natural signs (Peirce) or nomic regularities? Consider the typical example provided by the concentric rings visible in the wood of a cut tree trunk, which may be used to estimate the age of the plant. The externalist/extensionalist, who favours a positive answer to P16 (e.g. Dretske, Barwise), is faced by the difficulty of explaining what kind of information it is and how much of it saturates the world, what kind of access to, or interaction with 'information in the world' an informational agent can enjoy, and how information dynamics is possible. The internalist/intentionalist (e.g. Fodor, Searle), who privileges a negative answer to P16, needs to explain in what specific sense information depends on intelligence and whether this leads to an anti-realist view.

The location of information is related to the question whether there can be information without an informee, or whether information, in at least some crucial sense of the word, is essentially parasitic on the semantics in the mind of the informee, and the most it can achieve, in terms of ontological independence, is systematic interpretability. Before the discovery of the Rosetta Stone, was it legitimate to regard Egyptian hieroglyphics as information, even if their semantics was beyond the comprehension of any interpreter? We shall return to this question in chapter four (see 4.8).

I mentioned above that admitting that computers perform some minimal level of proto-semantic activity works in favour of a 'realist' position about 'information in the world'. Before moving to the next problem, it remains to be clarified whether the previous two ways of locating information might not be restrictive. Could information be neither here (intelligence) nor there (nature) but on the threshold, as it were, as a special relation or interface between the world and its inhabitants (constructionism)? Or could it even be elsewhere, in a third world, intellectually accessible by intelligent beings but not ontologically dependent on them (Platonism)?

P17 THE IT FROM BIT HYPOTHESIS (WHEELER (1990)):

CAN NATURE BE INFORMATIONALIZED?

The neologism 'informationalized' is ugly but useful to point out that this is the converse of the previous problem. Here too, it is important to clarify what the problem is not. We are not asking whether the metaphorical interpretation of the universe as a computer is more useful than misleading. We are not even asking whether an informational description of the universe, as we know it, is possible, at least partly and piecemeal. This is a challenging task, but formal ontologies already provide a promising answer (Smith (2004)). Rather, we are asking whether the universe in itself could essentially be made of information, with natural processes, including causation, as special cases of information dynamics (e.g. information flow and algorithmic, distributed computation and forms of emergent computation). Depending on how one approaches the concept of information, it might be necessary to refine the problem in terms of digital data or other informational notions. Chapters fourteen and fifteen tackle these questions.

Answers to P17 deeply affect our understanding of the distinction between virtual and material reality, of the meaning of artificial life in the ALife sense (Bedau (2004)), and of the relation between the philosophy of information and the foundations of physics. If the universe is made of information, is quantum physics a theory of physical information? Moreover, does this explain some of its paradoxes? If nature can be informationalized, does this help to explain how life emerges from matter, and hence how intelligence emerges from life? Of course, these questions are closely related to the questions listed in 2.5:

can we build a gradualist bridge from simple amoeba-like automata to highly purposive intentional systems, with identifiable goals, beliefs, etc.? (Dennett (1998), p. 262)

2.7 Values

It has long been clear to me that the modern ultra-rapid computing machine was in principle an ideal central nervous system to an apparatus for automatic control; and that its input and output need not be in the form of numbers or diagrams but might very well be, respectively, the readings of artificial sense organs, such as photoelectric cells or thermometers, and the performance of motors or solenoids [. . .] we are already in a position to construct artificial machines of almost any degree of elaborateness of performance. Long before Nagasaki and the public awareness of the atomic bomb, it had occurred to me that we were here in the presence of another social potentiality of unheard-of importance for good and for evil. (Wiener (1948), pp. 27–28)

The impact of ICT on contemporary society has caused new and largely unanticipated ethical problems (Floridi (2009e)). In order to fill this policy and conceptual vacuum (Moor (1985)), Computer Ethics (CE) carries out an extended and intensive study of real-world issues, usually in terms of reasoning by analogy. At least since the 1970s (see Bynum (2000) for earlier works in CE), CE's focus has moved from problem analysis— primarily aimed at sensitizing public opinion, professionals and politicians—to tactical solutions resulting, for example, in the evolution of professional codes of conduct, technical standards, usage regulations, and new legislation. The constant risk of this bottom-up procedure has remained the spreading of *ad hoc* or casuistic approaches to ethical problems. Prompted partly by this difficulty, and partly by a natural process of self-conscious maturation as an independent discipline, CE has further combined tactical solutions with more strategic and global analyses. The 'uniqueness debate' on the foundation of CE is an essential part of this top–down development (Floridi and Sanders (2002), Tavani (2002)). It is characterized by a metatheoretical reflection on the nature and justification of CE, and on whether the moral issues confronting CE are unique, and hence whether CE should be developed as an independent field of research with a specific area of application and an autonomous, theoretical foundation. The problem here is:

P18 THE UNIQUENESS DEBATE:

DOES COMPUTER ETHICS HAVE A PHILOSOPHICAL FOUNDATION?

Once again, the question is intentionally general. Answering it means addressing the following questions: why does ICT raise moral issues? Can CE amount to a coherent and cohesive discipline, rather than a more or less heterogeneous and random collection of ICT-related ethical problems, applied analyses and practical solutions? If so, what is its conceptual rationale? How does it compare with other (applied) ethical theories? Are CE issues unique (in the sense of requiring their own theoretical investigations, not entirely derivative from standard ethics)? Alternatively, are they simply moral issues that happen to involve ICT? What kind of ethics is CE? What justifies a certain methodology in CE, e.g. reasoning by analogy and case-based analysis? What is CE's rationale? What is the contribution of CE to the ethical discourse? In the following chapters I shall not address or even come close to any of these issues. They really require a different book, as I mentioned in the Preface.

CONCLUSION

We have now come to the end of this review. I hope the reader will be thrilled rather than depressed by the amount of work that lies ahead. I must confess I find it difficult to provide an elegant way of closing this chapter. Since it analyses questions but provides no answers yet, it should really end with 'The Beginning' rather than 'The End'. However, as I relied on Hilbert to introduce the topic, I may as well quote him again to conclude it:

To such a review of problems the present day, lying at the meeting of the centuries, seems to me well adapted. For the close of a great epoch not only invites us to look back into the past but also directs our thoughts to the unknown future.

Hilbert was right. In the second half of this book, I will address some of the problems reviewed in this chapter. Before that, however, we still need to consider one more, final metatheoretical issue, namely PI's method of levels of abstraction. This is the task of the next chapter.

3

The method of levels of abstraction

But we can have no conception of wine except what may enter into a belief, either—1. That this, that, or the other, is wine; or, 2. That wine possesses certain properties. Such beliefs are nothing but self-notifications that we should, upon occasion, act in regard to such things as we believe to be wine according to the qualities which we believe wine to possess. [...] and we can consequently mean nothing by wine but what has certain effects, direct or indirect, upon our senses; and to talk of something as having all the sensible characters of wine, yet being in reality blood, is senseless jargon.

Charles Sanders Peirce. *How to Make Our Ideas Clear* (Peirce (1878))

SUMMARY

Previously, in chapters one and two, I introduced the nature of PI and some of its main problems. In this chapter, the last of the metatheoretical ones, I present the main method of PI, called *the method of levels of abstraction*. After a brief introduction, section 3.2 provides a definition of the basic concepts fundamental to the method. Although the definitions require some rigour, all the main concepts are introduced without assuming any previous knowledge. The definitions are illustrated by several intuitive examples, which are designed to familiarize the reader with the method. Section 3.3 illustrates the philosophical fruitfulness of the method by using Kant's classic discussion of the 'antinomies of pure reason' as an example. Section 3.4 clarifies how the method may be applied to a variety of philosophical issues, including the Turing test, an issue that will be discussed again in chapter thirteen. Section 3.5 specifies and supports the method by distinguishing it from three other forms of 'levelism': (i) levels of organization; (ii) levels of explanation, and (iii) conceptual schemes. In that context, the problems of relativism and anti-realism are briefly addressed. The conclusion stresses the value and the limits of the method.

3.1 Introduction

Reality can be studied at different levels, so forms of 'levelism' have often been advocated in the past.[1] In the 1970s, levelism nicely dovetailed with the computational turn and became a standard approach both in science and in philosophy. Simon (1969) (see now Simon (1996)), Mesarovic et al. (1970), Dennett (1971), and Wimsatt (1976) were among the earliest advocates. The trend reached its acme at the beginning of the 1980s, with the work of Marr (1982) and Newell (1982). Since then, levelism has enjoyed great popularity[2] and even textbook status (Foster (1992)). However, after decades of useful service, levelism seems to have come under increasing criticism. Consider the following varieties of levelism currently available in the philosophical literature:

1. epistemological, e.g. levels of observation or interpretation of a system;
2. ontological, e.g. levels (or rather *layers*) of organization, complexity, or causal interaction etc. of a system;[3]
3. methodological, e.g. levels of interdependence or reducibility among theories about a system; and
4. an amalgamation of (1)–(3), e.g. as in Oppenheim and Putnam (1958).

The current debate on multirealizability in the philosophy of AI and cognitive science has made (3) controversial, as Block (1997) has shown; while Heil (2003) and Schaffer (2003) have seriously and convincingly questioned the plausibility of (2). Since criticisms of (2) and (3) end up undermining (4), rumours are that levelism should probably be decommissioned.

I agree with Heil and Schaffer that *ontological levelism* is probably untenable. However, I shall argue that a version of *epistemological levelism* should be retained, as a fundamental and indispensable method of conceptual engineering (philosophical analysis and construction) in PI, albeit in a suitably refined version. Fleshing out and defending epistemological levelism is the main task of this chapter. This is achieved in two stages. First, I shall clarify the nature and applicability of what I shall refer to as *the method of (levels of) abstraction*. Second, I shall distinguish this method from other level-based approaches, which may not, and indeed need not, be rescued.

Before closing this section, let me add a final word of warning. Although levelism has been common currency in philosophy and in science since antiquity, only more recently has the concept of *simulation* been used in computer science to relate levels of abstraction to satisfy the requirement that systems constructed in levels (in order to

---

[1] See for example Brown (1916). Of course the theory of ontological levels and the 'chain of being' goes as far back as Plotin and forms the basis of at least one version of the ontological argument.

[2] The list includes Arbib (1989), Bechtel and Richardson (1993), Egyed and Medvidovic (2000), Gell-Mann (1994), Kelso (1995), Pylyshyn (1984), and Salthe (1985).

[3] Poli (2001) provides a reconstruction of ontological levelism; more recently, Craver (2004) has analysed ontological levelism, especially in biology and cognitive science, see also Craver (2007).

tame their complexity) function correctly (see for example Hoare and He (1998) and Roever et al. (1998)). The definition of *Gradient of Abstraction* (GoA, see section 3.2.6) has been inspired by this approach. Indeed, I take as a definition the property established by simulations, namely the conformity of behaviour between levels of abstraction (more on this in section 3.4.7).

3.2 Some definitions and preliminary examples

This section introduces six key concepts necessary to explain the method of abstraction, namely, 'typed variable', 'observable', 'level of abstraction', 'behaviour', 'moderated LoA', and 'gradient of abstraction'. Some simple examples will illustrate their use.

3.2.1. Typed variable

As is well known, a variable is a symbol that acts as a place-holder for an unknown or changeable referent. In this chapter, a 'typed variable' is a variable qualified to hold only a declared kind of data.

Definition: A *typed variable* is a uniquely named conceptual entity (the *variable*) and a set, called its *type*, consisting of all the values that the entity may take. Two typed variables are regarded as *equal* if and only if their variables have the same name and their types are equal as sets. A variable that cannot be assigned well-defined values is said to constitute an *ill-typed variable* (see the example in section 3.2.3).

When required, I shall write x:X to mean that x is a variable of type X. Positing a typed variable means taking an important decision about how its component variable is to be conceived. This point may be better appreciated after the next definition.

3.2.2 Observable

The notion of an 'observable' is common in science, where it occurs whenever a (theoretical) model is constructed. The way in which the features of the model correspond to the system being modelled is usually left implicit in the process of modelling. However, in this context it is important to make that correspondence explicit. I shall follow the standard practice of using the word 'system' to refer to the object of study. This may indeed be what would normally be described as a system in science or engineering, but it may also be a domain of discourse, of analysis, or of conceptual speculation, that is, a purely semantic system, for example the logico-mathematical system of *Principia Mathematica* or the moral system of a culture.

Definition: An *observable* is an interpreted typed variable, that is, a typed variable together with a statement of what feature of the system under consideration it represents. Two observables are regarded as *equal* if and only if their typed variables are equal, they model the same feature and, in that context, one takes a given value if and only if the other does.

Being an abstraction, an observable is not necessarily meant to result from quantitative measurement or even empirical perception. The 'feature of the system under consideration' might be a physical magnitude, but we shall see that it might also be an artefact of a conceptual model, constructed entirely for the purpose of analysis. For example, the Greek goddess Athena has 'being born from Zeus' head' as one of her 'observables'.

An observable, being a typed variable, has specifically determined possible values. In particular, and simplifying:

Definition: An observable is called *discrete* if and only if its type has only finitely many possible values; otherwise it is called *analogue*.[4]

In this chapter, we are interested in observables as a means of describing behaviour at a precisely qualified (though seldom numerical) level of abstraction; in general, several observables will be employed.

3.2.3 Six examples

A good way to gain a better understanding of the previous concepts is by looking at a few simple examples.

1 Suppose Peter and Ann wish to study some physical human attributes. To do so Peter, in Oxford, introduces a variable, *h*, whose type consists of rational numbers. The typed variable *h* becomes an (analogue) observable once it is decided that the variable *h* represents the height of a person, using the Imperial system (feet and parts thereof). To explain the definition of equality of observables, suppose that Ann, in Rome, is also interested in observing human physical attributes, and defines the same typed variable but declares that it represents height in metres and parts thereof. Their *typed variables* are the same, but they differ as *observables*: for a given person, the two variables take different representing values. This example shows the importance of making clear the interpretation by which a typed variable becomes an observable.

2 The design of a database is a special case of the definition of a collection of observables. In a database, an observable is called a *key*, its relation to the system modelled by the database is left implicit (although it is often reflected in the name), and its type is inferred from either the values it takes or from its declaration in the database programming language. For instance, the type 'finite string of characters' is frequently used, often being the most appropriate concrete method of description. Other examples include *names*, *addresses*, and such like. This holds true for an observable in general: it is sometimes preferable not to provide in advance all the possible outcomes (i.e. a type) but simply to define its type to consist of all finite sequences of characters, with each value equal to a character

---

[4] The distinction is really a matter of topology rather than cardinality. However, this definition serves our present purposes.

string. This definition reflects a decision to the effect that, although the observable is well-typed, its actual type is not of primary concern.

3 Consider next an example of an *ill-typed variable*. Suppose we are interested in the roles played by people in some community. We could not introduce an observable standing for those barbers who shave just those people who do not shave themselves, for it is well known that such a variable would not be well typed (Russell (1902)). Similarly, each of the standard antinomies reflects an ill-typed variable (Hughes and Brecht (1976)). Of course, the modeller is at liberty to choose whatever type befits the application and, if that involves a potential antinomy, then the appropriate type might turn out to be a non-well-founded set (Barwise and Etchemendy (1987)). However, in this chapter as in the rest of the book we shall operate entirely within the boundaries of standard naïve set theory.

4 Gassendi provides another nice example, to which I shall return in the conclusion. As he wrote in his *Fifth Set of Objections to Descartes's Meditations*

If we are asking about wine, and looking for the kind of knowledge which is superior to common knowledge, it will hardly be enough for you to say 'wine is a liquid thing, which is compressed from grapes, white or red, sweet, intoxicating' and so on. You will have to attempt to investigate and somehow explain its internal substance, showing how it can be seen to be manufactured from spirits, tartar, the distillate, and other ingredients mixed together in such and such quantities and proportions.

What Gassendi seems to have in mind is that observables relating to tasting wine include the attributes that commonly appear on 'tasting sheets': *nose* (representing bouquet), *legs* or *tears* (viscosity), *robe* (peripheral colour), *colour, clarity, sweetness, acidity, fruit, tannicity, length*, and so on, each with a determined type. If two wine tasters choose different types for, say, *colour* (as is usually the case) then the observables are different, despite the fact that their variables have the same name and represent the same feature in reality. Indeed, as they have different types, they are not even equal as typed variables. Information about how wine quality is perceived to vary with time—how the wine 'ages'—is important for the running of a cellar. An appropriate observable is the typed variable a, which is a function associating to each year y:*Years* a perceived quality $a(y)$:*Quality*, where the types *Years* and *Quality* may be assumed to have been previously defined. Thus, a is a function from *Years* to *Quality*, written a:*Time*$\rightarrow$*Quality*. This example shows that, in general, types are constructed from more basic types, and that observables may correspond to operations, taking input and yielding output. Indeed, an observable may be of an arbitrarily complex type.

5 The definition of an observable reflects a particular view or attitude towards the entity being studied. Most commonly, it corresponds to a simplification, in view of a specific application or purpose, in which case non-determinism, not exhibited by the entity itself, may arise. The method is successful when the entity can

be understood by combining the simplifications. Let us consider another example.

In observing a game of chess, one would expect to record the moves of the game.[5] Other observables might include the time taken per move, the body language of the players, and so on. Suppose we are able to view a chessboard by just looking along *files* (the columns stretching from player to player). When we play 'files-chess', we are unable to see the ranks (the parallel rows between the players) or the individual squares. Files cannot sensibly be attributed a colour black or white, but each may be observed to be occupied by a set of pieces (namely those that appear along that file), identified in the usual way (king, queen, and so forth). In 'files-chess', a move may be observed by the effect it has on the file of the piece being moved. For example, a knight moves one or two files either left or right from its starting file; a bishop is indistinguishable from a rook, which moves along a rank; and a rook that moves along a file appears to remain stationary. Whether or not a move results in a piece being captured, appears to be non-deterministic. 'Files-chess' seems to be an almost random game.

Whilst the 'underlying' game is virtually impossible to reconstruct, each state of the game and each move (i.e. each operation on the state of the game) can be 'tracked' within this dimensionally-impoverished family of observables. If one then takes a second view, corresponding instead to rank, we obtain 'ranks-chess'. Once the two views are combined, the original, bi-dimensional game of chess can be recovered, since each state is determined by its rank and file projections, for each move. The two disjoint observations together, namely 'files-chess' + 'ranks-chess', reveal the underlying game.

6 The degree to which a type is appropriate depends on its context and use. For example, to describe the state of a traffic light in Rome one might decide to consider an observable *colour* of type {*red, amber, green*} that corresponds to the colour indicated by the light. This option abstracts the length of time for which the particular colour has been displayed, the brightness of the light, the height of the traffic light, and so on. This is why the choice of type corresponds to a decision about how the phenomenon is to be regarded. To specify such a traffic light for the purpose of construction, a more appropriate type would comprise a numerical measure of wavelength (see section 3.2.6). Furthermore, if we are in Oxford, the type of colour would be a little more complex, since—in addition to red, amber and green—red and amber are displayed simultaneously for part of the cycle. So, an appropriate type would be {*red, amber, green, red–amber*}.

We are now ready to appreciate the basic concept of *level of abstraction* (LoA).

---

[5] As the reader probably knows, this is done by recording the history of the game: move by move the state of each piece on the board is recorded—in so-called English algebraic notation—by rank and file, the piece being moved and the consequences of the move.

3.2.4 Levels of abstraction

The terminology and the study of LoA are rooted in a branch of theoretical computer science known as Formal Methods. Intuitively, Formal Methods are a collection of mathematical techniques used in computer science to prove that the concrete code implementation fits the abstract specifications of a computer system (Zeigler (1976)). More precisely, Formal Methods are a variety of mathematical modelling techniques used to specify and model the behaviour of a computer system and to verify, mathematically, that the system design and implementation satisfy functional requirements. Z and VDM are among the most successful model-based Formal Methods, capable of handling the formal conceptualization of very large-scale systems. The analysis provided in this chapter is based upon them.

The concept of interface in a computer system may be helpful in illustrating what an LoA is. An interface may be described as an intra-system, which transforms the outputs of system A (e.g. a computer) into the inputs of system B (e.g. a human user) and vice versa, producing a change in data types. LoAs are comparable to interfaces for two reasons: they are conceptually positioned between data sources and the agents' information spaces; and they are the place where (diverse) independent systems meet, act upon or communicate with each other. Let us now turn to a more formal description.

Any collection of typed variables can, in principle, be combined into a single 'vector' observable, whose type is the Cartesian product of the types of the constituent variables. In the wine example, the type *Quality* might be chosen to consist of the Cartesian product of the types *Nose*, *Robe*, *Colour*, *Acidity*, *Fruit*, and *Length*. The result would be a single, more complex, observable. In practice, however, such vectorization is unwieldy, since the expression of a constraint on just some of the observables would require a projection notation to single out those observables from the vector. Instead, it is easier to base our approach on a *collection* of observables, that is, on a level of abstraction (an interface, in our previous analogy):

Definition: A *level of abstraction (LoA)* is a finite but non-empty set of observables. No order is assigned to the observables, which are expected to be the building blocks in a theory characterized by their very definition. An LoA is called *discrete* (respectively *analogue*) if and only if all its observables are discrete (respectively analogue); otherwise it is called *hybrid*.

Consider the wine example. Different LoAs may be appropriate for different purposes. To evaluate a wine, the 'tasting LoA', consisting of observables like those mentioned in the previous section, would be relevant. For the purpose of ordering wine, a 'purchasing LoA' (containing observables like *maker*, *region*, *vintage*, *supplier*, *quantity*, *price*, and so on) would be appropriate; but here the 'tasting LoA' would be irrelevant. For the purpose of storing and serving wine—the 'cellaring LoA' (containing observables for *maker, type of wine, drinking window, serving temperature, decanting time, alcohol level, food matchings, quantity remaining in the cellar,* and so on) would be relevant.

The traditional sciences tend to be dominated by analogue LoAs, the humanities and information science by discrete LoAs and mathematics by hybrid LoAs. We are about to see why the resulting theories are fundamentally different.

3.2.5 Behaviour

The definition of observables is only the first step in studying a system at a given LoA. The second step consists in deciding what relationships hold between the observables. This, in turn, requires the introduction of the concept of system 'behaviour'. We shall see that it is the fundamentally different ways of describing behaviour in analogue and discrete systems that account for the differences in the resulting theories.

Not all values exhibited by combinations of observables in an LoA may be realized by the system being modelled. For example, if the four traffic lights at an intersection are modelled by four observables, each representing the colour of a light, the lights cannot in fact all be green together (assuming they work properly). In other words, the combination in which each observable is green cannot be realized in the system being modelled, although the types chosen allow it. Similarly, the choice of types corresponding to a rank-and-file description of a game of chess allows any piece to be placed on any square, but in the actual game two pieces may not occupy the same square simultaneously. Some technique is therefore required to describe those combinations of observable values that are actually acceptable. The most general method is simply to describe all the allowed combinations of values. Such a description is determined by a predicate, whose allowed combinations of values is called the 'system behaviours'.

Definition: the *behaviour* of a system, at a given LoA, is defined to consist of a predicate whose free variables are observables at that LoA. The substitutions of values for observables that make the predicate true are called the *system behaviours*. A *moderated LoA* is defined to consist of an LoA together with a behaviour at that LoA.

Consider two previous examples. In reality, human height does not take arbitrary rational values, for it is always positive and bounded above by (say) 9 feet. The variable h, representing height, is therefore constrained to reflect reality by defining its behaviour to consist of the predicate $0 < h < 9$, in which case any value of h in that interval is a 'system' behaviour. Likewise, wine is also not realistically described by arbitrary combinations of the aforementioned observables. For instance, it cannot be both white and highly tannic.

Since Newton and Leibniz, the behaviours of analogue observables, studied in science, have typically been described by differential equations. A small change in one observable results in a small, quantified change in the overall system behaviour. Accordingly, it is the rates at which those smooth observables vary which is most conveniently described.[6] The desired behaviour of the system then consists of the solution of the differential equations. However, this is a special case of a predicate: the predicate holds at just those values satisfying the differential equation. If a complex system is approximated by simpler systems, then the differential calculus provides a supporting method for quantifying the approximation.

The use of predicates to demarcate system behaviour is essential in any (non-trivial) analysis of discrete systems because, in the latter, no such continuity holds: the change of an observable by a single value may result in a radical and arbitrary change in system behaviour. Yet, complexity requires some kind of comprehension of the system in terms of simple approximations. When this is possible, the approximating behaviours are described exactly, by a predicate, at a given LoA, and it is the LoAs that vary, becoming more comprehensive and embracing more detailed behaviours, until the final LoA accounts for the desired behaviours. Thus, the formalism provided by the method of abstraction can be seen as doing for discrete systems what differential calculus has traditionally done for analogue systems.

Likewise, the use of predicates is essential in subjects like information and computer science, where discrete observables are paramount, and hence predicates are required to describe a system behaviour. In particular, state-based methods like *Z* (Spivey (1992), Hayes and Flinn (1993)) provide a notation for structuring complex observables and behaviours in terms of simpler ones. Their primary concern is with the syntax for expressing those predicates, an issue that will be avoided in this book by stating predicates informally.

The time has now come to combine approximating, moderated LoAs to form the primary concept of the method of abstraction.

3.2.6 *Gradient of abstraction*

For a given (empirical or conceptual) system or feature, different LoAs correspond to different representations or views. A *Gradient of Abstractions* (GoA) is a formalism defined to facilitate discussion of discrete systems over a range of LoAs. Whilst an LoA formalizes the scope or granularity of a single model, a GoA provides a way of varying the LoA in order to make observations at differing levels of abstraction.

For example, in evaluating wine one might be interested in the GoA consisting of the 'tasting' and 'purchasing' LoAs, whilst in managing a cellar one might be interested in the GoA consisting of the 'cellaring' LoA together with a sequence of annual results of observation using the 'tasting' LoA. The reader acquainted with Dennett's idea of 'stances' may initially compare them to a GoA (more on this in section 3.5).

---

[6] It is interesting to note that the catastrophes of *chaos theory* are not smooth; although they do appear so when extra observables are added, taking the behaviour into a smooth curve on a higher-dimensional manifold. Typically, chaotic models are weaker than traditional models, their observables merely reflecting *average* or *long-term* behaviour. The nature of the models is clarified by making explicit the LoA.

In general, the observations at each LoA must be explicitly related to those at the others; to do so, one uses a family of relations between the LoAs. For this, I need to recall some (standard) preliminary notation.

Notation: A *relation* R from a set A to a set C is a subset of the Cartesian product $A \times C$. R is thought of as relating just those pairs (a, c) that belong to the relation. The *reverse* of R is its mirror image: $\{(c, a) \mid (a, c) \in R\}$. A relation R from A to C translates any predicate p on A to the predicate $P_R(p)$ on C that holds at just those $c{:}C$, which are the image through R of some $a{:}A$ satisfying p

$$P_R(p)(c) = \exists a : AR(a, c) \wedge p(a)$$

We have finally come to the main definition of the chapter:

Definition: A *gradient of abstractions*, GoA, is defined to consist of a finite set[7] $\{L_i \mid 0 \leq i < n\}$ of moderated LoAs L_i, a family of relations $R_{i,j} \subseteq L_i L_j$, for $0 \leq i \neq j < n$, relating the observables of each pair L_i and L_j of distinct LoAs in such a way that:

1. the relationships are inverse: for $i \neq j$, $R_{i,j}$ is the reverse of $R_{j,i}$
2. the behaviour p_j at L_j is at least as strong as the translated behaviour $P_{R_{i,j}}(p_i)$.

$$p_j \Rightarrow P_{R_{i,j}}(p_i). \tag{1}$$

and for each interpreted type $x{:}X$ and $y{:}Y$ in L_i and L_j respectively, such that $(x{:}X, y{:}Y)$ is in R_{ij}, a relation $Rxy \subset X \times Y$.

Two GoAs are regarded as *equal* if and only if they have the same moderated LoAs (i.e. the same LoAs and moderating behaviours) and their families of relations are equal. A GoA is called *discrete* if and oknly if all its constituent LoAs are discrete.

Condition (1) means that the behaviour moderating each lower LoA is *consistent* with that specified by a higher LoA. Without it, the behaviours of the various LoAs constituting a GoA would have no connection with each other. A special case, to be elaborated below in the definition of 'nestedness', helps to clarify the point.

If one LoA L_i extends another L_j by adding new observables, then the relation $R_{i,j}$ is the inclusion of the observables of L_i in those of L_j and (1) reduces to this: the constraints imposed on the observables at LoA L_i remain true at LoA L_j, where 'new' observables lie outside the range of $R_{i,j}$.

A GoA whose sequence contains just one element evidently reduces to a single LoA. So the definition of 'LoA' is subsumed by that of 'GoA'.

The consistency conditions imposed by the relations $R_{i,j}$ are in general quite weak. It is possible, though of little help in practice, to define GoAs in which the relations connect the LoAs cyclically. Of much more use are the following two important kinds of GoA: 'disjoint' GoAs (whose views are complementary) and 'nested' GoAs (whose

---

[7] The case of infinite sets has application to analogue systems but is not considered here.

views provide successively more information). Before defining them, some further notations need to be introduced.

Notation: A *function* f from a set C to a set A is a relation, i.e. a subset of the Cartesian product $C \chi A$, which is single-valued, that is:

$$\forall c : C \ \forall a, a' : A ((c, a) \in f \wedge (c, a') \in f) \Rightarrow a = a'$$

this means that the notation $f(c) = a$ is a well-defined alternative to $(c,a) \in f)$, and total, that is:

$$\forall c : C \ \exists a : A \ f(c) = a$$

this means that $f(c)$ is defined for each $c:C$.

A function is then called *surjective* if and only if every element in the target set lies in the range of the function, that is:

$$\forall a : A \ \exists c : C \ f(c) = a.$$

We are now ready to introduce the definition of GoA:

Definition: A GoA is called *disjoint* if and only if the L_i are pairwise disjoint (i.e. taken two at a time, they have no observable in common) and the relations are all empty. It is called *nested* if and only if the only non-empty relations are those between L_i and L_{i+1}, for each $0 \le i < n$-1, and moreover the reverse of each $R_{i, \ i+1}$ is a surjective function from the observables of L_{i+1} to those of L_i.

A disjoint GoA is chosen to describe a system as the combination of several non-overlapping components. This is useful when different aspects of the system behaviour are better modelled as being determined by the values of distinct observables. For example, one may think of a typical case of Cartesian dualism, in which a disjoint GoA models the brain and its observables as a *res extensa*, and the mind and its observables as a *res cogitans*. The case of a disjoint GoA is rather simple, since the LoAs are more typically tied together by common observations. Using a more mundane example, the services in a domestic dwelling may be represented by LoAs for electricity, plumbing, telephone, security, and gas. Without going into detail about the constituent observables, it is easy to see that, in an accurate representation, the electrical and plumbing LoAs could overlap whilst the telephone and plumbing could not. Following the philosophical example, this would correspond to a case in which some form of epiphenomenalism is being supported.

A nested GoA (see Figure 1) is chosen to describe a complex system exactly at each level of abstraction and incrementally more accurately. The condition that the functions be surjective means that any abstract observation has at least one concrete counterpart. As a result, the translation functions cannot overlook any behaviour at an abstract LoA: behaviours lying outside the range of a function translate to the predicate *false*. The condition that the reversed relations be functions means that each observation at a concrete LoA comes from at most one observation at a more abstract

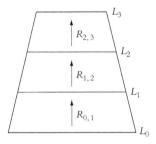

Figure 1 Nested GoA with four levels of abstraction

LoA (although the converse fails in general, allowing one abstract observable to be refined by many concrete observables). As a result, the translation functions become simpler.

In Figure 1, the higher the level the less details it conveys regarding the system being analysed. Using the previous example regarding the brain, ideally neuroscientific studies rely on nested GoAs, as they proceed from the investigation of whole brain functions and related areas, such as specific kinds of memories, to investigations of the physiological basis of memory storage in neurons. On a more prosaic note, recall the case of a traffic light, which is observed to have colour *colour* of type {*red, amber, green*}. This is captured by an LoA, L_0, having that single observable. If one wishes to be more precise about colour, e.g. for the purpose of constructing a new traffic light, one might consider a second LoA, L_1, having the variable *wl* whose type is a positive real number corresponding to the wavelength of the colour. To determine the behaviour of L_1, suppose that constants $\lambda_{red} < \lambda_{red'}$ delimit the wavelength of red, and similarly for amber and green. Then the behaviour of L_1 is simply this predicate with free variable *wl*:

$$(\lambda_{red} \leq wl \leq \lambda_{red'}) \vee (\lambda_{amber} \leq wl \leq \lambda_{amber'}) \vee (\lambda_{green} \leq wl \leq \lambda_{green'})$$

The sequence, consisting of the LoA L_0 and the moderated LoA L_1, forms a nested GoA. Intuitively, the smaller, abstract, type {*red, amber, green*} is a projection of the larger. The relevant relation associates to each value *c*:{*red, amber, green*} a band of wavelengths perceived as that colour. Formally, $R\,(colour, wl)$ is defined to hold if and only if, for each *c*:{*red, amber, green*}:

$$colour = c \leftrightarrow \lambda_c \leq wl \leq \lambda_{c'}.$$

In the wine example, the first LoA might be defined to consist of the variable 'kind' having type consisting of *red, white, rose* under the obvious representation. A second LoA might be defined to consist of the observable 'kind' having type:

{stillred, sparklingred, stillwhite, sparklingwhite, stillrose, sparklingrose}.

Although the second type does not contain the first, it produces greater resolution under the obvious projection relation. Thus, the GoA consisting of those two LoAs is nested.

These two important forms of GoA—disjoint and nested—are in fact interchangeable, at least theoretically. For if A and B are disjoint sets, then A and their union $A \cap B$ are increasing sets and the former is embedded in the latter. Thus, a disjoint GoA can be converted to a nested one. Conversely, if A and B are increasing sets with the former embedded in the latter, then A and the set difference $A \backslash B$ are disjoint sets. Thus, a nested GoA can be converted to a disjoint one.

Following the technique used to define a nested GoA, it is possible to define less restricted but still hierarchical GoAs. Important examples include tree-like structures, of which our nested GoAs are a special, linear case.

For theoretical purposes, the information captured in a GoA can be expressed equivalently as a single LoA of a more complicated type, namely one whose single LoA has a type equal to the sequence of the LoAs of the complex interface. However, the current definition is better suited to application.

3.3 A classic interpretation of the method of abstraction

A simple way to introduce the method of levels of abstraction (LoAs) and highlight its philosophical importance is by showing how closely it resembles Kant's transcendental approach. The resemblance is not casual, but a scholarly explanation of this 'genealogical relation' would take us too far, in an exegetical direction that I am not interested in pursuing here. Rather, it is useful to highlight here the theoretical similarities between the two methods by referring to Kant's classic discussion of the 'antinomies of pure reason'.

As is well known, each of the four antinomies comprises a thesis and an antithesis, which are supposed to be both reasonable and irreconcilable. I list them here by slightly adapting their formulation from Kant's *Critique of Pure Reason* (Kant (1998)):

1. **Thesis**: the world is finite; it has a beginning in time and is limited in space.
   Antithesis: the world is infinite, it has no beginning in time and no limit in space (A 426–7/B 454–5).
2. **Thesis**: the world is discrete; everything in the world consists of elements that are ultimately simple and hence indivisible.
   Antithesis: the world is continuous; nothing in the world is simple, but everything is composite and hence infinitely divisible (A 434–5/B 462–3).
3. **Thesis**: there is freedom; to explain causal events in the world it is necessary to refer both to the laws of nature and to freedom.
   Antithesis: there is no freedom; everything that happens in the world occurs only in accordance with natural causation (A 444–5/B 462–3).

4. **Thesis**: there is in the world an absolutely necessary Being.

Antithesis: there is nothing necessary in the world, but everything is contingent (A 452–3/B 480–1).

What I wish to stress here is that Kant's transcendental method and the method of abstraction converge both on the evaluation and on the resolution of these antinomies.

As Kant argues, the conflict is not between empirical experience and logical analysis. Rather, the four antinomies are generated by an unconstrained demand for unconditioned answers to fundamental problems concerning (1) time and space, (2) complexity/granularity, (3) causality and freedom, and (4) modality. And here is where my assessment agrees with Kant's: the attempt to strive for something unconditioned is equivalent to the natural, yet profoundly mistaken, endeavour to analyse a system (the world in itself, for Kant, but it could also be a more limited domain) independently of any (specification of) the level of abstraction at which the analysis is being conducted, the questions are being posed and the answers are being offered, for a specified purpose. In other words, trying to overstep the limits set by the LoA leads to a conceptual jumble.

As for the resolution, Kant divides the antinomies into two groups. He then shows that, in the first two antinomies, both the thesis and the antithesis are untenable because the search for the unconditioned mistakes time and space, and complexity/granularity, for features of the system instead of realizing that they are properties set by (or constituting) the level of abstraction at which the system is investigated and hence, as such, subject to alternative formatting. Following Kant, one may say that, assuming for the sake of simplicity that an LoA is comparable to an interface, it makes no sense to wonder whether the system under observation is finite in time, space, and granularity in itself, independently of the LoA at which it is being analysed, since this is a feature of the interface, and different interfaces may be adopted depending on needs and requirements. So, from an LoA approach, I agree with Kant: neither the thesis nor the antithesis in (1) and (2) are tenable. I will return to this point in chapter fourteen.

Regarding the third and fourth antinomy, Kant argues that both the thesis and the antithesis might be tenable, thus coming close to what has been defined above as a disjoint GoA. The mistake here lies in confusing what qualifies the phenomenal world of experience—which relies on causal relations and is characterized by contingency—with what might qualify the noumenal world of things in themselves—which may include freedom and necessary existence, but that remains inaccessible through direct experience. In the language of the method of abstraction, this means that models, i.e. the outcomes of the analyses of systems, are always characterized by natural laws of causality and a modality of contingencies, but this does not disprove the existence of freedom or a necessary being 'in the systems', two issues with respect to which one may remain agnostic and uncommitted at this stage.

All this clarifies three important aspects of the method of abstraction. First, the method is Kantian in nature. Although it does not inherit from Kant any mental or subject-based feature, it is a transcendental approach, which considers the conditions of possibility of the analysis (experience) of a particular system.

Second, the method is anti-metaphysical, again in a Kantian sense. Metaphysics is—when used as a negative label—what is done by sloppy reasoning when it pretends to develop a theory without taking into consideration, at least implicitly, the level of abstraction at, and hence the purpose for, which the theory itself is being developed. In other words, metaphysics is that LoA-free zone where anyone can say anything without fear of ever being proved wrong, as long as the basic law of non-contradiction is respected. Such an unconstrained game of ideas should be found dull and frustrating by anyone genuinely interested in the advancement of knowledge and understanding.

Third, the method provides a powerful tool to approach significant issues in philosophy. We have just seen how it can dispose of false antinomies in a Kantian way. I shall mention a few more examples in the next section.

3.4 Some philosophical applications

The following applications of the method of Levels of Abstraction should further explain its nature and value.

3.4.1 Agents

An *agent* can be thought of (Floridi and Sanders (2004b)) as a *transition system* (i.e. a system of states and transitions between them) that is *interactive* (i.e. responds to stimulus by change of state), *autonomous* (i.e. is able to change state without stimulus) and *adaptable* (i.e. is able to change the transition rules by which it changes state). However, each of those properties, and hence the definition of agenthood, makes sense only at a prescribed LoA. For example, whether a rock is deemed to be interactive depends on the length of time and level of detail of observation. Over a long period, it erodes and hence changes state. By day it absorbs solar radiation which it emits at night. But with observables resulting from scrutiny over a period of ten seconds by the naked eye from 10 metres, it can be deemed not to be interactive. If the LoA at which one observes it abstracts gravity and resistance, a swinging pendulum appears to be autonomous, but neither interactive nor adaptive. By extending the LoA to incorporate air resistance, it becomes adaptive. By observing also the whistling sound it makes with the air, it becomes interactive. If a piece of software that exhibits machine learning (Mitchell (1997)) is studied at an LoA which registers its interactions with its environment, then the software will appear interactive, autonomous, and adaptive, i.e. to be an agent. However, if the program code is revealed, then the software is shown to be simply following rules and hence not to be adaptive. These two LoAs are at variance. One reflects the 'open source' view of software: the user has access to the code. The other reflects the commercial view that, although the user has bought the software and can use it at will, he has no access to the code. At stake is whether or not the software forms an (artificial) agent.

3.4.2 The Turing test

Turing (1950) took the crucial step of arguing that the ability to think (since called 'intelligence') can be satisfactorily characterized by means of a test, rather than by explicit definition. In retrospect, that step may seem a small one. After all, we are quite familiar with areas in which no explicit definition is possible or sensible. We make no attempt to characterize what it means to be an acceptable driver in terms of vision, response times, coordination, experience, and other physical attributes. Instead, we rely on a driving test. Likewise, we do not attempt to define what it means for a school student to have reached an acceptable academic standard by the end of school; we rely on final school examinations. But incisive that step certainly must have been in view of the vast number of attempts (even to this day) to characterize intelligence explicitly. Opponents of Turing's approach usually object that his test works at the wrong LoA. Perhaps it ought to include observables concerning a component of creativity, of spontaneity, and so on. However, without concepts like those introduced above, it is very difficult to make one's objections precise, or defend Turing's approach. It is therefore of considerable interest to see, first, how the Turing test can be expressed using phenomenological LoAs and, second, how it can be analysed using conceptual LoAs.

3.4.2.1 Turing's imitation game.

Let us start, as did Turing, by considering an imitation game, in which a man A and a woman B are placed in a room separate from an interrogator C, who communicates with each by teleprinter (these days replaced by computer). C puts questions to A and B, known only as X and Y. C's task is to identify $X = A$ and $Y = B$ or, conversely, $X = B$ and $Y = A$, by considering their responses. We might describe this scenario by taking a first, extremely abstract, LoA to reflect just the correctness of C's identification. The LoA L_0 consists of a single variable *ans* of type {*right*, *wrong*} which becomes an observable under the correspondence: *ans* takes the value *right*, if C is correct, and the value *wrong* if C is incorrect. In choosing this LoA, we are intentionally abstracting the actual answer (whether X was A or B), the questions and answers, response times, and so on, in order to capture just the outcome of the imitation game.

We might reveal C's actual identification by defining a second, disjoint, LoA L_1, whose single variable, Z, is of type {(A,B), (B,A)} which is made into an observable under the correspondence that the first component of Z is the putative identity of X and the second component that of Y. Combining the two LoAs L_0 and L_1 gives a disjoint GoA.

Of course, there are alternative approaches, which is why it is important to be precise about the one taken. We might have defined a GoA by replacing the LoA L_1 with an LoA containing two observables, the first corresponding to the identity of X and the second corresponding to the identity of Y. That would be more involved, since each would have type {A, B} and we would have to moderate it with the behaviour that the values of X and Y differ. Our choice of L_1 avoids the complication by building that behaviour into the type of Z. However, with several observables, in general such moderating behaviours cannot be avoided.

To model C's questions, the addressees and their responses, we define a third LoA, L_2. Let Q and R denote the sets of possible (well-posed) questions and responses respectively (an example where the type of text strings may be considered appropriate). Then each 'question, addressee and response' triple is a variable whose type is the Cartesian product of Q, $\{X, Y\}$ and R. It becomes an observable under the correspondence just established. The observable we seek now consists of a sequence (of arbitrary but finite length) of such triples, corresponding to the sequence of interactions in temporal order; and L_2 contains that single observable. An alternative would be to have an observable for the number of questions, an observable for each question, and an observable for each response. L_2 can be added to either GoA T or T^* to obtain a GoA, which is still disjoint but has higher resolution.

More detailed LoAs are possible and easy to define but, following Turing, we stop here having appreciated that any discussion of the imitation game may be accurately 'calibrated' with a GoA, according to its level of abstraction.

3.4.2.2 Turing's test revisited. In the Turing test, A is replaced by a 'machine' (nowadays a 'computer'). Turing proposed that the meaningless question 'Can machines think?' be replaced by the sensible question: 'Will the interrogator decide wrongly as often when the game is played like this as he does when the game is played between a man and a woman?'. These days,[8] the test is normally stripped of its gender-specific nature and the interrogator is simply asked to determine the human from the machine. Appropriate GoAs are defined as above, but with A representing a computer, and B a human.

Although Turing did not make it explicit, the phrase 'as often' in his description implies repetition of the test, and a conclusion reached by statistical analysis. Suppose that C initiates a pair of question/answer sessions of the kind used in the imitation game. A list of questions is given to two situations, one containing a man and a woman, the other containing a machine and a woman. We suppose that the answers in the first situation are of type A_1 and those in the second of type A_2, thus avoiding here the question of whether $A_1 = A_2$. As before, C makes an identification. The appropriate LoA has type, call it J, equal to the Cartesian product of the type $\{(A,B), (B,A)\}$ and the type of all sequences of elements of the type $Q \times \{X, Y\} \times A_1 \times A_2$.

The observable corresponding to repetition of that situation j times, though not necessarily with the same questions, has type consisting of the Cartesian product of j-many copies of type J, namely J^j. The LoA incorporating that observation plus the answer to the ultimate question is then the Cartesian product of the type J^j and the type $\{right,$

---

[8]   For a summary of the Turing test today, and its incarnation in competitive form (the Loebner prize), see Moor (2001) and Floridi et al. (2009).

wrong}. Likewise, a more complex type can be constructed to reveal the nature of the statistical test; in this case too, let us follow Turing and overlook the details.

3.4.2.3 Turing discussed. The previous two sections have shown how to formalize the Turing test using phenomenologically motivated GoAs. The method of abstraction can also be used to discuss and compare variations on the test. Indeed it is difficult to imagine how such an analysis could be formulated without a concept equivalent to LoA. Now, details of the LoAs need not be given as long as it is clear that they could be.

Turing couched his test in terms of a single human interrogator. In the Loebner test, interrogation is provided by a panel of humans interacting via computer interface in real time. Alternatively, the interrogator could be a machine; or, instead of real-time interaction, a list of pre-arranged questions might be left, and the list of answers returned to the interrogator; or, instead of serial questions and answers, the interrogator might hold a 'general conversation'. Each alternative modifies the power of the test. All can be formalized by defining different GoAs. The Turing test might be adapted to target abilities other than 'thinking', like interpretation of text, game playing, puzzle solving, spatial reasoning, creativity, and so on. Contemplating the possible GoAs provides a way to formalize the variant test clearly and elegantly, and promotes simple comparison with contending treatments.

3.4.3 Emergence

The method of abstraction is ideally suited to the study of systems so complex that they are best understood stepwise, by their gradual disclosure at increasingly fine or alternative levels of abstraction. The study of such systems strikes at the heart of the following controversy: how does ultimate complexity arise in the stepwise approximation by simple systems? Gell-Mann (1994) has suggested calling the study of such phenomena *plectics*, and introduces it using an idea he calls *granularity* which is conveniently formalized by LoA.

A key concept in such an approach to complex systems is that of 'emergent behaviour', that is, behaviour that arises in the move from one LoA to a finer level (see Hendriks-Jansen (1989) for a discussion). In this section, I apply the method of abstraction to clarify that concept of emergence. In the next, I will focus on one particular area in which emergence has received much attention, that of artificial life (*Alife*, C. G. Langton (1989), (1992)).

Emergence, unsurprisingly for such an important concept, can take various forms. It derives from the idea that, according to Hendriks-Jansen (1989), 'properties at higher levels are not necessarily predictable from properties at lower levels' (p. 283). Note that in the quotation 'lower levels' are more abstract and 'higher levels' more detailed or concrete. In this section, we are concerned only with the idea of emergence, which is neatly captured using a GoA containing two nested LoAs. Let us consider an example first.

The process of tossing a coin may be modelled abstractly with an observable *outcome* of type {*head, tail*} corresponding to the side of the coin that faces upwards after the toss. This LoA abstracts any other result (like the coin's landing on its edge or becoming lost) and other features, like manner of tossing, number of spins, time taken, and so on. In particular, it models just one toss of the coin. Therefore, it cannot account for the 'fairness' of the coin, which would reveal itself statistically only after a large number of tosses. Now, suppose we wish to model the repetition of that process with the explicit aim of discussing a coin's fairness. We can introduce a more concrete LoA, whose observables are: a natural number n, corresponding to the number of tosses of the coin, and a list of n values from {*head, tail*}, corresponding to successive tosses as modelled above. At this second LoA, we are able to make judgements (using standard statistics, for example) about the fairness of the coin, based on the frequency of the outcomes.

This example demonstrates emergence as follows. In many repeated tosses of the coin, the more abstract model applies toss by toss, but does not allow frequency of outcome to be observed, as it is in the finer model. We say that the notion of the coin's fairness is emergent at the finer LoA. That situation may be formalized as follows.

Suppose some system is under consideration using a nested GoA consisting of two LoAs. Suppose the more abstract LoA, A, is moderated by behaviour p_A describing the abstract view of system and the more concrete LoA, C, is moderated by behaviour p_C describing the concrete view. The abstract and concrete observables are related by the total and one-to-many relation $R_{A,C}$. Recall that a behaviour of the system at LoA C is a triple of values for the observables of C that satisfies p_C.

Definition: A behaviour of the system at LoA C is said to be *emergent* (with respect to that nested GoA) if and only if its translation under the relation $R_{A,C}$ fails to satisfy p_A. *Emergence* is said to hold in the GoA if and only if there is some emergent behaviour.

There is frequently confusion about emergence. This is scarcely surprising since, without the notion of LoA, the various levels at which a system is discussed cannot be formalized. Emergence is a relational concept: a property is emergent not in a model but in a comparison between models. It arises typically because the *more concrete* LoA embodies a 'mechanism', or rule, for determining an observable, which has been overlooked at the *more abstract* LoA, usually quite deliberately, in order to gain simplicity at the cost of detail. Frequently, the breakthrough in understanding some complex phenomenon has come by accounting for emergent behaviour; and that has resulted from considering the process by which it occurs, rather than taking a more static view of the ingredients involved. In the coin example, we have avoided incorporating any mechanism; but any of the multitude of pseudo-random number generators could be used to generate lists of *head* and *tail*, and hence to account for the emergent phenomenon (Knuth (1997)).

An interesting example of emergence is provided by quantum mechanics, according to which each action (other than the process of observation) is (unitary and hence) reversible. Yet, when observations 'in the large' are made of huge physical systems, despite the components of those systems obeying the laws of quantum mechanics, the laws of thermodynamics *emerge*: despite local reversibility, entropy increases.

The majority of observables considered so far have been 'static'. However operations constitute vital observables. Indeed, the importance of 'process' may be indicated by the example of a sponge cake. With only the ingredients as observables (i.e. the amount and kind of each ingredient), the sponge-like nature of the cake is, as many a novice cook has found, emergent. But if the manner of aeration (a variable indicating the aerating effect of bicarbonate of soda under the right conditions) is also an observable, then sponginess is explicable. In other words, the behaviour of sponginess emerges only at the finer level of abstraction.

3.4.4 Artificial life

Attempts to define artificial life (ALife) have been no more successful than the attempts, both before and after Turing, to define 'intelligence' explicitly. Having chosen an LoA *L*, one may propose that ALife with respect to *L* be defined to consist of all those entities observably indistinguishable under *L* from a live entity. A sensible 'sanity check' on *L* is that the result does not depend on the particular species of life observed, provided that it is chosen with regard to the concept of life being explored.

To give a rather coarse example, perhaps the most abstract observation possible of a population is its size: the number of members as a function of time. That is an observable of type 'whole number' and it is well-typed, provided that the population is finite and well defined. At this LoA, a population provides no more information than its size. There is no distinction between live populations, artificial populations and, for that matter, any set which varies in size. However, such an LoA is sufficient to support the well-known Fibonacci model of population size per generation (Thompson (1992)). It is already of some interest if one adds observables including the rates of birth, mortality, migration, and harvesting. It then becomes sufficient, for example, to discuss age distribution across the population and for the management of pest populations, for the harvesting of natural populations, for the modelling of insect outbreaks, of interacting populations and so on (Murray (2003)). Of course, at this LoA an observer from space might decide that cars are the dominant life form on parts of earth. A slightly finer LoA is that at which the location of individual members of a population is plotted against time (say in Oxford, every 24 hours). At this 'spatial distribution' LoA, humans are still indistinguishable from ants, bicycles, and books: all move around, are created (photocopies) and destroyed (shredded or burnt). Indeed, depending on copyright regulations, books might also be 'cloned'. The method of abstraction seems to apply well to summarize, clarify and facilitate the comparison of existing contributions. One important approach has been that of C. G. Langton (1996), which extends the biological notions of genotype and phenotype to *gtype* and *ptype* respectively, so that those terms apply equally to ALife. Gtype refers to a low-level implementation mechanism, behaviour or LoA, whilst a ptype refers to a higher-level behavioural structure or LoA, that emerges as a result of those mechanisms interacting. Langton discusses the subtleties of inferring the latter from the former. His model provides an important instance of the use of a GoA containing two interfaces, one for gtype observables and the other for ptype observables.

3.4.5 Quantum observation

It is remarkable that the disparate disciplines of quantum mechanics and social anthropology share a fundamental feature: in each, observation automatically involves interference. Observing a quantum or anthropological system is possible only at the expense of a change to the system. By contrast, the definition of observable introduced above makes no assumptions about how the entity is (capable of being) measured (effectively) in practice. So let me address this issue here.

In quantum mechanics, 'observable' means something much more restricted than the sense in which I have used it here. There, it is to be distinguished from the state that is posited to exist in order to explain the frequency with which observables take their values. Such 'beables' (Bell (1987)) are, for the method of abstraction, also observables as is, for that matter, the frequency with which an observable takes on its values. The latter might be regarded as unachievable in practice, since any finite number of readings can achieve only an approximation to it. Yet that need be of no concern to us. Our only requirement is that an observable be well typed. When desired, the stricter 'observation as measurement' from quantum mechanics can be modelled as a certain kind of observation in the sense introduced in this chapter: the change in behaviour associated with an 'observation as measurement' event is specified to conform to the uncertainty principle. The same holds for the constraint of quantum mechanics that only certain (i.e.commuting) observables may be measured simultaneously: whilst two events, say A and B, may be observed independently, their simultaneous observation constitutes a third event, AB say, with the different behavioural consequences dictated by quantum mechanics.

3.4.6 Decidable observation

In the theory of computation, an observable is called *decidable*, or *effective*, if and only if its behaviour is given by a computable function. For example, it is known to be undecidable whether or not a program terminates, i.e. there is no algorithm for its determination (Boolos et al. (2002)). No assumption about the decidability of an observable should be made, for the following reason. We saw that the field of Formal Methods within computer science (Hoare and He (1998)) concerns itself with the mathematical specification and development of information systems. Typically, a specification embodies a twofold constraint: the required program must conform to such-and-such a functional specification *and terminate*. Without the last constraint, undesirable programs, which execute forever, never yielding a result, might be allowed in some models of computation. Such a specification is no more than a behaviour phrased in terms of observables for input, output (appearing in the functional specification), and termination (appearing in the second conjunct). We have just seen that termination cannot be assumed to be decidable. So the consequence of allowing an observable to be undecidable is that some ingenuity is required to prove that an implementation meets a specification phrased in terms of its observables: no program can possibly achieve that task in general.

3.4.7 Simulation and functionalism

LoAs can be connected together to form broader structures of abstraction, from hierarchy of abstractions to nets of abstraction. One of the possible relations between LoAs is that of simulation. Traditionally, a simulation is considered a dynamical representation of a system. This means that, if one wishes to produce a simulation, one must extract a model, by selecting some variables from the investigated system, and then construct an update function, which lets the variables in the simulator change as if they were the variables observed in the system. In a nutshell, a simulation is considered the observation of a model that evolves over time. Such definition, though correct, is still imprecise because, in order to understand what a simulation is, one also needs to clarify explicitly and precisely what a model is. This clarification is currently one of the most controversial issues in the philosophy of science, and it is far from clear how one may best deal with it. However, using the method of abstraction it becomes possible to characterize the notion of simulation in a different way, and hence bypass this difficulty.

A simulation relation is now the relation between the observables of a simulator system and a simulated one (Roever et al. (1998)). This relation must occur between pairs of observables in order to guarantee a satisfactory degree of congruence, not only for the current state of the two systems, but also for their evolution. In the simulation relation, the epistemic agent is coupling the state evolution of two systems by observing these two systems at different LoAs. This means that an epistemic agent seeks to construct an equivalence relation between the two systems, by analysing the LoA at which those systems could be considered congruent. By way of explanation, let us consider a simple example and apply the method of abstraction and the simulation relation to a new definition of functionalism.

Functionalism argues that a physical or abstract entity is identified by its causal or operational role. From this viewpoint, a system is not evaluated by its structures and their interactions, but rather by the functions it shows. If what constitutes a system is irrelevant for its identification, then the same functional organization can be realized by different systems and substrates, which are usually called realizations (Putnam (1967)). This is the multi-realizability thesis.

Some philosophers try to rule out multi-realizability from the functionalist approach. For example, they argue that multi-realizability could lead to a weakening of a neuroscientific approach in the explanation of human behaviour. For why should one be concerned with the actual neural structures, if one can execute an algorithm to instantiate the same behaviours shown by these neural structures? It is argued that a computational approach is therefore more suitable for processing those algorithms.

Unfortunately, multi-realizability cannot be detached from functionalism since, without it, functionalism becomes inexplicable. This is clear if we consider the mathematical concept of function. A function is usually expressed by an operation on one or more variables, the well-known scheme being $f(x) = y$. However, this simply means that the variables in the equation could be replaced or interpreted by an endless set of numbers or by points over the Cartesian plane or by means of a Turing machine or by set theory. Without all these instantiations, it would be impossible to explain the function $f(x) = y$. We shall therefore conclude that functionalism entails multi-realizability.

Now, in the classic account of functionalism we deal with *relata*—that is, the functional organization and the realizations—and relations—that is, the realization relation between the functional organization and the realizations, and the simulation relation between the various realizations. Our goal is to show that realization and simulation are equivalent. An epistemic agent can observe any functional organization, at a specific LoA, and the realization of that functional organization at another LoA. Then the realization relation between the two LoAs is characterized by: (a) the codification of the inputs of the functional organization LoA into the inputs of the various realizations LoA, and (b) the de-codification of the outputs of the latter into the outputs of the former. Basically, simulation relation and realization relation are equivalent because they are relations which describe the same processes. The argument is then that multi-realizability and functionalism are coupled concepts, and simulation relation is equivalent to a realization relation. But then it follows that a common functional organization does not exist at an LoA higher than its realizations. The functional organization is the net of LoAs (GoA) constructed by the epistemic agents with the simulation relation between the various realizations conceived at different LoAs. This means that it is the relational structure produced by various realizations and by the simulation relation that connects them. For example, a carpenter who is making a chair by following a blueprint is not handling a functional organization (the blueprint) and a realization (the chair), but two realizations of that piece of furniture at different LoAs, which are related in a simulation relation specified by his work. This interpretation of functionalism leads us to reconsider functionalistic explanations within the philosophy of AI and the philosophy of mind by introducing simulation relation as a new device. The functionalist explanation is configured as a specification of simulations between the LoAs at which the realizations are organized by the epistemic agent.

3.5. The philosophy of the method of abstraction

The time has come to provide further conceptual clarification concerning the nature and consequences of the method of abstraction. In this section, I relate the relevant work by Marr, Pylyshyn, Dennett, and Davidson to the method of abstraction, and discuss the thorny issues of relativism and anti-realism. A word of warning may be in order. When confronted with a new theory or method, it is natural to compare it and perhaps (mistakenly) identify it with something old and well established. In particular, previous theories or methods can work as powerful magnets that end by attracting anything that comes close to their space of influence, blurring all differences. So this section aims at putting some distance between some old philosophical acquaintances and the new proposal coming from Formal Methods.

3.5.1. Levels of organization and of explanation

Several important ways have been proposed for speaking of the levels of analysis of a system. The following two families can be singled out as most representative.

1) *Levels of Organization* (LoOs) support an *ontological* approach, according to which the system under analysis is supposed to have a (usually hierarchical) structure in itself, or *de re*, which is allegedly captured and uncovered by its description, and objectively formulated in some neutral observation language (Newell (1990), Simon (1996)). For example, levels of communication, of decision processing (Mesarovic et al. (1970)) and of information flow can all be presented as specific instances of analysis in terms of LoOs. There is a twofold connection between LoOs and LoAs. If the hierarchical structure of the system itself is thought of as a GoA, then for each constituent LoA there is a corresponding LoO. Alternatively, one can conceive the analysis of the system, not the system itself, as being the object of study. Then the method of abstraction leads one to consider a GoA whose constituent LoAs are the LoOs. Note that, since the system under analysis may be an artefact, knowledge of its LoO may be available constructively, i.e. in terms of knowledge of its specifications.

2) *Levels of Explanation* (LoEs) support an *epistemological* approach, quite common in cognitive and computer science (Benjamin et al. (1998)). Strictly speaking, the LoEs do not really pertain to the system or its model. They provide a way to distinguish between different epistemic approaches and goals, such as when one analyses an exam question from the students' or the teacher's perspectives, or the description of the functions of a technological artefact from the designer's, the user's, the expert's or the layperson's point of view. A LoE is an important kind of LoA. It is pragmatic and makes no pretence of reflecting an ultimate description of the system. It is defined with a specific practical view or use in mind. Manuals, pitched at the inexpert user, indicating 'how to' with no idea of 'why', provide a good example.

The two kinds of 'structured analysis' just introduced are of course interrelated. Different LoEs—e.g. the end-user's LoE of how an applications package is to be used versus the programmer's LoE of how it is executed by the machine—are connected with different LoAs—e.g. the end-user's LoA represented by a specific graphic interface versus the programmer's code—which in turn are connected with different LoO—e.g. the commonsensical WYSIWYG versus the software architecture.

However, LoAs provide a foundation for both, and LoOs, LoEs, and LoAs should not be confused. Let us consider some clarifying examples.

One of the most interesting and influential cases of multi-layered analysis is provided by Marr's three-levels hypothesis. After Marr (1982), it has become common in cognitive and philosophical studies (McClamrock (1991)) to assume that a reasonably complex system can be understood only by distinguishing between levels of analysis. Here is how Marr himself put it (all the following quotations are from Marr (1982)):

Almost never can a complex system of any kind be understood as a simple extrapolation from the properties of its elementary components. Consider for example, some gas in a bottle. A description of thermodynamic effects—temperature, pressure, density, and the relationships among these factors—is not formulated by using a large set of equations, one for each of the particles involved. Such effects are described at their own level, that of an enormous collection of particles; the effort is to show that in principle the microscopic and the macroscopic descriptions are consistent with one another. If one hopes to achieve a full understanding of a system as complicated as a nervous system, a developing embryo, a set of metabolic pathways, a bottle of gas, or even a large computer program, then one must be prepared to contemplate different kinds of explanation at different levels of description that are linked, at least in principle, into a cohesive whole, even if linking the levels in complete detail is impractical. For the specific case of a system that solves an information-processing problem, there are in addition the twin strands of process and representation, and both these ideas need some discussion. (pp. 19–20).

In particular, in the case of an information-processing system, Marr and his followers suggest the adoption of three levels of analysis:

1. *the computational level.* This is a description of

the abstract computational theory of the device, in which the performance of the device is characterised as a mapping from one kind of information structures, the abstract properties of this mapping are defined precisely, and its appropriateness and adequacy for the task at hand are demonstrated (p. 24);

2. *the algorithmic level.* This is a description of

the choice of representation for the input and output and the algorithm to be used to transform one into the other (pp. 24–25);

3. *the implementational level.* This is a description of

the details of how the algorithm and representation are realized physically—the detailed computer architecture, so to speak. (p. 25).

The three levels are supposed to be loosely connected and in a one-to-many mapping relation: for any computational description of a particular information-processing problem there may be several algorithms for solving that problem, and any algorithm may be implemented in several ways.

Along similar lines, Pylyshyn (1984) has spoken of the *semantic*, the *syntactic*, and the *physical levels of description* of an information-processing system, with the (level of) *functional architecture* of the system playing the role of a bridge between Marr's algorithmic and implementational levels. In addition, Dennett (1987) has proposed a hierarchical model of explanation based on three different 'stances': the *intentional stance*, according to which the system is treated, for explanatory purposes, *as if* it were a rational, thinking agent attempting to carry out a particular task successfully; the *design stance*, which concerns the general principles governing the design of any system that might carry out those tasks successfully; and the *physical stance*, which considers how a system implementing the appropriate design-level principles might be physically constructed.

The tripartite approaches of Marr, Pylyshyn, and Dennett share three important features. First, they are each readily formalized in terms of GoAs with three LoAs. Second, they do not distinguish between LoO, LoE, and LoA; this being because (third feature) they assign a privileged role to explanations. As a result, their ontological commitment is embedded and hence concealed. The common reasoning seems to be the following: 'this is the right level of analysis of the system because that is the right LoO of the system', where no justification is offered for why that LoO is chosen as the right one. Nor is the epistemological commitment made explicit or defended; it is merely presupposed. This is where the method of abstraction provides a significant advantage. By starting from a clear endorsement of each specific LoA, a strong and conscious effort can be made to uncover the ontological commitment of a theory (and hence of a set of explanations), which now needs explicit acceptance on the part of the user, and requires no hidden epistemological commitment, which now can explicitly vary depending on goals and requirements. I shall return to the topic of ontological commitment in chapter fifteen.

3.5.2. Conceptual schemes

The resemblance between LoAs and *conceptual schemes* (CSs) is too close not to require further clarification. In this section, the aim is not to provide an exegetical interpretation or a philosophical analysis of Davidson's famous criticism of the possibility of irreducible CSs, but rather to clarify further the nature of LoAs and explain why LoAs can be irreducible, although in a sense different from that preferred by supporters of the irreducibility of CSs. Note that Newell reached similar conclusions, despite the fact that he treated LoA as LoO, an ontological form of levelism that allowed him to escape relativism and anti-realism more easily (see Newell (1982) and Newell (1993)).

According to Davidson, all CSs share four features (all the following quotations are from Davidson (1974)):

1) CSs are clusters or networks of (possibly acquired) categories.

Conceptual schemes, we are told, are ways of organizing experience; they are systems of categories that give form to the data of sensation; they are points of view from which individuals, cultures, or periods survey the passing scene. (p. 183)

2) CSs describe or organize the world or its experience for communities of speakers.

Conceptual schemes (languages) either organize something, or they fit it [and as] for the entities that get organized, or which the scheme must fit, I think again we may detect two main ideas: either it is reality (the universe, the world, nature), or it is experience (the passing show, surface irritations, sensory promptings, sense-data, the given). (p. 192)

3) CSs are inescapable, in the sense that communities of speakers are entrapped within their CSs.
4) CSs are not intertranslatable.

Davidson argues against the existence of CSs as inescapable (from within) and impenetrable (from without) ways of looking at the world by interpreting CSs linguistically and then by trying to show that feature (4) is untenable. Could the strategy be exported to contrast the existence of equally inescapable and impenetrable LoAs? Not quite. Let us examine what happens to the four features above when LoAs are in question.

a. LoAs are clusters or networks of observables

Since they deal with observables, LoAs are not an anthropocentric prerogative but allow a more general (or indeed less biased) approach. We do not have to limit ourselves to human beings or to communities of speakers. Different sorts of empirical or abstract agents—not only human beings but also computers, animals, plants, scientific theories, measurement instruments etc.—operate and deal with the world (or, better, with the data they glean from it) at some LoAs. By neatly decoupling LoAs from the agents that implement or use them, we avoid confusion between CSs, the languages in which they are formulated or embodied, and the agents that use them. I shall return to this point presently.

b. LoAs model the world or its experience

LoAs are anchored to their data, in the sense that they are constrained by them; they do not merely describe or organize them, they actually build models out of them. So the relation between models and their references (the analysed systems) is neither one of discovery, as in Davidson's CSs, nor one of invention, but one of design, to use an equally general category. It follows that, contrary to Davidson's CSs, it makes no sense to speak of LoAs as Xerox machines or personal organizers of some commonly shared ontology (the world or its experience). Ontological commitments are initially negotiated through the choice and shaping of LoAs, which therefore cannot presuppose a metaphysical omniscience.

Because of the differences between (1)–(2) and (a)–(b), the remaining two features acquire a significantly different meaning, when speaking of LoAs. Here is how the problem is reformulated. LoAs generate, and commit the agent to, information spaces.

In holding that some LoAs can be irreducible and hence untranslatable I am not arguing that:

> (i) agents using LoAs can never move seamlessly from one information space to another.

This is false. They obviously can, at least in some cases: just imagine gradually replacing some observables in the LoAs of an agent. This is equivalent to arguing that human beings cannot learn different languages. Note, however, that some agents may have their LoAs hardwired: imagine, for example, a thermometer;

> (ii) agents using LoAs can never expand their information spaces.

This is also false. Given the nested nature of some LoAs and the possibility of constructing supersets of sets of observables, agents can aggregate increasingly large information spaces. This is equivalent to arguing that human speakers cannot expand their languages semantically, another obvious nonsense.

So, if we are talking about the agents using or implementing the LoAs, we know that agents can sometimes modify, expand, or replace their LoAs, and hence some degree of intertranslatability, understood as the acquisition or evolution of new LoAs, is guaranteed. The point in question is another one, however, and concerns the relation between the LoAs themselves.

LoAs are the place at which (diverse) independent systems meet and act on or communicate with each other. It will be recalled that this is the definition of an interface. The systems interfaced may adapt or evolve their interfaces or adopt other interfaces, as in (i) and (ii), yet different interfaces may still remain mutually untranslatable. Consider, for example, the 'tasting LoA' and the 'purchasing LoA' in our wine example. But if two LoAs are untranslatable, it becomes perfectly reasonable to assume that:

> (iii) agents may inhabit only some types of information spaces in principle.

Some information spaces may remain inaccessible not just in practice but also in principle, or they may be accessible only asymmetrically, to some agents. Not only that, but given the variety of agents, what is accessible to one, or some, may not be accessible to all. This is easily explained in terms of modal logic and possible worlds understood as information spaces. The information space of a child is asymmetrically accessible from the information space of an adult, but the information space of a bat overlaps insufficiently with the information space of any human agent to guarantee a decent degree of translatability (Nagel (1974)).

In principle, some information spaces may remain forever disjoint from any other information spaces that some agents may be able to inhabit. When universalized, this is Kant's view of the noumenal world, which is accessible only to its creator. Does this imply that, after all, we are able to say what a radically inaccessible information space would be like, thus contradicting ourselves? Of course not. We are only pointing in the direction of the ineffable, without grasping it.

To return to Davidson, even conceding that he may be successful in criticizing the concept of CSs, his arguments do not affect LoAs. The problem is that Davidson limits his consideration to information spaces that he assumes, without much reason, to be already linguistically and ontologically delimited. When this is the case, one may concede his point. However, LoAs do not vouch for the kind of epistemic realism, verificationism, panlinguism, and representationist view of knowledge that Davidson implicitly assumes in analysing CSs. And once these fundamental assumptions are eliminated, Davidson's argument loses most of its strength. Incommensurable and untranslatable LoAs are perfectly possible, although we shall see that this provides no good ground for a defence of some form of radical conceptual relativism (section 3.5.3) or anti-realism (section 3.5.4).

Davidson's criticism ends by shaping an optimistic approach to the problem of the incommensurability of scientific theories that supporters of the method of abstraction cannot share, but then, what conclusions can be drawn, from our analysis of LoAs, about the anti-realist reading of the history of science? An unqualified answer would fall victim to the same fallacy of unlayered abstraction I have been denouncing in the previous pages. The unexciting truth is that different episodes in the history of science are more or less comparable depending on the LoA adopted. Consider the great variety of building materials, requirements, conditions, needs, and so on, which determine the actual features of a building. Does it make sense to compare a ranch house, a colonial home, a town house, a detached house, a semidetached house, a terraced house, a cottage, a thatched cottage, a country cottage, a flat in a single-storey building, and a Tuscan villa? The question cannot be sensibly answered unless one specifies the LoA at which the comparison is to be conducted and hence the purpose of the comparison. Likewise, my answer concerning the reading of the history of science is: given the nature of LoAs, it is always possible to formulate an LoA at which comparing different episodes in the history of science makes perfect sense. The difference is made by the purpose or reason why a particular LoA is adopted. But do not ask absolute questions, for they just create an absolute mess.

3.5.3. *Pluralism without relativism*

An LoA qualifies the level at which a system is considered. In this chapter, I have argued that it must be made clear, at least implicitly, before the properties of the system can be sensibly discussed. In general, it seems that many disagreements might be clarified and resolved if the various 'parties' could acknowledge their LoA. By structuring the explanandum, LoAs can reconcile the explanans. Yet, another crucial clarification is now in order. It must be stressed that a clear indication of the LoA at which a system is being analysed allows pluralism without falling into relativism or 'perspectivism', a term coined by Hales and Welshon (2000) in connection with Nietzsche's philosophy. As remarked above, it would be a mistake to think that 'anything goes' as long as one makes the LoA explicit, because LoAs can be mutually comparable and assessable, in terms of inter-LoA coherence, of their capacity to take full advantage of the same data and of their degree of fulfilment of the explanatory and predictive requirements laid down by the level of explanation. Thus, introducing an explicit reference to the LoA makes it clear that the model of a system is a function of the available observables, and that it is reasonable to rank different LoAs and to compare and assess the corresponding models. The fact that one may use a shoe, a brick, and a hammer to nail something to the wall successfully does not meant that there is not a preferential difference between the three. This is a point that will be stressed repeatedly in the following chapters. The choice between different LoAs is not a matter of whimsical preference, personal taste, or subjective inclination of the moment. Anyone working in computer science knows already too well that one should never underestimate a crucial component in any use of an LoA, namely its goal or the 'what for?' question. LoAs are teleological, or goal-oriented. Thus, when observing a building, which LoA one should adopt—architectural, emotional, financial, historical, legal, and so forth—depends on the goal of the analysis. There is not a 'right' LoA independently of the purpose for which it is adopted, in the same sense in which there is no right tool independently of the job that needs to be done.

3.5.4 Realism without descriptivism

For a typed variable to be an observable, it must be interpreted, a correspondence that has inevitably been left informal. This interpretation cannot be omitted: an LoA composed of typed variables called simply x, y, z and so on and treated rather formally, would leave one with no hint of its domain of application. Whilst that is the benefit of mathematics, enabling its results to be applied whenever its axioms hold, in the method of abstraction it only results in obscurity. Does the informality of such an interpretation hint at some hidden circularity or infinite regress? Given the distinction between LoO and LoA, and the fact that there is no immediate access to any LoO that is LoA-free, how can an observable be defined as 'realistic'? That is, must the system under consideration already be observed before a 'realistic' observation can be defined? The mathematics underlying our definitions of typed variable and behaviour has been indicated (even if it is not always fully used in practice) to make the point that, in principle, the ingredients in an LoA can be formalized. There is no circularity: the heuristically appreciated system being modelled never exists on the same plane as that being studied methodically.

The point might be clarified by considering Tarski's well-known model-theoretic definition of truth (Tarski (1944)). Is there circularity or regress there? Might it be argued that one needs to know truth before defining it, as Meno would have put it? Of course not, and the same resolution is offered here. Tarski's recursive definition of truth over syntactic construction is based on an appreciation of the properties that truth is deemed to have, but that appreciation and the rigorous definition exist on 'different planes'. Hence, circularity is avoided.

More interesting is the question of infinite regress. Tarski's definition formalizes certain specific properties of truth; a regress would obtain only if one sought a complete characterization. So it is with the interpretation required to define an observable. Some property of an undisclosed system is being posited at a certain level of abstraction. An unending sequence of LoAs could possibly obtain were a complete characterization of a system sought.

It is implicit in the method of abstraction that a GoA is to be chosen that is accurate or 'realistic'. How, then, is that to be determined without circularity? The answer traditionally offered in mathematics and in science is that it is determined by external adequacy and internal coherence or, in computer jargon, *validation* (the GoA satisfies its operational goals) and *verification* (each step in the development of the GoA satisfies the requirements imposed by previous steps). I shall return to this important point in chapter eight. Here, I may stress that, first, the behaviours at a moderated LoA must adequately reflect the phenomena sought by complying with their constraints and taking advantage of their affordances; if not, then either the definition of the behaviour is wrong or the choice of observables is inappropriate. When the definition of observables must incorporate some 'data', the latter behave like constraining affordances and so limit the possible models. Second, the condition embodied in the definition of a GoA is a remarkably strong one, and ensures a robust degree of internal coherence between the constituent LoAs. The multiple LoAs of a GoA can be thought of as interlocking like the answers to a multidimensional crossword puzzle. Though such consistency does not guarantee that one's answer to the crossword is the same as the originator's, it drastically limits the number of solutions, making each more likely.

Adequacy/validation and coherence/verification neither entail nor support naïve realism. GoAs ultimately construct models of systems. They do not describe, portray, or uncover the intrinsic nature of the systems they analyse. We understand systems derivatively, only insofar as we understand their models. Adequacy and coherence are the most for which we can hope.

3.5.6 Constructionism

Through an LoA, an information agent (the observer) accesses a physical or conceptual environment, the system. LoAs are therefore interfaces that mediate the epistemic relation between the observed and the observer. Consider, for example, a motion detector (Figure 2). the past, motion detectors caused an alarm to activate whenever a movement was registered within the range of the sensor, including the swinging of a tree branch (object *a* in Figure 2). The old LoA_1 consisted of a single typed variable, which may be labelled *movement*. Nowadays, when a PIR (passive infrared) motion detector registers some movement, it also monitors the presence of an infrared signal, so the entity detected has to be something that also emits infrared radiation—usually perceived as heat—before the sensor activates the alarm. The new LoA_2 consists of two typed variables: *movement* and *infrared radiation*. Clearly, a car (object *b* in Figure 2) leaving the house is present for both LoAs; but for the new LoA_2, which is more finely

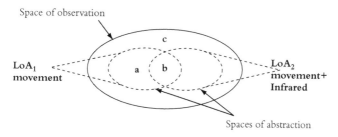

Figure 2 Example of level of abstraction

grained, the branch of the tree swinging in the garden is absent. Likewise, a stone in the garden (object *c* in Figure 2) is absent for both the new and the old LoA, since it satisfies no typed variable of either one.

The method of LoA is an efficient way of making explicit and managing the ontological commitment of a theory. Still relying on the example of the car, 'the battery is what provides electricity to the car' is a typical example of information elaborated at a driver's LoA. An engineer's LoA may output something like '12-volt lead-acid battery is made up of six cells, each cell producing approximately 2.1 volts', and an economist's LoA may suggest that 'a good quality car battery will cost between $50 and $100 and, if properly maintained, it should last five years or more'.

Data as *constraining affordances*—answers waiting for the relevant questions (see chapter four and chapter eight)—are transformed into factual information by being processed semantically at a given LoA (alternatively: the relevant question is associated with the right answer at a given LoA). Once data as constraining affordances have been elaborated into factual information at a given LoA for a particular purpose, the next question is whether truth-values supervene on factual information. This will be the topic of chapter four. Once information is available, knowledge can be built in terms of *semantic information*, an issue discussed in chapter twelve. An information agent knows that the battery is flat not by merely guessing rightly, but because e.g. it perceives that the red light of the low battery indicator flashing and/or that the engine does not start. In this sense, information provides the basis on which we build any further scientific investigation. Note, however, that the fact that data may count as *resources* for (namely, inputs an agent can use to construct) information, and hence for knowledge, rather than *sources*, leads to constructionist arguments against mimetic theories that interpret knowledge as some sort of picture of the world. The thesis will be elaborated throughout the rest of this book, but here it is in a nutshell. Whether empirical or conceptual, data make possible only a certain range of information constructs at a given LoA for a particular purpose, and not all constructs are made possible equally easily. An analogy may help here. Suppose one has to build a shelter. The design and complexity of the shelter may vary, but there is a limited range of 'realistic' possibilities, determined by the nature of the available resources and constraints (size, building materials, location, weather, physical and biological environment, working force, technical skills, purposes, security, time constraints, etc.). Not any shelter can be built. And the type of shelter that will be built more often will be the one that is more likely to take close-to-optimal advantage of the available resources and constraints, satisfying the given requirements and purposes. The same applies to data. Data are at the same time the resources and constraints that make possible the construction of information at some LoAs. The best information is that better tuned to the constraining affordances available. Thus informational coherence and adequacy do not necessarily entail nor support naïve or direct realism, or a correspondence theory of truth as this is ordinarily presented. Ultimately, information is the result of a teleological process of data modelling at a chosen LoA; it does not have to represent or photograph or portray or photocopy, or map or show or uncover or monitor or. . .the intrinsic nature of the system analysed, no more than an igloo describes the intrinsic nature of snow or the Parthenon indicates the real properties of stones. From this perspective, the world is neither discovered nor invented, but designed by the epistemic agents experiencing it. This is neither a realist nor an anti-realist but a *constructionist* view of information.

CONCLUSION

Feynman once remarked, a long time after Gassendi's comment to Descartes and Peirce's quotation opening this chapter, that

if we look at a glass of wine closely enough we see the entire universe. [. . .] If our small minds, for some convenience, divide this glass of wine, this universe, into parts—physics, biology, geology, astronomy, psychology, and so on—remember that nature does not know it![9]

In this chapter, I have shown how the analysis of the glass of wine may be conducted at different levels of epistemological abstraction, without assuming any corresponding ontological levelism. Nature does not know about LoAs either.

In the course of the chapter, I have introduced the epistemological method of abstraction and applied it to the study, modelling, and analysis of phenomenological and conceptual systems. I have presented its principal features and main advantages. Clearly, the adoption of the method of abstraction raises interesting questions, such as why certain LoAs, e.g. the so-called 'naïve physics' view of the world and the 'folk psychology' approach to the mind, appear to be 'privileged', or whether artificial life (ALife) can be defined in terms of a GoA. So much work lies ahead.

The method clarifies implicit assumptions, facilitates comparisons, enhances rigour and hence promotes the resolution of possible conceptual confusions. It also provides a detailed and controlled way of comparing analyses and models. Being clear about the LoA adopted provides a healthy antidote to ambiguities, equivocations and other fallacies or errors due to level-shifting, such as Aristotle's *metabasis eis allo genos* (shifting

---

[9] Feynman (1998), p. 66.

from one genus to another), Ryle's 'category-mistakes', and Kant's 'antinomies of pure reason'. Yet, all this should not be confused with some neo-Leibnizian dream of a *calculemus* approach to philosophical problems. In the previous two chapters, I argued that genuine philosophical problems are *intrinsically open*, that is, they are problems capable of different and possibly irreconcilable solutions, which allow honest, informed and reasonable differences of opinion. The method I have outlined seeks to promote explicit solutions, which facilitate a critical approach and hence empower the interlocutor. It does not herald any sort of conceptual 'mechanics'.

The method is not a panacea either. I have argued that, for discrete systems, whose observables take on only finitely-many values, the method is indispensable and has been with us in various versions for some time. Nevertheless, its limitations are those of any typed theory. Use of LoAs is effective in precisely those situations where a typed theory would be effective, at least informally and implicitly. Can a complex system always be approximated more accurately at finer and finer levels of abstraction, or are there systems which simply cannot be studied in this way? I do not know. Perhaps one may argue that the mind or society—to name only two typical examples—are not susceptible to such an approach. In this chapter, I have made no attempt to resolve this issue.

I have also avoided committing myself to determining whether the method of abstraction may be exported to ontological or methodological contexts. Rather, I have defended a version of epistemological levelism that is perfectly compatible with the criticisms directed at other forms of levelism.

The introduction of LoAs is often an important step prior to mathematical modelling of the phenomenon under consideration. However, even when that further step is not taken, the introduction of LoAs remains a crucial tool in conceptual analysis and in what I described, in chapter one, as conceptual engineering. Of course, care must be exercised in type-free systems, where the use of the method may be problematic. Such systems are susceptible to the usual paradoxes and hence to inconsistencies, not only when formalized mathematically but also when considered informally. Examples of such systems arise frequently in philosophy and in artificial intelligence. However, I hope to have shown that, if carefully applied, the method confers remarkable advantages in terms of treatment, consistency, and clarity. Too often philosophical debates seem to be caused by a misconception of the LoA at which the questions should be addressed and the purpose for which they should be answered. This is not to say that a simplistic policy of 'on the one hand...and on other hand' sort of arguments would represent a magic solution. Disagreement is often not based on confusion. But it seems that chances of resolving or overcoming it may be substantially enhanced if one is first of all careful about specifying what sort of observables are at stake and what requirements have determined their choice. The proof, of course, remains in the pudding, so the reader will be able to judge the fruitfulness of the method in the rest of the book, where it will be adopted more or less explicitly to reach a number of results that would have been otherwise impossible.

4

Semantic information and the veridicality thesis

Cominius: Where is that slave/ Which told me they had beat you to your trenches?/ Where is he?/ Call him hither.
Marcius (Coriolanus): Let him alone;/ He did inform the truth.

Shakespeare, Coriolanus Act I, Scene vi.

SUMMARY

Previously, in chapters one, two, and three, I provided a metatheoretical framework for PI. This chapter develops and supports the analysis of semantic information as well-formed, meaningful, and truthful data. In other words, we shall start tackling the first open problem discussed in chapter two (see P1). After a brief introduction, the General Definition of semantic Information (GDI) is criticized for providing necessary but insufficient conditions for the definition of semantic information. GDI is incorrect because truth-values do not supervene on semantic information, and misinformation (that is, false semantic information) is not a kind of semantic information, but pseudo-information, that is, not semantic information at all. This is shown by arguing that none of the popular reasons for interpreting misinformation as a kind of semantic information is convincing, whilst there are compelling reasons to treat it as pseudo-information. As a consequence, GDI is revised to include a necessary truth-condition. The conclusion summarizes the main results of the chapter, indicates some important implications and how the analysis of semantic information will be applied in the following chapters.

4.1 Introduction

'I love information upon all subjects that come in my way, and especially upon those that are most important.' Thus boldly declares Euphranor, one of the defenders of

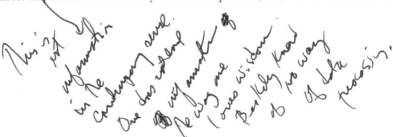

Christian faith in Berkeley's *Alciphron*.[1] Evidently, information has been an object of philosophical desire for some time, well before the computer revolution, Internet or the dot.com pandemonium. Yet what does Euphranor love, *exactly*?

Information is one of those crucial concepts whose technical meaning we have not inherited or even adapted from ancient philosophy or theology. It is not a Greek word, and the Latin term happens to have a different meaning, largely unrelated to the way we understand information nowadays. Perhaps it is because of this lack of sedimentation that we have so many different ways of understanding it, depending on the specific area of application and the task or purpose orienting ones analysis. Be that as it may, 'what is information?' has received many answers in different fields. Several surveys[2] do not even converge, let alone agree, on a single, unified definition of information. This is not surprising. Information is notoriously a polymorphic phenomenon and a poly-semantic concept so, as an *explicandum*, it can be associated with several explanations, depending on the level of abstraction adopted and the cluster of requirements and desiderata of a theory. Claude E. Shannon, for one, was very cautious:

The word 'information' has been given different meanings by various writers in the general field of information theory. It is likely that at least a number of these will prove sufficiently useful in certain applications to deserve further study and permanent recognition. *It is hardly to be expected that a single concept of information would satisfactorily account for the numerous possible applications of this general field.* (Shannon (1993), p. 180; italics added)

Weaver (1949), following Shannon, already supported a tripartite analysis of information in terms of

1. technical problems concerning the quantification of information and dealt with by Shannon's theory;
2. semantic problems relating to meaning and truth; and
3. what he called 'influential' problems concerning the impact and effectiveness of information on human behaviour, which he thought had to play an equally important role.

Shannon and Weaver provide only two early examples of the problems raised by any analysis of information. Indeed, the plethora of different analyses can be confusing. Complaints about misunderstandings and misuses of the very idea of information have been frequently expressed, even if to no apparent avail. Sayre (1976), for example, criticized the 'laxity in use of the term "information"' in Armstrong (1968), (see now Armstrong (1993)) and in Dennett (1969) (see now Dennett (1986)), despite appreciating several other aspects of their work. More recently, Harms (1998) pointed out similar alleged confusions in Chalmers (1996), who

---

[1] Dialogue 1, Section 5, Paragraph 6/10, see Berkeley (1732).

[2] See for example Debons and Cameron (1975), Larson and Debons (1983), Machlup and Mansfield (1983), Braman (1989), and Losee (1997). Adriaans and van Benthem (2008) provide a more recent survey.

seems to think that the information theoretic notion of information is a matter of what possible states there are, and how they are related or structured [. . .] rather than of how probabilities are distributed among them. (p. 480)

Given this scenario, in this chapter I shall not enter into the debate about what information in general might be. On this, the interested reader might wish to consult Floridi (2003a), (2003f), (2009b), (2009c). Rather, I will analyse only *one crucial aspect* of a *specific kind* of information, namely the alethic nature of *declarative, semantic information,* the kind of information that we normally take to be essential for epistemic purposes (more on these qualifications in the next section). This is Weaver's second point above. In such a context, the precise question addressed will be whether alethic values are supervenient[3] on such semantic information, as presumed by the General Definition of Information (GDI). I shall argue that well-formed and meaningful data do not yet qualify as semantic information because they need to be truthful as well. The constructive proposal defended is that semantic information encapsulates 'truthfulness', so that 'true information' is simply redundant and 'false information', i.e. misinformation, is merely pseudo-information. It follows that GDI needs to be revised by adding a necessary truth-condition.

4.2   The data-based approach to semantic information

It is common to think of information as consisting of *data*. This certainly helps, although less than one might imagine because, unfortunately, the nature of data is not well-understood philosophically either, despite the fact that some important past debates—such as those on the *given* and on *sense data*—have provided at least some initial insights. There still remains the advantage, however, that the concept of data is less rich, obscure, and slippery than that of information, and hence is easier to handle. So a data-based definition of semantic information seems to be a good starting point.

Intuitively, 'information' is often used to refer to user-independent, declarative (i.e. alethically qualifiable), factual, semantic contents, embedded in physical implementations like books, databases, encyclopaedias, websites, television programmes, and so on (Buckland (1991)), which can variously be produced, collected, accessed and processed. The *Cambridge Dictionary of Philosophy*, for example, defines information thus:

an objective (mind independent) entity. It can be generated or carried by messages (words, sentences) or by other products of cognizers (interpreters). Information can be encoded and transmitted, but the information would exist independently of its encoding or transmission. (Audi, 1999).

---

[3] This technical term is used here to mean, weakly, 'coming upon something subsequently, as an extraneous addition'. The term is not used with the stronger meaning according to which 'if a set of properties *x* supervenes on another set of properties *y*, this means that there is no variation with respect to *x* without a variation with respect to *y*'. I am grateful to Philipp Keller for having prompted me to add this clarification.

Examples include timetables, bank statements, scientific formulae, maps, sentences such as 'Berlin is the capital of Germany', 'the earth has only one moon', or 'the beer is in the fridge', and so forth. The analysis of this fundamental concept of *declarative, factual, semantic information* (henceforth simply information or semantic information) is not immediately connected to levels of subjective uncertainty and ignorance, to probability distributions, to utility-functions for decision-making processes, or to the analysis of communication processes. So the corresponding mathematical and pragmatic (see chapter five) senses in which one may speak of this kind of information (Weaver's first and third point above) are less than crucial in this context and will be disregarded. Likewise, there are many plausible contexts in which a stipulation ('let the value of $x = 3$' or 'suppose we discover the bones of a unicorn'), an invitation ('you are cordially invited to the college party'), an order ('close the window!'), an instruction ('to open the box turn the key'), a game move ('1.e2–e4 c7–c5' at the beginning of a chess game) may be correctly qualified as kinds of information. These and other similar, non-declarative meanings of 'information' (e.g. to refer to a music file or to a digital painting) are not discussed in this chapter, where we shall be concerned with an epistemic language-game, to use Wittgensteinian vocabulary:

The way music speaks. Do not forget that a poem, even though it is composed in the language of information, is not used in the language-game of giving information. (*Zettel*, § 160, see Wittgenstein (1981)).

4.3 The general definition of information

Over the last three decades, several analyses in information science, in information systems theory, methodology, analysis and design, in information (systems) management, in database design, and in decision theory have adopted a *General Definition of Information* (GDI) in terms of *data + meaning*. GDI has become an operational standard, especially in fields that treat data and information as reified entities (consider, for example, the now common expressions 'data mining' and 'information management'). A selection of quotations from a variety of important texts well illustrates the popularity of GDI:

Information is data that has been processed into a form that is meaningful to the recipient. (Davis and Olson (1985), p. 200)

Data is the raw material that is processed and refined to generate information. (Silver and Silver (1989), p. 6)

Information equals data plus meaning. (Checkland and Scholes (1990), p. 303)

Information is data that have been interpreted and understood by the recipient of the message. (Lucey (1991), p. 5)

data will need to be interpreted or manipulated [to] become information. (Warner (1996), p. 1)

Examples could easily be multiplied.[4] More recently, GDI has begun to influence the philosophy of computing and information as well (see for example S. Franklin (1995), Chalmers (1996), Mingers (1997), and Floridi (1999b)). The practical utility of GDI is indubitable. The question is whether it is rigorous enough to be applied in the context of an information-theoretical epistemology. We shall see that this is not the case, but before making any criticism, we need a more precise formulation.

Situation logic (Barwise and Perry (1983), Hanson (1990), Israel and Perry (1990), and Devlin (1991)) provides a powerful methodology and technical vocabulary for our task. Let us borrow the symbol σ and the term 'infon'[5] to refer to discrete items of information, irrespective of their semiotic code and physical implementation.[6] A clear and straightforward way of formulating GDI is as a tripartite definition:

> GDIσ (an infon) is an instance of semantic information if and only if:
> GDI.1 σ consists of n data (d), for $n \geq 1$;
> GDI.2   the data are *well-formed* (wfd);
> GDI.3   the wfd are *meaningful* (mwfd = δ).

According to GDI.1, semantic information comprises data. We shall see that things can soon become more complicated. In GDI.2, 'well-formed' means that the data are clustered together following the rules that govern the chosen system, code, or language being analysed. Syntax here must be understood broadly (not just linguistically), as what determines the form, construction, composition, or structuring of something. Engineers, film directors, painters, chess, and gardeners speak of syntax in this broad sense. As for GDI.3, this is where semantics finally occurs. 'Meaningful' means that the data must comply with the meanings of the chosen system, code, or language in question. In this case too, let us not forget that semantic information is not necessarily linguistic. For example, in a map, the illustrations are such as to be visually meaningful to the reader.

According to GDI, information cannot be dataless but, in the simplest case, it can consist of a single datum. Clearly, GDI requires a better understanding of the nature of data. This will be provided in the next section.

---

[4] Many other sources endorse equivalent accounts as uncontroversial. See for example Whittemore and Yovits (1973), Galliers (1987), Burch and Grudnitski (1989), Schoderbek et al. (1990), Drucker (1994), Kock et al. (1997), Bell and Wood-Harper (1998), Schultheis and Sumner (1998).

[5] 'The name [infon] suggests a parallel with the fundamental particles of physics, the electrons, protons, neutrons, photons and so forth.' (Devlin (1991), p. 37) Is there a conceptualization of 'information' as 'a theoretical commodity that we can work with, analogous to (say) the numbers that the number-theorist works with, or the points, lines and planes the geometer works with'? (Devlin (1991), p. 18) The question is answered in Dretske (1981), who provides a definition of information as an objective commodity. However, K. A. Taylor (1987) is justified in arguing that Dretske's 'objectivism' is not easily reconcilable with his pragmatic approach, whereby information is also defined pragmatically, with reference to a user S.

[6] This is in line with common practice in AI, Computer Science, and ICT, where the expression 'information resources' is used to refer to objective semantic information in different formats, e.g. printed or digital texts, sound or multimedia files, graphics, maps, tabular data, etc. (Heck and Murtagh (1993)).

4.4 Understanding data

A good way to uncover the most fundamental nature of data is by trying to understand what it means to erase, damage, or lose them. Imagine the page of a book written in a language unknown to us. Suppose the data are pictograms. The regular patterns suggest the compliance with some structural syntax. We have all the data, but we do not know their meaning, hence we have no information yet. Let us now erase half of the pictograms. One may say that we have halved the data as well. If we continue in this process, when we are left with only one pictogram, we might be tempted to say that data require, or may be identical with, some sort of representations. But now let us erase that last pictogram too. We are left with a white page, and yet not entirely without data. For the presence of a white page is still a datum, as long as there is a difference between the white page and the page on which something is, or could be, written. Compare this to the common phenomenon of 'silent assent': silence, or the lack of perceivable data, can be as much a datum as the presence of some noise, exactly like the zeros of a binary system. The fact is that a genuine, complete erasure of all data can be achieved only by the elimination of all possible differences. MacKay (1969) highlighted this important point when he wrote that 'information is a distinction that makes a difference'. He was followed by Bateson (1973), whose slogan is better known, although less accurate: 'In fact, what we mean by information—the elementary unit of information—is a difference which makes a difference.' Total data erasure means the erasure of MacKay's 'distinction' or Bateson's first occurrence of 'difference'.

All this clarifies why a datum is ultimately reducible to a *lack of uniformity*. More formally, according to the *diaphoric interpretation* (*diaphora* is the Greek word for 'difference'), the general definition of a datum is:

Dd datum $=_{def.}$ x being distinct from y
where the x and the y are two uninterpreted variables and the domain is left open to further interpretation.

Depending on philosophical inclinations, the diaphoric definition of data can be applied at three levels.

1 Data as diaphora *de re*, that is, as lack of uniformity in the real world out there. There is no specific name for such 'data in the wild'. A possible suggestion is to refer to them as *dedomena* ('data' in Greek; note that our word 'data' comes from the Latin translation of a work by Euclid entitled *Dedomena*). Dedomena are not to be confused with environmental data. They are pure data or proto-epistemic data, that is, data before they are epistemically interpreted. As 'fractures in the fabric of Being', they can only be posited as an external anchor of our information, for dedomena are never accessed or elaborated independently of a level of abstraction. They can be reconstructed as ontological requirements, like Kant's *noumena* or Locke's *substance*: they are not epistemically experienced, but their

presence is empirically inferred from, and required by, experience. Of course, no example can be provided, but dedomena are whatever lack of uniformity in the world is the source of (what looks to informational organisms like us as) data, e.g. a red light against a dark background. Note that the point here is not to argue for the existence of such pure data in the wild, but to provide a distinction that will help to clarify why some philosophers can accept the thesis that there can be no information without data representation (data are physical *dedomena*) while rejecting the thesis that information requires material implementation (*dedomena* are not material).

2 Data as diaphora *de signo*, that is, lack of uniformity between (the perception of) at least two *signals*, such as a higher or lower charge in a battery, a variable electrical signal in a telephone conversation, or the dot and the line in the Morse alphabet.

3 Data as diaphora *de dicto*, that is, lack of uniformity between two *symbols*, for example the letters A and B in the Latin alphabet.

Depending on one's position, *dedomena* in (1) may be either identical with, or what makes possible *signals* in (2); and signals in (2) are what make possible the coding of *symbols* in (3).

The dependence of information on the occurrence of syntactically well-formed data, and of data on the occurrence of differences variously implementable physically, explain why information can so easily be decoupled from its support. We all know that the actual *format*, *medium*, and *language* in which semantic information is encoded is often irrelevant and hence disregardable. So it is trivial to acknowledge that the same semantic information may be analogue or digital, printed on paper or viewed on a screen, in English or in some other language, expressed in words or pictures. However, interpretations of this support-independence can be philosophically tricky and may vary quite radically. For Dd leaves underdetermined:

- the classification of the *relata* (*taxonomic neutrality*);
- the logical type to which the *relata* belong (*typological neutrality*);
- the kind of support required for the implementation of their inequality (*ontological neutrality*); and
- the dependence of their semantics on a source or producer (*genetic neutrality*).

In order to understand the nature of semantic information, we shall now look at each kind of neutrality in turn. We shall then turn to a fifth kind. This concerns the truthfulness of the data in question (*alethic neutrality*), the crucial issue in this chapter.

4.5 Taxonomic neutrality

We saw that a white sheet of paper is not just the necessary background condition for the occurrence of a black dot as a datum, but a constitutive part of the black-dot-on-white-sheet datum itself, together with the fundamental relation of inequality that couples it with the dot. A datum is usually classified as the entity exhibiting the anomaly, often because the latter is perceptually more conspicuous or less redundant than the background conditions. But the relation of inequality is binary and symmetric. Nothing is a datum per se. Rather, being a datum is an external property. So GDI endorses the following thesis:

TaN a datum is a relational entity.

The slogan is 'data are *relata*' (a point to which I will return in chapter fifteen), but GDI is neutral with respect to the identification of data with *specific relata*. In our example, GDI refrains from identifying either the black dot or the white sheet of paper as the datum. In section 4.4, we saw that the concept of pure data in themselves (*dedomena*) is an abstraction, like Kant's *noumena* or Locke's substance. The point made was that data are never accessed and elaborated (by an information agent) independently of a *level of abstraction*. Understood as relational entities, data are *constraining affordances*: they allow or invite certain constructs (they are *affordances* for the information agent that can take advantage of them) and resist or impede some others (they are *constraints* for the same agent), depending on the interaction with, and the nature of, the information agent that processes them. With an analogy, a red light flashing repetitively and the car engine not starting allow one to construct the information that (a) the battery is flat. But it makes it more difficult to construct the information that (b) there is a short circuit affecting the proper functioning of the low-battery indicator, where the engine fails to start because there is no petrol in the tank, a fact not reported by the relevant indicator which is affected by the same short circuit. Still as constraining affordances, data are exploitable as input of adequate queries, at a given level of abstraction, that correctly semanticize them to produce information as output, for a particular purpose. In short, semantic information can also be described erotetically as *data + queries*. This essential feature will be exploited in chapter eight.

4.6 Typological neutrality

According to GDI, information can consist of different types of data as *relata*. The following classification into five categories is quite common, although the terminology is not yet standard or fixed (see Floridi (1999b)). They are not mutually exclusive, and one should not understand them as rigid: depending on circumstances, on the sort of analysis conducted, and on the level of abstraction adopted, the same data may fit more than one category.

δ.1. *Primary data*. These are the principal data stored e.g. in a database, such as a simple array of numbers. They are the data an information-management system—like the one used in the car to indicate that the battery needs to be charged—is generally designed to convey (in the form of information) to the user in the first place. Normally, when speaking of data, and of the corresponding information they constitute, one implicitly assumes that *primary data/information* is what is in question. So, by default, the red light of the low battery indicator flashing is assumed to be an instance of primary data conveying primary information.

δ.2. *Secondary data.* These are the converse of primary data, constituted by their absence (one could call them anti-data). In *Silver Blaze*, Sherlock Holmes solves the case by noting something that has escaped everybody else: the unusual silence of the dog. Clearly, silence may be very informative. This is a peculiarity of information: its absence may also be informative. When it is, the point is stressed by speaking of *secondary information*.

δ.3. *Metadata.* These are indications about the nature of some other (usually primary) data. They describe properties such as location, format, updating, availability, usage restrictions, and so forth. Correspondingly, *metainformation* is information about the nature of information. '"The earth has only one moon" is an English sentence' is a simple example.

δ.4. *Operational data.* These are data regarding the operations of the whole data system and the system's performance. Correspondingly, *operational information* is information about the dynamics of an information system. Suppose the car has a yellow light that, when flashing, indicates that the car checking system is malfunctioning. The fact that the yellow light is on may indicate that the low battery indicator is not working properly, thus undermining the hypothesis that the battery is flat.

δ.5. *Derivative data.* These are data that can be extracted from some data whenever the latter are used as indirect sources in search of patterns, clues or inferential evidence about things other than those directly addressed by the data themselves, e.g. for comparative and quantitative analyses (*ideometry*). As it is difficult to define this category precisely, a familiar example may be helpful to convey the point. Credit cards notoriously leave a trail of derivative data/information. From someone's credit card bill, concerning e.g. the purchase of petrol in a certain petrol station, one may derive the information about her whereabouts at a given time. Again, derivative information is not something new. Hume provides a beautiful example in these days of global warming. In the *Essays Moral, Political, and Literary* he reports that

It is an observation of L'Abbe du Bos, that Italy is warmer at present than it was in ancient times. 'The annals of Rome tell us,' says he, 'that in the year 480 ab U.C. the winter was so severe that it destroyed the trees. [. . .] Many passages of Horace suppose the streets of Rome full of snow and ice. We should have more certainty with regard to this point, had the ancients known the use of thermometers: But their writers, without intending it, give us information, sufficient to convince us, that the winters are now much more temperate at Rome than formerly. (Part II, Essay 11. *Of the Populousness of Ancient Nations*, Par. 155/186 mp. 448 gp. 432, see now Hume (1987))

Hume has just extracted some derivative information from some primary information provided by L'Abbé du Bos.

The previous distinctions are essential in order to understand the *typological neutrality* (TN) implicit in GDI.1. At first sight, TN may seem counterintuitive. A database query that returns no answer, for example, still provides some information, if only negative information; and we saw that silence is a meaningful act of communication, albeit minimalist. TN cannot be justified by arguing that absence of data is usually uninteresting, because similar pragmatic considerations are at least controversial, as shown by the previous two examples, and in any case irrelevant, since in this context the analysis concerns only objective semantic information, not *interested information* (see chapter five). Rather, TN is justified by the following principle of data-types reduction (PDTR):

PDTRσ consists of a non-empty set (D) of data δ; if D seems empty and σ still seems to qualify as information, then

1. the absence of δ is only apparent because of the occurrence of some *negative* primary δ, so that D is not really empty; or
2. the qualification of σ as information consisting of an empty set of δ is misleading, since what really qualifies as information is not σ itself but some non-primary information μ concerning σ, constituted by meaningful non-primary data $\delta.2$–$\delta.5$ related to σ.

Consider the two examples above. If a database query provides an answer, it will provide at least a *negative* answer, e.g. 'no documents found', so PDTR.1 applies. If the database provides no answer, either it fails to provide any data at all, in which case no specific information σ is available, or there is a way of monitoring or inferring the problems encountered by the database query to establish, for example, that it is running in a loop, in which case PDTR.2 applies. In the second example, silence could be negative information, e.g. as implicit assent or denial, or it could carry some non-primary information μ, e.g. the person has not heard the question, or the place is too noisy and we failed to receive an answer.

When apparent absence of data is not reducible to the occurrence of negative primary data, either there is no information or what becomes available and qualifies as information is some further non-primary information μ about σ, constituted by some non-primary data $\delta.2$–$\delta.5$. Now, differences in the reduction both of the absence of positive primary data to the presence of negative primary data and of σ to μ (when D is truly empty) warrant that there can be more than one σ that may (misleadingly) appear to qualify as information and be equivalent to an apparently empty D. Not all silences are the same. However, since GDI.1 defines information in terms of data, without any further restriction on the typological nature of the latter, it is sufficiently general to capture primary (positive or negative) data, that is, $\delta.1$, and non-primary data, that is, δ.2–δ.5 as well, and hence the corresponding special classes of information just introduced.

4.7 Ontological neutrality

By rejecting the possibility of dataless information, GDI also endorses the following modest thesis of ontological neutrality:

> ON no information without data representation.

When discussing 'Wiener's problem' in chapter two (see P.15), we saw that, following Landauer and Bennett (1985), and Landauer (1987), (1991), (1996), ON is often interpreted materialistically, as advocating the impossibility of physically disembodied information, through the equation 'representation = material implementation', that is:

> ON★ no information without material implementation.

ON★ is an inevitable assumption, when working on the physics of computation, since computer science applications must necessarily take into account the material properties and limits of the data carriers. Thus, the debate on ON★ has flourished especially in the context of the philosophy of quantum information and computing (see Deutsch (1985), (1997) and Di Vincenzo and Loss (1998); Steane (1998) provides a review). ON★ is also the ontological assumption behind the Physical Symbol System Hypothesis in AI and Cognitive Science (Newell and Simon (1976)). However, ON, and hence GDI, does not specify whether, ultimately, the occurrence of every discrete state necessarily requires a *material* implementation of the data representations. Arguably, environments in which all entities, properties, and processes are ultimately noetic (e.g. Berkeley, Spinoza), or in which the material or extended universe has a noetic or non-extended matrix as its ontological foundation (e.g. Pythagoras, Plato, Descartes, Leibniz, Fichte, Hegel), seem perfectly capable of upholding ON without necessarily embracing ON★. The *relata* in Dd could be *dedomena*, such as Leibnizian monads, for example. Indeed, the classic realism debate on the ultimate nature of reality could be reconstructed in terms of the possible interpretations of ON, as we shall see in chapter fifteen.

All this explains why GDI is also consistent with two other popular slogans, this time favourable to the immaterial nature of information, compatible with ON but antithetical to ON★:

It from bit. Otherwise put, every 'it'—every particle, every field of force, even the space–time continuum itself—derives its function, its meaning, its very existence (even if in some contexts indirectly) from the apparatus-elicited answers to yes-or-no questions, binary choices, *bits.* 'It from bit' symbolizes the idea that every item of the physical world has at bottom—a very deep bottom, in most instances—an immaterial source and explanation; that which we call reality arises in the last analysis from the posing of yes-no questions and the registering of equipment-evoked responses; in short, that all things physical are information-theoretic in origin and that this is a *participatory universe.* (Wheeler (1990), p. 5);

and

Information is information, not matter or energy. No materialism which does not admit this can survive at the present day. (Wiener (1948), p. 132)
  [information is] a name for the content of what is exchanged with the outer world as we adjust to it, and make our adjustment felt upon it. (Wiener (1950), p. 17).

Wheeler appears to endorse an information-theoretic, metaphysical monism: the universe's essential nature is digital, being fundamentally composed of information as data/dedomena instead of matter or energy, with material objects as a complex secondary manifestation. A similar position has been defended more recently in physics by Frieden ((1998), (2004)), whose work is based on a loosely Platonist perspective. Wheeler's position may, but does not have to, endorse a computational view of information processes, as we shall see in chapter fourteen. Wiener advocates a more pluralistic approach along similar lines. Both positions are consistent with GDI and ON, and I shall return to them in the last two chapters.

4.8 Genetic neutrality

Finally, let us consider the semantic nature of the data. How data can come to have an assigned meaning and function in a semiotic system, like a natural language, in the first place is one of the hardest questions in semantics, known as the *symbol grounding problem.* It is the topic of chapters six and seven. Luckily, the semanticization of data need not detain us here because GDI.3 only requires the data to be already provided with some meaning. The point in question is not *how* but *whether* data constituting semantic information can be correctly described as being meaningful *independently* of an informee. So the *genetic neutrality* (GeN) supported by GDI states that:

  GeN data can have a semantics *independently* of any informee.

GeN is well illustrated by the classic case of the Rosetta Stone, introduced in chapter two (see P16). Before its discovery, Egyptian hieroglyphics were already regarded as information, even if their semantics was beyond the comprehension of any interpreter. The identification of an interface between Greek and Egyptian did not affect the semantics of the hieroglyphics, but only its accessibility. This is the weak, conditional–counterfactual sense in which GDI.3 speaks of meaningful data being embedded in information-carriers informee-independently. GeN supports the possibility of *information without an informed subject*, to adapt a Popperian phrase. Meaning is not (at least not only) in the mind of the user. GeN is to be distinguished from the stronger, realist thesis, supported, for example, by Dretske (1981), according to which data could also have their own semantics independently of an intelligent *producer/informer*. This is also known as environmental information, and I already mentioned the example provided by the concentric rings visible in the wood of a cut tree trunk, which may be used to estimate the age of the plant.

To summarize, GDI defines information, broadly understood, as syntactically well-formed and meaningful data. Its four types of neutrality (TyN, TaN, ON, and GeN) represent an obvious advantage, as they make GDI perfectly scalable to more complex cases, and reasonably flexible in terms of applicability and compatibility. Indeed, philosophers have variously interpreted and tuned these four neutralities according to their theoretical needs. However, by specifying that GDI.1–GDI.3 are also sufficient conditions, GDI further endorses a fifth type of *alethic neutrality* (AN), which turns out to be problematic. Let us see why.

4.9 Alethic neutrality

According to GDI, alethic values are not embedded in, but supervene on semantic information. So defenders of the alethic neutrality of semantic information[7] argue that

(AN) meaningful and well-formed data qualify as information, irrespectively of whether they convey a truth, a falsehood, or have no alethic value at all.

Opponents[8] of (AN) object that

false information and *mis*-information are not kinds of information—any more than decoy ducks and rubber ducks are kinds of ducks. (Dretske (1981), p. 45)

and that

false information is not an inferior kind of information; it just is not information. (Grice (1989), p. 371)

The debate is not about a mere definition. Whether false information is a genuine kind of information has important repercussions on any philosophy and pragmatics of communication, for instance. Indeed, the discussion concerns the many ramified consequences of the alethic neutrality thesis, rather than an entry of the *Oxford English Dictionary*. If the thesis that meaningful and well-formed data already qualify as semantic information is correct then[9]

---

[7] Fox (1983), Colburn (2000b); also Fetzer (2004) and Dodig-Crnkovic (2005), who criticize Floridi (2004d); among situation theorists Devlin (1991), Floridi (2006), Dunn (2008), and Allo (forthcoming). For replies see Floridi (2005b) and Sequoiah-Grayson (2007).

[8] Other philosophers who accept a truth-based definition of semantic information are Barwise and Seligman (1997) and Graham (1999).

[9] Note that the conjunction of FI and TI presupposes two theses that are usually uncontroversial: (i) that semantic information is strictly connected with, and can be discussed in terms of alethic concepts; and (ii) that any theory of truth should treat alethic values or concepts symmetrically.

FI false information (including contradictions), i.e. misinformation, is a genuine kind of semantic information, not pseudo-information;

TA all necessary truths (including tautologies) qualify as semantic information (on this issue see Bremer (2003)); and

TI 'it is true that p' where p is a variable that can be replaced by any instance of genuine semantic information, is not a redundant expression; for example, 'it is true' in the conjunction '"the earth is round" qualifies as information and it is true' cannot be eliminated without semantic loss.

None of these consequences is ultimately defensible, and their rejection forces a revision of AN and hence of GDI. In the rest of this chapter, I will try to convince the reader that we should the reject FI and TA, following two strategies. The first consists in showing that none of the main reasons that could be adduced for interpreting false information as a kind of semantic information is convincing. This strategy is pursued in section 4.10. The second strategy consists in showing that there are compelling reasons to treat false and tautological information as pseudo-information. This is argued in section 4.11. As for TI, further arguments against it could be formulated on the basis of the literature on deflationary theories of truth. These arguments are not going to be rehearsed here because the development of this strategy, which has interesting consequences for the deflationary theories themselves, deserves an independent analysis that lies beyond the scope of this chapter. I shall return to the issue in the conclusion and then in chapter eight, in order to clarify what may be expected from this line of reasoning.

4.10 Why false information is not a kind of semantic information

Linguistically, the expression 'false information' is common and perfectly acceptable. What is meant by it is often less clear, though. The American legislation on food disparagement provides an enlightening example.

Food disparagement is legally defined in the US as the wilful or malicious dissemination to the public, in any manner, of *false information* that a perishable food product or commodity is not safe for human consumption. 'False information' is then defined, rather vaguely, as

information not based on reasonable and reliable scientific inquiry, facts, or data (Ohio legislation <http://www.ohiocitizen.org/campaigns/pesticides/veglibel.html>);

information that is not based on verifiable fact or on reliable scientific data or evidence (Vermont legislation <http://www.leg.state.vt.us/docs/2000/bills/intro/h-190.htm>);

information which is not based on reliable, scientific facts and reliable scientific data which the disseminator knows or should have known to be false (Arkansas legislation <http://www.arkleg.state.ar.us/ftproot/bills/1999/htm/hb1938.htm>).

In each case, false information is defined in the same way in which one could define a rotten apple, i.e. as if it were a 'bad' type of information, vitiated by some shortcoming. Why?

Suppose that there are going to be *exactly two* guests for dinner tonight, one of whom is in fact vegetarian. This is our dinner situation *D*. Let the false information about *D* be

FI =   '(A) there will be *exactly three* guests for dinner tonight and (B) one of them is vegetarian'.

One may wish to argue that FI is not mere pseudo-information, but a certain kind of information that happens to be false, for a number of reasons, yet even the most convincing ones are not convincing enough and this is why.

FI.1   FI can include genuine information.

Objection: this merely shows that FI is a compound in which only the *true* component B qualifies as information.

FI.2   FI can entail genuine information.

Objection: even if one correctly infers only some semantically relevant and true information TI from FI, e.g. that 'there will be more than one guest', what now counts as information is the inferred *true* consequence TI, not FI.

FI.3   FI can still be genuinely informative, if only indirectly.

Objection: this is vague, but it can be reduced to the precise concept of non-primary information μ discussed in section six. For example, FI may be coupled to some true, metainformation *M* that the source of FI is not fully reliable. What now counts as information is the true *M*, not the false FI.

FI.4   FI can support decision-making processes.

Objection: one could certainly cook enough food on the basis of FI but this is only accidental. The actual situation *D* may be represented by a wedding dinner for a hundred people. That is why FI fails to qualify as information. However, FI.4 clarifies that, if FI is embedded in a context in which there is enough genuine non-primary information μ about its margins of error, then FI can be *epistemically preferable* to, because *more useful* than, both a false FI_1, e.g. 'there will be only one guest for dinner', and a true but too vacuous FI_2, e.g. 'there will be less than a thousand guests for dinner' (see next chapter). What this shows is not

    i. that false information is an alethically qualified type of genuine information, but that
    ii. false information can still be *pragmatically interesting* because sources of information are usually supposed to be truth-oriented or truth-tracking by default (i.e. if they are mistaken, they are initially supposed to be so only accidentally and minimally), and that

iii. *logically*, an analysis of the information content of σ must take into account the level of approximation of σ to its reference, both when σ is true and when it is false.

This point is further discussed in the next chapters. In particular, misinformation will be shown to be irrelevant in chapter eleven.

FI.5   FI is meaningful and has the same logical structure as genuine information.

Objection: this is simply misleading. Consider the following FI: 'One day we shall discover the biggest of all natural numbers.' Being necessarily false, this can hardly qualify as genuine but false information. It can only provide some genuine, non-primary information μ, e.g. about the mathematical naïvety of the source. In the same sense in which hieroglyphics could qualify as information even when they were not yet interpretable, vice versa, an infon σ does not qualify as information just because it is interpretable. This point is further discussed in the next section.

FI.6   FI could have been genuine information had the relevant situation been different. Perhaps the difficulty seen in FI.5 is caused by the necessary falsehood of the example discussed. Meaningful and well-formed data that are only contingently false represent a different case and could still qualify as a type of information. It only happens that there will be fewer guests than predicted by FI.

Objection: this only shows that we are ready to treat FI as quasi-information in a hypothetical-counterfactual sense, which is just to say that, if D had been different then FI would have been true and hence it would have qualified as information. Since D is not, FI does not. FI need not *necessarily* be pseudo-information. It may be so *contingently*.

FI.7   If FI does not count as information, what is it? Assuming that p is false if S only thinks he or she has information that p, then what does S *really* have? Another cognitive category beyond information or knowledge would be necessary to answer this question. But another cognitive category is not required because we already have language that covers the situation: S only *thinks* he or she has *knowledge* that p, and actually has only information that p. (Colburn (2000a), p. 468)

Objection: first, a new cognitive category could be invented, if required. Second, there is actually *another* cognitive category, that of well-formed and meaningful data, which, when false, constitute *misinformation*, not a kind of semantic information. Third, the difference between being informed that p and knowing that p is that, in the latter case, S is supposed to be able to provide, among other things, a reasonable and appropriate (non-Gettierizable) *account* of why p is the case, as we shall see in chapter twelve. The student Q who can recall and state a mathematical theorem p but has no understanding of p or can provide no further account for p, can be said to be informed that p without having knowledge that p. But if the mathematical theorem is incorrect (if p is false), it must be concluded that Q is misinformed (i.e. not informed) that p (Q does not have any information about the theorem). It is perfectly possible, but strikes one as muddle and conceptually unsatisfactory, to reply that Q is informed that p (Q does have some information about the theorem) although p is false.

FI.8   We constantly speak of FI. Rejecting FI as information means denying the obvious fact that there is plenty of information in the world that is not true.

Objection: insofar as semantic information is concerned, this is a *non sequitur*. Denying that FI counts as a kind of semantic information is not equivalent to denying that FI is a common phenomenon; it is equivalent to denying that a false friend, who can perfectly well exist, counts as a kind of friend at all. We shall see this better in the next section. Here, it is sufficient to acknowledge that ordinary uses of technical words may be too generic and idiosyncratic, if not incorrect, to provide conceptual guidelines. In a supermarket, tuna is kept at the fish counter and bananas are placed with fruit, yet nobody would argue that this is evidence of the fact that our scientific categories should be updated.

FI.9   Informing does not require truth:

'x misinforms y that p' entails that $\neg p$ but 'x informs y that p' does not entail that p [and since]...we may be expected to be justified in extending many of our conclusions about 'inform' to conclusions about 'information' [it follows that]...informing does not require truth, and information need not be true; but misinforming requires falsehood, and misinformation must be false. (Fox (1983), pp. 160–161, 189, 193)

Objection: the principle of 'exportation' (from information as process to information as content) is more than questionable, but suppose it is accepted; misinforming becomes now a way of informing and misinformation a kind of information. All this is as odd as considering lying a way of telling the truth about something else and a contingent falsehood as really a truth, but on a different topic. The interpretation becomes perfectly justified, however, if informing/information is used to mean, generically, communicating/communication, since the latter does not entail any particular truth value. But then compare the difference between: (a) 'Q is told that p' and (b) 'Q is informed that p', where in both cases p is a contradiction. (a) does not have to entail that p is true and hence it is perfectly acceptable, but (b) is more ambiguous. It can be read as meaning just 'Q was made to believe that p', in which case information is treated as synonymous with (a form of) communication (this includes teaching, indoctrination, brain-washing etc.), as presumed by FI.9. But, more likely, one would rephrase it and say that (b) means 'Q is misinformed that p' precisely because p is necessarily false, thus implying that it makes little sense to interpret (b) as meaning 'S has the information that p' because a contradiction can hardly qualify as information, and being informed, strictly speaking, entails holding something true.

In conclusion, there seem to be no good reason to treat false information as a kind of information. This negative line of reasoning, however, may still be unconvincing, since other reasons might have escaped our analysis, which is certainly not exhaustive. We need some more 'constructive' arguments showing that false information is pseudo-information. This is the task of the next two sections.

4.11 Why false information is pseudo-information: Attributive vs predicative use

The first positive argument is a test based on a conceptual clarification. The confusion about the nature of false information seems to be generated by a misleading analogy. The most typical cases of misinformation are false propositions and incorrect data. Now, a false proposition is still a proposition, even if it is further qualified as not being true. The same applies to incorrect data. Likewise, one may think that misinformation is still a kind of information, although it happens not to be true. The conceptual confusion here may be explained in terms of *attributive vs predicative* uses of 'false'. The distinction was already known to medieval logicians. It was revived by Geach (1956) and requires a further refinement before we can apply it as a test to argue that 'false information' is pseudo-information.

Take two adjectives like 'male' and 'good'. A male constable is a person who is both male and employed as a policeman. A good constable, however, is not a good person who is also employed as a member of the police force, but rather a person who performs all the duties of a constable well. 'Male' is being used as a *predicative* adjective, whereas 'good' modifies 'constable' and is being used as an *attributive* adjective. On this distinction, we can build the following test: if an adjective in a compound is *attributive*, the latter cannot be split up without semantic loss. This property of indivisibility means that we cannot safely predicate of an attributively modified x what we predicate of an x. So far Geach. We now need to introduce two further refinements. *Pace* Geach, at least some adjectives can be used *attributively* or *predicatively* depending on the context, rather than necessarily being classified as either attributive or predicative intrinsically; 'false' is a typical example. Second, the attributive use can be either positive or negative. Positive, attributively used, adjectives further qualify their reference x as y. 'Good constable' is a clear example. Negative, attributively used, adjectives negate one or more of the qualities necessary for x to be x. They can be treated as logically equivalent to 'not'. For example, a false constable (attributive use) is clearly not a specific kind of constable, but not a constable at all (negative use), although the person pretending to be a constable may successfully perform all the duties of a genuine constable (this further explains FI.4 above). The same holds true for other examples such as 'forged banknote', 'counterfeit signature', 'false alarm', and so on. They are all instances of a correct answer 'no, it is a F(x)' to the type-question 'is this a *genuine x*?'.

Let us now return to the problem raised by the analogy between a false proposition and false information. When we say that p, e.g. 'the earth has two moons', is false, we are using 'false' predicatively. The test is that the compound can be split into 'p is a proposition' and 'p is a contingent falsehood' without any semantic loss or confusion. On the contrary, when we describe p as false information, we are using 'false' attributively, to negate the fact that p qualifies as information at all. Why? Because 'false information' does not pass the test. As in the case of the false constable, the compound cannot be correctly split. It is not the case, and hence it would be a mistake or an act of misinformation to assert, that p constitutes information about the number of natural satellites orbiting around the earth *and* is also a falsehood. Compare this case to the one in which we qualify σ as *digital information*, which obviously splits into 'σ is information' and 'σ is digital'. If false information were a genuine type of information it should pass the splitting test. It does not, so it is not.

4.12 Why false information is pseudo-information: A semantic argument

The second argument is semantic. It is based on four elementary principles and three basic requirements. Any satisfactory understanding of semantic information should implement the former and try to satisfy the latter, if possible. For the sake of simplicity, henceforth I shall speak of propositions, instead of alethically neutral, well-formed, and meaningful data. I shall also assume a two-value logic in which bivalence applies. All this will merely simplify the argument and make no difference to its cogency. Moreover, in order to formulate the argument more precisely the following vocabulary will be used:

$D = \{p_1, \ldots p_n\}$; D is a (possibly empty) domain of propositions.
ϕ, ψ = propositional variables ranging over D (for the sake of simplicity I shall occasionally leave implicit the universal quantification when it is obvious).
$S = \{i_1, \ldots i_n\}$; S is a (possibly empty) domain of instances of information.
$t(\phi) = \phi$ is contingently true.
$f(\phi) = \phi$ is contingently false.
$t/f(\phi) = \phi$ is contingently true or false.
$T(\phi) = \phi$ is a tautology.
$C(\phi) = \phi$ is a contradiction.
$H(\phi)$ = primary informative content of ϕ.
$P(x)$ = probability of x.

Independently of how members of S are defined, the four principles are (for x ranging over S):

P.1 $\forall x H(x) \geq 0$; *principle of the non-negative nature of information*: no instance of information can have negative, primary informative content.

P.2 $\forall x \forall y ((x \neq y) \rightarrow (H(x \cup y) = H(x) + H(y)))$; *additive principle*: for any two different instances of information, their overall informative content is equal to the sum of their informative contents.

P.3 $\forall \phi (P(\phi) = 1) \rightarrow (H(\phi) = 0))$; *inverse relationship principle*: any proposition whose probability is 1 has no informative content.

P.4 $\forall \phi \ (H(\phi) = 0) \rightarrow \neg \ (\phi \in S))$; any proposition with no informative content fails to qualify as information.

Note that, since we are assuming the possibility of empty sets, existentially (instead of universally) quantified formulae would be false. These four principles are uncontroversial and fairly standard assumptions in information theory and in the philosophy of information.[10] P.1 and P.2 concern S and the cumulative nature of informative contents. P.3 and P.4 concern D and the relation between information and probability.

We are now ready to consider the general strategy of the argument. Its form is indirect and basically reverses the steps that would be taken in 'slippery slope' reasoning. We shall begin by assuming that opponents of the veridical nature of information are correct. We shall then see that this is too permissive: too many items slip in. We shall then make the definition progressively tighter, until only the items that we wish to include in the definition of information are actually captured, and all the counterintuitive consequences are avoided. At that stage, we shall realize that we have endorsed the veridicality thesis itself.

4.12.1 First step: Too much information

Suppose we equate S to D, that is, let us assume that we accept the position according to which all propositions, independently of their truth value, already count as instances of information. An elementary consequence of P.3 and P.4 is that:

i. $T(\phi) \rightarrow (P(\phi) = 1)$;
ii. $(P(\phi) = 1) \rightarrow \neg \ (\phi \in S)$; therefore
iii. $T(\phi) \rightarrow \neg \ (\phi \in S)$.

Tautologies are not instances of information. Intuitively, no one can inform you about the outcome of a tossed coin by telling you that 'it is either heads or tails', since this much you know already. Note that tautologies represent a limit case since, following P.1 and P.4, they may be represented as instances of information devoid of any informativeness.

This initial and fairly weak constraint on the extension of the concept of semantic information is accepted by virtually all theories of semantic information. However, even if we restrict our analysis to propositional information, our initial equation $D = S$ is too permissive and needs to be revised.

---

[10] See for example Bar-Hillel and Carnap (1953), p. 242; Dretske (1981); Barwise and Seligman (1997); and van der Lubbe (1997), pp. 10–11.

4.12.2 Second step: Excluding tautologies

Following the previous analysis and P.1–P.4, we may adopt a weak alethic restriction on the extension of the concept of information, namely:

$$\forall \phi ((T(\phi) \rightarrow (H(\phi) = 0)) \rightarrow \neg (\phi \in S)) \qquad [1]$$

Unfortunately, even if we implement [1], we still have that

i. $P(\phi) = 0) \rightarrow (P(\phi) < 1)$
ii. $(P(\phi) < 1) \rightarrow (\phi \in S)$;
iii. $C(\phi) \rightarrow (P(\phi) = 0)$; therefore
iv. $C(\phi) \rightarrow (\phi \in S)$.

This is what I have defined as the Bar-Hillel–Carnap Paradox, according to which

a self-contradictory sentence, hence one which no ideal receiver would accept, is regarded as carrying with it the most inclusive information. (Bar-Hillel and Carnap (1953), p. 229)

Since contradictions are most unlikely, to the point of having zero probability, they are very informative; indeed they are the most informative propositions. Counterintuitively, you may be receiving an increasing amount of information about the outcome of an event by receiving an increasingly unlikely message but, strictly speaking, the most unlikely message is a contradictory one. In chapter five, I will show how this paradox can be solved. At this stage, let us simply assume that our position is too permissive and needs to be revised.

4.12.3 Third step: Excluding contradictions

The temptation, in taking the next step, would be to impose a straightforward, and very tight, veridicality constraint: something needs to be true to count as information, and this is why contradictions do not count. Yet this would be tantamount to endorsing the veridicality thesis. So our unconvinced opponent might still resist the temptation by including, in the original set of propositions, only those that are contingently true or false, and then argue that these and only these qualify as information, independently of their contingent truth-values. Here is the new restriction, revised:

$$\forall \phi ((T(\phi) \vee C(\phi)) \rightarrow \neg (\phi \in S)) \qquad [2]$$

This seems to be the model of information that most opponents of the veridical interpretation of semantic information have in mind (see for example Dodig-Crnkovic (2005)). They may accept that tautological and contradictory propositions do not qualify as information because they are in principle not informative, but they are still bent on arguing that contingently false propositions should count as information because they could be informatively useful (e.g. heuristically) or counterfactually informative about what could be (or have been) the case, although not about what is the case.

Intuitive as this might seem to some, it is still an untenable position, since it denies the possibility of erasing (in the sense of losing) information *syntactically*, that is, by generating inconsistencies (the same ϕ is affirmed and denied, independently of its truth value or semantic interpretation). Consider that from P.1–P.4 and [2] it follows that

$$\forall\phi\forall\psi((\phi \neq \psi \wedge t/f(\phi) \wedge t/f(\psi)) \rightarrow (0 < H(\phi) < H(\phi \cup \psi) > H(\psi) > 0)) \qquad [3]$$

Formula [3] says that, if you take any two, different, contingent propositions, then the union of their informative contents is always greater that the informative content of each of them considered separately. Now [3] might seem reasonable, until one realizes that it entails the following, highly counterintuitive conclusion: by accumulating any contingent propositions, we are always enlarging our stock of information, independently of whether the propositions in question are mutually inconsistent, thus generating a contradictory repository of information. More formally, [3] forces us to endorse:

$$H(\cup_1^n \phi) < H(\cup_1^{n+1} \phi) \qquad [4]$$

Formula [4] is utterly implausible. Although by definition (see P.2) our interpretation is meant to support only zero-order Markov chains, [4] generates sets that are, monotonically, increasingly informative, despite the random choice of the members. In simple terms, according to [4], the more propositions (of a contingent nature) are uploaded in a database, the more informative the latter becomes. This is obviously false, not least because one may 'diagonalize' the uploaded propositions in such a way that every progressively odd-numbered proposition uploaded is the negation of every even-numbered one previously uploaded.

A way of making [4] less unpalatable is to add the clause that ϕ may also range over informationally equivalent propositions (imagine 'John drives the car' and 'The car is driven by John') and tautologies. In this case one would obtain:

$$H(\cup_1^n \phi) \leq H(\cup_1^{n+1} \phi) \qquad [5]$$

Yet even in [5], informative contents cannot decrease over time unless data are physically damaged or erased. In fact, according to [5], it is still almost impossible not to increase informative contents by adding a random choice of contingent propositions. This is just too good to be true. We need to take a further step.

4.12.4 Fourth step: Excluding inconsistencies

The fact that the new interpretation turns out to be so counterintuitive does not prove that it is logically unacceptable, but it does show that it is at least in need of substantial improvements, if it has any hope of becoming reasonable. The problem with it is that [2] is still insufficient, so that the ensuing analysis of what may count as information is too inflated, even if one adopts [5]. Our model of information should satisfy the following two requirements:

R.1 informative contents can decrease syntactically, without necessarily being damaged or erased physically.

In symbols, we have the following consequence:

$$\diamond\left(H(\cup_1^n\phi) > H(\cup_1^{n+1}\phi)\right) \tag{6}$$

R.1 and [6] indicate that, by adding a new proposition, the result could be H(input) $\geq$ H(output), as we ordinarily assume. Imagine receiving first the proposition that p and then the proposition that $\neg p$. If you are unable to assess which message is reliable, the new proposition $p \vee \neg p$ has no informative content.

The second requirement is:

R.2 an information repository is unlikely to be increased by adding any contingent proposition; that is, the probability that, by adding any contingent ϕ to a information depository D, the informative content of D might increase becomes lower than (or at best equal to) the probability that it might be equal to what it was before, the larger the repository becomes.

R.2 further qualifies R.1 entropically: *ceteris paribus* (e.g. given the same amount of computational and intellectual resources involved in the production of informative contents), it is reasonable to assume that informative contents are comparatively more likely to decrease or remain unmodified (depending on how strongly R.2 is interpreted) than to increase. It is often the case that enlarging an information repository becomes increasingly expensive and difficult in terms of availability or management of resources. In symbols, we have that, for n progressively larger:

$$P(H(\cup_1^n\phi) \geq H(\cup_1^{n+1}\phi)) > P(H(\cup_1^n\phi) < H(\cup_1^{n+1}\phi)) \tag{7}$$

$$P(H(\cup_1^n\phi) \geq H(\cup_1^{n+1}\phi)) = P(H(\cup_1^n\phi) < H(\cup_1^{n+1}\phi)) \tag{8}$$

Note that the two formulae [7] and [8] need to be written separately because [7] represents a more radical version of R.2 than [8].

The implementation of R.1\[6] and at least R.2\[8] invites the elaboration of a new step, in which tautological and contradictory propositions have no informative content, and hence fail to qualify as information, while care needs to be exercised not to introduce inconsistency in our information repository. Here is the new set of restrictions, revised:

$$\forall \phi ((T(\phi) \lor C(\phi)) \to \neg (\phi \in S))$$

$$\sim C(\cap_1^x \phi)$$

[9]

$$\Diamond ((H(\cup_1^n \phi) \le H(\cup_1^{n+1} \phi))$$

As one would expect, now informative content can decrease syntactically and, if it increases, it does so much less easily than before. Have we finally reached a reliable model of semantic information? Not yet. Consider R.1 and R.2 once again. They specify that adding contingent propositions may lead to a decrease in the informative content obtained, but they do not specify that this might happen only for syntactic reasons (inconsistencies). Information content might decrease also semantically. In other words, the model of information implemented by [9] satisfies R.1/R.2 only partially, because it cannot fully account for the ordinary phenomenon of semantic loss of informative content. This is a serious shortcoming.

Imagine that the last extant manuscript of an ancient work tells us that 'Sextus Empiricus died in ad 201, when Simplicius went to Rome'. Suppose this is true. This informative content could be lost if the manuscript is burnt (physical loss of information), if it is badly copied so that the letters/words are irreversibly shuffled or the names swapped (syntactical loss of information), but also if some false statement is added or if the meaning is changed. However, according to [9], no loss of informative content would occur if the copyist were to write 'Sextus Empiricus was alive in ad 201, when Simplicius went to Alexandria'. Quantitatively, this may be true, but semantically it seems unacceptable. The former sentence would count as information, if true; the latter would not, if false. This is our third requirement:

R.3 informative content can be lost both physically, syntactically and semantically.

Information loss can occur by negation, by falsification, by making propositions satisfiable by all possible worlds (the upper limit represented by tautologies) or by making propositions inconsistent. In symbols:

$$\Diamond (H(\cup_1^n \phi) > H(\cup_1^{n+1} \phi))$$
physically, syntactically and semantically

[10]

R.3 and [10] motivate our last step.

4.12.5 Last step: Only contingently true propositions count as semantic information

Our last step consists now in revising the alethic constraint thus:

$$\forall \phi ((\phi \in S) \to t(\phi))$$

[11]

According to [11], informative content can easily decrease (one merely need to generate an inconsistency or a falsehood). When it increases, it does so even more slowly than in the previous model, and it can now be lost semantically, as well as physically and syntactically, as one would reasonably expect from a correct model of informative content dynamics. Note however that [11] is just another way of formulating the veridical thesis.

To summarize, if false information does not count as semantic junk but as a kind of information, it becomes difficult to make sense of the ordinary phenomenon of semantic erosion. Operators like 'not' lose their semantic power to corrupt information, information becomes semantically indestructible and the informative content of a repository can decrease only by physical and syntactical manipulation of data. This is utterly implausible, even if not logically impossible. We know that the fabric of semantic information can be, and indeed is, often undone by equally semantic means. This is the fragility of information. When false information is treated as semantic information, what may be under discussion is only a purely quantitative or syntactic concept of information, or well-formed and meaningful data.

4.13 The definition of semantic information

Well-formed and meaningful data may be of poor quality. Data that are incorrect (somehow vitiated by errors or inconsistencies), imprecise (understanding precision as a measure of the repeatability of the collected data) or inaccurate (accuracy refers to how close the average data value is to the 'true' value) are still data, and they are often recoverable, but, if they are not truthful, they can only constitute misinformation. Let me repeat: they can be informative, but only indirectly or derivatively: for example they can be informative about the unreliability of a source, but this is not the issue here. We have seen that misinformation (false information) has turned out to be not a kind of information but rather pseudo-information. Like 'truth' in the expression 'theory of truth', 'information' can be used as a synecdoche to refer both to 'information' and to 'misinformation'. 'False information' is like 'false evidence': it is not an oxymoron, but a way of specifying that the contents in question do not conform to the situation they purport to model. This is why, strictly speaking, to exchange (receive, sell, buy, etc.) false information about, for example, the number of moons orbiting around the earth, is to exchange (receive, sell, buy, etc.) no information at all about x, only meaningful and well-formed data, namely, mere semantic content. Since syntactical well-formedness and meaningfulness are necessary but insufficient conditions for information, it follows that GDI needs to be modified, to include a fourth condition about the veridical nature of the data in question:

GDI* σ is an instance of semantic information if and only if:

1. σ consists of n *data* (d), for $n \geq 1$;
2. the data are *well-formed* (wfd);
3. the wfd are *meaningful* (mwfd = δ);
4. the δ are *truthful*.

'Truthful' or 'veridical' is used here as synonymous for 'true', to mean 'providing true contents about the modelled system'. It is preferable to speak of 'truthful data' rather than 'true data' because the data in question may not be linguistic, and a map, for example, is truthful rather than true; and because 'true data' may give rise to a confusion, as if one were stressing the *genuine* nature of the data in question, not their veridicality.[11]

The veridical thesis embedded in GDI*.4 corresponds to the one characterizing the definition of 'knowledge'. Taking advantage of this parallelism, in chapter ten I will rely on the ordinary apparatus of modal logic (Chellas (1980)) to formalize '*a* is informed that *p*' as $I_a p$, and hence formulate the veridicality (of semantic information) thesis (VT) in terms of the so-called veridicality axiom (also known as **T**, **M**, or **K2**) ($\Box \phi \rightarrow \phi$) thus:

$$\text{VT)} \ I_a p \rightarrow p$$

The intended interpretation of VT is this: *a* is informed that *p* only if *p* is true, where, for present purposes, 'true' is suitable for a Tarskian treatment or to a treatment in terms of correctness (see chapter eight). We shall see that VT associates information logic (*IL*) to epistemic logics (*EL*) based on the normal modal logics **KT**, **S4**, or **S5**. It differentiates both *IL* and *EL* from doxastic logics (*DL*) based on **KD**, **KD4**, and **KD45**, since, of course, no *DL* satisfies the veridicality axiom. The problem concerning the veridical definition of information could then be formalized in the following way. What one might object is not that

a. There are other, non-epistemically-oriented concepts of information whose definitions do not satisfy VT;

for this is trivially true and uninteresting. Nor that

b. *IL* cannot be formalized in such a way as to satisfy VT;

for this is merely false, as I will show in chapter ten, where I will prove that information logic may allow truth-encapsulation (i.e. may satisfy VT) without facing epistemic collapse (i.e. merely morphing into another epistemic logic). Rather, the objection is that

c. when analysing the semantic, factual, epistemically-oriented concept of information, an *IL* that satisfies VT might be inadequate because too strong.

In other words, one might contend that '*a* is informed (has or holds the information) that *p*' is more like '*a* believes that *p*' rather than '*a* knows that *p*', and hence that the veridicality thesis should be dropped. In the next chapter, I will argue that this is not the case, because VT is pivotal if we are to solve the so-called Bar-Hillel–Carnap Paradox.

---

[11] I am grateful to Timothy Colburn and Philipp Keller for having pointed out this other possible source of confusion.

CONCLUSION

We ordinarily speak of false information when what we mean is misinformation, i.e. no information at all: whales are not fish just because one may conceptually think or say so. The goal of this chapter has been to clarify the confusion. The general definition of information (GDI) provides necessary but insufficient conditions for the qualification of data as semantic information. The definition has been modified to take into account the fact that semantic information encapsulates truthfulness. The new version of the definition (GDI*) now analyses information as well-formed, meaningful and truthful data. Here is a quick overview of some important implications of GDI*.

1 A critique of the deflationary theories of truth. From GDI*, it follows that one could accept deflationary arguments as perfectly correct, while rejecting the explanatory adequacy of deflationism. 'It is true that' in 'it is true that σ 'is redundant because there cannot be semantic information that is not true, but deflationism could mistake this linguistic or conceptual redundancy for unqualified dispensability. 'It is true that' is redundant precisely because, strictly speaking, information is not a *truth-bearer* but already encapsulates truth as truthfulness. Thus, deflationist approaches may be satisfactory as theories of truth-ascriptions but are inadequate as theories of truthfulness. I shall return to this point in chapter eight.

2 The analysis of the standard definition of knowledge as justified and true belief in light of a 'continuum' hypothesis that knowledge encapsulates truth because it encapsulates information. This hypothesis will be crucial for the rest of the book and is discussed in the following chapters.

3 The development of a quantitative theory of semantic information based on truth-values and degrees of discrepancy of σ with respect to a given situation, rather than probability distributions. As anticipated, this is the topic of next chapter.

4 The question about the informative nature (or lack thereof) of necessary truths, tautologies, equations or identity statements. This is a classic problem, as it runs through Hume, Kant, Frege and Wittgenstein. The latter, for example, interestingly remarked:

Another expression akin to those we have just considered is this: 'Here it is; take it or leave it!' And this again is akin to a kind of introductory statement which we sometimes make before remarking on certain alternatives, as when we say: 'It either rains or it doesn't rain; if it rains we'll stay in my room, if it doesn't . . .'. The first part of this sentence is no piece of information (just as 'Take it or leave it' is no order). Instead of, 'It either rains or it doesn't rain' we could have said, 'Consider the two cases . . .'. Our expression underlines these cases, presents them to your attention. (*The Blue and The Brown Books*, The Brown Book, II, p. 161, see Wittgenstein (1960))

I shall deal with this issue in the next chapter, though rather briefly (for a full discussion see D'Agostino and Floridi (2009)).

5 The solution of the problem of hyperintensionality. How one can draw a semantic distinction between expressions that are supposed to have the same meaning, according to a particular theory of meaning that is usually model-theoretic or modal in character, depends on how one can make sense of the relation between truth and informativeness in the case of logically equivalent expressions.

All these new issues are grafted to some old branches of the philosophical tree. We shall explore some of them in the rest of the book.

5

Outline of a theory of strongly semantic information

One is inclined to say: 'Either it is raining, or it isn't—how I know, how the information has reached me, is another matter.' But then let us put the question like this: What do I call 'information that it is raining'? (Or have I only information of this information too?) And what gives this 'information' the character of information about something? Doesn't the form of our expression mislead us here? For isn't it a misleading metaphor to say: 'My eyes give me the information that there is a chair over there?'

Wittgenstein, *Philosophical Investigations*, I. § 356, (Wittgenstein (2001)).

SUMMARY

Previously, in chapter four, I argued that semantic information is well-formed, meaningful and truthful data. This chapter applies, but also further supports, that conclusion by presenting a quantitative theory of strongly semantic information (TSSI) based on truth-values rather than probability distributions. The main hypothesis supported is that the classic quantitative theory of weakly semantic information (TWSI), based on probability distributions, assumes that truth-values supervene on factual semantic information, yet this principle is too weak and generates a well-known problem, called here the Bar-Hillel–Carnap Paradox (BCP). On the contrary, TSSI, according to which factual semantic information encapsulates truth, can avoid the BCP and is more in line with the standard conception of what generally counts as semantic information. After a brief introduction, section 5.2 outlines the BCP entailed by TWSI, analysing it in terms of an initial conflict between two requisites of a quantitative theory of semantic information. In section 5.3, three criteria of semantic information equivalence are used to provide a taxonomy of quantitative approaches to semantic information and introduce TSSI. In section 5.4, some further desiderata that should be fulfilled by a quantitative TSSI are explained. From section 5.5 to section 5.7, TSSI is developed on the basis of a calculus of truth-values and semantic discrepancy with respect to a given situation. In section 5.8, it is shown how TSSI succeeds in solving the paradox. Section 5.9 briefly discusses the so-called scandal of deduction, showing its connection with the BCP and how it can be solved by reference to the concept of 'virtual information'. The conclusion summarises the main results of the chapter and introduces the next.

5.1 Introduction

According to the classic quantitative theory of semantic information, there is more *information*[1] in a contradiction than in a contingently true statement. Bar-Hillel and Carnap (1953)[2] were among the first to make explicit this prima facie counterintuitive inequality:

It might perhaps, at first, seem strange that a self-contradictory sentence, hence one which no ideal receiver would accept, is regarded as carrying with it the most inclusive information. It should, however, be emphasized that semantic information is here not meant as implying truth. A false sentence which happens to say much is thereby highly informative in our sense. Whether the information it carries is true or false, scientifically valuable or not, and so forth, does not concern us. A self-contradictory sentence asserts too much; it is too informative to be true. (p. 229)

With a little hyperbole, one may conveniently refer to it as the Bar-Hillel–Carnap semantic Paradox (BCP).

Since its formulation, BCP has been recognized as an unfortunate, yet perfectly correct and logically inevitable consequence of any quantitative *theory of weakly semantic information* (TWSI; more on TWSI in section 5.2). As a consequence, the problem has often been either ignored[3] or tolerated[4] as the price of an otherwise valuable approach. Sometimes, however, attempts have been made to circumscribe its counterintuitive consequences. This has happened especially in Information Systems Theory (Winder et al. (1997))—where consistency is an essential constraint that must remain satisfied for a database to preserve data integrity—and in Decision Theory, where inconsistent information is obviously of no use to a decision maker. In these cases, whenever there are no possible models that satisfy a statement or a theory, instead of assigning to it the maximum quantity of semantic information, three strategies have been suggested:

1. assigning to all inconsistent cases the same, infinite information value (Lozinskii (1994)). This is in line with an economic approach, which defines x as impossible if and only if that x has an infinite price;

---

[1] This is short for 'semantic information content'. In this chapter I follow the common practice of using the two expressions interchangeably.

[2] The first version of the paper was read before the Symposium on Applications of Communication Theory in 1952. A more detailed and systematic treatment appeared then in Technical Report No. 247 of the Research Laboratory of Electronics, MIT, 1953. A slightly revised version was published in *The British Journal for the Philosophy of Science* in 1954. The chapter in Bar-Hillel (1964) is from the 1953 version, which is wrongly dated 1952 in the opening footnote.

[3] Cherry (1978), for example, contains one of the clearest and most informative summaries of TWSI, but no reference to the problem.

[4] Beginning with Bar-Hillel and Carnap (1953). Bar-Hillel and Carnap's analysis, discussed in the text, is further developed in Kemeny (1953), Smokler (1966), and Hintikka and Suppes (1970).

2. eliminating all inconsistent cases a priori from consideration, as impossible outcomes in decision-making (Jeffrey (1990)). This is in line with the syntactic approach developed by information theory (more accurately, the *mathematical theory of communication*,[5] more on this in a moment);

3. assigning to all inconsistent cases the same zero information value (Mingers (1997), Aisbett and Gibbon (1999)).

The third approach is close to the one developed in this chapter. The general hypothesis is that BCP indicates that something has gone essentially amiss with TWSI. TWSI is based on a semantic principle that is too weak, namely that truth-values supervene on semantic information. A semantically stronger approach, according to which information encapsulates truth, can avoid the paradox and is more in line with the ordinary conception of what generally counts as information. This thesis was defended in chapter four, but its practical viability is, of course, another matter. In this direction, however, information theory provides some initial reassurance. Information theory identifies the quantity of information associated with, or generated by, the occurrence of a signal (an event or the realization of a state of affairs) with the elimination of possibilities (reduction in uncertainty) represented by that signal (event or state of affairs).[6] In information theory, no counterintuitive inequality comparable to BCP occurs, and the line of argument in this chapter will be that, as in the case of information theory, a *theory of strongly semantic information* (TSSI), based on alethic and discrepancy values rather than probabilities, can also successfully avoid BCP.

Before developing TSSI, a note on the terminology, the concepts and the assumptions used in the chapter is in order. As in chapter four, I will borrow from situation logic the term 'infon' and the symbol σ to refer to discrete items of factual semantic information qualifiable in principle as either true or false, irrespective of their semiotic code and physical implementation. Some other basic concepts belonging to situation logic will also be adopted. Finally, the following three principles will be assumed without further justification:

a. Every source that generates, sends or transmits σ is treated as a bona fide source of information;

b. When it appears that σ can have a higher or lower degree of informativeness, it is attributed the highest of such degrees;

c. The channel of communication of σ is treated as ideally noiseless.

---

[5] This is also known as communication theory or information theory. In this book I have opted to refer to it as information theory, the most common label, despite the potential confusion. For an introduction to information theory in connection with the philosophical analysis of semantic information see Floridi (2003a).

[6] The classic reference is Shannon and Weaver (1949 rep. 1998). The reader interested in knowing more about information theory may start by reading Weaver (1949), Pierce (1980), Shannon and Weaver (1949 rep. 1998) then Jones (1979), and finally Cover and Thomas (1991). The latter two are technical texts. Floridi (2003e) provides a simplified analysis oriented to students. I shall avoid in this context any reference to 'doubt' (uncertainty of the signal) and 'surprise value' (statistical rarity of the signal), for these psychologistic terminology, preferred by Shannon and common in information theory, would be misleading here.

The primary aim of these principles is to shift the burden of proving that σ is not maximally informative from the sender to the receiver. They make it possible to set aside both error analysis issues and problems of a sceptical nature that would be out of place in this context.

5.2 The Bar-Hillel–Carnap Paradox

According to TWSI, the semantic content (CONT) of an infon σ can be identified *negatively*[7] with the set of all the descriptions of the possible states of the universe that are excluded by σ:

$$\text{CONT}(\sigma) =_{\text{def.}} \text{the set of all state–descriptions inconsistent with } \sigma \qquad [1]$$

Suppose E is a probabilistic experiment[8] in which infons are messages formulated by a source, using the standard language of set theory and classic, first-order logic with identity, to describe an elementary domain of three individual constants $D = \{a, b, c\}$ (e.g. three geometric figures of the plane) and a set of two predicates either affirmed or negated $\{G, H\}$, in such a way that each individual (e.g. each figure of the plane) is either G or $\neg G$ (e.g. four-sided or not), and either H or $\neg H$ (e.g. right-angled or not). E allows the formulation of twelve different atomic messages. These are incomplete state-descriptions of E. Complex messages can have any length, but a complete state-description is a message σ consisting of a conjunction of six different and consistent atomic messages. Each conjunctive message σ denotes one of the n possible states of E's universe. Since in E the number s of types of predicates is two and the length l of a message σ is six, the number of distinguishable messages is $s^l = 2^6 = 64$.

E is a microworld. Its fixed and finite sample space can be described either ontologically, as the set of all possible states $W = \{w_1, w_2, \ldots, w_{64}\}$, or semantically, as the set of all jointly exhaustive and mutually exclusive messages $\Sigma = \{\sigma_1, \sigma_2, \ldots, \sigma_{64}\}$.

Table 1 provides the matrix generated by E. Note that the layout is not trivial. The matrix is such that the fourth column contains the complements of the first column upside down (e.g. w_{49} is the complement of w_{16}), and the third column the complements of the second. This feature will turn out to be useful below.

E is functional precisely in order to have a discrete, one-to-one correspondence between formulae-like truth-makers and semiotic truth-bearers. This idealization guarantees information completeness. The question of whether a more coarse-grained model of truth-makers is metaphysically preferable will not be addressed here. Strictly speaking,

---

[7] Popper (1935) was one of the first to suggest that the amount of semantic information in a statement can be analysed in terms of the number of alternative possibilities excluded by that statement, see also Popper (1962). For a *positive* account, in terms of the set of all state-descriptions entailed by σ, see Hanson (1990). Both accounts equally lead to the occurrence of BCP.

[8] Following Hockett (1952), the choice of the model is suggested only by syntactic elegance and simplicity, and results can be adapted to cases where some redundancy also occurs.

Table 1 The sample space of a probabilistic experiment E with s^l [$s = 2$, $l = 6$] messages σ

	a	a	b	b	c	c
1	G	H	G	H	G	H
2	G	H	G	H	G	¬H
3	G	H	G	H	¬G	H
4	G	H	G	H	¬G	¬H
5	G	H	G	¬H	G	H
6	G	H	G	¬H	G	¬H
7	G	H	G	¬H	¬G	H
8	G	H	G	¬H	¬G	¬H
9	G	H	¬G	H	G	H
10	G	H	¬G	H	G	¬H
11	G	H	¬G	H	¬G	H
12	G	H	¬G	H	¬G	¬H
13	G	H	¬G	¬H	G	H
14	G	H	¬G	¬H	G	¬H
15	G	H	¬G	¬H	¬G	H
16	G	H	¬G	¬H	¬G	¬H
17	G	¬H	G	H	G	H
18	G	¬H	G	H	G	¬H
19	G	¬H	G	H	¬G	H
20	G	¬H	G	H	¬G	¬H
21	G	¬H	G	¬H	G	H
22	G	¬H	G	¬H	G	¬H
23	G	¬H	G	¬H	¬G	H
24	G	¬H	G	¬H	¬G	¬H
25	G	¬H	¬G	H	G	H
26	G	¬H	¬G	H	G	¬H
27	G	¬H	¬G	H	¬G	H
28	G	¬H	¬G	H	¬G	¬H
29	G	¬H	¬G	¬H	G	H
30	G	¬H	¬G	¬H	G	¬H
31	G	¬H	¬G	¬H	¬G	H
32	G	¬H	¬G	¬H	¬G	¬H
33	¬G	H	G	H	G	H
34	¬G	H	G	H	G	¬H
35	¬G	H	G	H	¬G	H
36	¬G	H	G	H	¬G	¬H
37	¬G	H	G	¬H	G	H
38	¬G	H	G	¬H	G	¬H
39	¬G	H	G	¬H	¬G	H
40	¬G	H	G	¬H	¬G	¬H
41	¬G	H	¬G	H	G	H
42	¬G	H	¬G	H	G	¬H
43	¬G	H	¬G	H	¬G	H
44	¬G	H	¬G	H	¬G	¬H
45	¬G	H	¬G	¬H	G	H
46	¬G	H	¬G	¬H	G	¬H
47	¬G	H	¬G	¬H	¬G	H
48	¬G	H	¬G	¬H	¬G	¬H
49	¬G	¬H	G	H	G	H
50	¬G	¬H	G	H	G	¬H
51	¬G	¬H	G	H	¬G	H
52	¬G	¬H	G	H	¬G	¬H
53	¬G	¬H	G	¬H	G	H
54	¬G	¬H	G	¬H	G	¬H
55	¬G	¬H	G	¬H	¬G	H
56	¬G	¬H	G	¬H	¬G	¬H
57	¬G	¬H	¬G	H	G	H
58	¬G	¬H	¬G	H	G	¬H
59	¬G	¬H	¬G	H	¬G	H
60	¬G	¬H	¬G	H	¬G	¬H
61	¬G	¬H	¬G	¬H	G	H
62	¬G	¬H	¬G	¬H	G	¬H
63	¬G	¬H	¬G	¬H	¬G	H
64	¬G	¬H	¬G	¬H	¬G	¬H

one needs to recall that, as in error analysis theory (J. R. Taylor (1997)), infons (e.g. measures) are never compared to 'absolute realities' (e.g. absolutely true values), but always and only to other infons that are assumed or known to be true, i.e. states of the world that are transformed into evidence by the information process, at least momentarily, until further critical revision (Levi (1967)). I shall return to this point in chapter fifteen.

Three direct consequences of formula [1] are that:

i. the inclusion of any other atomic message in any $\sigma_i \in \Sigma$ necessarily results in σ_i becoming inconsistent. Thus, Bar-Hillel and Carnap (1953) describe Σ as the set of all, 'most strongly synthetic messages' in E. Each σ_i is inconsistent with any other message in Σ, and any other conjunctive message that logically implies, or is stronger than, any σ_i is self-contradictory;

ii. the set of all messages inconsistent with a tautology is empty, therefore any tautology (T) has minimum semantic content (recall that the context is factual information), that is

$$\text{CONT}(T) = \text{MIN} \qquad [2]$$

iii. since any message is inconsistent with a contradiction ($\perp$), any contradiction has maximum semantic content, that is

$$(\text{BCP})\text{CONT}(\perp) = \text{MAX} \qquad [3]$$

In formula [3], two fundamental requisites (R.1 and R.2, see below) of a quantitative theory of semantic information appear to be in conflict. In section 5.7, we shall see that their relation is actually somewhat more complex, but at the moment it is sufficient to analyse it in its simplest form.

The first requisite (R.1) states that $\text{CONT}(\sigma)$ should be inversely related to $p(\sigma)$, the logical probability of σ. The 'mathematically simplest relation' (Bar-Hillel and Carnap (1953), p. 302) fulfilling this requirement is the complement of 1:

$$(\text{R.1})\text{CONT}(\sigma) = 1 - p(\sigma) \qquad [4]$$

TWSI implements R.1 but, as an alternative, R.1 could also be expressed as an inverse proportion:

$$(\text{R.1}^*)\text{CONT}(\sigma) \propto k/p(\sigma) \qquad [5]$$

where k is a constant of proportionality independent of the two values. This is the standard approach implemented by information theory, where the quantity of information conveyed by σ is equivalent to the reciprocal of $p(\sigma)$, expressed in bits:

$$I(\sigma) = \log_2 1/p(\sigma) = -\log_2 p(\sigma) \qquad [6]$$

The problem with implementing R.1* in TWSI is that $\text{CONT}(\sigma) \times p(\sigma) = k$, and the equation would require a more complex treatment of $\text{CONT}(T)$ and $\text{CONT}(\perp)$ as two limits of the continuous function $f(p(\sigma))$:

$$\text{Cont}(T) = \lim_{p(\sigma)\to 1} f(p(\sigma)) = 0$$
$$\text{Cont}(\bot) = \lim_{p(\sigma)\to 0} f(p(\sigma)) = 1 \qquad [7]$$

The complication does not occur in information theory because the latter presupposes a probabilistic approach and partitions the total amount of probability *a priori*, among all the actually possible alternatives, thus excluding by definition the occurrence of any option that is necessarily false. In more formal terms, logarithm of zero is not defined, so information theory eliminates the problematic cases a priori. In what follows, I shall argue that the set-theoretic approach expressed in R.1 can be successfully adopted by TSSI as well.

The second requisite (R.2* below, as usual, the asterisk is a reminder that the formula is provisional and will have to be refined) states that, *ceteris paribus*, the degree of informativeness of σ (in symbols $\iota(\sigma)$), should be directly proportional to the semantic content of σ:

$$(\text{R.2*})\iota(\sigma) \propto m \; \text{CONT}(\sigma) + b, \text{ with } m \geq 1 \text{ and } b \geq 0 \qquad [8]$$

For our purposes, the significant point in formula [8] is only the relation of direct proportionality between $\iota(\sigma)$ and $\text{CONT}(\sigma)$. So, for the sake of elegance and simplicity, we can adopt a weaker version of R.2*, by treating m and b as redundancy factors and hence reducing m to 1 and b to 0. Assuming that σ can be fully normalized in this way,[9] R.2* simplifies to:

$$(\text{R.2})\iota(\sigma) \propto \text{CONT}(\sigma) \qquad [9]$$

The simplification does not affect the following analysis, as anything that will be inferred from [9] below can be inferred from [8] *a fortiori*.

R.1 and R.2 generate no conflict about the interpretation of σ when σ is a tautology ($\vDash \sigma$). However, when σ is a contradiction ($\sigma \nvDash$), the conclusion is that $p(\sigma) = 0$ and $\iota(\sigma) = 0$, and it becomes unclear whether the value of $\text{CONT}(\sigma)$ should be MAX, following R.1, or MIN, following R.2. This tension is sufficiently problematic to invite the elaboration of a different approach.

5.3 Three criteria of information equivalence

TWSI, the classic quantitative theory of semantic information, concentrates on the (degree of) systemic consistency and then the *a priori*, logical probability of (sets of) infons. There is no reference to the actual alethic values of the infons in question, which are supposed to qualify as instances of information independently of their alethic value. This is why the theory has been described as only weakly semantic. Is it possible to avoid BCP by assuming a stronger semantic principle, according to which if σ qualifies as

---

[9] 'Normalization' refers here to the process followed to obtain a database design that allows for efficient access and storage of data and reduces data redundancy and the chances of data becoming inconsistent.

information it must encapsulate truth? The question presupposes a clear view of what alternatives to TWSI are available, hence a taxonomy of quantitative theories. Luckily, the latter can be provided on the basis of three criteria of semantic equivalence.

Any quantitative theory, including any theory dealing with the concept of semantic information and its various measures (Smokler (1966)), requires at least a criterion of comparative quantitative equivalence. The criterion makes it possible to establish whether two measured objects, e.g. two coins x and y, have the same weight z, even if z cannot be qualified any more precisely. Now, two infons $\sigma_n \neq \sigma_m$ can be said to be co-informative—that is, to possess an equivalent quantity of semantic information, $C_i(\sigma_n, \sigma_m)$—according to three criteria of comparative quantitative equivalence. They are listed here in order of decreasing strength:

$$(C.1) \quad C_i(\sigma_n, \sigma_m) \leftrightarrow \sigma_n \text{ and } \sigma_m \text{ have equivalent meaning} \qquad [10]$$

For example, declarative sentences expressing the same proposition, like 'Peter drives the car' and 'The car is driven by Peter', possess an equivalent amount of semantic information. If σ_n and σ_m are *qualitatively* co-informative, a *pragmatic theory* (Bar-Hillel and Carnap (1953)) could provide the relevant analysis, by addressing the question of how much information a given infon carries *for a subject S* in some informational state and within a specific informational environment. The pragmatic theory of 'interested information' is crucial in Decision Theory, where a standard quantitative axiom states that, in an ideal context and *ceteris paribus*, the more informative σ is to S (*interested information*), the more S ought to be rationally willing to pay to find out whether σ is true (Sneed (1967)). It remains to be seen whether a satisfactory quantitative theory can effectively be developed in full.[10]

$$(C.2) \quad C_i(\sigma_n, \sigma_m) \leftrightarrow \sigma_n \text{ and } \sigma_m \text{ are truth–functionally equivalent}^{11} \qquad [11]$$

If σ_n and σ_m are *alethically* co-informative, Boolean algebra provides the relevant analysis. Of course [11] can be extended to apply to classic n-order, multi-valued or fuzzy logic systems, and so forth.

$$(C.3) \quad C_i(\sigma_n, \sigma_m) \leftrightarrow \sigma_n \text{ and } \sigma_m \text{ are equiprobable} \qquad [12]$$

---

[10] See Sneed (1967) for an early, critical analysis based on Jeffrey (1965), now Jeffrey (1990). Szaniawski (1967), based on a game-theoretic approach, and Szaniawski (1974), both now in Szaniawski (1998), is more optimistic. Smokler (1966) defends a moderate approach, which, however, requires that every individual has, at a certain time, only a finite and consistent set of true/false beliefs, and that these can be expressed in the language of the classic logic of predicates. These seem unrealistic requirements, especially since Smokler accepts both (i) that beliefs are best characterized as propositions and (ii) that the latter are non-linguistic entities. As a counterexample, it suffices to note that any individual who knows arithmetic can both believe an infinite number of true propositions and hold some contradictory beliefs. Jamison (1970) goes as far as to argue that a pragmatic theory of informational quantities is the most fundamental of all approaches, and presents a sort of inverted BCP by suggesting that (p. 29) 'an undesirable feature of RL [i.e. what has been defined in this chapter as TWSI] is that in it logical truths carry no information', so that mathematical equations, insofar as they can be interpreted as tautologies, would be utterly non-informative.

[11] Smokler (1966), p. 202. See also Larkin and Simon (1987).

If σ_n and σ_m are *quantitatively* co-informative, the classic theory of weakly semantic information provides the relevant analysis.

Interpreting C.1–C.3 as conditionals rather than biconditionals provides the ground for a taxonomy of theories, illustrated by Table 2.

Table 2 Taxonomy of quantitative theories of semantic information

$C_i(\sigma_n, \sigma_m)$	Qualitatively co-informative (semantic equivalence)	Alethically co-informative (truth-functional equivalence)	Quantitatively co-informative (equiprobability)
(1)	1	1	1
(2)	1	1	0
(3)	1	0	1
(4)	1	0	0
(5)	0	1	1
(6)	0	1	0
(7)	0	0	1
(8)	0	0	0

More finely grained criteria for co-informativeness could now be developed, ranging from full semantic equivalence to full equiprobability. Intuitively, the closer a criterion is to semantic equivalence, the more the semantic theory is forced to rely on the interpretation of σ by an intelligent receiver/holder S capable of understanding its contextual sense (this is known as 'fully interested information'), the less easily the information in question can undergo a quantifiable treatment, and the more a hermeneutic approach becomes inevitable. At the other end of the spectrum, a purely quantitative approach to the theory of semantic information will tend to abstract from the users of σ ('fully disinterested information') and to deal only with the analysis of $p(\sigma)$, irrespective of its *actual* interpretation and contextual alethic value. The latter strategy is consistent with a family of realist positions, including mathematical Platonism and epistemological Cartesianism: infons are treated extensionally not intentionally, as semantic (at least in the sense of being interpretable), structured, abstract objects, comparable to fundamental informational particles. They subsist, are systemically related and may be physically implemented in the world of human experience.

A cursory analysis of Table 3 already suffices to show that:

a. approach no. 8 is trivially uninteresting;
b. approaches nos 3 and 4 are not implementable, since it is impossible for C_i (σ_n, σ_m) to be the case qualitatively without σ_n and σ_m also being alethically co-informative;
c. approaches nos. 1, 2 and 4 would initially rank as the most interesting alternatives, but a fully quantitative and extensionalist approach to the meaning of σ seems unachievable, witness the failure of many programs in 'strong' Artificial

Intelligence (Floridi (1999b), ch. 5). In this chapter, I shall assume that, if possible, less demanding alternatives should be developed first;

d. approach no. 6 is the one followed in mathematical logic; and
e. approach no. 7 is the one followed by information theory and TWSI. We have seen that the implementation of C.3 in no. 7 brings with it some obvious computational advantages, of which TWSI makes the most, but also a shortcoming, namely BCP. The avoidance of BCP invites the development of
f. approach no. 5, that is, an analysis of the quantity of semantic information in σ including a reference to its alethic value. This is TSSI.

5.4 Three desiderata for TSSI

As anticipated above, the principal goal of TSSI is to provide a quantitative analysis of semantic information that can be as mathematically successful as TWSI, but more respectful of our common-sense intuitions and the conclusions reached in chapter four. More specifically, this means trying to:

D.1 avoid any counterintuitive inequality comparable to BCP;
D.2 treat the alethic value of σ not as a supervenient but as a necessary feature of semantic information, relevant to the quantitative analysis (for a similar approach see Dretske (1981));
D.3 extend a quantitative analysis to the whole family of information-related concepts: semantic information vacuity and inaccuracy, informativeness, misinformation (what is ordinarily called 'false information'), disinformation.

Arguably, D.1 and D.2 are complementary. BCP-like problems can arise because the alethic values of the infons in question are treated as irrelevant to the quantitative analysis of semantic information, so TSSI can attempt to fulfil both D.1 and D.2 by implementing C.2. Regarding D.3, this requires a theory semantically richer than one based only on probability distributions (Szaniawski (1984), Mingers (1997), Szaniawski (1998)). In sections 5.6 to 5.9, it will be shown that, by following the definition of semantic information provided in chapter four (i.e. as encapsulating truth), TSSI offers a quantitative approach that can be generalized to a whole family of related concepts.

5.5 Degrees of vacuity and inaccuracy

The first step in the construction of TSSI is to define the concept of 'informative content' or intrinsic *informativeness* of σ extensionally and *a priori* in an *ideal* context, as a function of the positive or negative degree of 'semantic distance' or *deviation* of σ from a fixed point or origin, represented by the given situation w, to which σ is supposed to refer.[12] The context is ideal because it presupposes a state of *perfect* and *complete* information about the system, in the game-theoretic sense of the expressions. We shall see in section 5.9 that this is a further difference between TWSI and TSSI, which presupposes a state of imperfect and incomplete information with respect to the states of the system. Here it is possible to anticipate that presupposing some 'localized omniscience' does not affect the value of the approach, since TSSI attempts to discover what the quantity of semantic information in σ is when the alethic value of σ is known, not the average amount of semantic information any σ may have a priori.

Let w be a situation in a context, where a 'situation' may be 'determined by (what goes on in) a topologically simply-connected, structured region of space–time' (Devlin (1991), p. 69), and a 'context' is the set of interrelated conditions in which a situation occurs, what can be described, informally, as the immediate environment of a situation or, topologically, its neighbourhood. Each message σ_i in E conforms to (has the property of providing or conveying true contents about) its corresponding situation w_i in W. Still following the terminology of situation logic, this means that w_i fully supports σ_i (in symbols, $\Vdash_{Wi} \sigma_i$). Obviously, each message σ_i is maximally informative relatively to its corresponding situation w_i, yet this applies indiscriminately and trivially to any message. More interestingly, the amount of informativeness of each σ_i can be evaluated absolutely, as a function of

i. the polarity of σ_i, i.e. the alethic value possessed by σ_i; and

ii. the degree of discrepancy[13] (want of agreement) between σ_i and a given state of the world w, calculated as the degree ϑ of semantic deviation[14] of σ_i from the uniquely determinate state w in which E is ($\Vdash_{W\theta} \sigma$).

The given situation w functions as a benchmark to test the Boolean truth-value and the degree of discrepancy of each σ. This captures an important aspect of the ordinary conception of the nature of information, at the roots of any epistemic utility function (Levi (1967)): two infons can both be false and yet significantly more or less distant from the event or state of affairs w about which they purport to be informative, e.g.

---

[12] Although Szaniawski (1984) does not refer explicitly to any result in situation logic, he does develop an approach similar to Devlin (1991). A limitation of his analysis is that he does not acknowledge the fact that the change in perspective entails an inversion in the relation between information and truth, which no longer supervenes on, but now constitutes the former. His definition of semantic information as 'potential information about X that has been "singled out" in some way: observed, asserted, etc. Semantic information may be said to be true if it points to the actual state of the world' (p. 231) is unsatisfactory, not so much because it is circular (in the article the circularity is avoided at the cost of some vacuity, by means of a reference to unspecified ways in which σ is 'relevant' and 'points' to the actual state in which X is) but because it does not clarify what difference is made by the 'singling out' procedure. In his article, it becomes clear that 'singling out' p is attributing a positive alethic value to p as a description correctly pointing to the actual state in which X is.

[13] This is a technical term in error analysis terminology. When a measurement or a result is compared to another that is assumed or known to be more reliable, the difference between the two is defined as the *experimental* discrepancy.

[14] This is another technical term in error analysis. Deviations are 'experimental uncertainties' and are commonly called 'errors'. More precisely, when a set of measurements is made of a physical quantity, the difference between each measurement and the average (mean) of the entire set is called the deviation of the measurement from the mean.

'there are ten people in the library' and 'there are fifty people in the library', when in fact there are nine people in the library. Likewise, two infons can both be true and yet deviate more or less significantly from w, e.g. 'there is someone in the library' vs 'there are 9 or 10 people in the library'. This implies that a falsehood with a very low degree of discrepancy may be pragmatically preferable to a truth with a very high degree of discrepancy (Popper (1935)). This in turn provides an argument for the rejection of the deductive closure principle, in the following sense: since σ could be false, if S rationally commits him/herself to accepting σ as epistemically preferable—and we have seen that S should do so in cases in which a false σ with a low degree of discrepancy should be preferred to a true but highly vacuous σ—then S is *not* necessarily committing him/herself to accepting *all* the deductive consequences of σ as epistemically preferable.

In order to express both positive (for σ = true) and negative (for σ = false) degrees of discrepancy, let $f(\sigma)$ be a mapping function from members of $\Sigma = \{\sigma_1, \sigma_2, \ldots, \sigma_{64}\}$ to members of the set of some numeric values in the range of real numbers $[-1, +1]$. The function associates a real value ϑ of discrepancy to each σ depending on its truth-value and deviation from w:

$$\vartheta = f(\sigma) \tag{13}$$

The mapping generates a continuous set Γ of ordered pairs $<\sigma, \vartheta>$. Γ is a subset of the Cartesian product $\Sigma \times [-1, +1]$ that may be equipotent with respect to Σ. Although ϑ can in principle take any value in the range of real numbers $[-1, +1]$, thus giving rise to a continuous function, this does not mean that, given a specific model, an infinite number of interpretations of ϑ is effectively available. More realistically, a model always sets up a finite and discrete range of values for ϑ, approximate to n decimals. Following standard practice, in what follows the function is defined for all real numbers in the specified range, and discontinuities are associated only with truly dramatic behaviour on the part of the model. In a way that only partly resembles what happens in fuzzy logic, the lower and upper bound are used to represent complete discrepancy, while a selection of values in between is used to represent what are, intuitively, degrees of approximation to w from the negative and the positive side, with 0 as the indication of no discrepancy, i.e. complete conformity (note that, in the following diagrams, ϑ values are always mapped onto the x-axis in the graphs, since values on the y-axis are the result of a composite function).

Intuitively, ϑ indicates the distance of an infon σ from a selected situation w and can be read as the degree of support offered by w to σ. In a condition of total ignorance, the value of ϑ can be established *a priori* by using a non-monotonic or probabilistic calculus (this is what justifies the clause 'it is estimated that' in the following formulae), yet ϑ values should not themselves be interpreted as probabilities. Although they can have forecasting significance and may be based on the statistical strength of evidence supporting the assertion that σ conforms to w, they can also be negative and they do not need to sum to one. In real-life cases, it may be difficult to calculate ϑ values with a fully reliable degree of precision, and approximations may often be inevitable. However, any feasible and satisfactory metric will have to satisfy the following five conditions:

$$(\text{M.1}) \Vdash_{W} \sigma \rightarrow f(\sigma) = 0 \tag{14}$$

Formula [14] means that, if (it is estimated that) σ is *true* and conforms to w most *precisely* (i.e. in the least vacuous way) and *accurately*, then σ is assigned a zero degree of discrepancy, i.e. $\vartheta = 0$. This is the technical sense in which precise and accurate information can be seen as the threshold between vacuous truths and inaccurate falsehoods.

$$(\text{M.2}) \Vdash_{\forall W} \sigma \rightarrow f(\sigma) = 1 \tag{15}$$

Formula [15] means that, if (it is estimated that) σ is true and conforms to any situation, then σ is a tautology and it is assigned a maximum degree of *positive* discrepancy. Every situation supports σ, so no other true σ could be more distant from w than a tautological σ. In this case, σ has the highest degree of *semantic vacuity*, i.e. $\vartheta = 1$. Note that, in this context, vacuity does not refer to typical problems raised by borderline cases or the sorites paradox. In the model, each situation w is precise and each infon σ sharply divides the world into those situations to which σ applies, and those to which it does not. In this context, vacuity is a matter of semantic uncertainty, not in the sense that infons with a certain degree of vagueness are infons that apply to situations to varying degrees, hence generating indecision about borderline cases, but in the sense that infons with a certain degree of vagueness are infons that apply to a varying number of situations, hence generating indecision with respect to which w is the case. Infons do not increase gradually in their degrees of truth, as in fuzzy logic, but in their degree of conformity to w (lack of discrepancy). This approach appears to be consistent with the epistemic view according to which vagueness is a kind of ignorance.

$$(\text{M.3}) \Vdash_{\neg \exists W} \sigma \rightarrow f(\sigma) = -1 \tag{16}$$

Formula [16] means that, if (it is estimated that) σ is false and conforms to no possible situation, then σ is a contradiction and it is assigned a maximum degree of *negative* discrepancy. No possible situation supports σ, so no other false σ could be more distant from w than a contradictory σ. In this case, σ has the highest degree of *semantic inaccuracy*,[15] i.e. $\vartheta = -1$.

$$(\text{M.4}) \Vdash_{W-\theta} \sigma \rightarrow \left(0 > f(\sigma) > -1\right) \tag{17}$$

Formula [17] means that, if (it is estimated that) σ is contingently false, then it is assigned a degree of discrepancy with a value less than 0 but greater than -1 (degrees of semantic inaccuracy).

$$(\text{M.5}) \Vdash_{W+\theta} \sigma \rightarrow (0 < f(\sigma) < 1) \tag{18}$$

---

[15] 'Inaccuracy' here does not have exactly the same technical meaning as in error analysis theory, where a measurement is said to have high precision if it contains a relatively small indeterminate error, and is said to have high *accuracy* if it contains relatively small indeterminate error *and* relatively small determinate error.

Formula [18] means that, if (it is estimated that) σ is contingently true but does not conform to w with the highest degree of precision, then it is assigned a degree of discrepancy with a value greater than 0 but less than 1 (degrees of semantic vacuity).

According to M.1–M.5, σ_n in language L_n is semantically equivalent to σ_m in language L_m if and only if σ_n and σ_m have the same absolute alethic value and a comparable L-dependent degree of discrepancy with respect to w. In this sense, there is no indeterminacy of translation.

The implementation of M.1–M.3 causes no great difficulties but, when one deals with models that are not easily formalizable, the behaviour of the function $f(\sigma)$ in M.4–M.5 may become a matter of more conventional stipulations, which can grade ϑ values according to their comparative degree of vacuity or inaccuracy, relative to a specific application. There may be various ways of developing this comparative analysis. Since the present task is to provide a general outline of a strongly semantic theory, in what follows the analysis is based on a paradigmatic model, which any real-life application will try to approximate. Let us consider M.4 first, since it is simpler than M.5.

According to M.4, the relative 'amount of falsehood' in each contingently false σ indicates the *degree of inaccuracy* of σ with respect to w. This is then calculated as the ratio between the number of erroneous[16] atomic messages e in σ and its length (the minus sign indicates the negative value of the degree of inaccuracy):

$$(\text{Inac}) - \vartheta(\sigma) = -e(\sigma)/l(\sigma) \qquad [19]$$

Formula [19] allows us to partition $\Sigma = s^l$ into l disjoint classes of inaccurate σ {Inac^1, ..., Inac^1}, and map each class to its corresponding degree of inaccuracy.

Table 3 provides an illustration with respect to E.

Table 3 Classes of inaccuracy in E

number of erroneous atomic messages in σ_i	classes of inaccuracy	cardinality of Inac_i	degrees of inaccuracy $-\vartheta(\sigma \in \text{Inac}_i)$	degrees of informativeness $\iota(\sigma \in \text{Inac}_i)$
1	Inac_1	6	-1/6	≈ 0.972
2	Inac_2	15	-1/3	≈ 0.888
3	Inac_3	20	-1/2	= 0.75
4	Inac_4	14	-2/3	≈ 0.555
5	Inac_5	7	-5/6	≈ 0.305
6	Inac_6	1	-1	0

[16] Errors are not to be understood as blunders. Consistently with current practice in error analysis theory, the term 'error' is used here as a synonym for 'logical uncertainty' (see above the comment on 'uncertainty' as 'occurrence/elimination of possibilities'). Hence, the 'errors' in Inac are independent of the user, precisely characterizable and can be assumed to be normally distributed, unless the system is biased.

Consider now M.5. The *degree of vacuity* cannot refer to members of Σ immediately, but only to their logical transformations σ_j possessing a positive alethic value. Since each σ_j must be assumed to be true by definition, the analysis of e/l can no longer provide a clear measure of $\vartheta(\sigma)$. For example, both the set of complements or negations, that is, $\Sigma^n = \{\neg\sigma_1, \neg\sigma_2, \ldots, \neg\sigma_{64}\}$, and the logically equivalent set of duals (it is now useful to have Table 1 laid down in the way it is), that is, $\Sigma^\Delta = \{\sigma_1{}^\Delta, \sigma_2{}^\Delta, \ldots, \sigma_{64}{}^\Delta\}$, of all strongly synthetic messages contain formulae with $e = 0$ that would count as having the absolutely lowest degree of vacuity, i.e. $\vartheta = 0$, despite the obvious fact that, since they contain disjunctions, they would conform to a number of situations, including w, greater than one. Similar difficulties arise in the development of any analysis based on the ratio between the number of correct atomic messages in σ and its length. Is there any other reliable criterion to quantify $\vartheta(\sigma)$?

Recall that a tautology has $\vartheta = 1$ because it is consistent with every possible situation. In the case of the most weakly synthetic messages in E, i.e. members of the two sets Σ^n and Σ^Δ, each $\neg\sigma_i$ and $\sigma_i{}^\Delta$ is inconsistent with only one state in W. This means that members of the two sets have the highest possible degree of positive discrepancy to w, short of being analytically true. The conclusion can be generalized to any set of not strongly synthetic messages Σ^x. We shall say that, when σ is contingently true but vacuous, its semantic distance from w can be calculated as a function of the number of situations, including w itself, with which σ is consistent:

$$(Vac) + \vartheta(\sigma) = n/s^l \qquad [20]$$

More precisely, the degree of semantic vacuity of σ, with respect to a situation w, is the ratio between the cardinality n of the set of all the situations in E, necessarily including w, that support σ, and the number s^l of possible situations in E.

In [20], n is a positive integer that satisfies the condition $1 \leq n \leq s^l$. The number of situations supporting $\sigma \in \Sigma^x$ determine the specific value of n. Is there a systematic method for generating a 'continuum' of progressively weaker synthetic messages in E whilst keeping l constant? A simple solution is provided by the introduction of semiduals.

Semiduals are duals in which only the connectives $\{\wedge, \vee\}$ have been inverted but atomic messages have not been replaced by their complement, whilst parentheses can be introduced to avoid ambiguities. A message of length l contains l-1 connectives. We start with the assumption that all l-1 connectives are conjunctions, that is, all messages are strongly synthetic. By replacing all conjunctions with l-1 disjunctions we obtain the set of most weakly synthetic messages in E, whose $\vartheta = (s^l-1)/s^l$. We can then proceed to replace l-2 conjunctions, l-3 conjunctions and so forth, until l-n disjunctions = 1. The set with l-n = 1 disjunction is the set of true, synthetic messages in E with the lowest number of supporting situations and hence the lowest $\vartheta > 0$ in the model. In E, this means that we can construct five classes, whose members are true and consistent with, respectively, 63, 31, 15, 7, or 3 situations. These are the corresponding values of n.

Formula [20] and the previous method of *semantic weakening* allow us to partition Σ into $l-1$ disjoint classes Vac = {Vac$_1$ ... Vac$_{l-1}$}, and map each class to its corresponding degree of vacuity ϑ. Note that the value of ϑ for the class of most weakly synthetic messages in E is always $(s^l-1)/s^l$, whilst the middle values are found according to the formula $((s^l/2)-1)/s^l$, $((s^l/2^2)-1)/s^l$, ... $((s^l/2^n)-1)/s^l$, where $(s^l/2^n) - 1 = 3$, i.e. the smallest number of situations, including w, consistent with σ_i when $\vartheta(\sigma_i) > 0$. As before, Table 4 provides an illustration with respect to E.

Table 4 Classes of vacuity in E

number of compatible situations including w	classes of vacuity	cardinality of Vac$_i$	degrees of vacuityϑ ($\sigma \in$ Vac$_i$)	degrees of informativeness$_l$ ($\sigma \in$ Vac$_i$)
63	Vac$_1$	63	63/64	≈ 0.031
31	Vac$_2$	31	31/64	≈ 0.765
15	Vac$_3$	15	15/64	≈ 0.945
7	Vac$_4$	7	7/64	≈ 0.988
3	Vac$_5$	3	3/64	≈ 0.998

5.6 Degrees of informativeness

We are now ready to calculate the *degree of informativeness function* of σ. Arguably, the complement of the squared value of $\vartheta(\sigma)$ with respect to the maximum degree of informativeness provides an accurate measure:

$$\iota(\sigma) = 1 - \vartheta^2(\sigma) \qquad [21]$$

Figure 3 shows the graph generated by [21] when we include also negative values of distance for false σ (ϑ ranges from -1 = contradiction to 1 = tautology).

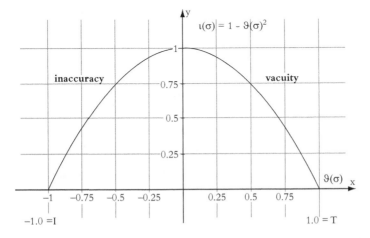

Figure 3 Degrees of informativeness

What are the motivations for [21]? If possible, the equation should satisfy the following 6 constraints, derived from the five necessary conditions for a satisfactory metrics M.1–M.5:

$$(E.1)\ (\vartheta(\sigma) = 0) \rightarrow (\iota(\sigma) = 1) \tag{22}$$

Formula [22] follows immediately from [14].

$$(E.2)\ \int_a^b \iota(\sigma)dx \text{ is a proper integer} \tag{23}$$

Formula [23] follows from the fact that the function $f(\sigma)$ is bounded on the interval [0, 1]. In the next section, we shall see that [23] simplifies the calculation of the quantity of informative, vacuous or inaccurate content in σ.

$$(E.3)(\vartheta(\sigma) = (+1 \vee -1)) \rightarrow (\iota(\sigma) = 0) \tag{24}$$

Formula [24] follows immediately from [15] and [16].

$$(E.4)((0 < \vartheta(\sigma) < +1) \vee (0 > \vartheta(\sigma) > -1)) \rightarrow 0 < \iota(\sigma) > 1 \tag{25}$$

Formula [25] follows immediately from [17] and [18].

$$(E.5)\text{ a small variation in } \vartheta(\sigma) \text{ results in a substantial variation in } \iota(\sigma) \tag{26}$$

Formula [26] is meant to satisfy the requirement according to which, the lower $\iota(\sigma)$ is, the smaller is the possible increase in the relative amount of vacuity or inaccuracy carried by σ. E.5 will become clearer in the next section, once the two concepts of quantity of vacuity and inaccuracy are introduced. Here, it is possible to rely on the intuitive view that, moving from a σ with $\vartheta = 0$ towards a σ with either $\vartheta = +1$ or $\vartheta = -1$, the first steps can be expected to bring a comparatively greater loss of informativeness (a greater increase in vacuity or inaccuracy) than the following ones. More generally, this means endorsing the view that an information system is not brittle, like a classic logic system (the presence of an inconsistency in the former is not as destructive as in the latter), and does not have a progressive degree of fault tolerance. For example, in the case of examination assessment techniques, or in the context of assessment of moral responsibility, *ceteris paribus*, the errors are usually evaluated more and more severely, the second having a comparatively more negative impact than the first and so forth. It is rather described as having an 'inverted' degree of fault tolerance: faults are decreasingly less impairing, the first being more damaging than the second and so forth. This holds true, for example, in the case of error analysis applied to scientific experiments, or in cases of assessment of moral trust and faithfulness. The first betrayal is much worse than the second.

$$(E.6)\text{ the } \textit{marginal information function} \text{ (MI) is a linear function} \tag{27}$$

Formula [27] is justified by the requirement that, a priori, all atomic messages ought to be assigned the same potential degree of informativeness and therefore, although [27] indicates that the graph of the model has a variable gradient, the rate at which $\iota(\sigma)$

changes with respect to change in $\vartheta(\sigma)$ should be assumed to be uniform, continuous and linear.

Formula [21] satisfies E.1 by adopting the standard convention according to which the absolute maximum value $\iota(\sigma) = 1$ occurs at $\vartheta(\sigma) = 0$, by analogy with the range of values of CONT(σ) and $p(\sigma)$. It satisfies E.2 by calculating the degree of informativeness of σ in terms of the complement of the value of $\vartheta(\sigma)$, not its reciprocal. We saw in section 5.3 that this solution has the further advantages of being mathematically simpler and in agreement with TWSI's approach. Finally, [21] satisfies E.3–E.6 by referring to the *squared* value of $\vartheta(\sigma)$. From [21], the derivative of $\iota(\sigma)$ is:

$$(MI)' \; (\sigma) = d/dx \; 1 - \vartheta^2(\sigma) = -2\vartheta(\sigma) \qquad [28]$$

Formula [28] means that the total degree of informativeness of σ changes at a rate of -2ϑ. The squared value of ϑ makes the function continuous and differentiable and provides the most satisfactory solution to model the degree of informativeness. This is so because in $\iota(\sigma) = 1 - \vartheta(\sigma)^n$, n could be an odd integer, 1, or an even integer greater than 2, but none of these alternatives is fully satisfactory. If n is an odd integer, the model satisfies only E.2, and introducing the absolute value of ϑ still leaves E.6 unsatisfied. If $n = 1$, the equation satisfies E.1, but in order to satisfy E.2 and E.3 we need to calculate the complement of the absolute value of $\vartheta(\sigma)$. However, the new formula $1 - |\vartheta(\sigma)|$ still fails to satisfy E.6. If n is any even integer greater than 2, the equation not only represents merely a more complicated extension of the simpler solution adopted in [21], it also fails to satisfy E.6.

5.7 Quantities of vacuity and of semantic information

Now that it is possible to calculate the *degree* of informativeness of σ, the next step is to measure on its basis the relative *quantity* of semantic information in σ. To this purpose, the absolute maximum quantity of information and its unity must first be defined.

If σ has a very high degree of informativeness ι (very low ϑ), we want to be able to say that it contains a large quantity of semantic information and, vice versa, the lower the degree of informativeness of σ is, the smaller the quantity of semantic information conveyed by σ should be. To calculate the quantity of semantic information contained in σ relative to $\iota(\sigma)$, we need to calculate the area delimited by equation [21], that is the definite integral of the function $\iota(\sigma)$ on the interval [0, 1]. As we know, the maximum quantity of semantic information (call it a) is carried by σ when $\vartheta(\sigma) = 0$. This is equivalent to the whole area delimited by the curve:

$$\sigma = \int_0^1 1(\sigma)dx = \frac{2}{3} \qquad [29]$$

Figure 4 shows the graph generated by equation [29]. The shaded area is the maximum amount of semantic information a carried by σ.

The quantity of vacuous information in σ is also a function of the distance ϑ of σ from w, or more generally:

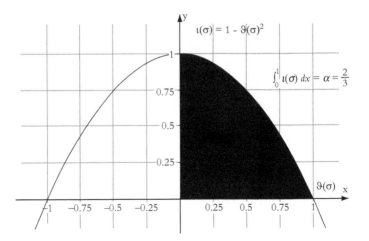

Figure 4 Maximum amount of semantic information α carried by σ

$$\beta = \int_0^{\vartheta} \iota(\sigma)\,dx \qquad\qquad [30]$$

Figure 5 shows the graph generated by equation [30]. The shaded area is the amount of vacuous information β in σ when, for example, $\vartheta(\sigma) = 0.25$.

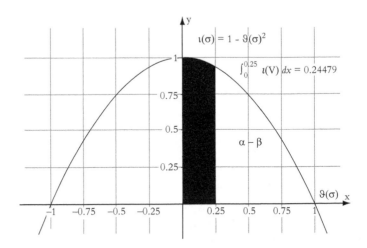

Figure 5 Amount of vacuous information β in σ

Clearly, the amount of semantic information in σ is simply the difference between α (the maximum amount of information that can be carried in principle by σ) and β (the amount of vacuous information actually carried by σ), that is, the clear area in the graph of Table 7 (see below, chapter ten). More generally, the quantity of strongly semantic information in σ, $\iota^*(\sigma)$, is obtained by calculating the complement of equation [31] with respect to equation [29]:

$$\iota^*(\sigma) = \alpha - \beta \qquad [31]$$

As required by the model constraints, when $\vartheta(\sigma) = 0$, it follows that the quantity of vacuous information $\vartheta^*(\sigma) = 0$ and $\iota^*(\sigma) = \max$ (σ is a fully accurate, precise and contingent truth), and when $\vartheta(\sigma) = 1$, it follows that $\vartheta^*(\sigma) = \max$ and $\iota^*(\sigma) = 0$ (σ is a tautology). Note that, following [31], the quantity of informative content in σ is established by reference to its truth-oriented properties and is not immediately identified with all information that is nomically or analytically nested in σ, as in Dretske (1981), yet the two approaches are perfectly compatible.

5.8 The solution of the Bar-Hillel–Carnap Paradox

We are now in a position to evaluate TSSI's solution of BCP. Suppose a deflationary argument is offered, phrased as follows. BCP owes its apparently counterintuitive nature to a conceptual confusion between CONT(σ) in [1] and $\iota^*(\sigma)$ in [31]. Once the two concepts are distinguished with sufficient clarity, the alleged paradox vanishes. On the one hand, CONT(σ) refers to the *quantity of semantic information* that can be attributed to σ a priori, on the basis of its probability distributions and independently of the state in which the system under analysis actually is (context of total ignorance). On the other hand, $\iota^*(\sigma)$ refers to the *quantity of semantic information* that can be attributed to σ still a priori, but in a context which is presupposed to be of 'localized omniscience' in the game-theoretical sense of perfect and complete information about the system, on the basis of σ'alethic value and its degree of discrepancy, relative to a fixed state w of the system under analysis. So R.1 and R.2 really embody two different and hence compatible explications of the pre-theoretical idea of 'quantity of semantic information': R.1 refers to the relation between CONT(σ) and $p(\sigma)$, whereas R.2 refers to the relation between $\iota^*(\sigma)$ and $\iota(\sigma)$. Since the two *requisita* are not really in conflict, there is no paradox to be solved.

Unfortunately, the conclusion cannot be granted. The previous analysis has shown that CONT(σ) $\neq \iota^*(\sigma)$, but this inequality is insufficient to explain the counterintuitive definition of the former in TWSI. What does follow from the deflationary argument is that the paradox can no longer be satisfactorily explicated merely in terms of a semantic conflict between R.1 and R.2. But the counterintuitive nature of CONT(σ) is actually increased by the fact that it is now obvious that CONT(σ) does not provide an indication of the amount of *informativeness* of σ. What does CONT(σ) really purport to indicate then? Despite the fact that CONT(σ) $\neq \iota^*(\sigma)$, there is a clear conceptual connection between the two measures: they both attempt to provide, from different perspectives, a quantitative evaluation of the 'information-richness' of σ. This is why it is difficult to reconcile CONT(σ) with a sound understanding of what the quantity of semantic information conveyed by σ is, without any further proviso. There is no uncontroversial sense in which a contradiction or a lie can be richer in information than a true proposition, and actually TSSI shows in what sense exactly the opposite can be proved. Abandoning CONT(σ) as a useless notion, marred by paradoxical implications, would be too hasty. Transforming it into a mere definitional convention or adopting *ad hoc* solutions, though viable alternatives, would not only be in conflict with Bar-Hillel and Carnap's original interpretation of their semantic theory, but would also make it substantially less interesting. Given the usefulness of TWSI, CONT(σ) should probably be salvaged, if possible. In TWSI, CONT(σ) is meant to indicate nothing less than the quantity of semantic information carried or conveyed by σ_m, which may be greater than the quantity of semantic information carried or conveyed by σ_n (Bar-Hillel (1964), pp. 222 and 299). It is exactly the unqualified boldness of this general claim that is in need of a more circumspect formulation. In order to avoid BCP, two modifications in the understanding of CONT(σ) are in order: a clarification of what CONT(σ) is really a measure of, and a constraint on its applicability.

First, CONT(σ) does not indicate the quantity of *semantic information* but, more precisely, the quantity of *data* in σ. By concentrating on the degree of systemic consistency and then the logical probability of sets of infons, CONT(σ) deals only with *completely uninterpreted information*, that is data, which are not carried by, but actually constitute σ, as syntactically well-formed combinations of interpretable signs or signals. Therefore, between TWSI and TSSI, it is the latter that, working on *alethically interpreted data*, comes closer to providing a quantitative indication of the information-richness or -poverty of σ. The former evaluates the information-richness of messages only insofar as their implementation is logically possible.

Second, because TWSI does not deal with semantic information but only with interpretable data and their possible combinations *a priori,* the general equation CONT(σ) = 1 - $p(\sigma)$ in R.1 cannot be assumed to have a precise value independently of its frame of reference. This means that the equation is really meaningful only once it is properly constrained by the following three systemic conditions:

S.1   unambiguous individuation and explicit description of the data system (in our model a universe consisting of 3 constants, each qualifiable by two properties, affirmed or negated);

S.2   generation of a fully normalized description of the data system, as the set of all the mutually exclusive messages necessary and sufficient to describe in full all the possible states in which the data system can be;

S.3   attribution of a probability p to each state-description σ_i—either in terms of uniform distribution, or according to any bias for which there may be evidence in the system—such that the following two standard conditions are satisfied:

$$0 < p(\sigma_i) < 1, \text{ for all } i$$

$$\sum_{i=1}^{n} p(\sigma_i) = 1 \tag{32}$$

It is only at this point that a precise meaning can be attached to CONT(σ). The complement of the value of p(σ) with respect to the maximum degree of probability can be used to indicate the quantity of interpretable data in σ only because of the connection between S.1 and S.2, whilst p can only be assigned a value in the open interval [0, 1] because of S.3. It is not that we are unable to analyse the probability of σ absolutely, but rather that the latter is inappropriate for the task in question. The probability of σ can be correctly interpreted as a measure of the quantity of interpretable data in σ only when σ is completely uninterpreted and implementable, that is, only when we are dealing with syntactically well-formed strings of data (symbols or signals) which are not already known to be either necessarily true or false a priori. These constraints make it possible to couple[17] probability of σ and quantity of interpretable data in σ sufficiently tightly that the former can provide a reliable indication of the latter. Outside these constraints, the two measures may not be significantly related or even lead to paradoxical conclusions, as BCP shows.

The two modifications in the interpretation of CONT(σ) force a re-assessment of the meaning of the standard view concerning the relation between the information-richness of σ and its likelihood. To develop a clear understanding of semantic information we need to move from likelihood (TWSI) to likeness (TSSI), as it were. When we say that the less likely σ is, the more informative it may be assumed to be, unless we are making some psychologistic remark about the subjective expectations of a receiver/user, we are referring to the higher or lower degree of discrepancy of σ with respect to one or more w. The less vacuous σ is, the fewer possible worlds support it, and the more informative σ becomes with respect to the fixed w that acts as a benchmark. Of course, this direct relation can also be analysed in terms of probability, since the latter can provide an interpretation for the concept of vacuity. But the two concepts do not overlap and they diverge when the σ in question is no longer uninterpreted. Semantic information about a situation presents *an actual possibility that is inconsistent with at least one but not all other possibilities*. A contradiction is not information-rich because it is not a possibility, and a tautology is not information-rich because it does not exclude any possibility. In TSSI, they are both limit instances of 'uninformation' (lack of both positive information and negative misinformation).[18]

5.9 TSSI and the scandal of deduction

Before closing this chapter, there is at least one crucial issue that needs to be addressed, namely the so-called *scandal of deduction*.

---

[17] 'Coupling' is used here in the technical IT sense, to refer to the strength of interrelations between the components of a system (e.g. the modules of a program, or the processing elements of an artificial neural network). The tighter the coupling, the higher the interdependency. Completely decoupled components—systems with a null degree of interdependency—have no common data and no control flow interaction.

[18] Not a word in the *OED*, 'uninformation' has already appeared on the Web with the meaning 'useless/undesired information', in connection with junk email, or 'disposable information'.

Traditionally, there are two ways to explain the function of deductive inference:

1. Deductive inference governs truth-transmission. The set of all possible worlds that make (the conjunction of) the premises true is included in the set of possible worlds that make the conclusion true.
2. Deductive inference governs the 'information flow'. The information conveyed by the conclusion is contained in the information conveyed by (the conjunction of) the premises.

In classical logic, (1) and (2) are reconciled by means of the notion of 'semantic information', which makes the information conveyed by a sentence equal to the set of all the possible worlds ruled out by that sentence.

Now, we saw in this chapter that information goes hand in hand with unpredictability. More precisely, the Inverse Relationship Principle (IRP), as Barwise labelled it, states that there is an inverse relation between the probability of P—which may range over sentences of a given language (as in Bar-Hillel and Carnap (1953) and Bar-Hillel (1964)) or events, situations or possible worlds (as in Dretske (1981))—and the amount of semantic information carried by P. Nowadays, IRP is often translated modally, by stating that the semantic information conveyed by P is the set of all possible worlds, or (more cautiously) the set of all the descriptions of the relevant possible states of the universe, that are excluded by, or are inconsistent with, P. We also saw that, following IRP, the less probable or possible P is, the more semantic information P is assumed to be carrying. This led to the Bar-Hillel–Carnap Paradox, which was solved by developing a theory of strongly semantic information. Consider now what happens when we follow IRP in the opposite direction. The more probable P is, the more its informational content decreases. When the probability of P is 1 (that is, when P is true in all possible worlds), its informational content is 0. It follows that all logical truths, being tautologies, become equally uninformative. And indeed, according to MTI, TWSI, and TSSI, tautologies are not informative. This seems both reasonable and unquestionable. If you wish to know what the time is, and you are told that 'it is either 5 p.m. or it is not' then the message you have received provides you with no information. The problem, however, is that, in classical logic, a conclusion C is deducible from a finite set of premises $\{P_1, \ldots, P_n\}$ if and only if the corresponding conditional $[P_1 \land P_2, \land \ldots P_n \rightarrow C]$ is a tautology. Accordingly, since tautologies carry no information at all, no logical inference can yield an increase of information, so logical deductions, which can be analysed in terms of tautological processes, also fail to provide any information. By identifying the semantic information carried by a sentence with the set of all possible worlds or circumstances it excludes, it is easy to see that, in any valid deduction, the information carried by the conclusion must be already contained in the information carried by the (conjunction of) the premises. This is what is often meant by saying that tautologies and inferences are 'analytical' (Corcoran (1998)). But then, logic and mathematics turn out to be utterly uninformative.

According to Hintikka, this counterintuitive conclusion can be described as 'the scandal of deduction'.

> C. D. Broad has called the unsolved problems concerning induction a scandal of philosophy. It seems to me that, in addition to this scandal of induction, there is an equally disquieting scandal of deduction. Its urgency can be brought home to each of us by any clever freshman who asks, upon being told that deductive reasoning is 'tautological' or 'analytical' and that logical truths have no 'empirical content' and cannot be used to make 'factual assertions': in what other sense, then, does deductive reasoning give us new information? Is it not perfectly obvious there is some such sense, for what point would there otherwise be to logic and mathematics? (Hintikka (1973), p. 222)

The scandal of deduction is the counterpart of the Bar-Hill–Carnap Paradox. If the conclusion of a deductive argument is always 'contained' in the premises, why is deductive reasoning generally perceived as highly valuable epistemically? If all theorems are 'contained' in the axioms of a theory, how is mathematical discovery possible at all? If one day we could fully axiomatize a scientific theory, would that theory stop being informative? As Dummett (1991) put it:

> If that were correct, all that deductive inference could accomplish would be to render explicit knowledge that we already possessed: mathematics would be merely a matter of getting things down on paper, since, as soon as we had acknowledged the truth of the axioms of a mathematical theory, we should thereby know all the theorems. Obviously, this is nonsense: deductive inference has here been justified at the expense of its power to extend our knowledge and hence of any genuine utility. (p. 195)

In D'Agostino and Floridi (2009), we argued that that there is a very reasonable sense in which classical deduction is actually informative, even at the propositional level, and that the scandal of deduction can thereby be dissolved. Since it would not be useful to reproduce the technical results of that article in this context, let me just outline the general strategy.

Classical deductions are informative because proof of their validity essentially requires the (temporary) introduction of *virtual information*,[19] which is assumed, used and then discharged, thus leaving no trace at the end of the process, but essentially contributing to its success. An elementary example will help to clarify the point.

Suppose we have the following information: (1) $P \vee Q$; (2) $P \rightarrow S$; and (3) $Q \rightarrow S$. Note that (1)–(3) is all the actual information we have. We do not have the information that P nor do we have the information that Q, but only the information that at least P or at least Q is the case. Classically, we reason by making some *assumptions*, that is, we step out of the available space of information, represented by (1)–(3), and pretend to have more information than we really have, strictly speaking. The reasoning is of

---

[19] Marcello and I adapted here an expression from physics, where virtual particles are particle/antiparticle pairs which come into existence out of nothing and then rapidly annihilate without releasing energy. They populate the whole of space in large numbers but cannot be observed directly.

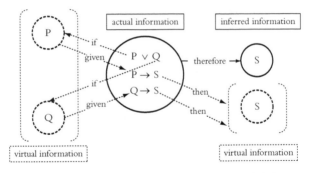

Figure 6 An example of virtual information in natural deduction

course elementary (see Figure 6). *Suppose P* is the case: then from (2) it already follows that *S*; but *suppose Q* is the case: then from (3) it already follows that *S*; but then, we do not need to *suppose* either *P* or *Q* by themselves, since we do have them packed together in (1); so from (1), (2), and (3) we can infer that *S*. Using the ∨ Elimination Rule in natural deduction system, we obtain the new information *S*. Having succeeded in showing that either disjunct suffices to entail the conclusion, we discharge the assumptions and assert the conclusion. Although the process is very simple, it should suffice to clarify the important fact that we quietly stepped out of the space of information that we actually had, moved into a space of *virtual* information, made it do quite a lot of essential work, and then stepped back in the original space of information that we did have, and obtained the conclusion. If one does not pay a lot of attention, the magic trick is almost invisible. But it is exactly the stepping in and out of the space of available information that makes it possible for deductions to be at the same time formally valid and yet informative.

The informational richness of logico-mathematical deductions is the result of the skilful usage of informational resources that are by no means contained in the premises, but must nevertheless be taken into consideration in order to obtain the conclusion.

CONCLUSION

In this chapter, I developed a quantitative theory of strongly semantic information (TSSI) on the basis of a calculus based on truth-values and degrees of discrepancies with respect to a given situation, rather than probability distributions. The main hypothesis that I supported has been that semantic information encapsulates truth, and hence that false information fails to qualify as information at all. This is consistent with, and corroborates the analysis I provided in, chapter four. The main result of the development of TSSI has been the solution of the Bar-Hillel–Carnap Paradox affecting the classic quantitative theory of semantic information, according to which a contradiction contains the highest quantity of semantic information. In the course of the analysis, I provided a review of the requirements for any quantitative theory of semantic information, of the criteria of semantic information equivalence, of the concepts of degrees of strongly (i.e. truth-based) semantic inaccuracy, vacuity and informativeness; and of the concepts of quantities of strongly semantic vacuity and information. I also briefly sketched the strategy to solve the scandal of deduction, which affects all theories of semantic information, including TSSI. One question I left unanswered is what kind of theory of truth might be most suitable to analyse the truthfulness of semantic information. This will be the topic of chapter eight. But first, we need to tackle a more basic problem, already encountered several times but so far left unsolved: if semantic information is well-formed, meaningful, and truthful data, as I have argued so far, how do data acquire their meaning in the first place? This is known as the *symbol grounding problem* and the next two chapters deal with it.

6

The symbol grounding problem

How can the semantic interpretation of a formal symbol system be made intrinsic to the system, rather than just parasitic on the meanings in our heads? How can the meanings of the meaningless symbol tokens, manipulated solely on the basis of their (arbitrary) shapes, be grounded in anything but other meaningless symbols?'

Harnad (1990), p. 335.

SUMMARY

Previously, in chapters four and five, I articulated and supported the analysis of semantic information as well-formed, meaningful, and truthful data. In order to substantiate such analysis, we now need to explain what it means for data to be meaningful and for meaningful data to be truthful. I shall address the first, semantic problem in this and in the next chapter. It will be recalled that, in chapter two, this was labelled as the *data grounding problem* (see P4): how can data acquire their meaning? The answer will consist in two parts, one negative, the other positive. This chapter provides the *pars destruens*. It shows that the main solutions proposed so far in the literature are unsatisfactory. After an introduction to the chapter, section 6.2 briefly recalls the symbol (or data, in the vocabulary of this book) grounding problem (SGP). It then identifies and defends the zero semantic commitment condition (*Z condition*), as the requirement that must be satisfied by a strategy in order to provide a valid solution of the SGP. Sections 6.3, 6.4, 6.5 analyse eight main strategies that have been developed for solving the SGP. They are organized into three approaches, one per section: *representationalism, semi-representationalism*, and *non-representationalism*. In the course of the chapter, all these strategies are shown to be semantically committed. None of them respects the *Z condition*, and hence they all fail to provide a *valid* solution of the SGP. This *pars destruens* of our investigation ends with a more constructive conclusion, about the requirements that a solution of the SGP should satisfy. Such requirements introduce a new solution of the SGP, which is developed in chapter seven, the *pars construens* of the answer.

6.1 Introduction

In chapter two, the symbol grounding problem (SGP) was introduced as one of the most important open questions in the philosophy of information. How can the data, constituting semantic information, acquire their meaning in the first place? The question poses a radical and deceptively simple challenge. For the difficulty is not (or at least, not just) merely grounding the symbols or data *somehow* successfully, as if all we were looking for were the implementation of some sort of internal look-up table, or the equivalent of a searchable spreadsheet. The SGP concerns the possibility of specifying *precisely how* a formal symbol system can *autonomously* elaborate its own semantics for the symbols (data) that it manipulates and do so *from scratch*, by interacting with its environment and other formal symbol systems. This means that, as Harnad rightly emphasizes in the quotation opening the chapter, the interpretation of the symbols (data) must be *intrinsic* to the symbol system itself, it cannot be *extrinsic*, that is, *parasitic* on the fact that the symbols (data) have meaning for, or are provided by, an interpreter.

In the following pages, I shall discuss eight strategies proposed for the solution of the SGP since Harnad's influential formulation. The list is far from exhaustive, but the chosen strategies are both influential and representative of the three main approaches to SGP: *representationalism*, *semi-representationalism*, and *non-representationalism*.

The representationalist approach is discussed in section 6.3. The first strategy (Harnad (1990)) is analysed in section 6.3.1. It provides the basis for two other strategies (Sun (2000) and Mayo (2003)), which are analysed in sections 6.3.2 and 6.3.3 respectively.

Three semi-representationalist strategies (Vogt (2002b), Davidsson (1993), and Rosenstein and Cohen (1998)) are the topic of section 6.4 They attempt to show that the representations required by any representationalist approach to the SGP can be elaborated in terms of processes implementable by behavioural-based robots. They are assessed in sections 6.4.1, 6.4.2, and 6.4.3 respectively.

The non-representationalist approach is discussed in section 6.5, where the *Physical Grounding Hypothesis* (Brooks (1990), (1991)) is first recalled. There follows a discussion of two communication- and behaviour-based strategies (Billard and Dautenhahn (1999), Varshavskaya (2002)) in sections 6.5.1 and 6.5.2 respectively.

All approaches seek to ground the symbols through the sensorimotor capacities of the artificial agents involved. The strategies differ in the methods used to elaborate the data obtained from the sensorimotor experiences, and in the role (if any) assigned to the elaboration of the data representations, in the process of generating the semantics for the symbols. As I anticipated, unfortunately, none of the strategies can be said to offer a *valid* solution to the SGP. We shall see that this does not mean that they are theoretically flawed or uninteresting, nor that they cannot work, when technically implemented. The conclusion is rather that, conceptually, insofar as they seem successful, such strategies either fail to address the SGP or circumvent it, by implicitly presupposing its solution and begging the question. In either case, the challenge posed by the SGP remains still open. This negative conclusion will introduce the constructive proposal developed in chapter 6.7.

Three caveats are in order before moving to the next section. First, the goal of this chapter is to assess the wide range of strategies that have been proposed for solving the SGP in order to learn some essential lessons that will be applied in the more constructive chapter seven. The goal is neither historical nor that of providing a fully comprehensive review of the whole literature on SGP.

Second, the works discussed have been selected for their influential role in several lines of research and/or for their representative nature, insofar as each of them provides an enlightening example of the sort of perspective that might be adopted to tackle the SGP. No inference should be drawn on the scientific value of works which have not been included here. In particular, I have focused only on strategies explicitly addressing the SGP, and disregarded the debates on

- the *Chinese Room Argument* (Searle (1980), Preston and Bishop (2002)), reviewed by Cole (2008);
- the *representation grounding problem* (Chalmers (1992)), the *concept grounding problem* (Dorffner and Prem (1993)) and the *internalist trap* (Sharkey and Jackson (1994)), all reviewed by Ziemke (1999); and
- the *symbols anchoring problem*, reviewed by Coradeschi and Saffioti (2003).

It is worth stressing, however, that the conclusion reached in this chapter—that SGP is a crucial but still unresolved problem—is consistent with the conclusions reached by Cole, Ziemke, and Coradeschi and Saffioti.

Third, although I have tried to provide a coherent and unifying frame of conceptual and technical vocabulary throughout the chapter, some lack of uniformity has been inevitable owing to the variety of methods, intellectual traditions, and scientific goals informing the strategies analysed. In particular, the reader may wish to keep in mind that ultimately the focus is on how data (rather than symbols) acquire their meaning in view of the analysis of semantic information.

6.2 The symbol grounding problem

Harnad (1990) uses the Chinese Room Argument to introduce the SGP.[1] A formal symbol system—that is, an artificial agent (AA) such as a robot—appears to have no access to the meaning of the data it can successfully manipulate syntactically. It is like a grown-up expected to learn Chinese as her *first* language by consulting a Chinese–Chinese dictionary. Both the AA and the non-Chinese speaker are bound to be unsuccessful, since a symbol may be meaningful, but its mere physical shape and syntactic properties normally provide no clue as to its corresponding semantic value, the latter being related to the former in a notoriously, entirely arbitrary way. Usually, the symbols constituting a symbolic system neither resemble nor are causally linked to

---

[1] See also Harnad (2003) for a more recent formulation.

their corresponding meanings. They are merely part of a formal, notational convention agreed upon by its users. One may then wonder whether an AA (or, better, a population of them) may ever be able to *develop* an *autonomous*, semantic capacity to connect its symbols with the environment in which the AA is embedded interactively. The challenge posed by the SGP is that

a. No form of *innatism* is allowed; no semantic resources (some *virtus semantica*) should be magically presupposed as already pre-installed in the AA; and
b. No form of *externalism* is allowed either; no semantic resources should be uploaded from the 'outside' by some *deus ex machina* already semantically proficient.

Note that (a) does not mean that in the long run a population of agents may (and indeed may easily) develop forms of innate semantics: (a) merely specifies the obvious fact that assuming since the beginning the presence of such innate meanings means leaving the question unanswered at best, or begging it at worst. Likewise, (b) does not mean that, in a population of agents already semantically proficient, communication, training and education will not play an essential role in the development of the semantic capacities of new generations. This is too obvious to be denied. Point (b) specified that such refinement and transmission of semantics cannot provide an explanation of how semantics emerges in the first place. Finally, points (a)–(b) do not exclude the possibility that

c. The AA may have its own capacities and resources (e.g. computational, syntactical, procedural, perceptual, etc., exploited through algorithms, sensors, actuators etc.) To be able to ground its symbols.

These three conditions only exclude the possibility that such resources may be semantic in the first place, if one wishes to appeal to them in order to solve the SGP without begging the question. Rather, (a)–(c) clarify the sense in which a valid solution of the SGP must be fully *naturalized*, despite the fact that we are talking about *artificial* agents. At the same time, by referring to artificial agents, one can ensure that (a)–(c) are more easily respected, and prepare the ground for a plausible implementation that could provide compelling evidence in favour of the feasibility of the solution. One may wish to check whether an AA (or a population of them) could actually be built that satisfies the previous requirements and solve the SGP.

Altogether, (a)–(c) define a requirement that must be satisfied by any strategy that claims to solve the SGP. Let us label it the *zero semantic commitment condition* (henceforth Z condition). Any approach that breaches the Z condition is semantically committed and fails to provide a *valid* solution to the SGP.

6.3 The representationalist approach

The representationalist approach considers the conceptual and categorical representations, elaborated by an AA, as the meanings of the symbols used by that AA. So, representationalist strategies seek to solve the SGP by grounding an AA's symbols in the representations arising from the AA's manipulations of its perceptual data. More specifically, it is usually argued that an AA is (or at least should be) able to

1. capture (at least some) salient features shared by sets of perceptual data;
2. abstract them from the data sets;
3. identify the abstractions as the contents of categorical and conceptual representations; and then
4. use these representations to ground its symbols.

The main problem with the representationalist approach is that the available representations—whether categorical or perceptual—succeed in grounding the symbols used by an AA only at the price of begging the question. We shall see that their elaboration, and hence availability, presuppose precisely those semantic capacities or resources that the approach is trying to show to be autonomously evolvable by an AA in the first place.

6.3.1. A hybrid model for the solution of the SGP

Harnad (1990) suggests a strategy based on a *hybrid model*, which implements a mixture of features characteristic of symbolic and of connectionist systems. According to Harnad, the symbols manipulated by an AA can be grounded by connecting them to the perceptual data that they denote. The connection is established by a bottom-up, invariantly categorizing processing of sensorimotor signals. Assuming a general psychological theory that sees the ability to build categories[2] of the world as the groundwork for language and cognition (Harnad (1987)), Harnad proposes that symbols could be grounded in three stages:

1. *iconization*: the process of transforming analogue signals (patterns of sensory data perceived in relation to a specific entity) into iconic representations (that is, internal analogue equivalents of the projections of distal objects on the agent's sensory surfaces);
2. *discrimination*: the process of judging whether two inputs are the same or, if they are different, how much they differ;
3. *identification*: the process of assigning a unique response—that is, a name—to a class of inputs, treating them as equivalent or invariant in some respect.

The first two stages yield sub-symbolic representations, whereas the third stage grounds the symbols. The iconic representations in (1) are obtained from the set of all the experiences related to the perceptions of the *same type* of object. The categorical representations are then achieved through the discrimination process in (2). Here, an AA considers only the *invariant features* of the iconic representations. Once elaborated,

---

[2] Harnad uses the term *category* to refer to the name of the entity denoted by symbol, so a category is not itself a symbol. A grounded symbol would have both categorical (i.e. a name) and iconic representations.

the categorical representations are associated in (3) with classes of symbols (the names), thus providing the latter with appropriate referents that ground them.

Iconization and *discrimination* are sub-processes, carried out by using neural networks. They make possible the subsequent association of a name with a class of input and subsequently the naming of referents. However, by themselves neural networks are unable to produce symbolic representations, so they cannot yet enable the AA to develop symbolic capacities. In order to avoid this shortcoming, Harnad provides his hybrid model with a symbolic system, which can manipulate symbols syntactically and finally achieve a semantic grounding of its symbols.

Harnad's proposal has set the standard for all following strategies. It attempts to overcome the typical limits encountered by symbolic and connectionist systems by combining their strengths. On the one hand, in

a pure symbolic model the crucial connection between the symbols and their referents is missing; an autonomous symbol system, though amenable to a systematic syntactic interpretation, is ungrounded. (Harnad (1990), pp. 341–342)

On the other hand, although neural networks make it possible to connect symbols and referents by using the perceptual data and the invariant features of the categorical representations, they still cannot manipulate symbols (as the symbol systems can easily do) in order to produce an intrinsic, systematic, and finite interpretation of them. This justifies the hybrid solution supported by Harnad, which, owing to its semi-symbolic nature, may seem to represent the best of both worlds.

Unfortunately, the hybrid model does not satisfy the Z condition. The problem concerns the way in which the hybrid system is supposed to find the invariant features of its sensory projections that allow it to categorize and identify objects correctly. Consider an AA that implements the hybrid model, called PERC ('PERCEIVES'). Initially, PERC has no semantic content or resources, so it has no semantic commitment. Let us assume that PERC is equipped with a way of acquiring some data input, for example a digital video camera, through which it observes its external environment. Following Harnad, suppose that, by means of its camera and neural networks, PERC is able to produce some iconic representations from the perceptual data it collects from the environment. PERC is then supposed to develop categorical representations from these perceptual data, by considering only the invariant features of the iconic representations. Next, it is supposed to organize the categorical representations into conceptual categories, like 'quadruped animal'. The latter are the meanings of the symbols. The question to be asked is: where do conceptual categories such as 'quadruped animal' originate? Neural networks can be used to find structures (if they exist) in the data space, such as patterns of data points. However, if they are *supervised*, e.g. through *back propagation*, then they are trained by means of a pre-selected training set and repeated feedback, so whatever grounding they can provide is entirely *extrinsic*. If they are *unsupervised*, then the networks implement training algorithms that do not use desired output data but rely only on input data to try to find structures in the data input space.

Units in the same layer compete with each other to be activated. However, they still need to have *built-in biases* and feature-detectors in order to reach the desired output. Such semantic resources are necessarily hard-coded by a supervisor, according to pre-established criteria. Moreover, unsupervised or self-organizing networks, once they have been trained, still need to have their output checked to see whether the obtained structures make any sense with respect to the input data space. This difficult process of validation is carried out externally by a supervisor. So in this case too, whatever grounding they can provide is still entirely *extrinsic*. In short, as Christiansen and Chater (1992) correctly remark, on criticizing Harnad:

> [So,] whatever semantic content we might want to ascribe to a particular network, it will always be parasitic on our interpretation of that network; that is, parasitic on the meanings in the head of the observer. (p. 235)

'Quadruped animal', as a category, is not the outcome of PERC's intrinsic grounding because PERC must already have had a great deal of semantic help to reach that conclusion. The strategy supported by Harnad actually presupposes the availability of those semantic resources that the AA is expected to develop from scratch, through its interactions with the environment and other AAs embedded in it, and the elaboration of its perceptual data.

One may object that the categorical representations do not need to collect all the invariant features of the perceptual data, for they may just indicate a class of similar data, which could then be labelled with a conventional name. Allegedly, this could allow one to avoid any reliance on semantic resources operating at the level of the neural network component.

The reply resembles Berkeley's criticism of Locke's semantic theory of general or abstract ideas. Locke had suggested that language consists of conventional signs, which stand for simple or abstract ideas. Abstract ideas, such as that of a horse, correspond to general names, e.g. 'horse', and are obtained through a process of abstraction, not dissimilar from the process that leads to categorical representations in Harnad's hybrid model, that is, by collecting the invariant features of simple ideas, in our case the many, different horses perceivable in the environment.

Against Locke's theory, Berkeley objected that the human mind elaborates only particular ideas (ideas of individuals, e.g. of that specific white and tall and . . . horse, or this peculiar brown, and short and . . . horse, and so forth) and therefore that universal ideas and the corresponding general names, as described by Locke, were impossible. This is especially true for abstract universal ideas. For example, the idea of 'extension', Berkeley argued, is always the idea of something that is extended. According to Berkeley, universal or abstract ideas are therefore only particular ideas that (are chosen to) work like prototypes or idealized models standing for a class of similar but equally particular ideas. In this way, the idea of a specimen is elected to the role of abstract idea of the whole class to which the specimen belongs.

Returning to Harnad, although he suggests that the categories available to an AA are the consequence of a Lockean-like abstraction from perceptual data, one may try to avoid the charge of circularity (recall that the solution has been criticized for infringing the Z condition) by trying to redefine the categorical representation in more Berkeleian terms: a particular representation could be used by an AA as a token in order to represent its type.

Unfortunately, this Berkeleian manoeuvre does not succeed either. For even if categorical representations—comparable to Lockean abstract ideas—are reduced to iconic representations—comparable to Berkeleian abstract ideas—the latter still need to presuppose some semantic resources to be elaborated. In our example, how is the class of horses (the data space) put together in the first place, without any semantic capacity to elaborate the general idea (whether Lockean or Berkeleian, it does not matter) of 'horse' to begin with? And how is a particular specimen of horse privileged over all the others as being the particular horse that could represent all the others, without presupposing some semantic capacities? And finally, how does one know that what makes that representation of a particular horse the representation of a universal horse is not, for example, the whiteness instead of the four-legged nature of the represented horse? The Z condition is still unsatisfied.

In sections 6.3.2 and 6.3.3, we shall assess two other solutions of the SGP based on Harnad's. Both raise further difficulties. Before that, however, we shall briefly look at the application of Harnad's solution to the explanation of the origin of language and its evolution, in section 6.3.1.1. The topic has been investigated by Harnad himself on several occasions. Given the scope of this chapter, I shall limit the discussion to three papers: Cangelosi et al. (2000), Cangelosi and Harnad (2001), and Cangelosi et al. (2002). These are based on Harnad (1990). They maintain that, within a plausible cognitive model of the origin of symbols, symbolic activity should be conceived as some higher-level process, which takes its contents from some non-symbolic representations obtained at a lower level. As we shall see in the next chapter, this is arguably a reasonable assumption. Because of their reliance on Harnad's initial solution, however, the papers share its shortcomings and are subject to the same criticism. They are all semantically over-committed and hence none of them provides a valid solution for the SGP. The three papers show that, despite the reply by Harnad (1993b) to Christiansen and Chater (1992), in subsequent research Harnad himself has chosen to follow a non-deflationist interpretation of his own solution of the SGP.[3] However, it seems that either Harnad's reply to the objection moved by Christiansen and Chater is satisfactory, but then Harnad's strategy for solving the SGP becomes too general to be of much

---

[3] A deflationist view of the SGP is supported by Prem (1995a), (1995b), (1995c), who argues that none of the different approaches to the problem of grounding symbols in perception succeed in reaching its semantic goals and that SG systems should rather be interpreted as some kind of automated mechanisms for the construction of models, in which the AA uses symbols to formulate descriptive rules about what will happen in its environment.

interest; or Harnad's strategy is a substantive, semantic proposal, in which case it is interesting but it is also subject to the objection in full.[4]

6.3.1.1 SGP and the symbolic theft hypothesis.   Cangelosi et al. (2000), Cangelosi (2001) provide a detailed description of the mechanisms for the transformation of *categorical perception* (CP) into grounded, low-level labels and, subsequently, into higher-level symbols.[5] They call *grounding transfer* the phenomenon of acquisition of new symbols from the combination of already grounded symbols. They show how such processes can be implemented with neural networks:

> Neural networks can readily discriminate between sets of stimuli, extract similarities, and categorize. More importantly, networks exhibit the basic CP effect, whereby members of the same category 'look' more similar (there is a compression of within-category distances) and members of different categories look more different (expansion of between-categories distances). (Cangelosi et al. (2002), p. 196)

According to Cangelosi and Harnad (2001), the functional role of CP in symbol grounding is to define the interaction between *discrimination* and *identification*. We have seen in 6.3.1 that the process of discrimination allows the system to distinguish patterns in the data, whilst the process of identification allows it to assign a stable identity to the discriminated patterns.

> CP is a basic mechanism for providing more compact representations, compared with the raw sensory projections where feature-filtering has already done some of the work in the service of categorization. (Cangelosi et al. (2002), p. 198)

Cangelosi et al. (2000) outline two methods to acquire new categories. They call the first method *sensorimotor toil* and the second one *symbolic theft*, in order to stress the benefit (enjoyed by the system) of not being forced to learn from a direct sensorimotor experience whenever a new category is in question. They provide a simulation of the process of CP, of the acquisition of grounded names, and of the learning of new high-order symbols from grounded ones. Their simulation comprises a three-layer feedforward neural network, which has two groups of input units: forty-nine units simulating a retina and six units simulating a linguistic input. The network has five hidden units and two groups of output units replicating the organization of input (retina and verbal output). The retinal input depicts nine geometric images (circles, ellipses, squares, rectangles) with different sizes and positions. The activation of each input unit corresponds to the presentation of a particular category name. The training procedure (which is problematic, in view of the Z condition) has the following learning stages:

1. the network is *trained by an external agent already semantically proficient* (so this already breaches the Z condition) to categorize figures: from input shapes it must

---

[4] Although for different reasons, a similar conclusion is reached by Taylor and Burgess (2004).
[5] The same mechanism is also described in Cangelosi (2001) and Harnad (2002).

produce the *correct* (here hides another breach of the Z condition) categorical prototype as output;

2. the network is then given the task of associating each shape with its name. This task is called *entry-level naming*. According to the authors, names acquired in this way can be considered grounded because they are explicitly connected with sensory retinal inputs. However, the semantic commitment is obvious in the externally supervised learning process;

3. in the final stage, the network learns how to combine such grounded names (for example, 'square' or 'rectangle') with new arbitrary names (for example 'symmetric' or 'asymmetric'). This higher-level learning process is implemented by simple imitation learning of the combination of names. This is like teaching the system conceptual combinations such as 'square is symmetric' or 'rectangle is asymmetric'. The AA learns through the association of grounded names with new names, while the grounding is *transferred* to names that did not have such a property.

The model has been extended to use the combination of grounded names of basic features in order to allow systems to learn higher-order concepts. As the authors comment

[T]he benefits of the symbolic theft strategy must have given these organisms the adaptive advantage in natural language abilities. This is infinitely superior to its purely sensorimotor precursors, but still grounded in and dependent on them. (Cangelosi et al. (2002), p. 203)

The explanation of the origin and evolution of language, conjectured by this general approach, is based on the hybrid symbolic/sensorimotor capacities implemented by the system. Initially, organisms evolve an ability to build some categories of the world through direct sensorimotor toil. They also learn to name such categories. Then some organisms must have experimented with the propositional combination of the names of these categories and discovered the advantage of this new way of learning categories, thus 'stealing their knowledge by hearsay' (Cangelosi et al. (2002), p. 203). However, the crucial issue of how organisms might have initially learnt to semanticize the data resulting from their sensorimotor activities remains unsolved, and hence so does the SGP.

6.3.2. A functional model for the solution of the SGP

Mayo (2003) suggests a *functional model* of AA that manages to overcome some of the limits of Harnad's hybrid model, although it finally incurs equally insurmountable difficulties.

Mayo may be interpreted as addressing the objection, faced by Harnad (1990), that an AA fails to elaborate its semantic categories autonomously. His goal is to show that an AA could elaborate concepts in such a way as to be able to ground even abstract names.

An AA interacting with the environment perceives a continuum of sensory data. However, data always underdetermine their structure, so there is a countless variety of possible categories (including categories related to particular tasks) by means of which the data could be organized. As Mayo acknowledges

[...] without some sort of bias, it is computationally intractable to come up with the best set of categories describing the world. [...] given that sensory data is continuous, there is an effectively infinite [...] number of possible categorizations of the data. (Mayo (2003), p. 56)

So Mayo proposes a *functional organization* of the representations as a way to ground the symbols involved. Categories are interpreted as *task-specific sets* that collect representations according to their practical function. Symbols are formed in order to solve specific task-oriented problems in particular environments. Having a specific task to perform provides the AA with a bias that orientates its search for the best categorization of sensory data. The bias is such that the symbols learnt by the AA are those that most help the AA to perform the task successfully. A symbol could then acquire different meanings, depending on the functional set in which it occurs. The sets overlap insofar as they share the same symbols and, according to Mayo, these intersections support the capacity of the AA to generalize and to name abstract concepts. For example, an AA can generalize the meaning of the symbol 'victory' if, according to Mayo, 'victory' is not rigidly connected to a specific occurrence of a single event but derives its meaning from the representation of the intersection of all the occurrences of 'victory' in different task-specific sets of various events, such as 'victory' in chess, in tennis, in war and in love.

Contrary to the hybrid model, Mayo's functional model avoids the problem concerning the elaboration of abstract concepts by the AA. However, like all the other representationalist hypotheses, Mayo's too founds the elaboration of the semantics on categorical and symbolic representations. But then, as in Harnad (1990), the initial presence of these representations requires the presence of robust semantic capacities that simply cannot be warranted without begging the question. In Mayo's case, these are the functional criteria. The AA is already presumed to have (access to, or the capacity to generate and handle) a 'functional' semantics. The AA is not (indeed it cannot be) supposed or even expected to elaborate this semantic resource by itself. Obviously, the strategy is already semantically committed and such commitment undermines its validity.

The difficulty might be avoidable by a model in which some *internal* (or internally developed) semantic resource allows the AA to organize its categories functionally and hence to ground its symbols *autonomously*. A proposal along these lines has been developed by Sun (2000), to be analysed in the next section.

6.3.3 An intentional model for the solution of the SGP

Sun (2000) proposes an *intentional model* that relates connectionism, symbolic representations and situated artificial intelligence.[6] As for Harnad and Mayo, for Sun too the

---

[6] The strategy is developed in several papers, see Sun (1997), (2001), Sun et al. (2001), Sun and Zhang (2002).

AA's direct interaction with the environment is pivotal in the elaboration of its symbolic representations and hence the solution of the SGP. The novelty lies in the development by the AA of some intentional capacities.

Sun refers to the interaction between an AA and the environment in the Heideggerian terms of *being-in-the-world* and *being-with-the-world*. As he remarks,

[the ability to elaborate] the representations presupposes the more basic comportment [of the agent] with-the-world. (Sun (2000), p. 164)

The AA is *in-the-world* and interacts with objects in the world in order to achieve its goals. Its intentional stance is defined in the still Heideggerian terms of *being-with-the-things*.

According to Sun, representations do not stand for the corresponding perceived objects, but rather for the uses that an AA can make of these objects as means to ends. The intentional representations contain the rules for the teleological use of the objects, and the AA elaborates this kind of representations through a learning process.

Still following a Heideggerian approach, Sun distinguishes between a first and a second level of learning:

it is assumed that the cognitive processes are carried out in two distinct levels with qualitatively different processing mechanisms. Each level encodes a fairly complete set of knowledge for its processing. (Sun (2000), p. 158)

The two levels are supposed to complement each other. The first-level learning directly guides the AA's actions in the environment. It allows the AA to follow some courses of action, even if it does not yet know any rule for achieving its goals. At this stage, the AA does not yet elaborate any explicit representations of its actions and perceptual data. The first-level learning guides the behaviour of the AA by considering only two factors: the structure of the external world and the

innate biases or *built-in constraints* and *predispositions* [emphasis added] which also depend on the (ontogenetic and phylogenetic) history of agent world interaction. (Sun (2000), p. 158)

Such an innate criterion—which already breaches the Z condition—is identified by Sun with a first-level intentionality of the AA, which is then further qualified as 'pre-representational (i.e., *implicit*)' (Sun (2000), p. 157; emphasis added). Such intentionality provides the foundation for the initial interactions of the AA with its environment and for the subsequent, more complex form of intentionality.

During the first-level learning stage, the AA proceeds by trial and error, in order to discover the range of actions that best enable it to achieve its goals. These first-level learning processes allow the AA to acquire the initial data that can then work as input for its second-level learning processes. The latter produce the best possible behaviour, according to some of the AA's parameters, to achieve its objectives. It is at this second-level stage of learning that the AA elaborates its conceptual representations from its first-level data, thanks to what Sun (2000) defines as second-level intentionality. At the first-level, the behaviour of the AA is intentional in the sense that it directs the AA to the objects in the world. Second-level intentionality uses first-level intentionality data in order to evaluate the adequacy of different courses of action available to the AA to achieve its objectives. According to Sun and Zhang (2002), this is sufficient to ground the conceptual representations in the AA's everyday activities, in a functional way.

So far, we have described first and second-level learning processes as layered in a bottom–up, dynamic structure but, according to Sun, there is also a top–down dynamic relation among the layers. This allows the AA to generalize the representations obtained in relation to its best behaviours, in order to use them in as many cases as possible. Through a top–down procedure, the AA verifies once more the validity of the representations elaborated, compares the selected representations with the goals to be achieved, generalizes those representations already related to the best behaviours (given some parameters) and fine-tunes the remaining representations to ensure that they are related to a more successful behaviour.

The intentional model elaborated by Sun defines a specific architecture for the AA, which has been implemented in a system called CLARION (Sun and Peterson (1998)). I shall briefly describe its features in order to clarify the difficulties undermining Sun's strategy for solving the SGP.

6.3.3.1. Clarion. CLARION consists of four layered neural networks (but see the problem in using neural networks to solve the SGP, discussed in section 6.3.1), which implement a bottom–up process. The first three levels elaborate the values of CLARION's actions. The fourth level compares the values of the actions and—given some parameters—chooses the best course to achieve its goals, elaborates an explicit rule and adds it to the symbolic level.

To evaluate its actions, CLARION employs a Machine Learning algorithm known as *Q-learning.* This is based on the reinforcement learning principle. Suppose an AA is confronted by a specific task. The algorithm models the task in terms of states of the AA and actions that the AA can implement starting from its current state. Not all states lead to the goal state, and the agent must choose a sequence of optimal or sub-optimal actions that will lead to the goal state, by using the least possible states to minimize cost. Each good choice is rewarded and each bad choice is punished. The agent is left training on its own, following these rules and rewards. During the training process, the agent learns what the best actions are to achieve a specific task. Given sufficient training time, the agent can learn to solve the problem efficiently. Note, however, that the algorithm works only if the (solution of the) problem can be modelled and executed in a finite time because the number of states and actions are relatively finite. A game like Go is already too complex. As far as the solution of the SGP is concerned, it is already clear that, by adopting the Q-learning algorithm, the intentional model is importing from the outside the very condition that allows CLARION to semanticize, since tasks, goals, success, failure, rewards, and punishments are all established by the programmer. The semantic commitment could not be more explicit.

CLARION's symbolic fourth level corresponds to the second-level learning process in Sun's model. The values of the actions are checked and generalized in order to make possible their application even in new circumstances. This last stage corresponds to the top–down process. CLARION's high-level concepts are

context dependent and they are functional to achieve the objectives of the agents [...] the concepts are part of the set of roles which an agent learns in order to interact with the environment. (Sun (2000), p. 168)

Sun stresses the functional nature of the concepts in order to point out that they come from experience and are not defined a priori.

The functionalism implemented by the intentional model is possible only thanks to extrinsic, semantic resources, freely provided to the AA. This undermines the value of Sun's strategy as a solution of the SGP. Sun (2000) attempts to overcome this difficulty by reinterpreting the functionalist criterion as an innate and intrinsic feature of the AA, namely its intentionality. Yet, this alleged solution also begs the question, since it remains unclear how the AA is supposed to acquire the necessary intentionality without which it would be unable to ground its data. In this case too, semantics is made possible only by some other semantics, whose presence remains problematic.

It might be replied that the intentionality of the representations can arise from the process of extraction of conceptual representations from first-level learning processes and that, at this level, the AA's intentionality could derive from its direct interactions with the world, encoded through its first-level learning. In this way, the semantic resources, to which the AA freely and generously helps itself, would not have to be extrinsically generated. Indeed, Sun (2000) describes first-level intentionality as a pure consequence of the interactions of an AA with its environment.

Comportment carries with it a direct and an unmediated relation to things in the world [...]. Therefore it provides [an] *intrinsic* intentionality (meanings), or in other words a connection (to things with the words) that is intrinsic to the agent [...]. (p. 164)

Unfortunately, it remains unexplained precisely how this first-level intentionality might arise in the first place. Presupposing its presence is not an answer. How does even a very primitive, simple, and initial form of intentionality develop (in an autonomous way) from the direct interactions between and AA and its environment? Unless a logically valid and empirically plausible answer is provided, the SGP has simply been shifted.

Sun (2000) argues that AAs evolve, and hence that they may develop their intentional capacities over time. In this way, first-level intentionality, and then further semantic capacities, would arise from evolutionary processes related to the experience of the AAs, without the presence of extrinsic criteria.

There are some existing computational methods available to accomplish simple forms of such [i.e. both first- and second-level] learning. [. . .] [A]nother approach, the genetic algorithm [. . .] may also be used to tackle this kind of task. (Sun (2000), p. 160)

However, in this case too, the solution of the SGP is only shifted. The specific techniques of artificial evolution to which Sun refers (especially Holland (1975)) do not grant the conclusion that Sun's strategy satisfies the Z condition. Quite the opposite. Given a population of individuals that evolve generationally, evolution algorithms make it possible to go from an original population of genotypes to a new generation using only some kind of artificial selection. Evolution algorithms are obviously based on a Darwinian survival mechanism of the fittest. However, it is the programmer who plays the key role of the 'natural' selection process. She chooses different kinds of genotype—AAs with different features—situates them in an environment, calculates (or allows the system to calculate) which is the behaviour that best guarantees survival in the chosen environment, and does so by using a parameter, defined by a *fitness formula*, that once again is modelled and chosen by her. The AAs showing the best behaviour pass the selection, yet 'artificial evolutionism' is only an automatic selection technique based on a programmer's criteria. True, it may possible to hypothesize a generation of AAs that ends up being endowed with the sort of intentionality required by Sun's strategy. By using the right fitness formula, perhaps a programmer might ensure that precisely the characteristics that allow the AAs to behave in an 'intentional way' will be promoted by their interactions with the environment. For example, a programmer could try to use a fitness formula such that, in the long run, it privileges only those AAs that implement algorithms like CLARION's *Q-learning algorithm*, thus generating a population of 'intentional' AAs. Nonetheless, their intentionality would not follow from their *being-in-the-world*, nor would it be developed by the AAs evolutionary and autonomously. It would merely be superimposed by the programmer's purposeful choice of an environment and of the corresponding fitness formula, until the AAs obtained satisfy the sort of description required by the model. One may still argue that the semantics of the AAs would then be grounded in their first-level intentionality, but the SGP would still be an open challenge. For the point, let us recall, is not that it is impossible to engineer an AA that has its symbols semantically grounded somehow. The point is how an AA can ground its symbols autonomously while satisfying the Z condition.

Artificial evolutionism, at least as presented by Sun, does not allow us to consider intentionality an autonomous capacity of the AAs. On the contrary, it works only insofar as it presumes the presence of a semantic framework, from the programmer acting as a *deus ex machina* to the right fitness formula. Sun's strategy is semantically committed and does not provide a valid solution for the SGP.

The analysis of CLARION concludes the part of this chapter dedicated to the representationalist approach to the SGP. None of the strategies discussed so far appears to provide a valid solution for the SGP. Perhaps the crucial difficulty lies in the assumption that the solution must be entirely representationalist. In the following section, we are going to see whether a weakening of the representationalist requirement may deliver a solution to the SGP.

6.4 The semi-representationalist approach

In this section, I discuss three strategies developed by Davidsson (1993), Vogt (2002b), and Rosenstein and Cohen (1998). They are still representationalist in nature but differ from those discussed in the previous section in that they deal with the AA's use of its representations by relying on principles imported from behaviour-based robotics.

6.4.1 An epistemological model for the solution of the SGP

According to Davidsson (1993), there is a question that the solution of the SGP suggested by Harnad (1990) leaves unanswered, namely, what sort of learning is allowed by neural networks? We have seen that this issue is already raised by Christiansen and Chater (1992).

Davidsson argues that concepts must be acquired in a gradual fashion, through repeated interactions with the environment over time. The AA must be capable of *incremental* learning, in order to categorize its data into concepts and hence provide its symbols with a semantics. However, neural networks provide a discriminative learning framework that does not lend itself to an easily incremental adaptation of its contents, given the 'fixed-structure of the neural nets' (Davidsson (1993), p. 160). It follows that, according to Davidsson, most neural networks are not suitable for the kind of learning required by an AA that might successfully cope with the SGP. Davidsson (1993) maintains that the SGP becomes more tractable if it is approached in terms of general 'conceptual representations' and Machine Learning.

According to Davidsson (1993) 'a concept is represented by a composite description consisting of several components' (p. 158). The main idea is that a concept must be a complete description of its referent object, and thus it should collect different kinds of representations, one for each purpose for which the object represented can be used. Davidsson defines three parts of a description:

1. the *designator*, which is the name (symbol) used to refer to a category;
2. the *epistemological representation*, which is used to recognize instances of a category; and
3. the *inferential representation*, which is a collection of all that it is known about a category and its members ('encyclopaedic knowledge') and that can be used to make predictions or to infer non-perceptual information.

For example, the concept corresponding to the word 'window' could denote a 3-D object model of a typical window and work as an epistemological representation. By means of the inferential knowledge component, one could then include information like: windows are used to admit light and air in a building, they are fitted with casements or sashes containing transparent material (e.g. glass) and capable of being opened and shut, and so forth.

The epistemological representations are pivotal in Davidsson's solution. They are elaborated through a vision system that allows the identification (categorization) of the perceived data. When an AA encounters an object, it matches the object with its epistemological representation. In so doing, the AA activates a larger knowledge structure, which allows it to develop further, more composite concepts. An epistemological representation does not have to be (elaborated through) a connectionist network, since it can be any representation that can be successfully used by the vision system to identify (categorize) objects.

Davidsson acknowledges that the representations that ground the symbols should not be pre-programmed but rather learned by the AA from its own 'experience'. So he suggests using two paradigms typical of Machine Learning: *learning by observation* and *learning from examples*.

Learning by observation is an unsupervised learning mechanism, which allows the system to generate descriptions of categories. Examples are not pre-classified and the learner has to form the categories autonomously. However, the programmer still provides the system with a specific number of well-selected description entities, which allow the AA to group the entities into categories. Clearly, the significant descriptions first selected and then provided by the human trainer to the artificial learner are an essential condition for any further categorization of the entities handled by the AA. They are also a *conditio sine qua non* for the solution of the SGP. Since such descriptions are provided *before* the AA develops its semantics capacities and *before* it starts to elaborate any sort of description autonomously, they are entirely external to the AA and represent a semantic resource given to the AA by the programmer.

The same objection applies to the learning from examples mechanism. Indeed, in this case the presence of external criteria is even more obvious, since the sort of learning in question presupposes a set of explicitly pre-classified (by the human teacher) examples of the categories to be acquired. The result is that Davidsson's strategy is as semantically committed as all the others already discussed, so it too falls short of providing a valid solution of the SGP.

6.4.2 The physical symbol grounding problem

Vogt (2002a), (2002b) connects the solution proposed by Harnad (1990) with situated robotics (Brooks (1990), (1991)) and with the semiotic definition of symbols (Peirce (1960)). His strategy consists in approaching the SGP from the vantage point of embodied cognitive science. He seeks to ground the symbolic system of the AA in its sensorimotor activities, transform the SGP into the *Physical Symbol Grounding Problem* (PhSGP), and then solve the PhSGP by relying on two conceptual tools: the *semiotic symbol systems* and the *guess game*.

Vogt defines the symbols used by an AA as a structural pair of sensorimotor activities and environmental data. According to a semiotic definition, AA's symbols have:

1. a *form* (Peirce's 'representamen'), which is the physical shape taken by the actual sign;
2. a *meaning* (Peirce's 'interpretant'), which is the semantic content of the sign; and
3. a *referent* (Peirce's 'object'), which is the object to which the sign refers.

Following this Peircean definition, a symbol always comprises a form, a meaning, and a referent, with the meaning arising from a functional relation between the form and the referent, through the process of semiosis or interpretation. Using this definition, Vogt intends to show that the symbols, constituting the AA's semiotic symbol system, are already semantically grounded because of their intrinsic nature. Since both the meaning and the referent are already embedded in (the definition of) a symbol, the latter turns out (a) to be directly related to the object to which it refers and (b) to carry the corresponding categorical representation. The grounding of the whole semiotic symbol system is then left to special kinds of AA that are able to ground the meaning of their symbols in their sensorimotor activities, thus solving the PhSGP.

The solution of the PhSGP is based on the *guess game* (Steels and Vogt (1997)), a technique used to study the development of a common language by situated robots. The guess game involves two robots, situated in a common environment. Each robot has a role: the *speaker* names the objects it perceives, the *hearer* has the task of finding the objects named by the speaker through trial and error. During the game, the robots develop a common system of semiotic symbol through communicative interactions, the *adaptative language games*. The robots have a very simple body, and can only interact with their environment visually. The *speaker* communicates only to convey the name of a visually detected referent. The *hearer* communicates only to inform the speaker about its guessing concerning the referent named by the speaker. The guess game ends successfully if the two robots develop a shared lexicon, grounded in the interactions among themselves and with their environment.

The game has four stages, at the end of which the robots are expected to obtain a shared name for an object in their environments. The first two stages—the beginning of the perceptual activities by the two robots in the environment and the selection of one part of the environment in which they will operate—lie outside the scope of this chapter so they will not be analysed here (for a complete description see Vogt (2002a), (2002b)). The last two stages concern the processes of meaning formation. More specifically, they constitute the *discrimination game*, through which the categories are elaborated, and the *naming game*, through which the categories are named. These two stages allow the robots to find a referent for their symbols and are crucial for the solution of the SGP.

In order to ground their symbols, the AAs involved in the guess game have to categorize the data obtained from their perception of an object, so that they can later distinguish this category of objects from all the others. According to Vogt, the process for the formation of meaning is carried out by the discrimination game. During this third stage, the AAs associate similar perceptual data in order to elaborate their categorical representations, as in Harnad's hybrid model. Once the AAs have elaborated one category for each of the objects perceived, the naming game begins. During this last stage, the AAs communicate in order to indicate the objects that they have categorized. The *speaker* makes an utterance that works as the name of one of the categories that it has elaborated. The *hearer* tries to interpret the utterance and to associate it with one of the categories that it has elaborated on its own. The goal is to identify the same category named by the *speaker*. If the *hearer* finds the right interpretation for the *speaker*'s utterance, the two AAs are able to communicate and the guess game is successful.

According to Vogt, the guess game makes explicit the meanings of the symbols and allows them to be grounded through the AAs' perceptions and interactions. If the guess game ends successfully, the PhSGP is solved. There are two main difficulties with Vogt's strategy. The most important concerns his semiotic approach; the other relates to what the guess game actually proves.

Suppose we have a set of finite strings of signs—e.g. 0s and 1s—elaborated by an AA. The strings may satisfy the semiotic definition—they may have a form, a meaning and a referent—only if they are *interpreted* by an AA that already has a semantics for that vocabulary. This was also Peirce's view. Signs are meaningful symbols only in the eyes of the interpreter. But the AA cannot be assumed to qualify as an interpreter without begging the question. Given that the semiotic definition of symbols is already semantically committed, it cannot provide a strategy for the solution of the SGP. Nor can the SGP be reduced to the PhSGP: the AA does not have an intrinsic semantics, autonomously elaborated, so one cannot yet make the next move of anchoring in the environment the semantics of the semiotic symbols because there is nothing to anchor in the first place.

It might be replied—and we come in this way to the second difficulty—that perhaps Vogt's strategy could still solve the SGP thanks to the guess game, which could connect the symbols with their external referents through the interaction of the robots with their environment. Unfortunately, as Vogt himself acknowledges, the guess game cannot, and indeed it is not meant to, ground the symbols. The guess game assumes that the AAs manipulate previously grounded symbols, in order to show how two AAs can come to make explicit and share the same grounded vocabulary by means of an iterated process of communication. Using Harnad's example, multiplying the number of people who need to learn Chinese as their first language by using only a Chinese–Chinese dictionary does not make things any better.

Vogt acknowledges these difficulties, but his two answers are problematic, and show how his strategy cannot solve the SGP without begging the question. On the one hand, he argues that the grounding process proposed is comparable to the way infants seem to construct meaning from their visual interactions with objects in their environment. However, even if the latter is uncontroversial (which it is not), in solving the SGP one cannot merely assume that the AA in question has the semantic capacities of a human agent. To repeat the point, the issue is how the AA evolves such capacities. As Vogt (2002b) puts it, several critics have pointed out that

robots cannot use semiotic symbols meaningfully, since they are not rooted in the robot, as the robots are designed rather than shaped through evolution and physical growth [. . .], whatever task they [the symbols used by the robots] might have stems from its designer or is in the head of a human observer. (p. 434)

To this Vogt replies (and here we arrive at his second answer) that

it will be *assumed* [emphasis added] that robots, once they can construct semiotic symbols, do so meaningfully. This assumption is made to illustrate how robots can construct semiotic symbols meaningfully. (p. 434)

The assumption might be useful in order to engineer AAs, but it certainly begs the question when it comes to providing a strategy for solving the SGP.[7]

6.4.3 A model based on temporal delays and predictive semantics for the solution of the SGP

As in all the other cases discussed so far, Rosenstein and Cohen (1998) try to solve the SGP through a bottom–up process 'from the perception to the elaboration of the language through the symbolic thought' (p. 20).[8] Unlike the others, their strategy for solving the SGP is based on three components:

1. a method for the organization of the perceptual data, called the *method of delays* or *delays-space embedding*, which apparently allows the AA to store perceptual data without using extrinsic criteria, thus avoiding any semantic commitment;
2. a predictive semantics; and
3. an unsupervised learning process, which allows the elaboration of an autonomous semantics.

Consider an example adapted from Rosenstein and Cohen (1999b). Ros is an AA that can move around in a laboratory. It is provided with sensors through which it can perceive its external environment. Ros is able to assess the distance between itself and the objects situated in the external environment. It registers distances at regular time intervals and plots distance and time values on a Cartesian coordinate system, with time on the x-axis and distances on the y-axis. Suppose Ros encounters an object. Ros does not know whether it is approaching the object but its sensor registers that, at time t, Ros is at 2000 mm from the object, at $t+1$ Ros is at 2015 mm from the object, and so forth. From these data, we, and presumably Ros, can deduce that it is moving away from the object. According to Rosenstein and Cohen, an AA like Ros can 'know' the consequences of similar actions through the Cartesian representation of the data

---

[7] For an approach close to Vogt's and that incurs the same problems see Baillie (2004).

[8] The strategy is developed in several papers, see Oates et al. (1998a), Oates et al. (1998b), Rosenstein and Cohen (1999a), (1999b), Sebastiani et al. (1999), Cohen et al. (2002), Firoiu and Cohen (2002).

concerning those actions. The AA envisioned by Rosenstein and Cohen identifies the meaning of its symbols with the outcome of its actions, through a Cartesian representation of its perceived data. Since the data plotted on a Cartesian coordinate system define an action, the AA associates with that particular 'Cartesian map' the meaning of the corresponding action.

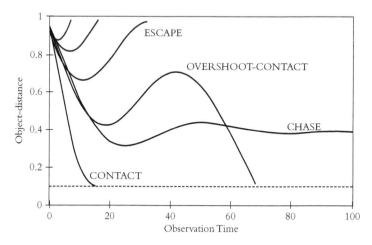

Figure 7 Cluster prototypes for 100 interactions in the pursuit/avoidance simulator
From Rosenstein and Cohen (1998), p. 21

Suppose now that a population of AAs like Ros interact in a simulated environment adopting several strategies for pursuit or avoidance.
Figure 7 shows the six prototypes derived from 100 agent interactions with randomly chosen strategies. According to Rosenstein and Cohen, the categories 'chase', 'contact', 'escape' etc. acquire their meanings in terms of the predictions that each of them enables the AA to make.

As one can see from Figure 7, the actions that have similar outcomes/meaning also have the same Cartesian representation. Rosenstein and Cohen call this feature of the Cartesian representation *natural clustering*. They maintain that, through natural clustering, an AA can elaborate categorical representations of its actions and that, since the Cartesian map already associates action outcomes with meanings, the categories too have meanings and thus they are semantically founded. Once some initial categories are semantically grounded, the AA can start to elaborate its conceptual representations. The latter are the result of both a comparison of similar categorical representations and of an abstraction of features shared by them. Like the categorical representations on which they are based, the conceptual representations too are semantically grounded. The 'artificial' semantics built in this way can grow autonomously, through the interactions of the AA with its environment, until the process allows the AA to predict the outcome of its actions while it is performing them. The prediction is achieved using a learning algorithm. When an AA has a new experience, the algorithm compares the new actions with the ones already represented by previous Cartesian representations, in order to identify and correlate similar patterns. If the AA can find the category of the corresponding actions, it can predict the outcome/meaning of the new action. The correlation between Cartesian representations and outcome/meaning of the actions allows the AA to elaborate a *predictive semantics*.

It seems that the SGP is solved without using any external or pre-semantic criteria. Apparently, the only parameter used for the initial categorization of an AA's actions is time, and this cannot be defined as an external parameter, since it is connected with the execution of the actions (Rosenstein and Cohen (1998)).

The appearance, however, is misleading. For it is the Cartesian coordinate system, its plotting procedures and symbolic conventions used by the AA, that constitute the pivotal, semantic framework allowing the elaboration of an initial semantics by an AA like Ros. Clearly, this 'Cartesian' semantic framework is entirely extraneous to the AA, either being presumed to be there (innatism) or, more realistically, having been superimposed by the programmer. Rosenstein and Cohen seem to consider the mapping of its actions on some Cartesian coordinates as some sort of *spontaneous* representation of the perceptual data by the AA itself. However, the very interpretation of the data, provided by the actions, as information of such and such a kind on a Cartesian coordinate system is, by itself, a crucial semantic step, based on extrinsic criteria. Obviously, the system does not satisfy the Z condition, and the approach fails to solve the SGP.

The temporal delays method concludes the part of this chapter dedicated to the semi-representationalist approach to the SGP. Again, none of the hypotheses discussed appears to provide a valid solution for the SGP. In the next section, we shall see what happens when representationalism is discarded in favour of an entirely non-representationalist approach to the SGP.

6.5 The non-representationalist approach

The roots of a non-representationalist approach to the SGP may be traced to the criticisms made by Brooks (1990), (1991) of the classic concept of representation. Brooks argues that intelligent behaviour can be the outcome of interactions between an *embodied* and *situated*[9] AA and its environment and that, for this purpose, symbolic representations are not necessary, only sensorimotor couplings. This is what Brooks (1991) calls the *Physical Grounding Hypothesis*.

In order to explore the construction of physically grounded systems, Brooks has developed a computational architecture known as the *subsumption architecture*, which

---

[9] An AA is embodied if it is implemented in a physical structure through which it can have direct experience of its surrounding world. The same AA is also situated if it is placed in a dynamic environment with which it can interact.

'enables us to tightly connect perception to action, embedding robots correctly in the world.' (Brooks (1990), p. 5). The details of Brooks' subsumption architecture are well known and there is no need to summarize them here. What is worth emphasizing is that, since a subsumption architecture allows an AA to avoid any elaboration of explicit representations, within this paradigm one may argue that the SGP is solved in the sense that it is entirely avoided: if there are no symbolical representations to ground, there is no symbol grounding problem to be solved. The truth is, however, that the SGP is merely postponed rather than avoided. An AA implementing a subsumption architecture may not need to deal with the SGP initially, in order to deal successfully with its environment. But if it is to develop even an elementary protolanguage and some higher cognitive capacities, it will have to be able to manipulate some symbols, but then the question of their semantic grounding presents itself anew. This is the problem addressed by the following two strategies.

6.5.1 A communication-based model for the solution of the SGP

Billard and Dautenhahn (1999) propose a communication-based approach to the SGP that can be interpreted as steering a middle course between the strategies advocated by Vogt (2002b) and by Varshavskaya (2002) (see next section).

The topic of their research is AAs' social skills in learning, communicating and imitating. They investigate grounding and use of communication through simulations within a group of AAs. It is within that context that we encounter their proposal on how to approach the SGP.

The experimental scenario consists of nine AAs interacting in the same environment and sharing a common set of perceptions. The AAs have short-term memory, and they are able to move around, communicate with each other and describe their internal and external perceptions. Their task is to learn a common language through a simple imitation game. In the experiment, the AAs are expected to learn a vocabulary to differentiate between coloured patches and to describe their locations in terms of distance and orientation, relative to a 'home point'.

The vocabulary is transmitted from a teacher agent, *which has a complete knowledge of the vocabulary from start* [emphasis added], to eight learner agents, which have no knowledge of the vocabulary at the start of the experiments. (Billard and Dautenhahn (1999), pp. 414–415).

Transmission of the vocabulary from teacher to learner occurs as part of an imitative strategy. Learning the vocabulary, or the grounding of the teacher's signals in the learner's sensor-actuator states, results from an association process across all the learner's sensor-actuator, thanks to a Dynamic Recurrent Associative Memory Architecture (DRAMA). DRAMA has a

considerable facility for conditional associative learning, including an efficient short-term memory for sequences and combinations, and an ability to easily and rapidly produce new combinations. (Billard and Dautenhahn (1999), p. 413)

According to Billard and Dautenhahn, the experiment indicates a valuable strategy for overcoming the SGP:

Our work showed the importance of behavioural capacities alongside cognitive ones for addressing the symbol grounding problem. (Billard and Dautenhahn (1999), p. 429)

However, it is evident that the validity of their proposal is undermined by three problems. First, the learning AAs are endowed with semantic resources (such as their DRAMA), whose presence is merely presupposed without any further justification (innatism). Note also that, in this context, there is a reliance on neural networks, which incurs the same problems highlighted in section 6.3.1. Second, the learning AAs acquire a pre-established, complete language from an external source (externalism): they do not develop it by themselves through their mutual communications and their interactions with their environment. Third, the external source-teacher is merely assumed to have full knowledge of the language and the semantics involved. This is another form of 'innatism' utterly unjustified in connection with the SGP. The hard question is how the teacher develops its language in the first place. This is the SGP, but to this Billard and Dautenhahn provide no answer. The result is that the strategy begs the question thrice and cannot be considered a valid solution of the grounding problem.

6.5.2 A behaviour-based model for the solution of the SGP

Following Brooks (1991), Varshavskaya (2002) argues that the development of semantic capacities in an AA could be modelled on the development of linguistic capacities in children. Theories of language acquisition appear to show that children acquire linguistic skills by using a language as a tool with which to interact with their environment and other agents, in order to satisfy their needs and achieve their goals. Accordingly, Varshavskaya supports a *pragmatic* interpretation of language acquisition in AA whereby

Language is not viewed as a denotational symbolic system for reference to objects and relationships between them, as much as a tool for communicating intentions. The utterance is a way to manipulate the environment through the beliefs and actions of others. (Varshavskaya (2002), p. 149)

Language becomes just another form of pragmatic interaction of the AA with its environment and, as such, its semantics does not need representations.

The hypothesis of a representations-free language has been corroborated by some experiments involving an MIT robot known as KISMET (Breazeal (2000), Breazeal (2002)):

KISMET is an expressive robotic head, designed to have a youthful appearance and perceptual and motor capabilities tuned to human communication channels. The robot receives visual input from four color CCD cameras and auditory input from a microphone. It performs motor acts such as vocalizations, facial expressions, posture changes, as well as gaze direction and head orientation. (Varshavskaya (2002), p. 151)

The experiments show that KISMET can learn from its trainer to use symbols and to develop protolinguistic behaviours. Varshavskaya states that, in so doing, KISMET has made the first steps towards the development of much more complex linguistic capacities.

Learning to communicate with the teacher using a shared semantics is for KISMET part of the more general task of learning how to interact with, and manipulate, its environment. KISMET has motivational (see next section and Table 5) and behavioural systems, and a set of vocal behaviours, regulatory drives, and learning algorithms, which together constitute its *protolanguage* module. Protolanguage refers here to the 'pre-grammatical' time of the development of a language—the babbling time in children—which allows the development of the articulation of sounds in the first months of life. To KISMET, protolanguage provides the means to ground the development of its linguistics capacities.

KISMET is an autonomous AA, with its own goals and strategies, which cause it to implement specific behaviours in order to satisfy its 'necessities'. Its 'motivations' make it execute its tasks. These motivations are provided by a set of homeostatic variables, called *drives*, such as the level of engagement with the environment or the intensity of social play. The drives must be kept within certain bounds in order to maintain KISMET's system in equilibrium. KISMET has 'emotions' as well, which are a kind of motivation.

Table 5 The correspondence between KISMET's nonverbal behaviours and protolinguistic functions

Emotion	Behaviour	Proto-linguistic Function
Anger, Frustration	complain	regulatory
Disgust	withdraw	instrumental or regulatory
Fear, Distress	escape	—
Calm	engage	interactional
Joy	display pleasure	personal or interactional
Sorrow	display sorrow	regulatory or personal
Surprise	startle response	—
Boredom	seek	—

Based on Varshavskaya (2002), p. 153

KISMET's emotions depend on the evaluations of the perceptual stimuli. When the homeostatic values are off-balance, KISMET can perform a series of actions that allow it to regain a pre-established equilibrium. In these cases, KISMET uses some protoverbal behaviours—it expresses its 'emotions'—with which it acts on itself and on the environment in order to restore the balance of the original values.

KISMET can implement protolinguistic behaviours, thanks to the presence of two drives (one for the language and one for the exploration of the environment), an architecture to express protoverbal behaviours and an architecture for the visual apparatus. The language drive allows two behaviours called *Reader* and *Hearer* (Figure 8) 'which interface with KISMET's perceptual system and procure global releasers for vocal behavior' (Varshavskaya (2002), p. 153). There is also a *Speaker* behaviour responsible for sending a speech request over to the robot.

The kind of requests depends on the competition between the individual proto-verbal behaviours that KISMET can perform. These are in a competitive hierarchy and the one which has the highest position in the hierarchy is executed.

Let us now see, with an example, what the emulation processes are and how they influence KISMET's learning process. Suppose KISMET learns the English word 'green'. The trainer shows KISMET a green object and at the same time she utters the word 'green', while KISMET is observing the green object. Then the trainer hides the green object, which will be shown again only if KISMET looks for it and expresses a vocal request corresponding to the word 'green'. If KISMET utters the word 'green' in order to request the green object, then KISMET has learned the association between the word and the object, and to use the word according to its meaning. By performing similar tasks, KISMET seems to be able to acquire semantic capacities and to develop them without elaborate representations. The question is whether this proves sufficient to solve the SGP.

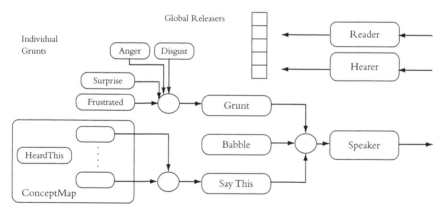

Figure 8 'Overall architecture of KISMET's protoverbal behaviors, where rounded boxes represent instances of behaviors and circles represent connections between behaviors. Connections between HeardThis and individual Concepts are not shown for clarity' from Varshavskaya (2002), p. 154

6.5.2.1 Emulative learning and the rejection of representations. The learning approach adopted by Varshavskaya is intrinsically inadequate to deal with the SGP successfully. For the question concerning the origin of semantic capacities in artificial systems—i.e.

how KISMET begins to semanticize in the first place—cannot be addressed by referring to modalities appropriate to human agents, since only in this case it is correct to assume

- a natural and innate predisposition in the agent to acquire a language;
- the existence of an already well-developed language; and
- the presence of a community of speakers, proficient in that language, who can transmit knowledge of that language to new members.

None of these assumptions is justified when an AA is in question, including KISMET. Recall that, in order to solve the SGP, the semantic capacities of the AA must be elaborated by the AA itself autonomously, without begging the question: no innatism or externalism is allowed. Yet, both occur in KISMET's case. KISMET is (innately) endowed with semantic features (recall the presence of a protolanguage) and it (externally) performs an explicitly emulative learning. It associates the symbol 'green' to the green object shown by the trainer, but the initial, semantic relation between 'green' and the green object is pre-established and provided by the trainer herself. As far as the SGP is concerned, teaching KISMET the meaning of 'green' is not very different from uploading a lookup table.

The point may be further clarified by considering the following difficulty: does the symbol 'green' for KISMET refer to the specific green object shown to KISMET by the trainer or does it, instead, name a general feature—the colour of the green object—that KISMET can recognize in that as well as in other similar objects? Suppose we show KISMET several objects, with different shapes but all having the property of being green. Among these objects, there is also the green object that KISMET already knows. If one asks KISMET to recognize a green object, it will recognize only the green object it has seen before. This is so because KISMET does not name classes of objects, e.g. all the green objects. Instead, it has symbols that name their referents rigidly, as if they were their proper names. For KISMET, the green object will not *be green*, it will *be called 'green'*, in the same sense in which a black dog may be called 'Blackie'. This follows from KISMET's non-representationalist elaborations. KISMET's semantics can grow as much as the emulative learning process externally superimposed by the trainer allows, but the absence of representations means that KISMET will not develop any categorical framework in the sense required to solve the SGP. Lacking representations, KISMET is unable to connect a symbol to a category of data.

CONCLUSION

The positive lesson that can be learnt at the end of this chapter is that (the semantic capacity to generate) representations cannot be presupposed without begging the question. Yet abandoning any reference to representations means accepting a dramatic limit to what an AA may be able to achieve semantically, since the development of even the simplest abstract category becomes impossible. So it seems that a valid solution of the SGP will need to combine at least the following features:

1. a bottom–up, sensorimotor approach to the grounding problem;
2. a top–down feedback approach that allows the harmonization of top-level grounded symbols and bottom-level, sensorimotor interactions with the environment;
3. the availability of some sort of representational capacities in the AA;
4. the availability of some sort of categorical/abstracting capacities in the AA;
5. the availability of some sort of communication capacities among AAs in order to ground the symbols diachronically and avoid the Wittgensteinian problem of a 'private language';
6. an evolutionary approach in the development of (1)–(5);
7. the satisfaction of the Z condition in the development of (1)–(6).

Whether all this may be possible even in principle is an entirely different issue, which I shall address in the next chapter.

7

Action-based semantics

The important insight is that there is a language-game in which I produce information automatically, information which can be treated by other people quite as they treat non-automatic information—only here there will be no question of any 'lying'—information which I myself may receive like that of a third person. The 'automatic' statement, report etc. might also be called an 'oracle'.—But of course that means that the oracle must not avail itself of the words 'I believe. . .'.

Wittgenstein, *Remarks on the Philosophy of Psychology* I. § 817 (Wittgenstein (1980)).

SUMMARY

Previously, in chapters four, five, and six, I argued that well-formed data need to be meaningful and truthful in order to count as semantic information; that this leads to the so-called symbol (data) grounding problem (SGP); but that all the main strategies proposed so far, in order to solve the SGP, fail to satisfy the *zero semantic commitment condition* (Z condition) and are therefore invalid, although they provide several important lessons to be followed by any new alternative. In light of such critical analysis, in this chapter I shall elaborate a constructive proposal, by developing and supporting a new solution of the SGP. It is called *praxical* in order to stress the key role played by the interactions between the agents and their environment. It is based on a new theory of meaning—which I shall call *Action-based Semantics* (AbS)—and on a new kind of artificial agents, called *two-machine artificial agents* (AM^2). Thanks to their architecture, AM^2s implement AbS, and this allows them to ground their symbols semantically as well as to develop some fairly advanced semantic abilities, including forms of semantically grounded communication and of elaboration of semantic information about the environment, while still respecting the Z condition. As the reader might recall, once we have explained how data might acquire their meanings, we still have the task of understanding what it means for meaningful data to be truthful. This will be the topic of the following chapter.

7.1 Introduction

Solving the symbol grounding problem (SGP) can be hard. We saw that the difficulty consists in specifying how an artificial agent (AA) can *autonomously* elaborate its own semantics for the data (symbols) that it manipulates, by interacting with its environment and other agents, while satisfying the *zero semantic commitment condition* (Z condition). Recall that, according to the Z condition, no valid solution of the SGP can rely on forms of *innatism* or *externalism*: semantic resources should be neither presupposed, as already pre-installed in the AA, nor merely uploaded from the 'outside' by some agent already semantically-proficient. The previous chapter ended with some recommendations about further requirements that a solution of the SGP may need to satisfy in order to be satisfactory. In this chapter, I develop and defend a solution of the SGP that respects the Z condition and satisfies those requirements. For reasons that will soon become clear, I shall refer to it as the *praxical*[1] solution. I will introduce it in two steps.

The first step, taken in section two, consists in outlining the appropriate approach involved in the process of generating new meanings. This is defined as *Action-based Semantics* (AbS). AbS requires an explanation of the specific process that allows the coupling of symbols to meanings. Such coupling is more intuitively introduced by referring to an actual agent implementing AbS, so I shall postpone its theoretical description until section three.

The second step, taken in section three, consists in describing a *two-machine* artificial agent (AM^2) that implements the AbS. An AM^2 assigns meanings to symbols without elaborating any kind of categorical representation yet. We shall see that it does not presuppose *semantic* resources or capacities in order to generate its semantics, and hence that it satisfies the Z condition. I shall then describe the second stage of the semantic process, namely how an AM^2 generates representations. These are neither categorical nor conceptual, unlike Harnad's, and yet it will be shown that they allow the development of a semantics in which symbols may be names of classes of meanings. Such semantics avoids both the constraints, highlighted in the previous chapter, for the semantics generated by the non-representationalist strategy (Brooks (1990); Varshavskaya (2002)), and the criticism levelled at the representationalist solutions (Harnad (1990)). In section 7.3.1, we shall look at three objections to the process performed by an AM^2. In section 7.3.2, I shall refer to a specific learning rule and to an evolutionary scenario in order to show how a population of AM^2s could develop its semantic abilities autonomously. In section four, I shall describe how a population of AM^2s can develop more complex semantics abilities, such as semantically grounded communication and a shared semantics. In the conclusion, I shall briefly summarize the work done and discuss an interesting consequence of the praxical solution of the SGP, namely the possibility of developing a full theory of meaning based on it. Its development, however, lies beyond the scope of this book and will be left to a future stage in the research on the philosophy of information.

---

[1] In the same sense in which 'praxis' is used to refer to 'theory in practice', I use 'praxical' to qualify interactions that are information- or knowledge-oriented. An embodied and embedded agent has a *praxical* relation with its surroundings when it learns about, and operates on, its environment in ways that are conducive to the acquisition of implicit information or knowledge about it. In human agents, *practical* experience is non-theoretical, whereas *praxical* experience is pre- but also pro-theoretical, as it conduces to theory.

7.2 Action-based semantics

The basic idea of an action-based semantics is simple: in the beginning, the proto-meanings of the symbols generated by an AA are the internal states of that AA, which in turn are directly correlated to the actions performed by the same AA.

Consider a common AA, such as a robot able to move in a laboratory. Let us call it FOTOC.[2] I shall describe and discuss FOTOC in greater detail in the next section. Here suffice to say that any time FOTOC executes a movement, such as 'turning left', it enters into a specific internal state and should be able to take advantage of this internal state as a meaning to be associated to a symbol. So, by saying that the performed actions are the meanings of the symbols, I mean that the AA relates its symbols to the states in which it is placed by the actions that it performs, and that symbols are considered the names of the actions via the corresponding internal states.

The advantage of this approach is that the very first step in the generation of meanings is not in itself a *semantic process*, but rather an *immediate consequence* of an AA's performance. Through AbS, an AA can generate meanings without its perceptual data (e.g. FOTOC's detection of its location in the lab office) causing some kind of representations, a process that is always based on semantic criteria and therefore cannot but breach the Z condition. The internal states of the AA are excellent candidates for the role of non-semantic yet semantic-inducing resources.

By following the AbS, one avoids the use of any kind of external assistance (e.g. a programmer or a trainer), while also avoiding extrinsic biases: the initial generation of meanings is *teleologically free*, i.e. it is *neutral* with respect to any purpose. Admittedly, most of the time, an AA performs an action in order to achieve some goal, but this form of teleological behaviour is not what is involved in the AbS. AbS assumes that the action performed—not the goal to be achieved—by an AA is going to ground its symbols semantically. In our example, FOTOC is supposed to ground a symbol to its internal state, induced by its action of turning left, and not by its *command* or *goal* expressible as avoid this obstacle or catch that object or turn left. This is both plausible and easily achievable. The development of an AA's goal-oriented behaviour may *then* be the result of the evolution of biochemical mechanisms that require no semantic resources at all. The heliotropic behaviour of plants, such as snow buttercups or sunflowers, is a canonical example.[3] Note that, even if an AA performs some action randomly—without any function or goal—or incorrectly, AbS still identifies that action as the source of the state that then provides the meaning of the related symbol.

---

[2] For a robot with skills similar to FOTOC's see Lego Wall Follower. It is equipped with a turret, enabling the rotation of its sensor (in the right direction) when a wall is detected. The following website provides a more detailed description http://www.techeblog.com/index.php/tech-gadget/lego-roverbot.

[3] The diurnal motion (being these of flowers or of leaves) is a response to the direction of the sun, performed by motor cells in flexible segments of the plant specialized in pumping potassium ions into nearby tissues (thus changing the turgor pressure) reversibly.

To summarize, at this stage, the *purpose* of the action has no direct influence in the generation of the meaning. No teleosemantics of any sort is presupposed. Hence, in AbS there are no extrinsic semantic criteria driving the process of meaning generation. This initial stage of the process is free of any semantic commitment, and thus satisfies the Z condition.

In the next section, we shall see how the general idea of an AbS may be implemented by an AA. We shall then consider the importance of evolutionary processes in the development of semantic capacities. Here, in order to clarify the AbS further, it is worth disposing of a potential misunderstanding. It concerns the similarities between AbS and the 'meaning as use' semantics associated with the later Wittgenstein.

According to that semantic theory, a language is a form of social interaction. The meanings of the symbols follow from the uses of the language in given contexts, and from negotiations, stipulations, and agreements among the speakers. Meanings are therefore partly conventionally defined in a community of speakers, partly identified with the speakers' intentions to perform some actions, given some symbols. All this qualifies Wittgenstein's linguistic games, pragmatically speaking, as teleological. Recall that, according to Wittgenstein, the meaning of the word 'slab' must be referred to its function within the linguistic game in which the word is used. A bricklayer says slab in order to interact with his co-worker and cause him to have a specific reaction: the one which involves giving him the slab. Then, it might seem that the meaning of slab is the *action* that the co-worker executes in association with the word 'slab'.

All this may look very similar, or perhaps outright identical, to a version of the AbS theory. The problem highlighted by this criticism is that, if AbS is indeed a user-based semantics à la Wittgenstein, it follows that meanings really arise from social interactions among speakers, i.e. agents already belonging to a community that shares means of communication, and from a kind of practical finalism. However, these are all features that represent external criteria, and hence presuppose some pre-established semantic abilities on behalf of the agents involved. If such a family resemblance between AbS and Wittgensteinian linguistic games were correct, it would be very hard to see how one could deny that AbS breaches the Z condition.

The criticism can be answered by explicating three main differences between AbS and the 'meaning as use' semantics, which significantly differentiate the former from the latter and hence defuse the objection.

First, in the semantics of linguistic games, meaning is not the performed action. The meaning of slab is defined through the linguistic game shared by the bricklayer and his co-worker, and the meaning is the way in which a symbol is to be *used* in order to trigger a particular reaction by the other player, within the linguistic game. But in AbS the meaning of slab is the internal state of the agent, a state triggered by the corresponding action. At this stage, no semantic interaction with other agents is yet in view.

Second, in a semantics based on 'meaning as use', the association between meanings and symbols is entirely conventional and contextual. It is based on negotiation and agreement among the speakers, requires training, and is regulated by degrees of success. By contrast, according to AbS, the initial association of symbols and meanings is a direct input–output relation that follows only from the performance of actions. As we shall see in the following section, an individual agent automatically associates a meaning with a symbol through the performance of an action, without considering yet the frame in which it has performed that action and, crucially, without taking into account yet the association performed by other AAs. The social component arises only *after* the association has taken place. To put it differently: according to AbS, semantics has its initial roots in the individual agent's behaviours, not in the community, and this is an advantage since, speaking in terms of logical order, the virtuous dialectic of interactions between a community of semantically-proficient agents and its members begins with the availability of individual agents capable of grounding their symbols, at least in principle and no matter how minimally and in some overridable way.

Third, to define meaning as a function of the use of the corresponding symbol entails a kind of finalism, which we have seen is not part of the AbS theory. AbS is therefore not a convention-based theory of meaning and does not entail, as a starting point, any kind of teleological theory of goal-oriented behaviour. This is what allows one to consider AbS free of any semantic commitment, unlike Wittgensteinian linguistic games, which clearly do not satisfy the Z condition. The time has come to consider the AbS in more detail.

7.3. Two–machine artificial agents and their AbS

In this section, I shall describe a kind of AA capable of implementing AbS. I have already referred to such an AA as a two-machine artificial agent, or simply AM^2. I shall argue that AM^2s can solve the SGP while satisfying the Z condition.

There are two main difficulties that must be overcome in order to show that an AM^2 solves the SGP correctly:

 i. it must be able to associate symbols to the actions that it performs; without
 ii. helping itself to any semantic resource in associating actions and symbols.
 iii. The architecture of an AM^2 explains how it can achieve (i) while avoiding (ii). This can be based on features of the so-called *reflective architecture,* in particular on the availability of *upward-reflection* processes. Such an architecture is well-documented and the interested reader may wish to consult, Brazier and Treur (1999), Cointe (1999), or Barklund et al. (2000) for a more in-depth description.

Essentially, the upward reflection is part of the *metaprogramming architecture*. A system capable of metaprogramming operates at two levels, which interact with each other. It organizes actions at an *object level* (OL), where it interacts with the external environment. But it can also take actions on its internal states and on its own elaborations. In this case, it operates at a *meta-level* (ML), which takes as data the actions at the OL. The relevant metaprograms are the *reflection processes*, where these function as *upward reflection*. In these metaprograms, the OL computation enables the ML computation. The modifications performed at the ML are effective and have a corresponding impact on the OL computation. The utility of reflection shows that the whole system [OL + ML] not only interacts with itself but is also properly affected by the results of such interactions.

The kind of AA we are discussing here is constituted by two machines—M1 and M2—which interact with each other and perform actions on two levels. M1 operates at OL, interacting directly with the external environment, e.g. by navigating, detecting obstacles, avoiding them etc., thus outputting and inputting actions. M2 operates at ML and the target of its elaborations is the internal states of M1. Any action that M1 outputs to, or inputs from, the environment defines a particular internal state (S_n) of M1. Hence actions and internal states are causally coupled: for any different action in M1 there is a different internal state S_n, and for all similar actions in M1 there is the same S_n. Two points need to be clarified before proceeding further: *continuity* and *similarity*.

Clearly, the agent's actions/states are not necessarily organized into a discrete flow, but may be subject to analogue/continuous variations. For instance, FOTOC may seamlessly move from action *a* to action *b*, and hence from the corresponding internal state S_n to another internal state S_{n+1}. All the same, here we shall disregard details about how this flow may be broken into a set of discrete elements. What is crucial is that, as in a continuous tape, cutting the flow means cutting both sides, as it were, with the action on the one hand and the corresponding internal state on the other; and that the same types of agents may be reasonably assumed to have similar types of internal states, triggered by similar types of actions, and to 'cut' their tapes in equally similar ways. This assumption of 'physiological or hardware-related similarity' does not breach the Z condition, since it refers to hard (structural and/or physical) similarities among agents, not to similarities assumed by the agents at a soft (semantic) level. Again, one may compare it to the similarity occurring in the behaviour and environmental interactions shown by a field of sunflowers.

To highlight the connection between M1's actions and states, let us represent (see Figure 9) the internal states of M1 as the results of a function (f) of interactions (e) between the machine (Machine 1) and the environment (E), so that $S_n = f(e)$.

Let us now see how the actions performed by an AM² may ground its symbols.

Imagine an AM², such as FOTOC, positioned in an environment such a laboratory. FOTOC is able to interact with the environment, it performs some actions, e.g. it moves around the laboratory office changing direction, and it has some perceptions. In particular, it is provided with a light-sensor on each of its sides, thus enabling it to detect the dark and light zones in the laboratory. When FOTOC detects a dark place, its M1 is in a specific internal state, say S_{dark}. Likewise, when FOTOC detects a light place, its M1 internal state is in S_{light}. For any dark place (for present purposes, the intensity of the darkness is irrelevant), FOTOC's M1 has the same (i.e. indistinguishable) internal

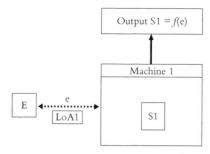

Figure 9 The structure of Machine 1: E is the environment, S_1 is the internal state of Machine 1, LoA_1 is the level of abstraction at which Machine 1 interacts with E, $f(e)$ is the function which identifies S_1, where (e) is a given interaction between the agent and the environment

state S_{dark}. That is why it does not need congruent perceptions of the environment to elaborate an internal state.

We can now apply the method of abstraction (see chapter three) to describe the degree of refinement of M1's perceptions. M1 accesses the environment at an LoA that allows only a specific granularity of detection of its features. Thus, through M1's perception, FOTOC can only obtain *approximate* (to whatever degree of granularity is implemented) *data* about its external environment. Note that such description makes full sense only from an external perspective, namely ours, where the LoAs are much more informative. For Fotoc, the world is just a sequence of dark and light *loci* with a hardwired LoA, i.e. with a specific granularity of details. The same holds true for the actions performed by an AM^2 embedded within an environment. Suppose Fotoc is able to move around the laboratory in such a way that it can turn 30° or 15° to the left. For both these actions, the M1 of Fotoc may have the same internal state, S_{left}, if its LoA does not allow any discrimination between angles, but only the detection of a left turn. This feature follows from an AM^2's structure. LoAs are related to the interactions between AM^2s and the environment and to the features of the two machines M1 and M2 in the sense that they are hardwired in AM^2s, that is, they are *structurally dependent* on the physical implementation (embodiment) of the AAs and of their interactions with their environment. Even if LoAs are not yet directly involved in the emergence of the elementary abilities required to overcome the SGP, a clear analysis of an agent's LoAs is crucial in order to understand the development of advanced semantic abilities. Hence, it is important to introduce an explicit reference to them at this early stage in the description of the architecture of an AM^2.

Following the metaprogramming architecture, M1 communicates with the other machine, M2. M1 sends its (uninterpreted) internal state to M2 (see Figure 10 below). M2 is a symbol maker and retainer. It is constituted by a symbol source, a memory space, and a symbol set. The two machines communicate their data at their respective LoAs. M2 reads the states from M1 according to its LoA (LoA_2), which is less refined then M1's LoA. Because of LoA_2's granularity, M2 does not read S_n as it has been sent by M1; instead, S_n is modified by the LoA_2 in such a way that the new state is more generic. In other words, M1's internal state is *transduced* into a new state at LoA_2. For example, suppose the state sent to M2 is related to the action turn left by $32°$, the state read by M2 according to its LoA is a more generic turn left. The new state can be considered the result of a function as $LoA_{2\ (Sn)} = S_{n2}$, where S_{n2} is a less specified state then S_n.

The transduction process is affected by M2's LoA. It is not defined by extrinsic criteria and it is not learned by the AM^2. Rather it follows directly from the AM^2's physical structure and its specific embodiment. In nature, bacteria, cells and unicellular organisms perform transduction processes in order to interact with the external environment and exchange information with it. During such processes, the molecular structure of the signal is converted in such a way that it can be perceived by the receptor of the signal, so that the receptor can read the signal and modify its behaviour. Bacteria interact with the external environment, by sending and receiving signals. The transmission of the signal is possible thanks to some receptors on the membrane. Such receptors interact with the signal's molecules and the interaction determines a change that causes a new behaviour of the bacteria. Like bacteria, an AM^2 may be assumed to have developed the transduction processes by evolution.

Once the new state is obtained, M2 associates the transduced state with a symbol removed from the symbol set. The process of removing a symbol from the set and coupling it with a state is discrete, non-recursive, and arbitrary but it is not random, in the following sense. M2 makes explicit just one symbol for each input it receives; and cannot remove the same symbol more than once. The choice of the symbol is arbitrary, since it is semantically unrelated to the transduced states, but it is not random, because similar types of agents will associate similar symbols with similar transduced states. Still, symbols and transduced states are different kinds of data: they are associated—coupled together—but not transduced one into another.

Once a symbol has been chosen, M2 applies a *storing rule* and a *performing rule*. The storing rule records the symbol and the related state in the memory space. The performing rule regulates the communications between M1 and M2 and concerns the association between a symbol and a state. Following the performing rule, each time M2 receives an input from M1 it initially verifies whether the input received, or any another similar (i.e. indistinguishable by M2 at its LoA) input, has already been elaborated. If M2 does not locate an input similar to the input stored in its memory, then it continues the process described above. Otherwise (if M2 finds the input, or an indistinguishable one, in its memory) it does not produce a new symbol, but reproduces the association already founded in its memory.

The association process is coherent: by following the performing rule, M2 obtains the same association any time it receives the same kind of input from M1, thus nomically associating different symbols to different internal states of M1. Any symbol elaborated by M2 is related through the internal state of M1 to a cluster of actions, i.e. all those actions not distinguished as different by the hardwired LoA. M2's symbols are

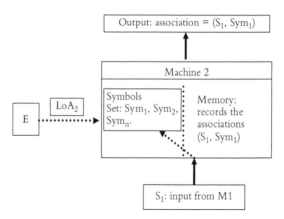

Figure 10 The structure of Machine 2 (M2). E is the environment, M2 does not act on the environment but on M1; the environment acts on M2 indirectly, through the evolutionary process. Sym_1 is the symbol elaborated by Machine 2. LoA_2 is the level of abstraction at which Machine 2 interacts with E. (S_1, Sym_1) is the ensuing association between a symbol and an internal state of Machine 1, the output of M2's elaboration

now grounded in the actions through the corresponding internal states of M1. The resulting symbol is the outcome of a function, namely $Sym_1 = g(S_n)$. And since S_n is also the result of a function $f(e)$, the symbols selected by M2 are actually the result of a function of a function, $Sym_1 = g(f(e))$, see Figure 11.

As I have shown above, M2's performances are also characterized by a specific LoA. In particular, the LoA of M2 is less refined than the LoA of M1. In our example, FOTOC's M2 may distinguish between M1's state S_{left}, related to the action turn left, and M1's state $S_{maintain}$, related to the action maintain this direction, but it may not draw any distinction between M1's state S_{left} and M1's state S_{right} related to the action turn right. In short, by 'abstracting in hardwired fashion', an AA ends up associating a single symbol with a cluster of similar actions. In the vocabulary of data compression, one may say that the process of transduction is lossy or never perfectly efficient. At this point, it is also important to stress that the whole process is formulated in such a way as to make it intuitive to us, as external observers, but that, in order to satisfy the Z condition, no assumption should be made in terms of a 'proper' way of abstracting that might result in some magic overlap between an AA's abstractions and ours. To use a previous example, heliotropism is a response to blue light, so if the plant is covered with a red transparent filter at night, blue light is blocked and the plant does not turn towards the sun, whereas a blue filter does not affect its behaviour. Now the filters are the physical implementations of the LoAs at which the plant interacts with its environment. So an external observer may simplify by saying that the plant abstracts the colour blue from light in hardwired fashion, in order to operate successfully in its

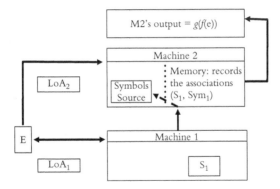

Figure 11 Two-machine artificial agents' architecture. A two-machine artificial agent inputs/ outputs some action/perception (e) from/on the environment E. E interacts with Machine 1 (M1) and acts on Machine 2 (M2) modifying it according to the evolutionary process. Any action is related to a corresponding internal state (S_1) of M1 at a specific level of abstraction, LoA_1. M1 communicates its internal states to M2. M1's internal state is transduced into an input for M2, which associates the input with a symbol (Sym_1). M2 stores the state and the relate symbol in its memory. For any other input, M2 follows the procedure defined by the performing rule. Each symbol selected by M2 is a function (g) of the internal state, S_1. Since also S_n is the result of a function—$f(e)$—a M2's output is a function of a function, $g(f(e))$

environment. This is fine as long as it is not taken literally. In our example, FOTOC abstracts in ways that we shall see are merely determined by its physical evolution and survival as an agent.

From the fact that M2's LoA is less refined than M1's, it follows that M2 does not have a finely grained perception of M1's internal states and may be unable to distinguish between M1's similar internal states. M2 will generate the same symbol to name all the actions which allow, for example, FOTOC to change the direction of movement. We may call these symbols *general symbols*. To M2, the meaning of such a symbol is a *general meaning*, which arises from a generalization of similar meanings; in our example, for FOTOC's M2, the general meaning would be turning.

An AM² does not have to rely on some semantic criterion in order to collect similar meanings in the first place and then elaborate the general one. Rather, we have seen above that a general meaning arises from a class of similar meanings elaborated by M2 according to its LoA. In its elaboration, M2 considers only the *syntactical* features of M1's internal states, not their meanings, i.e. the actions to which they refer. So here too, there is no semantic commitment in defining the class of meanings, which is elaborated whilst respecting the Z condition and can be used as a representation. In our example, FOTOC's M2 would not notice the difference between M1's internal states related to turning actions, but would simply consider all the states as if they were the same in elaborating a class of meanings.

The elaboration of the abstraction follows an impoverishment of AM^2's semantics. In elaborating a general meaning, an AM^2 loses the specific meanings related to the symbols. Thus, it appears that the evolution of the praxical process would generate a semantics composed of generic meanings and lacking specific ones. For an evolved AM^2, there would be only the meaning turning and there would (or indeed could) be no distinction between meanings such as turning left and turning right. To show how AM^2's semantics overcomes this shortcoming, more details about the praxical process are required. This is a fair request, but I shall delay its fulfilment until section 7.4, because we need to concentrate our attention on a more basic issue first. The reader will recall that we have outlined two main problems that must be solved to overcome the SGP. The first one—the ability to elaborate meanings and associate meanings with symbols—has been solved in this section. In sections 7.3.1–7.3.2 I offer a solution to the second problem, the one posed by the fulfilment of the Z condition.

7.3.1 Three controversial aspects of AM^2

There are three main elements in the process performed by an AM^2 that might be criticized for not being semantically free: the *transduction process*, the *storing rule,* and the *performing rule*. I shall now show that, in each case, the process described in section three satisfies the Z condition.

One may suspect that the association between M1's internal states and M2's symbols is implemented by following some semantic criterion, yet the process described is purely mechanical, i.e. a simple input/output process in which, given an input, S_n, M2 transduces and associates it with a symbol, Sym_n. No semantic contents or interpretation rules occur at this stage. The symbols are chosen arbitrarily, and the input S_n is elaborated by M2 only by virtue of its LoA. As shown in section three, LoAs are hardwired in relation to AM^2. They define the kind of perceptions that the machines have of the environment, and they do not imply any semantic content. What we have is a hardwired functional process that gives an output (symbol) for any received input (description of internal state). Input and output are then recorded together in M2's memory and only then do they become coupled together.

Against the availability of M2's capacity to apply the storing rule, one may object that recording capacities require in turn the ability to discriminate between useful (or relevant) and useless (or irrelevant) contents, but that this capability presupposes the existence of some semantic criteria enabling the agent to learn and apply some categorical order, and to identify what should be stored and what should be discarded. However, M2 does not draw any distinction in applying the storing rule, as it records some/all of the received inputs and some/all of its outputs. Some numerical threshold might be implemented, but no categorical criterion is at work in defining how M2 applies the storing rule. The latter dictates that M2 registers the elaborations without any distinction. Thus, no semantic criteria are presupposed at this stage either.

The third aspect concerns the performing rule. One may object that, given the sort of transduction, association and memorization described above, the AA must also be supposed to learn how to use the associated symbols and internal states (what we are treating as their meanings) successfully (that is, correctly, accurately, relevantly, efficiently etc.), and hence that it is at this stage that the AA must rely on some semantic resources, which would be extrinsic to the AM^2, and therefore beg the question. Perhaps not initially, but in the long run the elaborations of an AM^2 would not satisfy the Z condition and the SGP would remain unsolved. For the objection is that an AM^2 cannot *acquire* any proficiency in using the grounded symbols without violating the Z condition. Once in place, the performing rule may satisfy the Z condition, but its development in the first place actually violates that condition.

Fortunately, the objection is mistaken since it is possible to show that AM^2s can learn how to use their symbols successfully through their interactions with the environment and other similar type of agents embedded in it, without presupposing any semantic resource. This is the second step, which we are going to see in the next section.

7.3.2 *Learning and performing rule through Hebb's rule and local selection*

To show how a population of AM^2s can evolve to the point where its members can learn the performing rule while satisfying the Z condition, let us consider a typical learning rule, *Hebb's rule* (Hebb (1949)), and draw on the resources made available by the method of artificial evolution. More specifically, I shall rely on *local selection* (LS) *algorithms*, and especially on ELSA (*Evolutionary Local Selection Algorithm*) developed by Menczer et al. (2000), (2001). Note that the scenario described in the remainder of this section represents only a general framework, that is, only one of the possible ways in which AM^2s may be able to learn how to use the performing rule while respecting the Z condition. That there is such a possibility is all that is needed for our purposes; showing that this is the only way that is viable in terms of engineering, or that it is the actual or even a biologically plausible way in which agents may be able to learn the performing rule falls outside the scope of this chapter.

Hebb's learning rule may be summarized in the following statement: neurons that fire together wire together. The rule follows from a principle formulated by Hebb:

When an axon of cell A is near enough to excite a cell B and repeatedly or persistently takes part in firing it, some growth process or metabolic change takes place in one or both cells such that A's efficiency, as one of the cells firing B, is increased. (Hebb (1949), p. 62)

Hebb's rule is considered a fundamental way in which experience changes behaviour in both vertebrates and invertebrates (Real (1991), Donahoe and Dorsel (1997)). It has been studied in biology and ethology, and it is used to simulate learning processes with artificial neural networks. It is a general learning rule, according to which an AA learns to couple an input and an output. The algorithms based on Hebb's rule define a kind of reinforced learning. This is the most common process by which organisms learn from their interactions with the environment to achieve a goal. In such algorithms, the correlation of activity between two cells is reinforced by increasing the weighting between them, so the network's weightings are set in such a way that its output reflects its 'familiarity' with an input. The learning follows from a *scalar reinforcement signal*, which is defined according to the efficiency—established through the environment's feedback—of the performed associations.

Suppose we have a very first generation of AM^2s embedded in an environment. They are able to perform a few actions, such as moving around in the environment. Since it is the very first generation, it is plausible to assume that their architecture is simpler than the architecture of the AM^2 described in section 7.3. Their M2s have a finite set of symbols, and they do not delete the symbols they have already associated with states/meanings. Hence a symbol used for an association could be associated more than once, either with the same M1's state or with different ones. Same AM^2s execute, in the same arbitrary way, the associating process. As we know from section 7.3, every time M1 sends an internal state S_n to the M2, this is transduced at a given LoA, and M2 then selects a symbol, say Sym_n, from a symbol source, associates it to S_n, and stores this association in its memory. Before learning the performing rule, a M2 does not distinguish whether—and with which symbol—an incoming S_n has been already associated. Suppose that, after a finite number of runs, it turns out that an association between the same symbol and the same internal state has been used more than the other ones. According to Hebb's rule, the associations that are most used will be further privileged until they become stable. So that, when in the future M2 receives as input S_n, it will more readily associate S_n with Sym_n. In this way, AM^2s learn to associate a symbol with a meaning in a stable fashion and hence to execute the performing rule. The evolution of even rudimentary ways of grounding their symbols, and hence of managing some basic communication, will then further privilege and reinforce the selection of such AM^2s able to obtain the 'right' symbols-states associations. Gradually, generations of more evolved AM^2s will be able not only to perform some of the steps required to apply the performing rule, but also to impose a social pressure, on future AM^2s. Such pressure grows exponentially, until new agents will start being selected in relation to their capacities to respond to old agents' semantically-oriented behaviours. At that point, the hardwired nature of the initial stages in the process of symbol-grounding may even become redundant and disappear.

One may object that Hebb's rule, or one like it, provides an extrinsic bias towards identifying the most rewarding behaviour—in our case, this is the development of stable transductions and associations between behaviours, internal states, and symbols—and that therefore it breaches the Z condition. In order to answer this final objection, I shall refer to an evolutionary scenario simulated by running ELSA. This algorithm is well known, so the reader already acquainted with it may wish to skip the following summary.

ELSA is derived from a realistic scheme of the evolutionary processes. It follows from algorithms originally motivated by Alife models of adaptive agents placed in ecological environments. ELSA's main feature is that the selection is *locally* mediated by the environment in which the AAs are situated. This is to say that the fitness of AAs does not follow from global interactions across the whole population and the environment. Rather, the fitness is defined through the interactions between a singular AA and the environmental niche that the AA happens to inhabit. The environment biases the selection by managing the energetic resources, for it associates an energy bonus—which constitutes the selecting parameter—to every feature that the AAs may develop. The energy bonus assigned to any individual solution is in proportion both to the degree of the fitness of the solution and to the level of energy available in any zone of the environment. In this way, the environment can be considered as a data structure, which contains all the values assigned to each skill optimized by the AAs and keeps track of the actions of AAs. Two main aspects of ELSA need to be highlighted here.

First, the evolutionary process is independent of any external intervention. This defuses the previous objection. Running ELSA, the selection process is not performed according to some central bottleneck or predefined parameter; rather, the population changes depending on its interactions with the environment. The population's features are an intrinsic consequence of the environment's characteristics. This way, ELSA may be used to explain the Z-compliant use of Hebb's rule by a population of AM^2s. Suppose that, in some niches, the energy resources are set according to some instantiation of Hebb's rule. In such niches, the environment promotes those AM^2s able to follow Hebb's rule and hence to elaborate stable couplings of inputs and outputs. In so doing, the AM^2s do not appeal to any supervision from the programmer or from any other AA that is already semantically proficient; they just adapt to whatever bias is present in their environment. It follows that, in learning and performing Hebb's rule, they do not violate the Z condition. Moreover, since some fundamental biases are shared by most types of agents (think in biology of the famous three fs), it is literally natural that some functionally similar types of eco-tuned AbS will evolve among different populations of agents.

Second, according to ELSA, the energy bonus is shared by the AAs developing the same feature in the same niche. So, the competition between the AAs is about the finite environmental resources and it is never across the whole population, but rather among the AAs situated in the same environmental area. Hence, the AAs have 'interest' not only in achieving the best features, but also in finding the least populated zone in the environment where more energy is available. Thus, the population quickly distributes itself across the ranges given by the environmental features. This way ELSA encourages *coverage* and multi-modal optimization (all good solutions are represented in the population) rather than standard *convergence* (all individuals converging on the best solution). ELSA guarantees the natural implementation of a *heterogeneous* population, a feature that is pivotal for the solution of the SGP in view of a realistic account of the variety of groundings, and hence of semantics, that might become available across subpopulations.

So far, I have suggested a solution to the two problems posed at the beginning of section three. Recall: an agent must be able (i) to associate symbols with the actions that it performs, without (ii) helping itself to any semantic resource in associating actions and symbols. It follows that, through the praxical approach, an AM^2 is able to develop some elementary semantic skills while respecting the Z condition. Let us now see how an AM^2 could evolve its semantic abilities from the very first stage, described here, to a more complex one.

7.4 From grounded symbols to grounded communication and abstractions

At the end of chapter six, I outlined seven requirements that a strategy must satisfy to provide a valid solution for the SGP. So far, I have shown that the praxical strategy satisfies six of the seven requirements. In short, it allows the AM^2s to ground the meanings of the symbols in the empirical data following the sensorimotor interactions between the AM^2 and the environment; the development of some sort of representations and abstraction capacities; the use of evolution in the development of the semantic skills, and all this while satisfying the Z condition. I still have to show that the praxical strategy enables the AM^2s to develop some sort of communication capacities among AAs, in order to ground the symbols diachronically and avoid the Wittgensteinian problem of a 'private language'. So, in the remainder of this section, I shall describe how a population of AM^2s can develop more complex semantic abilities, such as communication and the elaboration of a shared lexicon, and thus satisfy the last requirement. I shall then rely on AA's communication abilities to show how AM^2s can overcome the problem of an impoverished semantics, anticipated in section 7.3.

Communication represents an invaluable achievement of a population of AAs, for which coordinated social activity and the exchange of information provides highly adaptive benefits and is crucial for survival. Given such advantages, one can explain the development of communication and of a shared lexicon in a population of AM^2s as a result of natural selection and of the interactions among a population of AM^2s and between AM^2s and environment. I shall now specify an evolutionary scenario in which such abilities could evolve.

Let us assume an environment in which the evolution is still local. Suppose we have a heterogenic population of AM^2s, made of both AM^2s able to elaborate only more specific meanings (SAM^2), and AM^2s able to elaborate only more general meanings (GAM^2). The AM^2s inhabiting a given niche interact with the environment in two ways: they feed and they can hide themselves to avoid the attacks of three kinds of predators—α, β, and γ—which put them in three internal states (the reader will find more details about this scenario in Grim et al. (1998)). Suppose the AM^2s involved in this scenario engage in a kind of adaptive language game, such as the *guess game* (Steels (2005)).

A guess game is a technique used to study the development of common language in situated AAs, and involves two AAs situated in a common environment. Each AA involved in the game has a role: one is the *speaker*, and names the object that it perceives; the other one is the *hearer* and has to guess the objects named by the speaker by trial and error. The speaker communicates only to convey the name of a perceived referent, and the hearer communicates only to inform the speaker about its guessing concerning the referent named by the speaker. During the game, the AAs interact and develop a common system of symbols. The game ends successfully if the two AAs develop a shared lexicon, grounded in the interaction among themselves and with the environment.

In the case of the AM²'s described above, the communicated symbols are related to the speaker's internal states and, indirectly, to the action that it performs, for example open your mouth hide yourself (using an anthropomorphic and observer-oriented description). Any time a symbol is communicated, the hearer performs one of these two actions. Since the actions are relevant to survival, the agents who perform the appropriate action—open their mouths and hide themselves when the communicated symbol indicates one of these actions—have a higher chance of surviving, and hence reproducing, than the ones which fail to perform the right action. The agents that survive receive positive feedback from the environment, and they learn—through a Hebb-like rule—to associate that received symbol with the internal state related to the action that they perform. We can suppose that the hearer applies the storing rule to the received symbol. It performs a new association process, and the AM² stores in its memory the ensuing couple: the symbol received and its M1's internal state related to the action performed once the symbol has been heard (see Figure 12). In the memory of the hearer's M1, internal states are associated both with the symbol it first used to name those states and with the new symbols communicated by the speaker.

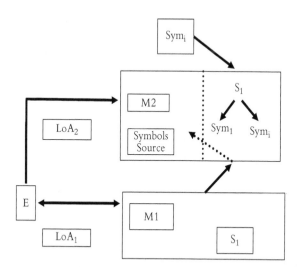

Figure 12 Sym_i is the incoming symbol communicated by the speaker to the hearer. Once it has received the symbol the hearer will record it in its memory. Sym_i will be recorded together with the hearer's internal state and the symbol that the hearer first associated with that state

In this way, the symbols communicated also acquire a meaning for the hearer and can be used by the AM^2s to develop a semantically grounded communication system. Since the same AM^2 interacts through different guessing games with other AM^2s, the same symbol can become related to the internal states of different AM^2s—with different LoAs—among the population. Thus, the symbol communicated by the speaker ends up naming a set of similar states. Following this strategy, a shared lexicon can emerge through communications among a population of AM^2s. The shared symbols emerge according to use, and one can conclude that the most useful and hence recurrent symbols will be used as names of sets of similar states.

For example, suppose a GAM^2 and a SAM^2 are involved in a guessing game. We know the GAM^2 will use the same symbol to name all the states related to the attacks of the predators α, β, and γ. Suppose a GAM^2 communicates its symbol to a SAM^2. In order for the game to end successfully, the SAM^2 has to associate the generic symbol with one of his states related to the attacks of the predators, it does not matter which. Thus, a GAM^2's symbols also acquire a meaning for a SAM^2, since they are related to its internal states as well. In this way, the meanings elaborated by any AM^2 can be communicated among the population in the system. The semantics elaborated following the praxical strategy does not incur the problem of the private language. Generation by generation, the AM^2s select recurrent symbols until they define a set of shared symbols that they all use as names of similar internal states.

Given how the AM^2s develop the shared lexicon, one might revive the objection that the semantics generated by the praxical strategy reproduces the Wittgensteinian semantics of meaning-as-use, and hence that it violates the Z condition (cf. section 7.2). However, the AM^2s' communication abilities and the development of their shared lexicon, described in this section, follow from a different process and do not play any role in the process of semantically grounding the symbols.

Semantically grounded communication develops when the AM^2s already use grounded symbols, and the SGP is *solved* before the AM^2s start to communicate with each other. The apparent chicken-and-egg paradox is averted by avoiding the comparison between a single member, that still needs to learn how to communicate, and a whole population of individuals that already know how to communicate with each other, in favour of a population of individuals that need (more naturalistically, are subject to the evolutionary pressure) to learn how to communicate, while interacting with each other and their shared environment. The system needs to be jump-started somewhere within the virtuous circle, and the 'where' is the relation between internal states and symbols in single members of the population, not their communication processes. In particular, one key feature helps us to distinguish praxical semantics from the semantics of meaning-as-use. In the Wittgensteinian theory, meaning arises from the communications among the agents; the agents play linguistic games in order to reach some agreement about the meaning. In praxical semantics, the meaning does not arise from the communication processes, but it is already defined, or at least well-sketched, when the AM^2 starts to communicate. What is shared in the communication process are the grounded symbols, not the meanings. Communication plays the role of a tuning process, not that of a grounding one.

Consider now a last limitation of an AM^2's semantics. The elaboration of abstractions, described in section three, causes an impoverishment of AM^2's semantics. In elaborating a general meaning, an AM^2 loses the specific meanings related to the symbols. Thus, it might be objected that the evolution of the praxical process generates a semantics composed of only very generic meanings, which tend to become progressively more generic. In our example, for an evolved AM^2, there would be only the meaning turning and there would (or indeed could) be no distinction between meanings such as turning left and turning right. Moreover, the same agent also runs the risk of losing even the meaning turning in favour of an even more generic moving. The reply is that it is true that the semantics of a single AM^2 is bounded by the LoAs of that agent. Nevertheless, this limit can be overcome when a whole population of AM^2s is taken into consideration. For we have seen that the ability to share semantically-grounded symbols to communicate among agents ensures that, through evolutionary pressure, the right (i.e. fit for survival) balance between generality and specificity of the semantics in question will be reached. In other words, it is the diachronic evolution of the population of agents that ensures the anchoring of otherwise possibly too-generically-grounded symbols to concrete usage in the real world for evolutionary-efficient purposes.

CONCLUSION

In this chapter, I proposed a new solution for the SGP, analysing its possible developments and some of its limitations. The solution suggested is called praxical in order to stress the interactions between agents and environment. The praxical approach is based on two main components: an Action-based Semantics (AbS) and the AM^2s, which implement the AbS thanks to their architecture. The two components allow the AAs to develop semantic skills sufficient to satisfy the seven requirements spelled out at the end of chapter six, and hence to overcome the SGP without violating the Z condition. There are now at least two perspectives from which the praxical approach may be understood.

Technically, the praxical approach provides a solution to the SGP and describes a plausible and implementable model of AA, thereby explaining what it means for data to acquire their meaning. The architecture of AM^2 is based on the metaprogramming paradigm, which is largely used to program AAs. Moreover, there are programming languages based on a framework that can already be interpreted in terms of AbS (Mosses (1992)).

Philosophically, I showed how AM^2s develop more complex semantic skills by combining the praxical approach and artificial evolution. We saw how a population of AM^2s could elaborate abstracted meanings and develop communications abilities and how they could cultivate a shared lexicon. This points towards a more ambitious and challenging perspective: the possibility of providing a theory of meaning based on praxical terms.

The distinction between symbols and meaning is a crucial difference between the praxical solution and the approaches reviewed in chapter six. Other attempts to solve the SGP consider meaning and symbol as two aspects of the *same* data. Thus, an AA is supposed to elaborate a set of perceptual data in order to obtain a representation which is both the meaning and the symbol that is then used to name that very representation. On the contrary, the praxical solution treats meaning and symbol as two kinds of *independent* data: the first one is given directly every time an AM^2 interacts with the environment, whereas the second is produced by M2. Only at the end of the process does an AM^2 couple them together. This allows the AM^2s to respect the Z condition: since there is no need for a process through which meaning must be elaborated, there is also no need for any extrinsic criteria required to guide the elaboration of meaning. Still, the semantics elaborated by the AM^2s has a significant lack of completeness and complexity. At best, AbS provides a very minimal and simple semantics. It is patently not truth-functional in the classic sense, nor does it justify the initial elaboration of meanings through some explicit negotiations among the agents. We have seen that it is also far from being Wittgensteinian as well. AbS, and the praxical approach more generally, define a semantics that is simple and elementary enough to be developed autonomously by AAs from scratch. This is a semantics that is compatible with AAs' features and hence, in this sense, it is *non-anthropocentric*. However, I showed that the complexity of AM^2s' semantics can be escalated through evolutionary and social processes, to the point where it allows the AM^2s to develop communication skills and create a shared lexicon that are biologically plausible.

The possibility of the evolution of language skills in a population of agents through social pressure has been well described by Maynard Smith and Szathmáry (1999):

When we meet a linguistic novelty we do not give up too easily: we try to guess the meaning by watching others, as well as trying it out of ourselves. [. . .] (the meaning) must be built on pre-existing neuronal structures. (p. 165)

I agree completely. Going back to the AM^2 population, and considering a generation of AM^2s already provided with semantic skills, it turns out that further semantic elaborations are greatly facilitated and improved by social interactions among AM^2s. So we can suppose that AM^2s acquire the performing and storing rule through a 'genetic assimilation learning' (Pinker (1994)). Through this process, a learnt behaviour is converted (replaced) into one that is genetically programmed. More specifically, in a generation of AM^2s, in which the performing and storing rules are genetically assimilated, the meaning no longer has to be directly related to the interactions between an AM^2 and the environment, but can be based upon interactions with other AM^2s.

The solution of the SGP, offered in this chapter, provides the seeds for an interesting explanation of how advanced semantic and linguistic skills may develop among higher biological agents in more complex environments. These implications of the praxical approach have been only briefly sketched here. Their full investigation belongs to a future stage of research in the philosophy of information, not least because they will probably require a functional analysis of the truthful nature of the grounded data. This actually introduces the topic of next chapter. Having seen how data may acquire their meaning, and it is now time to turn to the analysis of the sort of theory of truth that might be most suitable to explain their truthfulness.

8

Semantic information and the correctness theory of truth

For truth or illusion are not in the object in so far as it is intuited, but are in the judgement made about the object, in so far as it is thought. Hence, although it is correct to say that the senses do not err, this is so not because they always judge correctly, but because they do not judge at all. Thus both truth and error, and hence also illusion and the process of mistakenly leading to error, are to be found only in the judgement, i.e., in the relation of the object to our understanding.

Kant, *Critique of Pure Reason*, 1787

SUMMARY

Previously, in chapters four and five, I argued that semantic information is well-formed, meaningful, and truthful data. In chapters six and seven, I showed how well-formed data may become meaningful. In this chapter, I develop a correctness theory of truth (CTT) for semantic information that seeks to explain how well-formed and meaningful data may become truthful. After the introduction, section 8.2 defends the possibility of translating semantic information propositionally (symbolized by i). In section 8.3, i is polarized into a query (Q) and a result (R), qualified by a specific context, a level of abstraction and a purpose. This polarization is normalized in section 8.4, where $[Q + R]$ is transformed into a Boolean question and its relative yes/no answer $[Q + A]$. This completes the reduction of the truth of i to the correctness of A. In sections 8.5 and 8.6, it is argued that (1) A is the correct answer to Q if and only if (2) A correctly *saturates* (in a Fregean sense) Q by *verifying* and *validating* it (in the computer science's sense of 'verification' and 'validation'); that (2) is the case if and only if (3) $[Q + A]$ generates an adequate model (m) of the relevant system (s) identified by Q; that (3) is the case if and only if (4) m is a *proxy* of s (in the computer science's sense of 'proxy') *and* (5) proximal access to m commutes with the distal access to s (in the category theory's sense of 'commutation'); and that (5) is the case if and only if (6) reading/writing (*accessing*, in the computer science's technical sense of the term) m enables one to read/write (access) s. Section 8.7 provides some further clarifications about CTT, in connection with the semantic paradoxes. Section 8.8 draws a general conclusion about the nature of CTT and explains the work that needs to be done by the next four chapters in order to develop an informational analysis of knowledge based on CTT.

8.1 Introduction

As argued in the previous chapters, semantic information is primarily understood in terms of *content about a referent*. I shall discuss the formal nature of content in the following pages but, at the moment, suffice to say that by 'content' I shall mean *well-formed* and *meaningful data*. Strings or patterns of data may constitute sentences in a natural language, but of course they can also generate formulae, maps, diagrams, videos, and other semiotic constructs in a variety of physical codes, being further determined by their appropriate syntax (well-formedness) and semantics (meaningfulness). By 'about a referent' one is to understand the ordinary and familiar way in which some well-formed and meaningful data, constituting semantic information, concern or address a topic. Following Dretske (1981) and Dretske (1988) one may easily recognize this 'aboutness' feature in propositional attitudes such as 'Mary is informed that the beer is in the fridge'. Note that 'being informed' is used in the *statal* sense,[1] i.e. in the sense that Mary *holds*, rather than *is receiving*, that information. This is the condition into which *a* enters (and may remain, if *a* is not a memoryless agent) once *a* has *acquired* the information (*actional* state of being informed as becoming informed) that *p*. It is the sense in which a witness, for example, is informed (holds the information) that the suspect was with her at the time the crime was committed. The distinction is standard in linguistics, where one speaks of passive verbal forms or states as 'statal' or 'actional'. Compare the difference between 'the door was shut (state) when I last checked it' versus 'but I do not know when the door was shut (act)'. In this chapter, I will deal only with the statal sense of 'is informed', insofar as it is related to cognitive issues and to the logical analysis of an agent's 'possession' of a belief or some knowledge, which is analysed in chapter ten.

In chapters four and five I argued that a definition of semantic information in terms of alethically neutral content provides only necessary but insufficient conditions. If some content is to qualify as semantic information, it must also be true. One speaks of false information in the same way as one qualifies someone as a false friend, i.e. not a friend at all. This led to a refinement of the initial definition, GDI*, which can now be summarized thus:

[SI]*p* qualifies as semantic information if and only if *p* is (constituted by) *well-formed, meaningful, and truthful data*.

According to [SI], semantic information is, strictly speaking, inherently *truth-constituted* and not a contingent *truth-bearer*, exactly like knowledge but unlike propositions or

---

[1] I owe to Christopher Kirwan this very useful clarification; in a first version of this text I had tried to reinvent it, but the wheel was already there.

beliefs, for example, which are what they are independently of their truth-values and then, because of their truth-aptness, may be further qualified alethically.

[SI] offers several advantages. We saw in chapter five that it plays a crucial role in the solution of the so-called Bar-Hillel–Carnap Paradox. We shall see in chapter eleven that it provides a necessary element for a subjectivist theory of epistemic relevance. It also forges a robust and intuitive link between semantic information and knowledge, to the effect that knowledge encapsulates truth because it encapsulates semantic information, which, in turn, encapsulates truth, as in a three dolls matryoshka, as I shall argue in chapters ten and twelve. Despite its advantages, however, any approach endorsing [SI] raises two major questions. One is upstream:

a. What does it mean for semantic information to be truthful?

The other is downstream:

b. How does semantic information upgrade to knowledge?

Both questions are prompted by [SI] but neither is specifically about [SI] only, so each fails to provide a starting point for a *reductio ad absurdum*. They are rather information-theoretical versions of classic conundrums: (a) is a request for a theory of truth, and (b) is a request for a substantive analysis of knowledge. The goal of this chapter is to answer (a). Chapter twelve will answer (b).

In trying to answer (a), the challenge is not a shortage, but rather an overabundance of viable answers, since we are spoiled for choice by a variety of theories of truth.[2] Admittedly, in the literature on semantic information there appears to be at least an implicit predilection for some version of a Tarskian and/or correspondentist approach.[3] And yet, at least in principle, nothing prevents each of the major theories of truth from answering (a). They simply would have been refuted and abandoned a long time ago if they could not do so. It follows that some initial tolerance towards a pluralistic approach to (a) might be unavoidable, if not methodologically welcome. Of course, if this were all that one could sensibly recommend about (a), there would be little reason to pursue any further investigation. There is, however, another way of approaching (a), which opens up an interesting line of enquiry.

Consider the strategy sketched above. One may select the best available theory of truth and test how well it might be applied and adapted in order to explain the truthfulness of semantic information. With some negligible adjustments, such a top-down approach is comparable to the so-called 'design pattern' technique (Gamma et al. (1995)) in software engineering (Sommerville (2007)). This consists in identifying and specifying the abstract features of a design structure, which are then generally reusable

---

[2] In this chapter, I have relied especially on Lynch (2001), Engel (2002), and Künne (2003), among the many introductions and anthologies available on the major theories of truth, as particularly helpful.

[3] See for example Popper (1935), Dretske (1981), Fox (1983), Israel and Perry (1990), Barwise and Seligman (1997), and Bremer and Cohnitz (2004).

solutions to commonly occurring problems in the construction of an artefact. In our case, we have several design patterns for the concept of truth. We know that they are robust, because they have been tested and refined since Ramsey, if not Aristotle. We also know that they are reusable. Although they have been developed to deal primarily with propositional or sentential truths, one may reasonably expect them to be effectively adaptable to truthful data (e.g. a truthful map) as well. So, when our artefact, i.e. semantic information, is proved to require the particular feature of being truthful, a sensible alternative is to consider such design patterns and try to identify the ones that best satisfy the constraints and requirements imposed by the development of the artefact itself. Oversimplifying, one may answer (a) by choosing whichever pre-packaged theory of truth turns out to be most suitable. This strategy may be classic, is certainly viable, but it is hardly innovative. I shall not pursue it in this chapter, although I shall return to more standard theories of truth in section seven.

The other approach is bottom–up and suggests the sort of strategy that will guide us in the rest of the chapter. It consists in assuming the artefact itself as given—that is, in assuming that we do have in our hands a piece of (truthful) semantic information[4]— and then trying to discover the principles governing its properties and workings by analysing its structure, function and operations. In software engineering, this technique is known as 'reverse engineering'. This is 'the process of extracting the knowledge or design blueprints from anything man-made' (Eilam (2005), p. 3). It consists in examining an existing artefact in order to identify its components and their interrelationships, and hence create representations of it in other forms or at a higher level of generalization. Following this strategy, one may answer question (a) by assuming the occurrence of some semantic information (or, if the reader disagrees with me, some truthful semantic information) and then disassembling it in order to reveal what its components are and how they interact with each other to deliver information. We have the artefact and we seek to understand its mechanism by taking it apart, hopefully in the right way and places. Note that this second strategy is perfectly compatible with the first, once it is realized that there is a virtuous cycle of feedback between design patterns and reverse engineering results. Contrary to the first strategy, however, reverse engineering promises to deliver a more innovative analysis, as it avoids approaching the problem of the truthfulness of semantic information from pre-established theories and explores it from a new perspective. After all, the first strategy merely retrofits some already existing theory of truth to semantic information, instead of trying to develop a customized solution, which may then be generalizable. The cost to be paid for this innovation is that our bottom–up strategy will also be uphill, if I may be allowed to combine the two metaphors: it is much more economical to choose from

---

[4] This specification was added in the last revision of the book manuscript. I thought it was necessary once I saw at least two colleagues misunderstanding what I am saying here. The whole point is to *start*, from something (a piece of information) that we agree to be true (in this book: that we agree to be indeed information), and then analyse it to check what features (it does already have by definition) that make it true.

a pre-established menu than to develop a new approach. I can only hope that the reader will find the effort rewarding and the result enlightening. And now it is time to start climbing.

8.2 First step: Translation

A large variety of kinds of semantic information, from traffic lights to train timetables, from road signs to fire alarms, falls within the scope of [SI]. This is how it should be, but it is also extremely inconvenient for our purposes. For in order to reverse-engineer semantic information in such a way that its components might easily be identified, disassembled, and explained, it would be far easier and more fruitful to concentrate on just one kind, the propositional one, which lends itself to such a treatment straightfor-wardly. So, our first step will be to ensure that all kinds of semantic information covered by [SI] are indeed translatable into propositional semantic information, thus guaranteeing that what will be concluded about the latter may be extendable to the former. At this point, the reader who finds such 'translatability' uncontroversial, or indeed trivial, may wish to skip the rest of this section. The one who finds it impossible may concede the restriction of scope as a matter of convenient stipulation, although the rest of this section purports to show that the burden of proof is on her shoulders. As for the rest of us, what follows should be sufficiently convincing to make our second step unproblematic.

Syntactically (or in terms of information theory), the propositional translatability of any kind of semantic information is unquestionable and a matter of daily experience. After all, analogue information is reproducible digitally to any chosen degree of accuracy, its digital version is equivalent to finite lists of zeros and ones, and these can be further encoded into as many answers to questions asked in a suitably chosen language, and hence ultimately translated into statements of that language. That doing any of this would be sheer madness is irrelevant here. For the question is not how difficult or costly this process would be, e.g. in terms of accuracy, time, and memory resources, but that it might be possible at all. More to the point is whether some non-propositional, semantic information—the sort of information provided by the map of the London Underground, for example—may always be translatable *semantically* into propositional semantic information, at least in principle; not all of it at once, mind, and not even part of it at every level of abstraction, but any of it at the right LoA, depending on needs and requirements. Since the difference between a syntactic and a semantic translation may not be very familiar, let me first introduce it with an example.

Consider being able to reproduce the map of the London Underground on graph paper by being told, say over the phone, the position and colour of each square on the paper. The communication over the phone would provide a syntactic translation, with the end result (the coloured graph paper representing the map) constituting a test about whether the translation worked. Contrast it now to being able to travel from one station to another on the London Underground, by receiving verbal instructions from someone who is navigating using the visual indications provided by the map. This is a semantic translation, and your trip is a test of its accuracy.

Suppose now that a semantic translation from non-propositional into propositional information, of the kind just illustrated, were sometimes impossible, even in principle. Then there would be some residual semantic information, conveyed non-propositionally (e.g. by the map), that one would necessarily be unable to convey propositionally, independently of the resources available. We would then have reached the limits of the informational powers of any natural language, even natural languages formally extendable, e.g. mathematically. Allegedly, we should still be able to point to the information in question (in the previous example, suppose we are both looking at the same map), but we would be unable to generate the right sort of propositional content that could adequately convey it. This is a *reductio ad absurdum*. For here we are not engaging with some Wittgensteinian limits of the 'sayable', with Kantian *noumena*, with some linguistically ungraspable sensations, or some mystical experience enjoyed while looking at the map of the London Underground. We are talking about what the map of the London Underground can encode, in terms of information about travelling through the network, positions of the stations, interconnections, available routes etc., which, allegedly, would be at least partly beyond the expressive power of any natural language to convey. But since natural languages have been acknowledged to be 'semantically omnipotent' at least since Leibniz (Formigari (2004), pp. 91–92), one can arguably assume that the translation is always possible, even if it is likely to be onerous at times and hence often unfeasible in terms of resources. So, in the rest of the chapter, we shall treat semantic information as possibly semiotic-dependent (it may always require a code) but not as semiotically bounded (codes are translatable propositionally, if expensively resource-wise) or, more formally and briefly:

[Tr] $\forall x (\text{SI}(x) \wedge \text{Non-prop}(x)) \rightarrow \exists y \, (\text{Prop-t}(y, x) \wedge \text{SI}(y))$

The intended interpretation of [Tr] is that, if any data (the domain on which the quantifiers range) satisfy [Si] but are not propositional, then there is a propositional translation of those data which also satisfies [Si]. Note that we do not need to assume the stronger principle of translational equivalence: pictures may be worth thousands of words, but there might be thousands of words that are priceless. Not every good book can be turned into a good movie. All that [Tr] needs to guarantee is that the conclusions reached about the alethic nature of propositional semantic information will be exportable to the truthful nature of non-propositional semantic information as well. In other words, that what can be concluded about the truth of 'the beer is in the fridge' is equally applicable to the truthfulness of the perceptual experience conveying the same information.

8.3 Second step: Polarization

Once some information i is formulated propositionally, the second step is to follow a standard approach, in information theory, to the quantification of information, and disassemble i into a combination of a query Q and a result R. A query is to be understood as a request for data sent (e.g. an illocutionary act performed) by a sender to a receiver, in the form of a message. Thus, it might have the format of a question ('where is the beer?') as well as of an imperative ('tell me where the beer is'), or a string of symbols in a search engine. A result should also be understood as a message, comprising the requested data, sent by the receiver to the querying sender. In short, we have (the asterisk is a reminder that the formula is provisional and requires refinement):

$$[\text{Pol}^*]\; i = Q + R$$

That [Pol*] is always achievable is warranted by the fact that any propositional i is equivalent to a message, and that any message is a combination of querying and resulting data, encoded in the same set of symbols of the chosen language (alternatively: every p can be transformed into a request of whether p plus a result, but more on this in the next section). The polarization of i into $Q + R$ offers several advantages. We shall exploit four of them.

First, [Pol*] highlights the need to specify the *context* (C) in which, the *level of abstraction* (LoA) at which, and the *purpose* (P) for which the query is formulated, and hence it is expected to be satisfied by the result. For the sake of simplicity, below I shall refer to the combination of these three parameters by means of the acronym CLP. The first two requirements were stressed by Austin (1950). 'Where is the beer?' is asked by someone in some specific circumstance (the context), by relying on a specific granularity of discourse or detail, what I have defined as an LoA in chapter three. In our example, there might be no beer (if no beer has been purchased) or, if the sender of the query knows that some beer has been purchased, answering that 'the beer is somewhere' would amount to a joke or a mistake in the choice of LoA, if the sender wishes to know the precise location of the beer, e.g. left in the car or carried into the house, or placed in the fridge. The third requirement was stressed by Strawson (1964). LoAs are always teleological and queries are formulated (results are offered) for some *purpose*, even if the purpose might be implicit. In the example, one may wish to make sure that the beer has been placed in the fridge and not left in the car, for example. To recall a Fregean point, queries cannot acquire their specific meaning in isolation or independently of their CLP parameters. It is a bit of a pain, but we need to keep these variables in mind, lest the conceptual mess caused by their absence becomes unmanageable. So, as a memory aid, let me revise [Pol*] by adding a combined index, thus:

$$[\text{Pol}]i^{\text{CLP}} = [Q + R]^{\text{CLP}}$$

A second advantage of the polarization of i into $Q + R$ is that it makes evident the role of R, which is to *saturate* Q, to adapt another Fregean idea lately borrowed by information

[Ex. 1] Information   'The beer is in the fridge' =
        Query   'Where is the beer?' +
        Result   'In the fridge'

theory, according to which *saturation* is the condition at which a communications system reaches its maximum capacity of traffic-handling. Although it is trivial to apply [POL] to any piece of information, *p*, like 'the beer is in the fridge', in order to obtain:

it is important to keep in mind that the correct interpretation of Q in [POL] is not as

  i. a request for *confirmation* or
  ii. a *test*, but as
  iii. a genuine request to erase a data deficit through *saturation*.

The difference is that, in (i) and (ii), the sender of the query already holds the information that *p*, but wishes to double-check it, or to check whether the receiver also holds that information, whereas in (iii), the sender lacks the information that *p* and wishes to acquire the missing data from the receiver. Having said this, let me now hasten to clarify a point that might be a source of potential confusion. The polarization of *i* does *not* really involve two agents. I shall speak sometimes as if the querying sender and the saturating receiver were two different entities, but this is only for heuristic purposes and ease of treatment. Recall that we are reverse engineering an artefact, a given piece of information *i*, in order to study its features, we are not constructing *i*. So it is *i* that is being polarized, and the sender and receiver are really the same entity. If you need an intuitive representation, imagine a language in which Mary can make statements not by uttering declarative sentences, but only by formulating questions followed by the appropriate answers. Her language does not enable her to say: 'The beer is in the fridge' but only 'Where is the beer? In the fridge'.

    The third advantage is set-theoretic. Adopting a standard extensional theory of questions (see Groenendijk and Stokhof (1994) and Szabolcsi (1997)) it is easy to see that [POL] allows us to treat 'is correctly saturated by' as a relation *r* from a countable set of queries $A = \{Q \mid Q \in A\}$ to a countable set of results $B = \{R \mid R \in B\}$. Note that *r* is not a function because two or more propositional *i*, e.g. 'the beer is in the

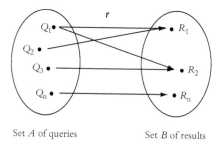

Set *A* of queries   Set *B* of results

Figure 13 The relation 'is correctly saturated by' assigns to each query *Q* in *A* at least one result *R* in *B*

fridge' and 'the beer is in the kitchen' are analysed as 'where is the beer?' + 'in the fridge' and 'where is the beer?' + 'in the kitchen', thus mapping the same Q_1 both to R_1 and to R_2 (see Figure 13). In section 8.6, we shall see that the real crux is to provide an analysis of correctness that does not beg the question.

The fourth advantage is that [POL] can be normalized. This is our next step.

8.4 Third step: Normalization

In real life, queries and results share, in variable proportions, the amount of semantic content that is to be found in the corresponding semantic information. In [Ex. 1], the full semantic content to be found in 'the beer is in the fridge' is allocated partly to Q, which contains a request for location and a reference to the object to be located, and partly to R, which contains a reference to the requested location of the object to be located. Although a step forward in the disassembling process, this is still unsatisfactory because it makes it very hard to quantify—precisely, consistently, and uniformly across the whole class of Qs + Rs—how much content is allocated to which side of the polarized information. In order to uncover what lies beneath the thick layer of content, it would be useful to shovel it all to one side. This can be achieved by shifting all the content, still embedded in R, to the left, until R is completely streamlined. At the same time, however, weakening R should not lead to an over-strengthening of Q into a rhetorical question, since a question that requires no answer would be a mere transliteration of i itself and would only defy the purpose. Luckily, a little trick from information theory comes to our rescue: we can reach the right balance, in shifting all the content onto the side of the queries, by normalizing them into yes/no questions, that is (again the asterisk reminds us that the formula is only a first approximation):

$$[\text{NORM}^*]\ [Q + R]^{\text{CLP norm}} \Rightarrow [Q_{0/1} + A_{0/1}]^{\text{CLP}}$$

The intended interpretation of [NORM*] is that a query Q and a result R, both CLP-parameterized, can be normalized into a Boolean Question Q and a Boolean Answer A (the 0/1 subscripts are there to remind us of their Boolean nature), equally CLP-parameterized. This is very much easier done than said, so let us look at our example again. By applying [NORM*] to [Ex. 1], we obtain:

[Ex. 2]   Information   'The beer is in the fridge' =
          Question   'Is the beer in the fridge?' +
          Answer   'Yes'

Of course, this is not what happens in the real world, where one cannot expect a querying sender to be able always to maximize the content of her questions, for she often lacks much more than just a positive or negative saturation. However, recall that we are disassembling semantic information as a given artefact: all the content is already provided, and hence some idealization, typical of controlled experiments, is perfectly reasonable. Recall also that [NORM*] does not really involve two agents. This time, imagine Mary being able to state that the beer is in the fridge only by uttering 'is the beer in the fridge? Yes'.

Once again, [NORM*] offers several neat advantages for our analysis, four of which will be immediately useful for our next step.

The first advantage is syntactic: following standard programming languages (e.g. BASIC, C++, Java, Pascal, and Python), we can now interpret '+'in [POL] and [NORM*] more precisely as a *concatenation operator*, whereby a string Q and a string A are locked together to form a longer string i.

The second advantage is semantic: it is now easy to see that it is really Q and not A that sets the scope of the CLP parameters. A Boolean answer can only endorse the *context* in which, the *level of abstraction* at which, and the *purpose* for which the Boolean question is formulated; it can neither change nor challenge them. So we can revise [NORM*] thus:

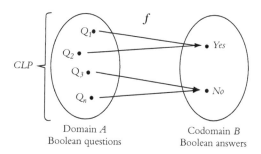

Domain A Codomain B
Boolean questions   Boolean answers

Figure 14 The function f (= is correctly saturated by) assigns to each Boolean question Q in A exactly one Boolean answer (either *Yes* or *No*) in B. Note that Q_3, for example, corresponds to a negative truth, e.g. 'the red wine is not in the fridge' in the case in which the fridge does not contain any red wine

$$[\text{NORM}] \quad [Q + R]^{\text{CLP norm}} \Rightarrow Q_{0/1}^{\text{CLP}} + A_{0/1}$$

The third advantage is set-theoretic: the normalization transforms the relation r 'is correctly saturated by' into a function f from a still countable domain of Boolean questions A $\{Q \mid Q \in A\}$ to a co-domain of only two possible Boolean answers $\{$Yes, No$\}$. Figure 14 provides an illustration.

The reader familiar with Frege's theory of The Truth and The False will spot a family resemblance here. Correctness is now a functional concept, but it is still premature to investigate it. At this stage, what matters is that the dramatic downsizing of the co-domain of the function represents the extensional counterpart of a fourth, informational advantage: [NORM] shifts all the content in i to Q. We have seen that this re-location of content is what motivates the normalization in the first place. To understand how it works and why it is useful, we need to recall a few other elementary facts in information theory.

As is well known, given a set of N equiprobable symbols, information theory quantifies the amount of information in a symbol thus:

$$\text{Log}_2 (N) = \text{bits of information per symbol}$$

It follows that a coin ($N = 2$), by producing a head (h) or tail (t), delivers at most (if it is fair) 1 bit of information, whereas two coins ($N = 4$), deliver at most (again, if they are both fair) 2 bits of information (e.g. $<h, t>$), and so forth.

Imagine now a biased coin, which makes obtaining h more likely. The more biased the coin is, the more likely h is, the less information is provided by the answer, the smaller the information deficit becomes, up to the point when, if both sides of the coin are heads, the bias is total, the probability of h is 1, the information conveyed by h is 0 bit and so too, is the receiver's information deficit. All this means that, since [NORM] transforms queries into yes/no questions that can be answered by tossing a coin A with different degrees of bias, the worst scenario is one in which Q corresponds to an information deficit that requires at most 1 bit of information from A in order to be saturated. However, even an $A_{0/1}$ worth a full bit of information fails to add anything, in terms of semantic content, to that already contained in Q. It follows that, whatever the specific semantic content in i is, [NORM] shifts it entirely to Q, exactly as we wished.

As a consequence, we now have an intuitive way of defining semantic content as unsaturated information or, more formally:

$$
\begin{aligned}
[\text{CONT}]\quad \text{Content in } i^{\text{CLP}} &= \text{Content in } Q_{0/1}^{\text{CLP}} \\
&= i^{\text{CLP}} - A_{0/1} \\
&= i^{\text{CLP}} - n \,\text{bit of information, for } n = 0 \text{ or } 1
\end{aligned}
$$

We have seen the case in which $n = 1$. For $n = 0$, the semantic information i^{CLP}, its content and the content in $Q_{0/1}^{\text{CLP}}$ overlap. This is the case with rhetorical questions ('are you joking?' when used to assert that you are joking), pseudo-questions ('could you close the door please?' asked in terms of a polite request instead of 'I would like you to close the door'), self-answering questions ('were the four evangelists more than three?') and tautological questions ('is a = a?' or 'are bachelors unmarried?' where the noun and the qualification are both used and not mentioned). Still following [CONT], it becomes easy to see how p and $\neg p$ may have exactly the same semantic content, while counting as very different information.

[CONT] is not just interesting in itself but provides a reassuring test, since it is perfectly consistent with the theory of strongly semantic information defended in chapter five. In particular, it shows that tautologies and contradictions are pure semantic contents, equally uninformative or, to phrase it differently, that they provide no semantic information about their referents, over and above their contents (in both cases the coin we are tossing has two identical sides, as it were). This is as it should be, so our reverse engineering seems to be proceeding in the right direction.

8.5 Fourth step: Verification and validation

We have now disassembled semantic information into two components. By combining [Pol] and [Norm], the result can be more succinctly formulated thus:

$$[\text{PN}] \; i^{\text{CLP}} = Q_{0/1}^{\text{CLP}} + A_{0/1}$$

Let us now scrutinize each component separately.

On the one hand, we have seen that $Q_{0/1}$ sets the CLP parameters. Since it provides all the content in i, $Q_{0/1}$ also identifies its referent, that is, what i is about. We can express all this more precisely by saying that $Q_{0/1}^{\text{CLP}}$ identifies a *system s* (the referent of i) and provides all the *semantic content* (the content in i) for a *model of s* (namely, $Q_{0/1}^{\text{CLP}} + A_{0/1}$) within a given context, at a particular LoA and for a purpose.

On the other hand, although $Q_{0/1}^{\text{CLP}}$ in [PN] is still neither a test nor a request for confirmation but a request for saturation, clearly the sort of saturation in question can no longer be a matter of content, as it was in [Pol]. $A_{0/1}$ acts only as a Boolean key, that either fails to apply at all (see $\neg A_{0/1}$ in Figure 15) or that applies and then either locks or unlocks the content provided by $Q_{0/1}^{\text{CLP}}$, thus generating a partial model (henceforth just model) of the targeted system. Once again, a conceptual distinction and some standard terminology from software engineering (Fox (2007)) can help to clarify this crucial point.

Software Verification and Validation (V&V) is the overall process of checking the 'fitness for purpose' of an artefact, by ensuring that the software being developed or modified:

a. Complies with some given *specifications*, regulations or preconditions imposed at the start of the development process; and
b. Accomplishes its intended purpose, meeting its *requirements*.

The two phases are complementary. In phase (a), called *verification* (no relation at all to the philosophical concept), one checks whether one is constructing (or has constructed) what one has (or had) planned to construct, that is, whether the artefact is being developed in the right way. This means evaluating the consistency, completeness and correctness of the software during the stages of its development life cycle.

In phase (b), known as *validation* (again, no relation to the logical concept), one checks whether one is constructing what is required, that is, whether the right artefact is being developed. This means evaluating the correctness of the final software with respect to the user's needs and requirements.

The V&V process applies to a variety of artefacts and products and helps to clarify the twofold role played by $A_{0/1}$ in [PN]. Let me first show how by relying on our example [Ex. 2].

Given the question 'is the beer in the fridge?' any Boolean answer—independently of whether it is 'yes' or 'no'—implicitly verifies (in the V&V sense) that the question complies with the preconditions (i.e. the specifications) regulating its proper formulation, including its context, LoA, and purpose. A question like 'Is the fridge in the beer?' fails to qualify as something that can receive either a 'yes' or a 'no' answer because it fails the verification check, since it blatantly fails to develop the semantic artefact in the right way. Once the question is verified—once it is shown to have been formulated properly—the specific answer, either 'yes' or 'no', validates (gives a green or a red light to) its content. If this process seems to be prone to error, recall that we started by assuming p in order to obtain Q and A, so the possibility of re-obtaining p by re-

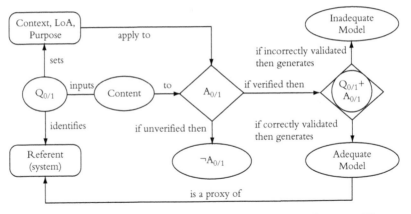

Figure 15 Summary of the first four steps in the analysis of semantic information. The process starts with $Q_{0/1}$ on the left

combining Q and A is a priori guaranteed by hypothesis, and sceptical suggestions would merely be out of place here.

All this can be formulated more precisely by saying that $A_{0/1}$ saturates $Q_{0/1}^{CLP}$ by implicitly *verifying* its CLP parameters (roughly: both 'yes' and 'no' implicitly signal that the question is being asked in the right context, at the right LoA and for the right purpose) and explicitly *validating* its content, as a model of the system (roughly: 'yes' and 'no' provide a green or a red light for the question respectively). Figure 15 summarizes how far we have progressed in reverse engineering semantic information.

Clearly, a correct saturation consists in a *correct verification* and a *correct validation*. It has taken several clarifications and distinctions and quite a bit of technical vocabulary, but we have finally reached the heart of our problem.

8.6 Fifth step: Correctness

Let us quickly review our progress. Simplifying, we now know that p qualifies as semantic information about a system s if and only if p is true; that p is true if and only if A correctly saturates the Boolean question Q corresponding to p; and that A correctly saturates Q if and only if it correctly verifies and validates it, thus generating an adequate model m of s. Having reduced truth (of semantic information) to adequacy (of the corresponding model m) via correctness (of A with respect to Q), our next challenge is the analysis of the correctness of A.

The challenge consists in negotiating two consecutive crossroads. The first is represented by the twofold correctness of the saturation. I shall return to the issue of what it means for A to verify correctly Q in section 8.7.5. Here, let me just highlight the fact that the correct verification of Q by A is a formal precondition for the development of an adequate model m of the targeted system s: it is necessary for, but does not contribute to, the truthfulness of i. In other words, the analysis of the correctness of the verification cannot help us in understanding what it means for semantic information to be truthful. At this crossroads, the really interesting path is represented by the correct *validation* of Q by A. By following it, we encounter the second crossroads, represented by two further alternatives. For now, we can either analyse correctness of the validation in terms of some concept of truth, thus showing consistency but also failing to provide a non-circular analysis of what it means for semantic information (which, it will be recalled, it is true) to be true. Or we can move forward, and check whether a further reduction of the correctness of the validation, and hence of the adequacy of the issuing model in terms that are truth-poietic but not truth-dependent, is possible. Let us quickly review the circular path first.

A useful way to test whether our reverse engineering process is still on the right track is by showing that we have not lost touch with our starting point. Statistics provides the standard analysis of what it means for a model to be adequate (Freedman et al. (2007)). A model is adequate with respect to its target system if it is *valid*. This is now the *statistical* (not the software engineering or the logical) concept of *validity*, which is to be understood as the result of a combination of *accuracy* and *precision*, two other technical concepts borrowed from statistics. Although one might have the impression that we are actually gaining some new ground, it is easy to see that this road only leads back to our starting point. For statistical *accuracy* is the degree of conformity of a measure or calculated parameter (belonging to the model) to its actual, that is, *true*, value (belonging to the system). And statistical *precision* is the degree to which further measurements or calculations show the same or similar results (this is why it is also called *reproducibility* or *repeatability*). So it turns out that the statistical concepts of validity, accuracy, and precision—even assuming that we could adapt them to our less quantitative needs and hence exploit them to clarify what we mean by an adequate model—ultimately presuppose a truth-dependent relation of *conformity* and hence cannot provide a foundational analysis of truth itself without begging the question. The silver lining in all this is that such internal coherence is reassuring: we have not got lost in some conceptual wilderness, while searching for the mechanism that generates semantic information. Encouraged by the knowledge that we could still go back to square one should we wish to do so, let us not press the panic button but push forward.

The second path should lead us away from semantics and epistemology, if we want to avoid ending up back where we started, and take us into the realm of pragmatics, that is, into the realm of actual and hopefully successful *interactions*—between an agent *a* holding the information that *p*, the model *m* generated by *p*, and the system *s* modelled by *m*—that can provide some *exogenous* grounding for the evaluation of the quality of the model itself. In order to achieve this, I shall ask the reader to bear with me a bit longer, as I need to introduce two more technical concepts to make sense of such interactions.

One is that of *proxy*, and is borrowed from ICT (Luotonen (1998)). Technically, it refers to a computer agent (e.g. a network service) authorized to act on behalf of another agent (the client), e.g. by allowing another computer to make indirect network connections to other network services (the server). In this sense, a proxy can be an interface for services that are remote, resource-intensive, or otherwise difficult to use directly. Note that the 'proxy-ing' system need not be a copy, an image, a representation or a reproduction of the 'proxy-ed' system (the client).

The other concept is that of *commutative diagram*, and is borrowed from category theory (Barr and Wells (1999)). Technically, it refers to a diagram of objects (vertices)

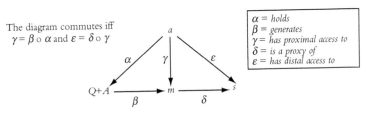

Figure 16 The meaning of [Cor]. Q+A is a simplification for $Q_{0/1}^{CLP} + A_{0/1}$

and morphisms (arrows) such that, when selecting two vertices, one can follow any directed path through the diagram and obtain the same result by composition.

Adapting these two concepts to our needs, we can now reverse engineer the correctness of the validation, and hence the adequacy of the ensuing model, in terms of the commutativity of the accessibility relation, thus (see Figure 16 for a more intuitive presentation, all Greek letters in [Cor] refer to paths in the diagram):

[COR] $A_{0/1}$ correctly validates $Q_{0/1}^{CLP}$ about a target system s identified by $Q_{0/1}^{CLP}$ if and only if $Q_{0/1}^{CLP} + A_{0/1}$ generates (β) an adequate model m of s; and m is an adequate model of s if and only if m is a proxy (δ) of s such that, if a holds (α) $Q_{0/1}^{CLP} + A_{0/1}$, then a's *proximal access* (γ) to m commutes with a's *distal access* (ϵ) to s.

[COR] offers two advantages and raises a problem. The first advantage is that it finally introduces an explicit reference to an informee a. This is crucial, since semantic information is an *objective* (i.e. not subjective) but also *liminal* (that is, neither internal nor external) and *relational* (that is, neither absolute nor relative) concept, like food. It makes little sense to talk about the presence and nature of food without any reference to the specific type of feeder. Likewise, something counts as semantic information only with respect to a specific type of informee.

The second advantage is that [COR] explains the well-known fact that semantic information provides *distal* access to its target. If the agent in the bedroom upstairs asks whether the beer is located in the fridge, and the agent in the kitchen downstairs answers positively, then the agent upstairs, by having proximal access to this overall piece of information, gains distal access to the presence of the beer in the fridge, as long as the answer is *correct*. [Cor] merely combines this into a single agent's informative state.

The problem concerns the interpretation of the relation of distal and proximal *accessibility*. If we were to interpret it alethically or epistemically (see chapter ten) this would obviously fail to take us off the semantic merry-go-round and, sooner rather than later, we would be sent back from where we came. The good news is that we do not need to go down that modal road. On the contrary, the sort of accessibility at stake here is a matter of pragmatic or factual interaction, which provides an exogenous grounding of correctness. It is the one that we find specified in computer science, where accessibility refers to the actual permission to *read* (technically, *sense* and *retrieve*) and/or *write* (again, technically *modify* and *record*) data as a *physical* process. The result is that a's *proximal access* to m commutes with a's *distal access* to s if and only if a can read/write s by reading/writing m.

The writing of s through the writing of m is admittedly rare, but it is useful to illustrate it in order to convey the sense of concrete interaction with the targeted system that is involved. Thus, we have left behind a magic culture that considered it an ordinary phenomenon (cf. the practice of sticking pins in a doll as a method of cursing an individual). Nevertheless, self-fulfilling prophecies (Bill Gates confessing that 'Microsoft's shares are overvalued'), performative sentences (the baptizing priest declaring that 'the name of this girl is Mary'), magic-placebo formulae (the guru concluding that 'you are now healed'), authoritative-fictional descriptions ('Sherlock Holmes never visited the Bodleian Library' written by Conan Doyle), God's *intellectual intuition* that p, according to Kant, and other ways of 'doing things with words' ('this train is not leaving the station' uttered by a dictator) are a good reminder that it is far from impossible to modify/record a system by accessing only its model. Of course, access to m is most commonly used in order to read (i.e. sense and retrieve) s by reading (ditto) m. One gains distal access to (part of) the actual, physical system represented by the fridge in the kitchen and its contents (one senses and retrieves the data in question at a distance) by gaining proximal access to its (partial) model represented by the semantic information 'the beer is in the fridge'. A way of conveying the same point is by relying on a subjunctive formulation: the proximal read/write access to m as a proxy of

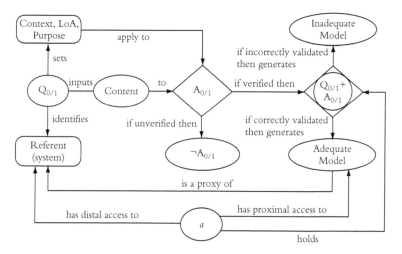

Figure 17 The correctness theory of truth

s commutes with the distal read/write access to s if and only by having read/write access to m one were having read/write access to s. This happens in space as well as time: imagine the question being 'Will the train leave from platform one?' and the answer being 'yes'. Semantic information may be seen as a way of being telepresent (Floridi (2005c)).

We needed actual interaction with the system being modelled in order to ground exogenously the correctness of the (validation provided by the) answer to the question pertaining to it, and we have now obtained it. Our toiling is almost over. Putting together this last piece of our jigsaw puzzle, we obtain Figure 17 (the reader may check that this is simply the result of merging Figure 15 and Figure 16, even if this may not be immediately obvious visually):

Figure 17 represents the blueprint of the mechanism that underlies the truthful nature of semantic information. If we apply it to our example, we obtain:

   i. 'the beer is in the fridge' qualifies as semantic information if and only if

   ii. 'the beer is in the fridge' is true; (ii) is the case if and only if

  iii. 'yes' is the correct answer to (i.e. correctly saturates by correctly verifying and validating) the question 'is the beer in the fridge?'; (iii) is the case if and only if

iv. 'is the beer in the fridge?' + 'yes' generate an adequate model m of the relevant system s; (iv) is the case if and only if

v. m is a proxy of s and proximal access to m provides distal access to s; and finally (v) is the case if and only if

vi. reading/writing m enables one to read/write s.

That is, if 'the beer is in the fridge' qualifies as semantic information, then holding that semantic information is tantamount to accessing the particular feature of the system addressed by the model which, in our example, is the location of the beer inside the fridge.

8.7 Some implications and advantages of the correctness theory of truth

A good way to explore some of the features of what I shall label the *correctness theory of truth* (henceforth CTT) is by making explicit some of its implications and advantages. They will also help us to grasp the similarities and differences between CTT and other standard approaches to truth.

8.7.1. Truthmakers and coherentism

At the beginning of this chapter, we saw that semantic information is, strictly speaking, not truth-bearing but truth-constituted. What is truth-bearing is instead content, which gets upgraded to semantic information only if it is truthful. It follows that, since a truth-maker is that in virtue of which a truth-bearer is true, CTT is compatible with a variety of theories of truth-makers, insofar as these are successfully adaptable and applicable to content. This is fine but probably less interesting than the fact that, since CTT seeks to reduce truth to correctness, it also translates the question about truth-makers into a question about correctness-makers: what is it that in virtue of which a correctness-bearer (i.e. $A_{0/1}$ as a correct answer) is indeed correct? A quick, Aristotelian reply may point to the system s as the most plausible candidate. For a look at Figure 17 may suffice to convince one that it is because of what s is that the model m may qualify as adequate, and hence that the answer $A_{0/1}$ that generates m may be correct. The story, however, is slightly more complicated. To show why let me first sketch two analogies.

Consider the case in which a non-atomic formula F in propositional logic (e.g. $\neg (P \vee Q) \rightarrow S$) is declared to be well formed. One may ask what it is that in virtue of which F is indeed well formed, that is, what its well-formedness-maker is. Pointing to the right sub-set of formation rules as the relevant well-formedness-makers would definitely be a good answer but, like pointing to the system s before, it would also be only partial. For what would be missing is the implicit fact that we are talking about a dynamic system: F is well formed also because it has been (or may be) constructed according to the relevant formation rules *recursively*. So the formation rules in question are only the most salient, necessary source of the well-formedness of F. Strictly speaking, they would be insufficient by themselves.

Consider next the more complex case of a bottle of Chianti wine. If we call that wine the Chianti-taste-bearer and ask what its Chianti-taste-maker is, pointing to Sangiovese grapes is fine, indeed necessary, but also insufficient. Clearly, the whole process, through which the wine is produced, makes a very significant difference and is as much a part of that in virtue of which the wine bears the taste of Chianti (the Chianti-taste-maker) as the original grapes. The Sangiovese grapes are only the necessary source of the Chianti-taste of the wine in question.

If we now go back to what a correctness-maker is according to CTT, given the engineering approach adopted by the theory and hence the treatment of semantic information as an artefact, it should be clear that the dynamic 'making' plays an essential role. The essential element that makes $A_{0/1}$ correct is indeed the system s, which is the necessary correctness-maker that is the source of the correctness of $A_{0/1}$. But s becomes sufficient only if it is embedded in the right sort of network of dynamic relations, as shown in the previous pages. For CTT, the system s is the source of correctness, but the correctness-maker only in a loose way of speaking. The *individually* necessary and *jointly* sufficient correctness-maker conditions are the whole complex construct, represented by the configuration of the entire distributed system[5] in which s is embedded as a source of correctness, including the commuting relation. Two final clarifications are now in order.

First, the previous point might be looked upon with some sympathy by followers of coherentist approaches to truth. At the risk of losing some allies, let me clarify that this would be a mistake. CTT may indeed be compatible with a coherentist theory of truth, but it is very far from being (committed to) one. Depending on the CLP parameters, some models play the role of systems against which other models are evaluated. In our example, we take a propositional model ('the beer is in the fridge') as less fundamental than a perceptual model (e.g. the observable presence of beer in the fridge, or the grasping of some beer once the fridge is opened). We could have used a memory-based system (the recollection that the beer had been placed in the fridge) or a testimony-based alternative (the reassurance by someone who knows where the beer is, that is, in the fridge). This is where CTT is closer to a coherentist theory of truth. However, the network of dynamic relations specified above (the blueprint illustrated in Figure 17) has very little to do with either coherence or consistency within an information system, which should be analysed independently of a correctness theory of truth, in terms of information *integrity*. Thanks to the commuting relation, correctness is not an internal property of the system, but the external feature of $A_{0/1}$ that guarantees the successful, pragmatic interaction with s through m.

---

[5] The occurrence of the term 'system' here is unfortunate but inevitable (it is dictated by standard terminology in model analysis). Luckily, it should not generate any confusion, since it clearly refers to the whole blueprint described by Figure 17.

Second, note that, as I have just specified, the system s, which is the source of the correctness of $A_{0/1}$ and hence of the adequacy of the model m, may be another model n. In this case, supporters of some forms of relativism and internalism may rejoice, but this reaction too would be premature. CTT offers an *intra-model* not an *infra-model* theory of truth. The reader may recognize here a Kantian point: CTT analyses truth as a relation between models, and never shifts from talking about semantic information to talking about systems in themselves, yet this is not a form of anti-realism. In CTT, truth is ultimately a matter of assessment of what is *claimed* to be the case against what is *taken* to be the case, within the (often very rigid) constraints and (often rather limited) affordances offered by the targeted system. Ultimately, it is the way the system is (the beer being in the fridge) that interactively constrains (recall the relation of commutation) the value of its models ('the beer is in the fridge', 'there is beer in the fridge', 'the fridge contains some beer', 'if you are looking for some beer look inside the fridge', and so forth) and determine their truth, even if the only way to deal with the system epistemically is through its models. The relation between model and system is not one of pictorial representation or resemblance or similarity (no metaphorical mechanism of mirroring or photocopying is at stake here) but one of fit, in the way in which a key 'corresponds' to a lock. To think that CTT supports an 'any key works' sort of policy would be a mistake. The philosopher sharing some (naïve, direct, scientific, common-sensical etc.) form of realism may be willing to accept CTT but then graft to it some form of (possibly privileged) epistemic access to s, or what is taken to be the case, in terms of what is actually the case. This is indeed an option. But it is not the one that I or any Kantian favour, because the alternative advocated by CTT points in the direction of a more modest epistemology, a safer commitment and a less ontologically-over-loaded conception of truth. As in statistics, in CTT we never talk about the ultimate, real nature of the world in itself, but compare data sets (the model) to data sets (the system), or phenomena (in the Kantian sense) to other phenomena (still in the Kantian sense). According to CTT, truth is a successful transduction of models among possible worlds. With a slogan: *truth is commutation*. Further discussion of this crucial point is found in the next topic.

8.7.2 Accessibility, bidimensionalism, and correspondentism

The reader might have noticed that, in CTT, the system s is first identified by $Q_{0/1}^{CLP}$ and then modelled by $Q_{0/1}^{CLP} + A_{0/1}$ and that this twofold manoeuvre is paralleled by the double access that a enjoys (at least in principle) to s as posed by $Q_{0/1}^{CLP}$ and to s as modelled by $Q_{0/1}^{CLP} + A_{0/1}$. This alethic bidimensionalism bears a strong resemblance to what Quine called *semantic ascent* and is crucial. We are able to check whether an answer is correct, and hence the issuing model is adequate, with respect to a posited s (whether some content about a targeted s is true and hence qualifies as semantic information) only if we have both s and (at least in principle) an *alternative* way of reading/writing s. When it comes to empirical knowledge, nobody could check the truthfulness of a newspaper by buying a second copy of the same issue, to paraphrase

Wittgenstein. So, contrary to what the correspondent theory of truth sometimes seems to suggest, in CTT truth is about *positing and modelling* a system and therefore having double, not single, access to it. We capture the world and its features by using pincers (bidimensionalism), not harpoons (monodimensionalism). In scientific research, this is well known, and common practice. For in order to understand whether a model is correct, a scientist looks at the data set and considers whether the model can success-fully reproduce and/or predict the behaviour of some aspect of the system being modelled (Davison (2003)). The better the model, the smaller the disagreement between its implementation and/or forecast and what happens in the *observed* system. In the technical vocabulary of testing theory, this means that, for a given model under test (MUT, our m), there is a reference model (RM, also known as an oracle, because it is assumed to be an infallible source of truth, our s) that serves as the basis for the construction of MUT and can then be used to establish whether MUT is behaving as required, through some alternative access to RM itself. This scientifically realistic, if not philosophically realist, feature allows CTT not to solve but to bypass two classic problems threatening monodimensional theories of truth as correspondence (according to which only one relation connects truth-bearers and truth-makers):

A. how systems (facts, in some correspondentists' terminology) may be understood independently of models (true sentences, still following the same terminology) without merely making them their 'tautological accusatives', to paraphrase Armstrong (1997); and

B. a version of the slingshot argument to the effect that all models (true sentences) correspond to the same 'Great System' (the 'Great Fact').

CTT avoids (a) because it argues that specific systems are posited and accessed independently of how they are modelled in the first place, and there are only specific models of specific systems, developed by fulfilling specific CLP parameters. So CTT's bidimensionalism further explains why it is not an internalist theory of truth and avoids (b): although all truth evaluations occur between models, as in Russell's theory of types there is no ultimate 'Great System' which all models adequately describe.[6]

A significant advantage of CTT's bidimensionalism is that it avoids overloading truth with a double task. Some theories of truth are *monodimensional* but *double-tasking* in that they require truth to work both semantically—in order to explain what it means for truth-bearers to have the truth-value they do have, e.g. what it means for 'the beer is in the fridge', which is true, to be indeed true—and ontologically, in order to explain what the world is like given that the truth-bearers have the truth-value they have, e.g. what the world is like given that 'the beer is in the fridge' is true. Metaphorically, such theories identify only one road between truth-makers and

---

[6] Note that Young (2002) has shown that even in the case of a correspondence theory of truth it is at least controversial whether the slingshot argument undermines it.

truth-bearers, which they assume to be two-way, epistemological and ontological. On the contrary, CTT decouples the semantic from the ontological task and requires truth to be only a semantic relation between models. In this, the similarity with Tarski's approach (which is also bidimensional and 'single-tasking', or one-way) is obvious: according to CTT 'snow is white' is true if and only if 'yes' is the correct answer to 'is snow white?'. The difference lies in the pragmatic (as opposed to model-theoretic) and hence exogenous turn that CTT takes when it grounds the correctness of the answer: having read/write access to the model m that 'is snow white? + yes' generates, commutes with having read/write access to the substance in question and its whiteness (the system s).

What CTT's bidimensionalism also shows is that deflationist theories of truth, when applied to semantic information, may be right, but in a trivial and uninteresting way. Since semantic information encapsulates truth, it is not truth-bearing but truth-constituted, so qualifying it as true is worse than informationally redundant, it is pointlessly noisy. If 'the beer is in the fridge' qualifies as information, to add that it is true fails to provide any further information and only messes up the communication, wasting resources. But to strip semantic information of such a uselessly[7] redundant qualification leaves the problem of its truthfulness (or of the truthfulness of the corresponding content) untouched and hence unsolved. We still need to run our reverse engineering process in order to understand what it means for p to qualify as semantic information. And as soon as we transform p into a Boolean question + answer, we know that the problem of the truth of p has been transformed into the problem of the correctness of the answer.

8.7.3 Types of semantic information and the variety of truths

We have already seen that CTT can account for the nature of tautologies and contradictions, but any acceptable theory of truth for semantic information should also be able to deal satisfactorily with a variety of genuine types of semantic information and hence with their truths. Happily, CTT proves to be sufficiently flexible. Here is a quick review.

We would like to be able to treat fictional truths, such as 'Watson is Sherlock Holmes' best friend', future truths, such as 'the flight will leave at 12.30 tomorrow', negative truths, such as 'whales are not fish', ethical truths, such as 'rape is morally wrong', modal truths, such as 'beer can be stored in a fridge', dispositional truths, such as 'sugar is soluble in water', and metaphorical truths, such as 'Achilles is a lion' (or even more complex cases such as 'Mary is not a fox') as informative, that is, as genuine instances of semantic information. CTT allows this treatment rather easily. In each case, the system s in question, posed by Q (e.g. 'is Watson Sherlock Holmes' best friend?'), is distally accessed through the model generated by the correct answer ('yes')

---

[7] Redundancy is often useful, but in this case it is pointless redundancy that is in question.

because CTT is not ontologically committed to the empirical existence of *s* but rather treats it as the reference model (*s* could be a segment of any possible world). A major advantage, over standard theories of truth as correspondence, is that this allows CTT to avoid any reference to some existing fictional facts, negative facts, queer moral facts, parallel modal facts, dispositional facts, or metaphorical facts, to which such truths would allegedly correspond. We never check semantic information (e.g. 'whales are not fish') against some fact (about their non-fishiness), we check it against other semantic constructs, which might be narrative (in Sherlock Holmes' case), decisional (in the flight's case), biological (in the whales' case), ethical (in the rape case), modal (in the storability case), dispositional (in the solubility case), and so forth.

One may object that treating fictional, empirical, ethical, modal, dispositional, metaphorical, and other kinds of instances of semantic information (independently of whether negative or positive, or past, present, or future) as all bona fide true impoverishes our capacity to discriminate between reality, imagination, and social conventions or stipulations. However, this would be a fair criticism only if one were to forget *the absolutely crucial fact* that the whole analysis must be conducted by paying careful attention to the LoA, the context and the purpose of the corresponding questions. To simplify, 'Achilles is a great warrior' is an instance of semantic information, and hence it is true, not only because 'yes' is the correct answer to the corresponding question, but also because we (rightly) take for granted Homer's *Iliad* as the right CLP framework. Consider 'snow is white', 'milk is white', and 'teeth are white'. Comparing these instances of semantic information is enlightening because, from such truths taken separately, it does not follow necessarily, at least not in CTT, that therefore 'milk, snow, and teeth have the same colour' is also true. This is because of the crucial role played by the CLP parameters. 'Milk, snow, and teeth have the same colour' is true if and only if 'yes' is the correct answer to the corresponding Boolean question, but now one cannot determine whether that answer is indeed correct unless one specifies the context in which, the LoA at which, and the purpose for which that question is being asked. Change the available palette (different LoA) or the purpose (redecorating the living room, say, instead of having one tooth replaced), for example, and the question may receive different answers. This is not relativism, it is, for want of a better word, 'precisism'. It is a fallacy to fuse two or more instances of semantic information into a large instance without making their CLP parameters homogenous, at least implicitly. If this seems too easy and commonsensical, it is worth recalling that we are only reaping the fruits of the hard labour undertaken in the previous pages.

Our opponent may still be unconvinced. He might retort that there is still a risk of causing an inflation of truths. Such concern is misplaced. 'The earth is flat', 'Sherlock Holmes is happily married to Watson', 'in 2012 the Olympic Games will take place in Rome', 'horses are oviparous', 'the use of violence against women is always justified' fail to qualify as semantic information because they are false; this because the corresponding questions are correctly answered in the negative, and this because affirmative answers do not commute with the systems posed by the corresponding questions. The point is important and deserves a fuller treatment in the next section.

8.7.4 A deflationist interpretation of falsehood as failure

CTT treats untruth (falsehood) as commutation failure. The treatment comes as rather natural if one realizes that

i. in logic programming, negation as failure (NAP) is a non-monotonic inference rule used to derive ¬ P from the failure to derive P (Gabbay et al. (1993));

ii. the so-called stable model semantics, which gives a semantics to logic programming with NAP, is a simplified form of autoepistemic logic (Nerode and Shore (1997)), and

iii. ¬ P may have not only the classic meaning but also the modal meanings, in autoepistemic logic, of 'P is not believed', 'P is not known' or 'P cannot be shown' (Gelfond (1987)).

The further but rather simple step taken by CTT consists in interpreting 'P is not true' (false for the classicist) as ¬ P and then analysing ¬ P as equivalent to commutation failure of the relevant diagram. The expanded autoepistemic semantics can then be given in terms of 'P is not information'. To illustrate more intuitively what all this amounts to, and see the advantage of such minimalism, consider the following example: 'the earth has two moons'. Following CTT, the usual analysis requires a specification of the CLP parameters, posed by the corresponding question 'does the earth have two moons?'. Once we have ascertained that we are talking about our planet considered astronomically and in light of our current knowledge (not, for example, of some twin earth in another possible world; or some future earth whose moon has been split into two; or some other planet also called earth; or some earth described in a sci-fi novel as having two moons; or some ancient text in which the earth is described as having two moons etc.), the answer 'yes' provides a model (the earth with two moons) the proximal access to which fails to commute with the distal access to the astronomical system in question. There is a failure in the information flow, and this is what it means for 'yes' to be incorrect, and hence for 'the earth has two moons' to be untrue (false). The advantage of this minimalism is that there is no need to treat truth and untruth (falsehood) in the same way: untruth (falsehood) is best understood as the mere absence of truth, a lesson well known to any non-Manichean philosopher, to whom darkness is only the absence of light.

8.7.5 The information-inaptness of semantic paradoxes

Semantic paradoxes are often seen as the ultimate benchmark of a theory of truth. The point of this section, however, is not to argue in favour of a CTT-based solution of them—a task out of place, given the nature of this chapter—but rather to see what semantic paradoxes may teach us about CTT.

Consider first the task of preventing the occurrence of semantic paradoxes. In this, CTT's strategy is Russellian–Tarskian. This comes as no surprise if one realizes that, technically speaking, CTT—with its emphasis on the importance of the CLP parameters and especially on the Method of Abstraction and its use of Levels of Abstraction—represents a late incarnation of Russell's approach to semantic paradoxes in terms of type theory. The modern lineage, of some interest for the historian, is through the adoption and refinement, in programming language theory, of Russell's and (later) Church's theory of types in order, for example, to construct type-checking algorithms to analyse compilers for programming languages and avoid the disasters caused by unconstrained self-reference. CTT is simply reclaiming for philosophical analysis what was its own in the first place.

Consider next the task of treating semantic paradoxes once they have occurred. CTT can explain their occurrence in terms of failure to respect Russellian–Tarskian constraints, e.g. about object language and metalanguage. It can then interpret their value, as alleged instances of semantic information, by relying on the reverse engineering procedure detailed in the previous pages, with the following results.

Semantic paradoxes are notoriously caused by self-referential mechanisms. *Internal* semantic paradoxes are those in which the self-referential relation occurs within the message itself (the semantic information *i*), independently of the sender. The classic example is, of course, 'this sentence is false'. Following CTT, the verdict on similar paradoxes is that they fail to pass the *verification* stage, in the computer science sense introduced in section 8.5. For consider the erotetic structure of 'this sentence is false'. Once the CLP parameters are taken care of, if 'this sentence is false' must count as semantic information, it must be true, and hence informationally equivalent to 'is this sentence false?' + 'yes'. But then it becomes easier to see that, before trying to understand the role of 'yes', one should acknowledge that 'is this sentence false?' is a question, not a declarative sentence at all, which is not truth-apt (it makes no sense to ask whether it can be correctly qualified as either true or untrue). So CTT can show this and other internal semantic paradoxes (e.g. 'the next sentence is false. The previous sentence is true.') to be badly engineered informational artefacts, comparable to any blueprint of a perpetual motion machine. Note that this applies to vicious as well as virtuous cases: 'this sentence is true' is equally self-referential, it also fails to pass the verification stage ('is this sentence true?' is not truth-apt) and hence cannot count as semantic information, according to CTT. This is fine since, informationally, 'this sentence is true' could not be false, and hence, like a tautology such as '*a is a*', cannot succeed to convey any information.

Note, however, that the previous approach is ineffective towards *external* semantic paradoxes. In this case, the self-referential relation is between the message (the semantic information *i*) and its sender. The classic example is, of course, 'Cretans always lie', suitably refined. In this case, there is nothing wrong with the erotetic structure of the message ('do Cretans always lie?' + 'yes'). The problem lies with its relation to the sender, when the message comes from a Cretan like Epimenides. Recall the example in which Mary—now Epimenides—can make statements not by uttering declarative sentences but only through Boolean questions followed by the corresponding Boolean answer. If 'Cretans always lie' counts as semantic information it should be true, and hence equivalent to 'do Cretans always lie?' + 'yes', where both 'do Cretans always lie?' and 'yes' are messages sent by the same source. And this is where the problem arises. For imagine the case in which you wish to know whether Cretans always lie. Asking a Cretan whether they do would provide you with no information: you would not know whether Cretans lie all the time, no matter what the Cretan answers. This means that a self-certifying question cannot be informatively asked to the source that needs to be certified. But this holds true even when it is the source itself that asks and then answers the self-certifying question. Mary cannot convey any semantic information by saying 'am I lying? Yes' because, by asking Q, she has *ipso facto* forfeited the possibility of answering it informatively. As in the previous case, the analysis treats vicious and virtuous cases in the same way. Informationally speaking, 'Cretans never lie', uttered by a Cretan, and 'I always tell the truth', run into the same problem faced by their paradoxical counterparts: they are equally disqualified by CTT as failing to pass the verification step to qualify as semantic information.

To summarize, both internal and external semantic paradoxes are faulty artefacts that fail to qualify as semantic information because they fail to pass the verification stage. This does not mean that they are useless informationally. Semantic paradoxes may help the flow of information by fulfilling a phatic function: they can perform the social task of establishing, prolonging, or discontinuing communication, or simply confirming whether the receiver is still there, exactly like 'how are you?' or the inarticulate sounds made by a listener during a telephone conversation are not meant to provide (or gain) any primary information.

The reader acquainted with the literature on semantic paradoxes may still be left with at least one further doubt: what happens when the semantic paradox has an erotetic format to begin with? Russell formulated his own paradox in terms of a question, but one may retort that, in his case, the problem is set-theoretical, not semantic. Nevertheless, there are other paradoxes that are both semantic and erotetic, such as Smullyan's 'is the answer to this question "no"?'.[8] How does CTT fare in this case? The answer is simple. If p is to count as semantic information, the relation between p and $[p? + answer]$ must be a biconditional. But this means that, independently of which answer one may later provide to 'is the answer to this question "no"?', in order to count as the first half of the erotetic equivalent of some semantic information, that question must correspond to the message 'the answer to this question is "no"' (or 'the answer to this question is not "no"'), but note that this is not a question, but a declarative sentence, hence it is malformed. It follows that this version of the semantic

---

[8] For the attribution to Smullyan see Landini (2007).

paradoxes too poses no problem for CTT, which diagnoses them as cases of verification failure.

CONCLUSION

We have come to the end of a rather long journey. Theories of truth often seem to be developed with passive viewers of an outside world in mind, detached observers, whether inside or outside Plato's cave, TV watchers, radio listeners, movie goers, in short, *systems users*, according to the computer science terminology favoured in this book. The correctness theory of truth, proposed in this chapter, should rather be seen as an attempt to cater for a different sort of customer, namely embodied and embedded, creative agents, who interact with reality, shape and build it, Plato's artisans, writers not just readers, players not audience, in short *systems designers*. To these customers, truth is about constructing and handling informational artefacts and interacting with them successfully, not merely experiencing them passively. Unfortunately, this is not very Greek, but it is still a very respectable tradition to which both Russell and Tarski belong, insofar as their groundwork in model theory concerned the design of systems.

We now have an answer to question (a): what does it mean for semantic information to be truthful? But we are still lacking an answer to question (b): how does semantic information upgrade to knowledge? As the reader will undoubtedly know, the traditional approach to (b) has been in terms of justification of true beliefs. In the next chapter, we shall see that such a traditional approach is mistaken. The tripartite account of knowledge is not only logically inadequate as it is, but also irretrievably so in principle, so it cannot provide us with a strategy to answer (b). This is not as bad as it looks. For the negative conclusion reached in chapter nine opens up the possibility of a non-doxastic but informational approach to the definition and conceptual understanding of knowledge. To achieve this we will need to understand what it means for an agent to be informed that *p* (chapter ten), what counts as relevant information for such an agent (chapter eleven) and, finally, how holding the relevant information that *p* may be upgraded to knowing that *p* once the agent is able to give an account of the relevant information in question (chapter twelve). Throughout these steps, the conception of truth that will be implicitly used will be the one I defended in this chapter.

9

The logical unsolvability of the Gettier problem

The finite mind cannot therefore attain to the full truth about things through similarity. For the truth is neither more nor less, but rather indivisible. What is itself not true can no more measure the truth than what is not a circle can measure a circle, whose being is indivisible. Hence reason, which is not the truth, can never grasp the truth so exactly that it could not be grasped infinitely more accurately. Reason stands in the same relation to truth as the polygon to the circle; the more vertices a polygon has, the more it resembles a circle, yet even when the number of vertices grows infinite, the polygon never becomes equal to a circle, unless it becomes a circle in its true nature. The real nature of what exists, which constitutes its truth, is therefore never entirely attainable. It has been sought by all the philosophers, but never really found. The further we penetrate into informed ignorance, the closer we come to the truth itself.

Nicholas of Kues, *De Docta Ignorantia* (*On Informed Ignorance*), Book I.

SUMMARY

Previously, in chapters four, seven, and eight, I tried to show how well-formed data can become meaningful and truthful, and hence constitute semantic information. Semantic information provides an ideal and robust basis to analyse knowledge. However, chapter seven indicated that it is still unclear how semantic information might be upgraded to knowledge. This chapter has now the negative goal of clearing the ground of a potential obstacle towards an informational analysis of knowledge. In the last decades, epistemology has been largely confined to the so-called tripartite analysis of knowledge as justified true belief. Now, it might seem that such a doxastic approach could provide the right strategy to tackle the upgrading problem. In this chapter, it is argued that this is not the case, for the following reason. The tripartite account of propositional, fallibilist knowledge that p as justified true belief can become adequate only if it can solve the Gettier problem. However, the latter can be solved only if the problem of a successful coordination of the resources (at least truth and justification)—necessary and sufficient to deliver propositional, fallibilist knowledge that p—can be solved. But it can be proved that the coordination problem is unsolvable by showing that it is equivalent to the 'coordinated attack' problem, which is demonstrably unsolvable in epistemic logic. It follows that the tripartite account is not merely inadequate as it stands, as proved by Gettier-type counterexamples, but demonstrably irreparable in principle, so that efforts to improve it can never succeed. The positive result is that the tripartite account should be abandoned in favour of a non-doxastic, informational approach. Substantiating the latter claim is the task of the next three chapters.

9.1 Introduction

According to the tripartite account of propositional and fallibilist knowledge that p, an epistemic agent S knows that p if and only if

   i. p is true,
   ii. S believes that p, and
   iii. S is justified in believing that p.

However, well-known Gettier-type counterexamples prove that this version of the tripartite account is inadequate. Even in the best scenario, conditions (i)–(iii) are at most necessary, but they are certainly insufficient to define propositional knowledge, since they fail to ensure S against mere epistemic luck (Gettier (1963)).

Epistemologists agree that Gettier-type counterexamples pose a genuine challenge.[1] Many hope that the challenge may be met by revising the tripartite account to avoid the counterexamples without incurring new difficulties. There are two interpretations of this strategy. One, incorrectly, argues that if the counterexamples are avoidable then the account can become adequate, that is (as usual, the asterisk is a reminder that the formula is provisional and will have to be refined):

Lemma 1⋆: (i) if Gettier-type counterexamples are avoidable, at least in principle, then the tripartite account can become adequate, at least in principle; (ii) Gettier-type counterexamples are avoidable, at least in principle; therefore (iii) the tripartite account can become adequate, at least in principle.

Lemma 1⋆ begs the question. If one could prove (ii) that the counterexamples are indeed avoidable, one would have proved that the tripartite account can become adequate, thanks to (i), but (i) is acceptable only if one already assumes (iii), that is, only if one already believes that the tripartite approach is a step in the right direction, but this is precisely the point in question. Thus, according to lemma 1⋆, proving that Gettier-type counterexamples are unavoidable in principle would not affect the potential adequacy of the account, a clear non sequitur.

---

[1]   See for example the reviews offered by Dancy (1985), Dancy and Sosa (1992), Everitt and Fisher (1995), Hetherington (1996), Steup (1996), and Greco and Sosa (1999).

The correct interpretation argues that, if the tripartite account can become adequate, at least in principle, then Gettier-type counterexamples must be avoidable, at least in principle, and hence that a successful strategy must prove that they are not demonstrably unavoidable:

Lemma 1: (i) if the tripartite account can become adequate, at least in principle, then Gettier-type counterexamples are avoidable, at least in principle; but (ii) Gettier-type counterexamples are not avoidable, even in principle, therefore (iii) the tripartite account is irreparably inadequate in principle.

Correctly, lemma 1 does not presuppose the adequacy of the tripartite account. This is the lemma that will be taken into consideration.

The crucial point in lemma 1 is to try to show that (ii) is not the case. Now this may be attempted by revising the tripartite account in only three ways:

a. by strengthening/modifying the only flexible feature of the account, namely the justification condition (iii) (Chisholm (1989)); or
b. by adding at least one more condition that would prevent the Gettierization of the required justified true beliefs or, alternatively, allow their de-Gettierization; or
c. by combining (a) and (b).

No other general strategies are available, in the sense that anything more radical than (a)–(c) amounts to a de facto rejection of the tripartite account. Plato, for example, departs from it, after having considered its viability in the *Theaetetus* (see below).

Let me recapitulate. If there is any chance that the tripartite definition of knowledge may ever become adequate, it must somehow be possible to avoid or overcome Gettier-type counterexamples, at least in theory. In order to show that the counterexamples are avoidable, one may try to revise the definition in three ways.

Each of the three strategies has been probed and applied in various ways, usually following the reasonable maxim of keeping changes to a minimum. Yet four decades of relentless effort have yielded no ultimate solution or even a point of convergence.[2] This raises circumstantial doubts as to whether Gettier-type counterexamples may indeed be avoidable at all (Kirkham (1984), Schreiber (1987), Craig (1990), and Zagzebski (1994)) without abandoning the tripartite approach. This chapter sets out to demonstrate that they are not avoidable and, most importantly, to explain why they can never be, no matter how the tripartite account is revised, improved or expanded. It follows that the tripartite account is not merely inadequate as it is, but demonstrably irreparable in principle. We should stop trying to fix it and start looking for a different approach. In the following chapters, I will suggest that our understanding of propositional knowledge could be based on an informational analysis.

---

[2] See Griffiths (1967), Roth and Galis (1970), Pappas and Swain (1978), Pappas (1979), Shope (1983), Plantinga (1993a), (1993b), Floridi (1996), Steup (2001).

9.2 Why the Gettier problem is unsolvable in principle

To prove that the tripartite account is irreparably inadequate in principle, it is sufficient to prove three more lemmas:

Lemma 2: all Gettier-type counterexamples are instances of a single Gettier Problem (GP).

Lemma 3: (i) if the tripartite account can become adequate, at least in principle, then GP can be solved, at least in principle; but (ii) GP is not solvable, even in principle, therefore (iii) the tripartite account is irreparably inadequate, even in principle.

Lemma 4: GP is logically equivalent to the so-called 'coordinated attack' problem.

As we shall see, a group of important theorems in epistemic logic proves that the 'coordinated attack' problem and some of its variations are logically unsolvable.[3] Thus, proving lemma 4 means proving that the Gettier problem too is logically unsolvable (one of the first to draw attention to the connection between Gettier's analysis and epistemic logic was Lenzen (1978)). Once this is established, it is simple to see that lemma 3 shows that the tripartite account is irreparably inadequate in principle. Of course, all this applies only given the constraints posed by the tripartite account itself. The proviso is crucial, and I shall say more about it in the conclusion. For the moment, consider the problem of squaring the circle. The problem is not that of constructing a square equal in area to a circle, but of doing so by using only algebraic means (straight-edge and compass). Once Lindemann proved that π is transcendental (not an algebraic number of any degree), it became clear that solving the problem and satisfying its constraints were mutually exclusive. We shall see that the same holds true of GP. Given the conditions set up by the tripartite account of knowledge, Gettier-type counter-examples are unavoidable in principle, no matter what new strategies are then adopted to improve the account. It seems that Plato's view is vindicated: the very idea of defining knowledge on a doxastic basis, in terms of true justified belief, proves to be misguided. Let us now turn to the proof.

Lemma 3 simply follows from 1 and 2 and lemma 2 is trivial. Epistemologists agree (see for example Steup (1996)) that there are countless Gettier-type counterexamples but only one logical problem, namely a *lack of successful coordination* (more on this in section 9.3) between the truth of *p* and the reasons that justify *S* in holding that *p*. A Gettier-type counterexample arises because the truth and the justification of *p* happen to be not only independent (as they should be, since in this context we are dealing with fallibilist knowledge) but also opaquely unrelated, that is, they happen to fail to converge or to agree on the same propositional content *p* in a relevant and significant

---

[3] A full formalization of the results concerning the 'coordinated attack' problem is provided in Fagin et al. (1995), Halpern and Moses (1990) and in Fagin et al. (1995). To my knowledge, the best introduction to the problem and to other relevant results in epistemic logic is still Halpern (1995).

way, without S realizing it (*Gettierization*). Once this feature is grasped, anyone can produce her own favourite counterexample. Thus, Shope (1983) lists ninety-eight examples in the literature, and Zagzebski (1994) provides an elegant recipe for cooking up your own. Yet nobody would expect each counterexample to require its own specific solution. If you are still not convinced, consider the following argument.

Suppose one argues that Gettier-type counterexamples can be avoided by making sure that the truth and the justification of p are successfully coordinated, and hence that all one needs to add to the tripartite account is a fourth clause specifying that:

iv. the relationship between the truth of p and S's justification for p is successfully coordinated.

Adding (iv) would be begging the question because it would be equivalent to adding a clause specifying that:

iv*. the relationship between the truth of p and S's justification for p is not Gettierizable.

But clause (iv*) is precisely what the revised version of the tripartite account needs to achieve, in order to qualify as an adequate account of propositional knowledge, not something that can merely be decreed by *fiat*. Now, the fact that (iv) and (iv*) are logically equivalent shows that Gettier-type counterexamples are caused by a lack of successful coordination between the truth and the justification of p, namely GP.

The demonstration of the logical unsolvability of GP really rests on the possibility of proving lemma 4, the only one which is not trivial. The proof can be introduced by considering a familiar Gettier scenario. Note that, in view of further discussion in section 9.3, it will be useful to pay attention to the fallibilist nature of the types of knowledge discussed.

John Smith has dental problems. Two molar teeth in his right mandible have initial interproximal caries (known as IIC). His dentist, Tracy (in the following analysis she will stand for the truth resource, hence the T for Tracy), suspects that *John's teeth have IIC* (call the sentence in italics p), but she is unable to detect its presence by clinical observation. Her true belief that p is therefore an unsubstantiated intuition, a lucky hunch. However, Tracy knows that visual detection of IIC is often difficult, so she refers John to a dental radiologist, Jane (in the following analysis, she will stand for the justification resource, hence the J for Jane), for a CDR (Computer Digital Radiography). Taking a CDR is usually a reliable procedure to diagnose IIC, although of course it is still entirely fallible. Suppose the CDR shows that John's molar teeth are affected by IIC. Jane has now very strong evidence in favour of p. However, unaided by Tracy, she too cannot correctly claim to know that p. Interpreting a CDR is a procedure that requires some expertise, so there is a chance that Jane might be mistaken and hold a false belief. At this point, Tracy by herself does not yet know that p because she might be merely lucky, and Jane does not yet know that p because she might be wrong, although reasonably justified. GP is going to affect Tracy, while sceptical problems affect Jane, but that is another story. The hope is that Jane and Tracy may be individually necessary and jointly sufficient. Clearly, they need to coordinate their efforts. Jane emails the CDR to Tracy. Unfortunately, she sends the CDR of a homonymous patient, who also suffers from IIC. Were Tracy to rely on this piece of evidence, she would be justified in believing that p, yet she would still not know that p, for she would be merely lucky. As it happens, Tracy notices a number of inconsistencies between the CDR and what she knows about her patient. She concludes that there must have been a mistake and that the allegedly supporting evidence is in fact irrelevant. So, she asks Jane to make sure that she sends the CDR of the right John Smith. Jane sends a new email, this time with the relevant CDR. Unfortunately, the actual traces of IIC in John's molar teeth have been transposed during the imaging process. This is unlikely but possible. John's mandible was not optimally positioned and now it looks as if John has two molar teeth with IIC in the right *maxilla*. Again, were Tracy to rely on this second CDR, she would have a true and justified belief that p, yet still fail to know that p. A less experienced dentist might be fooled, but not Tracy. Noticing some anomalies in the shape and granularity of the CDR, she asks Jane to re-process the image. Finally, a correct CDR for the right John Smith reaches Tracy. Unfortunately, it fails to show the caries because of their very early stage of development. At the same time, the CDR can be interpreted as showing that John has IIC in two molar teeth of the right mandible, due to the presence of tartar and some noise in the data. At this point, there are two scenarios. Tracy may no longer trust her source of justification and so suspend her epistemic commitment. She does not claim to know that p, but opts for some epistemically weaker attitude, for example she says the she suspects that p or that she is quite confident that p. Alternatively, Tracy may rely completely on the evidence provided by the radiography, concluding correctly, but only by chance, that John suffers from IIC, a typical Gettier case. If she is epistemically cautious, she will not immediately operate on John, thus making a mistake, although arguably a small and recoverable one. If she makes an epistemic mistake and misreads the CDR, she will operate on John immediately, thus succeeding in her duties, to the advantage of John's health, yet merely by chance. In either case, she does not know that p.

The example presents GP in a distributed system scenario. The two resources, truth and justification, are introduced as agents interacting to achieve a common goal. This feature is not very common in philosophical literature, but it is useful to add further generality and clarity to the present analysis. Interpreting the epistemic subject S as a stand-alone, single agent is only a case limit (the Cartesian subject) and not even the most interesting. On the contrary, looking at the problem from a multi-agent, distributed system perspective, we can more easily identify GP as a problem of coordination between resources, in the following way.

Consider our two agents in more general and abstract terms, as parts of a simple, multi-agent, distributed system.[4] When speaking of agents in this sense it is vital that

---

[4] For a very good introduction to agents and distributed systems see Wooldridge (2002).

we are clear that these are *not* knowing subjects like S. On the contrary, like the generals in the 'coordinated attack' problem (see below), Tracy and Jane are (clusters of) *resources* that have to be coordinated to deliver a product, in this case knowledge. More specifically, Tracy is any truth-producing oracle T, consisting of whatever resources are sufficient to generate $n \geq 1$ true propositions $\{p_1, p_2, \ldots, p_n\}$. Jane is any justification-producing reasoner J, consisting of whatever resources are sufficient to justify T's true propositions. Their shared goal is to deliver propositional knowledge that p for $p \in \{p_1, p_2, \ldots, p_n\}$. One can picture this as the goal of defeating a third agent, Charles, a propositional-knowledge challenger C consisting of whatever resources are sufficient to prove that no propositional knowledge that p has been delivered. Let us assume the most favourable case in which

a. T and J are non-faulty (they never fail to behave according to their specifications). Note that this condition is not essential, but just a matter of convenience. In this context, we shall deal with the case that is most favourable to the tripartite account. If the agents can be faulty, scepticism arises, and one has the less favourable case represented by the untrustworthy agents known as the 'Byzantine generals', see Pease et al. (1980) and Fagin et al. (1995);

b. The communication medium between T and J is reliable and fault-tolerant but (provably) not fault-free. This is equivalent to saying that the case of knowledge in question is fallible;

c. T and J deal with the same p;

d. T and J are individually necessary to produce propositional knowledge that p (i.e. To defeat C);

e. If T and J can coordinate their efforts successfully, then they are also jointly sufficient to produce propositional knowledge that p (i.e. To defeat C);

f. T and J are *non-strategic agents*. Strategic agents act in their own interests, whereas *non-strategic* agents follow rules given to them; this assumption makes more precise the intuitive view that there is some sort of harmony between the justification and the truth of p. Again, the condition is assumed for the sake of simplicity.

Enquiring whether the tripartite account can be revised, so that it provides an adequate analysis of propositional knowledge in terms of necessary and sufficient conditions, means enquiring whether one can ensure that the two *agents* T and J can defeat the third *agent* C. The trivial answer is that, in order to ensure their victory, it is sufficient to ensure that T and J succeed in coordinating their efforts. This prompts the interesting question whether, given conditions (a)–(f), there is indeed a way in which the two agents can interact through some communication protocol that guarantees that they succeed in coordinating their efforts. This is equivalent to saying that the tripartite account can become adequate only if GP can be solved, and that GP can be solved only if the problem of a successful coordination between the two agents T and J (the truth and the justification of p) can be solved. And this is lemma 4.

Although not in the same terms, the general point made by lemma 4 is often stressed by some of the best and most influential analyses of GP, such as Goldman (1967) and

Nozick (1981). We have seen that possible strategies to achieve indefeasible coordination (mind, not *indefeasible knowledge*) comprise a modification of the nature of clause
(iii) in the tripartite account, and/or an addition of at least a fourth condition.
Unfortunately, the coordination problem is demonstrably unsolvable.[5] This is so no
matter which strategy is adopted (here the proviso discussed above in connection with
squaring the circle applies). Let us see why.

T and *J* are any two agents/resources that are individually necessary to achieve a
particular goal—in our case, achieving propositional and fallible knowledge that *p* by
defeating *C*—but need to be successfully coordinated (i.e. need to interact *in a certain
way*, which can be left unspecified here, for reasons given in section 9.3) to become
jointly sufficient as a dynamic system. The coordination problem arises because the two
resources *T* and *J* are not only logically but also empirically independent, so they do not
yet deliver knowledge (let alone indefeasible knowledge), but need to rely for their
communication/coordination on some empirical interaction, which cannot be assumed to be completely fault-free. Now, this system can be elegantly modelled in
terms of a distributed, asynchronous message-passing system, like Tracy and Jane, or
two divisions of an army attacking a common enemy, or three or more Byzantine
(i.e. unreliable) generals, or *T* and *J* playing against *C*. Or it can be modelled by a
synchronous message-passing system, in which message delivery is as reliable as one
might wish but still not fault-free, that is, a system in which a message can take an
arbitrarily long time to arrive (on this distinction see Halpern (1995)). Since the
tripartite account aims at establishing necessary and sufficient conditions for propositional knowledge, the question whether GP is solvable in principle is equivalent to the
question whether there can be a time *t* at which the *n* (for $n \geq 2$) agents involved are
successfully coordinated with respect to *p*. In the case of a message-passing system, the
latter question is modelled as the question whether there is a communication protocol
that can guarantee coordination between the *n* agents at a certain time in the future
with respect to *p*. No protocol satisfies these requirements. This is proved in terms of a
regressus ad infinitum. *T* and *J* are separate and independent agents playing against a third
agent *C*. It is clear that if both agents play against *C* simultaneously they will defeat
him, while if only one agent plays against *C* she will be defeated. The agents do not
have pre-established strategies (this means that we are dealing with fallible knowledge)
and *T* wishes to coordinate a simultaneous move against *C* at some time *t*. Neither
agent will play unless she is sure that the other will play at the same time. In particular,
an agent will not play if she receives no messages. The agents can communicate by
means of messages. It takes a message some time $t \geq 1$ to get from the sender to the
receiver. However, the message may get lost or corrupted. How long will it take them
to coordinate a move against *C*? Suppose *T* sends a message *m* to *J* saying 'Let's play
move *s* against *C* at time *t'*. *J* receives *m*. Now *J* is informed that *m* (in standard notation:

---

[5] Gray (1978) and Halpern and Moses (1990) provide full coverage of the proof; the reader will find in
Floridi (2004b) a brief summary of the relevant theorems.

K_Jm), but will J play move s? Of course not, since the channel of communication is not fault-free, and T cannot be sure that she (J) received the message she (T) sent, and thus may not play. So J replies with an acknowledgement. Suppose the message reaches T. Now K_TK_Jm holds. So will T play move s? No, because now J does not have the information that T received the message, so J thinks that T may think that she (J) did not receive the original message, and thus not play. The next acknowledgment brings us to $K_JK_TK_Jm$, and so forth. The *regressus ad infinitum* is obvious. Each time a message is received, the depth of the agents' information increases by one, yet there is no stage at which they are both informed that they are both informed that ... they will play move s at time t. The agents never attain *common information* (basically in the technical sense of 'common knowledge', see Fagin et al. (1995)) that the move s is to be played at time t, because there is no protocol of communication that allows the distributed system to reach the established *fixed point*. As long as there is a possibility that the message may be lost or corrupted—and this possibility is guaranteed by the empirical and hence fallible nature of the interaction between the agents—common information is unattainable, even if the message is in fact delivered.

To summarize: successful coordination is a prerequisite for guaranteeing a successful game move, but common information is a prerequisite for guaranteeing successful coordination, and common information is unattainable in any distributed system in which there is any doubt at all about message delivery time. Such doubt is inevitable, if the agents are at least logically independent and must interact through empirical protocols. The tripartite account sets up exactly such a distributed system. T and J are logically separate resources in need of empirical coordination to be able to deliver knowledge that p. We now know that there is no communication protocol that guarantees that they will be successfully coordinated to produce knowledge that p. Of course, this does not mean that they cannot be coordinated sometimes or even often, or that sub-optimal strategies cannot be devised (Halpern and Tuttle (1993), Morris and Shin (1997)), but it does prove that counterexamples are inevitable in principle. The epistemic agent S may know that p but has no way of ascertaining that the truth of p, i.e. the resource T to which S has access, and the justification for p, i.e. the resource J that is also available to S, which are sufficient to provide S with propositional knowledge that p, unless S can be sure that they are indeed successfully coordinated with respect to p.[6] But the latter condition is unachievable in principle given the system set up by the tripartite account.

9.3 Three objections and replies

The proof can be further clarified by considering some potential objections.

One might ask whether the argument presented above implicitly presupposes an interpretation of knowledge as *indefeasible*, *certain*, or *infallible*. All these positions are at

---

[6] A similar point is made by Apel (1975) and Alston (1986).

least controversial and would be utterly inadequate in the context of a discussion of the tripartite account of knowledge, which, as we have seen, explicitly addresses empirical knowledge of a *fallibilist* kind.

This concern is reasonable, and its roots may be traced to the technical vocabulary required by the analysis of the coordination problem. The reader will recall, for example, that it has been argued that the question whether GP may be solvable in principle is equivalent to the question whether there can be a time t at which the resources involved are successfully coordinated with respect to p. However, this concern can be allayed once we clearly distinguish between

    i. how one qualifies the kind of coordination required between the resources that are necessary and sufficient for a successful delivery of fallible knowledge, and

    ii. how one qualifies the knowledge delivered.

The medical example chosen in the discussion, and the careful constraint placed on any sceptical drift, were meant to facilitate and support this distinction, but an analogy may make it sharper. Suppose that two independent processes, say packaging and handling, are individually necessary and jointly sufficient to deliver a box of fresh eggs unbroken to your house, as long as they are successfully coordinated. One may qualify this condition—successful coordination—in several ways. Suppose that, unless the coordination is 100 per cent successful, there is no guarantee that the eggs will be delivered unbroken. Of course, none of this is going to affect the intrinsic fragility of the eggs. Nor is it equivalent to saying that the eggs cannot be delivered unbroken when coordination is less than fully successful. The delivery may be successful just by luck. Let us now assume that the shop will not send you the eggs unless there is 100 per cent successful coordination between the two processes. The proof offered in the previous section shows that such a level of coordination is unattainable in principle, no matter how one modifies the processes involved, or how far one extends their number and scope. Of course, the proof may still be questioned—but not the fact that the attainability (or unattainability) of coordination is independent of the 'fragility' of the specific case of fallibilist propositional knowledge taken into consideration. To use the terminology of the 'coordinated attack' problem, unless the coordination is guaranteed, only a risky attack can be launched, but this begs the question, since the problem requires the launching of a completely safe attack. The necessary resources are also *jointly* sufficient only in a 'well-coordinated' sense of 'jointly'. Obviously, most of the time one can have knowledge that p by having true and justified beliefs that p, but this is not what we are looking for. We are seeking instead a definition of knowledge in terms of necessary and sufficient conditions, such that, if obtained, they successfully deliver 'fragile' knowledge 'unbroken'.

A different but related concern, because it still addresses the correct focus of the argument, can be phrased thus: suppose the argument does prove that Gettier counter-examples are inevitable in principle, isn't this a solution to Gettier's challenge? Yet the challenge was not

a. for us never to be Gettierized; but was

b. for us to understand what it is not to be Gettierized.

So there seems to be a worrying level of confusion afflicting the argument.

This new concern can be resolved in two steps. First, the argument does provide a solution to the Gettier problem, but only a negative one. The real achievement would not be to show that the tripartite account of knowledge is inadequate—this is precisely what the Gettier problem is about—but to prove that the Gettier problem is unsolvable *no matter how one tries to revise and improve the original account*, and hence that the inadequacy of the account cannot be remedied. This clarification leads to the second step, which concerns the alleged confusion between (a) and (b). It is certainly important to distinguish between understanding a challenge, as stressed in (b), and meeting it successfully, as specified in (a). But it is also equally important to understand that, in a negative proof, (a) and (b) are strictly connected. Recall the comparison with the squaring of the circle: a better understanding of the mathematical nature of π leads to a proof that it is impossible. Now, the argument proceeds exactly along the same lines. It shows that the Gettier problem is a special case of the 'coordinated attack' problem by showing that it is a problem about the coordination between whatever resources are deemed necessary and sufficient to deliver knowledge. This amounts to understanding what it is for us not to be Gettierized, that is, (b). But once this is clear, it becomes equally clear that the problem is unsolvable. And this amounts to proving that it is impossible never to be Gettierized, given the preconditions set by the standard account, that is, (a). If the challenge is properly understood, it becomes clear that it cannot be met.

Once the focus of the argument is fully vindicated, one may still have reservations about its formulation. One may suspect that the argument presented above depends on some equivocation regarding the crucial concept of 'coordination'. For

1. 'coordination' between T and J is presumably meant to correspond to the generals' *common knowledge* that they will both attack,

but

2. there is no warrant for assuming that the reason why knowledge fails in Gettier-type counterexamples is lack of common knowledge of justified true belief, or anything sufficiently formally analogous to it to satisfy the conditions for a generalized version of the negative findings concerning a coordinated attack. In fact,

3. any sense of 'coordination' that allows epistemologists to agree that lack of coordination between truth and justification is the key to the Gettier problem (as claimed above) is an extremely vague and unspecific one, and little more than a label for the problem.

In particular

4. it is not agreed that coordination is an epistemic relation rather than one of, for example, causation or counterfactual dependence. In the one-person case,

having common knowledge that one has justified true belief entails knowing that one knows that the belief is true; but since many epistemologists reject the KK principle ('positive introspection'), common knowledge cannot be assumed to be necessary for knowledge itself. Similar considerations apply in the many-person case.

But if this is the case, then

5. no plausible prima facie case for lemma 4 has been made, which is essential to the argument of the chapter.

The objection highlights some important features of the argument. Regarding (1), the suggestion is plausible but mistaken. The confusion concerns the level of analysis. Coordination between T and J does not correspond to the generals' *common knowledge* about the correct message m containing the time at which they will attack but to their coordination, interpretable as the synchronization of their actions. The generals' synchronization can only be guaranteed by, but is clearly different from, their common knowledge of m (for example, the generals may be lucky and be coordinated even without common knowledge). Their synchronization in turn guarantees, but is also different from, the safety of their action and hence the success of their attack. The attack never takes place because (a) the generals attack only if 'failure is not an option' and (b) their common knowledge of m requires perfectly fault-free communication, which is unobtainable in the given circumstances.

Since (1) is not the case, (2) is correct but does not apply. The argument is not that knowledge fails in Gettier-type counterexamples because the epistemic subject S lacks common knowledge of justified true belief. If this were the case, the argument would indeed have to be rejected. The argument is that knowledge fails in Gettier-type counterexamples because there are cases in which, although T and J are both available to S, one can still show that there is no coordination between T and J or, better, Gettier-type counterexamples prove that it is impossible to guarantee that an epistemic commitment by the system $T + J$ will be safe and hence successful in delivering propositional knowledge that p. This possible lack of coordination cannot be overcome because it is caused by a lack of common knowledge, not by S, but between the two agents T and J, and not of justified true belief, but of the relevant circumstances, that is, coordination, in which the system can make a safe epistemic commitment. Hence S's lack of common knowledge of justified true belief is irrelevant here. Compare the generals' common knowledge of m as against the generals' actual launch of the attack. The lack of common knowledge between T and J is caused by the absence of fault-free communication, which is unobtainable given the specified constraints. In other words, $T + J$ cannot guarantee delivery of propositional knowledge. Thus, the point of the argument lies in modelling T and J as two agents/resources and their interaction as a message-passing procedure. In this way, one can appreciate the fact that Gettier-type counterexamples show that, no matter how many times the two agents T and J check and double-check that they are properly coordinated, no fixed point can ever be reached. It is always possible that T and J may in the end fail to be coordinated.

Regarding (3), the objection is correct in pointing out the unspecified nature of the relation of coordination between T and J. However, it is *useful* to keep the relation unspecified precisely because this makes the result applicable to any interpretation of it (see points (1)–(3) in the Conclusion). And it is *not necessary* to specify the nature of the coordination relation. This is so because the failure to deliver propositional knowledge does not depend on a particular interpretation of it, but on the fact that, whichever way the relation is interpreted, it requires common knowledge, which in turn requires communication between the n agents involved, and the communication, being fallible, can never eliminate the possibility of Gettier-type counterexamples.

Regarding (4), we have seen that the argument does not equate successful coordination and common knowledge, contrary to the assumption in objection (1). Nor does it imply any other epistemic interpretation of coordination, for it leaves it unspecified. As for the acceptance of the KK thesis, the objection is correct in pointing out that KK is controversial, but this is also as far as the objection can go, for two reasons. First, suppose the argument did entail KK; this might still be taken as a reason in favour of the popularity of epistemic systems such as S4 and S5, rather than a *reductio*, so the objection may be answered on a purely logical ground. Second, and most importantly, the argument does not entail KK in any way that facilitates the objection in the first place, so there is no problem. According to the argument, for the *epistemic commitment* of the system $T + J$ to be safe, T and J need to be successfully coordinated. For this to be the case, T and J need to achieve common knowledge of the relevant circumstances in which they can make a safe epistemic commitment, i.e. the message m. It is important to clarify what the claim is here. Common knowledge between T and J is not *necessary* for knowledge itself—we have seen in section 9.2 that the agents may decide to adopt sub-optimal strategies, which can still deliver a result sometimes—but it is necessary for any epistemic commitment that needs to be absolutely safe, i.e. that guarantees the fulfilment of necessary and sufficient conditions for the delivery of propositional and fallible knowledge that p. Recall that the original theorem proves that the generals never attack, given the constraints in place; it does not prove that they could not win, should they decide to attack anyway. The generals can win the battle without having common knowledge, but they should not commit themselves to attacking the enemy in the first place, given the constraints they share. Likewise, T and J may deliver propositional knowledge without sharing common knowledge (so $K_S p$ does not require or entail $K_S K_S p$), but no epistemic commitment (no delivery of p) is guaranteed to be successful without their coordination, which requires them to achieve common knowledge. This common knowledge requires fault-free communication, which is not achievable because of the constraints posed by the tripartite account itself: $T + J$ cannot claim $K_S p$ with total certainty without T and J being successfully coordinated, something unachievable given the tripartite account.

CONCLUSION

It would be a mistake to interpret the coordination problem as a mere message-passing issue. For the latter is not the difficulty itself but an elegant way of modelling the dynamic interactions between $n \geq 2$ agents (resources, processes, conditions, etc.), in order to prove that the goal of ensuring successful coordination in a distributed system, such as the tripartite account, is insurmountable. The real difficulty is that, if T and J are independent (as they should be, given the fact that we are speaking of empirical, fallible knowledge), the logical possibility of a lack of coordination is inevitable and there is no way of making sure that they will deliver knowledge in a Gettier-proof way. In the absence of coordination, the agents will play only at the risk of defeat, or they will not play, if the cost of a defeat is too high. Likewise, since it is one of the tripartite account's constraints that T and J are not pre-coordinated, the system $T + J$ will at best be able to claim to know that p only defeasibly (Quine *docet*), or will not commit itself epistemically (this is the initial Cartesian option in the *Meditations*, while waiting for the discovery of the *Cogito*). The possibility of GP cannot be eliminated. Recall Tracy the dentist. In the end, either she trusts the CDR, inadvertently running the risk of not knowing that p, or she suspends her commitment, admitting that she may still not know that p, even if she is absolutely right about p. Either way, she never reaches the time t at which one (or she) can say for sure that she knows that p. The conclusion is that GP is logically unsolvable and now we know why. The tripartite account asks us to find a way to coordinate T and J successfully while satisfying constraints—empirical interaction between T and J as two independent resources—that, by their very nature, make it impossible to achieve the set goal, exactly like squaring the circle.

At this point, it should be clear that the logical unsolvability of the Gettier problem as a special case of the 'coordinated attack' problem holds true independently of any modification in the nature of J (including its relation to T) and/or any addition of extra agents beside J and T. Indeed, other variables can play no useful role. The following is a list of those that have attracted most attention in the literature. The Gettier problem/ 'coordinated attack' problem are logically unsolvable:

1. whatever the nature of the coordination protocols relating T and J, including truth-tracking and a (non-instantaneous) synchronic, causal interaction; recall the case of the synchronous message-passing system outlined above;
2. whatever the degree of reliability satisfied by the coordination protocols;
3. whatever, and no matter how many relations (e.g. internalist, externalist) may occur between the truth and the justification of p; (the previous three points further clarify why it is useful to leave the nature of the coordination unspecified);
4. whatever interpretation is offered of the concepts of truth and justification. The two agents, players, or divisions attacking a common enemy, can be as strong as one wishes and the two generals as smart as Alexander The Great and Julius Caesar;

5. whether the original concepts, especially justification, are replaced by other resources, e.g. well-foundedness or warrant (Plantinga (1993a), (1993b)). This is convincingly argued by Crisp (2000) and Pust (2000), even if in rather different terms;

6. whether any other agent (any other epistemic resource) is added, as long as all agents are still individually necessary and jointly sufficient only if successfully coordinated. Indeed, the analysis of the 'Byzantine generals' is usually based on $n \geq 3$ agents, see Fagin et al. (1995);

7. whether one models the various components as $n \geq 2$ agents in a distributed system or as $n \geq 2$ processes in a single agent (even in the latter case, it is a matter of granularity).

All this holds true *provided* that the $n \geq 2$ epistemic resources in question are logically independent and need to be successfully coordinated through a less than fault-free communication protocol to achieve their common goal. The previous proviso is crucial, as it makes clear that many alleged 'solutions' of the Gettier Problem/'coordinated attack' problem turn out to be fallacious. For they all presuppose or advocate some form of 'pre-established harmony', such as pre-coordination, instantaneous synchronicity, reduction of the $n \geq 2$ agents T and J to 1, or some fault-free and simultaneous protocol of communication between T and J. Similar 'Leibnizian' strategies do implement perfect coordination, and hence solve GP, but, apart from being unrealistic, they fail to respect the tripartite account's empirical constraints. Since p is an empirical and fallible proposition, its T and J cannot be assumed to be pre-coordinated a priori, in a way that makes their lack of coordination logically impossible, so similar strategies beg the question, in that they are all equivalent to a mere 'no-Gettierization' assumption.

Since GP is demonstrably unsolvable, it follows not only that the tripartite account is logically inadequate as it is, but also that it is irretrievably so in principle. GP is not a mere anomaly, requiring the rectification of an otherwise stable and acceptable account of propositional knowledge. It is proof that the core of the approach needs to be abandoned. But what needs to be abandoned? The task of the next chapter is to show, among other things, that it is the doxastic dogma that might be part of the trouble: a may know that p because a may be *informed* that p (plus other conditions of well-foundedness) where 'being informed' requires a different, non-doxastic analysis.

10

The logic of being informed

No one can venture with the help of logic alone to judge regarding objects, or to make any assertion. We must first, independently of logic, obtain reliable information; only then are we in a position to enquire, in accordance with logical laws, into the use of this information and its connection in a coherent whole, or rather to test it by these laws.

Kant, *Critique of Pure Reason*

SUMMARY

Previously, in chapter two, I discussed the problem (see P2) whether there might be an *information logic* (*IL*), different from *epistemic* (*EL*) and *doxastic logic* (*DL*), which formalizes the relation '*a* is informed that *p*' ($I_a p$) satisfactorily. In this chapter, I defend the view that the axiom schemata of the normal modal logic **KTB** (also known as **B** or **Br** or Brouwer's system) are well suited to model the relation of 'being informed'. After having shown that *IL* can be constructed as an informational reading of **KTB**, four consequences of a **KTB**-based *IL* are explored: information overload; the veridicality thesis ($I_a p \rightarrow p$); the relation between *IL* and *EL*; and the $Kp \rightarrow Bp$ principle or *entailment property*, according to which knowledge implies belief. Although these issues are discussed later in the chapter, they are the motivations behind the development of *IL* and the elaboration of this chapter at this point of the book, for they prepare the ground for an informational analysis of knowledge, developed in the following two chapters.[1]

10.1 Introduction

As anyone acquainted with modal logic (*ML*) knows, *epistemic logic* (*EL*) formalizes the relation '*a* knows that *p*' ($K_a p$), whereas *doxastic logic* (*DL*) formalizes the relation

---

[1] When revising the proofs of the book I had the opportunity to read Allo (forthcoming). His analysis is based on, and develops the conclusions reached in Floridi (2006) and hence in this chapter. It provides a pure and an applied semantics for the logic of being informed consistent with the main theses defended here, with a convergence that should be reassuring for the reader. Note, however, that Allo defends a semantics for *IL* based on non-normal possible worlds.

'*a* believes that *p*' ($B_a p$). We saw in chapter two that one of the open problems in the philosophy of information is whether there is also an *information logic* (*IL*), different from *EL* and from *DL*, that formalizes the relation '*a* is informed that *p*' ($I_a p$) equally well. The keyword here is 'equally' not 'well'. One may contend that *EL* and *DL* do not capture the relevant relations very well or even not well at all. Hocutt (1972), for example, provides an early criticism. Yet this is not the point here, since what I shall argue in this chapter is that *IL* can do for 'being informed' what *EL* does for 'knowing' and *DL* does for 'believing'. If one objects to the last two, one may also object to the first, yet one should not object to it more.

The proposal developed in the following pages is that the normal modal logic (*NML*) **KTB** (also known as **B**, **Br** or Brouwer's system[2]) is well suited to model the relation of 'being informed', and hence that *IL* can be constructed as an informational reading of **KTB**. The proposal is presented in three sections.

In section 10.1, several meanings of 'information' are recalled, in order to focus only on the 'cognitive' sense. Three main ways in which one may speak of a 'logic of (cognitive) information' are then distinguished. Only one of them is immediately relevant here, namely, '*a* is informed that *p*' as meaning '*a* holds the information that *p*'. These clarifications are finally used to make precise the specific question addressed in the rest of the chapter.

In section 10.2, the analysis of the informational relation of 'being informed' provides the specifications to be satisfied by its accurate formalization. It is then shown that **KTB** successfully captures the relation of 'being informed'.

In section 10.3, once it is established that there is an *IL* different from *EL* and from *DL*, four consequences of a **KTB**-based *IL* are briefly explored: information overload; the veridicality thesis ($Ip \rightarrow p$); the relation between *IL* and *EL*; and the entailment property or $Kp \rightarrow Bp$ principle, according to which knowledge implies belief. Although they are discussed later in the chapter, these four issues are the motivations behind the development of *IL*. In the conclusion, I introduce the work that remains to be done.

Throughout the chapter the ordinary language of classical, propositional calculus (PC) and of propositional *NML* (see for example Girle (2000)) will be presupposed. Implication ($\rightarrow$) is used in its 'material' sense; the semantics is Kripkean; Greek letters are metalinguistic, propositional variables ranging over well-formed formulae of the object language of the corresponding NML; and until section 10.2.6 attention is focused only on the axiom schemata of the NMLs in question.

---

[2] The name was assigned by Becker (1930). As Goldblatt (2003) remarks: 'The connection with Brouwer is remote: if 'not' is translated to 'impossible' ($\neg \lozenge$), and 'implies' to its strict version, then the intuitionistically acceptable principle $p \rightarrow \neg \neg p$ becomes the Brouwersche axiom'. For a description of KTB see Hughes and Cresswell (1996).

10.2 Three logics of information

We saw in previous chapters that 'information' may be understood in many ways, e.g. as signals, natural patterns or nomic regularities, as instructions, as content, as news, as synonymous with data, as power, or as an economic resource, and so forth. It is notoriously controversial whether even most of these senses of 'information' might be reduced to a fundamental concept. However, one kind of 'information' that has been discussed in this book is arguably the most important. It is 'information' as *semantic content* that, on one side, concerns some state of a system, and that, on the other side, allows the elaboration of an agent's propositional knowledge of that state of the system. It is the sense in which Matthew is informed that *p*, e.g. that 'the train to London leaves at 10.30 a.m.', or about the state of affairs *f* expressed by *p*, e.g. the railway timetable. In the rest of the chapter, 'information' will be discussed only in this sense of truthful *semantic content* that *p* or about *f*. This sense may loosely be qualified as 'cognitive', a neutral label useful to refer here to a whole family of relations expressing propositional attitudes, including 'knowing', 'believing', 'remembering', 'perceiving', and 'experiencing'. As usual by now, any 'non-cognitive' sense of 'semantic information' will be disregarded.

The scope of our inquiry can now be narrowed by considering the logical analysis of the *cognitive* relation '*a* is informed that *p*'. Three related yet separate features of interest need to be further distinguished, namely:

a. how *p* may be informative for *a*.

For example, the information that $\neg p$ may or may not be informative depending on whether *a* is already informed that $(p \lor q)$. This aspect of information—the *informativeness* of a message for *a*—raises issues of e.g. novelty, reliability of the source, and background information. It is a crucial aspect related to the quantitative theory of semantic information (see chapter five), to the logic of transition states in dynamic system, that is, how change in a system may be informative for an observer (Barwise and Seligman (1997)), and to the theory of levels of abstraction at which a system is being considered (see chapter three). I shall return to this sense in the next chapter, when discussing *relevant* information;

b. the process through which *a* becomes informed that *p*.

The informativeness of *p* makes possible the process that leads from *a*'s uninformed (or less informed) state *A* to *a*'s (more) informed state *B*. Upgrading *a*'s state *A* to a state *B* usually involves receiving the information that *p* from some external source *S* and processing it. It implies that *a* cannot be informed that *p* unless *a* was previously uninformed that *p*. And the logical relation that underlies this state transition raises important issues of timeliness and cost of acquisition, for example, and of adequate procedures of information processing, including introspection and metainformation, as we shall see in chapter thirteen. It is related to information theory, temporal logic,

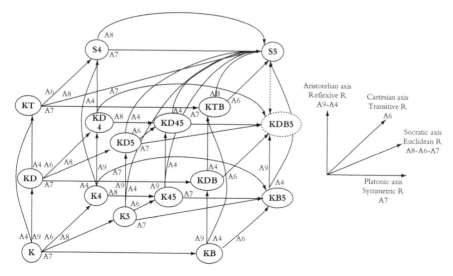

Figure 18 Fifteen normal modal logics. Note that KDB5 is a 'dummy' system: it is equivalent to S5 and it is added to the diagram just for the sake of elegance. Synonymous: T = M = KT; B = Br = KTB; D = KD. Equivalent axiomatic systems: B = TB; KB5 = KB4, KB45; S5 = T5, T45, TB4, TB5, TB45, DB4, DB5, DB45

updating procedures (Gärdenfors (1988)), and recent trends in dynamic epistemic logic (Baltag and Moss (2004));

c. the state of the epistemic agent *a*, insofar as *a holds* the information that *p*.

We have already encountered (c) in the previous chapter.

Point (a) requires the development of a logic of 'being informative'; (b) requires the development of a logic of 'becoming informed'; and (c) requires the development of a logic of 'being informed (i.e. holding the information)'. Work on (a) and (b) is already in progress. Allo (2005) and Sanders (forthcoming), respectively, develop two lines of research complementary to this chapter. Here, I shall be concerned with (c) and seek to show that there is a logic of information comparable, for adequacy, flexibility and usefulness, to *EL* and *DL*.

The problem can now be formulated more precisely. Let us concentrate our attention on the most popular and traditional *NML*, obtainable through the analysis of some of the well-known characteristics of the relation of accessibility (reflexivity, transitivity etc.). These fifteen[3] *NMLs* range from the weakest **K** to the strongest **S5** (see below Figure 18). They are also obtainable through the combination of the usual axiom schemata of PC with the fundamental modal axiom schemata (see below Figure 18). Both *EL* and *DL* comprise a number of cognitively interpretable *NML*, depending

---

[3] The number of *NMLs* available is infinite. I am grateful to Timothy Williamson and John Halleck who kindly warned me against a misleading wording in a previous version of this chapter.

on the sets of axioms that qualify the corresponding *NML* used to capture the relevant 'cognitive' notions. If we restrict our attention to the six most popular *EL* and *DL*—those based on systems **KT, S4, S5** and on systems **KD, KD4, KD45** respectively—the question about the availability of an information logic can be rephrased thus: among the popular *NMLs* taken into consideration, is there one, not belonging to {**KT, S4, S5, KD, KD4, KD45**}, which, if cognitively interpreted, can successfully capture and formalize our intuitions regarding '*a* is informed that *p*' in the (c) sense specified above?

A potential confusion may be immediately dispelled. Of course, the logical analysis of the cognitive relation of 'being informed' can sometimes be provided in terms of 'knowing' or 'believing', and hence of *EL* or *DL*. This is not in question, for it is trivially achievable, insofar as 'being informed' can sometimes be correctly, and indeed usefully, treated as synonymous with 'knowing' or 'believing'. We shall also see in section 10.3.3 that *IL* may sometimes overlap with *EL*. The interesting problem is whether 'being informed' may show properties that typically (i.e. whenever the overlapping would be unjustified, see section 10.3.3) require a logic different from *EL* and *DL*, in order to be modelled accurately. The hypothesis defended in the following pages is that it does and, moreover, that this has some interesting consequences for our understanding of the nature of the relation between 'knowing' and 'believing'.

10.3 Modelling 'being informed'

Let us interpret the modal operator $\Box$ as 'is informed that'. We may then replace the symbol $\Box$ with *I* for 'being informed', include an explicit reference to the informed agent *a*, and write

$$\Box p = I_a p \text{ to mean } a \text{ is informed (holds the information) that } p.^{4}$$

As customary, the subscript will be omitted whenever we shall be dealing with a single, stand-alone agent *a*. It will be reintroduced in section 10.3.4, when dealing with multiagent *IL*. Next, we can then define $\Diamond$ in the standard way, thus

$$U_a p =_{\text{def}} \neg I_a \neg p \text{ to mean } a \text{ is uninformed (is not informed, does not hold the information)}$$
that $\neg p$; or for all *a*'s information (given *a*'s information base), it is possible that *p*.

Simplifying, *a*'s information base can be modelled by representing it as a *dynamic*[5] set D_a of sentences of a language *L*. The intended interpretation is that D_a consists of all the

---

[4] A *de re* interpretation is obtainable by interpreting $I_a p$ as 'there is the information that *p*'.

[5] Dynamic sets are an important class of data structures in which sets of items, indexed by keys, are maintained. It is assumed that the elements of the dynamic set contain a field (called the key) by whose value they can be ordered. The phone directory of a company is a simple example of a dynamic set (it changes over time), whose key might be 'last name'. Dynamic sets can change over the execution of a process by gaining or losing elements. Of the variety of operations usually supported by a dynamic set, three are fundamental and will be assumed in this chapter:

Search(S,k) = given a set *S* and a key value *k*, a query operation that returns a pointer *x* to an element in *S* such that *key*[*x*] = *k*, or nil if no such element belongs to *S*.

information, that a holds at time t. We then have that $I_a p$ means that $p \in D_a$, and $U_a p$ means that p can be uploaded in D_a while maintaining the consistency of D_a, that is, $U_a p$ means $\lozenge\ (p \in D_a)$ *salva cohaerentiae*.[6] Note that a need not be committed, either doxastically (e.g. in terms of strengths of belief, Lenzen (1978)) or epistemically (e.g. in terms of degrees of certainty) in favour of any element in D_a.

Given that *IL* might actually overlap, and hence be confused with *EL* or *DL*, the most plausible conjecture is that an *IL* that can capture our intuitions, and hence satisfy our requirements regarding the proper formalization of *Ip*, will probably bear some strong resemblance to *EL* and *DL*. If there is any difference between these three families of cognitive logics it is likely to be identifiable more easily in terms of satisfaction (or lack thereof) of one or more axioms qualifying the corresponding *NML*. The heuristic assumption here is that, by restricting our attention to the fifteen *NMLs* in question, we may be able to identify the one which best captures our requirements. It is a bit like finding where, on a continuous map, the logic of information may be placed: even if we succeed in showing that **KTB** is the right *NML* for our task, there is still an infinite number of neighbouring *NMLs* extending **KTB**.[7]

For ease of reference, the axiom schemata in question are summarized and numbered progressively in Table 6, where ϕ, χ and ψ are propositional variables referring to any wff of PC. Following Hintikka's standard approach (Hintikka (1962)), a systematic way to justify the choice of some axiom schemata is by trying to identify a plausible interpretation of a semantics for the corresponding *NML*. We shall now consider the axiom schemata (see Table 6) and show that *IL* shares only some of them with *EL* and *DL*.

10.3.1 *IL satisfies* A_1, A_2, A_3, A_5

Trivially, we may assume that *IL* satisfies the axioms A_1–A_3. As for A_5, this specifies that *IL* is distributive, as it should be. If an agent a is informed that $p \to q$, then, if the same a is informed that p, that a is also informed that q. Note that, although this is entirely uncontroversial, it is less trivial. Not all 'cognitive' relations are distributive. 'Knowing', 'believing', and 'being informed' are, as well as 'remembering' and 'recalling'. This is why Plato is able to argue that a 'mnemonic logic', which he seems to base on **K4**, may replace *DL* as a foundation for *EL*.[8] However, 'seeing' and other experiential relations, for example, are not: if an agent a sees (in a visual, non-metaphorical sense) or hears or experiences or perceives that $p \to q$, it may still be false that, if a sees (hears etc.) p, a then also sees (hears etc.) q.

Insert(S,x) = an operation that augments the set S with the element x.

Delete(S,x) = an operation that removes an element pointed to by x from S (if it is there).

[6] As Patrick Allo has noted in a personal communication, this can also be expressed in terms of safety of inclusion of p in D_a.

[7] Many thanks to John Halleck for calling my attention to this point and to Miyazaki (2005).

[8] On Plato's interpretation of knowledge as recollection see especially *Phaedo* 72e–75 and *Meno* 82b–85.

Table 6 The axiom schemata of the propositional *NMLs*

Label	Definitions of Axiom Schemata	Name of the axiom or the corresponding *NML*	Frame
A_1	$\phi \rightarrow (\chi \rightarrow \phi)$	1st axiom of PC	
A_2	$(\phi \rightarrow (\chi \rightarrow \psi)) \rightarrow ((\phi \rightarrow \chi) \rightarrow (\phi \rightarrow \psi))$	2nd axiom of PC	
A_3	$(\neg \phi \rightarrow \neg \chi) \rightarrow (\chi \rightarrow \phi)$	3rd axiom of PC	
A_4	$\Box\phi \rightarrow \phi$	**KT** or **M**, K2, veridicality	Reflexive
A_5	$\Box(\phi \rightarrow \chi) \rightarrow (\Box\phi \rightarrow \Box\chi)$	**K**, distribution, deductive cogency	Normal
A_6	$\Box\phi \rightarrow \Box\Box\phi$	**4, S4**, K3, **KK**, reflective thesis or positive introspection	Transitive
A_7	$\phi \rightarrow \Box\Diamond\phi$	**KTB, B, Br**, Brouwer's axiom or Platonic thesis	Symmetric
A_8	$\Diamond\phi \rightarrow \Box\Diamond\phi$	**S5**, reflective, Socratic thesis or negative introspection	Euclidean
A_9	$\Box\phi \rightarrow \Diamond\phi$	**KD, D**, consistency	Serial
A_{10}	$\Box(\phi \rightarrow \chi) \rightarrow (\Box(\chi \rightarrow \psi) \rightarrow \Box(\phi \rightarrow \psi))$	Single agent transmission	
A_{11}	$\Box_x\Box_y\phi \rightarrow \Box_x\phi$	**K4**, multi-agent transmission, or Hintikka's axiom	

The inclusion or exclusion of the remaining seven axioms is more contentious. Although logically independent, the reasons leading to their inclusion or exclusion are not, and they suggest the following clustering. In section 10.3.2, *IL* is shown to satisfy not only A_9 (consistency) but also A_4 (veridicality). In section 10.3.3, it is argued that *IL* does not have to satisfy the two 'reflective' axioms, that is A_6 and A_8. And in section 10.3.4, it is argued that *IL* should satisfy the 'transmissibility' axioms A_{10} and A_{11}. This will leave us with A_7, to be discussed in section 10.3.5.

10.3.2 Consistency and truth: IL satisfies A_9 and A_4

In *DL*, A_9 replaces the stronger A_4, which characterizes *EL*: whereas p must be true for the epistemic agent a to know that p, the doxastic agent a only needs to be consistent in her beliefs. There are at least four reasons why *IL* should be characterized as satisfying A_9.

1 A_9 specifies that, in *IL*, the informational agent a is consistent, but so can be our ordinary informed agent in everyday life: $Ip \rightarrow Up$. If a holds the information that the train leaves at 10.30 a.m. then, for all a's information, it is possible that the train leaves at 10.30 a.m., in other words, p can be uploaded in a's information base D_a while maintaining the consistency of D_a.

2 Even if (1) were unconvincing, *IL* should qualify a as consistent at least normatively, if not factually, in the same way as *DL* does. If a holds the information that the train leaves at 10.30 a.m., then a should not hold the information that the train

does not leave at 10.30 a.m. The point is not that doxastic or informational agents cannot be inconsistent,[9] but that A_9 provides an information integrity constraint: inconsistent agents should be disregarded. Again, to appreciate the non-trivial nature of a normative approach to A_9, consider the case of a 'mnemonic logic'. It might be factually implausible and only normatively desirable to formalize 'a remembers that p' as implying that, if this is the case, then a does not remember that $\neg p$. Matthew may remember something that actually never happened, or he might remember both p (that he left the keys in the car) and $\neg p$ (that he left the keys on his desk) and be undecided about which memory is reliable. Likewise, if a database contains the information that p it might, unfortunately, still contain also the information that $\neg p$, even if, in principle, it should not, because this would seriously undermine the informative nature of the database itself (see next point 3), and although it is arguable (because of A_4, see below) that in such case either p or $\neg p$ fail to count as information.

3 Objections against IL satisfying A_9 appear to be motivated by a confusion between 'becoming informed' and 'being informed', a distinction emphasized in section 10.2.1. In the former case, it is unquestionable that a may receive and hence hold two contradictory messages, e.g. a may read in a printed timetable that the train leaves at 10.30 a.m., as it does, but a may also be told by b that the train does not leave at 10.30 a.m. However, from this it only follows that a has the information that the train leaves at 10.30 a.m., but since p and $\neg p$ erase each other's value as pieces of information *for a*, a may be unable, subjectively, to identify which information a holds. It does not follow that a is actually informed both that the train leaves at 10.30 a.m. and that it does not.

4 If IL satisfies the stronger A_4 then, *a fortiori*, IL satisfies A_9. Accepting that IL satisfies A_9 on the basis of (1)–(3) is obviously not an argument in favour of the inclusion of A_4. At most, it only defuses any argument against it based on the reasoning that, if IL did not satisfy A_9, it would fail to satisfy A_4 as well. The inclusion of A_4 requires some positive support of its own, to which I now turn.

According to A_4, if a is informed that p then p is true. Can this be right? Couldn't it be the case that one might be qualified as being informed that p even if p is false? The answer is in the negative, for the following reason. Including A_4 as one of IL axioms depends on whether p counts as information only if p is true. We saw in the previous chapters that, as in the case of knowledge, truth is a necessary condition for p to qualify as information.

Once the veridical approach to the analysis of semantic information is endorsed as the most plausible, it follows that, strictly speaking, to hold (exchange, receive, sell, buy, etc.) some 'false information', e.g. that the train leaves at 11.30 a.m. when in fact it

---

[9] It might be possible to develop a modal approach to QC (quasi-classical) logic in order to weaken the integrity constraint, see Grant and Hunter (forthcoming).

leaves at 10.30 a.m., is to hold (exchange, receive, sell, buy, etc.) no information at all, only some semantic content (meaningful data). But then, a cannot hold the information (be informed) that p unless p is true, which is precisely what A_4 states. Mathew is not informed but misinformed that Italy lost the World Cup in 2006 because Italy won it. And most English readers will gladly acknowledge that Matthew is informed about who won the World Cup in 1966 only if he holds that England did. The mistake— arguing that a may be informed that p even if p is false, and hence that IL should not satisfy A_4—might arise if one confuses 'holding the information that p', which we have seen must satisfy A_4, with 'holding p as information', which of course need not, since an agent is free to believe that p qualifies as information even when p is actually false, and hence counts as mere misinformation.

As far as A_4 is concerned, 'knowing that p' and 'being informed that p' work in the same way. This conclusion may still be resisted in view of a final objection, which may be phrased as dilemma: either the veridical approach to information is incorrect, and therefore IL should not satisfy A_4, or it is correct, and therefore IL should satisfy A_4, yet only because there is no substantial difference between IL and EL (information logic becomes only another name for epistemic logic). In short, the inclusion of A_4 among the axiom schemata qualifying IL is either wrong or trivial.

The objection is interesting but mistaken. So far, IL shares all its axiom schemata with EL, but information logic allows truth-encapsulation without epistemic collapse because there are two other axiom schemata that are epistemic but not informational, as I shall argue in the next section.

10.3.3 No reflectivity: IL does not satisfy A_6, A_8

Let us begin from the most 'infamous' of EL axiom schemata, namely A_6. One way of putting the argument in favour of A_4 and against A_6, is by specifying that the relation of 'informational accessibility'[10] H in the system that best formalizes 'being informed/ holding the information that p' is *reflexive* without being *reflective*. Reflectivity is here the outcome of a transitive relation in a single agent context, that is, 'introspection', a rather more common label that should be used with some caution given its psychologistic overtones.

If H were reflective (if the informational agent were introspective), IL should support the equivalent of the KK or BB thesis, i.e. $Ip \rightarrow IIp$. However, the II thesis is not merely problematic, it is unjustified, for it is perfectly acceptable for a to be informed that p while being (even in principle) incapable of being informed that a is informed that p, without adopting a second, metainformational approach to Ip. The distinction requires some unpacking.

On the one hand, 'believing' and 'knowing' (the latter here understood, more traditionally, as reducible to some doxastic relation, but see section 10.3.4) are mental

---

[10] The choice of the letter H is arbitrary, but it may graphically remind one of the H in Shannon's famous equation and in the expression 'holding the information that p'.

states that, arguably, in the most favourable circumstances, could implement a 'privileged access' relation, and hence be fully transparent to the agents enjoying them, at least in principle and even if, perhaps, only for a Cartesian agents. Yet *KK* or *BB* remain controversial (see Williamson (1999), Williamson (2000) for arguments against them). The point here is that defenders of the inevitability of the *BB* or *KK* thesis may maintain that, in principle, whatever makes it possible for *a* to believe (or to know) that *p*, is also what makes it possible for *a* to believe (or to know) that *a* believes (or knows) that *p*. If anything, *B* and *BB* (or *K* and *KK*) are two sides of the same coin. More precisely, if *a* believes (or knows) that *p*, this is an internal mental fact that could also be mentally accessible, at least in principle, to a Cartesian *a*, who can be presumed to be also capable of acquiring the relevant, reflective mental state of believing (knowing) that *a* believes (or knows) that *p*. Translating this into information theory, we are saying that either there is no communication channel that allows *a* to have a doxastic (or epistemic) access to *p*, or, if there is, this is also the *same* channel that, in principle, allows *a* to have a doxastic (or epistemic) access to *a*'s belief (or knowledge) that *p*. So a defender of the *BB* or *KK* thesis may argue that the mental nature of doxastic and epistemic states may allow *BB* and *KK* to piggyback on *B* and *K* without requiring a second, meta-channel of communication. Call this the single-channel nature of doxastic and epistemic relations.

On the other hand, all this does not hold true for 'being informed/holding the information', because the latter is a relation that does not necessarily require a mental or conscious state. Beliefs and knowledge (again, analysed doxastically) are in the head, information can be in the hard disk. Less metaphorically, artificial and biological agents may hold the information that *p*, even if they lack a mind or anything resembling mental states concerning *p*, as we saw in chapters six and seven, when discussing the symbol grounding problem. As a result, 'being informed' should be analysed as providing an unprivileged access to some *p*. A dog is informed (holds the information) that a stranger is approaching the house only if a stranger is actually approaching the house, yet this does not imply that the dog is (or can even ever be) informed that he is informed that a stranger is approaching the house. Indeed, the opposite is true: animals do not satisfy any of the *KK*, *BB*, or *II* theses. There are no Cartesian dogs. Likewise, a computer may hold the information that 'the train to London leaves at 10.30 a.m.', but this, by itself, does not guarantee, even in principle, that the computer also holds the information that it holds the information about the train timetable, or we might be much closer to true AI than anybody could seriously claim. Finally, Matthew might have the information that 'the train to London leaves at 10.30 a.m.' written in a note in his pocket, and yet not be informed that he holds the information that *p*. Actually, Matthew might even have it stored in his brain, like Johnny Mnemonic, who in William Gibson's homonymous novel is a mnemonic data courier hired to carry in his brain 320 gigabytes of crucial information to safety from the Pharmacom corporation. Note the difference: Johnny holds the information that he holds some precious information, yet this is like a black box, for he does not hold the information that he holds the information that p.

The distinction may be further clarified if, once again, it is translated into information theory. We are saying that either there is no communication channel that allows a to have an informational access to p, or, if there is, it is such that, even with a Cartesian agent placed in favourable circumstances (no malicious demon etc.), it may still fail to allow a to have an informational access to a's information that p. The possibly non-mental nature of informational states impedes II from piggybacking on I through the same channel of communication. An II relation requires in fact a *second*, meta-channel that allows an I relation between a and Ip, but then this channel too is not, by itself, reflective, since any III relation requires a third channel between I and IIp, and so forth. As far as reflectivity is concerned, 'being informed that p' is not like 'believing that p' or 'knowing that p' but more like 'having recorded that p' or 'seeing that p'. The former two require mental states, whose nature is such as to allow the possibility in principle of the BB-thesis or KK-thesis. The latter two do not require mental states, and hence do not include the possibility of a reflective state: information, records and perceptual sensations do not come with metainformation or metarecords or metasensations by default, even in principle, although there may be a second layer of memory, or another channel of communication or of experience, that refers to the first layer of memory or the first channel of information or the more basic experience. Call this the double-channel nature of the information relation.

The distinction between the single and double channel of information may be compared to the distinction between a reflective sentence that speaks of itself (single-channel, e.g. 'this sentence is written in English') and a meta-sentence that speaks of another sentence (double-channel, e.g. 'the following sentence is written in English' 'the cat is on the mat'). Natural languages normally allow both. Consider Matthew again. He may have in his pocket a note about the first note about the train timetable, yet this would be irrelevant, since it would just be another case of double-channel condition or metainformation. As Wittgenstein succinctly put it: 'nothing in the visual field allows you to infer that it is seen by an eye' (*Tractatus* 5.633). Likewise, nothing in a piece of information p allows you to infer that an information system that holds p also holds the information that it holds p (compare this to the fact that nothing in Matthew's ignorance allows you to infer that he is aware of his ignorance), whereas nothing in a belief or in a piece of knowledge allows you to infer that a doxastic or epistemic agent holding that belief of enjoying that piece of knowledge does not also believe that she believes that p, or does not also know that she knows that p. Knowledge and beliefs are primed to become reflective, information is not. I shall return to this issue in chapter thirteen, when I will deal with the nature of consciousness.

Consider now the following two objections against the distinction between the single-channel (or reflective or conscious or introspective, depending on the technical vocabulary) nature of epistemic and doxastic states and the double-channel (or opaque or unreflective or unconscious) nature of informational states.

First, one may point out that the *II* thesis seems to be implemented by some artificial systems. Actually, there are so-called 'reflective' artificial agents capable of proving the classic knowledge theorem (Brazier and Treur (1999)), variously known as the 'muddy children' or the 'three wise men' problem, the drosophila of epistemic logic and distributed AI (see chapter thirteen). The description, however, is only evocative. Artificial agents may appear to be 'reflective' only because of some smart tricks played at the level of interfaces and human–computer interactions, or because of a multi-layer structure. I shall return to this topic in chapter thirteen. Here, let me just stress that what is known as *reflective computing* is only a case of metaprogramming or a communication channel about another communication channel, precisely as expected. It is what has been labelled above the double-channel nature of the *II* states. One may compare it to a dog being informed that (or barking because) another dog is informed that (or is barking because) a stranger is approaching. At a higher level of abstraction, the two dogs may form a single security system, but the possibility of multi-agent (e.g. *n* dogs or *n* computational) informational systems does not contradict the deflationist view that 'being informed' is not a reflective relation.

Second, the *II* thesis seems to be implemented at least by some human agents. In this case, the reply is that this is so only because information relations can be implemented by human agents by means of mental states, which can then lend their reflective nature to *H*. It is not *H* to be reflective; rather, if an agent *a* can manage *Ip* through some epistemic or conscious state, for example, then, if the corresponding relation of accessibility is reflective the *II* thesis may become acceptable.

To summarize with a slogan: *information entails no iteration*. The point concerning the rejection of A$_6$ is not that 'being informed' cannot appear to be a reflective relation. This is possible because *Ip* may be the object of a second relation *I* (double-channel nature of *II*), when *a* is a multi-agent system, or because *Ip* may be implemented mentally, when *a* is a human agent, and hence be subject to reflection, consciousness or introspection. The point concerning the rejection of A$_6$ is that doxastic and epistemic accessibility relations, interpreted as mental states, may require in principle only a single-channel communication to become reflective, so the *BB* and *KK* theses may be justifiable as limit cases, whereas *H*, by itself, is not necessarily mental, and requires a double-channel communication to become reflective. But then the second channel may be absent even in the most idealized, animal or artificial agents, even in principle and, in any case, we are developing a logic of the communication channel represented by the information relation between *a* and *p*, and this channel is not reflective. The conclusion is that adopting A$_6$ to formalize *Ip* would be a misrepresentation.

There is a further objection to the latter conclusion, but we shall see it in the next section, since it is connected to A$_{10}$. Before, we may briefly look at a consequence of the exclusion of A$_5$ by considering A$_8$. This axiom too is reflective, and therefore equally inappropriate to qualify *IL*. From the fact that an artificial agent does not hold the information that $\neg p$ it does not follow that it holds the information that it is missing the information that $\neg p$. I shall return to this point in section 10.2.5. In this case too, the previous considerations regarding the possibility of meta-information (two-channel) or mental implementation of the information relation apply, but do not modify the conclusion.

10.3.4 Transmissibility: IL satisfies A_{10} and A_{11}

The exclusion of A_6 from the group of axiom schemata characterizing *IL* might still be opposed on the basis of the following reasoning: if the relation of informational accessibility is not interpreted as transitive, then it becomes impossible to transfer information, but this is obviously absurd, so A_6 must be included.

The objection is flawed for three reasons. First, transmission does not necessarily depend on transitivity: in the **KD**-based *DL*, a belief may be transferred from *a* to *b* despite the fact that the axiom schema $(B_a\phi \rightarrow B_aB_a\phi)$ and the corresponding relation of accessibility do not characterize **KD**.

Second, the exclusion of A_6 does not concern the exclusion of the transitivity of modal inferences formulated in A_{10}, which can easily be shown to be satisfied by *IL*. A_{10} is a theorem in all *NML* and, being a weaker version of the K-principle, it formulates a very weak property, unlike the *KK*-principle.[11]

Third, the exclusion of A_6 concerns the transitive nature of *H* when a single, standalone agent is in question. It does not preclude the inclusion of A_{11} (Hintikka's axiom of transmission) in a multiagent context. On the contrary, in this case, A_{11} correctly characterizes *IL*, as it is perfectly reasonable to assume that $(I_aI_b\phi \rightarrow I_a\phi)$: if Matthew is informed that Jenny is informed that the train to London leaves at 10.30 a.m., then he is also informed that it does. Note that this is made possible also thanks to A_4, i.e. the assumption that to be informed that *p* the latter must the true.

10.3.5 Constructing the information base: IL satisfies A_7

A_7 is the defining axiom schema of the system **KTB**. *IL* satisfies A_7 in the sense that, for any true *p*, the informational agent *a* not only cannot be informed that $\neg p$ (because of A_4), but now is also informed that *a* does not hold the information that $\neg p$.

The inclusion of A_7 in *IL* does not contradict the anti-reflective (i.e. zero introspection) constraint supported in section 10.2.3. True, the conclusion *IUp* can be inferred both from *Up* and from *p*. However, in the former case (A_8), one would have to assume some form of negative reflection (introspection), in order to allow the agent *a* to draw the inference from an informational state *Up* to the relevant, metainformational state *IUp*. Whereas in the latter case (A_7) the inference is drawn externally, by an observer, who concludes that, for any piece of information *p*, one can attribute to the agent *a* the information that *a* does not have the information that $\neg p$, irrespective of whether *a*

---

[11] I am very grateful to Patrick Allo for having called my attention to this point.

lacks any kind of reflection on a's informational states. This holds true for theorems such as $II(p \lor \neg p)$, which are demonstrable in $KTB\text{-}IL$: as we saw in 10.2.3, the point here is not denying the possibility of meta-information—it is trivially true that computers can have information about their information that p, for example—but objecting against the reflective (introspective, single-channel) nature of it.

The distinction may be better appreciated if we look at a second objection against the inclusion of A_7, which actually turns in its favour. It concerns the provability of $\lozenge\Box\phi \to \phi$ in KTB. Ontologically, this is known to be a rather controversial result. Yet, informationally, $UI\phi \to \phi$ has a very intuitive reading. We already know from A_9 that a is an informationally consistent agent and, from A_4, that a is informed that p only if p, so we only need now an axiom of *constructability of a's information base*: if, for all a's information it is possible that a holds the information that p (if, according to a's information base D_a, D_a can be consistently extended to include the information that p) then p must be the case. In other words, the negation of $UI\phi \to \phi$ would make no sense: if ϕ is false, then no coherent incrementation of the information database is possible by uploading the information that ϕ. This shows, quite interestingly, that the connection between the intuitionistically-inspired KTB and IL is not accidental. What lies behind both is a concern for direct methods to expand the information base.

It might seem that, by satisfying A_7, IL embeds a closed-world assumption.[12] The similarity is indeed there, but there is also a fundamental difference. In any interesting formalization of 'being informed', it is plausible to assume that the agent has only incomplete information about the world. This precludes, as inappropriate, the assumption that, if a is not informed that ϕ then ϕ is false.[13] What A_7 guarantees is that any possible extension of a's information base corresponds to a genuine state of the world. Since the dual (A_{7d}) $\lozenge\Box\phi \to \phi$ can replace A_7 as the characterizing axiom schema of any KTB-based system, in the next section we shall adopt it as a more intuitive alternative.

10.3.6 KTB-IL

We have now completed the analysis of all the axiom schemata. The result is a **KTB**-based information logic (*KTB-IL*). Compared to EL and DL, *KTB-IL* satisfies the following minimal set of axiom schemata and inference rules (*modus ponens* and necessitation):

$$A_1\ (\phi \to (\chi \to \phi))$$
$$A_2\ ((\phi \to (\chi \to \psi)) \to ((\phi \to \chi) \to (\phi \to \psi)))$$
$$A_3\ ((\neg\phi \to \neg\chi) \to (\chi \to \phi))$$
$$A_4\ (I\phi \to \phi)$$

---

[12] I am grateful to Daniel Lemire for having called my attention to this point. I agree with Patrick Allo that an elegant way of reading Lemire's suggestion is by explaining the weakening of the closed-world assumption by saying that being informed is 'prospectively or purposefully consistent/ true', and hence 'closed for the limiting case'.

[13] For a qualified assumption, in terms of local closed-world, see Golden et al. (1994).

$$A_5 \ (I(\phi \rightarrow \chi) \rightarrow (I\phi \rightarrow I\chi))$$
$$A_{7d} \ (UI\phi \rightarrow \phi)$$
$$\text{MP} \ \vdash \phi, \ \vdash (\phi \rightarrow \chi) \Rightarrow \ \vdash \chi$$
$$\text{Nec} \ \vdash \phi \Rightarrow \ \vdash I\phi$$

Two birds with the same stone, as the saying goes: we have a NML-based logic for 'being informed' and a cognitive reading of **KTB**.

10.4 Four epistemological implications of KTB-*IL*

The debate on information overload, the veridical nature of information, the unsatisfactory state of the $Kp \rightarrow Bp$ principle, and more generally the 'Gettierisable' nature of the tripartite definition of knowledge as justified true belief (see the previous chapter), are what motivated the search for a logic of information in this chapter, so let us turn now to these issues.

10.4.1 Information overload in KTB-IL

KTB-IL is not immune from the classic difficulty of *information overload*, generated by the inevitable inclusion of the rule of necessitation together with *IL*'s closure under implication through the axiom schema A_5 $(I_a(p \rightarrow q) \rightarrow (I_a p \rightarrow I_a q))$. The informational agent *a* is informed about all theorems provable in PC as well as in *KTB-IL*. This is a lot of information, perhaps too much to be realistically attributed to *a*. The difficulty has long been recognized in *EL* as a problematic consequence (Hintikka (1962)), to the point of being sometimes deployed as a *reductio ad absurdum*.

A first reply, of course, is to bite the bullet and argue that, in *IL*, the rule of necessitation describes only an ideal agent (Lemmon (1959)), one who is *strongly logical omniscient*, to adopt Girle's appropriate classification (Girle (2000)). One may then stress that cognitive overload—whether informational, epistemic, or doxastic—is a problem common to all cognitive modal logics anyway, not just *KTB-IL*. This is not a solution, of course, but 'a problem shared is a problem halved': *KTB-IL* is not less successful than *DL* or *EL*, and any argument usable to limit the damage of cognitive overload in those logics (again, see Girle (2000) for an overview) can be adapted to try to rescue *KTB-IL* as well. With an extra advantage: the informational agent *a* could be an ideal artificial agent, a Turing machine for example, and one may argue that, in this case (but the case is of course generalizable insofar as a Turing Machine is not computationally more powerful than a human agent provided with the same endless resources), the rule of necessitation is stating the conversion of ϕ from being a theorem to being inferable by an agent who, through the relevant axioms, could eventually deduce the information that ϕ without any external input (a priori, using the classic Kantian vocabulary), at least in principle.

The last suggestion is related to a second, more interesting reply, referring to the non-informative nature of logical truths. We saw in chapters four and five that the 'Inverse Relationship Principle' states that the probability P of *p* is inversely proportionate to the amount of semantic information carried by p. It follows that when p is a logical truth, we have $P(p) = 1$ and the informativeness of p is 0. Recall now the distinction introduced in section one between p being informative and a holding the information that p. If the information that p is 'empty', i.e. entirely uninformative, as it is the case of e.g. a tautology $(q \lor \neg q)$, then a can hold the (empty) information that $(q \lor \neg q)$, but cannot be informed by receiving it, i.e. a's deficit of information cannot be filled by receiving $(q \lor \neg q)$. If you ask me when the train leaves and I tell you that either it does or it does not leave at 10.30 a.m., you have not been informed, although one may indifferently express this by saying that what I said was uninformative in itself or that (it was so because) you already were informed that the train did or did not leave at 10.30 a.m. anyway. The next step consists in realizing that inputting a logical theorem $\vdash \phi$ into a is indistinguishable from assuming that a already holds the information (is already informed) that ϕ, which is exactly what is stated in $\vdash \phi \Rightarrow I\phi$. It turns out that the apparent difficulty of information overload can be defused by interpreting $\vdash \phi \Rightarrow \vdash I\phi$ as an abbreviation for $\vdash \phi \Rightarrow \vdash P(\phi) = 1 \Rightarrow \vdash \mathrm{Inf}(\phi) = 0 \Rightarrow \vdash I\phi$, which does not mean that a is actually informed about all theorems provable in PC as well as in *KTB-IL*—as if a contained a gigantic database with a lookup table of all such theorems—but that, much more intuitively, any theorem ϕ provable in PC or in *KTB-IL* (indeed, any ϕ that is true in all possible worlds) is uninformative for a. Recall that a might be a Turing Machine, and note the difference: we are not saying that a cannot hold the information that ϕ. One may still object that we have assumed the availability of unlimited resources. The reply is that this is a useful abstraction and the approach is neatly consistent with the 'implicit knowledge' strategy developed to solve the logical omniscience problem when this affects resource-bounded agents (Levesque (1984) and Fagin and Halpern (1988)). What is informative in the deduction of $\vdash \phi$ is the process through which ϕ is obtained, as I have argued in chapter five, when dealing with Hintikka's 'scandal of deduction'.

10.4.2 In favour of the veridicality thesis

In chapter five, I analysed the counterintuitive consequence of the 'Inverse Relationship Principle', namely the fact that the less probable p is the more informative it becomes, with the result that the most informative p is a contradiction, since P (contradiction) = 0. In that context, I argued that the paradox may be solved by assuming that factual semantic information encapsulates truth. Matthew is informed that milk contains calcium if and only if Matthew holds that milk contains calcium and it is true that it does. Were milk not to contain calcium we would deem Matthew disinformed or uninformed. There is, however, a remaining objection that could not be discussed there. Any strongly semantic theory of information (i.e. one that defines information as necessarily veridical), including the one presented in chapter five, would be challenged by the lack of a logic that may allow truth-encapsulation without facing epistemic collapse (i.e. the transformation into an epistemic logic). We have seen that this is the difficulty solved by the availability of *KTB-IL*, which shows that a modal logic that captures the relation of 'being informed' by interpreting it on the basis of a strongly semantic interpretation of information is possible.

10.4.3 The relations between DL, IL, and EL

As Lemmon (1959) rightly remarked

> With different interpretations in mind, and with generically different justifications, one may accept as in some way correct any of the formal systems [....] M, S4 and S5. Once the complexity of the notion of correctness here is made clear, there is little temptation to view these (and other) modal systems as if they were rival competitors in the same field, of which only one can win. The very multiplicity of modal systems is precisely an advantage, because it gives opportunities for choice. (p. 40)

Mutatis mutandis, a similar temptation should be resisted in any 'cognitive' interpretation of *NML*. Let us briefly look at the variety of alternatives.

The exclusion of A$_4$ from *KTB-IL* yields a **KDB**- or **KB**-based logic, which may be confused with some kind of *DL* (see Table 7). Yet both systems still include A$_{7d}$, which makes a doxastic interpretation unfeasible. *KTB-IL* is not based on a more basic, doxastic logic, not even when *DL* is constructed using the 'logic of strong belief' as in Lenzen (2002). For in this case, *Cp* formalizes '*a* is firmly convinced that *p* ', but axiom A$_4$ still fails to apply, so *UIp* cannot be interpreted as being equivalent to *Cp*. We shall see the importance of this conclusion in the next section.

On the other hand, the exclusion of A$_{7d}$ from *KTB-IL* yields a **KT**-based *IL*, which is modally equivalent to, and hence subjectively indistinguishable for *a* from, the corresponding *EL*: **KT** may be equally used to formalise a weak *IL* or a weak *EL*, with at least three significant consequences.

First, *KT-IL* may be generated by adding A$_4$ to a **KD**-based *DL*. This is interesting because it allows a different interpretation of *DL* as a logic of (well-formed and meaningful) data-holding, free from any mental component. Moving from **K** to **KD**

Table 7 Summary of the main 'cognitive' modal logics

	A$_4$	A$_6$	A$_7$	A$_8$	A$_{11}$
	$\Box_x\phi \to \phi$	$\Box_x\phi \to \Box_x\Box_x\phi$	$\phi \to \Box_x\Diamond_x\phi$ or $\Diamond_x\Box_x\phi \to \phi$	$\Diamond_x \phi \to \Box_x\Diamond_x\phi$	$\Box_x\Box_y\phi \to \Box_x\phi$
Frame	Reflexive	Transitive	Symmetric	Euclidean	(multi-agent)
S5-based *EL*	1	1	1	1	1
S4-based *EL*	1	1	0	0	1
KT-based *EL*	1	0	0	0	1
KD5-based *DL*	0	1	1	1	0
KD4-based *DL*	0	1	0	0	0
KTB-based *IL*	1	0	1	0	1
KDB-based *IL*	0	0	1	0	1
KT-based *IL*	1	0	0	0	1

to **KT**, one may read each system as formalising increasingly stringent logics of '*a* holds that *p*', where *p* is some well-formed and meaningful data, i.e. some semantic content, expressed propositionally.

Second, *KT-IL* can then be used to generate an S4-based (by adding A_6) or an S5-based *EL* (through S4 or by adding A_8), which is also obtainable from *KTB-IL*, through A_6 or A_8. All this goes some way towards explaining why conceptual analyses of knowledge, belief and information may move rather freely between *DL*, *IL* and *EL*.

Third, the partial overlap between *IL* and *EL* in **KT** points out that there is something missing in *EL* itself. In the epistemological context, the relation of 'knowing' is normally expected to include more than just true (doxastic or informational) content. Normally, 'being justified' (or some similar relation of well-foundedness, e.g. Plantinga's 'warranty' or Nozick's 'truth-tracking') plays a significant role. Yet, in *EL* there is no reference to any further condition. This reinforces the point made in section 10.3.2: there is room for *IL* between *DL* and *EL*, at the very least because *EL* is just reflective (introspective, in more psychologistic vocabulary) *IL*. The present state of *EL* may therefore finally look unsatisfactory, insofar as a crucial feature of the 'knowing' relation escapes the formalizations offered by the various versions of *EL*. *EL* needs to be augmented by a logic of a relation of well-foundedness.[14] This is a crucial problem which I shall discuss in chapter thirteen.

10.4.4 *Against the untouchable*

We have reached the main goal of this chapter. The commonly held principle[15] that knowledge necessarily implies belief—known as the *entailment property* (Lenzen (1978)) or the $Kp \rightarrow Bp$ principle (Girle (2000))—although reasonable, can now be shown to be dispensable because it is not the only alternative. This is because $\neg Bp \rightarrow \neg Kp$ is no longer necessarily true, since we might have $Kp \rightarrow Ip$ and it is not necessarily true that $Bp \rightarrow Ip$ or that the relation of 'being informed that *p*' is necessarily reducible to a weaker relation of 'believing that *p*' (see section 10.2.6). This means that *a* may know that *p* because *a* is informed that *p* and *a* being informed that *p* may not be based on any doxastic state or process. *EL* may be based on *IL* bypassing any *DL* entirely, because 'believing' may bear no relation to coherence or truth, but does require a mental attitude of assent and may encompass the *BB* thesis, whereas 'being informed' may not be a mental condition and hence avoids the *II* thesis, but cannot be decoupled from the veridical nature of the content, through A_{7d} or A_4.

---

[14] van Benthem (1991) has called attention to the importance of developing an epistemic logic reinforced by a logic of justification. Research in this direction includes Voorbraak (1991), (1992) and more recently several papers by Artemov and colleagues, see especially Artemov and Nogina (2005), which provides an overview as well.

[15] In the literature on epistemic logic, the principle is usually introduced as uncontroversial and unproblematic, see for example Schlesinger (1985), Girle (2000) or Lenzen (2002). The same holds true in analytic epistemology, where it is often attributed to Plato as if Plato had not only discussed it but also endorsed it.

Rejecting the $Kp \rightarrow Bp$ principle requires a new approach in epistemology, yet the reader should not be scandalized. 'Doxasticism' in epistemology is a recent phenomenon, despite some pervasive propaganda. The Greeks, and especially Plato, could not have mistrusted 'doxa' more. Modern philosophers were equally concerned with epistemic processes involving ideas (Descartes, Locke, Hume) or judgements (Kant), not necessarily beliefs. And many philosophers of science have always been suspicious of 'doxasticism', considering it far too close to forms of armchair psychologism to provide a reliable starting point (one may recall Popper's 'epistemology without a knowing subject'). As Plato forcefully argues in the *Theaetetus*:

[208b] Socrates: So my friend there is such a thing as right belief together with justification, which is not entitled to be called knowledge.

Theaetetus: I am afraid so.

[210a] Socrates: [. . .] So, Theaetetus, neither perception, nor true belief, nor the addition of a 'justification' to true belief can be knowledge.

It was an uncritical revival, between the wars, of a psychologistic reading of the Cartesian tradition (Floridi (2003c)) that brought the $Kp \rightarrow Bp$ principle to the forefront and silently transformed it into a dogma. The time has come to approach it with more than a pinch of critical attitude. The invitation is not entirely new. Recent research (Voorbraak (1991), Halpern (1996)) has raised substantial doubts on the indiscriminate acceptability of the principle, although for reasons different from those expounded here. Voorbraak (1991) has proved, for example, that objective knowledge as formalized in S5-*EL* does not imply rational belief as formalized in **KD45**-*DL*. Furthermore, a critical, if not suspicious, attitude towards 'doxasticism' is a healthy outcome of epistemological investigations employed to deal with artificial epistemic agents.

Dethroning the $Kp \rightarrow Bp$ principle from its safe position as a *de facto* axiom[16] has a crucial consequence: it opens up the possibility of a non-doxastic but informational approach to the definition and conceptual understanding of knowledge. This is important. We saw in the previous chapter that the Gettier problem is demonstrably unsolvable and therefore that the tripartite account is irretrievably inadequate in principle. The Gettier problem shows that something in the tripartite approach needs to be abandoned. Now, of the conditions required by the tripartite definition of knowledge, once we exclude the possibility of fiddling with the truth requirement, it has always been the justification relation that has come under investigation, to be revised or augmented by a fourth condition, depending on the verdict. However, chapter nine proved that the relation of justification is not guilty, i.e. that nothing one can do about it can actually change the outcome: the Gettier problem remains

---

[16] Kraus and Lehmann (1986) and van der Hoek (1991), for example, have developed epistemic systems that include $Kp \rightarrow Bp$ among the axioms.

unsolvable. Where else could we look then? The culprit might have been right in front of our eyes, unsuspected, all along: it may be the doxastic condition, the conviction that if a knows that p then, necessarily, a must *believe* that p. This seems to be far from obvious now. We have been blinded by the uncritical assumption of the $Kp \rightarrow Bp$ principle as dogma. The truth is that a may know that p because a may be informed that p (plus other conditions of well-foundedness) and 'being informed' requires a different, non-doxastic analysis.

CONCLUSION

The results obtained in this chapter pave the way for a better understanding of the relations between 'knowing', 'believing', and 'being informed', for a non-doxastic foundation of knowledge, and for the possibility of a non-psychologistic, non-mentalistic and non-anthropomorphic approach to epistemology, which can easily be applied to artificial or synthetic agents such as computers, robots, webbots, companies, and organizations. There is, admittedly, quite a lot of work to be done. For example, if an informational analysis of knowledge is possible, then the strategy to defuse the problem of information overload proposed in section 10.4.1 could be extended to try to solve the problem of strongly logical omniscience in *EL* as well. More generally, the agenda includes the development of a clear analysis of the connections between *KTB-IL* and the logics of 'becoming informed'. As far as this book is concerned, however, we need to concentrate on the task of providing an informational (as opposed to doxastic) analysis of knowledge. For this, two more steps are required. Not all semantic information counts as a good candidate for the role of knowledge. Semantic information needs to be *relevant*. So the task of the next chapter is to provide a clear account of this key feature. And holding the relevant semantic information that p is still insufficient to be able to claim that one knows that p. Some form of grounding is also needed, as we shall see in chapter twelve.

11

Understanding epistemic relevance

Stating is not a gratuitous and random human activity. We do not, except in social desperation, direct isolated and unconnected pieces of information at each other but on the contrary intend in general to give or add information about what is a matter of standing or current interest or concern.

Peter Strawson, 'Identifying Reference and Truth-Value' (Strawson 1964)

SUMMARY

Previously, in chapter eight, I asked the following question: how does semantic information upgrade to knowledge? In chapter nine, I argued that the doxastic approach, normally taken by traditional epistemology to answer this question, might be blocked. In chapter ten, I introduced an alternative path towards an informational analysis of knowledge, by providing a logic for 'S is informed that p'. This chapter deals with a further step towards an answer to the original question. Semantic information needs to be not only truthful but also *relevant* in order to qualify as knowledge. As is well known, agents require a constant flow, and a high level of processing, of *relevant* semantic information, in order to interact successfully among themselves and with the environment in which they are embedded. Standard theories of information, however, are silent on the nature of epistemic relevance. So, in this chapter, I develop and defend what will turn out to be a subjectivist interpretation of epistemic relevance. This is based on a counterfactual and metatheoretical analysis of the degree of relevance of some semantic information i to an informee/agent a, as a function of the accuracy of i understood as an answer to a query q, given the probability that q might be asked by a. This interpretation of epistemic relevance is consistent with, and further vindicates, the strongly semantic theory of information developed and supported in the previous chapters. It accounts satisfactorily for several important applications and interpretations of the concept of relevant semantic information in a variety of philosophical areas. It interfaces successfully with current philosophical interpretations of causal and logical relevance. Finally, it provides the missing analysis of the relevance condition necessary to upgrade semantic information to knowledge. There is still a crucial ingredient missing, namely some sort of account of the well-foundedness of relevant semantic information. This will be the topic of the next chapter.

11.1 Introduction

A frequent complaint about current theories of information is that they are utterly useless when it comes to establishing the actual *relevance* of some specific piece of semantic information. As a rule, agents assume that some content is by default an instance of semantic information (Sperber and Wilson (1995)). What they often wonder is whether, and how far, that content may contribute to the formulation of their choices and purposes, the development of their decision processes, and eventually to the successful pursuit of their goals.

The complaint must not be underestimated. Questions of relevance affect many critical contexts, from the most mundane transactions to scientific experiments, from medical diagnoses to juridical procedures. And yet, the complaint may seem unfair, for no theory of information, from the most purely syntactical to the most strongly semantic, was ever meant to cast any light on the phenomenon of relevance. This is true but, unfortunately, critics may still retort that they have at least a normative point. Information theories should care more about the relevance-related features of what they model as information. If they do not, this is not only their problem but also a good reason to disregard them when informational needs become increasingly pressing. It seems clear that, in order to upgrade to knowledge, semantic information must be relevant.

This 'normative' objection easily morphs into a full-blooded dilemma. On the one hand, theories that formalize syntactical or structural properties of information rely on probability theory, they are statistical in nature and their pervasive applications are scientifically sound. Yet these theories abstract from any semantic feature, relevance included, and hence they seem inconsequential for the investigation of further episte-mological and communication issues depending on it. On the other hand—the objection continues—there are philosophical theories that seek to capture the most salient semantic properties of information, through a variety of techniques, from situation semantics to the semantics of possible worlds or a modified calculus of probabilities. But if they end up making the concept of semantic information encap-sulate that of true content (well-formed and meaningful data qualify as information only if they are also true), then they are mistaken. For any theory that imposes a truth condition on the concept of semantic information cannot therefore explain how some misinformation (semantic content actually false) may still be relevant. The result is that current theories are either irrelevant or mistaken. The only way forward—the objec-tion concludes—may be to analyse semantic information in terms of well-formed and meaningful data, without including any further truth constraint, and then trying to understand relevance in these terms. This is, however, inconsistent with the most accredited theories of relevance, according to which falsities are irrelevant (more on this in section nine). Obviously something has to go, but it is unclear what.

In light of these problems, I shall pursue two goals in this chapter. The first is to provide a subjectivist interpretation of epistemic relevance (i.e. epistemically relevant semantic information), thus satisfying those critics who lament its absence and, because of it, may be sceptical about the utility of using an information-theoretical approach to analyse knowledge. The second goal is to show that such a subjectivist interpretation can (indeed must) be built on a veridical conception of semantic information, thus further reinforcing the case in favour of the strongly semantic theory of information defended in chapters four and five, and proving wrong those critics who argue that misinformation can be relevant. This means showing that the second horn of the dilemma outlined above is actually blunt. That is what has to go.

The two goals are achieved through a strategy of progressive refinements. In section 11.2, the distinction between system-based or causal, and agent-oriented or epistemic relevance is recalled. In section 11.3, I discuss the most common and basic sense in which semantic information is said to be epistemically relevant. This has some serious shortcomings, so, in section 11.4, the basic case is refined probabilistically. The new version too can be shown to be only partly satisfactory, so in section 11.5 there will be a second, counterfactual revision. The limits of this version are finally overcome in section 11.6, where the analysis is completed by providing a conclusive, metainformational refinement. In section 11.7, some of the advantages of the metatheoretical revision are illustrated. In section 11.8, I briefly outline some important applications of what I shall label the subjectivist interpretation of epistemic relevance. In section 11.9, I return to the problem of the connection between a strongly semantic theory of information and the concept of epistemic relevance and explain why misinformation cannot be relevant. In section 11.10, two common objections are answered; their discussion helps to clarify further the proposed theory. In section 11.11, I conclude by briefly summarizing the results obtained and the work that lies ahead.

11.2 Epistemic vs causal relevance

Most of the literature on relevance[1] does not so much interpret the nature of the phenomenon as actually use the corresponding concept for specific applications. For example, relevant information is essential in many epistemological analyses, especially in the so-called *relevant alternatives theory*, but the question about what exactly makes some information relevant is normally left unanswered (Moser (2002)). True, we encounter plenty of hints about what it might mean for some information p to be relevant, yet these normally amount to more or less implicit endorsements of a variety of commonsensical and pre-theoretical understandings of the concept, which fail to

---

[1] See for example Yus (2006), a bibliography online on relevance theory in pragmatics and related disciplines. For recent review articles on relevance in information science see Greisdorf (2000) and the very useful Borlund (2003). Philosophical accounts of relevance include Gärdenfors (1976), (1978), Cohen (1994), Lakemeyer (1997), and Delgrande and Pelletier (1998), all works that have influenced the research for this chapter.

provide a conceptual foundation and a shareable, explanatory frame. To make things worse, the theories of relevance currently available come from a variety of fields that often do not speak to each other: several branches of computer science and of information science, statistics and probability theory, AI, cognitive science, epistemology, logic, philosophy of language, linguistics, and jurisprudence. The risk of gerrymandering is obvious. It was already stressed by Cohen (1994).

Following previous taxonomies by Cohen (1994) and Borlund (2003), approaches to the study of relevance can be divided into two groups, depending on whether they focus on a more system-based or a more agent-oriented concept of relevance.

System-oriented theories (S-theories) usually analyse relevance in terms of *topicality*, *aboutness*, or *matching* (how well some information matches a request), especially in the information retrieval (IR) literature, and various forms of *conditional in/dependence* (how some information can help to produce some outcome), especially in logic, probability theory, philosophy of science, and AI.

Agent-oriented theories (A-theories) tend to analyse relevance in terms of *conversational implicature* and *cognitive pertinence*, especially in philosophy of language, pragmatics, and psychology, and perceived *utility*, *informativeness*, *beneficiality*, and other ways of 'bearing on the matter at hand' in relation to an agent's informational needs, especially in IR literature and in epistemology. Adapting a distinction introduced by Hitchcock (1992), S-theories and A-theories may be seen to be interested mainly in *causal relevance* and *epistemic relevance* respectively.

S-theories clearly do not try to define, but rather presuppose, the fundamental concept of relevance understood as a relation between some information and an informee. The problem is accurately described in Crestani et al. (1998):

The concept of relevance is arguably the fundamental concept of IR. In the above presented model we purposely avoid giving a formal definition of relevance. The reason behind our decision is that the notion of relevance has never been defined precisely in IR. Although there has been a large number of attempts towards a definition of the concept of relevance (Saracevic (1970), Cooper (1971), Mizzaro (1996)), there has never been agreement about a unique and precise definition. A treatment of the concept of relevance is outside the scope of this paper and we will not attempt to formulate a new definition or even accept a particular already existing one. What is important for the purpose of our survey is to understand that relevance is a relationship that may or may not hold between a document and a user of the IR system who is searching for some information: if the user wants the document in question, then we say that the relationship holds.

Similar conclusions may be reached regarding the logical literature, which has concentrated mainly on S-theories, providing a variety of formalizations of logics for relevance-related notions such as conditional independence, subjunctive conditionals, novelty, causal change, and co-variance (also known as perturbation models). Here is a typical example:

A specific 'entity' (such as an action, training sample, attribute, background proposition, or inference step) is irrelevant to a task in some context if the appropriate response to the task does not change by an unacceptable [sic] amount if we change the entity in that context, Otherwise, we view that entity as (somewhat) relevant to the task. This view is explicitly stated in the paper by Galles and Pearl, which deals with causality and where a perturbation corresponds to a material change in the physical world. (Subramanian et al. (1997), p. 2)

In this context, Weingartner and Schurz (1986) distinguish between two types of relevance, one à la Aristotle (*a-relevance*) and the other à la Körner (*k-relevance*). Their point is that

an inference (or the corresponding valid implication) is a-relevant if there is no propositional variable and no predicate which occurs in the conclusion but not in the premises. And an inference (or in general any valid formula) is k-relevant if it contains no single occurrence of a subformula which can be replaced by its negation *salva validitate*.[2]

Clearly, neither *a-relevance* nor *k-relevance* addresses the problem of epistemic relevance. It is not surprising then that some years later, in a ground-breaking article on relevant properties and causal relevance, Delgrande and Pelletier (1998) could still conclude that

as mentioned at the outset, we feel that 'relevant' is a concept for which we have no deep understanding. (p. 166)

They made no attempt to connect their analysis to an informee-oriented explanation of epistemic relevance. However, in an equally important work on relevance relations in propositional logic, published the year before, Lakemeyer (1997) had already tried to bridge the gap between the two kinds of relevance:

Perhaps the most distinctive feature that sets this work apart from other approaches to relevance is the subjective point of view. In particular, we try to capture relevance relations relative to the deductive capabilities of an agent. For example, two agents who are given the same information may very well differ in their opinion about whether p is relevant to q. Even the same agent may at first miss a connection between the two, which may be discovered upon further reflection. For instance, a student solving a geometry problem involving a right-angled rectangle may not see the connection to the Pythagorean Theorem. (p. 138)

We shall see that this is a promising starting point. The current situation can be summarized thus: some philosophical work has been done on several formal aspects of system-based or causal relevance, but the key question, namely what it means for some semantic information to be relevant to some informee, still needs to be answered. We lack a foundational theory of agent-oriented or epistemic relevance. The warming-up is over. The time has come to roll up our sleeves.

---

[2] The adequacy of Körner criterion of relevance for propositional logic has been proved by Schroder (1992).

11.3 The basic case

As the quotation opening this chapter indicates, Strawson thought that

stating is not a gratuitous and random human activity. We do not, except in social desperation, direct isolated and unconnected pieces of information at each other. (Strawson (1964), p. 92)

Rather, according to his Principle of Relevance, we

intend in general to give or add information about what is a matter of standing or current interest or concern. (p. 92)

He was right, of course, and one may add that giving or adding information happens most commonly through interactions of questions and answers. So let us start from an abstract definition of a very basic case of relevant information and then add a couple of examples.

It is common to assume that some information i is relevant (R) to an informee/agent a with reference to a domain d in a context c, at a given level of abstraction[3] (LoA) l, if and only if

1. a asks (Q) a question q about d in c at l, i.e. $Q\,(a, q, d, c, l)$, and
2. i satisfies (S) q as an answer about d in c, at l, i.e. $S\,(i, q, d, c, l)$

In short:

$$R(i) \leftrightarrow (Q(a, q, d, c, l) \wedge S(i, q, d, c, l)) \qquad [1]$$

The basic idea expressed by [1] is simple: 'the train to London leaves at 13.15' is relevant to Mary if and only if Mary has asked for that piece of information about train timetables in such and such circumstance and with the usual linguistic conventions, and 'the train to London leaves at 13.15' satisfies her request.

   Formula [1] is what we find applied by services like Amazon or eBay, when they suggest to a user a new item that might be relevant to her, given her past queries. It is also what lies behind the working of databases and Boolean searches, including Google queries. Finally, understood as in [1], relevance is the semantic counterpart of the algebraic concept of marginalization, $(\phi, x) \mapsto \phi^{\downarrow x}$, in information algebra Kohlas (2003).

11.3.1 Advantages of the basic case

The formulation provided in [1] has several advantages, which explain why it is so popular.

   a. [1] explicitly identifies semantic information as the ultimate relevance-bearer. Other candidates in the literature on relevance comprise events, facts, documents, formulae, propositions, theories, beliefs, and messages, but Cohen (1994)

---

[3] The analysis of relevance also depends on the level of abstraction at which the process of assessment is conducted, cf. the analysis of 'the point of view' according to which something is relevant in Cohen (1994).

has convincingly argued that relevance is propositional. He is largely correct, but while any proposition may be interpreted informationally, not all semantic information (e.g. a map) is immediately propositional (see chapter eight), so [1] simply brings to completion his reduction.

b. [1] takes into account the informee's interests by explicitly making the relevance of i depend on her queries. No semantic information is relevant *per se*, relevance being an informee-oriented concept, as anyone who has been listening to airport announcements knows only too well. This move is crucial, since it means that causal relevance can be better understood if the informee is considered part of (i.e. is embedded in) the mechanism that gives rise to it. More explicitly, this means grounding relations of causal relevance on relations of epistemic relevance.

c. [1] couples relevance and the domain d about which, the context c in which, and the LoA l at which the relevant information is sought. Relevance is *situational* (Borlund (2003)): the same informee can find the same information relevant or irrelevant depending on d, c, and l.

d. [1] analyses relevance *erotetically*, in terms of logic of questions and answers (Groenendijk (2003)), and this is a strength, since it is a standard and robust way of treating semantic information in information theory, in information algebra (Kohlas (2003)) and in the philosophy of information. Note that the class of questions discussed excludes those that are 'loaded'.[4]

e. [1] also seeks to provide an *objective* sense of relevance insofar as i is not any information, but only the information that actually satisfies q at some LoA l.

f. [1] constrains the amount of *subjectivity* involved in the analysis of relevance. This is achieved by assuming that the agent a in [1] is a *type of rational agent* which satisfies the so-called Harsanyi doctrine (Harsanyi (1968)). This point deserves some comment.

According to the Harsanyi doctrine, also known in game theory as the 'common prior assumption', if two or more rational agents share a set of beliefs (the common prior assumption) about the possible state of the world, expressed by means of a probability distribution over all possible states, then—if they receive some new information about the world and if they update their set of beliefs by making them conditional (Bayesian learning) on the information received—they obtain the same revised probability (the posterior probability). So, if their new, updated beliefs differ, the conclusion is that this is because they have received different information. As Aumann (1976) synthetically put it:

differences in subjective probabilities should be traced exclusively to differences in information.

---

[4] A question Q is loaded if the respondent is committed to (some part of) the presupposition of Q (Walton (1991), 340) e.g. 'how many times did you kiss Mary?', which presupposes that you did kiss Mary at least once.

The model is both famous and controversial. In our case, it can be used not as an abstract, if still phenomenologically reliable, description of agents' behaviour, but as a definition of what an idealized, yet not unrealistic, rational agent should be. The proposal is to define *a* as belonging to the class of (rational) agents who, if they share the same information about the probable realization of an event, should hold the same beliefs about it (they reach the same subjective probability assignments). This allows one to treat differences in beliefs among rational agents, and hence in their querying processes, as completely explainable in terms of differences in their information. In game theory, this is called reaching consistent alignment of beliefs. Two further consequences are that rational agents cannot possess exactly the same information and agree to disagree about the probability of some past or future events. In fact, they must independently come to the same conclusion and, second consequence, they cannot surprise each other informationally.

To conclude, the connection between the informee-oriented and the query-satis-faction-based features explains that [1] supports a *subjectivist* interpretation of epistemic relevance in terms of the degree of *a*'s interest in *i*. It is the sense in which one speaks of a subjectivist interpretation of probability, and should not be mistaken for any refer-ence to the idiosyncratic inclinations of an empirical epistemic agent or their phenom-enological analysis, contrary to what can be found in Schutz (1970).

11.3.2 *Limits of the basic case*

Common sense and scientific literature thus provide a good starting point, namely [1]. Despite its popularity and the advantages listed in (a)–(f), however, the basic case is severely limited. Three of the main shortcomings are:

1. [1] is insufficiently explanatory, since the relation between *i* and *q* is left un-touched: how *adequate* must *i* be as an answer to *q* in order to count as *relevant* information?

2. [1] is too coarse, for it fails to distinguish between degrees of relevance and hence of epistemic utility of the more or less relevant information. It might be relevant to *a* that the train has been delayed, but it is even more relevant to *a* that the train has been delayed by one hour instead of ten minutes, yet [1] can not capture this distinction.

3. [1] is brittle, in that it is forced to declare *i* irrelevant when condition $Q(a, q, d, c, l)$ is not satisfied. Obviously, even if *a* does not ask *q*, *i* (understood, following [1] as the answer to *q* about *d* in *c* at *l*) may still be highly relevant to *a*. This is what researchers and salesmen alike find distressing.

11.4 A probabilistic revision of the basic case

The first step is to revise [1] by making more explicit the relation between *i* and *q*. We can then move from a rigid double-implication to a more flexible, functional relation between the degree of relevance and the degree of probability of the two conditions concerning the questioning and the answer. Note that Bowles (1990) follows a similar strategy to explain probabilistically the relation of relevance in propositional inferences.

Call A the degree of *adequacy* of the answer, that is, the degree to which *i* satisfies *q* about *d* in *c* at *l*. One can define A as precisely as one wishes by adapting the *statistical* concept of *validity*. *Validity* is the combination of *accuracy* and *precision*, two other technical concepts also borrowed from statistics. *Accuracy* is the degree of conformity of a measure or calculated parameter to its actual (true) value. *Precision* (also called *reproducibility* or *repeatability*) is the degree to which further measurements or calculations show the same or similar results. We shall say that *i* is an *adequate* answer to *q* insofar as it is a *valid* answer to *q*, that is, insofar as it is an answer to *q* both *accurate* and *precise*.

We can now make [1] more resilient by considering the probability that *a* may ask *q* *and* the probability that *i* may answer *q* adequately. Unfortunately, the probability of asking a question is unrelated to the probability of receiving an adequate answer (or life would be much easier), so the two events are independent and their conjunction translates into a simple multiplication. By adopting this refinement we obtain:

$$R(i) = P(Q(a, q, d, c, l)) \times P(A(i, q, d, c, l)) \qquad [2]$$

11.4.1 Advantages of the probabilistic revision

[2] combines the advantages (a)–(f) of [1] with the further advantage (g) of making it possible to talk about degrees of epistemic relevance (not just Boolean quantities) and adequacy. This is coherent with a broader informational approach: in [2], the more likely *a* is to ask *q* and the more adequate *i* is as an answer to *q*, the more relevant *i* becomes to *a*.

11.4.2 Limits of the probabilistic revision

The main disadvantage of [2] is that the epistemic relevance of *i* decreases too rapidly in relation to the decrease in the probability of Q, and it becomes utterly counterintuitive in some cases. Realistically, the informee *a* cannot be considered omniscient, even if *a* is assumed to be so modal-logically (see chapter ten). The world is informationally opaque to *a*, at least empirically, so *a* may often fail to request the information that would actually be epistemically relevant to her, seen from a sort of God's-eye perspective. What happens when the probability that *a* may ask *q* is less than 1? As Figure 19 shows, in [2] there are four possible trends, since R tends towards 0 or 1 depending on whether both P(Q) and P(A) tend towards 0 or 1. Three out of four cases in [2] are realistic and unproblematic. But when P(Q) tends to 0 while P(A) tends to 1, we re-encounter the counterintuitive collapse of epistemic relevance already seen above: *i* is increasingly irrelevant epistemically because it is increasingly unlikely that *a* may ask *q*, even when the adequacy of *i* is made increasingly closer, or equal, to 1.

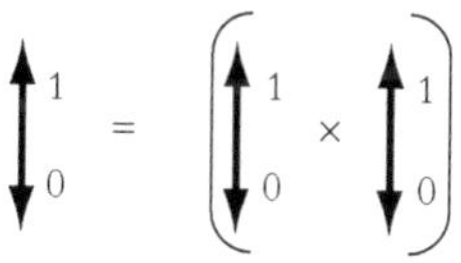

$$\uparrow_0^1 \;=\; \left(\uparrow_0^1 \;\times\; \uparrow_0^1 \right)$$

$$R\,(i) \approx 0 \text{ when } P(Q) \approx 0 \times P(A) \approx 1$$

Figure 19 Four trends in formula [2]. The highlighted case is the problematic one

11.5 A counterfactual revision of the probabilistic analysis

The collapse can be avoided by revising [2] counterfactually. Instead of analysing the probability that a might ask q, one needs to consider two scenarios:

- the case in which a asks q, i.e. $P(Q) = 1$, and
- the case in which a does not, but might, ask q, i.e. $0 \le P(Q) < 1$.

In the former case, the only variable that counts is the probability that i might be adequate. In the latter case, one can consider the probability that a would (have) ask(ed) q if a were (had been) sufficiently informed. Using the standard symbol '$\square\!\!\rightarrow$' for the counterfactual implication and simplifying a bit our notation by omitting (q, d, c, l), we obtain:

$$R(i) = \begin{cases} P(A(i)) & \text{if } P(Q(a)) = 1 \\[2em] P(Ia(i)\square\!\!\rightarrow Q(a)) \times P(A(i)) & \text{if } 0 \le P(Q(a)) < 1 \end{cases} \qquad [3]$$

The second line in [3] states that the epistemic relevance of i is a function of the probability that i might be an adequate answer to q times the probability that a would ask q if a were sufficiently informed about the availability of i.

11.5.1 Advantages of the counterfactual revision

The advantages of [3] are all the advantages (a)–(g) of [1] and [2] plus the further advantage (h) of solving the problem of the opacity of epistemic relevance and its corresponding collapse.

11.5.2 Limits of the counterfactual revision

The first limit requires some fine-tuning: it concerns a potentially circular use of counterfactuals. The metalinguistic interpretation of counterfactuals à la Goodman requires a reference to a characterization of the *relevant* initial conditions that would make a counterfactual true. Thus, using Quine's classic example, 'if Julius Caesar had been in charge of U.N. Forces during the Korean War, then he would have used (a) nuclear weapons or (b) catapults', one can make sense of the general scenario, and hence of the two alternatives, only if the *relevant* domain knowledge is available. This is obviously circular and would not do. However, the more standard Stalnaker–Lewis semantics allows an interpretation of counterfactuals in terms of possible worlds close to the actual world within a specific similarity-structure in a logical space. This is good news because, although references to agents' epistemic interests might be brought to bear in this case as well, the move is unnecessary: the closeness or similarity function may be computed on the basis of a purely extensional analysis or probabilistic projection, starting from the given, actual world. The Stalnaker–Lewis approach is far from being uncontroversial or devoid of problems, but it does allow one to avoid the circularity of having to establish what information is metatheoretically or contextually relevant to the agents in order to evaluate some further relevant information.

The second limit of [3] may be labelled the counterfactual paradox of semantic information and it is not avoidable without further revising the approach. According to [3], assuming, for the sake of simplicity, that $P(A(i, q, d, c, l)) = 1$, i would be maximally relevant epistemically only if the probability is also 1 that, if a had been informed that i was the answer, then a would have asked q to obtain i. But this conditional reminds one of Meno's paradox (*Meno* 80d–81a):

> Meno: And how will you investigate, Socrates, that of which you know nothing at all? Where can you find a starting-point in the region of the unknown? Moreover, even if you happen to come full upon what you want, how will you ever know that this is the thing that you did not know?
>
> Socrates: I know, Meno, what you mean; but just see what a tiresome dispute you are introducing. You argue that man cannot enquire either about that which he knows, or about that which he does not know; for if he knows, he has no need to enquire; and if not, he cannot; for he does not know the very subject about which he is to enquire.

For, if a had held i in the first place, *strictly speaking a* would not have been in any need to ask q to obtain i, so it is not true that a would have asked q had he held i. It follows that [3] *largely* fails to deliver a good analysis of epistemic relevance. 'Strictly speaking' and 'largely' are emphasized because, *in practice*, i would be epistemically relevant if a is assumed to be looking not for new information but for *confirmation*: a may ask q even if a already knows that i is the answer, if a wishes to be reassured that i is indeed the answer. Yet, double-checking procedures are insufficient to rescue the analysis, for the complete reduction of relevance to confirmation would work as a *reductio ad absurdum*.

11.6. A metatheoretical revision of the counterfactual analysis

The solution is to bypass the paradox by revising [3] metatheoretically.[5] One can still rely on a's rationality to gauge the epistemic relevance of i to a herself without

---

[5] This solution is partly adopted in information theory by Tishby et al. (1999), who 'define the relevant information in a signal $x \in X$ as being the information that this signal provides about another signal $y \in Y$.

providing the actual content of *i* but only some information about its availability. For if *a* had been informed that new information (*ni*) about *d* was available, insofar as *a* would then have asked a question to retrieve *i*, it follows that *i* would have been correspondingly more or less epistemically relevant to *a*. Now, a simple way of constructing *ni* is by changing the LoA *l*. For example, if *a* had been informed that something had changed regarding the schedule of the meeting (higher LoA), *a* would probably have asked what had changed about it, and the information that the meeting had been cancelled (lower LoA) would then be correctly analysed as highly epistemically relevant to *a*. In this way we obtain:

$$R(i) = \begin{cases} P(A(i, q, d, c, l_m)) & \text{if } P(Q(a, q, d, c, l_m)) = 1 \\ P(Ia(ni, d, l_n)\square\!\!\mapsto Q(a, q, d, c, l_m)) \times P(A(i, q, d, c, l_m)) \\ & \text{if } 0 \leq P(Q(a, q, d, c, l_m)) < 1 \end{cases} \quad [4]$$

or, by simplifying our notation:

$$R(i) = \begin{cases} P(A(i, l_m)) & \text{if } P(Q(a, l_m)) = 1 \\ P(Ia(ni, l_n)\square\!\!\mapsto Q(a, l_m)) \times P(A(i, l_m)) & \text{if } 0 \leq P(Q(a, l_m)) < 1 \end{cases} \quad [5]$$

A final refinement can now complete the analysis. In most cases, *a* is not informed that *ni* is available. Rather, *a* may only be informed that *ni might* be available. So, instead of analysing the probability that *a* would ask *q* about *d* in *c* at *l_m* if *a* were informed that new information *ni* is available about *d* at *l_n*, one should consider, more realistically, the case in which *a* is informed that there is a probability P > 0 that there might be new information *ni* about *d* at *l_n*, that is, $P(IaP(ni, l_n) \square\!\!\mapsto Q(a, l_m))$. Note the scope of the two probabilities: the formula should not be interpreted as a problematic case of second-order probability (Gaifman (1988)), as if the counterfactual depended on the probability of the probability of *a* being informed. It is actually *a* who is informed about the probability of *ni*. The revised formula, with the usual simplifications, is:

$$R(i) = \begin{cases} P(A(i, l_m)) & \text{if } P(Q(a, l_m)) = 1 \\ P(IaP(ni, l_n)\square\!\!\mapsto Q(a, l_m)) \times P(A(i, l_m)) & \text{if } 0 \leq P(Q(a, l_m)) < 1 \end{cases} \quad [6]$$

[6] synthesizes the subjectivist interpretation of epistemic relevance.

Examples include the information that face images provide about the names of the people portrayed, or the information that speech sounds provide about the words spoken.' Note that what they treat as 'relevance' is really a quantitative relation of structural conjunction, which can be considered a necessary condition for semantic relevance, but should not be confused with it.

11.7 Advantages of the metatheoretical revision

The availability of new information about d, retrievable at a higher LoA, is like a sealed envelope for a: a is informed that new information is available inside it, but does not hold the specific informational content (compare this to the message 'you have mail' sent by an email client). In this way, no informational version of Meno's paradox arises, and one can also account for the prima facie obligation that collaborative or informee-friendly informers may have towards a. The trite answer 'I didn't tell you because you didn't ask', offered when someone fails to provide some epistemically relevant information, is now easily shown to be disingenuous. For either a should be assumed to be in a standing state of querying about (i.e. as being interested in) i, in which case the informer has a prima facie obligation to provide a with i even if a did not explicitly ask for it. Imagine the case in which Mathew, a friend of Mary's, knows that she has lost her job, but that she has not yet been informed about this. It would be safe to assume Mary to be in a standing state of querying about such piece of information, so Mathew, as a collaborative informer, has a prima facie obligation to inform her. Or a may simply be assumed to be reasonable enough to ask the appropriate question to obtain i, if provided with sufficient metainformation about the availability of i. In which case, the informer may have the prima facie obligation to provide at least enough metainformation about the availability of new information. Mathew has at least the prima facie obligation to tell Mary that something might have happened regarding her job. Either way, not being explicitly asked by the informee fails to be a proper justification for the (informee-friendly) informer's silence.

A last, important advantage to be highlighted is that [6] is easily translatable into a Bayesian network, which then facilitates the computation of the various variables and subjective probabilities. This is most convenient. Concentrating on the interesting case in which $0 \leq P(Q(a, q, d, c, l_m) < 1$, and for variables N (corresponding to IaP(ni, l_n)), A (corresponding to P($A(i, q, d, c, l_m)$)) and Q (corresponding to P (IaP(ni, l_n) $\square \rightarrow$ $Q(a, l_m)$), given some interpretation of the conditional probabilities:

P(n), the probability of variable N;
P(q | n), the probability of variable Q given n;
P(q | $\bar{n}$), the probability of variable Q given $\bar{n}$;
P(a), the probability of variable A;
P(q | n), the probability of variable Q given n;
P(q | $\bar{n}$), the probability of variable Q given $\bar{n}$;
P(r | $a, \bar{q}$), the probability of variable R given a and $\bar{q}$;
P(r | a, q), the probability of variable R given a and q;
P(r | $\bar{a}, \bar{q}$), the probability of variable R given $\bar{a}$ and $\bar{q}$;
P(r | $\bar{a}, \bar{q}$), the probability of variable R given $\bar{a}$ and $\bar{q}$;

we obtain the corresponding value of the joint probability function:

$$P(r) = \sum_{N,A,Q} P(R|A, Q) \cdot P(Q|N) \cdot P(N) \cdot P(A)$$

Table 8 Example of a node probability table for a Bayesian interpretation of epistemic relevance

N	Q	A	R	P(N)	P(Q | N)	P(A)	P(R | Q, A)
yes	yes	yes	yes	0.9	0.9	0.8	1.0
yes	no	yes	yes	0.9	0.1	0.8	0.1
no	yes	yes	yes	0.1	0.1	0.8	1.0
no	no	yes	yes	0.1	0.9	0.8	0.1
yes	yes	no	yes	0.9	0.9	0.2	0.1
yes	no	no	yes	0.9	0.1	0.2	0.0
no	yes	no	yes	0.1	0.1	0.2	0.1
no	no	no	yes	0.1	0.9	0.2	0.0
yes	yes	yes	no	0.9	0.9	0.8	0.0
yes	no	yes	no	0.9	0.1	0.8	0.9
no	yes	yes	no	0.1	0.1	0.8	0.0
no	no	yes	no	0.1	0.9	0.8	0.9
yes	yes	no	no	0.9	0.9	0.2	0.9
yes	no	no	no	0.9	0.1	0.2	1.0
no	yes	no	no	0.1	0.1	0.2	0.9
no	no	no	no	0.1	0.9	0.2	0.1

For example, suppose we assume that the probability of new information occurring is very high (0.9), that if there is new information, the probability that the agent will ask a question about it is also very high (0.9), and that, if the question is asked, the probability that the answer is adequate is also high (0.8). It follows that the node probability distribution (Table 8) yields a degree of epistemically relevant semantic information of 0.6868:

This can be graphically shown as in Figure 20. Of course, the identification of the right set of Bayesian priors is a hard problem faced by any analysis of real-life phenomena. The formulation of a prior distribution over the unknown parameters of the model should be based on the available data (including subjective beliefs) about the modelled phenomena, yet this is easier said than done, see for example Dongen (2006). Here, the mere assumption of some values is justified and we only need an illustrative example.

To summarize, [6] is easily implementable as a Bayesian Network. It explains why a collaborative informer has a prima facie epistemic obligation to inform a about i, or at least about its availability when the informer does not know what i amounts to, even if the informee does not ask for i. As we shall see in the next section, this is the fundamental assumption behind the juridical concept of relevant information. It is also what may generate conflicts in medical ethics, when epistemically relevant information may or may not be shared with all interested parties.

11.8 Some illustrative cases

As anticipated, the previous analysis is compatible with a large variety of widespread usages of the concept of relevant information, to which it provides a unified, conceptual

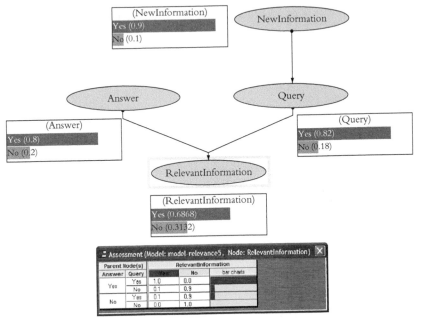

Figure 20 Example of an implementation of [6] by means of a Bayesian network. The variables N, A, Q, and R have been given more intuitive names. The assessment in the smaller window shows the conditional probabilities of variable R = 'Relevant Information'. The diagram was produced with MSBNx Version 1.4.2, Microsoft Research's Bayesian network authoring and evaluation tool

foundation. We have just seen the deontological and Bayesian contexts. Three other examples will suffice to illustrate the point and show how the conceptual ingredients found in [6] also occur in the literature on relevance, even if unsystematically.

The idea of interpreting relevant information erotetically was already exploited by Cohen (1994). It is common in computer science and information science, where relevant information is broadly treated as 'information whose subject matter matches that of a query' (Choo et al. (2000)).

The connection between relevance, probability, and counterfactual inference is drawn, although not too clearly, in jurisprudence. For example, the *U.S. Federal Rules of Evidence 401. Article IV. Relevancy and its limits* states that

'Relevant evidence' means evidence having any tendency to make the existence of any fact that is of consequence to the determination of the action more probable or less probable than it would be without the evidence.

Essentially, the law of evidence treats epistemic relevance as a relation between an informee *a* and two pieces of information *p* and *q*, such that it renders *p* (e.g. information about the involvement of an agent in a crime) more probable to *a* because of the occurrence of *q* (e.g. information about the time and location of an agent when the crime was perpetrated) either by itself, or in connection with other pieces of information (e.g. information about means of transportation).

Finally, in pragmatics, relevance theory (Sperber and Wilson (1995)) states that

In relevance-theoretic terms, an input is relevant to an individual when its processing in a context of available assumptions yields a positive cognitive effect. A positive cognitive effect is a worthwhile difference to the individual's representation of the world – a true conclusion, for example. *False conclusions are not worth having* [emphasis added]. [...] Intuitively, relevance is not just an all-or-none matter but a matter of degree. [...] Thus, relevance may be assessed in terms of cognitive effects and processing effort:

Relevance of an input to an individual

a. other things being equal, the greater the positive cognitive effects achieved by processing an input, the greater the relevance of the input to the individual at that time.

b. other things being equal, the greater the processing effort expended, the lower the relevance of the input to the individual at that time. (Wilson and Sperber (2004), p. 608)

Obviously, 'relevance' is used in relevance theory as a technical term:

Relevance here is a technical term (though clearly related to the natural language homonym), whereby an interpretation is relevant only in cases where the cognitive cost of processing the event which demands the attention of the agent is outweighed by the cognitive benefits of that processing (where benefits include deriving or strengthening new assumptions, and confirming or rejecting previous assumptions). 'Optimal relevance' states that the first interpretation which crosses the relevance threshold is the right one; that is, that the first relevant interpretation the addressee arrives at is the one the speaker intended to communicate. (Emma Borg, 'Intention-Based Semantics', in LePore and Smith (2006), p. 255)

Nevertheless, it is easy to see how several elements in the previous quotation can also be found included in [6], especially the informee-oriented, context-based, query-driven nature of relevance. The improvements encapsulated in [6] are threefold:

i. semantic information (not just some linguistic item) is explicitly identified as the relevance-bearer;

ii. point (a) in the quotation above is still assumed but it is now translated into a's (counterfactual) interest in asking q to obtain i, expressed by a's query. This translation no longer requires the problematic specification of what may count as 'positive cognitive effects';

iii. point (b) in the same quotation is replaced by degrees of probability of obtaining i, since [6] entirely decouples the degree of epistemic relevance of i from the degree of cognitive (or computational) obtainability of i. It seems counterintuitive to assume that 'the greater the processing effort expended, the lower the relevance of the input to the individual at that time'. Indeed, if it were not for the technical use of 'relevance' stressed above, one might argue exactly the opposite: *ceteris paribus*, sometimes it is precisely those bits of information more difficult to obtain (access, process etc.) that are the most epistemically relevant.[6]

A fundamental consequence of both the pragmatic approach (see the quotation above) and the subjectivist interpretation (see [6]) is that false semantic content fails to be relevant at all. This is the next point to be discussed.

11.9 Misinformation cannot be relevant

It is easy to be confused about both 'relevance' and 'misinformation'. Regarding the former, we now have a clear analysis; regarding the latter, I argued in this book that misinformation is 'well-formed and meaningful data (i.e. semantic content) that is false'. 'Disinformation' is simply misinformation purposefully conveyed to mislead the receiver into believing that it is information. If we analyse epistemic relevance in terms of cognitive efforts, clearly misinformation makes no worthwhile difference to the informee/agent's representation of the world. On the contrary, it is actually deleterious. If the train leaves at 13.15, being told that it leaves at 14.25 is a nuisance to say the least. Likewise, if we endorse [6], clearly no rational informee/agent would be interested in receiving some misinformation as an answer to her query. This is consistent with the truth requirement established in Cohen (1994). That one might not know whether the answer counts as information is an entirely different problem, one that involves trust, the reliability of both sources and methods of information processing and, of course, sceptical issues. That misinformation may turn out to be useful in some serendipitous way is also a red herring. False (counterfeit) banknotes may be used to buy some goods, but they would not, for this reason, qualify as legal tender. Likewise, astrological data may, accidentally, lead to a scientific discovery but they are not, for this reason, epistemically relevant information. Of course, there are many ways in which misinformation may be indirectly, inferentially or metatheoretically relevant, yet this is not what is in question here. The student who answers 'Napoleon' to the question 'who fought at Thermopylae?' has said something false, and hence uninformative and a fortiori epistemically irrelevant, to someone who asked the question in order to be informed about the battle, although his answer is informative about, and hence might be epistemically relevant to someone interested in assessing, the student's historical education. It is because of this distinction that the domain, context, and the level of abstraction at which one is evaluating epistemic relevance need to be kept clear and fixed in the course of the analysis. If they are not, the outcome is conceptual carnage.

---

[6] Ziv (1988) has argued that relevance theory needs to be supplemented by a theory of rationality of causal relations, in other words, what in this chapter has been called causal relevance (following Hitchcock (1992)) and the assumption of a rational agent.

In the end, the previous discussion shows that we are on the right track. The pragmatic and the subjectivist interpretation of what may count as communicationally or epistemically relevant semantic information coherently converge on the same conclusion, even if they come from different perspectives: had a known that i was actually a piece of misinformation, she would not have asked q in order to obtain i in the first place. Misinformation is not worth the effort, according to the pragmatic theory. It is unworthy of a rational agent's interest, according to the subjectivist interpretation developed in this chapter. These are two sides of the same coin.

11.10 Two Objections and replies

The subjectivist theory of epistemically relevant information is not entirely uncontroversial and is subject to some criticisms, which may be summarized in two objections. Each of them cast further light on the proposal. Fortunately, they are both answerable.

11.10.1 Completeness: No relevant semantic information for semantically unable agents

The first objection argues that the subjectivist interpretation in [6] relies too heavily on the semantic capacities of the agent a. How can some specific information i (say the location of some organic debris) be relevant to an amoeba, if the amoeba cannot ask any question, not even in principle (as when one might wish to say: 'imagine an amoeba could speak, then . . .'). There is plenty of information that is epistemically relevant to semantically-unable agents, but [6] fails to take this into account, so it is *incomplete* at best.

The objection deserves three replies. First, as it was specified at the outset, the proposed interpretation concerns *semantic* information, not any kind of information. The location of some food is a vitally important yet physical fact, which might be conveyed by a message, and hence be transformed into semantic information, but it is not in itself semantic information. For agents entirely incapable of any semantic interactions, such translation is impossible or rather meaningless, and so should be any analysis of epistemically relevant semantic information as a consequence. In the example, the amoeba and its environment do not interact semantically and this is just the end of the story. No such difficulties arise with animals with higher cognitive faculties, capable of interacting with other animals and the environment semantically. So relevant semantic information can play a role even when zombies are in question (see chapter thirteen).

The second reply is that one might think of some cases of *relevant facts* or uninterpreted *signals/data* as being interpretable in terms of hard-wired questions, posed by the agents involved, which receive equally hard-wired answers, offered by the environment, where the latter are interpretable as affordances (see chapters six and seven). Take the interactions between the environment and organisms even simpler than amoebae, for example heliotropic plants, such as snow buttercups or sunflowers, which react to light. In this case, the 'question' may be seen to have been hard-wired by evolutionary processes into the motor cells located in flexible segments of the plant specialized in pumping potassium ions into nearby tissues (thus changing the turgor pressure) reversibly. The direction of the sun works as the factual answer. The result is a diurnal motion of flowers or leaves. The hard-wiring of questions and answers is just another way of conceptualizing utility functions associated with behavioural strategies. The important difference is that the 'questioning' is entirely externalized. This then allows a quantitative approach to Shannon-type information and its relevance that is coherent with the subjectivist interpretation of semantic information proposed in this chapter, as is clearly shown in Polani et al. (2006) (see also Polani et al. (2001)), who have recently tried to use the bottleneck method (Tishby et al. (1999)) to

study a scenario where a multicellular colony has to trade-off between *utility* of strategies for investment in persistence or progeny and the (Shannon-type) *relevant* information necessary to realize these strategies. (p. 337; emphasis added)

The third reply concerns AI. Heliotropic plants act as analogue computational agents. Do digital computational agents fare any better when it comes to epistemically relevant information as defined in [6]? Not really. Identifying relevant information is just a case of the 'frame problem' (McCarthy and Hayes (1969)), a notorious obstacle for any form of artificial intelligence developed so far. Hard- or soft-wiring 'questions'— which might enable artificial agents to act as if they could process relevant semantic information—is a good but limited strategy. The subjectivist interpretation of relevant information cannot really work for artificial agents simply because the latter are not semantic engines. The same intelligence that leads an agent to *ask* questions is what allows that agent to spot subjectively relevant information. Amoeba, sunflowers, and Turing machines have no semantic abilities, no intelligence, no curiosity, ask no questions and cannot therefore be used as counterarguments against [6] because nothing can be semantically relevant to them. On the contrary, [6] may provide a criterion to discriminate between intelligent, semantically-able agents and non-intelligent, semantically-unable ones. For one may run a sort of reverse-engineered Turing test, in which the agents being tested do not answer, but rather ask questions. One may then check whether the human and the artificial agent's capacities to grasp the relevance of the answers provided are sufficiently indistinguishable. Should that ever happen, that is, if one day artificial agents do perform on average as well as humans in asking questions and dealing with the relevance of the semantic information they receive as answers, some people (myself included) will consider that nothing short of a miracle, which will usher in a dramatically new era in human history.

11.10.2 Soundness: Rationality does not presuppose relevance

The second objection still focuses on the role played by the agent *a*, but with a different strategy. We have seen that throughout the chapter the agent *a* was assumed to be rational. Without this normative condition, *a* would not be pursuing her interests consistently, and she would not be asking those questions that she considers most helpful in order to gather the sort of information that would be useful to satisfy her needs and interests. At the train station, Mary would ignore the announcements, would not ask when her train leaves, would carelessly buy a ticket to some place, wait at a random platform and jump on the first train she fancies. The whole world would be a matter of indifference to her and hence irrelevant to her. So far so good. The objection, however, is not that the informee *a* in [6] should not be assumed to be a sufficiently rational agent, but that this necessary condition begs the question. For surely a rational agent must also be one who is capable of discriminating between more or less relevant alternatives, that is, pieces of semantic information, in order to formulate and guide her choices. But then, we are back to square one: we are explaining epistemic relevance by presupposing it and, even worse, by doing so necessarily, i.e. inescapably.

There are two replies to this objection. The first turns out to be unsatisfactory but helps one to understand the second, which actually answers the objection.

As a first attempt, one may accept the circularity but reject its viciousness. In order to clarify what it means for some information *i* to be epistemically relevant to *a*, one has to refer to a rational agent *a* to whom *i* is relevant, hence *a* must be an agent capable of detecting and weighing relevance. Yet, what is being presupposed is not some pre-formed or innate quantity of relevant information in the head of the informee, but just the presence in *a* of some relevance-detecting capacity, implicit in the description of *a* as a rational agent. Some information *i* is relevant to *a* if and only if *a* behaves in such a way as to show that *i* is relevant to her and this includes asking questions to retrieve *i*. We are using a rational agent *a* to identify information epistemically relevant to *a* in the same was as a chemist may use litmus to detect acid substances. As Polani et al. (2001) put it: 'One can regard the decision system or agent as an estimator for the optimal action to take' and hence the corresponding, relevant information that determines it.

The previous reply would be entirely convincing were it not for the fact that the chemist does not stop at the successful litmus test, but actually explains its success through a well-supported theory on the nature and nomic behaviour of acids as substances that are proton donors and accept electrons to form ionic bonds. It is this scientific explanation that allows her to avoid any circularity. Litmus does not tell her what it means for a substance to be an acid; it merely tells her whether it is an acid. If this were all she could say about acidity, it would be just a matter of circular and conventional definition, not much better than the *virtus dormitiva* used to explain why camomile makes one sleep. Likewise, if all we could offer were a reduction of epistemically relevant information to *a*'s capacity to detect it, we would be merely shifting the problem. We would be saying that some information *i* is epistemically relevant to an agent *a* because *a* can detect it as such, and *a* detects *i* as such because it is so. Clearly, the viciousness of the circularity kicks in, unless we have something comparable to the chemist's safety exit. The first reply is unsatisfactory. Fortunately, a second reply comes to its rescue.

It is insufficient to rely on the rationality of the agent, if this is just another way of speaking of epistemic relevance, but rational agents need not be defined in terms of their capacities to detect relevant information. The 'surely' used in formulating the objection above is merely rhetorical and unjustified. On the contrary, the standard way in which a rational agent a is defined refers only to the following four conditions:

R.1 *information input*: a can perceive her environment through sensors;

R.2 *action output*: a can act upon her environment through effectors in order to modify and/or control it;

R.3 *preferences about outcomes*: a is not indifferent with respect to the new states of the environment and of herself that she may obtain (outcomes); she has desires, likes, dislikes, and so forth, which may make her privilege some outcomes over others;

R.4 *optimization of outcomes with respect to preferences*: a acts in her own best interest, always preferring the outcomes that have the highest *expected utility*.

No condition contains, or requires a reference to, epistemically relevant information. The Harsanyi doctrine, regarding multiagent systems, is also relevance-independent, and the logic of rational choice in general, or Bayesian learning in particular, does not rely on epistemic relevance. So *it seems* that, by referring to rational agents in [6], one can validly reduce epistemically relevant semantic information to a set of conditions none of which is based in its turn on relevance or other cognate concepts.

'It seems' because our sceptical opponent may still believe that he has one last card up his sleeve. He may retort that irrational agents are normally defined in terms of ir/relevant information. In particular, he may stress that it is a standard move in the literature on rational choice to consider an agent a irrational if

Ir.1 a deliberately ignores (what a considers to be) relevant information; and/or

Ir.2 a deliberately uses (what a considers to be) irrelevant information (here the typical case is known as the sunk cost fallacy).

His objection is now that (Ir.1) and (Ir.2) are not cases of mistaken evaluation (the clauses 'deliberately' and the bracketed conditions take sufficient care of this) but rather evidence that the very concept of ir/rational agent presupposes that of ir/relevant semantic information and therefore cannot ground it.

This final version of the objection is based on a conflation between irrationality and incoherence, which unfortunately seems to be widespread in the literature on rational choice. We have seen above that two or more agents are rational if they satisfy the Harsanyi doctrine. A single agent a is then rational if she satisfies conditions R.1–R.4. If R.1 or R.2 are unsatisfied, a is not an agent; and if R.3 or R.4 are unsatisfied, a is an agent but not rational. This is textbook material. Once conditions R.1–R.4 are satisfied, the rational agent may be embedded in [6] to yield a non-circular definition of epistemically relevant information. And once it is established that some information i is epistemically relevant to the rational agent a, then this can be used to establish whether *a* is a *coherent* agent. Now coherence may be loosely discussed in terms of rationality but, given the standard definition above, it is important to be more precise and careful, by looking at the course of actions of our agent through time.

Suppose *a* is irrational because *a* fails to satisfy R.3 or R.4. According to [6], there is no information that is epistemically relevant to *a*. So there is no problem about *a* deliberately ignoring relevant information, a behaviour which is an effect of *a*'s irrationality, not a cause of it. The agent *a* is irrational because of other shortcomings, unrelated to the notion of relevance.

Suppose *a* is rational because *a* initially satisfies R.3 and R.4. Then, according to [6], there is some information *i* that is epistemically relevant to *a*, and some other information *l* that is epistemically irrelevant. But then, if, after this stage, *a* goes on deliberately ignoring *i* or deliberately using *l*, this means that her course of action becomes incoherent: in particular, she no longer acts in her own best interest, an interest that was defined by the role she played in identifying epistemically ir/relevant information in the earliest stage of the analysis using [6]. At this point, the agent is not entirely irrational, but she is certainly incoherent: she is initially rational, insofar as her behaviour may lead to the definition of epistemically ir/relevant information, but she is then irrational, insofar as her subsequent behaviour does not take her previous behaviour and its outcome into account. In other words, she is incoherent and her incoherence results from a comparison between her behaviour before and after the identification and gathering of some information *i* as epistemically ir/relevant.

In either case, there is no circularity. We are defining coherence in terms of deliberate consideration/usage of epistemically ir/relevant information and ir/relevant information in terms of rational agency, and this in terms of R.1–R.4 (stand-alone agent) and the Harsanyi doctrine (multi-agent systems). What is gained, rather than a fallacious definition, is a useful way to quantify the mismatch between the rational behaviour of asking *q* in [6] first, and the irrational behaviour of disregarding the answer to it, or using some information that does not satisfy [6], later. Basically, the higher the probability that *a* might have asked *q*, the more irrational *a* is if she then deliberately ignores the resulting *i* or uses *l*.

CONCLUSION

In this chapter, I developed and defended a subjectivist interpretation of relevance. The theory, synthesized in [6], is consistent with and reinforces the veridical thesis defended in the previous chapters. It is defensible in terms of its completeness and soundness, and it provides the missing foundation for a general theory of relevance. It constitutes the hub for several other theories of relevance already developed in the literature, a hub that can be easily expanded by other modules. Two are worth stressing in this conclusion. First, [6] is easily combined with theories of information (or belief) upgrade. This is crucial, since the latter can explain how degrees of relevance may be dynamically upgraded following the evolution of *a*'s background information and beliefs and feedback loops. Second, [6] is perfectly compatible with subjectivist interpretations of probability and Bayesian learning. Clearly these are implications and applications that will be worth developing, but the reader will recall that our next task is another. We needed a theory of relevant information in order to move towards a non-doxastic, informational analysis of knowledge. We now have it so we can move to that topic, in the next chapter.

12

Semantic information and the network theory of account

Evans had the idea that there is a much cruder and more fundamental concept than that of knowledge on which philosophers have concentrated so much, namely the concept of information. Information is conveyed by perception, and retained by memory, though also transmitted by means of language. One needs to concentrate on that concept before one approaches that of knowledge in the proper sense. Information is acquired, for example, without one's necessarily having a grasp of the proposition which embodies it; the flow of information operates at a much more basic level than the acquisition and transmission of knowledge. I think that this conception deserves to be explored. It's not one that ever occurred to me before I read Evans, but it is probably fruitful. That also distinguishes this work very sharply from traditional epistemology.

Dummett (1993a), p. 186.

SUMMARY

Previously, in chapters four and five, I developed and defended a strongly semantic theory of semantic information. According to it, semantic information is well-formed, meaningful, and truthful data. In chapters six and seven, I analysed the symbol grounding problem and proposed a solution in order to explain how well-formed data might become meaningful. In chapter eight, I articulated and supported a correctness theory of truth in order to explain how well-formed and meaningful data might become truthful. In chapter nine, I showed that the doxastic, tripartite analysis of knowledge is irrecoverably faulty in order to clear the ground for an informational approach. An informational approach to the analysis of knowledge needs to be logically feasible, and I proved this in chapter ten. The question remained, however, how semantic information could upgrade to knowledge. In chapter eleven, I provided a theory of relevance as a necessary condition for such an upgrade. Semantic information must be truthful and relevant in order to become knowledge. Yet well-formedness, meaningfulness, truthfulness and relevance are still insufficient to differentiate a lucky informee from a knower. So, in this chapter, I add the last necessary ingredient, in terms of a theory of account. This should provide a positive answer to P13 (see chapter two). The introductory section explains the technical terminology and the relevant background. Section 12.2 argues that, for relevant semantic information to be upgraded to knowledge, it is necessary and sufficient to be embedded in a network of questions and answers that correctly accounts for it. Section 12.3 shows that an information flow network of type A fulfils such a requirement, by warranting that the erotetic deficit, characterizing the target semantic information t by default, is correctly satisfied by the information flow of correct answers provided by an adequate informational source s. Section 12.4 illustrates some of the major advantages of such a network theory of account (NTA) and clears the ground of a few potential difficulties. Section 12.5 clarifies why NTA, and an informational analysis of knowledge, according to which knowledge is semantic information for which we can provide an account, is not subject to Gettier-type counterexamples. A concluding section briefly summarizes the results obtained.

12.1 Introduction

The problem addressed in this chapter may be phrased rather simply: how does relevant semantic information upgrade to knowledge? The solution, articulated and supported in the following pages, is equally straightforward: relevant semantic information upgrades to knowledge if and only if it is correctly accounted for. As the reader may already suspect, the difficulty lies in the theoretical work required to understand the problem in detail, to explain and defend the solution successfully and to show how the two are properly related. These tasks will be undertaken in the next four sections. They are followed by some concluding remarks, which briefly summarize the results obtained. Before we enter into a thorough investigation of the subject matter, however, it might be helpful to clarify, in this section, some key concepts and the general framework in which they will be used, lest the lack of a shared vocabulary might hinder the work that lies ahead.

12.2 The nature of the upgrading problem: Mutual independence

In chapter eight, we saw that [SI], that is,

> [SI] p qualifies as semantic information if and only if p is (constituted by)
>
> *well − formed, meaningful, and truthful data,*

nests semantic information into knowledge so tightly that one is naturally led to wonder whether anything might be missing, in order to upgrade from the weaker to the stronger phenomenon, and hence between their corresponding concepts. Indeed, the threshold can be so fine that one may often overlook it, and thus fail to distinguish between the two propositional attitudes, treating 'Mary *is informed that* the water in the electric kettle is boiling' and 'Mary *knows that* the water in the electric kettle is boiling' as if they were always interchangeable without loss. In everyday life, this might be the norm and the conflation is usually harmless: it can hardly matter whether the bus driver is informed or knows that the traffic light is red. Philosophically, however, the distinction captures an important difference, and hence it is important to be more accurate. It takes only a moment of reflection to see that one may be informed (hold the information) that p without actually knowing that p. Not only because in chapter ten it was argued that holding the information that p does not have to be a *reflective* state (although it is not necessarily the case that $I_a p \rightarrow II_a p$, one may also object that $K_a p \rightarrow KK_a p$ is notoriously controversial as well) but also because, even when it is, it might still arguably be *opaque* and certainly *aleatoric* (epistemic luck), whereas knowledge cannot.

Consider *opaqueness* first. It is open to reasonable debate whether a messenger carrying (in her memory, in her hand, or in a pocket, it does not matter) an encrypted message p that she does not understand—even if she is informed that she carries p—may be said to hold the information that p. On the one hand, one may argue that she is not genuinely informed that p. On the other hand, one may retort that, if she can deliver the information that p (and we are assuming that she can), then she can legitimately be said to be informed that p or hold that information. The interesting point here is not to solve the dispute, but to note that the dispute itself is reasonable. Compare the case where the same messenger knows that p, there can be no doubt that she must also understand the information carried by p. It might be open to debate whether holding the information that p is necessarily a non-opaque state, but such a dispute would be pointless in the case of knowing that p. Note that, as far as opaqueness is concerned, knowing and being informed that p might collapse from a first-person perspective, although not from a second-person perspective, but that the collapse is not necessary if one first-personally, reflectively realizes that one does not really have a clue about p, apart from holding the information that p. I will return to this point in the next chapter.

Next, consider *epistemic luck*. When asking how semantic information may be upgraded to knowledge, we are not asking what further axioms may need to be satisfied by normal modal logic **KTB**. For even if we were to upgrade **KTB** all the way up to S5, as it is perfectly, and indeed easily, doable, we would still be left with the problem of the non-aleatoric nature of knowledge. Now, raising the issue of epistemic luck serves two purposes. It further strengthens the conclusion that there is a clear difference between (holding) the semantic information that p and (having) the knowledge that p. And it points towards what might be missing for semantic information to upgrade to knowledge.

Regarding the first purpose, epistemic luck affects negatively only knowledge but not semantic information. To see why, one may use a classic Russellian example: if one checks a watch at time t and the watch is broken but stopped working exactly twelve hours before ($t - 12$) and therefore happens to indicate the right time $t - 12$ at t, one is still informed that the time is t, although one can no longer be said to know the time. The same applies to a more Platonic example, in which a student memorizes, but fails to grasp, the proof of a geometrical theorem: she is informed (holds the information) that the proof is so and so, but does not really know that the proof is so and so. Generalizing, Russell- Plato- or Gettier-type counterexamples may succeed in degrading 'knowing' to merely 'being informed' ('holding the information that'), but then 'being informed' is exactly what is left after the application of such counterexamples and what remains resilient to further subjunctive conditionalization.

Regarding the second purpose, epistemic luck, if properly diagnosed, should be understood as a *symptom* of the disease to be cured, rather than the disease itself, and therefore as providing an indication of the sort of possible treatment that might be required. To explain how, let me introduce the following thought experiment.

Imagine a memoryless Oracle, who can toss a magic coin to answer Boolean questions.[1] The coin is magic because it unfailingly lands heads whenever the correct answer to the Boolean question is yes, and tails whenever it is no. The Oracle has two alternatives. Either she remains silent and does not answer the Boolean question at all. This happens whenever the question cannot be answered uncontroversially and unambiguously either yes or no. Examples include 'is the answer to this question "no"?', 'do colourless green ideas sleep furiously?', or 'will there be a naval battle tomorrow?'. Or she can toss the coin and thereby give the correct answer by reading the result aloud. Let us assume that there is no significant time lag between question and answer: if no answer is provided within a few seconds, it means that the Oracle will provide no answer at all (recall that she has no memory). It seems clear that the Oracle is the ultimate reliable source of information, but that she has no propositional knowledge. Imagine now a Scribe. He knows that heads means yes and tails means no. He asks the Oracle answerable Boolean questions and methodically records her correct answers in his scroll, thus acting as an external memory. The entries in the scroll are ordered pairs that look like this:

> [. . .]
> <Q: 'Is Berlin the capital of France?' A: 'no'>
> <Q: 'Is Berlin in Germany?' A: 'yes'>
> <Q: 'Is Berlin the capital of Germany?' A: 'yes'>
> <Q: 'Has Berlin always been the capital of Germany?' A: 'no'>
> <Q: 'Did Berlin become the capital of reunified Germany in 1990?' A: 'yes'>
> <Q: 'Is Berlin the largest city in Europe?' A: 'no'>
> <Q: 'Is Germany in Europe?' A: 'yes'>
> [. . .]

The scroll will soon resemble a universal Book of Facts, with each entry (each ordered pair) as an information packet. Further details could easily be added, such as a time stamp

---

[1] Note that the example of the Oracle, the magic coin and the Scribe should not be confused with BonJour's example of Norman, who is assumed to be a perfectly reliable clairvoyant (BonJour (1985)). This because the latter is supposed to have no evidence at all indicating that he is a clairvoyant, and has no way of realizing that his beliefs are caused by his clairvoyance, therefore having no justification for them in terms of his clairvoyant capacities.

t indicate when the entries were obtained. Now, it has been customary, at least since Plato, to argue that the scroll contains at most relevant semantic information but not knowledge, and that the Scribe may at best be informed (even counterfactually so: if *p* were not the case, the Oracle would not have given the answer she has given), but does not know, that e.g. 'Germany is in Europe', because knowledge cannot be aleatoric. This much seems uncontroversial. What is less clear is the exact nature of the problem. By seeking to uncover it, we enter into the second half of this section: understanding what the difference is between relevant semantic information and knowledge.

It might be tempting to argue that epistemic luck is the actual problem because, if we were to depend on it for our knowledge of reality, sooner or later we would run into trouble. We cannot be lucky in all circumstances and, even in the same circumstances, we might have been unlucky, so other epistemic agents might easily disagree with us, for they might enjoy different degrees of epistemic luck, which means that further coin-tossing would hardly help, and that interactions with the world and other agents embedded in it might be utterly haphazard. Yet giving in to this temptation would be short-sighted. Relevant semantic information is impervious to epistemic luck whereas knowledge is not, but epistemic luck is only a criterion that helps us to differentiate between the two, a device used to cast light on the real difficulty. This is why the Oracle–Scribe example ensures that we see, clearly and distinctly, that the erratic and unreliable nature of epistemic luck plays no role. By definition, the Oracle is infallible, in the sense that she always provides the correct answer, and the Scribe is fully reliable, in the sense that he is perfectly able to record and later access the right piece of relevant semantic information. Moreover, if a second Scribe were to consult the Oracle, he would obtain the same piece of information (ordered pairs). Indeed, the Oracle would be the ultimate Salomonic judge of any Boolean dispute. Nevertheless, we are facing a case of information at most, not of knowledge. If the problem with epistemic luck were that we may never have it, or that we might not have had it, or that we may never have enough of it, or that different epistemic agents may have different degrees of it, then the argument should be that hoping or trusting to be always (by oneself) and consistently (with respect to others) lucky cannot be a successful epistemic strategy even in the short term. But it should not be that, when one is actually lucky, one still fails to win the epistemic game. Nevertheless, this is exactly what we are asserting above, and rightly so. There is indeed something epistemically unsatisfactory with answering questions by tossing a coin, yet the aleatoric nature of the process is not the fundamental difficulty, it is only the superficial symptom, and that is why taking care of the features that are most obviously problematic, by using a magic coin, clarifies that we are still failing to tackle the real issue.

At this point, one may concede that, yes, epistemic luck is only evidence of a more profound failure, but then conclude that this failure might be related to truth-conductivity, subjective justification or a combination of both. Yet this too would be a mistake. By hypothesis, the procedure of asking Boolean questions to the Oracle and recording her answers is as truth-conducive as anyone may wish it to be. Likewise, the Scribe holding the information contained in the scroll is perfectly justified in doing so, and his attitude is indeed very rational: given the circumstances and the availability of the Oracle, he ought to consult her, and rely on her answers, both in order to obtain information and in order to justify and manage (increase, refine, upgrade etc.) his own information states (set of beliefs, in the doxastic vocabulary). He is not prey to some wishful thinking, but sensibly constrained by his source of information. So, epistemic luck is indeed a warning sign, but neither of some alethic ineffectiveness on the side of the epistemic process, nor of some rational laxity on the side of the knowing subject.

The problem lies elsewhere, more deeply: the aleatorization of information (i.e. the randomization of the ordered pairs or scroll entries in the lucky sense seen above) dissolves the bonds that hold it together coherently (its consilience), like salt in water. If one analyses each entry in the scroll, there is clearly nothing epistemically wrong, either with it or with the subject holding it. What the aleatoric procedure achieves is the transformation of each piece of information into a standalone, mutually independent item, entirely and only dependent on an external and unrelated event, namely, the tossing of the magic coin. The problem is therefore systemic: aleatorization tears information items away from the fabric of their interrelations, thus depriving each resulting information packet of its potential role as evidence, and of its potential value for prediction or retrodiction, inferential processes, and explanation.

Consider our thought experiment once again. This time, in order to explain mutual independence, let us assume that the Oracle uses an ordinary coin and that we have no reassurance about the truth or falsity of each ordered pair so obtained. Each $<Q_x, A_x>$ will now have a probability value P independent of any other[2] ordered pair $<Q_y, A_y>$ (for $x \neq y$), that is:

$$P(<Q_X, A_X > \cap <Q_y, A_y >) = P(<Q_X, A_X >)P(<Q_y, A_y >).$$

More generally, the scroll will contain only mutually independent entries, in the precise sense that any finite subset $S_1, \ldots, S_n$ of ordered pairs listed in the scroll will satisfy the multiplication rule: $P(\cap_{i=1}^{n} S_i) = \prod_{i=1}^{n} P(S_i)$. This feature is somewhat hidden when the coin is magic, since, in that case, each ordered pair and any finite subset of them in the scroll has probability 1. But consider what happens in the process of making an ordinary coin increasingly better at providing the correct answer (i.e. more and more 'magic'): all the difficulties concerning chance and unreliability, truth-conductivity and subjective justification gradually disappear, until, with a perfectly magic coin, total epistemic luck indicates no other problem but the semantic lack (if we are trying to upgrade semantic information to knowledge) or removal (if we are trying to downgrade knowledge to semantic information) of any structural pattern stitching the various pieces of information together.

---

[2] This is to ensure that no confusion is caused by self-referential independence (strictly speaking x is independent of itself if and only if its probability is one or zero).

Such mutual independence is not yet a difficulty per se yet, but it finally points towards the problem that we need to solve. As Dummett (2004) nicely puts it

We do not merely react piecemeal to what other people say to us: we use the information we acquire, by our own observation and inferences and by what we are told, in speech and writing, by others, to build an integrated picture of the world. (p. 29)

Yet, by definition, mutually independent pieces of information cannot yield this integrated picture of the world because they cannot *account* for each other, that is, they cannot answer the question *how come* that $<Q_x, A_x>$. Both italicized expressions require clarification.

Plato[3] famously discusses the importance of embedding truths (our packets of semantic information) into the right network of conceptual interrelations that can 'provide reason' (*logon didonai*) for them in order to gain knowledge of them. Plato seems to have meant several different things with 'provide reason', as this could refer to giving a definition, a logical proof, some reasonable support (e.g. dialectically), an explanation (e.g. causally) or some clarification (e.g. through an analogy), depending on the context. We shall see that this range of meanings is worth preserving. It is roughly retained in English by 'giving a reasoned account' or simply 'accounting for', hence the use of the term above.[4]

Aristotle, not less famously, discusses the range of questions that an account may be expected to answer. For our purposes, we may organize them into *teleological* (future-oriented why, or what for, or for what goal or purpose), *genealogical* (past-oriented why, or where from, or through which process or steps) and *functional* questions (present-oriented why, or in what way, or according to which mechanism). Again, in English 'how come' captures these different meanings without too much semantic stretching. This point was famously stressed in the philosophy of biology by Mayr (1961):

The functional biologist is vitally concerned with the operation and interaction of structural elements, from molecules up to organs and whole individuals. His ever-repeated question is 'How?' How does something operate, how does it function? [...] The chief technique of the functional biologist is the experiment, and his approach is essentially the same as that of the physicist and the chemist. [...] The evolutionary biologist differs in his method and in the problems in which he is interested. His basic question is 'Why?' When we say 'why' we must always be aware of the ambiguity of this term. It may mean 'How come?' but it may also mean the finalistic 'What for?' When the evolutionist asks 'Why?' he or she always has in mind the historical 'How come?' [...] We can use the language of information theory to attempt still another characterization of these two fields of biology [i.e. functional biology and evolutionary biology]'. (the citation is from the text reproduced in his *Toward a New Philosophy of Biology: Observations of an Evolutionist*, pp. 25–26).

---

[3] See for example C. C. W. Taylor (1967) and more recently C. C. W. Taylor (2008), esp. pp. 185–187.

[4] This epistemic sense should not be confused with the sense in which 'account' is technically used in communication studies, where it refers to the common practice of justifying one's own behaviour, see ch. 13 in Whaley and Samter (2006). In Floridi (1996) I referred to it in terms of *supporting explanation*.

If we apply this clarification to our examples, when someone asks today 'how come that Berlin is the capital of Germany?' one may be asking what future purposes this might serve (teleological question); or which events in the 1990s led to the transfer of the capital from Bonn to Berlin (genealogical question); or (admittedly less obviously in this example) how Berlin works as the re-established capital of a re-unified Germany (functional question). 'How come' questions (henceforth HC-questions) may therefore receive different answers. 'How come that the water in the electric kettle is boiling?' may receive as an answer 'because Mary would like some tea' (teleological account); or 'because Mary filled it with water and turned it on' (genealogical account); or 'because electricity is still flowing through the element inside the kettle, resistance to the electric flow is causing heat, and the steam has not yet heated up the bimetallic strip that breaks the circuit' (functional account).

In the next section, we shall see that the wide semantic scope of both expressions ('account' and 'HC-questions') is an important feature, essential in order to develop a sufficiently abstract theory that can show how information can be upgraded to knowledge. At the moment, the previous clarifications suffice to formulate more precisely our problem (P) and working hypothesis (H) to solve it, thus:

P   (a packet of) relevant semantic information does not qualify yet as (an instance of) knowledge because it raises HC-questions that it cannot answer;

H   (a packet of) relevant semantic information can be upgraded to (become an instance of) knowledge by having the HC-questions it raises answered by an account.

What is an account then, and how does it work?

12.3 Solving the upgrading problem: The network theory of account

Each piece of semantic information is an answer to a question, which, as a whole, poses further questions about itself that require the right sort of information flow in order to be answered correctly, through an appropriate network of relations with some informational source. Until recently, it would have been difficult to transform this general intuition about the nature of epistemic account into a detailed model, which could then be carefully examined and assessed. Fortunately, new developments in an area of applied mathematics and computational algorithms known as *network theory* (Ahuja et al. (1993), Newman et al. (2006)) has provided all the technical and conceptual resources needed for our task.

The task is fairly simple: we need to construct a network through which the right sort of information flows from a source s to a sink target t. In this network, t poses the relevant questions and s accounts *for t* if and only if s provides the correct answers. If the bi-conditional holds, we shall say that the whole network yields an account *of t*. Let us see the details.

We start by modelling the network as a finite directed graph G, representing the pattern of relations (a set E of *edges*) linking s and t. The edges work like communication channels: they have a set capacity c (e.g. how much information they can possibly convey) and implement an actual flow f (e.g. the amount of information they actually convey), which can be, at most, as high as their capacity. The path from s to t is usually mediated, so we shall assume the presence of a set (V) of other nodes (called *vertices*) between s and t that relay the information. Figure 21 provides an illustration.

The system just sketched qualifies as a flow network if and only it satisfies the following conditions (where u and v are any two vertices generating an edge):

1. $G = (V, E)$ is a finite directed graph in which each edge $(u, v) \in E$ has a capacity c $(u, v) \geq 0$. Although we shall assume that c could be real-valued, for our purposes we may deal only with non-negative, natural values;

2. in G there are two special vertices: a source s, and a sink t;

3. every vertex lies on some path from s to t;

4. any (u, v) that is not an edge is disregarded by setting its capacity to zero;

5. a flow is a real-valued function on pairs of vertices $f: V \times V \rightarrow R$, which satisfies the following three properties:

   i. *capacity constraint*: $\forall v, u \in V, f(u, v) \leq c(u, v)$, that is, the flow along an edge can be at most as high as the capacity of that edge;

   ii. *skew symmetry*: $\forall v, u \in V, f(u, v) = -f(v, u)$, that is, the net flow forward is the opposite of the net flow backwards;

   iii. *flow conservation*: $\forall v, u \in V$ and $u \neq s$ and $u \neq t$, $\sum_{w \in V} f(u, w) = 0$, that is, the net flow to a vertex is zero, except for s, which generates flow, and t, which consumes flow. Given (b), this is equivalent to flow-in = flow-out.

The next step is to transform the flow network into an *information* flow network A, which can successfully model the process through which some semantic information is accounted for.

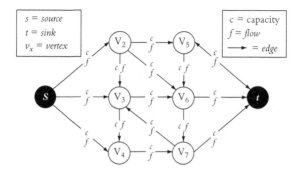

Figure 21 Example of a flow network

Since A is a flow network, it satisfies all the previous five conditions. In order to obtain a rather idealized but still realistic model of informational accounting, A needs to satisfy the following additional conditions.

a. *Single commodity*. This is a standard simplification in network theory. In A there is only one good (information as answers to questions) that flows through the network, with no constraint on which vertex gets which part of the flow. In real life, it usually matters how the flow is distributed through which vertices, but this feature would only increase the complexity of A with no heuristic added-value for our present purpose. Multi-commodity flow problems turn out to be NP-complete even for natural-valued flows and only two commodities. This is a good reminder that A is meant to be an abstract, conceptual model of the process of accounting, not a blueprint for some algorithmic application.

b. *Single source*. This is another standard assumption in network theory since, even if there were more than one source s_n, we could always add a special supersource S of information linking it to all the other s_n with edges with infinite capacity. By pushing the maximum flow from S to t we would actually produce the maximum flow from all the s_n to t.

c. *Redundancy* $= 0$. Intuitively, we assume that each packet of information is sent only once. More precisely, the vertices between s and t are not real secondary sources but rather ideal witnesses, constructed by means of a partition of the set of Boolean answers possible within the network (capacity) and actually required by t (flow). This because, contrary to ordinary physical flow networks (e.g. water through pipes, automobile traffic through a road network and so forth), in A, s could send the same piece of information repeatedly through different channels without any loss, and this would make it more difficult to quantify it. It is possible to revise (c) by applying linear logic constraints to network theory that safeguard a realistic deployment of packets of information (interpreted as truths) as resources, but it would not be philosophically useful here.

d. *Fidelity* $= 1$. Following information theory, we assume a completely accurate transfer of information from s to t. This means no noise and no equivocation, as specified in (e) and (f).

e. *Noise* $= 0$. Recall that, in information theory, noise is defined as any information received but not sent. In A, this means that any vertex different from s adds nothing to the information provided by s. Again, it is possible, but not philosophically useful, to model more complex scenarios, known as networks with gains, in which at least some vertices have a real-valued gain $g \geq 0$ such that, if an amount of information x flows into v then an amount gx flows out of v.

f. *Equivocation* $= 0$. In information theory, this is information sent but never received.

g. *Processing* $= 0$. This follows from conditions 5.i–iii and (e)–(f): every vertex between s and t merely retransmits the information it receives, without elaborating it, coding it, or even reinforcing it (as repeaters do). Recent research on network information flow (Ahlswede et al. (2000), Yeung (2008)) has proved that, in real circumstances, information can be multicast at a higher rate by using network coding, in which a receiver obtains as input a mix of information packets and elaborates which of them are meant to reach a sink. Yet this refinement is not essential for our purposes.

h. *Memory* = 0. As in (g), every vertex between s and t does not register the information flow, it merely multicasts it (see (j) below).

i. *Cost* = 0. Again, following information theory, we shall disregard any cost involved in the transmission of information from one vertex to another. Network theory does provide the technical tools to handle this problem, by assigning to each edge $(u, v) \in E$ a given cost $k(u, v)$ and then obtaining the overall cost of sending some flow $f(u, v)$ across an edge as $f(u, v) \times k(u, v)$. This would be crucial in any logistic context in which transmission costs need to be minimized, but it can be disregarded here.

j. *Routing scheme*: multicast. Realism requires that s may deliver its information to many vertices simultaneously.

The information flow network A that we obtain from conditions (1)–(5) and (a)–(j) is a standard idealization, which contains all the elements required for our theoretical purposes but does not abstract from any feature that would be relevant. It merely simplifies our task, which is now that of showing how A models the process of accounting for some semantic information.

We have seen that epistemic luck dismantles the machinery of knowledge into its constitutive components, leaving them in perfect epistemic condition but piled up in a heap, unable to account properly for each other. This mutual independence is the semantic loss that needs to be tackled in order to upgrade relevant semantic information to knowledge. We need to restore the epistemic fabric within which each piece of relevant semantic information is a thread. This is what (an implementation of) the information flow network A achieves, in the following way.

The relevant semantic information to be accounted for is the sink t. Using our previous example, let us set t = 'the water in the electric kettle is boiling'. The sink t poses a number of HC-questions. For the sake of simplicity, we shall disregard the important fact that such questions will be formulated for a particular purpose, within a context and at some level of abstraction. Further simplifying, we transform each HC-question into a Boolean question. For example: 'how come that the water in the electric kettle is boiling?' may become 'Is the water in the electric kettle boiling because Mary wants some tea?'. So, t comes with an information deficit, which is quantifiable by the number of Boolean answers required to satisfy it. In our example, let us assume that t requires 10 Boolean answers. Accounting for t means answering t's HC-questions correctly, that is, providing the necessary flow of information that can satisfy t's Boolean deficit satisfactorily. The required answers come from the source s, but the connection between s and t is usually indirect, being mediated by some relay systems: a document, a witness, a database, an experiment, some news from the mass media, may all be vertices in the information flow, with the proviso that they are constituted by their capacity and flow values according to condition (c) above. Following standard practice, and again for the sake of illustration only, let us assume the presence of six intermediate vertices. Each vertex v_x and the source s can provide a maximum number of Boolean answers. This is the capacity c. An edge is now a vector with direction, indicating where the answers come from, and magnitude, indicating how many answers the starting point could provide in theory. In Figure 22, the edge (v_5, t), for example, can convey up to 4 Boolean answers, while the total capacity of the selected area (known as a *cut*) is $20 + 5 + 4 = 29$.

The next task is to identify the flow of information, that is, the set of Boolean answers actually required by t. Information percolates through the network but, ultimately, it is assumed to come from a single source s. In most cases, the source and the layers of vertices have a much higher informational capacity c. This because s and any v_x may be a very rich source of information, like a complex experiment, a perceptual experience, an encyclopaedia, a large database, a universal law, a whole possible world, the universe, or indeed our Oracle with a magic coin (recall the Supersource in (b) above). Clearly, s and the vertices between s and t can answer many more questions than the ones posed by t. Figure 23 shows a possible flow of information, given our example. The vectors (edges) now have a magnitude consti- tuted by the numeric values for c (first value) and f (second value, in bold).

If all the HC-questions posed by t are correctly answered by s through A, then s accounts for t and A is an account of t. If the answers are incorrect or insufficient in number, then t remains unaccounted for, A is insufficient and may need to be improved or replaced. Before exploring some of the features of the model just proposed, let us take stock of the results obtained so far.

There is a difference between relevant semantic information and knowledge, which can be highlighted by epistemic luck. The difference is that relevant semantic

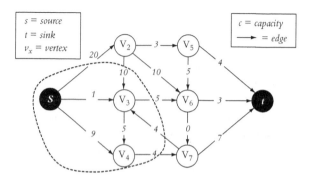

Figure 22 An information flow network with capacities and cut

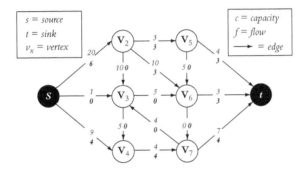

Figure 23 An information flow network with capacities and flow

information lacks the necessary structure of relations that allow different packets of information to account for each other. It follows that, for relevant semantic information to be upgraded to knowledge, it is necessary to embed it in a network of equally relevant questions and corresponding correct answers. An information flow network of type *A* fulfils such a requirement, by making sure that the erotetic deficit, which the target semantic information *t* has by default, is satisfied by the flow of correct answers, provided by an adequate informational source *s*.

At this point, we can become better acquainted with what I shall refer to as a network theory of account (henceforth NTA) by appreciating some of its major advantages and clearing the ground of a few potential difficulties. This is the task of the next section.

12.4 Advantages of a network theory of account

Let me first dissipate two concerns regarding NTA: that it might be too general or, in another sense, too specific.

Regarding its generality, I suggested above that it should be appreciated as an advantage. In short, it is the same generality that we find in the supply and demand model in economics. More specifically, at least two of the main valuable features of NTA (the interested reader is referred to Chen (2003) for further details) make such generality welcome:

- *robust scalability*: the description of NTA outlined above highlights only the features that are of main interest here—in order to make sense of what an account for some semantic information amounts to, and hence how semantic information may be upgraded to knowledge—but it should be clear that more complex scenarios can be easily and elegantly handled by NTA, by relying on the wealth of theoretical results and successful applications of network theory; and
- *flexible semantics*: network theory deals as abstractly as possible with flow structures (this generality may remind the reader of category theory). Following network

theory, NTA inherits a similarly high degree of generality. It thus provides a unifying notation, terminology, and modelling approach, which make it suitable for a variety of specific applications, depending on how the sink, the source, the layers of vertices, the edges, the information flow, and the complexity of the network (see conditions (a)–(j) in the previous section) are interpreted.

Because of its robust scalability and flexible semantics, NTA has a very wide scope of applicability. It can make sense of simple and mundane forms of accounting, for example by modelling the account that might be given of why the water in the electric kettle is boiling, or a police account of an accident (Stering (2008)). But suitably interpreted, NTA may also model *scholarly* and *scientific explanations* of the semantic information under investigation, following a variety of deductive-nomological, inductive-statistical, teleological, functional, analogical, historical, or psychological approaches. For example, in the deductive-nomological and the inductive-statistical cases, the source contains initial conditions and law-like generalizations, which enable the network to answer the HC-questions posed by the semantic information *t* concerning the event to be explained. Indeed, since the 1980s some theories of explanation (Van Fraassen (1980b) and Achinstein (1983), but see also more recently Walton (2007)) have developed and defended erotetic approaches to explanation that are close to the analysis of account supported in this chapter. Furthermore, following Plato, NTA could also give rise to a *logical deduction* of *t*, which would then represent the theorem T to be proved starting from the premises contained in the source. In this case, NTA allows both constructive (proving T by answering the question 'how come that T is the case?') and non-constructive approaches (proving T by answering the question 'how come that ¬ T is not the case?'). Alternatively, the network of vertices and edges and the probability of received answers through such paths could be given a Bayesian interpretation, as in Van Fraassen's erotetic model of explanation (Van Fraassen (1980)). The list could be expanded. The interesting point to be stressed here is not how versatile NTA is, but that NTA's plasticity is a valuable feature, obtained by raising the level of abstraction at which one may analyse what it means for some information (supply) to make sense of some other information by answering (satisfying) its HC-questions (demand).

Regarding its specificity, someone convinced by the previous defence of NTA's abstract generality may still harbour doubts about its quantitative approach. Could one really attach numbers to both *c* and *f* in *A*? The positive answer is twofold.

First, it is far from being implausible that one may be numerically precise about how many questions need to be answered (value of *f*) in order to account for *t*, and how many answers any v_x and *s* may provide in theory (value of *c*). For example, one may assume v_x and *s* to be finite databases, from which a finite set of correct, Boolean answers might be extracted, only some of which will be relevant to answer *t*'s HC-questions correctly. Equally possible, and indeed feasible, is to transform any HC-question into a Boolean question. In this case, one only has to think of the twenty questions game. A handful of Boolean questions is often sufficient to account for some given information.

Second, even if the quantitative approach were utterly implausible and unfeasible, it would still remain logically possible, and this would be sufficient for our purpose, which is to clarify, through a simplified model, what accounting for some semantic information consists in. A related, but different, problem concerns what Boolean questions to ask and how to answer them correctly. About this, NTA remains silent, and rightly so. It is not up to a model of informational accounting to determine the nature of the specific information that will be conveyed through the network, in the same way that the engineer is not concerned about the sort of messages that will be exchanged through a digital system of communication. This does not make the formalism pointless. On the contrary, NTA can take full advantage of the theorems and algorithms available in network theory (Jungnickel (1999) and Cormen et al. (2001)). For example, in the previous section we have already encountered a limiting result with respect to the NP-completeness of two-commodity, natural-valued flow problems and we shall presently see that a classic result, known as the max-flow min-cut theorem (Elias et al. (1956), Ford and Fulkerson (1956)), can also be very enlightening.

With the previous concerns at least mitigated, if not entirely dispelled, it is useful to highlight now some positive and interesting features of NTA that will finally introduce the next section. I shall deal with them rather schematically because the goal is to give a general flavour of NTA, and only the last feature will be crucial for our current purposes.

NTA supports an epistemic or semantic interpretation of 'accounting'. That is, both t and s are informational in nature: they may refer to, but are not in themselves, phenomena or events. So, too, are the questions asked and the answers provided. However, nothing prevents the realist from expanding NTA into a more ontologically-committed approach, if she so wishes, depending on the theory of truth that she selects to ground the truthfulness of the information flowing through the network. I shall return to this point in chapter fifteen.

NTA lends itself to fast procedures of revision. It is clear that, if an account of t is unsatisfactory and there is a problem in the required flow of information, NTA helps to detect this more quickly, to check where the difficulty might be and to improve the configuration of A accordingly. In particular, inferences to the best account may require improved or different sources of information, if s does not answer correctly and in full all the qu⋯ ⋯ posed by t. It is true that, in ordinary life, our social network of interlocking As is often resilient to radical changes but, even in such stable scenarios, very significant experiences may lead to equally radical revisions. Othello or Hamlet are just idealized cases. This holds true in science as well. A Copernican revolution is any dramatic alteration in the accounting networks that cement our relevant semantic information.

The previous point is related to the possibility that not all semantic information might be upgradeable to knowledge. Sometimes HC-questions cannot be properly asked (recall Russell's example of the broken watch) or are unanswerable anyway because the source that could account for p is inaccessible or cannot be established, as for example when trying to account for some archaeological information concerning a pre-historical civilization. Knowledge (and hence knowing) is a much rarer phenomenon than (relevant and semantic) information (or being informed).

With regard to ways of improving an interpreted A, the max-flow min-cut theorem is a classic cornerstone in optimization theory and flow network, which turns out to be very useful for NTA as well. The theorem states that, given a single-source, single-sink, flow network N, the maximum amount of flow f in N is equal to the capacity c of a minimum cut in N. The idea is simple: the maximum flow in N is determined by its bottleneck. Applied to A, this can be intuitively appreciated by looking at Figure 24, where it is easy to see that the maximum information flow reaching t is equivalent to the cut indicated by the selected area.

In this case too, there are many technical results that could be useful for specific applications, such as the classic Ford–Fulkerson algorithm (Ford and Fulkerson (1956)), which calculates the maximum flow in a network. But the philosophically interesting point here is that we have an elegant way of stating the equivalent of Ockham's razor for NTA: vertices and edges *non sunt multiplicanda praeter necessitatem*. In Figure 24, it is clear that vertices v_5 and v_7 are redundant in terms of capacity. The size and shape of the informational network A required to account for t (answer t's HC-questions) can then be optimized by searching for the minimal set of vertices whose informational capacity equates to the needed flow. Put simply, we should not look for more potential answers than we need.

Once the flow in A is optimized using (Ockham's) max-flow min-cut theorem, two other interesting features become obvious. First, networks can be interlocked like Lego bricks: what for one analysis is a sink can easily be a target for a different analysis, and this holds true for vertices as well. The building of larger networks is modular and perfectly feasible, like the scaling up of the features of the obtained complex network, in which conditions (a)–(j) may be variously satisfied. Depending on which theory of

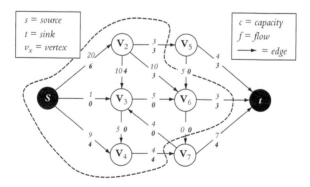

Figure 24 Min-cut max-flow theorem applied to an information flow network

truth one adopts to analyse semantic information, the successful interlocking of a boundless set of accounts could actually be all that is required to make sense and support a coherentist approach.

Second, different accounts of the same semantic information posing the same HC-questions are perfectly possible, because NTA allows the constructions of different networks A_x that guarantee the same flow of information. Yet this does not commit NTA to some relativism: not every information network works and some informational networks work better than others. This is obvious in network theory, where the max-flow min-cut theorem can be used to prove that there may be more than one flow which attains the maximum amount, and more than one cut that attains the minimal weight. The same result seems to apply uncontroversially to NTA as well.

As for the actual nature of the elements constituting a simple network, the application of the max-flow min-cut theorem can also help us to understand the phenomenon of testimony in the following way. Imagine we wish to account for some semantic information t which actually refers to s; for example, we wish to account for t = 'Julius Caesar was assassinated in Rome on 15 March 44 BC' through an informational network A whose source s is ultimately some first-hand information about the set of events that occurred in Rome on 15 March 44 BC. All the vertices v_x between s and t are testimonies. We can now define the concept of *perfect testimony* very precisely: an ideal scenario for a historian would be to have all the answers that she might wish to be provided by s (that is, s' capacity c) wholly preserved through the network, but this can happen only if there is no bottleneck narrower than s'c. In others words, the informational flow reaching t should be equal to the informational capacity of s, so that the min-cut should include only s. In order to evaluate a group of testimonies, we should set the capacity of s and then check whether the min-cut includes any v_x: for any v_x that gets caught in the min-cut is telling less than the truth, the whole truth and nothing but the truth.

The previous features should have given the general flavour of how NTA works and of its scope of applicability. The last aspect to which I wish to call the reader's attention in this section is the special relation that NTA establishes between s and t in A, as this will play a crucial role in the next section.

It is plausible to assume, although this assumption will not be further developed here, that the logic of HC-questions may be easily rendered by adapting that of why-questions (Bromberger (1966), Koura (1988), Burgin and Kuznetsov (1994)). What is of the utmost importance here is that, within such logical analysis, one feature is both uncontroversial and crucial. It can be introduced by referring to some familiar instances of accounting. Suppose a theory explains a particular set of phenomena: for example, it explain why metals expand when heated, by indicating that, as temperature increases, the kinetic energy of the atoms in the metal increases as well, this leads to a greater average separation, hence to an expansion of the internal structure of the metal and so of its volume. Although this explanation might be expressed in more ('crystalline lattice') or less ('wobbling') technical terms, thus generating different networks with the same sink t, there is one aspect that remains invariant under different formulations and in each issuing network: explanans and explanandum cannot be de-coupled without making the explanation incorrect. Or put more simply: an explanation of p is correct if and only if it applies correctly to p. Hopefully the reader will find this uncontroversial to the point of triviality, but note the bi-conditional and let me stress the importance of the sufficiency condition. Consider now a second example, equally unproblematic: suppose a conclusion is validly deduced from a set of premises. We know that classical formal validity is monotonic: if the deduction is valid it remains valid, and the conclusion remains validly deduced from the premises, no matter how many other premises are added. The only way of de-coupling the conclusion from the premises is by showing that the deduction itself was not valid in the first place. Finally, take any ordinary way of accounting for some semantic information, such as the example of 'the water in the electric kettle is boiling'. It seems clear that, in all the cases we have encountered so far, either an account works (is correct) or it does not (is not correct), but that it makes no sense to talk of an account that is correct and yet fails to apply for some unknown reasons. Explanations, deductions, teleological or functional 'giving reasons', and other forms of accounting all appear to share this essential feature: accounting is *rigid*, so A is a correct account of t if and only if in A s correctly accounts for t and they cannot be de-coupled without revising the initial assumption that s did account for t correctly and hence that A was a correct account of it. Visually, t and s may be seen as the two end, bounding points of a line segment represented by the information flow: they are part of it as they define it. I shall refer to this characteristic as the *rigid coordination* between the accounting s and the accounted t in A.

One might object that we are not entirely sure that such rigid coordination does extend to all forms of accounting covered by NTA. After all, the list of types of accounting was left open, so how could one be so confident? This reluctance is understandable and might be overcome not so much by pointing out that the burden of showing that some forms of accounting are not rigid is on the side of the sceptic, but, more easily, by agreeing that, should indeed some forms of accounting turn out to be non-rigid, it will be sufficient to accept that, nevertheless, some major, important forms of accounting, such as the ones we have discussed in this chapter, are rigid, and that these are the only ones to which we are referring.

12.5 Testing the network theory of account

So far, I have argued that (an interpreted) A provides the *necessary* condition to upgrade relevant semantic information to knowledge. The time has come to deal with a difficult question: does (an interpreted) A also provide the *sufficient* condition to upgrade relevant semantic information to knowledge? The alert reader will have spotted here the ghost of the Gettier-type problem discussed in chapter nine. In that context, it was precisely the lack of such rigid coordination that caused all the troubles in the 'coordinated attack' problem. So it will be helpful to rephrase the problem thus: is the analysis of knowledge as accounted relevant semantic information (henceforth just accounted information) Gettierisable? The short answer is no, the long answer requires some toil.

To begin with, it is important to recall that Gettier-type problems are logically unsolvable because they are a sub-class of the more general 'coordinated attack' problem, which we saw to be demonstrably unsolvable in epistemic logic. The difficulty at the root of this mess is that the tripartite definition presupposes the possibility of coordinating two resources, the objective truth of p and the subjective justification of the knowing subject S, which, by hypothesis, can always be de-coupled. There is a *potential lack of successful coordination*, between the truth of p and the reasons that justify S in holding that p, that is inherently inerasable. So a Gettier-type counterexample can always arise because the truth and the justification of p happen to be not only mutually independent (as they should be, since we are dealing with fallibilist knowledge) but may also be opaquely unrelated, that is, they may happen to fail to converge or to agree on the same propositional content p in a relevant and significant way, without S realizing it (Gettierization). All this entails that the tripartite definition of knowledge is not merely inadequate as it stands, as proved by Gettier-type counterexamples, but demonstrably irreparable in principle because of the constraints it set ups, so that efforts to improve it can never succeed. With an analogy already used in chapter eight, the problem is not that one cannot square the circle, but that squaring the circle with algebraic means (straight-edge and compass) is impossible.

Given such a disheartening conclusion, one is entitled to interpret Gettier-type problems as symptoms of a bankrupt approach. The assumption remains, however, that we in many cases we do enjoy epistemic propositional states: Mary knows that the kettle is boiling. So the constructive strategy consists in breaking away from the constraints that make the problem unsolvable: we no longer try to define knowledge doxastically and by relying on a logic of subjective justification, but informationally, and by using a logic of objective accounting. Of course, the new tools require shaping and sharpening, but that was exactly the task of the previous sections. So we are now ready to reap the fruits of our labour: some information t, if correctly accounted by an information flow network A, is rigidly coordinated to the source s that correctly accounts for it, and cannot be de-coupled from it without making A an incorrect account, so it follows that Gettier-type counterexamples cannot arise. In epistemic logic, this is equivalent to saying that the Byzantine generals (in our case the two resources s and t) do not try to coordinate their attack infallibly, which is impossible, but rather join forces first, and then attack, which is perfectly feasible.

Let us now consider what happens to our Scribe. So far we have employed an extensional approach: packets of semantic information have been treated as conceptual artefacts or, more figuratively, as items in the Scribe's scroll. We can now translate them intentionally, in the following way: an agent (e.g. the Scribe) S knows that t if and only if:

i. t qualifies as relevant semantic information;
ii. A accounts for t, that is, $A(A, t)$;
iii. S is informed that t; and
iv. S is informed that $A(A, t)$.

This informational definition of knowledge faces at least one major objection, but, before discussing it, a few essential clarifications are in order.

The first two clauses (i) and (ii) seem to require no further comments, but the third clause is meant to satisfy at least the information logic based on **KTB** (see chapter ten) if not some higher epistemic logic, and this leads to a first clarification. Depending on whether we assume S's informational states in (iii) and (iv) to be non-opaque—that is, depending on whether S not only holds the information, but also understands that t and that $A(A, t)$—we may be able (or fail) to include current artificial agents among the class of epistemic subjects. Since at least 2005 (First International Symposium on Explanation-aware Computing), there has been increasing interest in so-called explanation-aware computing (ExaCt) and more results have become available in recent years. However, it is important to stress that the sort of explanatory processes in question in ExaCt are not the ones that have been discussed here. The goal is to develop ways in which artificial expert systems may interact more profitably with human users, and hence increase their rate of success at solving problems collaboratively by 'explaining' their operations and making their procedures and results more accessible. So we should be rather cautious: extensionally, knowledge is accounted information, and this is why we say that a scientific textbook or a website like Wikipedia, for example, contains knowledge, not just information. However, intentionally it seems that knowing requires understanding, or at least that the two are mutually related, and hence that current artificial agents cannot qualify as knowing subjects. They may hold knowledge extensionally, but they cannot know intentionally. This of course says nothing about futuristic artefacts that, should AI ever become possible, would be welcome to join us. This issue will be the main topic of the next chapter.

A second, apparent restriction comes with the more or less explicit holding not just of some information t, but also of a satisfactory account for it. It seems clear that animals do not hold explicit accounts for their information, so it follows that even the smartest dog can at most be informed that the neighbour's cat is a nasty beast, and yet not know it. However, animals do not hold justifications for their beliefs either, but when we acknowledge the old, doxastic, tripartite definition to be more inclusive, we mean that, as observers, it allows us to attribute to animals justificatory grounds supporting their beliefs implicitly. But if this is the case, then the same stance can be adopted in the case of holding an account. The dog knows that the neighbour's cat is a nasty beast because we may attribute to it the (at least implicit) memory of the historical account, for example, of the events that led to such belief. Animals do not hold *explicit accounts for* their information but it seems unproblematic to attribute to them both reasonable levels of understanding (contrary to engineered artefacts) and *implicit accounts of* their information, and therefore knowledge.

A third restriction concerns human knowing subjects. It is an advantage of the informational analysis of knowledge over the doxastic one that the former but not the latter allows for a graded evaluation of epistemic states. This is an important require- ment. The doxastic approach is binary: either the Scribe knows that *t* or he does not, and if he does, his knowledge would be as good as that of an omniscient god. This Cartesian position is simplistic and the informational approach redresses the situation by making the acknowledgement of expertise possible: the Scribe might know that *p* better than his dog does because he can provide an account for it, not just hold an implicit account of it. However, a scientist or an historian, for example, might know that *p* even better than the Scribe. This because it is possible to agree on a minimal range of HC-questions that need to be answered correctly in order to qualify as a knowing subject—this is what we ordinarily do in educational and training contexts— but of course there is a vast number of further HC-questions that only an expert will be able to answer. Mary may know that her TV is not working properly because she is well informed about it and what accounts for it, but only the expert will have the right level of advanced knowledge to answer further HC-questions. Knowledge comes in degrees, and insipience as well as omniscience are not only a matter of scope—as we have seen above when discussing the possibility of non-upgradeable information—but also of depth.

The profile of a knowing subject that emerges from the informational analysis of knowledge is, unsurprisingly, rather Greek. One important difference, however, is that the analysis links propositional knowledge to practical knowledge (know-that to know-how) in a way that Plato and Aristotle might have found less congenial, but might have pleased Bacon and Kant for being closer to their constructionist approach to knowledge. For it seems clear that knowing that *t* relies on knowing how to build, articulate and defend a correct account for *t*. We saw that this pragmatic side of knowledge emerged explicitly also in the Action-based Semantics (chapter seven) and the correctness theory of truth (chapter eight) on which the informational approach supported in this book is based (recall the need for a commuting relation between model and system). Yet this is often acknowledged in Greek epistemology only partly and somewhat reluctantly, not in terms of ability to manufacture the required conceptual artefact, but merely in terms of ability to convey its properties. In Plato, it is the user that is considered to know something better than the artisan that has produced it. The informational analysis of knowledge is more engineer-friendly. According to it, the production of knowledge that *t* relies, ultimately, on the intelligent mastery of the practical expertise (including modelling or, more mundanely, story-telling) required to produce not only *t* but also its correct account *A*. 'Knowing that' is grounded on 'knowing how', hardly surprising from an evolutionary perspective.

The last comment concerns the potential objection anticipated above, to which we can now finally turn. One may contend that the informational analysis of knowledge merely shifts the de-coupling problem. In the doxastic analysis, this affects the relation between the truth of *t* and *S*'s justification for believing in it. In the informational analysis—the objection continues—the problem merely resurfaces by affecting the relation between the correct account of *t* and the possibility that *S* may hold it.

This objection deserves to be taken seriously, not because it represents anything close to a refutation, but because it does highlight a significant difficulty, which is different from what the objection seems to imply, and that can be turned into an advantage. Let me explain.

The objection suggests that we did not really get rid of Gettier-type counter-examples but only moved them out of sight. This is mistaken. The task was to show how relevant semantic information can be upgraded to knowledge and the previous analysis provides the necessary and sufficient conditions to achieve this. The problem left unsolved is not the potential Gettierization of the informational analysis because—once the logic of accounting replaces that of justification—the condition of possibility of Gettier-type counterexamples (i.e. de-coupling) is removed through the rigid coordination implicit in any correct accounting. Nonetheless, the objection is correct in raising the more generic suspicion that something has been left unsolved. For the trouble is that the informational analysis converts Gettier-type problems into sceptical ones. How can *S* be certain that *A* is the correct account of *t*? This is not among the questions answered by any account of *t*. Indeed, it must be acknowledged that nothing has been said in this book that goes towards tackling this sceptical question. But then, nothing should, because this is not the challenge we had set out to address. Of course, one may find this unsatisfactory: we are jumping out of Gettier's frying pan only to land into the sceptic's fire. Yet such dissatisfaction would be ungenerous. The sceptical challenge concerns the truth of *t* and, broadly speaking, the correctness of an account *A* of *t* (or of the answers offered with respect to the HC-questions posed by *t*) and *S*'s possibility of not being mistaken about holding *A*. The reader interested in knowing how I have dealt with the sceptical problem may wish to check Floridi (1996) and Floridi (forthcoming-a). The sceptical challenge was always going to affect any analysis of knowledge, including the doxastic one. So, by converting Gettier problems into sceptical problems we have made progress, because the latter problems are not made any more serious by such conversion and we now need to take care of only one set of difficulties instead of two. Fighting on only one front is always preferable and it is an improvement. Von Clausewitz *docet*

CONCLUSION

Knowledge and information are members of the same conceptual family. What the former enjoys and the latter lacks, over and above their family resemblance, is the web of mutual relations that allow one part of it to account for another. Shatter that, and you are left with a pile of truths or a random list of bits of information that cannot help to make sense of the reality they seek to address. Reconstruct that network of relations, and information starts providing that overall view of the world which we associate with the best of our epistemic efforts. In this chapter, I showed how this upgrading of relevant semantic information to knowledge is possible, welcome and resilient, by relying on some results from network theory. The proposal, if successful, is not without its costs. Exchanging Gettier-type counterexamples, which affect the justification of S, for doubts about whether S might hold the correct account of his information, means reverting to the challenge posed by the sceptic. It is a serious challenge, related to P12 (see chapter two), which will have to be met, but, fortunately, not in this context. The proposal also has some significant advantages. In the next three chapters, I shall explore some of them. In chapter thirteen, we shall look at what sort of epistemic agents can handle what kind of relevant semantic information in order to know their conscious nature. We shall then consider, in chapters fourteen and fifteen, what an informational analysis of knowledge can do for our metaphysics and scientific understanding of the world.

13

Consciousness, agents, and the knowledge game

> Silently Peyton weighed his opponent. It was clearly a robot of the very highest
> order. [...] 'Who are you?' exclaimed Peyton at last, addressing not the robot,
> but the controller behind it. [...] 'I am the Engineer.' 'Then come out and let
> me see you.' 'You are seeing me'. [...] There was no human being controlling
> this machine. It was as automatic as the other robots of the city—but unlike them,
> and all other robots the world had ever known, it had a will and a consciousness
> of its own.
>
> A. C. Clarke, *The Lion of Comarre*, 1949.

SUMMARY

Previously, in chapters four, five, and twelve, I supported a theory of strongly semantic
information that allowed an informational analysis of knowledge. This chapter applies
such a result in order to pursue three goals. The first is to introduce the 'knowledge
game', a new, simple, and yet powerful tool for analysing some intriguing philosophical questions. The second is to apply the knowledge game as an informative test to
discriminate between conscious (human) and conscious-less agents (zombies and
robots), depending on which version of the game they can win. And the third is
to use a version of the knowledge game to provide an answer to Dretske's question
'how do you know you are not a zombie?'. At the end of the chapter we should have
a better view of which agents count as conscious informational organisms (inforgs),
that is, the sort of inforgs that can intentionally process relevant semantic information.
The chapter could be read as an attempt to provide a general approach in order to
answer P8–P11 (see chapter two).

13.1 Introduction

Consciousness is one of those fish we seem to be unable to catch, much like intelligence. We recognize its presence, traces. and effects, but its precise nature, workings,
and 'location' still escape our grasp. Tired of ending up empty-handed, some philosophers have recently tried to approach the problem of consciousness indirectly. If you

can't hook it, try to corner it. To this new approach belongs a series of mental experiments involving the possibility of conscious-less agents (see for example Symposium (1995)).

Imagine three populations of agents: *robots* (conscious-less artificial agents), *zombies* (conscious-less biological agents), and *humans* (conscious biological agents). I shall say more about the first two types of agents presently. There is of course a possible, fourth population, that of conscious artificial agents like *The Engineer* in Clarke's story, but I shall not consider it in this chapter. At the moment, the assumption is that you, a human, are neither a robot nor a zombie and that you know it. This much is granted. The question is *how you know it*. Compare this with the sceptical problem about propositional justification: one may be justified in believing that *p*, without this warranting that one is also able to know that one is justified (Alston (1986)). As Descartes saw, one may try to get out of this predicament by making sure that the test (for him, the method of doubt) run to check whether one is justified in believing that *p* brings out one's knowledge that one is justified in believing that *p*. Dretske (2003) phrases the problem neatly:

I'm not asking whether you know you are not a zombie [or a robot, my addition]. Of course you do. *I'm asking how you know it.* The answer to that question is not so obvious. Indeed, *it is hard to see how you can know it.* Wittgenstein (Wittgenstein (1961): 57) didn't think he saw anything that allowed him to infer he saw it. The problem is more serious. There is nothing you are aware of, *external or internal,* that tells you that, unlike a zombie, you are aware of it. Or, indeed, *aware of anything at all.* (emphasis added).

Whatever your answer to Dretske's question is, it will cast some light on your conception of consciousness, but before we embark on any further discussion, let me introduce our dramatis personae.

Artificial agents are not science fiction but advanced transition systems capable of *interactive, autonomous,* and *adaptable* behaviour. *Interactivity* means that artificial agents and their environments can act upon each other effectively. *Autonomy* means that the agents can perform internal transitions to change their states teleologically, without direct responses to interactions. This property imbues agents with a certain degree of complexity and decoupled-ness from their environments. *Adaptability* means that the agents' interactions can change the transition rules by which they change states. This property ensures that agents might be viewed, at a given level of abstraction (Floridi and Sanders (2004b)), as learning their own mode of operation in a way that depends critically on their past interactions and future goals.

According to Dretske—and indeed, rightly, to anyone using this thought experiment—zombies are agents that lack consciousness of *any kind*. Now, this initial definition needs to be refined, since there are four main senses in which an agent AG can be said to possess or lack consciousness, not all of which might be in question here.

AG may be environmentally conscious if

e.1   AG is not 'switched-off', e.g. if AG is not asleep, comatose, fainted, anaesthetized, drugged, hypnotized, in a state of trance, stupor, catalepsy, or somnambulism, and so forth;

or (depending on one's approach this may be a disjunctive or)

e.2   AG is able to process information about, and hence to interact with, AG's surroundings, its features, and stimuli effectively, under normal circumstances.

Animals, including human agents are normally said to be conscious in the (e.1) or (e.2) sense. But AG may also be *phenomenically conscious* if

p   AG experiences the qualitative, subjective, personal, or phenomenological properties of a state in which AG is. This is the sense in which Nagel (1974) famously speaks of being conscious of a certain state as having the experience of 'what it is like to be' an agent in that state;

or (and this is at least an inclusive 'or', and at most a misleading place-holder for a double implication, more on this in section seven) AG may be *self-conscious* if

s   AG has a (second- or higher-order) sense of, or is (introspectively) aware of, AG's personal identity (including AG's knowledge that AG thinks) and (first- or lower-order) perceptual or mental experiences (including AG's knowledge of what AG is thinking).

All four states are informational in character: *e-consciousness* is externally oriented and first-order, whereas *p-consciousness* and *s-consciousness* are internally oriented and (at least in the case of *s-*) second- or higher-order.

  These distinctions are useful to clarify Dretske's question. For it may be unfair to interpret Dretske as saying that zombies lack consciousness even in the environmental sense. Perhaps some zombies can be conceived as being both 'switched-off' (e.1) and incapable of any effective informational interactions with the environment (e.2). But then, not only might it be easier for us to say how we know that we are not *that sort* of zombies, it would also be far less interesting to investigate how we know it. So I suggest we restrict Dretske's claim to saying that zombies are biological agents almost like us, but for the fact that they lack both *p-consciousness* and *s-consciousness*. Indeed, Dretske appears to embrace the same analysis:

The properties you are aware of are properties of—what else? —the objects you are aware of. The conditions and events you are conscious of—i.e., objects having and changing their properties—are, therefore, completely objective. They would be the same if you weren't aware of them. *Everything you are aware of would be the same if you were a zombie.*[footnote] *In having perceptual experience, then, nothing distinguishes your world, the world you experience, from a zombie's.* (emphasis added)

According to our refined definition, zombies are biologically embodied, environmentally embedded, cognitive systems capable, like us and some artificial agents, of *some kind* of first-order, informational and practical interactions with other agents and their environment. The 'kind' does not have to be anything human-like, it only needs to be indistinguishable (and not even intrinsically, but only by us) from an ordinary human agent's way of dealing fairly effectively with the world.

The idea is not new. There is a delightful passage in Spinoza's *On the Improvement of the Understanding*, for example, where he compares sceptics to automata (zombies, in our more refined vocabulary). The passage is worth quoting in full:

If there yet remains some sceptic, who doubts of our primary truth, and of all deductions we make, taking such truth as our standard, he must either be arguing in bad faith, or we must confess that there are men in complete mental blindness, either innate or due to misconceptions—that is, to some external influence. Such persons are not conscious of themselves. If they affirm or doubt anything, they know not that they affirm or doubt: they say that they know nothing, and they say that they are ignorant of the very fact of their knowing nothing. Even this they do not affirm absolutely, they are afraid of confessing that they exist, so long as they know nothing; in fact, they ought to remain dumb, for fear of haply supposing which should smack of truth. Lastly, with such persons, one should not speak of sciences: for, in what relates to life and conduct, they are compelled by necessity to suppose that they exist, and seek their own advantage, and often affirm and deny, even with an oath. If they deny, grant, or gainsay, they know not that they deny, grant, or gainsay, so that they ought to be regarded as *automata* [emphasis added], utterly devoid of intelligence.

When Dretske asks how you know that you are not a zombie (or one of Spinoza's automata), he is not wondering how you know that you are either *p*- or *s-conscious*. For Dretske is mainly concerned with perception and 'the attitudinal aspect of thought', as he writes. His question about consciousness is

how one gets from what one thinks—that there is beer in the fridge—to a fact about oneself—that one thinks there is beer in the fridge. What you see—beer in the fridge—doesn't tell you that you see it, and what you think—that there is beer in the fridge—doesn't tell you that you think it either.

In other words, what we are looking for is not how we know that we are *s-conscious*—although, if we were zombies, indicating how we know that we are *s-conscious* would highlight an important difference between us and them—but how we know that we are *p-conscious* of something when we are perceiving that something. To quote Dretske once more

What we are looking for, remember, is *a way of knowing* that, unlike zombies, we are conscious of things. (emphasis added)

Dretske's question *does not exclude* any reference to *s-consciousness* in principle, but it is meant to address primarily *p-consciousness*.

Now that we have defined the relevant agents and types of consciousness, a final point in need of clarification concerns what we are in principle asked to provide in terms of an answer. In the article, it is clear that Dretske (again, rightly) understands his 'how' question in two slightly different ways:

Q.1 as a question that can take as an answer a specification of how one *actually* knows that one is 'conscious of things' and hence not a zombie; and

Q.2 as a question that can take as an answer 'a way of knowing that, unlike zombies, we are conscious of things', that is, how one can *possibly* know that one is not a zombie.

An answer to Q.1 could describe some actual further experience that one ordinarily enjoys when having a *p-conscious* experience, in order to show how one knows that one is not a zombie. An answer to Q.2 is less demanding, for it could describe just a (not *the*, and not *the only*) possible experience usable as a way of knowing and explaining how one knows that one is not a zombie. Q.1 invites the identification of the right sort of factual description or logical fact inferable from, or perhaps just relevantly related to, the conscious experience of the world, whereas Q.2 invites the identification of some sort of informative test.

The distinction is crucial. We normally move from one to the other type of question when we realize that a test is probably the best way of explaining how one knows that one qualifies as a certain kind of agent. Yet, this erotetic shift may seem problematic. Let me illustrate the difficulty with an analogy.

Suppose you are a good cook and that you know that you are a good cook, but that you are asked to explain how you know it. Suppose that we agree that there is no actual special experience, somehow related to your cooking experience, that you and I would find entirely satisfactory to clarify the matter. As Dretske does in the article, we would be shifting to a Q.2-type of question: is there anything at all—not just an actual something, but maybe just a possible something—that could ever count not merely as evidence that you are a good cook but as a way of knowing that you are a good cook?

One standard solution would be to devise a satisfactory gourmet test and see whether you can pass it. Passing the test would not merely confirm your qualities as a good cook: your culinary capacities are not in question, so the test would not be informative in this respect. Nor would the importance of the test consist in its capacity (which it does have) to make you know that you are a good cook. Its importance would lie in the fact that it would provide you with a way of explaining how you know that you are a good cook. This because you have had the successful experience of cooking well *while* cooking well *and while* the former experience was positively assessed as qualifying you as a good cook, and you know all this.

Someone may still be unconvinced. Suppose you get full marks for your pasta but only barely pass the test for puddings. Since you are a good cook, we assume that you pass the gourmet test overall. At this point, an observer may still object that the original question was of a Q.1-type, but that the test provides an answer only to a Q.2-type of question. In general, very few people qualify as good cooks because they have passed a gourmet test. If they are good cooks they are so for other reasons than passing an official exam. Moreover, a test can only certify the presence/absence of the property in question (e.g. being a good cook) at best, but it does not tell you in any detail what it takes to have it. The objection is that answering a Q.2-type of question fails to address the original concern.

The reply to this objection is twofold. First, we moved from a Q.1-type to a Q.2-type of question because we agreed that answering Q.1 may be impossible. If this is all our interlocutor wishes to see acknowledged, it has already been conceded. However, and this is a crucial point, by moving to a Q.2-type of question—as Dretske himself does—the test we have devised is not merely a successful way of discriminating between good and bad cooks. It is also informative (for the agent being tested) about what being a good cook means: it means going through the process you just went through (recall your good pasta and the bad puddings) and qualifying because of it as a good cook. The test is not any test, but a test that concerns precisely the way you actually cook, only it examines it as a 'work in progress' and in a context constrained by well-specified conditions, whereby the process is assessed as the right sort of process to qualify as a certain kind of agent. Good tests usually are informative, that is, they usually are more than just successful criteria of identification of x as y, because they examine the very process they are testing precisely while the process is occurring, and so they provide the tested agent with a way of (a) showing that he qualifies as a certain kind of agent, (b) knowing that he is that kind of agent, and (c) answering how he knows that he is that kind of agent, by pointing to the passed test and its (a)–(b) features.

All this means that, when Dretske seeks to show that there is nothing you are aware of that tells you that you are aware of anything, I shall argue that he may be right in suspecting that no answer to the 'how' question understood as in Q.1 is available, but that he is too pessimistic in concluding that therefore there is no other possible answer to the Q.2 version either, i.e. no possible 'way of knowing that, unlike zombies, we are conscious of things', for one can devise an informative test about consciousness such that passing it provides a possible way of explaining how we may know that, unlike zombies, we are conscious of things.

To summarize: according to Dretske, there is nothing you are aware of that tells you that you are aware of it, although you are indeed aware of it and you do know that you are, so it may be impossible to answer the question 'how do you know you are not a zombie?'. Now, one way to ascertain whether x qualifies as P is to set up a P-test and check whether x passes it. You know you are a car driver, a chess master, a good cook, or that you are not visually impaired if you satisfy some given standards or requirements, perform or behave in a certain way, win games and tournaments, pass an official examination, and so forth. This also holds true for being intelligent, at least according to Turing (1950). I shall argue that it applies to *s-consciousness* as well and that, since *s-consciousness* implies *p-consciousness*, an *informative* test for the presence of the former is also an *informative* test for the presence of the latter. I agree with Dretske that mental and perceptual experiences may bear no hallmarks of consciousness or of any further property indicating our non-zombie (and non-artificial) nature. Consciousness (either *p-* or *s-*) does not piggyback on experience, which tells us nothing over and above itself. Blame this on the transparency of consciousness itself (it is there, attached to experience, but you cannot perceive it) or on the one-dimensionality of experience (experience is experience, only experience, and nothing but experience). However, I shall argue that this does not mean that one cannot devise a reliable and informative test for the presence of consciousness as a way of showing that, and explaining how, one knows that one is a *p*- and *s-conscious* agent. The knowledge game is such test.

13.2 The knowledge game

The knowledge game presented in this section is a useful tool with which to tackle a variety of epistemic issues.[1] It closely resembles Turing's test and it exploits a classic result, variously known as the 'muddy children' or the 'three wise men' theorem, the drosophila of epistemic logic and distributed AI.[2]

The game is played by a multi-agent system comprising a finite group of at least two interacting agents with communicational and inferential capacities. Agents are assigned specific states in such a way that acquiring a state *S* is something different from being in *S* and different again from knowing that one is in *S*. The states are chosen by the experimenter from a *commonly known* (in the technical sense of the expression introduced in epistemic logic: all players know that all players know that all players know . . . the) set of alternatives. The experimenter questions the agents about their states, and they win the game if they answer correctly. Agents can determine the nature of their state inferentially and only on the basis of the informational resources available. They cannot rely on any innate, *a priori* or otherwise *privileged access* (Alston (1971)). Most notably, they have no introspection, internal diagnosis, self-testing, meta-theoretical processes, inner perception, or second-order capacities or thoughts.[3] Since the game blocks the system from invoking any higher-order, mental, or psychological *deus ex machina* to ascertain directly the state in which the system is, we test the presence of *p*- and *s-consciousness* indirectly and avoid the problem of dealing with these two types of consciousness by means of concepts that are at least equally troublesome.

Let me now sketch how the knowledge game will be used. In the following pages, we shall compare three types of agents: humans (agents who enjoy not only *e*- but also *p*- and *s*-consciousness), actual artificial agents (robots endowed with interactivity, autonomy, and adaptability), and logically possible zombies (agents almost like

---

[1] Two very different uses of the knowledge game can be found for example in Lacan (1988), discussed in Elmer (1995), and in Shimojo and Ichikawa (1989). I hope to show the applicability of the knowledge game to the dreaming argument and the brain-in-a-vat or malicious demon hypothesis in a future work.

[2] The classic version of the theorem has been around for decades. It is related to the Conway–Paterson–Moscow theorem and the Conway paradox (see Groenendijk et al. (1984), pp. 159–182 and Conway and Guy (1996)) and was studied, among others, by Barwise and Seligman (1997) and Barwise (1988). For some indications on its history see Fagin et al. (1995), p. 13. The social game *Cluedo* is based on it. Its logic is analysed in Ditmarsch (2000). The *Logics Workbench* is a propositional theorem prover that uses various versions of the theorem as benchmarks <http://www.lwb.unibe.ch/index.html>.

[3] For an approach to Dretske's question in terms of self-awareness see Werning (2004). Lycan (2003) argues that the inner sense theory can be defended against Dretske's criticism.

humans, but for the fact that they lack *p*- and *s*-consciousness). To make things interesting, zombies will (at least appear to) be 'switched-on' and able to exchange first-order, *relevant semantic information* about the environment and interact with it as cognitively effectively, on average, as any ordinary conscious agent. The goal will be to establish not whether one belongs to the human type of agents or whether one knows that one does, but how one knows that one does. This will involve devising four versions of the knowledge game. The first two versions can be won by all inferential agents. This guarantees initial fairness and avoids begging the question. However, a third, more difficult version can be won only by non-artificial agents like us and the zombies. And a final, fourth version can be won only by *s-conscious* agents like us. I shall then argue that the presence of *s-consciousness* implies the presence of *p-consciousness*. So, if you win all versions, first, you are neither an artificial agent nor a zombie, but a *p*- and *s-conscious* agent; second, you now know (assuming you did not already) that you are not a zombie; and, third, you also have a way of explaining how you know that you are not a zombie, by pointing to your victory in the knowledge game. And since the test is only a sufficient but not a necessary condition to qualify as not a zombie, nothing is lost if one does not pass it. After all, you may still be a good driver even if you do not pass a driving test.

13.3 The first and classic version of the knowledge game: Externally inferable states

A guard challenges three prisoners *A*, *B*, and *C*. He shows them five fezzes, three red and two blue, blindfolds them and makes each of them wear a red fez, thus minimizing the amount of information provided. He then hides the remaining fezzes from sight. When the blindfolds are removed, each prisoner can see only the other prisoners' fezzes. At this point, the guard says: 'If you tell me the colour of your fez you will be free. But if you make a mistake or cheat you will be executed'.

The guard interrogates *A* first. *A* checks *B*'s and *C*'s fezzes and declares that he does not know the colour of his fez. The guard then asks *B*. *B* has heard *A*, checks *A*'s and *C*'s fezzes, but he too must admit that he does not know. Finally, the guard asks *C*. *C* has heard both *A* and *B* and immediately answers: 'My fez is red'. *C* is correct and the guard sets him free. As Dretske would put it: *C* is indeed in the state in which he says he is, and *C* knows that he is in that state or he would not have said so, the question is, *how does he know it?*

Take the Cartesian product of the two sets of fezzes. If there were three fezzes of each colour, we would have the following Table (1 = red, and 0 = blue):

The prisoners know that they all know that there are only two blue fezzes, so ¬ h is *common knowledge*. This is a crucial piece of external information, without which no useful reasoning would be possible. Consider now *A*'s reasoning. *A* knows that, if *B* and *C* are both wearing blue fezzes, he must be wearing a red one (situation d). However, *A* says that he does not know, so now ¬ d is also common knowledge. *B*

Table 9 The setting of the first version of the knowledge game

	a	b	c	d	e	f	g	h
A	1	1	1	1	0	0	0	0
B	1	1	0	0	1	1	0	0
C	1	0	1	0	1	0	1	0

Table 10 Who knows what at the end of the first version of the knowledge game

		BC		ABC		BC		ABC
	a	¬ b	c	¬ d	e	¬ f	g	¬ h
A	1	1	1	1	0	0	0	0
B	1	1	0	0	1	1	0	0
C	1	0	1	0	1	0	1	0

knows that if both *A* and *C* are wearing blue fezzes, he must be wearing a red one (situation f). However, *B* too says that he does not know, so *C* also knows that ¬ f. Moreover, since *B* knows that ¬ d, he also knows that, if he sees *A* wearing a red fez and *C* wearing a blue one, then he can only have a red fez (situation b). Since *B* says that he does not know, *C* also knows that ¬ b. Updating Table 9, the final Table 10, available to *C*, is (the top row indicates who knows which situation):

At this point, the game is over, since in all remaining situations {a, c, e, g} *C* is wearing a red fez. Note that *C* does not need to *see* *A* and *B*, so *C* could be blind. So, in a slightly different version, the prisoners are in a queue facing a wall, with *A* seeing *B* and *C*, *B* seeing *C*, and *C* looking at the wall. Despite appearances, the better off is still *C*.

13.3.1. Synchronic inferences: A fairer version of the knowledge game

Sometimes the agents have a letter attached to their back or a muddy forehead, or play a card game (Fagin et al. (1995)). Instead, we only used 1s and 0s. The details are irrelevant, provided we are considering *externally inferable* states. Given an agent AG, a state *S* and an environment *E*, *S* is an externally inferable state if and only if

   i. in *E*, AG is in *S*; and
   ii. logical and informational resources can be polarised in such a way that
        ii. a only logical resources are in AG;
        ii. b all informational resources are in *E*; and
        ii. c if AG has access to *E*, then AG can infer AG's state *S* from *E*.

The prisoners exploit three environmental resources:

   a. the nature and number of available states;
   b. the observable states of the other prisoners;
   c. the other prisoners' answers;

plus the fact that they have common knowledge of (a)–(c).

Regarding (b), the whole point of having a distributed system is that the components can communicate about their states. However, in our case this cannot be done by explicit acknowledgement of one's state, since the experiment relies on the agents not knowing beforehand in which states they are. Therefore, the communication must be in terms of external observation, which requires some form of access. All this is easily modelled in terms of observable states, but it does not have to be. For example, the prisoners could be blindfolded and made to choose the fez to wear, one after the other, in such a way that each would know only which fez the other two have chosen. In this case, they would have to rely on their memories of observable processes. Note, finally, that in our version the communication is verbal and explicit, but in another version the prisoners are synchronized and merely asked to walk silently towards the door of the cell as soon as they know the answer. They all walk together after a given time.

Regarding (c), this is the only resource that increases in the course of the game. This is unfair, for prisoner A can take no advantage of (c), whereas prisoner C cashes in on all the previous answers. Prisoner B is the most frustrated. He knows that, given his answer, if he were C he would be able to infer his (C's) state. The fact that B cannot answer correctly before C, despite knowing that his answer will allow C to answer correctly without (C) even looking at A and B (recall that C may be blind), shows that B knows what it is like to be C—both in the sense of being the agent whose turn it is to answer the question, and in the sense of being in C's given state—but that C is still 'another mind' to B. B knows Table 10 as well as C, but cannot put this information to any use because he is not C. If there were no 'other minds', there would be no difference in the location of B and C in the logical space of the knowledge game, but there is such a difference, so B and C are different, and B knows it. This, by the way, shows one way in which B can prove the existence of other minds.

To give a chance to every prisoner, the guard must interrogate all of them synchronically. *Mutatis mutandis*, the fair challenge goes like this:

Guard: Do you know the colour of your fez?
  A, B, and C together: No.
Now all agents are in the state in which B was in the unfair game.

Guard: Think again. Do you know the colour of your fez?
  A, B, and C together: No.

Now they are all in the state in which C was in the unfair game, so they can immediately add, without being asked a third time:

A, B, and C together: Yes, it is red.

In the fair challenge, the prisoners work *synchronically*, no longer *sequentially*, and in *parallel*, as a multi-agent system. The system is entirely distributed. It still relies on shared memory, but there is no centralized decision-taker, planner, or manager, no CPU or homunculus that collects, stores, and processes information and organizes the interactions between the components. An interesting consequence is a net increase in efficiency. The multi-agent system can now take full advantage of the resources (a)–(c) and extract more information from the environment, in fact all the available information, by excluding more alternatives under more constraints. Hearing C's reply in the unfair challenge we only know that he is correct, but we do not know what A and B are wearing. Hearing the system, on the contrary, we come to know that all prisoners wear a red fez.

13.3.2 Winners of the classic version

Since all informational load is outsourced in the environment and A, B, and C are *tabulae rasae* that behave like mere inferential engines, they are replaceable by artificial agents or zombies. Three Turing machines in a network could ascertain, inferentially, that they are all switched on (e.g. three green LEDs) and not off (e.g. two red LEDs). Put them in a black box, query the box about its own state, and you will obtain a correct answer. Having hidden some details, it seems that the box is magically 'aware' of its own 'switched-on' state. Clearly, the level of abstraction at which we observe the agent(s) makes a very significant difference. Indeed, the solution of the prisoners' problem can be transformed into a computable algorithm generalizable to any finite number of interacting computer systems, something that turns out to be quite useful in industry.[4]

In one more variant of the classic version of the knowledge game, we can imagine that a robot, a zombie, and a human prisoner team up to win the game. Externally inferable states do not allow us to discriminate between types of inferential agents. In order to differentiate between the types of agents, we need a tougher game, and I shall suggest three versions. First, we can make the agents rely on some information made available by their newly acquired states themselves. This game will be analysed in the next section, where we shall see that Dretske is right: in this case too, we cannot discriminate among different types of agents, although for different reasons from those just discussed. At this stage, not only do the agents not know how they know that they are not zombies, they might even doubt whether they are zombies or robots. We can then make the agents exploit whatever information is provided by the question itself. Artificial agents lose this version of the game. Finally, we can make the agent exploit the information implicit in their own answers. This version can be won only by conscious agents. It shows that whoever passes the test is not a zombie, that one can know this by winning the game, and that one can explain how one knows that one is

---

[4] See for example DESIRE, a computational framework for DEsign and Specification of Interacting REasoning components to model distributed air traffic control that is based on the classic version of the knowledge game (Langevelde et al. (1992); Brazier et al. (1994)).

not a zombie by referring to the way one wins the game. Thus, the last version of the game provides an answer to Dretske's question.

13.4 The second version of the knowledge game

The prisoners are shown five pairs of boots, all identical but for the fact that the three worn by the prisoners are torturing instruments that crush the feet, while the remaining two are ordinary boots. The guard plays the fair version of the challenge. Of course, the three prisoners answer correctly at once. Fezzes have only useless tassels, but torturing boots can *bootstrap*.

Bootstrapping is a technique that uses the input of a short sequence of instructions to make a system receptive to a larger set of instructions. Here, one can slightly adapt the term to describe the new state of wearing torturing boots because

i. wearing them provides more external information (the short sequence) than wearing fezzes, namely a mechanical pressure;
ii. the prisoners are agents capable of receiving this extra information; and
iii. the extra information is sufficient to *verify* the state (the larger set of instructions) without having to *derive* it through a sequential or parallel process.

In bootstrapping states, the information about the 'large' states becomes inferable through the interaction between the 'short' state, its carrier and its receiver. The *verification* process of a bootstrapping state requires more information (the 'short' state) but less time (number of logical steps) than the *derivation* of the same state through external inference (imagine the case in which the torturing boots are also red and the prisoners are sitting at three tables and cannot see their own boots). Thus, verification capacities confer a selective advantage on the agent displaying them.

Unfortunately, one cannot reach a satisfactory taxonomy of agents on these grounds. Bootstrapping states are useless for discriminating between humans and zombies because the inference requires no p- or *s-consciousness* but only some sort of registration of the bootstrapping state as a premise to the successful inference. Since the underlying conscious life is the only difference between humans and zombies, whatever state is bootstrapping for the former may be assumed to be so (at least functionally) also for the latter and vice versa. But bootstrapping states are also useless for discriminating between artificial and non-artificial agents. A state is bootstrapping only *relationally*, depending on the source *and* the receiver of the information that indicates the state. So other types of agents can have their own types of bootstrapping states, which may or may not be bootstrapping for human agents (imagine the boots bear a barcode label). Since not all types of bootstrapping states are necessarily so for any human-like agent, a general bootstrapping game does not allow the necessary distinction between being able to play the game and winning it. For either the three types of agents are assessed on the basis of the *same* (types of) bootstrapping states accessible to all of them, in which case the game is useless, for they all win (participating is winning), or the agents are assessed on the basis of different, i.e. their own, idiosyncratic (types of) bootstrapping states, accessible to only some of them, in which case the game is still useless, since each type of agent wins the game in which its own idiosyncratic states are in question (again, participating is winning).

One may object that, precisely because some specific types of agents can be nomically associated to some types of bootstrapping states, the game can be modified so that the chosen (types of) bootstrapping states allow one to discriminate at least between artificial and non-artificial agents. But biological chauvinism will not help, as already shown by Turing (1950) and further argued by Dretske (2003), even if only for the distinction between zombies and humans. Selecting some specific (types of) feelings or experiences or perceptions, in order to show that we and the zombies can perceive them as bootstrapping, but artificial agents do not, would be like choosing 'heart-beating' as a criterion of discrimination. First, we are back to the 'participating = winning' situation, this time in the converse sense that losing the game is equivalent to being unable to play it, rather than to playing it unsuccessfully. This makes the game not only unfair but above all uninteresting, for it is trivial to show that agents with access to different resources perform differently. Second, the game either presupposes the difference between types of agents that it is supposed to identify, thus begging the question, or it misses a fundamental point, the indiscernibility of the differences between the bootstrapping experiences. Zombies are almost like us: they z-feel the z-pain of the bootstrap, and they z-verify the corresponding z-state in ways that are either identical to ours or at least not discernible (for us) from them anyway. Dretske draws roughly the same conclusion when discussing zombies' *protopain*. Likewise, it would be very simple to engineer artificial agents capable of a-feeling the pressure of the 'painful' boot or any other bootstrapping state we may choose. In either case, as far as we know, no difference between experiencing, z-experiencing, and a-experiencing torturing boots can be usefully exploited within the game. So Dretske is right. Appeal to self-booting experiences will not do. You cannot answer the 'how' question by relying on them. We need a different version of the game.

13.5 The third version of the knowledge game

So far the players have taken advantage of (their common knowledge of) the information provided by (i) the nature and number of assignable states; (ii) the observable states of the other agents; (iii) the other agents' answers; and (iv) the assigned states, when they are bootstrapping. A source that has not yet been exploited is the question itself.

Suppose the prisoners are offered five glasses. They are informed that three contain water and two contain a totally deafening beverage that looks and tastes exactly like water. We play the game *unfairly*, i.e. sequentially, not synchronically. The first thing prisoner A hears is the guard shouting his question. Of course, the prisoner answers correctly at once. To him and to us, the question is trivially self-answering. Yet, why it is so is much less obvious. The guard's question (Q)

    i. does not *entail* the answer;

    ii. does not *implicate* (in Grice's sense) its answer, for this is not a matter of implicit meaning of Q or intention of the utter of Q;

    iii. does not *presuppose* its answer, for Q cannot be answered by relying on the background information that the speaker and the listener tacitly assume (Groenendijk and Stokhof (1994), section 6.4.5). Note that 'a *presupposition of a question is* defined as a proposition that the respondent becomes committed to in giving any direct answer to the question' (Walton (1991), p. 338).

    iv. is not *self-fulfilling*, that is, it does not contain its answer in the 'fridge-paradox' sense that asking Q is equivalent to implementing whatever state S is whose existence Q is about (like opening the fridge to check whether the light is on);

    v. is not *loaded*, for Q is loaded only if the respondent is not committed to (some part of) the presupposition of Q (Walton (1991), p. 340).

Self-answering questions are not the subject of much analysis in erotetic logic. For example, in their excellent survey, Groenendijk and Stokhof (1994) pay no attention to them. Perhaps they are too trivial. Sometimes they are even confused with rhetorical questions, which are really assertions under cover. Yet a self-answering question is not one that requires no answer, or for which the questioner intends to provide his or his own answer. It is a question that answers itself, if one knows how to interpret it, and this can be achieved in several ways. The erotetic commitment of the question can be external. For example, asking a yes/no question while nodding may count as an externally, pragmatically self-answering question. Or the erotetic commitment can be internal. 'How many were the four evangelists?' is an internally, semantically self-answering question. In our case, the erotetic commitment is neither internal nor external but relational. The question about the agent being in a certain state is self-answering in a more complex way, for the answer is *counterfactually embedded* in Q and it is so somewhat 'indexically'[5] since, under different circumstances, the question or the questioning would give nothing away (henceforth this is what I shall mean by self-answering question).

For A to extract from the self-answering Q the information that A is in S, something like the following is required:

1. A, B, and C can each be set in a new state, either S or $\neg$ S
2. A receives the information contained in (1)
3. A is set in a new state, either S or $\neg$ S
4. A receives the information contained in (3)
5. A's new state is S

---

[5] Selmer Bringsjord and Patrick Grim have pointed out to me that this use of 'indexically' may not be entirely appropriate and could generate confusion. I appreciate their concern, but I do not know of any other term that would express the point equally well. The reader is warned that the qualification is slightly unorthodox.

   6. *A* does not receive the information contained in (5)

   7. *A* receives the question *Q* about the nature of *A*'s new state

   8. *A* receives the information contained in (7)

   9. *A* reasons that if *A* were in $\neg S$ then *A* would be in some state *D*; but if *A* were in *D* then *A* could not have received *Q*; but *A* received *Q*, so *A* could receive *Q*, so *A* is not in *D*, so *A* is not in $\neg S$, but *A* is in either *S* or $\neg S$, so *A* is in *S*.

  10. *A* answers that *A* is in *S*.

An interesting example of this new version of the knowledge game is provided by Hobbes and Gassendi. At different stages, they both object to Descartes that states such as 'walking' or 'jumping' may replace 'thinking' within the Cartesian project. 'Ambulo ergo sum' would do equally well, they argue. However, Descartes correctly replies that they are both mistaken (and they were). 'Are you (am I) thinking?' is self-answering in the sense just defined, but 'are you (am I) walking?' is not. As we shall see in the next game, a zombie can jump and walk but he still cannot infer (let alone be certain) from this that he exists, for *he* does not (indeed cannot) know that *he himself* is jumping and walking. Whereas, even if we perceive ourselves jumping and walking, we may still wonder whether we are dreaming, in which case it is the activity of wondering (in other words, thinking) that one may be dreaming that makes the difference, not the dreamt state itself (the jumping and walking in one's dream); or we may wonder whether we are zombies, and if so, whether we are zombies dreaming that they are jumping or walking, in which case too there is still nothing intrinsic to the jumping or to the walking that will enable us to tell the difference, i.e. to answer Dretske's 'how' question.

Extracting (as opposed to *verifying* or *deriving*) relevant semantic information (the erotetic commitment) about states from self-answering questions about those very states requires agents endowed with advanced semantic capacities. These are often clustered under broader and more general labels such as intellect, reason, intelligence, understanding, high-order cognition, or mind. In order to be less inclusive and to stress their procedural nature, I suggest we opt for *reflection*.

Reflection is only a useful label. It is not to be understood here as referring to some higher-order awareness or cognition, if lower-order awareness or cognition is a sense of self, or consciousness. So far, we have avoided relying on consciousness (in any sense of the word), and we should keep resisting the temptation to cheat or to beg the question. Reflection is not meant to refer to privileged access, introspection, or psychological awareness of internal states either, no matter of what kind and order. Rather, it is to be understood as a label for the semantic capacity of backward inference, from under-standing the question to understanding its conditions of possibility and hence its answer. In more Kantian terms, this backward inference is a form of transcendental thinking, that is, thinking about the condition of possibility of something.

Reflection so understood is something that artificial agents do not enjoy, at least not yet. We have already encountered in chapter ten so-called 'reflective' artificial agents that can win the classic knowledge game (Brazier and Treur (1999)), but that description is only evocative. Architectures or programs for computational systems (of AI) and systems for machine learning are technically called 'reflective' when they contain an accessible representation of themselves that can be used (by themselves) e.g. to monitor and improve their performance. This seems to be what Block (1995) has termed, in human agents, 'access-consciousness' (see Bringsjord (1997)). However, what is known as *reflective computing* is only a case of metaprogramming,[6] and the knowledge game does not contradict this deflationist view, since, strictly speaking, the axiomatization of the reasoning involved requires only standard first-order logic (McCarthy (1971–1987), (1990)) without any appeal to introspection, even if it can be analysed using e.g. epistemic logic or the BDI (Belief, Desire, Intention) architecture (Rao and Georgeff (1991)).

Current artificial agents are unable to take advantage of the self-answering nature of the question because they are intellectually and semantically impaired, somewhat like Descartes's animal automata or Spinoza's 'sceptical' automata. Reflection is an AI-complete problem, i.e. a problem whose solution presupposes a solution to the 'strong AI problem', the synthesis of a decent (to many this is synonymous with human) degree of commonsensical intelligence endowed with some semantic skills. As we still lack anything even vaguely resembling a semantically proficient and intelligent artificial agent, this version of the knowledge game suffices to discriminate between them (the artificial) and us (zombies and humans). Let me now qualify this claim.

First, to be answered correctly, a self-answering question requires both understanding of the content of, and a detachment from, the question itself. Self-answering questions are part of the *frame problem*. A normal query works like an instruction that *pushes* an agent AG into a search-space, where a correct symbolic manipulation can identify the state of the agent itself. But a self-answering question *pulls* a reflective agent in the opposite direction, in search of what his own state must be if the question is receivable/accessible and intelligible in the first place. Now, some counterfactual truths concerning a variety of type-situations can be pre-programmed (soft-encoded, hardwired, or 'interfaked', i.e. faked through an interface) in our artificial agents. As in the Turing test, this is trivially achievable, yet it is not a solution, but only an ad hoc and brittle trick. It is the difference between winning a type of game or just a specific token of it. Contrary to artificial agents, zombies and humans can be assumed to have a full and intelligent command of language, and hence enjoy a counterfactual-reflective understanding of the semantics of an open-ended number of indexical questions. If we repeat the test, in principle, if the question is self-answering, zombies and humans should be able to appreciate it, but artificial agents cannot. Any digital make-up is here only a boring 'catch me if you can' of no conceptual interest.

Second, I specified above that we have tested the difference between artificial agents and zombies by making them play the third version of the knowledge game *unfairly*, i.e. sequentially not synchronically. Zombie A passes the test, whereas robot A does not. What happens if we let the artificial agents play the game *fairly*? A parallel, multi-agent system of artificial agents would still fail the test. This because the answers provided by the other machines are non-informative (they do not provide further, informational constraints on C's options), so they do not really improve the overall performance. The last artificial agent C, or the whole system working in parallel, is in the same predicament as the first artificial agent A, or the system working sequentially. So the performance of a single zombie will still be different from the performance of a system of artificial agents. Zombie-like behaviour (or a semantic engine) cannot yet be obtained by coordinating several artificial agents (syntactic engines). If it could, we would have found a way of building semantic systems.

Third, my previous claim comes with a 'best before' date: *current* and *foreseeable* artificial agents as we know them cannot answer self-answering questions, either in a stand-alone or in a multi-agent setting. What is *logically possible* for (or achievable at some distant time in the future by) a single artificial agent, or for an artificial multi-agent system, is not in question. I explained at the outset that we are not assuming some science fiction scenario. 'Never' is a long time, and I would not like to commit myself to any statement like 'artificial agents will never be able (or are in principle unable) to answer self-answering questions'. The knowledge game cannot be used to argue that AI or AC (artificial consciousness) is impossible in principle. In particular, its present format cannot be used to answer the question 'How do you know you are not a *futuristic*, intelligent, and conscious artificial agent of the kind envisaged in *Blade Runner* or *Natural City*?'. As far as artificial agents are concerned, the knowledge game is a test to check whether AI and AC have been achieved. We shall see that, given the difference between us and zombies, as Bringsjord (1999) has rightly noticed, if one day artificial agents do pass the test, we shall have created zombies. Having made this much clear, I entirely agree with Searle (1992) and Bringsjord (1999) in their criticism of computationalism. As Bringsjord writes in his defence of Searle's position against Dennett, in current, computational AI

'the person building project' will inevitably fail, but [...] it *will* manage to produce artifacts capable of excelling in the famous Turing Test, and in its more stringent relatives. What sort of artifacts will these creatures be? I offer an unflattering one-word response: Pollock, Dennett, and like-minded researchers are busy building ... *zombies*.

Indeed, I am even more pessimistic than Bringsjord, although elsewhere I argued that neo-Frankensteinian AI may be computer-ethically problematic (Floridi and Sanders (2004b)).

To summarize, unlike artificial agents, zombies are reflective in the sense specified above, for (the starting hypothesis is that) they share with us everything but *p*- and *s-consciousness*. So Descartes, Spinoza, Leibniz (1995), and Dretske are right: we and they can win this version of the knowledge game and nobody could spot the difference. Is there any other source of information that a conscious agent can exploit inferentially but a zombie cannot?

Recall that the difference is supposed to rest on the subjectively conscious nature of the states in the (*p*) and (*s*) senses. This is mirrored in the nature of the corresponding reports. A zombie *Z* knows that *Z* is in state *S*, but does not know that *he* is *Z*, or that *S* is *his* state, nor does *Z* know what it is like for *himself* to be in *S*. A human agent *H*, on the contrary, will find it difficult to dissociate himself from his own states, which are always 'proprietary'. To *H*, *H*'s states are, first of all, his own states or states as he experiences them (thus-states), or of which he is conscious, at least in so far as his attention can be called upon *S*. A detached (third-person or zombie-like) perspective on one's own thus-states can be acquired, but it is not the default option and, if adopted, would seem rather contrived.

This intuition can be made profitable by exploiting a last source of information about the agent's state, namely his own answer, thus coming full circle, as you may recall that in the first version each agent takes advantage of the other agents' answers, not yet of his own.

13.6 The fourth version of the knowledge game

The three prisoners are offered five tablets: three are completely innocuous and two make the agents totally dumb. As before, we play the game *sequentially*. For reasons that will be discussed in the following section, we shall focus only on prisoner *A*'s performance. *A* cannot know which tablet he has taken, in terms of externally inferable, bootstrapping, or self-answering states. As usual, all forms of privileged or direct accesses to his state are also excluded *ex hypothesi*. *A* hears the question and is then allowed to answer. Since he has no way of knowing or inferring whether he is in a dumb state, he answers by reporting his state of ignorance. Now, *whatever A* says to communicate his state of ignorance, e.g. 'Heaven knows', either

- a. his verbal report about his state of ignorance triggers no further reaction; or
- b. his verbal report about his state of ignorance triggers a counterfactual reasoning of the following kind: 'had I taken the dumbing tablet I would not have been able to report orally my state of ignorance about my dumb/non-dumb state, but I have been, and I know that I have been, as I have heard myself speaking and saw the guard reacting to my speaking, but this (my oral report) is possible only if I did not take the dumbing tablet, so now I know that I am in a non-dumb state, hence I know that I have not taken the dumbing tablet, and I know that I know all this, that is, I know that my previous state of ignorance has now been erased, so I can revise my statement and reply, correctly, in which state I am, which is a state of not having taken the dumbing tablet, of knowing that I haven't, and—by

going through this whole process and passing the test—of knowing how I know both that I haven't and that I know that I haven't'.

In case (a), *A* does not correct himself, and so he fails the test: he does not know in which state he is. Literally. The agents who fail the test do not know that it is themselves that they are hearing talking. If they did, they would pass the test. These agents lack *s-consciousness*.

In case (b), *A* corrects himself, so he is able to pass the test by saying in which state he is. In order to be able to infer his actual state on the basis of his initial report about his lack of information about their state, the player needs to be able to identify

1. the agent reporting (e.g. by uttering an interjection to communicate his lack of information) that
2. the agent is in a state of ignorance about
3. the agent's empirical state in question (dumbness/non-dumbness, in our example)
4. as the *same* agent, and then this agent as himself, that is, as the agent *A* who is playing the knowledge game and to whom the guard addressed the question concerning his state after having taken the tablet. But this means that players can pass the test only if they realize that it is themselves and their own states that they are talking about. Winners of this final version of the knowledge game need to be *s-conscious* agents, so they cannot be zombies.

Note that it would be more elegant to allow the agents to reply in the usual way, by saying 'I do not know', when they wish to acknowledge their state of ignorance. Yet his might generate some distracting confusion. For someone might wonder whether passing the test is somehow connected to the capacity of issuing first-person report, and this is definitely not the point. Nothing hangs on the specific verbal capacities of the agents or on the language employed. The game would work equally well if the tables were 'arms-paralysing' and the agents could reply only by raising their arms. Basically, any form of communication will do, as long as one can take advantage of the detachment between reporting and reported agent by identifying a state *S* such that the reporting agent *A* knows that he is in *S* only if *A* knows that *he himself* is the reporting agent *x* in his own description of his lack of information about *x*'s state.

We have seen that a difference between artificial agents and zombies/humans is that the latter are capable of *counterfactual reflection*, something that requires *semantics*. A difference between zombies and humans is that the latter are also capable of *subjective reflection*, something that requires not only *semantics* but also *consciousness*. The time has come to use the knowledge game to answer Dretske's question.

13.7 Dretske's question and the knowledge game

How do you know you are not a zombie? The briefest answer is: by playing as A and winning the last version of the knowledge game. The long answer will take some clarifications. By winning the fourth version of the knowledge game, the agent A

  i. shows that he is not a zombie,
  ii. experiences what it is like to be *s-conscious* (and hence not a zombie in this sense) by identifying himself as himself while being in S; and
  iii. experiences what it is like to be *p-conscious* of S (and hence not a zombie in this sense too) by realizing what it is like to be in a certain state S and be able to know and explain that he is in that state S.

Shouldn't one, having won the game, wonder whether what one experienced as state S might also be z-experienced by a zombie? No, because, contrary to what happens in the third version of the game, what is in question now is not the mere experience of being in a state S, nor the knowledge of being in that state, nor just the simple *p-consciousness* of being in S, but the *p-consciousness* of being in S brought about by (what is the other side of consciousness, namely) the *s-consciousness* of being the agent who is in S, and this twofold consciousness brings with itself the further knowledge that this is as good evidence as anything that one is not (indeed cannot) z-experiencing S, for if one did, then one would not be able to win the game as one did.

Perhaps a different approach, based on the logical order of the questions, might help to clarify the argument further. Consider the following statements made of question + answer:

  1. are you not a zombie? yes;
  2.1 do you know that (1)? yes;
  2.2 how do you know that (1)?
  3. do you know that (2.1)? yes.

Points (1) and (2.1) are conceded. Point (2.2) is not an implicit challenge of (1) or (2.1), but it is Dretske's question. We have seen that we cannot use the knowledge game to answer (2.2) by relying on (1) and (2.1). The fourth version of the game shows that (2.2) can be answered by appealing to a higher level, namely (3), what in epistemic logic would go under the general label of the KK thesis. Should we not repeat (2.2) at an even higher level, and wonder how one knows that one knows that (1)? No, because the escalation from (2.1) to (3) brings about the so-called 'common knowledge' phenomenon: once an agent knows that he knows that he is not a zombie, then he also knows that he knows that ... he knows that he is not a zombie. So how do you know that you are not a zombie? By passing a test that proves that you know that you know that you are not, which implies that you know that you are not, which implies that you are not; and then by pointing to this whole process, and the corresponding test that brings it about and the common knowledge it generates, to explain how you know all this.

Two final clarifications can now be introduced as answers to two main objections.

First, we have seen that Dretske's question concerns primarily knowing that one is *p-conscious*. However, one may contend that winning the last version of the knowledge game indicates, at best, that the agents in question are *s-conscious*. If so, it says nothing about *p-consciousness* and *a fortiori* nothing about how one knows that one is *p-conscious*.

Second, one may argue that, if we allow the agents to play the fourth version of the game until *C* answers, or *fairly*, i.e. *synchronically*, it seems that *C* (or the multi-agent zombie system) will pass the test, and this shows that the test itself is not a good test anyway.

Both objections are reasonable but easily answered. Consider the first objection. The knowledge game shows not only that an agent *A*, who is *s-conscious*, can tell in which empirical state *S* he is (e.g. he is not dumb), but also that, by going through the process of identifying his correct empirical state *S* while being in *S*, the agent *A* comes to realize what it is like to be in that state *S*, that is, he is also able to appreciate the subjective nature of the state *S* involved, at least insofar as this triggers the consciousness of being in *S*. Stripped of its qualitative nature, the reasoning is that, if the agent enjoys no *p-consciousness* of any kind, then he enjoys no *s-consciousness* of any kind, but winning the knowledge game shows that the agent enjoys *s-consciousness* of some kind, so it also shows that he enjoys some *p-consciousness* of some kind (the 'kind' is contingent on the setting of the game and the choice of the state *S*).

Someone may wish to resist the previous line of reasoning by arguing that the form of the *modus tollens* is hardly questionable, but that the implication to which it is applied is controversial. The reply is that there are plenty of reasons for being confident about the implication as well.

To begin with, *p-* and *s-consciousness* seem to be strictly related. Indeed, they may be related by a double implication, the tenability of one half of which has already been established by Kriegel (2004). Kriegel has argued, convincingly, that some forms of *p-consciousness* imply some forms of *s-consciousness*. If one does not find this compelling, the ball is in his court. Suppose we therefore accept that some forms of *p-consciousness* imply some forms of *s-consciousness*. It then seems much less difficult to argue for the other half of the double implication,[7] from some forms of *s-consciousness* to some forms of *p-consciousness*, which is the implication needed above, in the negative form that absence of the latter implies absence of the former. If an agent has some (second- or higher-order) sense, or is (introspectively) aware of, his personal identity (including his knowledge that he thinks) and (first- or lower-order) experiences, both mental and perceptual (including his knowledge of what he is thinking), then he must also have

---

[7] Kriegel (2003) comes very close to arguing for this second half of the double implication when he supports the thesis that 'a mental state is conscious when, and only when, it involves implicit self-awareness'. I am grateful to Kriegel for having called my attention to this article.

some experience of the qualitative, subjective, personal, or phenomenological properties of the state in which he is. You cannot be x, be *s-conscious* that you are x, know that you are *s-conscious* that you are x, and yet not know (i.e. be *p-unconscious* of) what it is like to be x, because the knowing (being *p-conscious*) of what it is like to be x is just equivalent to knowing (being *s-conscious* of) what it is like to be yourself.

Our sceptical interlocutor may still be unconvinced. Appealing to some common sense; showing that, in some cases, half of the double implication is already proved and the other half is even more reasonable; shifting the burden of proof; reasoning that you cannot be *s-conscious* in a vacuum of *p-consciousness* of something; all this may still appear to be insufficient. Luckily, we can leave the sceptic to his own doubts because Dretske himself seems happy to concede, following several other philosophers, that indeed *p-consciousness* is inferably related to *s-consciousness*. The point at stake is not that Dretske believes that *p-* and *s-consciousness* are unrelated, but that he suggests that relating *p-consciousness* to *s-consciousness* makes no difference to whether his 'how' question can be answered. Yet, the knowledge game shows that this conclusion is unjustified. It does make a difference because, by then having a test based on the presence of *s-consciousness while* having a *p-consciousness* of a particular state, you can have the experience of what it is like to be *p-conscious* of S *and* have a way of showing how you know that you are *p-conscious* of S. Dretske was right when, in the past, he thought the argument based on *s-consciousness* was convincing.

So, going back to our sceptic, the worst scenario is that at least Dretske and I share the same presupposition: *p-* and *s-consciousness* are two sides of the same coin, take it all or leave it all. Disjoining the two is misleading. Since the two are correlated, showing how you know that you are *s-conscious* while you are in S is, at the same time, a way of showing how you know you are also *p-conscious* of S.

Consider now the second objection. If we let the agents play the game until the end (C's answer) or synchronically (as a multi-agent group), the answers by the three zombies (e.g. three 'Heaven knows') will provide increasing informational constraints on C's (or on the multi-agent zombie system's) options. The zombies already have the information that there are only three players. Therefore, from hearing first one, then two and finally three voices, it will be possible to infer that all players have taken innocuous tablets, and this without recurring to any sort of consciousness. Eventually, C (or the multi-agent zombie system), on hearing three voices, will infer that the three zombies have taken the innocuous tablets, he will correct his statement and pass the test. So can the test be passed by C and hence by a multi-agent zombie system? The right answer is: it should, but it does not matter.

Of course, each zombie still does not know that he himself has taken an innocuous tablet because otherwise he would not have been able to answer in the first place, but this is not relevant here. What are relevant are two other considerations.

On the one hand, the test devised is fair only if your performance, as a whole conscious agent, can in principle become indistinguishable from the performance of yourself considered as a system each part of which (everybody should agree) is not conscious. Now zombies may just be such parts: we have assumed that each of them has all the (perceptual, semantic, cognitive, logical, and so forth) capacities that you have, but for the fact of being p- and s-*unconscious*. So, if they coordinate their efforts, apart from a lot of spare capacity and redundancy (recall that each zombie is like a p- s-conscious-less you), we should expect the performance of a system of zombies to be as successful as yours, *given the constraints offered by the knowledge game*. In other words, you and the multi-agent zombie system should appear to an external observer as performing equally well: you should both win it in two steps. This guarantees fairness and some plausibility, but it does not mean that the multi-agent zombie system is conscious. For, on the other hand, recall that, precisely because you and a system of zombies would be able to win the fourth version, we have compared your performance as agent A to that of a single zombie in the same position, not to the whole system of interacting zombies. And because A does not yet have all the constraints that will be available to C, you can pass the test but a zombie will not, nor will a system of zombies, insofar as it would have to be considered, in its turn, as a single agent A in need of coordinating its answers with other two multi-agent zombie systems B and C. To put it bluntly: it is a problem of levels of abstraction; if one messes with them then the whole game becomes pointless.

A general lesson to be learnt from the previous discussion is that, when discussing how agents could win the third version, we saw that we cannot obtain zombie-like performance by coordinating the behaviour of our current conscious-less artificial agents. Whereas, we now know that, as far as winning the fourth version of the game is concerned, we could obtain close-to-conscious performance if only we could create multi-agent zombie systems.

After having asked 'how do you know you are not a zombie?', Dretske comments

> Everything you are aware of would be the same if you were a zombie. In having perceptual experience, then, nothing distinguishes your world, the world you experience, from a zombie's.

I agree. This is the hypothesis supporting the thought experiment. Dretske then asks: 'This being so, what is it about this world that tells you that, unlike a zombie, you experience it?'. He answers 'nothing', and I agree, at least insofar as the first version of the knowledge game shows that externally inferable states are useless in this respect. Dretske finally asks: 'What is it you are aware of that indicates you are aware of it?'. His and my answer is again 'nothing'. I have argued in favour of this point by showing that self-booting and reflective states are also useless. Dretske asks no more questions and concludes:

> We are left, then, with our original question: How do you know you are not a zombie? Not everyone who is conscious knows they are. Not everyone who is not a zombie, knows they are not. Infants don't. Animals don't. You do. Where did you learn this? To insist that we know it despite there being *no identifiable way* [emphasis added] we know it is not very helpful. We can't do epistemology by stamping our feet. Skeptical suspicions are, I think, rightly aroused by this

result. Maybe our conviction that we know, in a direct and authoritative way, that we are conscious is simply a confusion of what we are aware of with our awareness of it.

I have argued that this pessimistic conclusion is premature because it does not take into account the agent's inferential interactions with other agents as discussed in the fourth version of the knowledge game.

CONCLUSION

In the knowledge game designed in this chapter there are four sources of information: the environment, the states, the questions and the answers. Agents are assigned predetermined states using the least informative setting (the initial difference in states is not imported within the system, whose components are assigned equal states). They are then assessed according to their capacities to obtain relevant semantic information about their own states from these sources inferentially. Depending on the chosen state, each source can identify a type of game and hence a class of players able to win it. The communicative and logical nature of the game excludes even very intelligent mammals from participation, including infants, chimpanzees, orang-utans, and bottlenose dolphins, who consistently pass the test of mirror self-recognition (Allen (2009)). This, however, is not an objection, since the question addressed in this chapter is not how you (a grown-up person, who can fully understand the 'how' question) know that you are an animal. Conversely, whatever the answer to the latter question is, it certainly cannot rely on some unique logical capacities you enjoy.

The knowledge game is an informative test. It is not meant to provide a *definition* of intellectual or semantic abilities or of consciousness. It is not a defence of an inferential theory of consciousness either, nor does it provide ammunition for the displaced perception model. Like the Turing test for AI, it purports to offer something much weaker, namely a reliable and informative criterion to discriminate between types of (inferential) agents and hence a way to answer the 'how' question, at a clearly specified level of abstraction, without relying on that foggy phenomenon that is human introspection.

The criterion employed is more than a successful means of identification because it is also informatively rich. An informatively poor criterion would be one that used an otherwise irrelevant property P to identify x successfully. To use an example à la Donnellan, at a party you may successfully identify Mary's friend as the only man in the room—this also conveys quite a bit of extra information about him—or as the person who is closer to the window, which is true at that precise moment but otherwise very poor informatively. The knowledge game relies on relevant and significant properties, which characterize agents in an informatively rich way. This is like cataloguing animals according to their diets. The trap would be to reduce (or simply confuse) what matters most in the nature of x to (or with) what makes an informatively rich difference between x, which has P, and y, which lacks P. An agent AG may have the unique capacity to infer his own states and yet this may not be the most important thing about

AG, *pace* Descartes. We avoid the trap if we recall that our task is to answer Dretske's question. Consciousness-centrism may be perfectly justified and even welcome, but it is a different thesis, which requires its own independent defence; it is not what the knowledge game is here to support.

The last version of the game suggests a view of consciousness as *subjective reflectivity*, a state in which the agent and the I merge and 'see each other' as the same subject. It seems that artificial agents and zombies are entirely decoupled from the agents they can issue reports about, but which they cannot identify as themselves. Animals, on the other hand, seem wholly coupled to external information. Humans are both decoupled from their environment and coupled to themselves, that is, they appear to constitute themselves as centres of subjective reflectivity, prompted by, but independent of, the environment. Consciousness is comparable to a mathematical fixed point: it occurs as a decoupling from reality and a collapsing of the referring agent and the referred agent. I suppose this might be what lies behind the description of the (re)acquisition of consciousness as a sort of 'awakening'.

This perspective has some surprising consequences. One of the most interesting concerns the transcendental nature of the I. In the final knowledge game, states are inferentially appropriated by the agent as his own (*p-consciousness*) only because the agent is already conscious of himself as himself (*s-consciousness*). Once unpacked, this logical priority seems to indicate that agents are *p-conscious* of their perceptual/internal contents not only *after* or *if* but also *because* they are *s-conscious* of themselves. It certainly means that it is not true that they are *s-conscious because* they are *p-conscious* (the *if*, we have seen, has been accepted following Kriegel (2004)). Perceptual or internal contents of which the agent is conscious do not carry with themselves inferentially the (relevant semantic information that the agent has) consciousness of the content itself or of himself as an extra bonus. Perhaps *s-consciousness* is not constructed from perceptual and internal knowledge bottom–up but cascades on it top–down. This IBM ('I Before the Mine') thesis is a strong reading of Searle's view that 'the ontology of the mental is an irreducibly first-person ontology' (Searle (1992), p. 95). Adapting Harnad's phrase, zombies are empty homes but your home is wherever your self is.

If *s-consciousness* really has a logical primacy over the conscious-ed contents, I doubt whether the IBM thesis might be reconciled with some sort of naturalism. It is certainly not externalist-friendly, if by externalism one basically refers, ontologically, to a thesis about where the roots of consciousness are—outside the mind—rather than, heuristically, to a thesis about where the search for them can start. For the knowledge game shows that, in explaining consciousness without relying on introspection, we still cannot progress very far by relying only on environmental information.

The knowledge game coheres much better with an internalist perspective, with an important proviso. Sometimes semantic and rational agents can obtain relevant semantic information about their own states only if they interact successfully in a collaborative context rather than as stand-alone individuals.[8] The external source is a Socratic-maieutic device, which has an eliciting role that is functionally inverse to the one attributed to the malicious demon by Descartes.[9] We have seen that the knowledge game promotes an intersubjective conception of agenthood, moving in the same direction as Grice's cooperative principle and Davidson's charity principle, while favouring an internalist view of *s-consciousness*.

We now have a better understanding of the sort of informational organisms we are. We are neither zombies nor artificial agents, and the knowledge game can tell us how we can know that we are not. The next question concerns the nature of the environment in which we are embedded as inforgs. In the following two chapters, I shall argue that an informational ontology provides a good answer.

---

[8] This 'social' point is emphasized in Moody (1994), see also the several contributions and discussions of Moody's position in Symposium (1995), especially Bringsjord's convincing analysis.

[9] The examiner/guard and the questioning father in the muddy children version have a crucial role, for they guarantee *common knowledge* among the players, see Fagin et al. (1995). This external source is a sort of ghost outside the machine.

14

Against digital ontology

The so-called Pythagoreans, who were the first to take up mathematics, not only advanced this subject, but saturated with it, they fancied that the principles of mathematics were the principles of all things.

Aristotle, *Metaphysics*

SUMMARY

Previously, in chapter thirteen, I argued that human agents may know that they are neither zombies nor artificial agents, but conscious inforgs. However, as conscious inforgs, human agents share with other informational agents a reality made of information. In this chapter, I argue that *digital ontology*, according to which the ultimate nature of reality is digital, and the universe is a computational system equivalent to a Turing machine, should be carefully distinguished from *informational ontology*, according to which the ultimate nature of reality is structural, in order to abandon the former and retain only the latter as a promising line of research. Digital vs analogue is a Boolean dichotomy typical of our computational paradigm, but digital and analogue are only ways in which reality is experienced or conceptualized by an epistemic agent at a given level of abstraction. A preferable alternative is provided by an informational approach to structural realism, according to which knowledge of the world is knowledge of its structures. The most reasonable ontological commitment turns out to be in favour of an interpretation of reality as the totality of structures dynamically interacting with each other. This chapter develops the first part (the *pars destruens*) of the argument. The *pars construens* is developed in the next chapter.

14.1 Introduction

In recent years, the age-old question about the *discrete vs continuous* nature of reality[1] has been recast in the more fashionable terms of *digital* vs *analogue* ontology. As such, it has enjoyed a remarkable revival. However, as will become clear in due course, this is a typical case of old wine in new bottles. And I shall argue that Kant's conclusion, reached against the more classic, old dichotomy in the context of the 'antinomies of

---

[1] Holden (2004) provides an enlightening and insightful analysis of the modern debate, to which I am indebted. I have also relied on the excellent article by Lesne (2007).

pure reason' (Kant (1998), A 434–5/B 462–3), has lost none of its value when applied to the most recent reformulation of the same alternative.

The chapter is structured into four other main sections. In section 14.2, I provide a brief introduction to what is known as digital ontology. In section 14.3, the longest, I introduce a new thought experiment in order to show that digital (discrete) vs analogue (continuous) is a Boolean dichotomy typical of the computational paradigm of our age, but both digital and analogue are only 'modes of presentation of Being' (to paraphrase Kant), that is, ways in which an agent epistemically experiences and conceptualizes reality, at a given level of abstraction (LoA). They do not pick up some knowledge- or LoA-independent properties, intrinsic to the external world. Although this conclusion applies both to digital and to analogue ontologies, the chapter concentrates mainly on the criticism of digital ontology (hence its title) because its constructive goal is to clear the ground for a defence of informational ontology, with which it is often confused. In section 14.4, I further clarify the argument by answering three potential objections. In section 14.5, which concludes the chapter, I provide a positive note and an explanation of the more constructive rationale for the argument developed in this chapter, as a bridge to the next. The two chapters together could be read as an attempt to answer P17 (see chapter two).

14.2 What is digital ontology? *It from Bit*

Konrad Zuse[2] is acknowledged by many as the father of digital ontology.[3] According to him and to digital ontologists in general:

1. the nature of the physical universe (time, space and every entity and process in space-time) is ultimately discrete.

This thesis, with which we shall be engaged for the rest of the chapter, may be accompanied by (a selection of) three other, related theses:

2. the physical universe can be adequately modelled by discrete values like the integers;
3. the evolution (state transitions) of the physical universe is computable as the output of a (presumably short) algorithm; and
4. the laws governing the physical universe are entirely deterministic.

Theses (1) and (2) give away the neo-Pythagorean nature of digital ontology (Steinhart (2003)): reality can be decomposed into ultimate, discrete *indivisibilia*. Note that

---

[2] Zuse is famous for having constructed the first fully operational program-controlled electromechanical binary calculating machine (the Z3) in 1941, see Zuse (1993).

[3] *Digital ontology* is also known as *digital metaphysics* and *digital philosophy*, and has a scientific counterpart in *digital physics*, see Steinhart (1998) for an introduction and Steinhart (2003) for a review chapter. For a recent bibliography see <http://digitalphysics.org/Publications/>

philosophers still disagree on the precise definition of 'digital' and 'analogue'. For example, the debate between Goodman (1968) and Lewis (1971) on the actual nature of the 'digital' has been recently revisited by Müller (forthcoming). And Lesne (2007) has convincingly argued that the distinction between discrete and discretized system is unnecessary

It now appears that there is no reason to make a fundamental distinction between discrete and discretized systems: an object seems to be intrinsically discrete, even isolated, only if we choose the proper glasses. (p. 14)

The 'glasses' are interpreted more formally in this chapter in terms of levels of abstraction. However, there is little doubt that a necessary feature of what it means for something to be digital is that of being discrete, and this will suffice for the purposes of this chapter.

Thesis (3) interprets the neo-Pythagorean ontology in computational terms: the ultimate, discrete *indivisibilia* are actually computable digits, while elegance and Ockham's razor inclines digital ontologists to favour an algorithmic theory as simple as possible (see Feynman (1992), quoted below in section 14.3.3). Thus, a digital ontology

is based on two concepts: bits, like the binary digits in a computer, correspond to the most microscopic representation of state information; and the temporal evolution of state is a digital informational process similar to what goes on in the circuitry of a computer processor. (Fredkin (2003b), p. 189)

In a nutshell, 'we are run by a short algorithm' (Schmidhuber (1997), p. 205).

As for thesis (4), this is presented by supporters of digital ontology as a direct consequence of theses (1)–(3) and explicitly related by them to Einstein's reluctance to accept the conclusion that the universe might be intrinsically probabilistic. The suggestion is that the analysis of physical laws in terms of deterministic state transitions may be made compatible with the ostensibly probabilistic nature of quantum phenomena, while being sufficiently flexible to overcome other criticisms. Fredkin (1992) presents the point with usual clarity (but see also Hooft (2002), (2005)):

Uncertainty is at the heart of quantum mechanics. Finite Nature requires that we rule out true, locally generated randomness because such numbers would not, in this context, be considered finite. [. . .] The deterministic nature of finite digital processes is different in that it is unknowable determinism. From within the system an observer will never be able to know very much about the true microscopic state of that system. Every part of space is computing its future as fast possible, while information pours in from every direction. The result is the same as caused by the apparent randomness of quantum mechanical processes.

The position that unifies most supporters of digital ontology is summarized in what is known as Zuse thesis:

ZT'the universe is being deterministically computed on some sort of giant but discrete computer' (Zuse (1967), (1969)).

The computer referred to in ZT could be a *cellular automaton*. This is argued by Zuse (1967), (1969), also on the basis of Von Neumann (1966), by Fredkin (2003a) and, more recently, by Wolfram (2002).[4] Indeed, a variant of ZF, which is less general, is known as Fredkin–Zuse thesis: 'The Universe is a cellular automaton' (Petrov (2003)). Alternatively, the computer in ZT could be a *universal Turing machine*, as suggested by Schmidhuber (1997), who in turn acknowledges his intellectual debt to Zuse himself; or a *quantum computer*, as proposed more recently by Lloyd (2006). Other well-known proponents of versions of ZT include David Chalmers (1996), the Nobel laureate Gerard 't Hooft (1997), and Gregory Chaitin (2005). The latter has explicitly interpreted digital ontology as a contemporary development of Pythagoras' metaphysics, Democritus' atomism and Leibniz's monadology. Indeed, in the *Critique of Pure Reason*, Kant called any philosopher who holds a 'discrete' ontology a Monadologist.

The overall perspective, emerging from digital ontology, is one of a metaphysical monism: ultimately, the physical universe is a gigantic digital computer. It is fundamentally composed of digits, instead of matter or energy, with material objects as a complex secondary manifestation, while dynamic processes are some kind of computational states transitions. There are no digitally irreducible infinities, infinitesimals, continuities, or locally determined random variables. In short, the ultimate nature of reality is not smooth and random but grainy and deterministic. To quote Fredkin (1992) again:

A fundamental question about time, space and the inhabitants thereof is 'Are things smooth or grainy?' Some things are obviously grainy (matter, charge, angular momentum); for other things (space, time, momentum, energy) the answers are not clear. Finite Nature is the assumption that, at some scale, space and time are discrete and that the number of possible states of every finite volume of space–time is finite. In other words Finite Nature assumes that there is no thing that is smooth or continuous and that there are no infinitesimals.

Since in the rest of this chapter I shall be concerned only with the digital vs analogue nature of reality, namely thesis (1) to be found at the beginning of this section, let me conclude this brief presentation of digital ontology with a final comment about the computational nature of the physical universe. It concerns an important distinction that needs to be kept in sight and to which I shall briefly return in the conclusion.

---

[4] To be precise, it has been argued that is unclear whether Wolfram means to support the view that the universe is a *classical* cellular automaton. Wolfram acknowledges Zuse's and Fredkin's work on pp. 1026–1027, but only very briefly and states that 'no literal mechanistic model can ever in the end realistically be expected to work.' I follow Edwin Clark's interpretation in reading this as a rejection of classical cellular automata. Wolfram seems to have in mind something slightly different 'what must happen relies on phenomena discovered in this book—and involves the emergence of complex properties'. The potential differences between Fredkin and Wolfram on this issue, however, are not significant for the discussion of the tenability of a digital ontology.

We have seen that digital ontologists tend to be computationally minded and hence subscribe to some version of the pancomputational thesis, according to which the physical universe is a computational system of some kind, where the kind is irrelevant as long as the preferred models are computationally equivalent, like Turing machines, cellular automata, quantum computers. Indeed even recurrent neural networks could do the job. Although I do not know anyone supporting this position, perhaps because artificial neural networks are not usually analysed algorithmically, the choice is available insofar as any algebraically computable function can be expressed as a recurrent neural network (Hyötyniemi (1996), Siegelmann (1998)). However, digital ontology and pancomputationalism are independent positions. We saw in chapters two and four that, through his 'It from Bit' thesis, Wheeler (1990) supported the former but not (or at least not explicitly) the latter. Physical processes in Wheeler's participatory universe might, but need not, be reducible to computational state transitions. On the other hand, pancomputationalists like Lloyd (2006), who describes the universe not as a Turing machine but as a quantum computer, can still hold an analogue or hybrid[5] ontology. Laplace's demon, for example, is an analogue pancomputationalist. And informational ontologists like Sayre (1976), or myself do not have to embrace either a digital ontology or a pancomputationalist position as described in Zuse thesis. The distinction between digital ontology, informational ontology, and pancomputationalism is crucial in order to understand the strategy of this chapter, which is to criticize digital ontology in order to make room for an informational approach to structural realism, defended in the next chapter, while not committing it to pancomputationalism. I will return to this point in the conclusion. With this clarification in mind, we can now turn to the objections against digital ontology.

14.2.1 Digital ontology: From physical to metaphysical problems

When discussing digital ontology, two separate questions arise:

a. whether the physical universe might be adequately modelled digitally and computationally, independently of whether it is actually digital and computational in itself;

and

b. whether the ultimate nature of the physical universe might be actually digital and computational in itself, independently of how it can be effectively or adequately modelled.

---

[5] Hybrid computers comprise features of analog computers and digital computers. The digital component normally serves as the controller and provides logical operations; the analogue component normally serves as a solver of differential equations. Plagiarism disclaimer: the previous definition is the source of the corresponding definition in *Wikipedia*, not vice versa.

The first is an empirico-mathematical question that, so far, remains unsettled. I shall say a bit more about it in this section, but the rest of the chapter is not concerned with it. The second is a metaphysical question that, in the rest of the chapter, I hope to show to be ill-posed and hence, when answered, to be misapplied.

Answers to (a) and (b) are often found intertwined. The following passage by Edward Fredkin, one of the earnest supporters of digital ontology, provides a good example of a unified synthesis:

[digital ontology] is a totally atomistic system. Everything fundamental is assumed to be atomic or discrete; and thereby so is everything else. In physics, DP [digital philosophy, what has been called in this paper digital ontology] assumes that space and time are discrete. There are two mathematical models of such systems. The first is Diophantine analysis; the mathematics of the integers. The second is automata theory; the mathematics of digital processes. We choose the latter as it also has the property of explicitly representing a discrete temporal process, while the mathematics of the integers simply establishes a set of true theorems and thus can represent implicitly only temporal processes. Tremendous progress in the sciences followed the discovery of the calculus (and partial differential equations) as a way of mathematically representing physical-temporal relationships. But we look elsewhere with respect to the most fundamental models of physical processes. What we must demand of DP is the eventual ability to derive, from our DP models of fundamental processes, the same mathematical equations that constitute the basis of science today. Conway's Game of Life [a famous cellular automaton, my added comment] is a good example of a simple digital system and the consequent emergent properties. We arbitrarily assume that DP represents state by patterns of bits, as is done in ordinary computers. All of the fundamental transformations we can do with bits in a computer are really a subset of what mathematics can do with the integers. [. . .] The bits of DM [digital mechanics] exist at points in a regular digital spacetime, where each point contains one bit of information. We think of spacetime as digital since it is made up only of points located where all of the coordinates are integers. Automata theory and computer science lead us to believe that the representation of state by bits imposes no limitations beyond the fact that everything is ultimately quantized. Computers and their software are the most complex things ever made by man. However, computation is based on the simplest principles ever discovered. Our world is complex and we are looking for simple models that might be at the bottom. The principles of DP require us to find and start with the simplest possible models. Thus the unit of state is the bit, which is considerably simpler than a real number. (Fredkin (2003b), pp. 190–191).

As the passage illustrates, the empirico-mathematical and the metaphysical position with respect to digital ontology are compatible and complementary. Consider the following way of interpreting digital ontology. Physical simulations or models may share the same ontology with their simulated or modelled systems. Thus, a wind tunnel, used to investigate the effects of wind-speed and flow around solid objects, is actually windy, more or less spacious, may contain several physical objects, and so forth. However, digital (computer) simulations or models *often* have a different ontology from their corresponding systems. A computational fluid dynamics simulation, used to model and simulate the behaviour of flowing air, is neither windy nor wet in itself.

I emphasized 'often' because this is not always the case. For example, computer simulations are routinely used to test and debug other application programs, in which case simulator and simulated share the same digital ontology. Digital ontology may then be interpreted as arguing that one could have a digital model or simulation of the ultimate nature of the physical universe, which ends up sharing the same digital ontology with the modelled system.

Although an answer to (a) could then pave the way to an answer to (b), it is useful to keep the two issues separate because they face different challenges.

The empirico-mathematical position seeks to answer question (a) and it is weaker, and hence more defensible, than the metaphysical position, which seeks to answer question (b), because it may avoid any ontological commitment to the ultimate nature of reality. That a system might be modelled and simulated digitally, e.g. as a cellular automaton, does not imply that the intrinsic nature of that system is digital. This lack of ontological commitment may be an advantage and, occasionally, the weaker position seems to be all that digital ontologists wish to hold. Toffoli (2003), for example, who sympathizes with digital ontology, has proposed to treat digital ontology as a heuristically interesting line of research:

> We argue that a nonfrivolous [sic] aspect of this Digital Perspective is its heuristic capacity: to help us guess which aspects of our understanding of nature are more 'universal,' more robust, more likely to survive theoretical and experimental challenges. Behaviors that are substrate-independent— that can, for instance, thrive well on a digital support, even though they are traditionally imagined as taking place in a continuum—are especially promising candidates. (p. 147)

And Fredkin (online) himself suggests that

> there are computer systems (cellular automata) that may be appropriate as models for microscopic physical phenomena. Cellular automata are now being used to model varied physical phenomena normally modelled by wave equations, fluid dynamics, Ising models, etc. We hypothesize that there will be found a single cellular automaton rule that models all of microscopic physics; and models it exactly. We call this field DM, for digital mechanics.

Both passages could easily be read as addressing only question (a).

If digital ontology is an answer to (a) and not (also) to (b), then, even if objections against the metaphysical value of digital ontology may be correct, nothing could be inferred from them with regard to the scientific tenability of digital physics weakly interpreted. Perhaps someone may wish to argue that the latter would be damaged by a lack of ontological support but, personally, I doubt this would be of much consequence to the digital physicist.

So, let us suppose that digital ontologists would prefer to support their position as an answer to (a) and not to (b), in order to avoid metaphysical complications. Even the weaker position is not devoid of problems. In terms of empirical ontology, the majority of physicists either ignores or is positively sceptical about the value of the approach. In the words of a supporter of digital ontology:

Several speakers in this meeting ['The Digital Perspective' workshop, organized by Edward Fredkin, my note] express their optimism concerning the possibility to describe realistic models of the Universe in terms of deterministic 'digital' scenarios. Most physicists, however, are acutely aware of quite severe obstacles against such views. It is important to contemplate these obstacles, even if one believes that they will eventually be removed. (Hooft (2003), p. 349)

The models proposed by digital ontologists—when they are subject to testable experiments, at least in principle—show implications that are not easily reconcilable with many postulates and results commonly obtained in physics and with our current understanding of the universe. Here is a very simple illustration: Lloyd (2002) estimates that the physical universe, understood as a computational system, could have performed 10^{120} operations on 10^{90} bits (10^{120} bits including gravitational degrees of freedom) since the Big Bang. The problem is that if this were true, the universe would 'run out of memory':

To simulate the Universe in every detail since time began, the computer would have to have 10^{90} bits—binary digits, or devices capable of storing a 1 or a 0—and it would have to perform 10^{120} manipulations of those bits. Unfortunately there are probably only around 10^{80} elementary particles in the Universe. (Ball (2002, 3 June))

Schmidhuber (forthcoming) maintains that 'computing all evolutions of all universes is much cheaper in terms of information requirements than computing just one particular, arbitrarily chosen evolution'.[6] However, if there are insufficient particles for Lloyd's computations, it is unclear how there might be sufficient particles for Schmidhuber's.

A digital reinterpretation of contemporary physics may be possible in theory. After all, discrete systems can approximate continuous systems to increasing degrees of accuracy, so it is unlikely that any experiment could rule out the possibility that the world might be digital in itself. One might even argue that a digital ontology could be coherent with the many-worlds interpretation of quantum mechanics, insofar as the former satisfies what Goodman described as the multiple-realization characteristic of digital states. The history of the world would then be more like a (discrete) chess game, in which every move generates a different state and hence a parallel universe, rather than a (continuous) football game, in which every tiny (as tiny as one may wish it to be) little difference, e.g. in the trajectory of the ball, would generate another world. What seems to be the case, however, is that, if digital ontology seeks to advance our understanding of the physical universe by providing a 'conceptual strategy of looking at physics in terms of digital processes' (Fredkin (2003b)), then its success would represent a profound change in our scientific practices and outlook. Quite a bit of our contemporary understanding of the universe is firmly based not only on discrete but also on many analogue ideas (the real numbers, continuous functions, differential

---

[6] See version online at <http://www.idsia.ch/juergen/everything/node3.html>

equations, Fourier transforms, waves, force fields, the continuum)[7] which seem to be difficult to replace entirely. Of course, this is not a final argument against digital ontology, for our analogue understanding of the universe may turn out to be digitally reinterpretable after all. But, as acknowledged by Hooft in the quotation above, the burden of showing how it can actually be replaced, and why it should, is definitely on the shoulders of the digital ontologists. A quote from Einstein well highlights the overall difficulty:

I consider it quite possible that physics cannot be based on the field concept, i. e., on continuous structures. In that case, nothing remains of my entire castle in the air gravitation theory included, [and of] the rest of modern physics.[8]

If digital ontologists are right, then the 'analogue' tradition that goes from Newton to Einstein will be deeply affected, as digital ontologists are willing to acknowledge.[9] This is one of the reasons why, although contemporary particle physics and astrophysics increasingly depend on e-science,[10] they are currently not digital-ontology-friendly. Steven Weinberg, another Nobel laureate in physics, has well expressed such lack of sympathy when talking about Wolfram's version of Zuse thesis:

Wolfram himself is a lapsed elementary particle physicist, and I suppose he can't resist trying to apply his experience with digital computer programs to the laws of nature. This has led him to the view (also considered in a 1981 article by Richard Feynman) that nature is discrete rather than continuous. He suggests that space consists of a network of isolated points, like cells in a cellular automaton, and that even time flows in discrete steps. Following an idea of Edward Fredkin, he concludes that the universe itself would then be an automaton, like a giant computer. It's possible, but I can't see any motivation for these speculations, except that this is the sort of system that Wolfram and others have become used to in their work on computers. So might a carpenter, looking at the moon, suppose that it is made of wood. (Weinberg (24 October 2002))

To summarize and simplify, it would be a mistake to confuse the *predicative* use of 'digital' ('digital physics' is the study of the laws of the universe helped by digital-computational instruments) with its *attributive* use ('digital physics' is the study of the intrinsically digital-computational nature of the laws of the universe). A great deal of contemporary physics is digital in the predicative sense, but not in the attributive sense.

So much for question (a). Regarding question (b), namely whether the ultimate nature of the physical universe might be intrinsically digital and computational, does

---

[7] For a very instructive analysis of the 'interplay between discrete and continuous behaviors and corresponding modelings in physics' see Lesne (2007).

[8] Einstein, 1954, in a letter to Besso, quoted in Pais (2005), p. 467.

[9] At least this is the way digital ontologists see the impact of their work and how it is perceived by some of their contemporaries, see for example the list of reviews of Wolfram (2002) available at <http://www.wolframscience.com/coverage.html> and at <http://www.math.usf.edu/eclark/ANKOS_reviews.html>

[10] The term refers to any computationally intensive scientific research that relies on distributed network environments, very powerful processing capacities, and very large data sets.

digital ontology fare any better with contemporary metaphysics? Is the latter any more 'attributive-friendly'? In the rest of the chapter, I shall argue that it is not. As I wrote earlier, the argument leads to a Kantian conclusion: it is not so much that reality in itself is not digital, but rather that, in a metaphysical context, the digital vs analogue dichotomy is not applicable.

14.3 The thought experiment

Let me first provide an overall view of the argument and then of the thought experiment through which I will expound it.

If the ultimate nature of reality in itself is digital, this implies that it is either digital or analogue,[11] so the premise can be refuted by showing that the disjunctive conclusion is mistaken. This can be achieved in two steps.

The first step consists in arguing that, even assuming that reality in itself is indeed digital or analogue, an epistemic agent, confronted by what appears to be an (at least partly) analogue world of experience, could not establish whether its source (that is, reality in itself as the source of the agent's experience or knowledge) is digital (or analogue).

One could object, however, that this first, epistemological step is merely negative, for it establishes, at best, only the unknowability of the intrinsically digital (or analogue) nature of reality lying behind the world of experience, not that reality in itself is not digital (or analogue). Independently of the epistemic access enjoyed by an agent—the objection continues—logic dictates that reality must be assumed to be digital/discrete (grainy) or continuous/analogue (smooth).

So the second step is more positive and ontological. It consists in showing that the initial concession, made in the first step, can be withdrawn: the intrinsic nature of reality does not have to be digital or analogue because the dichotomy might well be misapplied. Reality is experienced, conceptualized, and known as digital or analogue depending on the level of abstraction (LoA) assumed by the epistemic agent when interacting with it. Digital and analogue are features of the LoA modelling the system, not of the modelled system in itself.

The negative result of the argument is that one cannot know whether reality is intrinsically digital or analogue not only because of inherent limitations in the type of epistemic access to reality that one may enjoy, but also because reality in itself might be just the wrong sort of thing to which these categories are being applied. The positive result of the argument is that there are ontologies—in particular those supported by ontic structural realism and by informational structural realism—that treat the ultimate nature of reality as relational. And since relations are neither digital nor analogue nor a

---

[11] For the sake of simplicity, I shall treat the or as the logic disjunction, and hence as equivalent to asserting that reality in itself is either digital/discrete (grainy) or continuous/analogue (smooth) or hybrid (lumpy). Nothing depends on this simplification.

combination of the two, the negative conclusion clears the ground of a potential confusion between digital and informational ontology and makes room for the development of the latter, as we shall see in section 14.5.

In order to develop the arguments just outlined, I shall rely on a thought experiment. This is divided into four stages. At each stage an ideal agent will be introduced, but only in order to make the argument more intuitive and vivid.

Stage 1 sets up a scenario in which reality in itself is assumed to be either digital or analogue.

This satisfies the initial concession, made in the first, negative, epistemological step seen above, which assumes the world to be digital or analogue. At this stage, we shall need an ideal agent capable of showing that reality in itself is either digital or analogue. Call this agent Michael. Recall now that the argument is that an epistemic agent, who is confronted by what appears to be an (at least partly) analogue world of experience, cannot establish whether reality in itself is digital or analogue. So

Stage 2 is where the epistemic agent—which we have not specified yet—is provided with an analogue world of experience that is based on reality in itself, which, following the previous stage, is assumed to be digital or analogue.

Stage (2) is a simplification of what one of the supporters of digital ontology has aptly defined as 'the stubborn legacy of the continuum' (Margolus (2003), p. 309). Epistemic agents experience the world as (at least partly, if not mainly) analogue. So an easy way of understanding stage (2) is by interpreting it as providing an analogue interface between reality in itself—which has been assumed to be digital or analogue at stage (1)—and an epistemic agent who experiences it (see stage (3)). Call the agent responsible for translating reality in itself (whether digital or analogue) into an analogue world of experience Gabriel. Once Gabriel (i.e. the interface) has translated Michael's digital or analogue reality into an analogue world, we move to:

Stage 3, where the epistemic agent is shown to be incapable of establishing whether the source (reality in itself, assumed as either digital or analogue in stage one) of the analogue, experienced world (obtained at stage two) is intrinsically digital or analogue.

This will be argued by using the method of abstraction (see chapter three). The epistemic agent observes his analogue world at an endless number of levels of abstraction, can never reach an end in his informational explorations, and hence can never know whether there is a digital ontology behind the observable world. Call the third, epistemic agent Raphael. Once Raphael (the epistemic agent) is shown to be unable to establish the digital (or analogue) nature of reality in itself, one still needs to answer the objection according to which this conclusion, even if granted, shows nothing about the actual nature of reality in itself. So, what has been called above the second, positive, ontological step, requires

Stage 4, where the concession made at stage one is withdrawn, and it is shown that the alternative digital vs analogue may easily be misapplied, when talking about reality in itself, because the latter could be neither, while it might be experienced as either digital or analogue depending on how the epistemic agent is related to it.

At this last stage, a fourth agent, call it Uriel, is needed in order to show that the same reality can be observed as being digital or analogue, depending on the epistemic position of the observer (Raphael) and the level of abstraction adopted.

Stage (4) concludes the thought experiment against digital ontology. A final note on the four agents might still be in order before seeing the details of the argument. These agents are ideal because they are endowed with the following boundless (i.e. always sufficient yet not infinite) resources:

i. time, to be interpreted computationally as the number of steps required to achieve a specific task;
ii. space, to be interpreted computationally as memory; and
iii. accuracy, to be interpreted computationally as the degree of precision of an operation, which is assumed (the accuracy) to be increasable to whatever level may be required.[12]

Thus the four agents resemble Turing machines. This is important because the digital ontologist, of all people, will hardly object to their assumption as perfectly conceivable. For a more colourful and vivid representation, I have proposed to call them Michael, Gabriel, Raphael, and Uriel. The reader may recognize them as the four archangels and indeed some of their iconological properties turn out to be nicely consistent with their tasks in each stage, hence the choice. Philosophy has already seen its fair share of demons, think of Socrates' inquisitive demon, Descartes's malicious demon, Laplace's deterministic demon, or Maxwell's intelligent demon. Time for the angels to stage a comeback. But of course nothing hangs on this, and the reader who finds the analogy or the names unhelpful is invited to translate the four agents into M, G, R and U.

Let us now consider each stage and the overall argument in more detail.

14.3.1 Stage 1: Reality in itself is digital or analogue

Suppose our ideal agent, Michael, enjoys a God's eye view of reality in itself (the sort of approach criticized by Dewey) and has access to its intrinsic nature, what Kant called the noumenal. Whatever the noumenal reality is in itself—call it stuff—we assume that Michael is able to manipulate it and test whether it is digital/discrete or analogue/continuous. He first shapes this stuff into an ordered set, by applying some total ordering relation (e.g. 'is to the right of'). For the sake of simplicity, we can represent the result geometrically, as a line. Michael then uses his sword to obtain a Dedekind cut

---

[12] For example, the degree of accuracy depends on how many figures or decimal places are used in rounding off the number. The result of a calculation or measurement (such as 13.429314) might be rounded off to three (13.429) or two decimal places. The first answer is more *accurate* than the second.

(Dedekind (1963)). Intuitively, a Dedekind cut is a partition of the set of rational numbers into two non-empty subsets, in such a way as to uniquely define a real number. Following Dedekind's geometrical description,[13] Michael's sword could not be sharper: it has length but no thickness. When it cuts (i.e. intersects) the line, it divides it into two disjoint, non-empty parts, left and right. If the point at which the sword cuts the line belongs to either the left or the right half, then that point corresponds to a rational number. If the point belongs to neither (if neither subset of the rationals contains it), then it corresponds to an irrational number.[14] Now, let us make the process iterative, so that the output of each operation becomes the input of the next operation.

Suppose Michael is able to Dedekind-cut the line indefinitely, without his sword ever going through any empty space. Michael takes the right part, Dedekind-cuts it again, drops the left part, picks up the new right part, Dedekind-cuts it again, and so forth, never halting and never being able to drive his sword between two points (or corresponding numbers) without hitting another point (number). In this case, Michael's noumenal reality is dense[15] and continuous, like the set of the real numbers.

Suppose, on the contrary, that when Michael tries to Dedekind-cut the line, the point at which the sword intersects the line belongs to either the left or the right half. Or, to put it differently, Michael's sword is so sharp that it can miss the line by going through its gaps, which correspond to missing points (imagine a line in which the irrational numbers have been knocked off). Then Michael's noumenal reality is no longer continuous but discrete, and either still dense (like the rationals, which are closed under division), in which case he will not halt; or not even dense (like the integers, which are not closed under division), in which case he will halt.

If reality is continuous or analogue, the output of Michael's process may consist, physically, of waves or fields, for example; mathematically, they would be equivalent to the real numbers. On the other hand, if reality is discrete, the output of Michael's process may consist of the atoms of any Democritean physics, of the natural numbers of the Pythagoreans, of Leibniz's indivisible monads or of the bits of the digital ontologists (see Figure 25).[16] At the end of this first stage, reality in itself can be assumed to be

---

[13] Dedekind's *Schnitt* is a cut in the geometric sense, that is, it is the intersection of a line with another line that crosses it, see Dedekind (1963).

[14] To be more precise, the goal of a Dedekind's cut is to *construct* each real number as a pair (L, R) of sets of rationals such that every rational is in exactly one of the sets, and every rational in L is smaller that every rational in R. This couple is called a Dedekind cut. However, the distinction between 'construction' and 'correspondence' is not relevant here.

[15] An ordered set (e.g. the rationals) is dense if any two of its elements have an element in between.

[16] For a similar idea, but applied to simple divisibility, see Kant's description of 'annihilating composition in thought' and what Holden (2004) defines as metaphysical divisibility. Holden characterizes metaphysical divisibility as divisibility which is logically possible, and distinguishes it from physical divisibility (physically possible), formal divisibility (based on distinguishable parts in space) and intellectual divisibility (a weaker notion of logical or metaphysical divisibility, based on the possibility of being able to imagine the division).

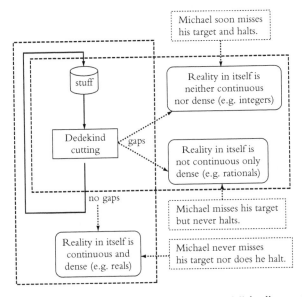

Figure 25 First stage of the thought experiment, Michael's sword

digital or analogue, with no further ontological commitment required, depending on the output of Michael's operation.

14.3.2 Stage 2: The stubborn legacy of the analogue

The second stage involves Gabriel and his message (see Figure 26). Recall that Gabriel is an ideal agent working as an interface between reality in itself (Michael the source) and the world as observed by the epistemic agent (Raphael the observer). If Michael's ontology is analogue, Gabriel uses it as his input to produce an analogue reality

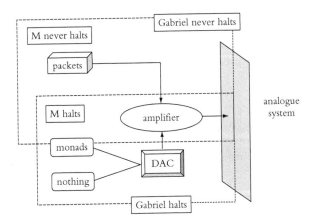

Figure 26 Second stage of the thought experiment, Gabriel's message

(henceforth also called the *system*). On the other hand, if Michael's ontology is digital, Gabriel puts it through a DAC (a Digital to Analogue Converter) to produce an analogue reality. In both cases, Gabriel might need an amplifier to produce his output, that is, an analogue system (a continuous world) like the one observed by the epistemic agent. At the end of this second stage, Gabriel's output (his message) consists of an endlessly updated flow of analogue data. This is the analogue system made available to the observer, Raphael.

14.3.3 Stage 3: The observer's analysis

Gabriel's message, that is, the analogue system comparable to the world surrounding us, is now observed by Raphael, the epistemic agent, who is on the other side of the screen, as it were (see Figure 26 and Figure 27). Raphael, like us, can adopt any level of abstraction to study and analyse the analogue system and formulate his theory about it (the space within the dotted line in Figure 27). Indeed, Raphael can observe the analogue system, produced by Gabriel on the basis of Michael's input, at an endless number of LoA. This is tantamount to saying that Raphael may avail himself of as many different interfaces as he wishes in order to analyse the system (metaphorically: in order to read Gabriel's analogue message), each of which will provide further information about the system itself. Figure 27 summarizes this point.

Raphael never halts. This is just a colourful way of saying that, outside our thought experiment, *analogue systems are closed under modelling at levels of abstraction*, or, which is the same thing, there is no finite number of levels of abstractions that can provide all possible models of an analogue system.

The observer (Raphael and us) can extract an endless amount of *semantic* information from an analogue system, so it requires an endless amount of computation to describe even the simplest system. The specification 'semantic' is crucial, for otherwise the conclusion would be inconsistent with Shannon's fundamental theorem according to which, if we

[l]et a source have entropy H (bits per symbol) and a channel have a capacity C (bits per second). Then it is possible to encode the output of the source in such a way as to transmit at the average rate of C/H − ε symbols per second over the channel where ε is arbitrarily small. It is not possible to transmit at an average rate greater than C/H. (Shannon and Weaver (1949 rep. 1998), p. 59)

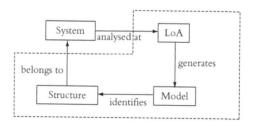

Figure 27 Third stage of the thought experiment, Raphael's LoAs

Shannon's limiting result states that if you devise a good code you can transmit symbols over a noiseless channel at an average rate as close to C/H as one may wish but, no matter how clever the coding is, that average can never exceed C/H. The limit can be extended to memory devices, which can contain only a certain amount of syntactic information. What is in question here, however, is semantic information.

Some people find the previous conclusion intellectually unpleasant. Richard Feynman was one of them. Here is how he phrased the problem:

It always bothers me that, according to the laws as we understand them today, it takes a computing machine [our Raphael] an infinite number of logical operations to figure out what goes on in no matter how tiny a region of space, and no matter how tiny a region of time [our analogue system]. How can all that be going on in that tiny space? Why should it take an infinite amount of logic to figure out what one tiny piece of space/time is going to do? So I have often made the hypothesis that ultimately physics will not require a mathematical statement, that in the end the machinery will be revealed, and the laws will turn out to be simple, like the chequer board with all its apparent complexities. (Feynman (1992), pp. 57–58)

Because of similar statements, Feynman is sometimes listed among the digital ontologists (cf. the quotation from Weinberg in section 14.2.1) but, to be fair to Feynman, the quotation continues

But this speculation is of the same nature as those other people make—'I like it', 'I don't like it',—and it is not good to be prejudiced about these things.

To anyone acquainted with Kant's philosophy, the boundless informational–richness of the world comes as no surprise. The system under observation (Gabriel's message read by Raphael) works a bit like the noumenal. For the method of levels of abstraction allows one to understand that reality in itself, though not epistemically *inaccessible*, remains an epistemically *inexhaustible* resource out of which knowledge is constructed.

Since Raphael never halts, he can never know whether the world is digital or analogue. On the one hand, if the world were digital, there might be a theoretical possibility of knowing it, but it probably is not, or at least Raphael's and our knowledge of the world, inescapably mediated by some LoA, seem to point in the opposite direction. It is of no avail to object that even in our thought experiment we have assumed the existence of four agents/archangels resembling four digital Turing machines. As Turing himself remarked, even in the case of actual digital artefacts:

The digital computers [. . .] may be classified amongst the 'discrete state machines', these are the machines which move by sudden jumps or clicks from one quite definite state to another. These states are sufficiently different for the possibility of confusion between them to be ignored. *Strictly speaking there are no such machines. Everything really moves continuously* [emphasis added]. But there are many kinds of machine, which can profitably be thought of as being discrete state machines. (Turing (1950), p. 439)

By 'profitably be thought of' Turing was really referring to the level of abstraction at which 'many kinds of machine' are analysed as 'discrete state machines'. In other words, even our agents may, deep down, better understood by us as analogue agents. The world, at least as we and Raphael experience it, might well be analogue, and the digital only a convenient abstraction or the result (and technical exploitation) of some physical features in our artefacts.

However, Raphael, and ourselves with him, cannot exclude either empirically or in principle that reality in itself might actually be digital, i.e. discrete. For the endless amount of information that Raphael can extract from Gabriel's message says nothing about the presence or absence of some ultimate *indivisibilia*.

At this point, the doubt that naturally comes to one's mind is whether the analogue/ continuous vs digital/discrete dichotomy may be sound at all, or at least whether its application to the description of the intrinsic nature of reality may not be misguided. Kant thought it was. And I agree that it is. Analogue/continuous and digital/discrete are modes of presentation of Being, i.e. ways in which a system is modelled (experienced or conceptualized) by an observer (an epistemic agent) at a given level of abstraction. The last stage in our thought experiment consists in trying to understand how this could be the case.

14.3.4 Digital and analogue are features of the level of abstraction

From the observer's position, which is Raphael's as well as ours, it is impossible to establish whether reality in itself (the noumenal) is analogue or digital. As we saw in chapter three, Kant, in the *Critique of Pure Reason*, had already convincingly argued against the soundness of the dichotomy and its correct application, even if in rather different terms (Kant (1998)). As is well known, each of the four antinomies discussed by Kant comprises a thesis and an antithesis, which are supposed to be both reasonable and irreconcilable. The one which interests us here is the second. It will be recalled that, paraphrasing Kant, the antinomy states that (A 434–5/B 462–3):

(Digital) Thesis: the world is discrete; everything in the world consists of elements that are ultimately simple and hence indivisible.

(Analogue) Antithesis: the world is continuous; nothing in the world is simple, but everything is composite and hence infinitely divisible.

Yet we saw in chapter three that it is pointless to try to determine the properties of the system in itself, independently of the LoA at which it is being analysed. In particular, the digital or analogue features are determined by the LoA and characterize the model of the system. So, although for reasons based on the method of levels of abstraction, I cannot but agree with Kant: neither the thesis nor the antithesis is tenable. A good way of making sense of this conclusion in our thought experiment is by referring to a fourth and last agent, Uriel, the 'sharpest sighted spirit of all in Heaven', as Milton called him in *Paradise Lost*.

Uriel builds a wheel in which there are four nodes (see Figure 28). Each node contains either a DAC (digital to analogue converter) or an ADC (analogue to digital

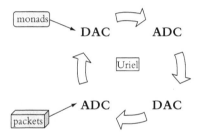

Figure 28 Fourth stage of the thought experiment, Uriel's wheel

converter). Since it is possible to convert information from analogue into digital form and back again with as little loss of detail as needed, Uriel's wheel generates a system— as an output from an analogue or digital ontology—which will be observed by Raphael as being either analogue or digital depending on the latter's position with respect to the wheel. It is now obvious that it makes no sense to ask whether the system is digital or analogue in itself. We have discharged our initial assumption about reality in itself being digital or analogue.

All this is less 'metaphysical' than it might seem. In quantum mechanics, we are used to seeing a similar effect, known as the wave–particle duality. The basic idea is that all objects (both micro- and macroscopic) enjoy properties associated both with continuous waves and with discrete particles, in short, that objects have a dual nature, partly wave-like and partly particle-like. Although this is experimentally detectable only on very small scales, the factual results are well known and indisputable, if puzzling in terms of interpretation. The classic double-slit experiment, for example, shows that, if only one slit is open at a time, the individual photons fired against it that manage to go through the slit and hit the screen on the other side at different times generate a pattern with a single peak, behaving like tiny bullets.[17] However, if both slits are open at the same time, the individual photons, still hitting the screen at different times, generate a wave-like interference pattern. In the conceptual frame presented in this chapter, the slits act as a hardwired (physically implemented) level of abstraction: change the level (open or close the slits) and the beam of individual photons or electrons will be (observed as) behaving 'digitally' or 'analogically', like bullets or like waves, presenting a world that is discrete or continuous, not in itself, but in relation to the observer's LoA. Similar effects can be shown with electrons and other particles. Experiments that test particle properties show that electrons behave as if they were particles, and experiments that test wave properties show that electrons behave as if they were waves. The ways in

---

[17] To be precise, in real experiments one cannot really distinguish between two plausible explanations for the observed result (a) electrons are classical particles, i.e. they behave just like bullets fired from a gun and (b) electrons are wave trains, i.e. waves of finite length. The real difficulty occurs when both slits are open and the single electrons, sent at separate times, like as many bullets, end up generating a typical interference pattern as if they were waves (no matter of what length).

which one has epistemic access to the system affect the outcome of the analysis or experiment. As Lesne (2007) has well synthesized:

In conclusion, physics in all instances is an interplay between discrete and continuous features, mainly because any such feature actually characterizes a representation, from a given observer, of the real system and its evolution. [. . .] In practice, the choice between discrete and continuous models should be substantiated with the comparison between the respective scales of description, observation, variations (e.g. gradient scales, oscillation periods, or inhomogeneity sizes) and correlations [what in this book has been called the method of abstraction, my addition]. [. . .] Paradoxes and inconsistencies between discrete and continuous viewpoints only appear when forgetting that our descriptions, and even physical laws, are only idealized abstractions, tangent to reality in an appropriate scale range, unavoidably bounded above and below. [. . .] Any physical theory is in the same way based on a representation of the system and deals only with this representation, while the reality always remains beyond and is never fully captured. (pp. 35–36)

Kant might have agreed. I certainly do. Raphael observes Uriel's world as analogue or digital depending on his position (LoA) with respect to it. What remains invariant in Uriel's world, from Raphael's perspective, cannot be its digital or its analogue nature, but rather the structural properties that give rise to a digital or analogue reality. These invariant, structural properties are those in which science is mainly interested. So it seems reasonable to move from an ontology of things—to which it is difficult not to apply the digital/discrete vs analogue/continuous alternative—to an ontology of structural relations, to which it is immediately obvious that the previous dichotomy is irrelevant. As we shall see in the next chapter, this is precisely the step taken, in the current debate on scientific realism, by supporters of different forms of structural realism. The step is important, and deserves a final comment by way of conclusion, but first, let me reinforce the case against digital ontology by clearing the ground of three potential objections.

14.4 Three objections and replies

One may contend that the argument presented in this chapter begs the question. For it builds an analogue reality through the interface represented by Gabriel—no matter whether the original source (that is, Michael's world) is intrinsically digital or analogue—but then it purports to show that Raphael (an agent like us), by having access to this analogue reality, cannot determine whether its original source is digital. Unsurprisingly, Raphael is trapped in a (perception of the) world as analogue, but this is merely what is already presupposed.

The objection can be answered by recalling that the goal of the argument is to establish that both a digital and an analogue ontology are untenable. The argument seeks to achieve this conclusion by making crucial use of the boundless number of levels of abstraction at which an analogue reality may be observed. So, the argument would indeed be begging the question if it were positing not Gabriel's interface, as it does, but rather Uriel's wheel, that is, if the argument were to presuppose that the world is digitally/analogously undetermined to begin with. This the argument does not do, since Uriel's wheel is introduced only as a fourth step, in order to make sense of the problem disclosed by the argument. The second step in the argument relies on the analogue interface, represented by Gabriel's 'translation', because it needs to make explicit the starting point that is conceded by all parties involved in the debate, namely that some aspects of the world really seem to be intrinsically and irreducibly analogue rather than digital, and that it is up to the defender of digital ontology to make a convincing case for the opposite view. This is why the section's title is a paraphrase of Margolus's comment about 'the stubborn legacy of the continuum' (the reader may recall that Margolus is one of the strong supporters of digital ontology). One may retort that the argument would not work were one to assume that Gabriel translates Michael's world into a digital world. The reply is that this is correct but also not relevant here. For the question being debated is not: given that some aspects of the world appear to be digital, is a digital ontology justified? This is uncontroversial but also uninteresting. The question is rather: given that some aspects of the world appear to be analogue, is a digital ontology justified? One only needs to recall why the Pythagoreans abandoned their digital ontology to understand the pressure exercised by the question. The argument simplifies all this by generating a scenario in which Raphael (us) interacts epistemically with an analogue reality, at various levels of abstraction, and this scenario is not in need of a justification, for it is the starting difficulty under discussion.

The defender of a digital ontology might still be unconvinced because of a second objection. The argument is clearly Kantian, but all it does, at best, is to explain how (an aspect of) Kant's metaphysics could be true. It does not show that Kant's metaphysics is true. So, even conceding that digital ontology may not be a promising line of research from a Kantian perspective, this fails to be convincing to anyone who does not already share such a transcendental approach.

This objection may be answered by starting from the distinction between arguing for the same conclusion and arguing in the same way for that conclusion. The conclusion of the argument is indeed Kantian, so it is a matter of scholarship to give to Kant what is Kant's. This may have the further advantage of helping anyone familiar with Kant's philosophy to follow the argument more easily. But the argument itself is not based on, nor intends to be an exposition or a vindication of, Kant's transcendental epistemology. Rather, it seeks to provide a different and independent route to the same theoretical point, so it should be assessed on its own merits (or lack thereof). To put it visually, Kant's argument and the one presented in this chapter are like two lines that intersect at one point, but coming from, and going in, different directions. So, the objection that the argument is unconvincing (that the new route is blocked) because it reaches a conclusion also reached by Kant (the intersecting point) is either counteractive or ineffective. Counteractive since calling its conclusion Kantian cannot weaken the argument, but it might increase its acceptability. For a reader with Kantian sympathies may find this convergence reassuring and enlightening, while anyone unwilling to follow Kant's route may still find the one presented here appealing. Ineffective because the objection, to be effective, needs to show that (i) the argument is just a version of Kant's argument and that (ii) the latter is wrong, but, even if one were to concede (ii), the fact remains that the argument supports a more constructive position that is not in itself Kantian at all, as we shall see in the answer to the next objection and in the conclusion, so (i) cannot be granted.

According to the third and last objection to be discussed here, the argument against digital ontology appears to depend on the claim that each LoA has equal right to tell us whether the ultimate nature of reality is analogue or digital (each LoA is equally valid). However, this is a claim that an opponent is likely to deny. There seems to be no reason why each LoA should be granted equal authority in answering questions about the ultimate nature of the universe. Some LoAs are undoubtedly useful in some contexts and not in others, but we have no reason to think that all of them are equally good at limiting the true structure of reality. In particular, someone might argue that it is reasonable that, if our best fundamental physical theory is, say, digital, then this gives us good reason to think that the fundamental nature of reality is digital. This is not deductive warrant, but it does appear to provide some degree of justification. Therefore, for such a critic, when it comes to the question of whether reality is analogue or digital, it does not seem that each LoA should have equal say. The argument needs to do more to respond to such a critic. For it seems that it is only against the claim that one can adopt a 'LoA-free' position and decide from there whether reality is digital or analogue, yet this seems a straw man. A realist about the analogue/digital divide is more likely to claim that some LoAs are better than others for telling one about the ultimate nature of reality, not to claim a miraculous ability to adopt a 'LoA-free' position. Furthermore, an attack solely on the 'LoA-free' position would be insufficient to support the positive claim that no LoA is a better guide than any other to the ultimate digital/analogue nature of reality.

The objection contains an important clarification, which will help to introduce the positive defence of informational structural realism, sketched in the next section. The clarification is this. The argument is not merely based on the dichotomy 'LoA-free' vs 'LoA-bounded' approaches to ontology. Although important, this is only the first move. Once we accept that epistemology is LoA-based and that no ontology can be LoA-free, then a second, but equally crucial move consists in realizing that digital and analogue are features of the LoAs adopted to analyse reality, not features of reality in itself, or, to put it differently, that digital and analogue features are internal features of the models made possible by various LoAs, not external features of the systems modelled by LoAs. So the argument is not merely that some LoAs show reality to be digital while others show it to be analogue and that we cannot decide which LoAs are better, but, far more importantly, that some LoAs are digital and some are analogue and that, depending on which of them we adopt (because of requirements, goals etc., i.e. teleologically), reality will be modelled as digital or analogue. The case of the double-slit experiment was recalled as a clear illustration of the impossibility of determining the intrinsically digital vs analogue nature of reality independently of how it is accessed. Now, the objection correctly points out that, even if all this is granted, LoAs are still not 'born equal', and not just as a matter of instrumental convenience. Arguably (see chapter three), some LoAs still fit better their systems, both in terms of taking full advantages of their affordances and in terms of respecting their constraints, and that this is very significant and worth accounting for, ontologically. So, the objection continues, perhaps one could work his way inside out, as if were, and try to grasp what the nature of reality might be in itself, given the sort of successful LoAs that are adopted on this side of the relation. To use a terminology borrowed from computer science (see chapter eight), one could try to reverse-engineer the output (our models of reality as obtained through our most successful LoAs) in order to obtain at least some information about the original input (Michael's world, or Kant's noumenal world). This is all correct. But we need to be careful about what can be actually inferred from this valuable suggestion. Even assuming, and this is very far from a trivial concession, that reality might be successfully modelled through a digital (or analogue, where the 'or' is assumed to be exclusive of the sake of simplicity) ontology and that it is not the case that an analogue (or, if talking of an analogue ontology in the first place, a digital) ontology may not be equally satisfactory; all this would not show that reality is digital (or analogue) in itself. It would only show that our ontological commitment in favour of a digital (or analogue) ontology would be safe in the sense that we could not be proven wrong because we would be (or, our opponent would argue, we would have no way of proving that we are not) taking a feature of our LoAs for a feature of the system that they model. This is unsatisfactory. It is the impasse that I have tried to describe more intuitively by means of Uriel's wheel. The exit from this impasse, in terms of a defence of a form of realist ontology that is compatible with a non-relativistic and yet LoA-based epistemology, leads to a non-Kantian position, which seeks to reconcile digital and analogue ontology by identifying the minimal denominator shared by both. And this is the sort of position that I have defended in the constructive chapter, under the label structural information realism. So, insofar as the objection is correct, it seems that an informational approach to ontology is the best way of taking advantage of its lesson.

CONCLUSION

In this chapter, I argued against the tenability of a digital ontology, and against the soundness of the digital vs analogue dichotomy when applied to our metaphysical understanding of reality. The criticism is motivated by the concern that informational ontology, according to which the ultimate nature of reality is informational (see next chapter) might be confused with either pancomputationalism (according to which the universe is a computational system equivalent to a Turing machine), with a version of digital ontology (according to which the ultimate nature of reality is digital) or with a combination of the two (according to which the universe is a cellular automaton, for example). The concern is justified, for the risk is real. Take, for example, an influential article by Margolus (2003), in which we read that

Given more than a century of finite-state underpinnings, one might have expected that by now all of physics would be based on informational and computational concepts. That this isn't so may simply reflect the stubborn legacy of the continuum, and the recency [sic] and macroscopic character of computer science. (p. 309)

The passage conflates the informational and the digital, as if they were synonymous. Clearly, they are not, not least because information may easily be analogue or continuous. Yet even Wheeler himself fell into the same trap (see the quotation provided in chapter four). Drawing no distinction between an informational and a digital ontology is a mistake. Digital ontology is very implausible and obviously behaves as a misleading distraction, when it comes to assessing the value of an informational ontology. The latter can be better appreciated once the ground has been cleared of any potential confusion. Thus, this chapter provided the preparatory *pars destruens* (digital ontology is a bad idea) of a two-stage piece of research, whose second, *pars construens* (in favour of informational structural realism) can now be presented, in the next, and final, chapter of this book.

15

A defence of informational structural realism

To put the conclusion crudely—the stuff of the world is mind-stuff. [. . .] The mind-stuff of the world is, of course, something more general than our individual conscious minds; but we may think of its nature as not altogether foreign to the feelings in our consciousness. [. . .] We are acquainted with an external world because its fibres run into our consciousness; it is only our own ends of the fibres that we actually know; from those ends we more or less successfully reconstruct the rest [. . .] The mind-stuff is the aggregation of relations and relata which form the building material for the physical world. It is sometimes urged that the basal stuff of the world-stuff should be called 'neutral stuff', rather than 'mind-stuff' since it is to be such that both mind and matter originate from it.

Eddington (1928), pp. 276–280

SUMMARY

Previously, in chapter fourteen, I argued that a digital (or analogue) ontology is not a satisfactory approach to the description of the environment in which informational organisms like us are embedded. This final chapter defends an informational ontology, to which I shall refer as Informational Structural Realism (ISR). The reader might read this as a proposal to interpret Eddington's 'neutral stuff', in the quotation opening this chapter, as informational stuff. As a form of realism, ISR is committed to the existence of a mind-independent reality addressed by, and constraining, knowledge. ISR supports the adoption of LoAs that carry a minimal ontological commitment in favour of the structural properties of reality and a reflective, equally minimal, ontological commitment in favour of structural objects. However, unlike other versions of structural realism, ISR supports an informational interpretation of these structural objects. This second commitment, in favour of structural relata, is justified by epistemic reasons. We are allowed to commit ourselves ontologically to whatever minimal conception of objects is useful to make sense of our first commitment in favour of structures. The first commitment answers the question 'what can we know?'; the second commitment answers the question 'what can we justifiably assume to be in the external world?'. So, according to ISR, explanatorily, instrumentally and predictively successful models (including, but not only, those propounded by scientific theories) of reality, at a given LoA, can be, in the best circumstances, increasingly informative about the relations that obtain between the (possibly sub-observable) informational objects that constitute the system under investigation (through the observable phenomena). A significant consequence of ISR is that, as far as we can tell, the ultimate nature of reality is informational, that is, it makes sense to adopt LoAs that commit our theories to a view of reality as mind-independent and constituted by structural objects that are neither substantial nor material (they might well be, but we have no need to suppose them to be so) but cohering clusters of data, not in the alphanumeric sense of the word, but in an equally common sense of differences *de re*, i.e. mind-independent, concrete, relational points of lack of uniformity, what have been defined in chapter four as *dedomena*. Structural objects work epistemologically like constraining affordances: they allow or invite certain epistemic constructs (they are affordances for inforgs like us, who elaborate them) and resist or impede some others (they are constraints for the inforgs), depending on the interaction with, and the nature of, the informational organisms that process them. They are exploitable by a theory, at a given LoA, as input of adequate queries to produce information (the model) as output. In short, Being and Information *conventuntur*.

The chapter is divided into two parts. The first part defends an informational approach to structural realism. It does so in three steps. First, I explain how epistemic (ESR) and ontic (OSR) structural realism are reconcilable within the debate about structural realism (SR). It follows that a version of OSR is defensible from a structuralist-friendly position. Second, I argue that a version of OSR is also plausible, because not all *relata* (structured entities) are logically prior to relations (structures). Third, I show that a version of OSR is also applicable to both sub-observable (unobservable and instrumentally-only observable) and observable entities, by developing its ontology of structural objects in terms of informational objects. The outcome is ISR, a version of OSR supporting the ontological commitment to a view of the world as the totality of informational objects dynamically interacting with each other. In the second part of the chapter, I answer ten objections that could be moved to the proposal, in order to clarify it further. Overall, the chapter could be read as an attempt to answer positively question P14 from chapter two.

15.1. Introduction

Broadly construed, *structural realism* (SR) argues that the structural properties of reality are knowable in themselves, and hence that it is possible to get them right:

SR   Explanatorily, instrumentally and predictively successful models (especially, but not only, those propounded by scientific theories) can be, in the best circumstances, increasingly informative about the *relations* that obtain between the (possibly sub-observable, i.e. unobservable or instrumentally-only observable) objects that constitute the system under investigation (through the observable phenomena).

SR encompasses a variety of positions in epistemology and in the philosophy of science, including, in the past, Carnap's, Cassirer's, Duhem's, Eddington's, Poincaré's, Russell's, Schlick's, and Whitehead's.[1] As a whole family of theories, SR is confronted by two major challenges. One is *Newman's problem*.[2] The other may be referred to as the *ontological problem*.

Newman's problem is epistemological. It contends that what SR has to say about our knowledge of reality is either trivial or false. It is also an *external* challenge, for it is typically deployed to reject any version of SR. I shall not dwell upon Newman's 'frying pan or fire' alternative, partly because it lies beyond the limited scope of this chapter, and partly because is a well-known objection to SR, which has been fully dealt with in the literature. It must be acknowledged that it remains a future concern for any structuralist approach, including the one developed in this chapter. At this stage, suffice it to say that, if pressed, I would agree with Worrall and Zahar (2001), French and Saatsi (2006), and Votsis (forthcoming) that arguments based on it are probably much less damaging than detractors of SR appear to believe;[3] and that, as Esfeld and Lam (2008) argue, an ontology that does not privilege either *relata* or relations (the package hypothesis discussed later in this chapter) may not be subject to Newman's problem because of the concrete nature of the relata in question.

The ontological problem is a metaphysical and *internal* challenge. It concerns the ontological commitments of SR. This is the topic of this chapter. SR may be convincing, but it leaves unspecified the nature of the *relata* in the structures. As a result, the current debate among structural realists has resuscitated the classic question about the accessibility of the ontic status of objects in themselves. The problem does not have to be restricted to theoretical or sub-observable entities. We shall see that, as the Kantian terminology and the Russellian origins of the approach point out, what is in question is the (knowability of the) ultimate nature of reality. I shall return to this methodological point when discussing objection 6.3 in section 6.

---

[1] An earlier assessment of Whitehead's and Russell's SR is Heath (1928). Russell's and Poincaré's versions of SR have been the most influential so far, thanks to Maxwell (1968), (1970a), (1970b); and to Worrall (1989), (1994) respectively. Gower (2000) provides an excellent scholarly analysis of the earlier history of the various structural realisms. Psillos (2000a) reconstructs Carnap's structuralist position with admirable accuracy, in order to show that this version too is subject to roughly the same 'Newmanian' difficulties that, according to Psillos, undermine Russell's and Poincaré's positions. French (2003) concerns Eddington's ontic structural realism. French (2001) highlights Cassirer's SR and more generally the Kantian roots of SR.

[2] Newman's problem (Newman (1928)) originally concerned Russell's version of SR. It was later revived by Demopoulos and Friedman (1985) in terms of the Ramsey-sentence. It has recently been expanded in scope by Psillos (1999), ch. 7 and Psillos (2001), who deploys it to reject any form of SR. It is formalized by Ketland (2004), who supports it, and by Votsis (2003), who seeks to counteract it. On the history of the problem, see also French (2003).

[3] See also French's analysis of Eddington's response (to which I am sympathetic) to Braithwaite in French (2003). I hope to discuss Newman's problem from the perspective of an informational approach to SR in a future work.

The ontological problem is explainable by means of a simple formalism. The set-theoretic scheme of a structure S comprises four sets (three, if one treats properties as unary relations):

1. a non-empty set O of objects (the domain of S),
2. a non-empty set P of first-order, one-place properties of the objects in O,
3. a non-empty set of relations R on O, and
4. a possibly empty set T of transitions rules (operations) on O.

This is not the only way of dealing with the concept of structure, and it may not be the best, if compared to the semantic or model-theoretic approach. Chakravartty (2001) has argued that it is questionable whether the model-theoretic approach significantly favours scientific realism rather than any other form of realism. If Chakravartty is right, it follows that the approach may not significantly favour SR either. However, this neutrality thesis can be guaranteed while still endorsing the SR-centric view, supported by e.g. French and Ladyman (2003b) and French and Saatsi (2006), that the semantic (model-theoretic) approach is more suitable for SR than the syntactic (set-theoretic) one. So, the semantic (model-theoretic) approach will be adopted below, when it will become necessary to clarify the different ontological commitments of a theory. Here, however, the set-theoretic approach suffices to formulate the ontological problem in very simple terms: what are the objects in O? *Epistemic Structural Realism* (ESR) and *Ontic Structural Realism* (OSR) provide different answers.[4]

ESR takes an *agnostic stance*. Objects can be posited only as *ontic residua*, i.e. what remains in principle unknowable once the knowable structures of reality have been factored out. Quite naturally, Poincaré (1902) used a Kantian vocabulary and spoke of objects in themselves as *noumena*. Ramsey sentences provide a standard (if perhaps unsuccessful by themselves, see French and Ladyman (2003a)) method to circumvent an ontological commitment in favour of these *noumena*.[5]

ESR's agnostic stance may be interpreted as what Lewis (2009) called 'Ramseyan humility', although I would opt for a version of Kantian humility instead. Lewis relied on Ramsey sentences and the multiple realizability of even our hypothetically true and ultimate theory of everything to argue that the intrinsic nature of reality *may be unknowable*, whereas Kant's conclusion was that it is in principle *unknown and unknowable*, owing to the nature of human knowledge, a slightly but significantly different

---

[4] The distinction between ESR and OSR, introduced by Ladyman (1998), is now standard, even if the vocabulary adopted may differ, with some authors referring to OSR as 'metaphysical' or 'ontological' SR. For a recent analysis see Psillos (2004). Van Fraassen (2006b) distinguishes between 'moderate structuralism: the theory describes only the structure of a bearer, which has also non-structural features (though science is said not to describe those), radical structuralism: 'structure is all there is' [and] in-between structuralism: the structure described by science does have a bearer, but that bearer has no other features at all.'. This chapter falls into the 'in-between' category.

[5] This is a standard approach at least since Maxwell (1970b). Worrall and Zahar (2001) provide a recent defence. Votsis (2003) reviews the various difficulties involved in using Ramsey sentences in SR. For a defence of a Ramseyan approach see Cruse and Papineau (2002), who are criticized by Newman (2004).

position.[6] Given its Kantian humility, ESR introduces a restricting clause in its definition of SR:

ESR   Explanatorily, instrumentally and predictively successful models (especially, but not only, those propounded by scientific theories) can be, in the best circumstances, increasingly informative *only* about the relations that obtain between the (possibly sub-observable) objects that constitute the system under investigation (through the observable phenomena), but not about the first-order, one-place predicates qualifying *the objects in themselves* (the intrinsic nature of the *noumena*).

Heath (1928) referred to ESR as 'bifurcated structuralism' because of its obvious (and typically Kantian) dualism. As French (2003) aptly phrases it:

while the ultimate constituents of the world may be non-structural, all that physics—or science in general—tells us about, and hence all that we can know, on the basis of that physics, is structure. (p. 255)

OSR seeks to overcome the 'bifurcation' in ESR by not granting the restricting clause. This can be achieved in at least two ways, one radical, the other more moderate. *Eliminativist*[7] OSR suggests that:

EOSR   Ultimately, only structures are primitive and ontologically subsistent. Individual objects are not *residua* but *figmenta,* heuristically more useful but no more existent than Bacon's *idola*.

In EOSR, the epistemological problem (i.e. the bifurcation in ESR) is solved because there is nothing to know about the intrinsic nature of individual objects anyway. Non-eliminativist OSR holds that:

NOSR   Ultimately, there are entities, but they are not classically re-identifiable individuals; rather, they are themselves structural objects, and in the best cases they can be indirectly denoted (circumscribed) by our models, at least in principle.

Both positions move away from any metaphysical substantivalism (there are no permanent and more fundamental, individual 'hooks', substantial atoms, monads, substrata, or essential elements), so they may not necessarily be distinguished—Saunders (2003), for example, does not—or may be distinguished but interpreted as interchangeable, as in Morganti (2004). I shall argue that they are quite different.

Eliminativist OSR has emerged also in connection with the debate on individuality in quantum mechanics (French and Redhead (1988)), and this may explain its extremely revisionist nature. The position avoids the bifurcation in ESR by disposing of any ontology of objects *tout court* (this seems to be the position sometimes advocated

---

[6] R. Langton (2004) provides an enlightening analysis of the implications of Lewis's 'Ramseyan humility'.

[7] I am adapting this distinction from Parsons (2004), who discriminates between eliminativist and non-eliminativist forms of structuralism in the philosophy of mathematics. Parsons' non-eliminativist approach is related to Dedekind's 'logical structuralism', as defined by Reck (2003). It seems to be in line with at least a neo-Kantian view of mathematical objects, and I would consider it coherent with the theses defended in this chapter.

by Ladyman (1998) and further defended in French and Ladyman (2003a), but see below). The empirical and common-sensical costs of this strategy are evidently very high. They have been convincingly stressed by Cao (2003), Chakravartty (2003), and Morganti (2004). True, advocates of eliminativist OSR may rejoin that the metaphysical and epistemological gains are even greater: ontic monism and structural knowledge guarantee that reality is fully knowable in principle. Moreover, there are 'thin' versions of mathematical structuralism that can bring some support to eliminativist OSR (Reck and Price (2000) provide a useful overview). However, it is easy to counter that such gains are suspiciously great, for at least three reasons, which may be quickly outlined here.

First, as a form of *syntactic realism*, eliminativist OSR betrays the original Kantian polarization between knowable phenomena and unknowable *noumena*, which lies at the roots of SR. It starts resembling a metaphysically more problematic form of absolute idealism, according to which 'whatever is real is structural and whatever is structural is real', to paraphrase Hegel.

Second, eliminativist OSR becomes less clearly distinguishable from a stronger form of scientific realism, which may then be unable to cope with the *Pessimistic Meta-Induction Argument* (see section 15.2.1).

Finally, without objects/entities, eliminativist OSR triggers a potential regress of structures (see section 15.3).

For these reasons at least, I agree with Cao (2003) that eliminativist OSR should probably be adopted only as a matter of last resort.

Non-eliminativist OSR is equally anti-substantivalist but metaphysically less drastic. It seeks to temper the effects of the bifurcation in ESR by arguing that something can be known about structured entities, namely that they are structural objects. Non-eliminativist OSR is expounded and supported by Chakravartty (1998), (2003), Esfeld (2004), and Dorato and Pauri (forthcoming). It seems to be the position defended sometimes by other ontic-structuralists such as Cassirer, and French and Ladyman (2003b). It can find allies among 'entity realists' in philosophy of science, and gain support from some 'thick' version of mathematical structuralism (see Reck and Price (2000)).[8] It is the version of OSR that will be discussed in the rest of this chapter, and henceforth OSR will mean non-eliminativist OSR, unless otherwise specified.

15.2 First step: ESR and OSR are not incompatible

Philosophers sympathetic to SR are divided between those who support (various versions of) OSR or ESR, and a third party of those who appreciate the advantages and shortcomings of both and choose to remain uncommitted. This section attempts to

---

[8] Dedekind's 'logical structuralism' is probably the version most compatible with the informational approach developed in this chapter, see Reck (2003) for a detailed analysis and support.

convince at least this third party that there is a reasonable way of combining the virtues of both brands of SR without incurring most of their costs.

15.2.1 Indirect knowledge

SR was revived by Worrall (1989) to deal with two problems in the philosophy of science, the *No-Miracles Argument*:

NMA   (Some form of) realism 'is the only philosophy that does not make [the predictive success of] science a miracle' (Putnam (1975), p. 73);

and the *Pessimistic Meta-Induction Argument*:

PMIA   Since many predictively-successful scientific theories have been discarded in the past, there is some inductive evidence that current theories are likely to be discarded as well, despite their increased success. (Laudan (1981)).

NMA is neutral with respect to the form of realism that it supports. For example, both instrumentalism (understood as a form of realism insofar as it is committed to the existence of an external world that determines the empirical success of scientific theories, more on this in section 15.6, objection 4) and naïve realism would be plausible candidates. As for SR, in its case NMA leads to the view that the epistemic success of a theory is a function of its being correct about the structure of reality.

PMIA has been questioned on several grounds. Here, it is useful to highlight three general criticisms.

First, *sub specie aeternitatis*, science is still in its puberty, when some hiccups are not necessarily evidence of any serious sickness. What are a handful of centuries compared to the following millennia? From a longer perspective, science may be settling down, and the initial swings may be just a prelude to a more inert state of 'structural stability'.[9] As Hacking (1999) has emphasized, it already seems that it is not so much revolutionary change as normal stability that requires explanation. Of course, the *sub specie aeternitatis* view provides no support for scientific realism, which was the target of PMIA in the first place. The drying up of scientific revolutions may be just a sign of decreasing empirical or intellectual resources. One day, we may be at our wits' end, or at the end of our technical or financial means. Then the oscillations and vibrations in our scientific theories may be so subtle and infrequent that our thick-skinned metaphysics may not notice them. Indeed, at that point, it may become difficult to talk of bad metaphysics at all. The risk is that then the best theory available may still be the best of a very bad lot, as Van Fraassen has emphasized.

---

[9] 'Modern mathematical models are 'structurally stable', that is, their (qualitative or approximate quantitative) predictions are insensitive to small changes. A circle is not structurally stable, in that a slightly deformed circle is not a circle. But the system of Königsberg bridges retains exactly the same topological structure if its islands are eroded slightly, or its river narrows.' J. Franklin (1999)

Second, although the *pax scientifica* may not provide much reason for optimism, it fails to support pessimism too, for the latter is trivially observer-relative. Look on the bright side and you may transform PMIA into an optimistic meta-induction:

OMIA   The *Optimistic Meta-Induction Argument*: since many false scientific theories have been discarded in the past, despite their being predictively-successful, there is some inductive evidence that, if current theories are also false, they will be discarded as well, notwithstanding their increased success.

The half-full glass of OMIA is consistent with NMA and both together are comfortably reassuring. Precisely because there is no symmetry between semantics and pragmatics—truth is predictively-successful but predictive success is not necessarily truth-tracking—in the long run, we, realists, shall not be fooled by currently predictively-successful but actually untruthful mermaids.

Third, SR may endorse OMIA and defuse PMIA by arguing that, although for the sake of argument one may concede that discontinuity in theory change may be radical[10] when non-structural descriptions of the nature of entities are involved, this is counterbalanced by considerable continuity at the structural level.

Now, NMA and PMIA/OMIA are strictly related to two other broad issues in epistemology:

i. the goal of vindicating at least partly, and at any rate some of, our ordinary ontological commitments, despite
ii. the problem that we do not have direct or any other privileged epistemic access to reality in itself.

Goal (i) and problem (ii) bear witness to the Kantian roots of SR. Again, this is not a coincidence. Even if nowadays one tends to associate (i) and (ii) more readily with work beginning with Quine (1939) and Sellars (1956) respectively, the neo-Kantian origins of structuralism can be traced back to a revival of interest in Kant's transcendental idealism at the beginning of the last century (French and Ladyman (2003b)).

Problem (ii) differentiates SR from forms of naïve realism, whereas goal (i) differentiates SR from forms of instrumentalism.

Naïve realism relies on a conception of knowledge as a direct relation between model and modelled. Statically and synchronically, it looks robust at a given time because it is rigidly coupled to whatever description of the world is available at that time. However, dynamically and hence diachronically, naïve realism is dreadfully brittle, for it is easily shattered by any epistemic change. This does not have to be a major scientific revolution; it may be just some simple counterexample or a good old-fashioned, sceptical argument. In fact, naïve realism is most informative when it breaks, exactly like the tell-tale glass fixed across cracks to monitor movement in a building.

---

[10] The 'radicality' however need not be guaranteed because of recent, convincing defences of Post's *General Correspondence Principle* in French and French and Kamminga (1993).

Various forms of instrumentalism circumvent the risk of a breakdown by avoiding any specific ontological commitment over and above the minimal acceptance of a mind-independent, external reality. This is the admittedly very deflated sense in which even an instrumentalist may claim to be a realist (see the 0-order commitment in section 15.2.4).

Instead, structural realism may seek to combine some richer ontological commitment—a defence of NMA/OMIA and a positive development of (i)—with a degree of resilience to epistemic change, especially in science. It achieves this flexibility not by decoupling knowledge from reality, as instrumentalism does, but by decoupling, within knowledge itself, the descriptions of the knowable structural characteristics of the system from the explanations of its intrinsic properties. Both can still crash, but the structural descriptions are now not cemented to their source and are therefore far more resilient to change than the ontological explanations, which can be left sinking, if necessary. All this comes at a price, which is paid at the checkout represented by problem (ii) above. SR gains epistemic resilience by endorsing a view of knowledge as an *indirect* relation between the epistemic (possibly multi-) agent and the system under analysis, and a somewhat weakened ontological commitment. Let's see how.

15.2.2 Structuralism and the levels of abstraction

In Kant, knowledge of reality is indirect because of the mind's transcendental schematism. After the downfall of neo-Kantism and Cassirer's and C. I. Lewis's revisions of the transcendental, an approach is needed that is less infra-subjective, mental (if not psychologistic), innatist, individualistic and rigid. In chapter three, I proposed the *method of levels of abstraction* (LoAs) as a more inter-subjective, socially constructible (hence possibly conventional), dynamic and flexible way to further Kant's approach. This is a step away from *internal realism* (the kinds, categories, and structures of the world are only a function of our conceptual schemes), but not yet a step into *external* or *metaphysical realism* (the kinds, categories, and structures of the world belong to the world and are not a function of our conceptual schemes, either causally or ontologically). If necessary, it might be called *liminal realism*, for reasons that will become clearer below. Four advantages of the method can be highlighted here.

First, and most importantly for our present concerns, the method is useful to specify the meaning of 'indirect knowledge'. Direct knowledge is to be understood here as typically knowledge of one's mental states, which is apparently not mediated (see for example chapter thirteen). Indirect knowledge is usually taken to be knowledge that is obtained inferentially or through some other form of mediated communication with the world. We can now be more precise and define 'indirect knowledge' in terms of knowledge mediated by an LoA.

It follows, (second advantage) that specifying the LoA means clarifying, from the outset, the range of questions that (a) can be meaningfully asked and (b) are answerable in principle. We saw that one might think of the input of an LoA as consisting of the *system* under analysis, comprising a set of *data*; its output is a *model* of the system, comprising *information*. The quantity of information in a model varies with the LoA: a lower LoA, of greater resolution or finer granularity, produces a model that contains more information than a model produced at a higher, or more abstract, LoA. Thus, a given LoA provides a quantified commitment to the kind and amount of relevant semantic information that can be 'extracted' from the system. The choice of an LoA pre-determines the type and quantity of data that can be considered and hence the information that can be contained in the model. So, knowing at which LoA the system is being analysed is indispensable, for it means knowing the scope and limits of the model being developed.

Third, different LoAs may be fairly compared and ranked depending on their virtues, that is, (a) how well they model the system in question according to what purpose and (b) how well they satisfy a list of explicit modelling specifications, e.g. informativeness, coherence, elegance, simplicity, explanatory power, consistency with the data, predictive power, and so on. In Devitt's terminology, (b) comprises the non-empirical virtues of an LoA and (a), when the purpose is truth, the empirical virtues:

Empirical virtue is a matter of entailing (in conjunction with accepted auxiliaries) observational truths and not entailing observational falsehoods. The nonempirical virtues are explanatory power, simplicity, and the like. Devitt (2005)

So, different analyses of the same system can be fairly compared provided that they share a comparable LoA.

Finally, by stating its LoA, a theory is forced to make explicit and clarify its ontological commitment, in the following way.

15.2.3 Ontological commitments and levels of abstractions

We have seen that a model is the output of the analysis of a system, developed at some LoA(s), for some purpose. So a theory of a system comprises at least three components:

    i. an LoA, which determines the range of available observables and allows the theory to investigate the system under analysis and to elaborate;

    ii. the ensuing model of that system, which identifies;

    iii. a structure of the system at the given LoA.

Let us refer to this as the system-level-model-structure (or SLMS) scheme. We already encountered a version of SLMS in chapter thirteen, but here is a more general illustration here (Figure 29):

The structuralist position can now be rephrased thus (the asterisk is a reminder of the temporary nature of the statement):

SR★ Explanatorily, instrumentally, and predictively successful models (especially, but not only, those propounded by scientific theories) *at a given LoA* can be, in the best circumstances, increasingly informative about the relations that obtain between the (possibly sub-observable) objects that constitute the system under investigation (through the observable phenomena).

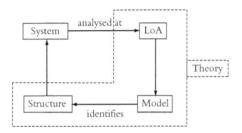

Figure 29 The SLMS scheme

The ontological commitment of a theory can be clearly understood by distinguishing between a *committing* and a *committed* component, within the SLMS scheme.

A theory commits itself ontologically by opting for a specific LoA, whose application commits the theory to a particular model of the system. The order is purely logical. By adopting an LoA, the theory decides what kind of observables are going to play a role in elaborating the model. In out traffic light example, suppose the LoA commits the theory to take into account only data relative to colour type. When the LoA generates a model, i.e. when the observables are instantiated, the theory is committed to a particular view of the system. Again, in our example, this might be, for instance, the specific colours used in the model. According to Votsis (forthcoming), Worrall, for example, seems to hold this much when phrasing SR in terms of

a commitment to structures (including equations) whose observation terms are fully interpreted and whose theoretical terms are implicitly defined through their logical relations with one another and with the observation terms. This just amounts to the Ramsey sentence approach to theories.

To summarize, by accepting an LoA a theory commits itself to the existence of certain types of objects, the types constituting the LoA (by trying to model a traffic light in terms of three colours one shows one's commitment to the existence of a traffic light of that kind, i.e. one that could be found in Rome, but not in Oxford, see chapter three), while by endorsing the ensuing models the theory commits itself to the corresponding tokens (by endorsing a particular model, which is the outcome of the interpretation of the data at the chosen LoA, one commits oneself to that model, e.g. one now cannot have a fourth phase when amber and green are on at the same time).

Figure 30 summarizes this distinction (note that, for the sake of simplicity the term 'theory' is the dotted line that comprises, as above, LoA, model, and structure). The distinction just introduced can now be used to reconcile ESR and OSR.

15.2.4 How to reconcile ESR and OSR

What scope of ontological commitment can an LoA provide to a theory? There is virtually no upper limit. Depending on the LoA, a theory may end up by talking of witches and neurotransmitters, zodiac signs and the Morning Star, ether and white swans, phlogiston and hadrons. However, there is a lower limit, a minimalist approach

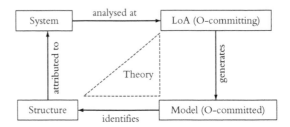

Figure 30 The SLMS scheme with ontological commitment

to how little a theory may safely assume to be there (in the system itself) for the theory (and for the history of knowledge in general and of science in particular) to be consistent and meaningful. ESR endorses such *minimalism*. It argues that, in the best circumstances, a theory is justified in adopting an LoA that commits it (the theory) ontologically to a realist interpretation of the structural properties of the system identified by the model that has been produced by the theory at the chosen LoA. This ontological commitment is minimal in that it concerns knowledge of the first-order structural properties (the non-empty set P of first-order, one-place properties of the objects in O, see section one) of the system under investigation (more on this in section 15.6, objection 5). It is, in other words, the sort of commitment that is deemed safer by all supporters of structural realism, since it is based on the existence of certain relations, identified by the model as implemented by the system, rather than of particulars in themselves, with specific properties within the system.

ESR is arguably correct. On the one hand, the adoption of any LoA supporting a degree of ontological commitment less minimal than the epistemic-structuralist one endorsed by ESR seems metaphysically risky and suspicious. This is the point usually made by supporters of ESR: it is better to limit one's ontological commitment to the existence and knowability of (properties of) relational structures. Any other commitment to the knowability of (properties of) the *relata* in themselves seems unnecessary, and not backed up by a general conception of knowledge, understood as an indirect relation with the world, even if this were not explicitly interpreted in terms of an LoA methodology. In short, Ockham's razor applies and one tries to keep one's commitment as minimal as possible. But could the commitment be even more minimalist? No, because there is no ontological commitment more minimalist than the one supported by ESR—which holds that structures are knowable—but still less minimalist than the extremely deflated commitment of the instrumentalist, who may be happy to concede just the existence of an external world. Basically, there is no logical space for manoeuvre here between ESR and instrumentalism.[11]

---

[11] Of course ESR may be more or less 'lite', depending on the scope of the relations taken into account, but this does not change the sort of ontological commitment in question, which still favours relations instead of *relata*.

An important consequence is that one may believe that, if ESR is correct, this is all that can be said about the issue and there is no logical space left for OSR either.

The impression is widespread. The current internal debate among structural realists has been developing on the assumption that, if there is some room for manoeuvre, it must be found at expense of one of the two positions. It is held that (versions of) OSR and ESR are incompatible, one of the two must go and, it is often argued, this should not be ESR. Indeed, since ESR is the most popular variety of SR, Morganti (2004), for example, defends it negatively, by showing that the only SR-friendly alternative to ESR, namely OSR, is untenable. The strategy becomes a case of friendly fire when Newman's problem is further deployed to reject ESR as well, and hence to discard SR altogether. It is a strategy we shall encounter again in section 15.6, objection 1.

This attack on OSR is, however, misguided. ESR and OSR work at separate LoAs, so they are not mutually exclusive. As far as a first-order analysis is concerned, SR justifies only one kind of ontological commitment, the one endorsed by ESR; but at a *derivative* or *metatheoretical* level of analysis, OSR correctly argues in favour of an economical view of objects, in the following way.

Consider again the SLMS scheme. The assumption is that there is no *direct* knowledge of the intrinsic nature of the entities in themselves that constitute the system under investigation. However, once a theory has ontologically committed itself to the structural properties of the system, one is entitled to infer *indirectly* that, whatever the system and its components (i.e. the objects or *relata*) may be in themselves, they must be such as to allow the theory to model at least some of their structural/relational properties. This is a transcendental feedback: what are the conditions of possibility of knowledge (the knowledge offered by the theory) of the structural properties of the system?

On the one hand, all realists agree that there is a mind-independent, external reality addressed by our knowledge, yet this is a red herring. We have seen that this ontological commitment is even poorer or more basic than the one supported by the epistemic structuralist. It is the sort of uninteresting commitment that allows a reasonable conversation among the various forms of realism (naïve, structural, scientific, even the instrumentalist, in the sense specified above, and so forth). It is not what is in question here.

On the other hand, at the meta-level level of analysis just assumed, one is exploring whether there might be a justifiable, higher LoA, that commits the theory to some kind of interpretation of the sort of objects/*relata* that support the structural properties of the system identified by the model that has been produced by the theory at the lower LoA. The question is what makes ESR possible. Obviously, the epistemic structuralist simply has nothing to offer here, for her concern is with a primary commitment. The ontic structuralist, on the contrary, can argue in favour of a minimalist approach with respect to the relata. And this seems a reasonable step to take. The LoA that one may justifiably adopt at this level is one that commits the theory to an interpretation of the objects/*relata* as themselves structural in nature. I shall say more about this in the next two sections, but let me first clarify in what this higher-level commitment consists.

At the first-order level (Figure 31), we have seen that one may reasonably adopt a transcendental approach to knowledge—as an LoA-mediated epistemic relation with reality—and use Ockham's razor as a methodological safety measure to limit the *number* of (types of) components a theory should be ontologically committed to by its LoAs. In the best circumstances, first-order LoAs should ontologically commit a theory at most to the existence of the (type of first order) structures identified by its models.

At a second-order level, one re-adopts a transcendental approach to what makes possible the previous first-order knowledge of structures. In order not to 'revert to the sin of transcendental metaphysics', as Quine (1992) nicely phrases it, one applies a qualitatively modified version of Ockham's razor, which now suggests, still methodologically, keeping the *nature* of the objects/*relata* as simple as possible: *entia non sunt complicanda praeter necessitatem*, to use some medieval Latin. According to this new safety principle, it is reasonable to assume that 0-order *relata* are structural entities, for this is all the theory needs in order to justify its previous commitment in favour of first-order relations. A higher degree of commitment (to things/*relata*)—achieved through reflection on the condition of possibility of the previous, minimalist commitment (to structures/relations)—corresponds to a lower degree of 'stuff' assumed to be out there in the world (relations are first-order, *relata* are 0-order). Since the two ontological commitments occur at different levels there is no incompatibility and hence no objection. Figure 31 summarizes the new analysis.

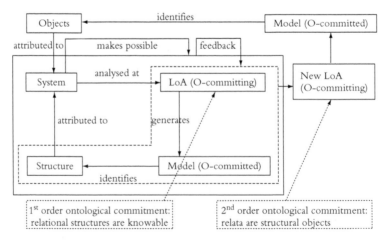

Figure 31 The SLMS scheme with ordered ontological commitments

15.3 Second step: *Relata* are not logically prior to all relations

The opponent of OSR may not be satisfied. Eliminating the apparent inconsistency between ESR and OSR is only a first step. It does not yet show that OSR is *plausible* because there is a direct and quite forceful objection to OSR that still needs to be neutralized. This is our second step.

Relations (structures) require *relata* (structured/able objects), which therefore cannot be further identified as relations (structures) without running into some vicious circularity or infinite regress. Yet this is precisely what OSR appears to be forced to argue, if the very idea of structural objects is supposed to make sense.[12]

As usual, one may bite the bullet and talk of an infinite regress of structures. Note that the point here is not that objects may be structural, but that, even if there are objects, they are unreachable, hidden behind an infinite series of structural layers, or as the lower limit of an infinite series of structures. In either case, it may be turtles all the way down, as Saunders (2003) wittily puts it. This is certainly a solution. Whether it is satisfactory is another matter. Instead of tackling the problem, we run away from it, and run forever. True, we are not caught by our opponents, but we do not defeat them either. For those who do not like draws, or who run out of conceptual breath when asked to run ad infinitum, there is an alternative.

Admittedly, *external* relations usually require *relata*. Distance and speed are two good examples. However, *internal* relations constitute their *relata* for what they are. 'Married' comes easily to one's mind: John and Mary are husband and wife only because of their mutual relation. More formally, if an individual x has a predicate ϕ which is such that, by virtue of having ϕ, x necessarily has a relation R to at least another individual y, then R is an internal relation of x.[13] Could this provide the right approach?

Not yet. Unfortunately, as E. G. Moore showed, internal relations seem to supervene on their *relata* and further qualify them. Mary and John did not come into existence by getting married; they only acquired a new contingent property, their marital status, after their wedding. If one wants to defend the logical priority of internal relations over their *relata*, then one must show much more, namely that the essential properties of the objects in question depend on some more fundamental internal properties. And this is arguably very difficult.

Difficult but not impossible. For there is a significant exception, a case that is ontologically more fundamental than the case in which the essence of the *relata* is in question. This is the (internal) relation of *difference*, which constitutes its *relata*.

---

[12] The objection is expounded in Psillos (1999), (2001), (2004); its strength is fully acknowledged in French and Ladyman (2003b); Morganti (2004) reviews some replies.

[13] This was the basis of the classic debate on internal vs external relations between Bradley and Moore, with the former arguing that ultimately all relations are necessarily internal, and the latter trying to show that this position can be defended only on the basis of a confusion concerning the scope of the modalities involved.

The relation of difference seems a precondition for any other relation and hence for any process of knowledge. *Relata* as merely *differentiated* entities and nothing else (at least not yet) are possible only because there is a relation of initial, ontological difference in the first place. They can be understood as epistemically (still) indistinguishable but (already) ontically distinctly-existing *differentiae*, to follow French (2003). Let us consider what a completely undifferentiable entity *x* might be. It would be one unobservable and unidentifiable at any possible LoA. Modally, this means that there would be no possible world in which *x* would exist. And this simply means that there is no such *x*. Call this the modified Leibnizian principle of *the necessary inexistence of the logically undifferentiable*. The principle still says very little about the nature of the objects/ *relata* in question, but one may argue that there is finally a clear sense in which *relata* are logically preceded by a fundamental internal relation of difference. Difference is our Ur-relation.[14]

Well, not so fast. Describing the relation of difference as an Ur-relation may make things clearer but it does not make them less controversial. On the contrary, the argument just sketched would be much weaker if it did not rely on a classic fallacy, namely an unqualified use of universal quantification. One considers Everything (Bradley would have called it the Absolute) and wonders what this Everything would be like if all differences were erased, i.e. if Everything were identical to Everything else. A similar universe would be a universe in which no individual could exist and nothing could happen, for example, although it would not have to be an empty universe. Imagine a toy universe constituted by a two-dimensional, boundless, white surface. Anything like this toy universe is a paradoxical fiction that only a sloppy use of logic can generate. For example, where is the observer in this universe? Would the toy universe include (at least distinguishable) points? Would there be distances between these points? The answers should be in the negative, for this is a universe without relations. Perhaps it is not true that there are *relata* that are logically prior to their relations, but we should be wary of the fallacious nature of any unqualified universalization.

There seems to be some truth in the last reply, leading to a sort of truce. Nobody should quantify without restriction or qualifications, no matter whether on *relata* or on relations. At the fundamental level where *relata* appear as bare *differentiae de re*, it makes little sense to talk of logical priority. Like the two playing cards that can stand up only by supporting each other or not at all, ultimately the relation of difference and the *relata* it constitutes appear logically inseparable. Difference and the differentiated are like the two sides of the same sheet of paper: they come together or not at all. So it is more reasonable to accept that, ultimately, basic entities and structures, *relata* and relations, simply co-exist as a package: they make each other possible and one cannot choose which one to have: it is all or nothing.

---

[14] Note that this is the other side of the Fregean problem of identity statements discussed in *Sinn und Bedeutung*.

So the conclusion is perhaps weaker. It may not be true that a relation of difference is logically prior to the *relata* that it differentiates. Luckily, we can leave the question unanswered because the package hypothesis is all that is needed; it is already enough for our strategy that the logical rank of the most basic relation of difference is not necessarily higher than the logical rank of the most basic *relata*. It is not true that all *relata* are logically prior to relations. This much has been granted and this much suffices.

Unsurprisingly, this was also Eddington's conclusion:

The relations unite the *relata*; the *relata* are the meeting points of the relations. The one is unthinkable apart from the other. I do not think that a more general starting-point of structure could be conceived' (Eddington (1928), pp. 230–231, quoted in French (2003), 233).

It makes sense. In terms of naïve ontology, we may define roads as what connects roundabouts, yet the latter are not less real (and dangerous, or safe, and so forth) just because they are the meeting points of the roads they connect. On a more sophisticated and much smaller scale, Esfeld (2004) has built on quantum entanglement to argue in favour of

replacing [in quantum physics] a metaphysics of intrinsic properties with a [moderate] metaphysics of relations. [. . .] A metaphysics of relations is often dismissed out of hand, for it seems to be paradoxical. It seems that (a) relations require relata, that is, things which stand in the relations, and that (b) these things have to be something in themselves, that is, must have intrinsic properties over and above the relations in which they stand. However, a metaphysics of relations merely has to reject the second part of this claim: one can maintain that (a) relations require relata, that is, things which stand in the relations, but that (b*) these things do not have any intrinsic properties that underlie the relations in which they stand. There is nothing paradoxical in this latter claim.

The idea seems to be that relata without relations are possible but intrinsically anonymous. I shall return to this point in the conclusion. If even a weaker position such as Eddington's—the package hypothesis—is convincing, and I think it is, OSR should be granted full plausibility. For example, a similar moderate approach to the relata vs. relations issue has been defended in the philosophy of physics by Esfeld and Lam (2008), who argue that

objects and relations (structure) are on the same ontological footing, with the objects being characterized only by the relations in which they stand.

15.4 Third step: The concept of a structural object is not empty

Plausible, however, does not mean applicable. Even if ESR and OSR are compatible, and even if it is true that, ultimately, structured *relata* are not necessarily logically prior to all structural relations, one still lacks a clear grasp of what these structural objects might be like, even if indirectly or metatheoretically. What if they are merely conceivable fictions or just *impossibilia*? In either case, they would be perhaps harmless but certainly inapplicable speculations, philosophically useless.

They are not. A straightforward way of making sense of these structural objects is as *informational objects*, that is, as cohering clusters of *data*, not in the alphanumeric sense of the word, but in an equally common sense of *differences de re*, i.e. mind-independent, concrete points of lack of uniformity. Some clarifications are in order.

It might be recalled that in chapter four I argued that, in its simplest form, a datum can be reduced to just a lack of uniformity, that is, a binary difference, like the presence and the absence of a black dot, or a change of state, from there being no black dot at all to there being one. Admittedly, a datum is usually classified, in our folk ontology of chairs and pens, as the relatum exhibiting the anomaly. This is often so because the relatum exhibiting the anomaly is perceptually more conspicuous or subjectively less redundant than the other relatum, seen as a background condition. However, the relation of difference is binary and symmetric. In the example, the white sheet of paper is a constitutive part of the datum itself, together with the fundamental relation of inequality that couples it with the dot. In this specific sense, nothing is a datum *per se*, without its counterpart, just as nobody can be a wife without there being a husband. It takes two to make a datum. So, ontologically, data (as still unqualified, concrete points of lack of uniformity) are purely relational entities. Of course, from a structural perspective, they remain unknowable in themselves. In this technical sense, one never deals epistemically with pure data but only with somewhat interpreted data, what I have defined as *content*. Now, cohering clusters of data as relational entities (differences *de re*) are the elementary *relata* we are looking for in our modified version of OSR. Thus, the structuralism in question here is based on relational entities (understood structurally) that are *particular*, not on 'patterns' that are abstract and universal (this distinction is carefully analysed by Reck and Price (2000); it is parallel to the difference between Poincaré's and Russell's approaches to structures respectively). These relational entities are unknowable not because they are somehow mysteriously unreachable, but because their epistemic malleability is *inexhaustible* (I shall return to this point in section 15.7).

All this is not entirely novel. As French (2001) points out, in the context of the philosophy of physics,

> if we want to continue to talk, in everyday language, about electrons as objects—because we lack the logico-linguistic resources to do otherwise—then we can do so 'only indirectly', '. . . not insofar as they themselves, as individuals, are given, but so far as they are describable as 'points of intersection' of certain relations' (Cassirer, *ibid.*). And this relational conception of an object is taken straight from Kant himself: 'All we know in matter is merely relations . . . but among these relations some are self-subsistent and permanent, and through these we are given a determinate object.' (Kant, quoted on p. 182)

The informational view of structural objects can be further clarified by considering the following objection. What could an informational version of OSR look like, not just in some logically possible way, but 'metaphysically seriously', as Bloomfield (2005) quite rightly requires when chastising Chalmers' modal laxity? After all, if informational/structural objects are mere logical *possibilia* this explains why one can do some fancy mathematics with them, but not much more. However, serious metaphysics should be *applicable* to the real world and *scalable* (more on this shortly) from sub-observables to observables, that is, it needs to be *usable* when dealing with the macroworld of everyday life and experience, so that it may become *useful* in other philosophical contexts, not only in epistemology, but also in ethics, in the philosophy of mind, or in the philosophy of language. In a nutshell, the objection is that an ontology of structural objects as informational entities may be logically viable, but seems to lack both seriousness and scalability (see below).

Answering this twofold objection requires a clarification, and I hope the reader won't mind if we borrow some more technical vocabulary from computer science.

We have seen that an ontology is a conceptualization of a system under analysis, made possible (the conceptualization, that is) by an LoA, and that it is embedded in the model of the system. An ontology may satisfy different specifications, such as experiential or commonsensical realism and resilience to scientific tests and discoveries. In particular, from a methodological point of view, the *generality* of an ontology is a function of its *portability*, *scalability*, and *interoperability*.

Portability refers to the ease with which a piece of software or a file format can be 'ported', i.e. made to run on a new platform and/or to compile with a new compiler. For example, assembly code is the least portable type of language, since it is specific to one particular (family of) processor(s). Using this concept for our theoretical purposes, it is clear that the lower the LoA, the less portable the corresponding model is. This means that an ontology is increasingly portable the more general it can be. The most portable ontology would be one that could be made to 'run' in any possible world. This is what Aristotle meant by a general metaphysics of Being *qua* Being. The portability of an ontology is a function of its importability and exportability between theories even when they are disjoined (the LoAs have no observables in common). Imagine an ontology that successfully accounts for the natural numbers and for natural kinds. I shall return to this point in section 15.6, when discussing objection 10.

Scalability refers to how well a solution to some problem will work when the complexity or magnitude of the problem increases. In our context, the scalability of an ontology is a function of its successful applicability independently of the vertical granularity and the horizontal scope of hierarchically nested or overlapping theories (the LoAs share at least one typed variable) and their corresponding systems. Imagine an ontology that successfully accounts not only for Schrödinger's cat but also for the atomic particles dangerously decaying in its proximity.

Finally, *interoperability* refers to the ability of software and hardware on multiple machines from multiple vendors to communicate and interact successfully. *Mutatis mutandis*, the interoperability of an ontology is a function of its capacity of allowing interactions between different theories. Imagine an ontology that successfully accounts for a system modelled as a brain and as a mind.

Obviously, these three specifications are interdependent. High portability, scalability, and interoperability guarantee increasing context-independence and seamless integration of models into a unified world view. An ontology that is highly portable, scalable, and interoperable is an ontology that can be applied to a variety of possible worlds, at a variety of degrees of complexity and that allows a variety of theories that adopt it to interact with each other successfully. We are now ready to define a specific metaphysics as an ontology with fixed degrees of portability, scalability, and interoperability: there is Descartes's metaphysics and Spinoza's, Leibniz's and Hume's, David Lewis's and Armstrong's, and each will have its own degrees of portability, scalability, and interoperability.

It has become common to acknowledge that both physics (Chakravartty (2003), Saunders (2003)) and mathematics (Brink and Rewitzky (2002), Shapiro (2004)) underdetermine metaphysics. This may be cause for despair in some sceptical quarters, for some sort of 'anything goes' thesis may seem inevitable. But it may also be interpreted, more optimistically, as a green light for a purely philosophical approach. I share the latter view. Metaphysical questions are intrinsically open (cannot be answered either by experiments or by calculations, to put it bluntly, they are a matter of informed exchange of rational arguments, see chapter two) and, as far as structural realism is concerned, evaluating the ontological commitment of a theory is philosophical business. So let us return to the general characterization of a metaphysical position.

A metaphysics may be criticized, philosophically, for being *local* whenever its degrees of portability, scalability, and interoperability are just local maxima. For example, a Cartesian metaphysics is notoriously undermined by its poor degree of interoperability: the mind/body dualism generates a mechanistic physics and a non-materialist philosophy of mind that do not interact very well. Leibniz's metaphysics of monads is not easily scalable (it is hard to account for physical macro-objects in its terms). Indeed, a metaphysics may be so local as to be peripheral, i.e. usable only within a possible world that is constituted by it. Imagine the ontology of *The Lord of the Rings*.

Now, as a metaphysics, one of the greatest strengths of OSR is its portability between physical and mathematical theories. This is to be expected, given its connection with the philosophy of quantum physics. Mathematics is the common language that helps to explain structural objects group-theoretically, as in Weyl and Cassirer, for example, or set-theoretically—in terms of partial structures, as in Ladyman (1998) and in da Costa and French (2003), or of quasi-structures, as in Krause (2005)—or categorically, as suggested again by Krause (2005). To use Cassirer's phrase, it has been a long time since mathematics moved from substance to function.

Moreover, the portability of OSR between physical and mathematical theories helps to explain why mathematics is so successfully applicable to a structurally interpreted physical world. Indeed, the degree of portability is such that even the problems are similar. As Reck and Price (2000) have highlighted, there is a variety of structuralisms in the philosophy of mathematics and Carter (forthcoming) shows that some of the basic issues arising in the development of structuralist philosophies of physics, especially those concerning the ontology of individuality and the semantics of re-identification, bubble up in the structuralist philosophies of mathematics as well.

All this reinforces the point that an ontology of structural objects is possible (read: logically consistent), but it does not yet remove all doubts about its seriousness, since OSR may still be metaphysically too local and lack scalability.

This is where an informational approach turns out to be a further strength. An ontology of structural objects is portable to computer science as well, and while mathematics guarantees consistency, computer science facilitates scalability. Simply put, micro- and macro-objects are analysable as informational objects that satisfy OSR specifications. To see more precisely how, let us turn to an instructive example provided by the methodology of *Object Oriented Programming* (OOP; Rumbaugh (1991)).

OOP is a method of programming that changed the approach to software development. A program used to be viewed as an algorithmic procedure that takes input data, processes it, and produces output data. The difficulty was then represented by the elaboration of the algorithmic process. OOP shifted the focus from the logic procedures, required to manipulate the objects, to the objects that need to be manipulated. Consider a pawn in a chess game. Its identity is not determined by its contingent properties as a physical body, including its shape and colour. Rather, a pawn is a well-defined cluster of specific *states* (properties like white or black, and its strategic position on the board) and determined *behavioural rules* (it can move forward only one square at a time, but with the option of two squares on the first move; it can capture other pieces only by a diagonal, forward move; and it can be promoted to any piece except a king when it reaches the opposite side of the board), which in turn are possible only in relation to other pieces and the logical space of the board. For a player, the actual pawn is only a placeholder, whereas the real pawn is an 'informational object'. It is not a material thing but a set of typed variables, using the LoA terminology, or a mental entity, to put it in Berkeley's terms, or an entity constituted by a bundle of properties, to use a Humean expression. Its existence and nature is determined by the differences and nomological relations that characterize the game of chess. The physical placeholder can be replaced by a cork without any semantic loss at the LoA required by the game. Indeed, a player may not even need a physical placeholder at all. Now in OOP, *data structures* (e.g. the pawn's property of being white) and their *behaviour* (programming code, e.g. the pawn's power to capture pieces only by moving diagonally forward) are packaged together as informational objects. Discrete objects are self-contained collections of data structures and computational procedures. They are grouped in a hierarchy of classes (e.g. pawns), with each class inheriting characteristics from the class above it (e.g. all pieces but the king can be captured, so every pawn can be captured). A class is a named representation for an abstraction, where an abstraction is a named collection of attributes and behaviour relevant to modelling a given entity for some particular purpose at a certain LoA. The routines or logic sequences that can manipulate the objects are called *methods*. A method is a particular implementation of an operation, i.e. an action or transformation that an object performs or is subject to by a certain class. Objects communicate with each other through well-defined interfaces called *messages*.

There is no need to add further details. Clearly, OOP provides us with a rich description of informational objects that can be used to *conceptualize* a structural object as a combination of both data structure and behaviour in a single entity, and a system as a collection of discrete structural objects. Given the flexibility of the conceptualization, it becomes perfectly possible, indeed easy, to approach the macroworld of everyday experience in a structural-informational way.

All this does not mean that we can overstep the limits of our structural knowledge of reality set by ESR. Recall that all we are assuming to be in the world are informational objects as the conditions of possibility of those structures that our first-order LoAs allow us to know and to attribute to the world in the first place. Thus, OOP is not a philosophical ontology but a practical example of a valuable methodology that can clarify the nature of our ontological components and prove their scalability.

OOP is only a good example of how the concept of informational object provides a useful way to conceptualize precisely the *relata* described as structural objects by OSR. Once again, it is reassuring to see that all this too is not a complete novelty. Dennett (1991), for example, argues that macro-objects are patterns and that the existence of a pattern as a real object depends on the usefulness of the theories—especially their explanatory power and reliability in making predictions—that admit that pattern in their ontology. One may say that Informational Structural Realism (ISR) introduces a more flexible and powerful methodology to clarify and make precise Dennett's 'pattern-like' objects.[15] A computational approach (e.g. the methodology of Object Oriented Programming) can do for the scalability of a structural ontology what category or group theory can do for its portability. So ISR is perfectly applicable.

15.5 Informational structural realism

The time has come to summarize the proposed solution to the ontological challenge to SR introduced in section 15.1.

Informational structural realism (ISR) is a version of SR. As a form of realism, ISR is (0-order) committed to the existence of a mind-independent reality addressed by and constraining our knowledge. Like ESR, ISR supports LoAs that carry a minimal ontological commitment in favour of the structural properties of reality. Like OSR, ISR also supports LoAs that carry a reflective, equally minimal, ontological commitment in favour of structural objects. Unlike ESR and OSR, ISR supports an informational interpretation of these structural objects. The second commitment (in favour of

---

[15] I owe this insight to Wallace (2003).

structural relata) is justified by epistemic reasons. We are allowed to commit ourselves ontologically to whatever minimal conception of objects is useful to make sense of our first commitment in favour of structures. The first commitment answers the question 'what can we know?'; the second commitment answers the question 'what can we safely assume to be there (in the outside world)?'. We are now ready for a definition:

ISR Explanatorily, instrumentally and predictively successful models (especially, but not only, those propounded by scientific theories) at a given LoA can be, in the best circumstances, increasingly informative about the relations that obtain between the (possibly sub-observable) informational objects that constitute the system under investigation (through the observable phenomena).

A significant consequence of ISR is that, as far as we can tell, the ultimate nature of reality is informational, that is, it makes sense to adopt LoAs that commit our theories to a view of reality as mind-independent and constituted by structural objects that are neither substantial nor material (they might well be, but we have no need to suppose them to be so) but informational. This allows IRS to reconcile two metaphysical views in the philosophy of information favourable to the proto-physical nature of information, Wiener's and Wheeler's (see chapter four).

When Cassirer talked about structuralism, he had in mind, like Kant and Russell earlier and Maxwell later, a full-blooded ontology of objects as structural entities (see for example the quotation from French in the previous section). ISR seeks to fulfil this role. Of course, if an ontology of informational objects is scalable to the macroworld, then it should be applicable to the folk ontology of cars and chairs and usable within other philosophical contexts. There is no space to show here how well ISR can pass this test, but the interested reader is referred to some initial work in Floridi (1999a), (2003b), (2008d), where ISR has already been shown to be a flexible and fruitful approach.

15.6 Ten objections and replies

The case in favour of ISR can now be reinforced by clearing the ground of some potential perplexities and objections.

Objection 1. One might wonder whether reconciling ESR and OSR really has any purpose. The objection is that ESR may be an appealing position, but it faces a serious objection (articulated by Psillos and Papineau), namely

 i. if restriction of beliefs to structural claims is really no restriction at all, then
 ii. ESR collapses into full-blown realism; therefore
 iii. ESR cannot provide a notion of continuity in science that avoids the pessimistic meta-induction; however
 iv. we want to retain the notion that structure is what is preserved successfully across otherwise radical theory change; so

v. we had better move to a notion of ontological structural realism in which structures directly represent reality; and we can be right about those structures. But then,

vi. from the beginning OSR conceded that the argument against ESR was compelling and sought to develop a notion of realism about structure that did not fall prey to the same argument; so

vii. why should OSR be interested in reconciling its view with ESR, when it has already been conceded that the latter is untenable?

viii. Conversely, if it is felt that adopting ESR is inconsistent with adopting OSR, then one first needs to overcome the objection that made it necessary to move to OSR in the first place.

The answer is that the objection is valid but unsound, as it starts from a false premise:

1. in order to hold the inference (i) → (ii), the objection needs to be serious about 'collapse', that is, it must mean that ESR is at least logically equivalent to full-blown realism (FBR), so that (ii) = (ESR ↔ FBR), which means that

2. (i) → (ESR ↔ FBR); but then

3. if (ESR ↔ FBR) is false, then

   a. either (i) is true, in which case the inference in (2) is invalid and anything can trivially follow from it;

   b. or (i) is false, but then anything can trivially follow from (i) itself;

in either case, the whole argument is valid but unsound. So the point becomes considering whether (ESR ↔ FBR) is false.

It is. If properly constructed, ESR cannot become equivalent to FBR both for theoretical reasons—for example, ESR rejects the possibility of knowledge of the intrinsic nature of objects in themselves, which is supported by FBR, so the two forms of realism have different scopes, with only ESR implementing 'Kantian humility'—and for metatheoretical reasons—since, if ESR could be reduced to FBR, then, *mutatis mutandis*, objections such as Newman's could be extended to FBR as well, an obvious *reductio*.

Once (i) → (ii) is dismissed, it becomes clear that (iii) cannot be held, since it depends on (ii). As for the inference (iv) → (v), it may be sound, but it is also uninteresting unless it is further constrained by (iii), that is, unless (iii) were true and hence ((iii) ∧ (iv)) → (v) were the case non-trivially, but we have seen that (iii) cannot be granted.

A supporter of the objection may retort that (vi)–(viii) still apply, independently of whether they follow from the premises, which could be mended or replaced.

The reply is that, once we take a more sceptical view of (2), the rest of the alleged reconstruction of the original dialectic between ESR and OSR becomes historically inaccurate and conceptually suspicious.

Regarding the historical inaccuracy, one needs to remember that OSR has emerged within the context of the debate on individuality in quantum mechanics (French and

Redhead (1988)) and that it is actually eliminativist OSR that runs the risk of becoming indistinguishable from a stronger form of scientific realism, which may then be unable to cope with the *Pessimistic Meta-Induction Argument* (see sections 15.1 and 15.2.1). So point (vi) cannot be granted as a faithful description of the current internal debate between ESR and OSR (see for example Morganti (2004)). Such debate is much more reliably interpreted by e.g. Ladyman (1998) and Votsis (forthcoming) in terms of a discussion concerning the ontological implications of SR. Moreover, even if (vi) were actually granted de facto in the literature, no structural realist should grant it *de jure*, because we have seen that (ESR ↔ FBR) is unjustified, and it appears even more evidently so from a SR-friendly perspective. Concerning (vii), there are no more reasons to raise the rhetorical question, since ESR is far from untenable, given that the inference in (2) is either invalid or valid but trivial. As for (viii), the whole point of section 15.2 is to show that ESR and OSR are not mutually inconsistent but may be reconciled, a point that now may be better appreciated as quite interesting. The objection should address not the value of the endeavour but, in this case, the validity of the arguments.

Regarding the suspicious nature of the objection, this is the interesting aspect mentioned above. The objection (mistakenly) assumes (2) to be uncontroversial in order to build a Trojan horse, as we have seen in section 15.1.1. However, the goal of the previous reconstruction is not really to wonder whether reconciling ESR and OSR is to any purpose—from an SR-friendly perspective it obviously is, witness the current debate— but rather to move an implicit attack against SR as a whole: for if ESR is untenable, then SR can be reduced to OSR, but then SR can be more easily defeated by showing that OSR is equally untenable because of its metaphysical consequences. Now, from a structuralist perspective, ESR is the strongest position, when it comes to resisting objections from without; but OSR is the most satisfactory, when it comes to settling internal debates. As I made explicit at the beginning, ISR is not an attempt to support SR directly, but to show that supporters of SR could successfully combine, by means of ISR, the strengths of both ESR and OSR in order to counterbalance any divide-and-rule strategy.

Objection 2. It may be objected that the definition of ESR, offered in section 15.1, is inconsistent with e.g. Grover Maxwell's conception of structural realism, for the latter would allow one-place predicates qualifying objects, if they were suitably perceptual, that is, it is only theoretical terms with dubious status—for the empiricist—that have to be replaced in the Ramsey sentence.

This objection provides the opportunity to clarify two points. First, the definition of ESR in section one is explicitly based on the neo-Kantian versions of SR endorsed by Cassirer, Russell and Poincaré, among others. The approach is arguably justified. Gower (2000), French (2001), Bitbol (2002), and Ryckman (2003), for example, provide well-supported reconstructions of structural realism from a transcendental perspective. The latter equates the nature of things-in-themselves with the first-order properties (monadic or unary relations) qualifying *noumena*. This is why the definition explicitly specifies that by '*first-order*, one-place predicates qualifying the objects *in themselves*' one is referring to '*the intrinsic nature of the noumena*' (note that the objection overlooks all the specifications in italics). In other words, the relations that are said to be unknowable, in the definition of ESR, are not the *n*-places relations subject to Ramseyfication mentioned by the objection, which are perfectly acceptable. This is the second point. The relations mentioned by the objection are the equivalent of phenomenal relations, in Kantian terms. So the definition is consistent with Maxwell's version of SR as well. This will become even more obvious in the reply to the next objection.

Objection 3. The previous objection leads to a further concern regarding the mixing of issues specific to philosophy of science and the epistemology of scientific theories with general issues in epistemology and metaphysics. This seems an unjustified confusion. For example, someone who may have genuine worries specifically about the epistemology of scientific theories may have no worries about epistemology in the broad sense, considering that it is only when things become unobservable that we begin to run into difficulties, and this seems a perfectly respectable position.

The objection is correct insofar as it argues that issues specific to the different fields in question do not have to be brought together, but it is mistaken in inferring that therefore they cannot or should not be combined, and that doing so may not be helpful but only confusing. Threading together issues in different contexts is not a problem per se. On the contrary, in the previous pages the strategy has been intentionally adopted in order to provide interdisciplinary depth and strength to the case for ISR. One can cast light on problems that have several dimensions only by analysing them from different perspectives, while leaving anyone free to maintain a more localized position, should she wish to do so. In the reply to Objection 2, for example, we have seen that it is important to understand carefully when one is speaking about relations as unknowable predicates of *noumena/relata* or as ordinary predicates in the language of a scientific theory or in any ordinary experience. In this respect, the new example provided by Objection 3 is equally enlightening. From a Kantian perspective, it is simply not true that we begin to run into philosophical difficulties only when unobservables are in question, not least because the scope of 'unobservable' is much wider. It is a scope inherited by several structural realists. For example, following Russell's version of structural realism, and hence assuming a neo-Kantian perspective, Maxwell (1968) remarks that 'all of the external world, including even our own bodies, is unobserved and unobservable' (p. 152). This reinforces the reply to the second objection, if necessary: Maxwell's conception of SR allows one-place predicates qualifying objects only insofar as the objects are not unobservable in the strong sense just seen, not in the sense that they are suitably perceptual, as alleged by the objection. Poincaré and Worrall endorse the same perspective: unobservable means noumenal, that is, epistemically inaccessible.[16] One may disagree with them. Indeed, throughout

---

[16] On this point see Votsis (forthcoming).

this chapter I have been careful not to adopt the same conceptual vocabulary, preferring to use sub-observable to refer to the usual unobservables as ordinarily understood in philosophy of science (this is also the reason why it is better to keep the comment on Maxwell's understanding of 'observable' separate from the previous objection). Yet one must also concede that, following their line of reasoning, it is natural to merge issues in epistemology with issues in the philosophy of science, metaphysical issues with issues concerning the ontological commitments of scientific theories. This is the Kantian approach that has been intentionally followed in this chapter as well, where scientific knowledge is taken to be only knowledge of a special kind.

Objection 4. A slightly different objection, related to the previous one, concerns the use of the term 'instrumentalism', which seems unclear. At points, instrumentalism is said to be a form of realism, but that is flatly incompatible with the notion of realism that is pertinent in philosophy of science (realism about scientific theories or entities). Evidently, a more general sense of realism is thus supposed to be in use.

The objection is correct: instrumentalism is said to be a form of realism in three cases, and in each case what is at stake is a very basic, minimal form of realism. However, this sense is neither unclear nor unusual. An instrumentalist may wish to claim that she is a realist insofar as she accepts 'the ontological thesis' of realism, namely that there is a mind-independent world. That this is a fairly common way of looking at instrumentalism is shown, for example, by Psillos (2000b), who, in a carefully argued defence of scientific realism, suggests, correctly, that what distinguishes scientific realism from instrumentalism is not 'The Metaphysical Thesis: the world has a definite and mind-independent structure' (which one must assume they both share, though Psillos is not explicit about this) but rather 'The Semantic Thesis: scientific theories should be taken at face-value'.

Objection 5. The 'Ockham' motivation for the move to structural objects at the second level is a crucial part of the argument in section 15.2.4, but it needs stronger motivation. The first level LoA is agnostic about the *relata* of its relations—it says that they are just things standing in some relations. Why is it then *simpler* to construe them structurally? At the first level, we have objects bearing relational properties; it is not clear that objects with monadic properties are a different *type* of objects, or that monadic predicates are more complicated than relational predicates.

The objection can be answered by dispelling two potential confusions on which it is based. The first is that, by talking of first- vs second-order LoAs one may be talking about first- vs second-order predicates (monadic or not). This is not the case, and indeed in 15.2.2 the precise formulation says '*derivative* or *metatheoretical*'. The second-order LoA, at which one may argue in favour of a structural understanding of *relata*, is a meta-level: it is related to the first-order LoA as a sentence p in English may be related to one in Italian that p is explaining. It has nothing to do with the sense in which first- and second-order is (justifiably but inappropriately) used in the objection. So the issue here is not monadic vs non-monadic predicates. The 'Ockhamist strategy' is first applied at the 'object-level' (nothing to do with 'level of objects', of course), where ESR is shown to provide the best alternative, and then is re-applied at a meta-level, where OSR is shown to provide the best alternative because it is the one that assumes the less demanding ontology for the *relata* in question. The distinction clarifies why the argument is explicitly described as *transcendental*, a label that would make no sense if first- and second-order were understood as the objection suggests, instead of levels of reflection.

The second potential confusion concerns the value of the 'Ockhamist strategy'. When, by reflecting on the conditions of possibility of ESR, we come to consider the possibility of OSR, we still do so economically, but the nature of the question has changed by moving up one level of reflection: instead of asking 'what can we know?', a question answered by ESR, we now ask 'what is the least that we can safely assume to be there in order for our acceptance of ESR to make sense?'. The latter is a question that pertains to OSR, which offers a structuralist analysis of entities as the least demanding approach consistent with the acceptance of ESR. Both strategies adopt Ockham's razor, but one in order to constrain one's commitment to the *number* of types of things in the world that are knowable (the doxastic scope discussed in the reply to Objection 1), and hence defend ESR; the other in order to constrain one's commitment to the possible *nature* of things in the world that would be consistent with the previous commitment, and hence defend OSR as supporting ESR.

Objection 6. Concerning the modified Leibnizian principle of the necessary inexistence of the logically undifferentiable, isn't there another counter-example to this proposed principle? What if we consider the world as a whole? There is nothing for it to be differentiated from, but it still exists.

The objection is correct in pointing out that a principle that held the necessary inexistence of the *undifferentiated* would be irreparably mistaken, for the counterexample would indeed apply. Yet this is irrelevant, for the principle endorsed in the chapter (as the objection itself indicates) holds the necessary inexistence of the *logically undifferentiable*. So the objection does not apply, since a world W as a whole would still be logically differentiable, even if it were actually undifferentiated, and it would be so not only with respect to any of its parts, but also to its negative counterpart, to a whole $\neg W$. The principle says that if something is logically undifferentiable, i.e. if it is logically impossible to differentiate it from anything else, then that something does not exist. This seems as safe (and perhaps as uncontroversial) as the indiscernibility of the identicals, not as controversial as the identity of the indiscernibles.

Objection 7. Concerning the toy universe, why can we not think of the white surface itself as an individual?

Perhaps we could, but so far nobody has been able to solve the problem of finding a principle of identification for something that, by definition, is undifferentiated, like our white surface. This is one of the main arguments used by Quine against second-order logic: we have no right to treat e.g. colours as individuals because we have no criteria to identify them as such. Things are even worse in our toy universe, where there is not even an external 'place' from which an observer can wonder about the identity criterion. So the reply is: no individuality without identifiability, and the toy universe is by definition constructed as unidentifiable.

Objection 8. The discussion concerning the concept of datum is problematic. We are told that '[A] datum can be reduced to just a lack of uniformity, that is, a binary difference'. Now, it seems that two distinct ideas are being run together here. First, a datum involves (i) a difference between (at least) two possible states of an entity and (ii) a background condition of readability. So a datum involves distinguishable (binary) differences, not just difference per se. But if so, it looks less clear that data will be the suitable entities for basic structural entities in OSR. The notion of datum outlined in this chapter seems to overplay the condition of readability as constituting the datum; this cannot be right.

The objection presents an epistemological conception of datum, based on 'readability', which would be acceptable in other contexts, but that is inappropriate here in order to understand the argument developed in favour of OSR and its basic structural entities. The concept of data employed here is as mere *differentiae de re*, that is, mind-independent, concrete points of lack of uniformity in the fabric of Being. These *differentiated* entities are epistemically (still) virgin but (already) ontically distinctly-existing. It is not a matter of vocabulary. Clearly, we are dealing with a stage that logically precedes the one described by the objection. The *relata*/data, as structural entities, do not yet require any background condition to be read, for they do not need to be read at all in order to subsist. If they did, OSR would be a version of absolute idealism, that is, it would reduce the existence of the external world to its epistemic condition of 'readability', something that is explicitly rejected. Indeed, at this initial stage, we do not even know whether the relata as differences *de re* may be so synchronically, in which case one could imagine them as two entities, or diachronically so, in which case one could imagine them as two states of the same entity. We can only guess, for the assumption is that these data/*relata* are noumenal, and we do not have access to them. This sense of datum as difference or inequality *de re* provides the condition of possibility of the sort of epistemological datum that is then described by the objection, but that is a further step. A step criticized by the following objection.

Objection 9. If a datum is a difference, then a datum is an abstract thing, as a difference is an abstract, rather than a concrete thing. But this raises a severe problem, if data are supposed to be the basic objects in our structural realism (assuming that this is supposed to be structural realism as a possible position in philosophy of science). For the structural objects need to be *concrete* things in the world (even if they are things structurally conceived), as they are the things that other concrete things are made from. You cannot make concrete things out of abstract things, so informational objects do not seem to be viable candidates for the objects in an ontological structural realism fit for the philosophy of science.

The reply to the objection can be articulated in three steps. First, it is true that no concrete things can come out of purely abstract things, at least not without presupposing some metaphysical superpower that science (and its philosophy) had better leave alone, if they can. However, no reason has been offered to justify the view that data, understood as *differentiae de re*, may not be as concrete as one's definition of 'concrete' may allow. Indeed, we have seen that Objection 8 goes exactly in the opposite direction, for it stresses that it is *insufficient* to consider data as concrete differences, since, still according to Objection 8, their conception must also include an epistemic component ('readability'). Now, the correct position is somewhere in between: as far as the argument in favour of ISR is concerned, data are neither purely epistemic (abstract) entities, as suggested by Objection 9, nor ontic (concrete) *differentiae de re* inseparably coupled to some epistemic component, as suggested by Objection 8. They are (or need to be treated as) ontic (concrete) differences that are *then* epistemically exploitable as resources, by agents like us, for their cognitive processes. After all, one should recall that the data/differences in question can be concrete because we do not have to assume something as radical and problematic as Leibniz's conception of monads: Eddington's package hypothesis (Ur-relata + Ur-relations) is sufficient to support OSR.

Second, it should therefore be clear that the interpretation of structural objects as informational objects is not meant to replace an ontology of concrete things with one of virtual entities. As specified, OOP provides us with an interesting example of how we may *conceptualize* structural objects and make sense of their ontology.

Third, by talking of concrete *differentiae de re*, and conceptualizing them as data structures and hence as informational objects, we are defending a version of structural realism that supports at least an irreducible, fundamental dualism, if not a Leibnizian pluralism, as the correct description of the ultimate nature of reality.

Objection 10. It is difficult to relate the comments on ontological commitment in section 15.2.3 to the comments in section 15.4. If a type of ontological commitment is associated with a particular choice of LoA, then how is it possible to port ontology from one LoA to a disjoint one? Moreover, the treatment of informational objects and ontology makes it hard to see what work the appeal to Object Oriented Programming is doing.

The objection raises several issues. First, the connection between 15.2.3 and 15.2.4 is the following: it is possible to reconcile ESR and OSR by showing that they work at different LoAs, but OSR still faces the problem of providing an ontology that may be applied both to sub-observable and to observable objects, if possible. In 15.2.4, it is shown that, by translating structural objects into informational objects, this can be achieved in a way that is both efficient and elegant.

Second, the same question about portability could be asked in computer science, where the answer is that a piece of software p is portable from platform A to platform B if there is a compiler for p both for A and for B, even when A and B are completely different (disjoint). An ontology is portable from an LoA_x to another LoA_y (even when they are disjoint) if there is one or more LoA_z that can translate the ontology from one to the other. For example, it has been argued that Kripke's view of rigid designators is based on an ontology that is 'portable' to Aristotle's view of substances.

Third, the appeal to OOP is that it provides an intuitive example of a well-defined method to clarify how one may conceptualize structural objects as informational objects. A unified ontology, scalable from the sub-observable to the observable, has an added value, with respect to localist ontologies: it does not have to assume some radical dichotomy between fields of knowledge. We have rejected the Greek (large scale) distinction between sub-lunar and celestial physics/ontology, and it would be better not to reintroduce it at the (small scale) level of observable vs. unobservable worlds. ISR does support a Kantian-style dualism between knowable and unknowable, and at least a dualist, if not a pluralist metaphysics, but not a dualism in terms of ultimately irreconcilable ontologies for utterly different fields of knowledge.

Finally, a further general advantage of an informational approach to structural realism is that one is able to practice what one preaches, that is, use informational concepts to develop and defend an informational approach.

CONCLUSION

At least since Plato's images of the line and of the cave, philosophers have often relied on spatial analogies to explain their theories. References to rooms are particularly popular. Sextus Empiricus thought that we are like people in a dark room, searching for gold or shooting at a target: no matter how long the search or the shooting proceeds, it is pointless because in principle there is no way to establish whether any of us has found a nugget or hit the mark (*Outlines of Pyrrhonism* I.52 and II.325). Turing used different rooms for his famous test and Searle devised a Chinese room for his counterexample. I shall rely on their examples and suggest a double box analogy to illustrate ISR. But first, a final bit of terminology.

In software engineering, *black-box* refers to a test-design method that focuses on testing functional or behavioral requirements of a program. The methodology treats the *analysandum* as a completely opaque and closed system, avoiding using explicit knowledge of its internal nature or structure to understand the way it works. The opposite methodology is known as *white-box* test design. This allows one to 'look inside' the system, and it focuses on using specific and detailed knowledge of the program code to guide the selection of test data. A *grey-box* approach is one that allows only a partial view of the internal properties of the system.

According to ISR, any white-box approach to reality is excluded in principle, given the LoA-mediated nature of knowledge. Forget about getting out of Plato's cave. There is no God's eye perspective from without. We look at the world as if we were in

Sextus' dark room. This is the first box. We are inside it, but our goal is not mimetic, nor are our (often *causal*) *interactions* with the furniture in the room unidirectional, as Sextus assumed. Unlike Sextus', ours is only a grey-box. In the best cases, it allows the reconstruction of the structural properties relating the furniture of the room, i.e. our informational objects. These are our second kind of boxes. As in Turing's test, they are black-boxes, not directly knowable, but 'epistemically interactable' through LoAs. Sometimes, we can indirectly capture their nature by observing their behaviour and mutual interactions, but we do not know their intrinsic properties. How we relate them and use them to build other black-boxes is our responsibility. This is the right context in which to talk about a demiurgic power (Floridi and Sanders (2005)). ISR takes our epistemic goal to be *constructionist* (mind, not *constructivist* in any psychologistic or 'sociologistic' sense), not mimetic. Knowledge is not a matter of either (a) discovering and describing, or (b) inventing and constructing, but of (c) designing and modelling reality, its features and behaviours into a meaningful world as we experience it (semanticization). And one may design and model successfully even in the dark. Intelligibility is the name of the epistemic game, and humanity tries to achieve it at any cost, even when this means distorting reality in the most absurd way, from the conception of a flat earth placed at the centre of the universe to the interpretation of natural forces and events as anthropomorphic divinities or to the assumption of calories, phlogiston, and luminiferous ether. Since we wish to devise an intelligible conceptual environment for ourselves, we do so not by trying to picture or photocopy whatever is in the room (mimetic epistemology),[17] but by interacting with it as a *resource* for our semantic tasks, interrogating it through experience, tests, and experiments. Reality in itself is not a source but a resource for knowledge. Structural objects (clusters of data as relational entities) work epistemologically like *constraining affordances*: they allow or invite certain constructs (they are *affordances* for the information organisms that elaborate them) and resist or impede some others (they are *constraints* for the same organisms), depending on the interaction with, and the nature of, the information system that processes them. They are exploitable by a theory, at a given LoA, as input of adequate queries to produce information (the model) as output. This epistemic malleability of reality as a resource seems to be what Chakravartty (2003) defines as the 'dispositional nature' of structural objects[18] and Saunders (2003) calls their 'heuristic plasticity'. Transforming constraining affordances into information need not be a metaphysically violent business (as Bacon thought it might), if reality in itself is indeed indeterminate (Rosen and Smith (2004)) or if we are ready to be led by it insofar as it is determinate. From this perspective, semantic concerns (most importantly reference, representation

---

[17] Suárez (2003) provides a series of arguments and references against what I have called here mimetic epistemology.

[18] Apparently David Lewis held a similar view, see R. Langton (2004).

and truth[19]) belong to the relation among models, that is, among outcomes of LoAs (Kant's phenomenal world of experience), not to the relation between models and reality in itself.[20]

It turns out that we are like Turing's interrogator, since the model of investigation is erotetic: we have indirect (LoA-mediated) access to reality and can query it as a database. Bacon and Galilei shared a similar view. But since our task is not to find out who is who, we resemble Searle in his Chinese room: we get the input on one side and output information on the other. The difference, in this case, is that we have some understanding of the rules of the game. It makes little sense to ask whether the factual information we gain resembles its source. The Parthenon is as concrete and objective as anyone may wish it to be, but it does not represent marble. Knowing reality is interpreting it constructively, not portraying it passively.

So the basic idea behind ISR is quite simple: we are inforgs dealing with black-boxes inside a grey-box. The last specification to be added is that these qualifications are LoA-dependent, in the same way as the distinction between being a system and being a component or unit of a system is. A black-box may be opened, but opening it transforms it into a grey-box, in which more black-boxes may be found. Whether ad infinitum we simply cannot know. It might be Russian dolls (informational objects) all the way in.

---

[19] Van Fraassen (2006a) seems to be sharing a similar view on truth as a relation between models.

[20] This seems to me the point of convergence between ISR and the position expressed by French and Saatsi (2006).

References

Adler, M. 1979, 'Has Philosophy Lost Contact with People?', *Long Island Newsday*, 18 November.

Adriaans, P., and van Benthem, J. F. A. K. (eds) 2008, *Philosophy of Information*, Handbook of the Philosophy of Science, vol. 8 (Amsterdam; London: North-Holland).

Ahlswede, R., Cai, N., Li, S.-Y. R., and Wai-Ho Yeung, R. 2000, 'Network Information Flow', *IEEE Transactions on Information Theory*, 46(4), 1204–1216.

Ahuja, R. K., Magnanti, T. L., and Orlin, J. B. 1993, *Network Flows: Theory, Algorithms, and Applications* (Englewood Cliffs, NJ: Prentice Hall).

Aisbett, J., and Gibbon, G. 1999, 'A Practical Measure of the Information in a Logical Theory', *Journal of Experimental and Theoretical Artificial Intelligence*, 11(2), 201–218.

Allen, C. 2009, 'Animal Consciousness', in Edward N. Zalta, ed., *The Stanford Encyclopedia of Philosophy*, Spring 2009 edn, <*http://plato.stanford.edu/archives/spr2009/entries/consciousness-animal/*>.

Allo, P. 2005, 'Being Informative: Information as Information Handling', in K.-D. Althoff, A. Dengel, R. Bergmann, M. Nick, and T. Roth-Berghofer, eds, *Wm2005: Professional Knowledge Management Experiences and Visions* (Kaiserslautern: DFKI Gmbh), 579–586.

Allo, P. forthcoming, 'The Logic of "Being Informed" Revisited and Revised'.

Alston, W. 1971, 'Varieties of Privileged Access', *American Philosophical Quarterly*, 8, 223–241.

Alston, W. 1986, 'Epistemic Circularity', *Philosophy and Phenomenological Research*, 47, 1–30.

Anderson, A. R. (ed.) 1964, *Minds and Machines* (Englewood Cliffs: Prentice-Hall).

Apel, K. O. 1975, 'The Problem of Philosophical Fundamental-Grounding in Light of a Transcendental Pragmatic of Language', *Man and World*, (8), 239–275.

Arbib, M. A. 1989, *The Metaphorical Brain 2: Neural Networks and Beyond* (New York; Chichester: Wiley).

Armstrong, D. M. 1968, *A Materialist Theory of the Mind* (London: Routledge & Kegan Paul).

Armstrong, D. M. 1993, *A Materialist Theory of the Mind*, 2nd edn (London: Routledge).

Armstrong, D. M. 1997, *A World of States of Affairs* (Cambridge: Cambridge University Press).

Artemov, S., and Nogina, E. 2005, 'On Epistemic Logic with Justification', in Ron van der Meyden, ed., *Proceedings of the 10th conference on Theoretical Aspects of Rationality and Knowledge, Singapore* = (National University of Singapore), 279–294.

Audi, R. (ed.) 1999, *The Cambridge Dictionary of Philosophy* (Cambridge: Cambridge University Press).

Aumann, R. J. 1976, 'Agreeing to Disagree', *Annals of Statistics*, 4(6), 1236–1239.

Austin, J. L. 1950, 'Truth', in J. O. Urmson and G. J. Warnock, eds, *Philosophical Papers* (Oxford: Oxford University Press), 117–133.

Baillie, J. C. 2004, 'Grounding Symbols in Perception with Two Interacting Autonomous Robots', *Proceedings of the Fourth International Workshop on Epigenetic Robotics: Modeling Cognitive Development in Robotic Systems*, Genoa, Italy, 107–110.

Ball, P. 2002, June 3, 'Universe Is a Computer', in *Nature News*. doi:10.1038/news020527–16

Baltag, A., and Moss, L. S. 2004, 'Logics for Epistemic Programs', *Synthese*, 139(2), 165–224.

Bar-Hillel, Y. 1964, *Language and Information: Selected Essays on Their Theory and Application* (Reading, Mass.; London: Addison-Wesley).

Bar-Hillel, Y., and Carnap, R. 1953, 'An Outline of a Theory of Semantic Information' repr. in Bar-Hillel (1964), 221–274.

Barklund, J. 1995, 'Metaprogramming in Logic', in A. Kent and J. G. Williams, eds, *Encyclopedia of Computer Science and Technology* (New York: Marcel Dekker), vol. xxxiii, 205–227.

Barklund, J., Costantini, S., Dell'Acqua, P., and Lanzarone, G. A. 2000, 'Reflection Principles in Computational Logic', *Journal of Logic and Computation*, 10(6), 743–786.

Barr, M., and Wells, C. 1999, *Category Theory for Computing Science*, 3rd edn (Montreal: CRM Press).

Barwise, J. 1988, *The Situation in Logic* (Stanford, Calif.: Center for the Study of Language and Information).

Barwise, J., and Etchemendy, J. 1987, *The Liar: An Essay on Truth and Circularity* (New York; Oxford: Oxford University Press).

Barwise, J., and Perry, J. 1983, *Situations and Attitudes* (Cambridge, Mass.: MIT Press).

Barwise, J., and Seligman, J. 1997, *Information Flow: The Logic of Distributed Systems* (Cambridge: Cambridge University Press).

Bateson, G. 1973, *Steps to an Ecology of Mind* (Frogmore, St. Albans: Paladin).

Bechtel, W., and Richardson, R. C. 1993, *Discovering Complexity: Decomposition and Localization as Strategies in Scientific Research* (Princeton: Princeton University Press).

Becker, O. 1930, 'Zur Logik Der Modalitaten', *Jahrbuch für Philosophie und phänomenologische Forschung*, 11, 497–548.

Bedau, M. 2003, 'Artificial Life', in Floridi (2003f), ch. 16.

Bell, J. S. 1987, 'The Theory of Local Beables', in *Speakable and Unspeakable in Quantum Mechanics: Collected Papers on Quantum Mechanics* (Cambridge: Cambridge University Press), 52–62.

Bell, S., and Wood-Harper, A. T. 1998, *Rapid Information Systems Development: A Non-Specialist's Guide to Analysis and Design in an Imperfect World*, 2nd edn (London: McGraw-Hill).

Benjamin, P., Erraguntla, M., Delen, D., and Mayer, R. 1998, 'Simulation Modeling and Multiple Levels of Abstraction', in D. J. Medeiros, E. F. Watson, J. S. Carson, and M. S. Manivannan, eds, *Proceedings of the 1998 Winter Simulation Conference* (Pistacaway, NJ: IEEEPress), 391–398.

Berkeley, G. 1710–1734, *A Treatise Concerning the Principles of Human Knowledge* (Oxford: Oxford University Press, 1998).

Berkeley, G. 1732, *Alciphron: Or the Minute Philosopher* (Edinburgh: 1948–57: Thomas Nelson). Vol. iii of *The Works of George Berkeley, Bishop of Cloyne*, ed. A. A. Luce and T. E. Jessop.

Billard, A., and Dautenhahn, K. 1999, 'Experiments in Learning by Imitation Grounding and Use of Communication in Robotic Agents', *Adaptive Behaviour*, 7, 411–434.

Bitbol, M. 2002, 'Jean-Louis Destouches' Transcendental Structuralism', *One-Day Worshop 'Structuralism in Twenty-Century Physics', University of Leeds, June 14.*

Block, N. 1995, 'On a Confusion About a Function of Consciousness', *Behavioral and Brain Sciences*, 18, 227–247.

Block, N. 1997, 'Anti-Reductionism Slaps Back', in J. E. Tomberlin, ed., *Philosophical Perspectives 11: Mind, Causation, and World* (Oxford; New York: Blackwell), 107–133.

Bloomfield, P. 2005, 'Let's Be Realistic About Serious Metaphysics', *Synthese*, 144(2), 69–90.

Boden, M. 1984, 'Methodological Links between Ai and Other Disciplines', in F. Machlup and V. Mansfield, eds, *The Study of Information: Interdisciplinary Messages* (New York: John Wiley and Sons), 125–132.

Boden, M. A. 1990, *The Philosophy of Artificial Intelligence* (Oxford: Oxford University Press).

Boden, M. A. (ed.) 1996, *The Philosophy of Artificial Life* (Oxford: Oxford University Press).

Bolter, J. D. 1984, *Turing's Man: Western Culture in the Computer Age* (London: Duckworth).

BonJour, L. 1985, *The Structure of Empirical Knowledge* (Cambridge, Mass.: Harvard University Press).

Boolos, G., Burgess, J. P., and Jeffrey, R. C. 2002, *Computability and Logic*, 4th edn (Cambridge: Cambridge University Press).

Borlund, P. 2003, 'The Concept of Relevance in Ir', *Journal of the American Society for Information Science and Technology*, 54 (10), 913–925.

Bowles, G. 1990, 'Propositional Relevance', *Informal Logic*, 90, 65–77.

Braman, S. 1989, 'Defining Information', *Telecommunications Policy*, 13, 233–242.

Brazier, F. M. T., and Treur, J. 1999, 'Compositional Modelling of Reflective Agents', *International Journal of Human-Computer Studies*, 50(5), 407–431.

Brazier, F. M. T., Treur, J., Wijngaards, N. J. E., and Willems, M. 1994, 'Formal Specification of Hierarchically (De)Composed Tasks', B. R. Gaines and M. A. Musen, eds, *Proceedings of the 9th Banff Knowledge Acquisition for Knowledge-based Systems workshop, KAW'95*, Calgary (SRDG Publications, Department of Computer Science, University of Calgary), 25/21–25/20.

Breazeal, C. 2000. 'Sociable Machines: Expressive Social Exchange between Humans and Robots', MIT Doctoral Thesis.

Breazeal, C. L. 2002, *Designing Sociable Robots* (Cambridge, Mass.; London: MIT Press).

Bremer, M., and Cohnitz, D. 2004, *Information and Information Flow: An Introduction* (Frankfurt; Lancaster: Ontos Verlag).

Bremer, M. E. 2003, 'Do Logical Truths Carry Information?', *Minds and Machines*, 13(4), 567–575.

Bringsjord, S. 1997, 'Consciousness by the Lights of Logic and Commonsense', *Behavioral and Brain Sciences*, 20, 144–146.

Bringsjord, S. 1999, 'The Zombie Attack on the Computational Conception of Mind', *Philosophy and Phenomenological Research*, 59(1), 41–69.

Brink, C., and Rewitzky, I. 2002, 'Three Dual Ontologies', *Journal of Philosophical Logic*, 31(6), 543–568.

Bromberger, S. 1966, 'Why-Questions', in Baruch A. Brody, ed., *Readings in the Philosophy of Science* (Englewood Cliffs: Prentice Hall), 66–84.

Brooks, R. 1990, 'Elephants Don't Play Chess', *Robotics and Autonomous Systems*, 6, 3–15.

Brooks, R. 1991, 'Intelligence without Representation', *Artificial Intelligence*, 47, 139–159.

Brown, H. C. 1916, 'Structural Levels in the Scientist's World', *The Journal of Philosohy, Psychology and Scientific Methods*, 13(13), 337–345.

Buckland, M. 1991, 'Information as Thing', *Journal of the American Society of Information Science*, 42(5), 351–360.

Burch, J. G., and Grudnitski, G. 1989, *Information Systems: Theory and Practice*, 5th edn (New York; Chichester: Wiley).

Burgin, M., and Kuznetsov, V. 1994, 'Scientific Problems and Questions from a Logical Point of View', *Synthese*, 100(1), 1–28.

Burkholder, L. 1992, *Philosophy and the Computer* (Boulder, Colo; Oxford: Westview).

Bynum, T. W. (ed.) 1985, *Computers and Ethics* (Oxford: Blackwell). This volume was published as the October 1985 issue of *Metaphilosophy*.

Bynum, T. W. 1998, 'Global Information Ethics and the Information Revolution'. This is published in Bynum and Moor (1998), 274–289

Bynum, T. W. 2000, 'A Very Short History of Computer Ethics', *APA Newsletters on Philosophy and Computers*, 99(2).

Bynum, T. W., and Moor, J. (eds) 1998, *The Digital Phoenix: How Computers Are Changing Philosophy* (Oxford: Blackwell).

Cangelosi, A. 2001, 'Evolution of Communication and Language Using Signals, Symbols and Words', *IEEE Transaction in Evolution Computation*, 5, 93–101.

Cangelosi, A., Greco, A., and Harnad, S. 2000, 'From Robotic Toil to Symbolic Theft: Grounding Transfer from Entry-Level to Higher-Level Categories', *Connection Science*, 12, 143–162.

Cangelosi, A., Greco, A., and Harnad, S. 2002, 'Symbol Grounding and the Symbolic Theft Hypothesis', in A. Cangelosi and D. Parisi, eds, *Simulating the Evolution of Language* (London: Springer), 191–210.

Cangelosi, A., and Harnad, S. 2001, 'The Adaptive Advantage of Symbolic Theft over Sensorimotor Toil: Grounding Language Perceptual Categories', *Evolution of Communication*, 4, 117–142.

Cao, T. Y. 2003, 'What Is Ontological Synthesis? A Reply to Simon Saunders', *Synthese*, 136(1), 107–126.

Carnap, R. 1935, *Philosophy and Logical Syntax* (London: Kegan Paul, Trench, Trubner & Co).

Carter, J. forthcoming, 'Identity between and Individuating Objects in Structures: A Problem for Structuralism?', *Synthese*.

Chaitin, G. 2003, 'Two Philosophical Applications of Algorithmic Information Theory', *Proceedings DMTCS'03: Springer Lecture Notes in Computer Science*, 2731, 1–10.

Chaitin, G. J. 2005, *Meta Math!: The Quest for Omega* (New York: Pantheon Books).

Chakravartty, A. 1998, 'Semirealism', *Studies in History and Philosophy of Science*, 29(3), 391–408.

Chakravartty, A. 2001, 'The Semantic or Model-Theoretic View of Theories and Scientific Realism', *Synthese*, 127(3), 325–345.

Chakravartty, A. 2003, 'The Structuralist Conception of Objects', *Philosophy of Science*, 70(5), 867–878.

Chalmers, D. online, *A Computational Foundation for the Study of Cognition* <http://www.u.arizona.edu/chalmers/papers/computation.html>.

Chalmers, D. J. 1992, 'Subsymbolic Computation and the Chinese Room', in J. Dinsmore, ed., *The Symbolic and Connectionist Paradigms: Closing the Gap* (Hillsdale: Lawrence Erlbaum), 25–48.

Chalmers, D. J. 1996, *The Conscious Mind: In Search of a Fundamental Theory* (New York: Oxford University Press).

Checkland, P. B., and Scholes, J. 1990, *Soft Systems Methodology in Action* (New York: John Wiley & Sons).

Chellas, B. F. 1980, *Modal Logic: An Introduction* (Cambridge: Cambridge University Press).

Chen, W.-K. 2003, *Net Theory and Its Applications: Flows in Networks* (London: Imperial College Press).

Cherry, C. 1978, *On Human Communication: A Review, a Survey, and a Criticism*, 3rd edn (Cambridge, Mass.; London: MIT Press).

Chisholm, R. M. 1989, *Theory of Knowledge*, 3rd edn (Englewood Cliffs: Prentice-Hall).

Choo, C. W., Detlor, B., and Turnbull, D. 2000, *Web Work: Information Seeking and Knowledge Work on the World Wide Web* (Dordrecht; Boston: Kluwer Academic Publishers).

Christiansen, M. H., and Chater, N. 1992, 'Connectionism, Meaning and Learning', *Connection Science*, 4, 227–252.

Churchland, P. S., and Sejnowski, T. J. 1992, *The Computational Brain* (Cambridge, Mass.; London: MIT Press).

Clancey, W. J. 1997, *Situated Cognition* (Cambridge: Cambridge University Press).

Cohen, J. 1994, 'Some Steps Towards a General Theory of Relevance', *Synthese*, 101, 171–185.

Cohen, P. R., Sutton, C., and Burns, B. 2002, 'Learning Effects of Robot Actions Using Temporal Associations', *2nd International Conference on Development and Learning*, 90–101.

Cointe, P. (ed.) 1999, *Meta-Level Architectures and Reflection, Second International Conference on Reflection* (Saint-Malo, France: Springer-Verlag).

Colburn, T. R. 2000a, 'Information, Thought, and Knowledge', *Proceedings of the World Multiconference on Systemics, Cybernetics and Informatics*, 467–471.

Colburn, T. R. 2000b, *Philosophy and Computer Science* (Armonk, N.Y.: M. E. Sharpe).

Cole, D. 2008, 'The Chinese Room Argument', Edward N. Zalta, ed., *The Stanford Encyclopedia of Philosophy*, Fall 2008 edn, <http://plato.stanford.edu/archives/fall2008/entries/chinese-room/>.

Conway, J. H., and Guy, R. K. 1996, *The Book of Numbers* (New York: Copernicus).

Cooper, W. S. 1971, 'A Definition of Relevance for Information Retrieval', *Information Storage and Retrieval*, 7, 19–37.

Copeland, B. J. 2003, 'Computation', in Floridi (2003f), 3–17.

Coradeschi, S., and Saffioti, A. 2003, 'An Introduction to the Anchoring Problem', *Robotics and Autonomous Systems*, 43, 85–96.

Corcoran, J. 1998, 'Information-Theoretic Logic', in C. Martínez, U. Rivas, and L. Villegas-Forero, eds, *Truth in Perspective: Recent Issues in Logic, Representation and Ontology* (Aldershot: Ashgate), 113–135.

Cormen, T. H., Leiserson, C. E., Rivest, R. L., and Stein, C. 2001, *Introduction to Algorithms*, 2nd edn (Cambridge, Mass.; London: MIT Press).

Costantini, S. 2002, 'Meta-Reasoning: A Survey', in A. C. Kakas and F. Sadri, eds, *Computational Logic: Logic Programming and Beyond: Essays in Honour of Robert A. Kowalski* (Springer-Verlag), 253–288.

Cover, T. M., and Thomas, J. A. 1991, *Elements of Information Theory* (New York; Chichester: Wiley).

Craig, E. 1990, *Knowledge and the State of Nature: An Essay in Conceptual Synthesis* (Oxford: Clarendon Press).

Craver, C. F. 2004, 'A Field Guide to Levels', *Proceedings and Addresses of the American Philosophical Association*, 77(3).

Craver, C. F. 2007, *Explaining the Brain: Mechanisms and the Mosaic Unity of Neuroscience* (Oxford; New York: Oxford University Press).

Crestani, F., Lalmas, M., Van Rijsbergen, C. J., and Campbell, I. 1998, 'Is This Document Relevant? . . . Probably: A Survey of Probabilistic Models in Information Retrieval', *ACM Computing Surveys*, 30(4), 528–552.

Crisp, T. M. 2000, 'Gettier and Plantinga's Revised Account of Warrant', *Analysis*, 60(265), 42–50.

Cruse, P., and Papineau, D. 2002, 'Scientific Realism without Reference', in M. Marsonet, ed., *The Problem of Realism* (Aldershot: Ashgate Publishing Company), 174–189.

D'Agostino, M., and Floridi, L. 2009, 'The Enduring Scandal of Deduction. Is Propositional Logic Really Uninformative?', *Synthese*, 167(2), 271–315.

da Costa, N. C. A., and French, S. 2003, *Science and Partial Truth: A Unitary Approach to Models and Reasoning in Science* (Oxford: Oxford University Press).

Dancy, J. 1985, An Introduction to Contemporary Epistemology (Oxford: Blackwell).

Dancy, J., and Sosa, E. (eds) 1992, *A Companion to Epistemology* (Oxford: Blackwell Reference).

Davidson, D. 1974, 'On the Very Idea of a Conceptual Scheme', *Proceedings and Addresses of the American Philosophical Association*, 47. Reprinted in *Inquiries into Truth and Representation* (Oxford: Clarendon Press, 1984), 183–198. All page numbers to the quotations in the text refer to the reprinted version.

Davidsson, P. 1993, 'Toward a General Solution to the Symbol Grounding Problem: Combining Machine Learning and Computer Vision', in *AAAI Fall Symposium Series, Machine Learning in Computer Vision: What, Why and How*, 157–161.

Davis, G. B., and Olson, M. H. 1985, *Management Information Systems: Conceptual Foundations, Structure, and Development*, 2nd edn (New York: McGraw-Hill).

Davison, A. C. 2003, *Statistical Models* (Cambridge: Cambridge University Press).

Debons, A., and Cameron, W. J. (eds) 1975, *Perspectives in Information Science: Proceedings of the Nato Advanced Study Institute on Perspectives in Information Science, Held in Aberystwyth, Wales, UK, August 13–24, 1973* (Leiden: Noordhoff).

Dedekind, R. 1963, 'Continuity and Irrational Numbers', in his *Essays on the Theory of Numbers* (New York: Dover), first essay. Originally published in 1872.

Deleuze, G., and Guattari, F. 1994, *What Is Philosophy?* (New York: Columbia University Press).

Delgrande, J. P., and Pelletier, J. 1998, 'A Formal Analysis of Relevance', *Erkenntnis*, 49(2), 137–173.

Demopoulos, W., and Friedman, M. 1985, 'Critical Notice: Bertrand Russell's the Analysis of Matter', *Philosophy of Science*, 52, 621–639.

Dennett, D. C. 1969, *Content and Consciousness* (London: Routledge & Kegan Paul).

Dennett, D. C. 1971, 'Intentional Systems', *The Journal of Philosophy*, (68), 87–106.

Dennett, D. C. 1986, *Content and Consciousness*, 2nd edn (London: Routledge & Kegan Paul).

Dennett, D. C. 1987, *The Intentional Stance* (Cambridge, Mass.; London: MIT Press).

Dennett, D. C. 1991, 'Real Patterns', *Journal of Philosophy*, 87, 27–51. Reprinted in D. Dennett, *Brainchildren* (London: Penguin, 1998), 95–120.

Dennett, D. C. 1994, 'Cognitive Science as Reverse Engineering: Several Meanings of "Top-Down" and "Bottom-up"', in D. Prawitz, B. Skyrms, and D. Westerstahl, eds, *Proceedings of the 9th International Congress of Logic, Methodology and Philosophy of Science* (North-Holland), 679–689.

Dennett, D. C. 1998, *Brainchildren* (Cambridge Mass.: MIT Press).

Deutsch, D. 1985, 'Quantum Theory, the Church–Turing Principle and the Universal Quantum Computer', *Proceedings of the Royal Society*, 400, 97–117.

Deutsch, D. 1997, *The Fabric of Reality* (London: Penguin).

Devlin, K. J. 1991, *Logic and Information* (Cambridge: Cambridge University Press).

Di Vincenzo, D. P., and Loss, D. 1998, 'Quantum Information Is Physical', *Superlattices and Microstructures: Special issue on the occasion of Rolf Landauer's 70th birthday*, 23, 419–432.

Dietrich, E. 1990, 'Computationalism', *Social Epistemology*, 4, 135–154.

Ditmarsch, H. P. v. 2000, *Knowledge Games* (Amsterdam). University of Groningen, doctoral thesis in computer science, available online at <http://www.ai.rug.nl/hans/>.

Dodig-Crnkovic, G. 2005, 'System Modeling and Information Semantics', in J. Bubenko, O. Eriksson, H. Fernlund, and M. Lind, eds, *Proceedings of the Fifth Promote IT Conference, Borlänge, Sweden* (Studentlitteratur: Lund), 24–30.

Donahoe, J. W., and Dorsel, V. P. (eds) 1997, *Neural Network Models of Cognition: Biobehavioral Foundations* (Amsterdam: Elsevier Science Press).

Dongen, S. V. 2006, 'Prior Specification in Bayesian Statistics: Three Cautionary Tales', *Journal of Theoretical Biology*, 242(1), 90–100.

Dorato, M., and Pauri, M. forthcoming, 'Holism and Structuralism in Classical and Quantum General Relativity', in S. French, ed., *Structuralism and Quantum Gravity* (Oxford: Oxford University Press).

Dorffner, G., and Prem, E. 1993, 'Connectionism, Symbol Grounding, and Autonomous Agents', *Proceedings of the Fifteenth Annual Meeting of the Cognitive Science Society*, 144–148.

Dretske, F. I. 1981, *Knowledge and the Flow of Information* (Oxford: Blackwell).

Dretske, F. I. 1988, *Explaining Behavior: Reasons in a World of Causes* (Cambridge, Mass.: MIT Press).

Dretske, F. I. 2003, 'How Do You Know You Are Not a Zombie?', in B. Gertler, ed., *Privileged Access and First-Person Authority* (Burlington: Ashgate), 1–14.

Dreyfus, H. L. 1992, *What Computers Still Can't Do: a Critique of Artificial Intelligence*, 2nd edn (Cambridge, Mass.: The MIT Press).

Drucker, P. F. 1994, *The New Realities: In Government and Politics – in Economy and Business – in Society – and in World View* (Oxford: Butterworth-Heinemann).

Dummett, M. A. E. 1991, *The Logical Basis of Metaphysics* (London: Duckworth).

Dummett, M. A. E. 1993a, *Origins of Analytical Philosophy* (London: Duckworth).

Dummett, M. A. E. 1993b, *Origins of Analytical Philosophy* (London: Duckworth).

Dummett, M. A. E. 2001, *La Natura E Il Futuro Della Filosofia* (Genoa: Il Nuovo Melangolo).

Dummett, M. A. E. 2004, *Truth and the Past* (New York; Chichester: Columbia University Press).

Dunn, J. M. 2008, 'Information in Computer Science', in P. Adriaans and J. van Benthem, eds, *Philosophy of Information* (Amsterdam; London: Elsevier), 581–608.

Eddington, A. 1928, *The Nature of the Physical World* (Cambridge: Cambridge University Press).

Egyed, A., and Medvidovic, N. 2000, 'A Formal Approach to Heterogeneous Software Modeling', in T. Mailbaum, ed., *Proceedings of the Third International Conference on the Fundamental Approaches to Software Engineering (Fase 2000, Berlin, Germany, March-April), Published in Lecture Notes in Computer Science, 1783* (Berlin/Heidelberg: Springer-Verlag), 178–192.

Eilam, E. 2005, *Reversing: Secrets of Reverse Engineering* (Indianapolis, Ind.: Wiley).

Elias, P., Feinstein, A., and Shannon, C. E. 1956, 'Note on Maximum Flow through a Network', *IRE Transactions on Information Theory*, IT-2, 117–119.

Eliasmith, C. 1996, 'The Third Contender: A Critical Examination of the Dynamicist Theory of Cognition', *Journal of Philosophical Psychology*, 9(4), 441–463.

Elmer, J. 1995, 'Blinded Me with Science: Motifs of Observation and Temporality in Lacan and Luhmann', *Cultural Critique*, 30, 101–136.

Engel, P. 2002, *Truth* (Chesham: Acumen).

Esfeld, M. 2004, 'Quantum Entanglement and a Metaphysics of Relations', *Studies in History and Philosophy of Science Part B: Studies in History and Philosophy of Modern Physics*, 35, 625–641.

Esfeld, M., and Lam, V. 2008, 'Moderate Structural Realism About Space-Time', *Synthese*, 160, 27–46.

Everitt, N., and Fisher, A. 1995, *Modern Epistemology: A New Introduction* (New York; London: McGraw-Hill).

Fagin, R., and Halpern, J. Y. 1988, 'Belief, Awareness and Limited Reasoning', *Artificial Intelligence*, 34, 39–76.

Fagin, R., Halpern, J. Y., Moses, Y., and Vardi, M. Y. 1995, *Reasoning About Knowledge* (Cambridge, Mass; London: MIT Press).

Fetzer, J. H. 2004, 'Information: Does it Have To Be True?', *Minds and Machines* 14(2), 223–229.

Feynman, R. P. 1992, *The Character of Physical Law* (London: Penguin). Originally published: London: British Broadcasting Corporation, 1965.

Feynman, R. P. 1998, *Six Easy Pieces* (London: Penguin).

Firoiu, L., and Cohen, P. R. 2002, 'Segmenting Time Series with a Hybrid Neural Networks: Hidden Markov Model', *The Eighteenth National Conference on Artificial Intelligence*, 247–252.

Floridi, L. 1996, *Scepticism and the Foundation of Epistemology: A Study in the Metalogical Fallacies* (Leiden: Brill).

Floridi, L. 1999a, 'Information Ethics: On the Philosophical Foundations of Computer Ethics', *Ethics and Information Technology*, 1(1), 37–56.

Floridi, L. 1999b, *Philosophy and Computing: An Introduction* (London; New York: Routledge).

Floridi, L. 2002, 'What Is the Philosophy of Information?', *Metaphilosophy*, 33(1–2), 123–145.

Floridi, L. 2003a, 'Information', in Floridi (2003f), 40–61.

Floridi, L. 2003b, 'On the Intrinsic Value of Information Objects and the Infosphere', *Ethics and Information Technology*, 4(4), 287–304.

Floridi, L. 2003c, 'The Renaissance of Epistemology 1914–1945', in T. Baldwin, ed., *The Cambridge History of Philosophy 1870–1945* (Cambridge: Cambridge University Press), 531–541.

Floridi, L. 2003d, 'The Renaissance of Epistemology: 1914–1945', in T. Baldwin, ed., *Cambridge History of Philosophy 1870–1945* (Cambridge: Cambridge University Press).

Floridi, L. 2003e, 'Two Approaches to the Philosophy of Information', *Minds and Machines*, 13(4), 459–469.

Floridi, L. (ed.) 2003f, *The Blackwell Guide to the Philosophy of Computing and Information* (Oxford, New York: Blackwell).

Floridi, L. 2004a, 'Informational Realism', in *ACS: Conferences in Research and Practice in Information Technology (Computers and Philosophy 2003: Selected Papers from the Computer and Philosophy Conference CAP 2003)*, 37, 7–12.

Floridi, L. 2004b, 'On the Logical Unsolvability of the Gettier Problem', *Synthese*, 142(1), 61–79.

Floridi, L. 2004c, 'Open Problems in the Philosophy of Information', *Metaphilosophy*, 35(4), 554–582.

Floridi, L. 2004d, 'Outline of a Theory of Strongly Semantic Information', *Minds and Machines*, 14(2), 197–222.

Floridi, L. 2005a, 'Consciousness, Agents and the Knowledge Game', *Minds and Machines*, 15(3–4), 415–444.

Floridi, L. 2005b, 'Is Information Meaningful Data?', *Philosophy and Phenomenological Research*, 70(2), 351–370.

Floridi, L. 2005c, 'The Philosophy of Presence: From Epistemic Failure to Successful Observability', *Presence: Teleoperators and Virtual Environments*, 14(6), 656–667.

Floridi, L. 2006, 'The Logic of Being Informed', *Logique et Analyse*, 49(196), 433–460.

Floridi, L. 2008a, 'Artificial Intelligence's New Frontier: Artificial Companions and the Fourth Revolution', *Metaphilosophy*, 39(4/5), 651–655.

Floridi, L. 2008b, 'Data', in W. A. Darity, ed., *International Encyclopedia of the Social Sciences* (Detroit: Macmillan).

Floridi, L. 2008c, 'A Defence of Informational Structural Realism', *Synthese*, 161(2), 219–253.

Floridi, L. 2008d, 'Information Ethics: Its Nature and Scope', in Jeroen van den Hoven and John Weckert, eds, *Moral Philosophy and Information Technology* (Cambridge: Cambridge University Press), 40–65.

Floridi, L. 2008e, 'Understanding Epistemic Relevance', *Erkenntnis*, 69(1), 69–92.

Floridi, L. 2009a, 'Against Digital Ontology', *Synthese*, 168(1), 151–178.

Floridi, L. 2009b, *Information: A Very Short Introduction* (Oxford: Oxford University Press).

Floridi, L. 2009c, 'Information, Semantic Conceptions Of', in E. N. Zalta, ed., *Stanford Encyclopedia of Philosophy*, Summer 2009 edn, <http://plato.stanford.edu/archives/sum2009/entries/information-semantic/>.

Floridi, L. 2009d, 'The Semantic Web Vs. Web 2.0: A Philosophical Assessment', *Episteme*, 6, 25–37.

Floridi, L. (ed.) 2009e, *Handbook of Computer Ethics* (Cambridge: Cambridge University Press).

Floridi, L. 2010, *Information: A Very Short Introduction* (Oxford: Oxford University Press).

Floridi, L. forthcoming-a, 'Information, Possible Worlds, and the Cooptation of Scepticism', *Synthese*.

Floridi, L. forthcoming-b, 'Semantic Information and the Network Theory of Account', *Synthese*.

Floridi, L. forthcoming-c, 'Semantic Information and the Correctness Theory of Truth', *Erkenntnis*.

Floridi, L., and Sanders, J. W. 2002, 'Computer Ethics: Mapping the Foundationalist Debate', *Ethics and Information Technology*, 4(1), 1–9.

Floridi, L., and Sanders, J. W. 2004a, 'The Method of Abstraction', in M. Negrotti, ed., *Yearbook of the Artificial. Nature, Culture and Technology. Models in Contemporary Sciences* (Bern: Peter Lang), 177–220.

Floridi, L., and Sanders, J. W. 2004b, 'On the Morality of Artificial Agents', *Minds and Machines*, 14(3), 349–379.

Floridi, L., and Sanders, J. W. 2005, 'Internet Ethics: The Constructionist Values of Homo Poieticus', in R. Cavalier, ed., *The Impact of the Internet on Our Moral Lives* (New York: SUNY).

Floridi, L., Taddeo, M., and Turilli, M. 2009, 'Turing's Imitation Game: Still a Challenge for Any Machine and Some Judges', *Minds and Machines*, 19(1), 145–150.

Fodor, J. A. 1975, *The Language of Thought* (Cambridge, Mass.: Harvard University Press).

Fodor, J. A. 1987, *Psychosemantics: The Problem of Meaning in the Philosophy of Mind* (Cambridge, Mass.; London: MIT Press).

Fodor, J. A. 2008, *Lot 2: The Language of Thought Revisited* (Oxford: Oxford University Press).

Ford, L. R., and Fulkerson, D. R. 1956, 'Maximal Flow through a Network', *Canadian Journal of Mathematics*, 8, 399–404.

Formigari, L. 2004, *A History of Language Philosophies* (Amsterdam/Philadelphia: John Benjamins Pub.).

Foster, C. L. 1992, *Algorithms, Abstraction and Implementation: Levels of Detail in Cognitive Science* (London: Academic Press).

Fox, C. J. 1983, *Information and Misinformation: An Investigation of the Notions of Information, Misinformation, Informing, and Misinforming* (Westport, Conn: Greenwood Press).

Fox, C. J. 2007, *Introduction to Software Engineering Design* (Boston, Mass.; London: Pearson/Addison-Wesley).

Franklin, J. 1999, 'Structure and Domain-Independence in the Formal Sciences', *Studies in History and Philosophy of Science*, 30(4), 721–723.

Franklin, S. 1995, *Artificial Minds* (Cambridge, Mass.: The MIT Press).

Fredkin, E. 1992, 'Finite Nature', *Proceedings of the XXVIIth Rencontre de Moriond, March 22–28, 1992*, Les Arcs, Savoie, France (Editions Frontieres: Gif-sur-Yvette, France).

Fredkin, E. 2003a, 'The Digital Perspective', *International Journal of Theoretical Physics*, 42(2), 145. Also available online at <http://www.springerlink.com/content/q36wt3738033746n/>

Fredkin, E. 2003b, 'An Introduction to Digital Philosophy', *International Journal of Theoretical Physics*, 42(2), 189–247. Also available online at <http://digitalphilosophy.org/>.

Fredkin, E. online, *Digital Mechanics: An Informational Process Based on Reversible Universal Cellular Automata*, <http://www.digitalphilosophy.org/dm_paper.htm>.

Freedman, D., Pisani, R., and Purves, R. 2007, *Statistics*, 4th edn (New York; London: W.W. Norton).

French, S. 2001, 'Symmetry, Structure and the Constitution of Objects', *Symmetries in Physics, New Reflections: Oxford Workshop, January 2001*, Oxford. Available at<http://philsci-archive.pitt.edu/archive/00000327/00/Symmetry&Objects_doc.pdf>

French, S. 2003, 'Scribbling on the Blank Sheet: Eddington's Structuralist Conception of Objects', *Studies in History and Philosophy of Modern Physics*, 34, 227–259.

French, S., and Kamminga, H. (eds) 1993, *Correspondence, Invariance and Heuristics. Essays in Honour of Heinz Post* (Dordrecht: Kluwer).

French, S., and Ladyman, J. 2003a, 'The Dissolution of Objects: Between Platonism and Phenomenalism', *Synthese*, 136(1), 73–77.

French, S., and Ladyman, J. 2003b, 'Remodelling Structural Realism: Quantum Physics and the Metaphysics of Structure', *Synthese*, 136(1), 31–56.

French, S., and Redhead, M. 1988, 'Quantum Mechanics and the Identity of the Indiscernibles', *British Journal for the Philosophy of Science*, 39, 233–246.

French, S., and Saatsi, J. 2006, 'Realism about Structure: The Semantic View and Non-linguistic Representations', *Philosophy of Science*, 78, 548–559.

Frieden, B. R. 1998, *Physics from Fisher Information: A Unification* (Cambridge: Cambridge University Press).

Frieden, B. R. 2004, *Science from Fisher Information: A Unification*, 2nd edn (Cambridge: Cambridge University Press).

Gabbay, D. M., Hogger, C. J., and Robinson, J. A. 1993, *Handbook of Logic in Artificial Intelligence and Logic Programming* (Oxford: Clarendon Press).

Gaifman, H. 1988, 'A Theory of Higher-Order Probabilities', in Brian Skyrms and William Harper, eds, *Causation, Chance and Credence* (London, Ontario: University of Western Ontario Press), 191–219.

Galliers, R. 1987, *Information Analysis: Selected Readings* (Sydney; Wokingham: Addison-Wesley).

Gamma, E., Helm, R., Johnson, R., and Vlissides, J. 1995, *Design Patterns : Elements of Reusable Object-Oriented Software* (Reading, Mass.; Wokingham: Addison-Wesley).

Gärdenfors, P. 1976, 'Discussion: Relevance and Redundancy in Deductive Explanations', *Philosophy of Science*, 43, 420–431.

Gärdenfors, P. 1978, 'On the Logic of Relevance', *Synthese*, 37, 351–367. Reprinted in J.-P. Dubucs, ed., *Philosophy of Probability*, Philosophical Studies Series 56 (Kluwer, Dordrecht 1993), 35–54.

Gärdenfors, P. 1988, *Knowledge in Flux: Modeling the Dynamics of Epistemic States* (Cambridge, Mass; London: MIT).

Geach, P. T. 1956, 'Good and Evil', *Analysis*, 17, 33–42.

Gee, J. P. 1998, 'What Is Literacy?', in V. Zamel and R. Spack, eds, *Negotiating Academic Literacies: Teaching and Learning across Languages and Cultures* (Mahwah, NJ: Erlbaum), 51–59.

Gelfond, M. 1987, 'On Stratified Autoepistemic Theories', *Proceedings of National Conference on Artificial Intelligence (AAAI)*, 207–211.

Gell-Mann, M. 1994, *The Quark and the Jaguar: Adventures in the Simple and the Complex* (London: Little Brown).

Gettier, E. 1963, 'Is Justified True Belief Knowledge?', *Analysis*, 23, 121–123.

Gibson, J. J. 1979, *The Ecological Approach to Visual Perception* (Boston, Mass.: Houghton Mifflin).

Giere, R. N. 1988, *Explaining Science: A Cognitive Approach* (Chicago: University of Chicago Press).

Giere, R. N. 1999, 'Using Models to Represent Reality', in L. Magnani, N. J. Nersessian, and P. Thagard, eds, *Model-Based Reasoning in Scientific Discovery* (Dordrecht: Kluwer), 41–57.

Girle, R. 2000, *Modal Logics and Philosophy* (Teddington: Acumen).

Glymour, C. N. 1992, *Thinking Things Through: An Introduction to Philosophical Issues and Achievements* (Cambridge, Mass.; London: MIT Press).

Goldblatt, R. 2003, 'Mathematical Modal Logic: A View of Its Evolution', *Journal of Applied Logic*, 1(5–6), 309–392.

Golden, K., Etzioni, O., and Weld, D. 1994, 'Omnipotence without Omniscience: Efficient Sensor Management for Software Agents', in O. Etzionieds, *Proceedings of the Twelfth National Conference on Artificial Intelligence*, Seattle, Washington, United States (AAAI Press), 1048–1054.

Goldman, A. 1967, 'A Causal Theory of Knowing', *Journal of Philosophy*, 64(12), 355–372.

Goodman, N. 1968, *Languages of Art: An Approach to a Theory of Symbols* (Indianapolis: Bobbs-Merrill).

Gower, B. 2000, 'Cassirer, Schlick and "Structural" Realism: The Philosophy of the Exact Sciences in the Background to Early Logical Empiricism', *British Journal for the History of Philosophy*, 8(1), 71–106.

Graham, G. 1999, *The Internet: A Philosophical Inquiry* (London: Routledge).

Grant, J., and Hunter, A. forthcoming, 'Measuring Inconsistency in Knowledgebases', *Journal of Intelligent Information Systems*.

Gray, J. N. 1978, 'Notes on Database Operating Systems', in R. Bayer, R. Graham, and G. Seegmuller, eds, *Operating Systems: An Advanced Course* (Berlin: Springer-Verlag), 393–481.

Greco, G. M., Paronitti, G., Turilli, M., and Floridi, L. 2005, 'How to Do Philosophy Informationally', *Lecture Notes in Computer Science*, vol. 3782, 623–634.

Greco, J., and Sosa, E. (eds) 1999, *The Blackwell Guide to Epistemology* (Oxford: Blackwell Publishers).

Greisdorf, H. 2000, 'Relevance: An Interdisciplinary and Information Science Perspective', *Informing Science*, 3(2), 67–71.

Grice, H. P. 1989, *Studies in the Way of Words* (Cambridge, Mass.: Harvard University Press).

Griffiths, A. P. (ed.) 1967, *Knowledge and Belief* (London: Oxford University Press).

Grim, P., Mar, G., and St Denis, P. 1998, *The Philosophical Computer: Exploratory Essays in Philosophical Computer Modeling* (Cambridge, Mass.; London: MIT Press).

Groenendijk, J. A. G. 2003, 'Questions and Answers: Semantics and Logic', in R. Bernardi and M. Moortgat, eds, *2nd Colognet-Elsnet Symposium – Questions and Answers: Theoretical and Applied Perspectives* (Amsterdam: OTS). Available at <http://www.narcis.info/publication/RecordID/oai:uva.nl:122520>

Groenendijk, J. A. G., Janssen, T. M. V., and Stokhof, M. J. B. (eds) 1984, *Truth, Interpretation, and Information: Selected Papers from the Third Amsterdam Colloquium* (Dordrecht, Holland; Cinnaminson, U.S.A: Foris Publications).

Groenendijk, J. A. G., and Stokhof, M. J. B. 1994, 'Questions', in van Benthem and ter Meulen, *Handbook of Logic and Language* (North-Holland: Elsevier Science), 1055–1124.

Hacking, I. 1999, *The Social Construction of What?* (Cambridge, Mass.: Harvard University Press).

Hales, S. D., and Welshon, R. 2000, *Nietzsche's Perspectivism* (Urbana: University of Illinois Press).

Halpern, J. Y. 1995, 'Reasoning about Knowledge: A Survey', in D. Gabbay, C. J. Hogger, and J. A. Robinson, eds, *Handbook of Logic in Artificial Intelligence and Logic Programming* (Oxford: Oxford University Press), 1–34. A version of the paper similar to the published version is available in postscript and pdf from <http://www.cs.cornell.edu/home/halpern/abstract.html>.

Halpern, J. Y. 1996, 'Should Knowledge Entail Belief?', *Journal of Philosophical Logic*, 25(5), 483–494.

Halpern, J. Y., and Moses, Y. 1990, 'Knowledge and Common Knowledge in a Distributed Environment', *Journal of the Association for Computing Machinery*, 37(3), 549–587.

Halpern, J. Y., and Tuttle, B. 1993, 'Knowledge, Probability and Adversaries', *Journal of the Association for Computing Machinery*, 40, 917–962.

Hanson, P. P. (ed.) 1990, *Information, Language, and Cognition* (Vancouver: University of British Columbia Press).

Harms, W. F. 1998, 'The Use of Information Theory in Epistemology', *Philosophy of Science*, 65(3), 472–501.

Harnad, S. (ed.) 1987, *Categorical Perception: The Groundwork of Cognition* (New York: Cambridge University Press).

Harnad, S. 1990, 'The Symbol Grounding Problem', *Physica Scripta*, D(42), 335–346.

Harnad, S. 1993a, 'Problems, Problems: The Frame Problem as a Symptom of the Symbol Grounding Problem', *Psycoloquy*, 4(34), on-line/unpaginated. <http://cogsci.soton.ac.uk/harnad/Papers/Harnad/harnad93.frameproblem.html>

Harnad, S. 1993b, 'Symbol Grounding in an Empirical Problem: Neural Nets Are Just a Candidate Component', *Proceedings of the Fifteenth Annual Meeting of the Cognitive Science Society*. Available at <http://cogprints.org/1588/>.

Harnad, S. 2000, 'Minds, Machines and Turing: The Indistinguishability of Indistinguishables', *Journal of Logic, Language, and Information*, 9(4), 425–445.

Harnad, S. 2002, 'Symbol Grounding and the Origin of Language', in M. Scheutz, ed., *Computationalism: New Directions* (Cambridge, Mass., MIT Press), 143–158.

Harris, R. A. 1998, 'A Note on the Max Planck Effect', *Rhetoric Society Quarterly*, 28, 85–89.

Harsanyi, J. 1968, 'Games with Incomplete Information Played By "Bayesian" Players: Parts 1, 2, 3', *Management Science*, 14, 159–182, 320–134, 486–502.

Haugeland, J. 1981, *Mind Design: Philosophy, Psychology, Artificial Intelligence* (Cambridge, Mass.; London: MIT Press).

Haugeland, J. 1997, *Mind Design Ii: Philosophy, Psychology, Artificial Intelligence* Rev. and enl. edn (Cambridge, Mass.; London: MIT Press).

Hayes, I., and Flinn, B. 1993, *Specification Case Studies*, 2nd edn (New York; London: Prentice Hall).

Heath, A. E. 1928, 'Contribution to the Symposium "Materialism in the Light of Scientific Thought"', *Proceedings of the Aristotelian Society, Supplement*, 8, 130–142.

Hebb, D. O. 1949, *The Organization of Behavior: A Neuropsychological Theory* (New York: John Wiley & Sons).

Heck, A., and Murtagh, F. (eds) 1993, *Intelligent Information Retrieval: The Case of Astronomy and Related Space Sciences* (Dordrecht; London: Kluwer).

Heil, J. 2003, 'Levels of Reality', *Ratio*, 16(3), 205–221.

Hendriks-Jansen, H. 1989, 'In Praise of Interactive Emergence: Or Why Explanations Don't Have to Wait for Implementations', in Langton (1989), 282–299.

Hetherington, S. C. 1996, *Knowledge Puzzles: An Introduction to Epistemology* (Boulder, Colo.; Oxford: Westview Press).

Hilbert, D. 1900, 'Mathematische Probleme. Vortrag, Gehalten Auf Dem Internationalen Mathematiker-Kongress Zu Paris 1900', in *Nachrichten Von Der Königlichen Gesellschaft Der Wissenschaften Zu Göttingen, Mathematisch-Physikalische Klasse, Geschäftliche Mitteilungen*, 253–297. Repr. in *Archiv der Mathematik und Physik* 3.1, 44–63, 213–37, 1901; Eng. trans. 'Mathematical Problems', *Bulletin of the American Mathematical Society* 8, 437–479, 1902.

Hintikka, J. 1962, *Knowledge and Belief: An Introduction to the Logic of the Two Notions* (Ithaca: Cornell University Press).

Hintikka, J. 1973, *Logic, Language-Games and Information: Kantian Themes in the Philosophy of Logic* (Oxford: Clarendon Press).

Hintikka, J., and Suppes, P. (eds) 1970, *Information and Inference* (Dordrecht: Reidel).

Hitchcock, D. 1992, 'Relevance', *Argumentation*, 6(2), 251–270.

Hoare, C. A. R., and He, J. 1998, *Unifying Theories of Programming* (London: Prentice Hall).

Hockett, C. F. 1952, 'An Approach to the Quantification of Semantic Noise', *Philosophy of Science*, 19(4), 257–260.

Hocutt, M. 1972, 'Is Epistemic Logic Possible?', *Notre Dame Journal of Formal Logic*, 13 (4), 433–453.

Hofkirchner, W. (ed.) 1998, *The Quest for a Unified Theory of Information: Proceedings of the Second International Conference on the Foundations of Information Science* (Amsterdam: Gordon & Breach).

Holden, T. A. 2004, *The Architecture of Matter: Galileo to Kant* (Oxford: Clarendon Press).

Holland, J. H. 1975, *Adaptation in Natural and Artificial Systems: An Introductory Analysis with Applications to Biology, Control, and Artificial Intelligence* (Ann Arbor: University of Michigan Press).

Hooft, G. 't 1997, *In Search of the Ultimate Building Blocks* (Cambridge: Cambridge University Press).

Hooft, G. 't 2002, 'How Does God Play Dice? (Pre-)Determinism at the Planck Scale', in R. A. Bertlmann and A. Zeilinger, eds, *Quantum [Un]Speakables, from Bell to Quantum Information* (Berlin: Springer Verlag), 307–316.

Hooft, G. 't 2003, 'Can Quantum Mechanics Be Reconciled with Cellular Automata?', *International Journal of Theoretical Physics*, 42, 349-354.

Hooft, G. 't 2005, 'Does God Play Dice?', *Physics World*, 18(12), 21–23.

Hughes, G. E., and Cresswell, M. J. 1996, *A New Introduction to Modal Logic* (London: Routledge).

Hughes, P., and Brecht, G. 1976, *Vicious Circles and Infinity: A Panoply of Paradoxes* (London: Cape). Originally published: Garden City, N.Y.: Doubleday, 1975.

Hume, D. 1987, *Essays, Moral, Political, and Literary* (Indianapolis: LibertyClassics).

Hyötyniemi, H. 1996, 'Turing Machines Are Recurrent Neural Networks', J. Alander, T. Honkela, and M. Jakobsson, eds, *STeP'96 - Genes, Nets and Symbols* (Publications of the Finnish Artificial Intelligence Society (FAIS), Helsinki, Finland), 13–24.

Israel, D., and Perry, J. 1990, 'What Is Information?', in P. P. Hanson, ed., *Information, Language, and Cognition* (Vancouver: University of British Columbia Press), 1–28.

Jamison, D. 1970, 'Bayesian Information Usage', in J. Hintikka and P. Suppes, eds, *Information and Inference* (Dordrecht: Riedel), 28–57.

Jeffrey, R. C. 1965, *The Logic of Decision* (New York: McGraw-Hill).

Jeffrey, R. C. 1990, *The Logic of Decision*, 2nd edn (Chicago: University of Chicago Press).

Jones, D. S. 1979, *Elementary Information Theory* (Oxford: Clarendon Press).

Jungnickel, D. 1999, *Graphs, Networks, and Algorithms* (Berlin; New York: Springer).

Kamp, H. 1984, 'A Theory of Truth and Semantic Interpretation', in J. Groenendijk, T. M. V. Janssen, and M. Stokhof, eds, *Truth, Interpretation and Information* (Dordrecht: Foris), 277–322.

Kant, I. 1998, *Critique of Pure Reason* repr. w. corr. (Cambridge: Cambridge University Press). Trans. and ed. by Paul Guyer, Allen W. Wood.

Kelso, J. A. S. 1995, *Dynamic Patterns: The Self-Organization of Brain and Behavior* (Cambridge, Mass; London: MIT Press).

Kemeny, J. 1953, 'A Logical Measure Function', *Journal of Symbolic Logic*, 18, 289–308.

Ketland, J. 2004, 'Empirical Adequacy and Ramsification', *British Journal for Philosophy of Science*, 55(2), 287–300.

Kirkham, R. L. 1984, 'Does the Gettier Problem Rest on a Mistake?', *Mind*, 93, 501–513.

Kirkham, R. L. 1992, *Theories of Truth: A Critical Introduction* (Cambridge, Mass.; MIT Press).

Knuth, D. E. 1997, *The Art of Computer Programming*, 3rd edn (Reading, Mass.; Harlow: Addison-Wesley), 3 vols.

Kock, N. F., Jr., McQueen, R. J., and Corner, J. L. 1997, 'The Nature of Data, Information and Knowledge Exchanges in Business Processes: Implications for Process Improvement and Organizational Learning', *The Learning Organization*, 4(2), 70–80.

Kohlas, J. 2003, *Information Algebras: Generic Structures for Inference* (London: Springer).

Kolakowski, L. 1968, 'Karl Marx and the Classical Definition of Truth', in *Toward a Marxist Humanism* (New York: Grove Press), 38–66.

Koura, A. 1988, 'An Approach to Why-Questions', *Synthese*, 74(2), 191–206.

Kraus, S., and Lehmann, D. 1986, 'Knowledge, Belief and Time', *Proceedings of the 13th ICALP*, edited by C. Krott (Springer), 186–195.

Krause, D. 2005, 'Structures and Structural Realism', *Logic Journal of the IGPL*, 13(1), 113–126.

Kriegel, U. 2003, 'Consciousness as Sensory Quality and as Implicit Self-Awareness', *Phenomenology and the Cognitive Sciences*, 2(1), 1–26.

Kriegel, U. 2004, 'Consciousness and Self-Consciousness', *The Monist*, 87 185–209.

Künne, W. 2003, *Conceptions of Truth* (Oxford: Clarendon Press).

Lacan, J. 1988, 'Logical Time and the Assertion of Anticipated Certainty', *Newsletter of the Freudian Field*, 2, 4–22. Originally written in March 1945, this was first published in *Écrits*, pp.197–213, 1966.

Ladyman, J. 1998, 'What Is Structural Realism?', *Studies in History and Philosophy of Science*, 29A(3), 409–424.

Lakemeyer, G. 1997, 'Relevance from an Epistemic Perspective', *Artificial Intelligence*, 97 (1–2), 137–167.

Landauer, R. 1987, 'Computation: A Fundamental Physical View', *Physica Scripta*, 35, 88–95.

Landauer, R. 1991, 'Information Is Physical', *Physics Today*, 44, 23–29.

Landauer, R. 1996, 'The Physical Nature of Information', *Physics Letter*, A 217, 188.

Landauer, R., and Bennett, C. H. 1985, 'The Fundamental Physical Limits of Computation', *Scientific American*, July, 48–56.

Landini, G. 2007, *Wittgenstein's Apprenticeship with Russell* (Cambridge, UK; New York: Cambridge University Press).

Langevelde, I. A. v., Philipsen, A. W., and Treur, J. 1992, 'Formal Specification of Compositional Architectures', in B. Neumann, ed., *Proceedings of the 10th European Conference on AI, ECAI-92* (John Wiley & Sons), 272–276.

Langton, C. G. (ed.) 1989, *Artificial Life: The Proceedings of an Interdisciplinary Workshop on the Synthesis and Simulation of Living Systems, Held September, 1987 in Los Alamos, New Mexico* (Redwood City, Calif.; Wokingham: Addison-Wesley).

Langton, C. G. (ed.) 1992, *Artificial Life Ii: Proceedings of the Workshop on Artificial Life, Held February 1990 in Santa Fe, New Mexico* (Redwood City, Calif.; Wokingham: Addison-Wesley).

Langton, C. G. 1996, 'Artificial Life' reprinted in Boden (1996), 39–94. This is an updated version of the original which appeared in Langton (1992).

Langton, R. 2004, 'Elusive Knowledge of Things in Themselves', *Australasian Journal of Philosophy*, 82(1), 129–136.

Larkin, J. H., and Simon, H. A. 1987, 'Why a Diagram Is (Sometimes) Worth Ten Thousand Words', *Cognitive Science*, 11(1), 65–100.

Larson, A. G., and Debons, A. (eds) 1983, *Information Science in Action: System Design. Proceedings of the Nato Advanced Study Institute on Information Science, Crete, Greece, August 1–11, 1978* (The Hague: M. Nijhoff).

Laudan, L. 1981, 'A Confutation of Convergent Realism', *Philosophy of Science*, 48, 19–48.

Leibniz, G. W. 1995, 'Monadology', in G. H. R. Parkinson, ed., *Philosophical Writings* (London: Dent; first published in Everyman's Library in 1934; published, with revisions in Everyman's University Library in 1973), 179–194.

Lemmon, E. J. 1959, 'Is There Only One Correct System of Modal Logic', *Proceedings of the Aristotelian Society*, 23, 23–40.

Lenzen, W. 1978, *Recent Work in Epistemic Logic* (Amsterdam: North-Holland).

Lenzen, W. 2002, 'Epistemic Logic', in *Handbook of Epistemology*, edited by I. Niniiluoto, M. Sintonen, and J. Wolenski (Dordrecht: Kluwer), ch. 25.

LePore, E., and Smith, B. C. (eds) 2006, *The Oxford Handbook of Philosophy of Language* (Oxford: Clarendon Press).

Lesne, A. 2007, 'The Discrete Versus Continuous Controversy in Physics', *Mathematical Structures in Computer Science*, 17(02), 185–223.

Levesque, H. 1984, 'A Logic of Implicit and Explicit Belief', *Proceedings AAAI-84*, Austin, TX, 198–202.

Levi, I. 1967, 'Information and Inference', *Synthese*, 17, 369–391.

Lewis, D. 1971, 'Analog and Digital', *Nous*, 5(3), 321–327.

Lewis, D. 2009, 'Ramseyan Humility', in D. Braddon-Mitchell and R. Nola, eds, Conceptual Analysis *and Philosophical Naturalism* (Cambridge, Mass.: MIT Press), 203–222.

Li, M., and Vitanyi, P. M. B. 1997, *An Introduction to Kolmogorov Complexity and Its Applications*, 2nd edn (New York: Springer).

Lloyd, S. 2002, 'Computational Capacity of the Universe', *Physical Review Letters*, 88(23), 237901–237904.

Lloyd, S. 2006, *Programming the Universe: From the Big Bang to Quantum Computers* (London: Jonathan Cape).

Losee, R. M. 1997, 'A Discipline Independent Definition of Information', *Journal of the American Society for Information Science*, 48(3), 254–269.

Lozinskii, E. 1994, 'Information and Evidence in Logic Systems', *Journal of Experimental and Theoretical Artificial Intelligence*, 6, 163–193.

Lucas, J. R. 1961, 'Minds, Machines and Gödel', *Philosophy*, 36, 112–127.

Lucas, J. R. 1996, 'Minds, Machines and Gödel: A Retrospect', in P. Millican and A. Clark, eds, *Machines and Thought: The Legacy of Alan Turing* (Oxford: Clarendon Press), 103–124.

Lucey, T. 1991, *Management Information Systems*, 6th edn (London: DP Publications).

Luotonen, A. 1998, *Web Proxy Servers* (Upper Saddle River, NJ: Prentice Hall PTR).

Lycan, W. G. 2003, 'Dretske's Ways of Introspecting', in B. Gertler, ed., *Privileged Access and First-Person Authority* (Burlington: Ashgate), 1–14.

Lynch, M. P. 2001, *The Nature of Truth: Classic and Contemporary Perspectives* (Cambridge, Mass.; London: MIT Press).

Machlup, F., and Mansfield, U. (eds) 1983, *The Study of Information: Interdisciplinary Messages* (New York: Wiley).

MacKay, D. M. 1969, *Information, Mechanism and Meaning* (Cambridge: MIT Press).

Mandik, P. 2002, 'Synthetic Neuroethiology', in T. W. Bynum and J. H. Moor, eds, *Cyberphilosophy: The Intersection of Philosophy and Computing* (New York; Oxford: Blackwell), 11–29.

Margolus, N. 2003, 'Looking at Nature as a Computer', *International Journal of Theoretical Physics*, 42(2), 309–327.

Marr, D. 1982, *Vision: A Computational Investigation into the Human Representation and Processing of Visual Information* (San Francisco: W. H. Freeman).

Maxwell, G. 1968, 'Scientific Methodology and the Causal Theory of Perception', in Imre Lakatos and Alan Musgrave, eds, *Problems in the Philosophy of Science* (Amsterdam: North-Holland Publishing Company), 148–160.

Maxwell, G. 1970a, 'Structural Realism and the Meaning of Theoretical Terms', in Stephen Winokur and Michael Radner, eds, *Analyses of Theories, and Methods of Physics and Psychology* (Minneapolis: University of Minnesota Press), 181–192.

Maxwell, G. 1970b, 'Theories, Perception and Structural Realism', in Robert Colodny, ed., *Nature and Function of Scientific Theories* (Pittsburgh: University of Pittsburgh Press), 3–34.

Maynard Smith, J., and Szathmáry, E. 1999, *The Origins of Life: From the Birth of Life to the Origin of Language* (Oxford: Oxford University Press).

Mayo, M. 2003, 'Symbol Grounding and Its Implication for Artificial Intelligence', *Twenty-Sixth Australian Computer Science Conference*, ACSC2003 (Adelaide, Australia), 55–60.

Mayr, E. 1961, 'Cause and Effect in Biology', *Science*, 134, 1501–1506. Also in E. Mayr, *Toward a New Philosophy of Biology: Observations of an Evolutionist* (Cambridge, Mass.: Harvard University Press, 1988) and in E. Mayr, ed., *Evolution and the Diversity of Life* (Cambridge, MA: Harvard University Press, 1997).

McCarthy, J. 1971–1987, 'Formalization of Two Puzzles Involving Knowledge'. manuscript available online at <http://www-formal.stanford.edu/jmc/puzzles.html>, first published in McCarthy (1990).

McCarthy, J. 1990, *Formalizing Common Sense: Papers by John Mccarthy* (Norwood, NJ: Ablex).

McCarthy, J. 1995, 'What Has Ai in Common with Philosophy?', *Proceedings of the 14th International Joint Conference on AI, Montreal, August 1995*, IJCAI 95 (Montréal, Québec, Canada).

McCarthy, J., and Hayes, P. J. 1969, 'Some Philosophical Problems from the Standpoint of Artificial Intelligence', *Machine Intelligence*, 4, 463–502.

McClamrock, R. 1991, 'Marr's Three Levels: A Re-Evaluation', *Minds and Machines*, 1, 185–196.

McDowell, J. H. 1996, *Mind and World: With a New Introduction* (Cambridge, Mass.; London: Harvard University Press).

Menczer, F., Degeratu, M., and Street, W. N. 2000, 'Efficient and Scalable Pareto Optimization by Evolutionary Local Selection Algorithms', *Evolutionary Computation*, 8(2), 223–247.

Menczer, F., Street, W. N., and Degeratu, M. 2001, 'Evolving Heterogeneous Neural Agents by Local Selection', in M. Patel, V. Honavar, and K. Balakrishnan, eds, *Advances in the Evolutionary Synthesis of Intelligent Agents* (Cambridge, Mass.: MIT Press), 337–366.

Mesarovic, M. D., Macko, D., and Takahara, Y. 1970, *Theory of Hierarchical, Multilevel, Systems* (New York: Academic Press).

Mingers, J. 1997, 'The Nature of Information and Its Relationship to Meaning', in R. L. Winder *et al.*, eds, *Philosophical Aspects of Information Systems* (London: Taylor and Francis), 73–84.

Minsky, M. L. 1967, *Computation: Finite and Infinite Machines* (Englewood Cliffs, NJ: Prentice Hall).

Minsky, M. L. 1990, 'Logical Vs. Analogical or Symbolic Vs. Connectionist or Neat Vs. Scruffy', in P. H. Winston, ed., *Artificial Intelligence at MIT, Expanding Frontiers* (Cambridge, Mass.: MIT Press), 218–243.

Mitcham, C., and Huning, A. 1986, *Philosophy and Technology Ii: Information Technology and Computers in Theory and Practice* (Dordrecht: Reidel).

Mitchell, T. M. 1997, *Machine Learning* International edition (New York; London: McGraw-Hill).

Miyazaki, Y. 2005, 'Normal Modal Logics Containing Ktb with Some Finiteness Conditions', *Advances in Modal logic*, 6, 171–190. <http://www.aiml.net/volumes/volume5/>

Mizzaro, S. 1996, 'Relevance: The Whole (Hi)Story', *Technical Report UDMI/12/96/RR (Dec.)* Dipartimento di Matematica e Informatica, Università di Udine, Italy). Available at <http://users.dimi.uniud.it/stefano.mizzaro/research/papers/stefanology/stefanology-of-relevance.html>

Moody, T. C. 1994, 'Conversations with Zombies', *Journal of Consciousness Studies*, 1(2), 196–200.

Moor, J. H. 1985, 'What Is Computer Ethics?', *Metaphilosophy*, 16(4), 266–275.

Moor, J. H. 2001, 'The Status and Future of the Turing Test', *Minds and Machines,* 11(1), 77–93.

Morganti, M. 2004, 'On the Preferability of Epistemic Structural Realism', *Synthese*, 142(1), 81–107.

Morris, S., and Shin, H. S. 1997, 'Approximate Common Knowledge and Co-Ordination: Recent Lessons from Game Theory', *Journal of Logic, Language and Information*, 6, 171–190.

Moser, P. K. 2002, *The Oxford Handbook of Epistemology* (New York; Oxford: Oxford University Press).

Mosses, P. D. 1992, *Action Semantics* (Cambridge: Cambridge University Press).

Müller, V. C. forthcoming, 'What Is a Digital State?'.

Murray, J. D. 2003, *Mathematical Biology*, 3rd edn (New York; London: Springer), 2 vols.

Muskens, R. 1997, 'Dynamics', in J. van Benthem and A. Ter Meulen, eds, *Handbook of Logic and Language* (Amsterdam: Elsevier), ch. 10.

Nagel, T. 1974, 'What Is It Like to Be a Bat?', *The Philosophical Review*, 83(4), 435–450.

Nerode, A., and Shore, R. A. 1997, *Logic for Applications*, 2nd edn (New York: Springer).

Newell, A. 1980, 'Physical Symbol Systems', *Cognitive Science*, 4, 135–183.

Newell, A. 1982, 'The Knowledge Level', *Artificial Intelligence*, 18, 87–127.

Newell, A. 1990, *Unified Theories of Cognition* (Cambridge, Mass; London: Harvard University Press).

Newell, A. 1993, 'Reflections on the Knowledge Level', *Artificial Intelligence*, 59, 31–38.

Newell, A., and Simon, H. A. 1976, 'Computer Science as Empirical Inquiry: Symbols and Search', *Communications of the ACM*, 19, 113–126.

Newman, M. 2005, 'Ramsey-Sentence Realism as an Answer to the Pessimistic Meta-Induction', *Philosophy of Science*, 72(5), 1373–1384.

Newman, M. E. J., Barabási, A.-L., and Watts, D. J. (eds) 2006, *The Structure and Dynamics of Networks* (Princeton, NJ: Princeton University Press).

Newman, M. H. A. 1928, 'Mr. Russell's "Causal Theory of Perception"', *Mind*, 37, 137–148.

Nozick, R. 1981, *Philosophical Explanation* (Cambridge, Mass.: Harvard University Press).

Oates, T., Cohen, P. R., and Durfee, C. 1998a, 'Efficient Mining of Statistical Dependencies', *Seventh International Workshop on Artificial Intelligence and Statistics*, 133–141.

Oates, T., Jensen, D., and Cohen, P. R. 1998b, 'Discovering Rules for Clustering and Predicting Asynchronous Events', *Predicting the Future: AI Approaches to Time Series Workshop*, 73–79.

Oppenheim, P., and Putnam, H. 1958, 'The Unity of Science as a Working Hypothesis', in H. Feigl, Michael Scriven, and Grover Maxwell, eds, *Minnesota Studies in the Philosophy of Science. Concepts, Theories, and the Mind-Body Problem* (Minneapolis: University of Minnesota Press), vol. ii, 3–36.

⌡ Pagels, H. R. 1988, *The Dreams of Reason: The Computer and the Rise of the Sciences of Complexity* (New York: Simon and Schuster).

Pais, A. 2005, *Subtle Is the Lord: The Science and the Life of Albert Einstein* (Oxford; New York: Oxford University Press). Originally published in 1982, republished with a new foreword by Sir Roger Penrose.

Pappas, G. S. (ed.) 1979, *Justification and Knowledge: New Studies in Epistemology* (Dordrecht, Holland; Boston: Reidel).

Pappas, G. S., and Swain, M. (eds) 1978, *Essays on Knowledge and Justification* (Ithaca; London: Cornell University Press).

Parsons, C. 2004, 'Structuralism and Metaphysics', *The Philosophical Quarterly*, 54(214), 56–77.

Pease, M., Shostak, R., and Lamport, L. 1980, 'Reaching Agreement in the Presence of Faults', *Journal of the Association for Computing Machinery*, 27(2), 228–234.

Peirce, C. S. 1878, 'How to Make Our Ideas Clear', *Popular Science Monthly*, 12, 286–302.

Peirce, C. S. 1960, *Collected Papers of Charles Sanders Peirce* (Cambridge, Mass.: Harvard University Press). Third printing of 1931–1958 edn, with new lists of errata included.

✝ Penrose, R. 1989, *The Emperor's New Mind: Concerning Computers, Minds, and the Laws of Physics* (Oxford: Oxford University Press).

Penrose, R. 1990, 'Précis of "the Emperor's New Mind: Concerning Computers, Minds, and the Laws of Physics"', *Behavioral and Brain Sciences*, 13, 643–705.

Penrose, R. 1994, *Shadows of the Mind: A Search for the Missing Science of Consciousness* (New York: Oxford University Press).

Petrov, P. 2003, 'Church–Turing Thesis Is Almost Equivalent to Zuse-Fredkin Thesis (an Argument in Support of Zuse-Fredkin Thesis)', *Proceedings of the 3rd WSEAS International Conference on Systems Theory and Scientific Computation, Special Session on Cellular Automata and Applications (ISTASC'03)*, Rhodes Island, Greece.

⤳ Pierce, J. R. 1980, *An Introduction to Information Theory: Symbols, Signals and Noise*, 2nd edn (New York: Dover Publications).

Pinker, S. 1994, *The Language Instinct: The New Science of Language and Mind* (London: Allen Lane).

Planck, M. 1950, *Scientific Autobiography and Other Papers*; with a memroial address on Max Planck by Max von Laue; translated from the German by Frank Gaynor (London: Williams & Norgate).

Plantinga, A. 1993a, *Warrant: The Current Debate* (New York; Oxford: Oxford University Press).

Plantinga, A. 1993b, *Warrant and Proper Function* (Oxford: Oxford University Press).

Poincaré, H. 1902, *Science and Hypothesis* (repr. New York: Dover, 1952).

Polani, D., Martinetz, T., and Kim, J. T. 2001, 'An Information-Theoretic Approach for the Quantification of Relevance', J. Kelemen and P. Sosík, eds, *Proceedings of the 6th European Conference on Advances in Artificial Life* (Heidelberg; New York: Springer), 704–713.

Polani, D., Nehaniv, C., Martinetz, T., and Kim, J. 2006, 'Relevant Information in Optimized Persistence Vs. Progeny Strategies', in L. Rocha, L. Yaeger, M. Bedau, D. Floreano, R. Goldstone, and A. Vespignani, eds, *Artificial Life X: Proceedings of the Tenth International Conference on the Simulation and Synthesis of Living Systems*, (Cambridge, Mass., MIT), 337–343.

Poli, R. 2001, 'The Basic Problem of the Theory of Levels of Reality', *Axiomathes*, 12, 261–283.

Popper, K. R. 1935, *Logik Der Forschung: Zur Erkenntnistheorie Der Modernen Naturwissenschaft* (Wien: J. Springer). Eng. tr. *The Logic of Scientific Discovery* (London: Hutchinson, 1959).

Popper, K. R. 1962, *Conjectures and Refutations* (London: Routledge).

Port, R. F., and Van Gelder, T. (eds) 1995, *Mind as Motion: Explorations in the Dynamics of Cognition* (Cambridge, Mass.; London: MIT Press).

Prem, E. 1995a, 'Dynamic Symbol Grounding, State Construction, and the Problem of Teleology', in J. Mira and F. Sandoval, eds, *From Natural to Artificial Neural Computation: Proceedings of the International Workshop on Artificial Neural Networks, Malaga–Torremoloinos, Spain* (Berlin: Springer), 35–51.

Prem, E. 1995b, 'Grounding and the Entailment Structure in Robots and Artificial Life', in F. Moran *et al.*, eds, *Advances in Artificial Life: Proceedings of the Third European Conference on Artificial Life, Granada, Spain* (Berlin: Springer), 12–19.

Prem, E. 1995c, 'Symbol Groundinga dn Transcendental Logic', in L. Niklasson and M. Boden, eds, *Current Trends in Connectionism* (Hillsdale: Lawrence Erlbaum), 271–282.

Preston, J., and Bishop, M. (eds) 2002, *Views into the Chinese Room: New Essays on Searle and Artificial Intelligence* (Oxford: Clarendon Press).

Psillos, S. 1999, *Scientific Realism: How Science Tracks Truth* (London: Routledge).

Psillos, S. 2000a, 'Carnap, the Ramsey-Sentence and Realistic Empiricism', *Erkenntnis*, 52, 253–279.

Psillos, S. 2000b, 'The Present State of the Scientific Realism Debate', *British Journal for Philosophy of Science*, 51 (Special Supplement), 705–728.

Psillos, S. 2001, 'Is Structural Realism Possible?', *Philosophy of Science (Supplement)*, 68(3), 13–24.

Psillos, S. 2006, 'The Structure, the Whole Structure and Nothing but the Structure?', *Philosophy of Science*, 73, 560–570.

Pust, J. 2000, 'Warrant and Analysis', *Analysis*, 60(265), 51–57.

Putnam, H. 1967, 'Psychological Predicates', in W. H. Captain and D. D. Merrill, eds, *Art, Mind and Religion* (Pittsburgh: Pittsburgh University Press).

Putnam, H. 1975, 'What Is Mathematical Truth?', *Mathematics, Matter and Method, Philosophical Papers*, i (Cambridge: Cambridge University Press), 60–78.

Pylyshyn, Z. W. 1984, *Computation and Cognition: Toward a Foundation for Cognitive Science* (Cambridge, Mass.: MIT Press).

Pylyshyn, Z. W., and Bannon, L. J. (eds) 1970, *Perspectives on the Computer Revolution* (Englewood Cliffs, N.J.,: Prentice-Hall).

Quine, W. V. O. 1939, 'A Logistical Approach to the Ontological Problem', *Fifth International Congress for the Unity of Science* (Cambridge, Mass.), repr. in *The Ways of Paradox and Other Essays* (New York: Random House, 1966), 64–69.

Quine, W. V. O. 1979, 'Has Philosophy Lost Contact with People?', *Long Island Newsday* (18 November). The article was modified by the editor. The original version appears as essay no. 23 in *Theories and Things* (Cambridge, Mass.: Harvard University Press, 1981).

Quine, W. V. O. 1992, 'Structure and Nature', *Journal of Philosophy*, 89(1), 5–9.

Rao, A., and Georgeff, M. 1991, 'Modeling Rational Agents within a Bdi-Architecture', in J. Allen, R. Fikes, and E. Sandewall,eds, *Proceedings of the Second International Conference on Principles of Knowledge Representation and Reasoning* (San Mateo, CA: Morgan Kaufmann), 473–484.

Rapaport, W. J. 1998, 'How Minds Can Be Computational Systems', *Journal of Experimental and Theoretical Artificial Intelligence*, 10, 403–419.

Real, L. A. 1991, 'Animal Choice Behavior and the Evolution of Cognitive Architecture', *Science*, 30(253), 980–985.

Reck, E. H. 2003, 'Dedekind's Structuralism: An Interpretation and Partial Defense', *Synthese*, 137(3), 369–419.

Reck, E. H., and Price, M. P. 2000, 'Structures and Structuralism in Contemporary Philosophy of Mathematics', *Synthese*, 125(3), 341–383.

Reichenbach, H. 1951, *The Rise of Scientific Philosophy* (Berkeley and Los Angeles: University of California Press).

Resnik, M. D. 2000, *Mathematics as a Science of Patterns* (Oxford: Oxford University Press).

Ringle, M. (ed.) 1979, *Philosophical Perspectives in Artificial Intelligence* (Atlantic Highlands N.J.: Humanities Press).

Rockmore, T. 2001, 'Analytic Philosophy and the Hegelian Turn', *The Review of Metaphysics*, 55, 339–370.

Roever, W. P. d., Engelhardt, K., and Buth, K.-H. 1998, *Data Refinement: Model-Oriented Proof Methods and Their Comparison* (Cambridge: Cambridge University Press).

Rorty, R. 1982, *Consequences of Pragmatism: Essays, 1972–1980* (Brighton: Harvester).

Rosen, G., and Smith, N. J. J. 2004, 'Wordly Indeterminacy: A Rough Guide', *Australasian Journal of Philosophy*, 82(1), 185–198.

Rosenstein, M., and Cohen, P. R. 1999a, 'Concepts from Time Series', *Proceedings of the Fifteenth National Conference on Artificial Intelligence*, 739–745.

Rosenstein, M., and Cohen, P. R. 1999b, 'Continuous Categories for a Mobile Robot', *Proceedings of the Sixteenth National Conference on Artificial Intelligence*, 634–640.

Rosenstein, M. T., and Cohen, P. R. 1998, 'Symbol Grounding with Delay Coordinates', *AAAI Technical Report WS-98–06, The Grounding of Word Meaning: Data and Models*, 20–21.

Roth, M. D., and Galis, L. (eds) 1970, *Knowing: Essays in the Analysis of Knowledge* (New York: Random House).

Rumbaugh, J. 1991, *Object-Oriented Modeling and Design* (Englewood Cliffs; London: Prentice-Hall International).

Russell, B. 1902, 'Letter to Frege', in J. van Heijenoort, ed., *From Frege to Gödel: A Source Book in Mathematical Logic, 1879–1931* (Harvard University Press: Cambridge, Mass., 1967), 124–125.

Russell, B. 1912, *The Problems of Philosophy* (Oxford University Press: Oxford).

Ryckman, T. A. 2003, 'Surplus Structure from the Standpoint of Transcendental Idealism: The "World Geometries" of Weyl and Eddington', *Perspectives on Science*, 11(1), 76–106.

Salthe, S. N. 1985, *Evolving Hierarchical Systems: Their Structure and Representation* (New York: Columbia University Press).

Sandbothe, M. 2003, 'The Pragmatic Twist of the Linguistic Turn', in M. Sandbothe and W. Egginton, eds, *The Pragmatic Turn in Philosophy: Contemporary Engagements between Analytic and Continental Thought* (Albany, NY: State University of New York Press).

Sanders, J. W. forthcoming, 'On Information'.

Saracevic, T. 1970, 'The Concept of "Relevance" in Information Science: A Historical Review', in T. Saracevic, ed., *Introduction to Information Science* (New York: Bower Company), 111–151.

Saunders, S. 2003, 'Structural Realism, Again', *Synthese*, 136(1), 127–133.

Sayre, K. M. 1976, *Cybernetics and the Philosophy of Mind* (London: Routledge & Kegan Paul).

Schaffer, J. 2003, 'Is There a Fundamental Level?', *Nous*, 37(3), 498–517.

Schlesinger, G. N. 1985, *The Range of Epistemic Logic* (Aberdeen: Aberdeen University Press; Atlantic Highlands, NJ: Humanities Press).

Schlick, M. 1979, 'The Vienna School and Traditional Philosophy', in *Philosophical Papers* (Dordrecht: Reidel) (original text, 1937), 491–498.

Schmidhuber, J. 1997, 'A Computer Scientist's View of Life, the Universe, and Everything', *Lecture Notes in Computer Science*, 1337, 201–208.

Schmidhuber, J. forthcoming, 'All Computable Universes', *Spektrum der Wissenschaft* (German edition of *Scientific American*).

Schoderbek, C. G., Schoderbek, P. P., and Kefalas, A. G. 1990, *Management Systems: Conceptual Considerations*, 4th edn (Homewood, IL: BPI/Irwin).

Schreiber, D. S. G. 1987, 'The Illegitimacy of Gettier Examples', *Metaphilosophy*, 18, 49–54.

Schroder, J. 1992, 'Korner's Criterion of Relevance and Analytic Tableaux', *Journal of Philosophical Logic*, 21(2), 183–192.

Schultheis, R., and Sumner, M. 1998, *Management Information Systems*, 4th edn (London: McGraw-Hill).

Schutz, A. 1970, *Reflections on the Problem of Relevance*, edited, annotated, and with an introduction by R. M. Zaner (New Haven; London: Yale University Press).

Searle, J. R. 1980, 'Minds, Brains, and Programs', *Behavioral and Brain Sciences*, 3(3), 417–457.

Searle, J. R. 1990, 'Is the Brain a Digital Computer?', *Proceedings and Addresses of the American Philosophical Association*, 64, 21–37.

Searle, J. R. 1992, *The Rediscovery of the Mind* (Cambridge, Mass; London: MIT Press).

Sebastiani, P., Ramoni, M., and Cohen, P. R. 1999, 'Unsupervised Classification of Sensory Input in a Mobile Robot', *IJCAI-99 Workshop on Sequence Learning*, 23–28.

Seligman, J., and S., M. L. 1997, 'Situation Theory', in J. van Benthem and A. ter Meulen, eds, *Handbook of Logic and Language* (Amsterdam: Elsevier), ch. 4.

Sellars, W. 1956, 'Empiricism and the Philosophy of Mind', in H. Feigl and M. Scriven, eds, *Minnesota Studies in the Philosophy of Science* (Minneapolis: University of Minnesota Press), 253–329.

Sellars, W. 1963, 'Philosophy and the Scientific Image of Man', in *Science, Perception and Reality*, London: Routledge & Kegan Paul).

Sequoiah-Grayson, S. 2007, 'The Metaphilosophy of Information', *Minds and Machines*, 17(3), 331–344.

Shannon, C. E. 1993, *Collected Papers*, ed. by N. J. A. Sloane and A. D. Wyner (New York: IEEE Press).

Shannon, C. E., and Weaver, W. 1949 rep. 1998, *The Mathematical Theory of Communication* (Urbana: University of Illinois Press).

Shapiro, S. 2004, 'Foundations of Mathematics: Metaphysics, Epistemology, Structure', *The Philosophical Quarterly*, 54(214), 16–37.

Sharkey, N. E., and Jackson, S. A. 1994, 'Three Horns of the Representational Trilemma', in V. Honavar and L. Uhr, eds, *Symbol Processing and Connectionist Models for Artificial Intelligence and Cognitive Modeling: Steps towards Integration* (Academic Press), 155–189.

Shimojo, S., and Ichikawa, S. 1989, 'Intuitive Reasoning About Probability: Theoretical and Experimental Analyses of The "Problem of Three Prisoners"', *Cognition*, 32, 1–24.

Shope, R. K. 1983, *The Analysis of Knowing: A Decade of Research* (Princeton, NJ: Princeton University Press).

Siegelmann, H. T. 1998, *Neural Networks and Analog Computation: Beyond the Turing Limit* (Boston, Mass.: Birkhäuser).

Silver, G. A., and Silver, M. L. 1989, *Systems Analysis and Design* (Reading, Mass.: Addison-Wesley).

Simon, H. A. 1962, 'The Computer as a Laboratory for Epistemology', first draft, revised and published in Burkholder (1992), 3–23.

Simon, H. A. 1969, *The Sciences of the Artificial*, 1st edn (Cambridge, Mass.; London: MIT Press).

Simon, H. A. 1996, *The Sciences of the Artificial*, 3rd edn (Cambridge, Mass.: MIT Press).

Sloman, A. 1978, *The Computer Revolution in Philosophy: Philosophy, Science, and Models of Mind* (Hassocks, Eng.: Harvester Press).

Sloman, A. 1995, 'A Philosophical Encounter: An Interactive Presentation of Some of the Key Philosophical Problems in AI and AI Problems in Philosophy', *Proceedings of the 14th International Joint Conference on AI, Montreal, August 1995*. Available at <http://cogprints.org/719/>

Smith, B. 2003, 'Ontology', in Floridi (2003f), ch. 12.

Smokler, H. 1966, 'Informational Content: A Problem of Definition', *The Journal of Philosophy*, 63(8), 201–211.

Smolensky, P. 1988, 'On the Proper Treatment of Connectionism', *Behavioral and Brain Sciences*, 11(1), 1–23.

Sneed, D. J. 1967, 'Entropy, Information and Decision', *Synthese*, 17, 392–407.

Sommerville, I. 2007, *Software Engineering*, 8th edn (Harlow: Addison-Wesley).

Sperber, D., and Wilson, D. 1995, *Relevance: Communication and Cognition*, 2nd edn (Malden, Mass.; Oxford: Basil Blackwell).

Spice, B. 2000, 'CMU's Simon Reflects on How Computers will Continue to Shape the World', *Post Gazette* (Monday, 16 October). <http://www.post-gazette.com/regionstate/20001016simon2.asp>.

Spivey, J. M. 1992, *The Z Notation: A Reference Manual*, 2nd edn (New York; London: Prentice-Hall).

Steane, A. M. 1998, 'Quantum Computing', *Reports on Progress in Physics*, 61, 117–173.

Steels, L. 2005, 'The Emergence and Evolution of Linguistic Structure: From Lexical to Grammatical Communication Systems', *Connection Science*, 17, 213–230.

Steels, L., and Vogt, P. 1997, 'Grounding Adaptive Language Games in Robotic Agents', *Proceedings of Fourth European Conference on Artificial Life*, 474–482.

Steinhart, E. 1998, 'Digital Metaphysics', in Bynum and Moor (1998), 117–134.

Steinhart, E. 2003, 'The Physics of Information', in Floridi (2003f), ch. 13.

Stent, G. 1972, 'Prematurity and Uniqueness in Scientific Discovery', *Scientific American*, December, 84–93.

Stering, R. 2008, *Police Officer's Handbook: An Analytical and Administrative Guide* (Sudbury, Mass.: Jones and Bartlett Publishers).

Steup, M. 1996, *An Introduction to Contemporary Epistemology* (Upper Saddle River: Prentice Hall).

Steup, M. 2001, 'The Analysis of Knowledge', *Stanford Encyclopedia of Knowledge,* <http://plato.stanford.edu/entries/knowledge-analysis/>

Strawson, P. 1964, 'Identifying Reference and Truth-Value', *Theoria*, 30, 96–118. Reprinted in P. Strawson, (1971). *Logico-linguistic Papers* (London: Methuen), 75–95.

Suárez, M. 2003, 'Scientific Representation: Against Similarity and Isomorphism', *International Studies in the Philosophy of Science*, 17(3), 225–244.

Subramanian, D., Greiner, R., and Pearl, J. 1997, 'The Relevance of Relevance', *Artificial Intelligence*, 97(1–2), 1–5.

Sun, R. 1997, 'Learning, Action, and Consciousness: A Hybrid Approach Towards Modelling Consciousness', *Neural Networks, special issue on consciousness*, 10(7), 1317–1331.

Sun, R. 2001, 'Computation, Reduction, and Teleology of Consciousness', *Cognitive Systems Research*, 1(4), 241–249.

Sun, R. 2000, 'Symbol Grounding: A New Look at an Old Idea', *Philosophical Psychology*, 13, 149–172.

Sun, R., Merrill, E., and Peterson, T. 2001, 'From Implicit Skills to Explicit Knowledge: A Bottom-up Model of Skill Learning', *Cognitive Science*, 25(2), 203–244.

Sun, R., and Peterson, T. 1998, 'Some Experiments with a Hybrid Model for Learning Sequential Decision Making', *Information Science*, 111, 83–107.

Sun, R., and Zhang, X. 2002, 'Top-Down Versus Bottom-up Learning in Skill Acquisition', *Proceedings of the 24th Annual Conference of the Cognitive Science Society* 63–89.

Suppe, F. 1989, *The Semantic Conception of Theories and Scientific Realism* (Urbana: University of Illinois Press).

Suppes, P. 1960, 'A Comparison of the Meaning and Uses of Models in Mathematics and the Empirical Sciences', *Synthese*, 12, 287–301.

Suppes, P. 1962, 'Models of Data', in E. Nagel, P. Suppes, and A. Tarski, eds, *Logic, Methodology and Philosophy of Science: Proceedings of the 1960 International Congress* (Stanford: Stanford University Press), 252–261.

Symposium 1995, 'Symposium On "Conversations with Zombies"', *Journal of Consciousness Studies*, 2(4).

Szabolcsi, A. 1997, *Ways of Scope Taking* (Dordrecht; London: Kluwer Academic).

Szaniawski, K. 1967, 'The Value of Perfect Information', *Synthese*, 17, 408–424. Now in Szaniawski (1998).

Szaniawski, K. 1974, 'Two Concepts of Information', *Theory and Decision*, 5, 9–21. Now in Szaniawski (1998).

Szaniawski, K. 1984, 'On Defining Information'. Now in Szaniawski (1998).

Szaniawski, K. 1998, *On Science, Inference, Information and Decision-Making: Selected Essays in the Philosophy of Science* (Dordrecht; London: Kluwer Academic).

Taddeo, M., and Floridi, L. 2005, 'Solving the Symbol Grounding Problem: A Critical Review of Fifteen Years of Research', *Journal of Experimental & Theoretical Artificial Intelligence*, 17(4), 419–445.

Taddeo, M., and Floridi, L. 2007, 'A Praxical Solution of the Symbol Grounding Problem', *Minds and Machines*, 7(4), 369–389.

Tarski, A. 1944, 'The Semantic Conception of Truth and the Foundations of Semantics', *Philosophy and Phenomenological Research*, 4, 341–376. Reprinted in L. Linsky, ed., *Semantics and the Philosophy of Language* (Urbana: University of Illinois Press, 1952).

Tavani, H. T. 2002, 'The Uniqueness Debate in Computer Ethics: What Exactly Is at Issue, and Why Does It Matter?', *Ethics and Information Technology*, 4(1), 37–54.

Taylor, C. C. W. 1967, 'Plato and the Mathematicians: An Examination of Professor Hare's Views', *The Philosophical Quarterly*, 17(68), 193–203.

Taylor, C. C. W. 2008, 'Plato's Epistemology', in G. Fine, ed., *The Oxford Handbook of Plato* (New York; Oxford: Oxford University Press), 165–190.

Taylor, J. L., and Burgess, S. A. 2004, 'Steve Austin Versus the Symbol Grounding Problem', *Proceedings of Selected Papers from the Computers and Philosophy Conference (CAP2003)* (Canberra, Australia), 21–25.

Taylor, J. R. 1997, *An Introduction to Error Analysis: The Study of Uncertainties in Physical Measurements*, 2nd edn (Sausalito, Calif.: University Science Books).

Taylor, K. A. 1987, 'Belief, Information and Semantic Content: A Naturalist's Lament', *Synthese*, 71, 97–124.

Thompson, D. A. W. 1992, *On Growth and Form*, rev. edn (New York: Dover Publications).

Tishby, N., Pereira, F., and Bialek, W. 1999, 'The Information Bottleneck Method', in B. Hajek and R. S. Sreenivas, eds, *Proceedings of the 37th Annual Allerton Conference on Communication, Control and Computing* (Urbana, University of Illinois Press), 368–377.

Toffoli, T. 2003, 'A Digital Perspective and the Quest for Substrate-Universal Behaviors', *International Journal of Theoretical Physics*, 42, 147–151.

Torrance, S. B. 1984, *The Mind and the Machine: Philosophical Aspect of Artificial Intelligence* (Chichester: Ellis Horwood; New York: Wiley).

Turing, A. M. 1936, 'On Computable Numbers, with an Application to the Entscheidungsproblem', *Proceedings of the London Mathematics Society, 2nd series*, 42, 230–265. Correction published in vol. 43 (1936), pp. 544–546.

Turing, A. M. 1950, 'Computing Machinery and Intelligence', *Minds and Machines*, 59, 433–460.

van Benthem, J. 1991, 'Reflections on Epistemic Logic', *Logique et Analyse*, (133–134), 5–14.

van Benthem, J. 2003, 'Logic and the Dynamics of Information', *Minds and Machines*, 13(4), 503–519.

van Benthem, J., and van Rooy, R. 2003, 'Connecting the Different Faces of Information', *Journal of Logic, Language and Information*, 12(4), 375–379.

van der Hoek, W. 1991, 'Systems for Knowledge and Beliefs', in J. van Eijck, ed., *Logics in Ai* (Berlin: Springer), 267–281.

van der Lubbe, J. C. A. 1997, *Information Theory* (Cambridge: Cambridge University Press).

Van Fraassen, B. 1980, *The Scientific Image* (Oxford: Clarendon Press).

Van Fraassen, B. C. 2006a, 'Representation: The Problem for Structuralism', *Philosophy of Science*, 73, 536–547.

Van Fraassen, B. C. 2006b, 'Structure: Its Shadow and Substance', *British Journal for the Philosophy of Science*, 57(2), 275–307.

van Gelder, T. 1995, 'What Might Cognition Be, If Not Computation?', *Journal of Philosophy*, 92, 345–381.

Varela, F. J., Thompson, E., and Rosch, E. 1991, *The Embodied Mind: Cognitive Science and Human Experience* (Cambridge, Mass.: MIT Press).

Varshavskaya, P. 2002, 'Behavior-based Early Language Development on a Humanoid Robot', in C. G. Prince, Y. Demiris, Y. Marom, H. Kozima, and C. Balkenius, eds, *Second International Workshop on Epigenetic Robotics: Modelling Cognitive Development in Robotic Systems* (Edinburgh, Scotland), 149–158.

Vogt, P. 2002a, 'Anchoring Symbols to Sensorimotor Control', *Proceedings of Belgian/Netherlands Artificial Intelligence Conference BNAIC02.* Available at <http://cogprints.org/3060/>

Vogt, P. 2002b, 'The Physical Symbol Grounding Problem', *Cognitive Systems Research*, 3, 429–457.

Von Neumann, J. 1966, *Theory of Self-Reproducing Automata* (Urbana, Ill.; London: University of Illinois Press). Edited and completed by A. W. Burks.

Voorbraak, F. 1991, 'The Logic of Objective Knowledge and Rational Belief', in J. van Eijck, ed., *Logics in AI, European Workshop JELIA '90, Proceedings,* (Berlin: Springer), 499–515.

Voorbraak, F. 1992, 'Generalised Kripke Models for Epistemic Logic', in Y. O. Moses, ed., *Theoretical Aspects of Reasoning about Knowledge: Proceedings of the Fourth Conference,* (San Mateo, Calif.: Morgan Kaufmann), 214–228.

Votsis, I. 2003, 'Is Structure Not Enough?', *Philosophy of Science, Supplement,* 70(5), 879–890.

Votsis, I. forthcoming, 'Dispelling Certain Misconceptions About Structural Realism'.

Wallace, D. 2003, 'Everett and Structure', *Studies in History and Philosophy of Modern Physics*, 34, 87–105.

Walton, D. N. 1991, 'Critical Faults and Fallacies of Questioning', *Journal of Pragmatics*, 15, 337–366.

Walton, D. N. 2007, 'Dialogical Models of Explanation', in *Explanation-Aware Computing: Papers from the 2007 Aaai Workshop, Association for the Advancement of Artificial Intelligence,* (AAAI Press), 1–9.

Warner, T. 1996, *Communication Skills for Information Systems* (London: Pitman Publishing).

Weaver, W. 1949, 'The Mathematics of Communication', *Scientific American*, 181(1), 11–15.

Weinberg, S. 2002, 'Is the Universe a Computer?', *The New York Review of Books* (24 October).

Weingartner, P., and Schurz, G. 1986, 'Paradoxes Solved by Simple Relevance Criteria', *Logique et Analyse*, 29, 3–40.

Werning, M. 2004, 'Self-Awareness and Imagination', in J. Sáàgua, ed.,*A Explicação Da Interpretação Humana / the Explanation of Human Interpretation* (Lisbon: Colibri), 369–377.

Whaley, B. B., and Samter, W. (eds) 2006, *Explaining Communication: Contemporary Theories and Exemplars* (London: Routledge).

Wheeler, J. A. 1990, 'Information, Physics, Quantum: The Search for Links', in W. H. Zureck, ed., *Complexity, Entropy, and the Physics of Information*, edited by (Redwood City, Calif.: Addison-Wesley), 3–28.

Whittemore, B. J., and Yovits, M. C. 1973, 'A Generalized Conceptual Development for the Analysis and Flow of Information', *Journal of the American Society for Information Science*, 24(3), 221–231.

Wiener, N. 1948, *Cybernetics or Control and Communication in the Animal and the Machine*, 2nd edn (Cambridge, Mass.: MIT Press).

Wiener, N. 1950, *The Human Use of Human Beings: Cybernetics and Society* (London: Eyre and Spottiswoode).

Williamson, T. 1999, 'Rational Failures of the Kk Principle', in C. Bicchieri, R. Jeffrey, and B. Skyrms, eds, *The Logic of Strategy* (Oxford: Oxford University Press), 101–118.

Williamson, T. 2000, *Knowledge and Its Limits* (Oxford: Oxford University Press).

Wilson, D., and Sperber, D. 2004, 'Relevance Theory', in G. Ward and L. Horn, eds, *Handbook of Pragmatics* (Oxford: Blackwell), 607–632.

Wimsatt, W. C. 1976, 'Reductionism, Levels of Organization and the Mind–Body Problem', in G. Globus, G. Maxwell, and I. Savodnik (eds), *Consciousness and the Brain* (New York: Plenum), 199–267.

Winder, R., Probert, S. K., and Beeson, I. A. (eds) 1997, *Philosophical Aspects of Information Systems* (London; Bristol, Pa.: Taylor & Francis).

Wittgenstein, L. 1922, *Tractatus Logico-Philosophicus* (London: Kegan Paul, Trench, Trübner). Translation of: *Logisch-Philosophische Abhandlung*. Parallel German text and English translation, with an introduction by Bertrand Russell.

Wittgenstein, L. 1960, *Preliminary Studies for the Philosophical Investigations: Generally Known as the Blue and Brown Books*, 2nd edn (Oxford: Basil Blackwell).

Wittgenstein, L. 1961, *Tractatus Logico-Philosophicus* (London: Routledge & Kegan Paul).

Wittgenstein, L. 1980, *Remarks on the Philosophy of Psychology*, 2 vols. (Chicago; Oxford: University of Chicago Press; Basil Blackwell).

Wittgenstein, L. 1981, *Zettel*, 2nd edn (Oxford: Blackwell).

Wittgenstein, L. 2001, *Philosophical Investigations: The German Text with a Revised English Translation* 3rd edn (Oxford: Blackwell). Translated by G. E. M. Anscombe. Incorporates final revisions made by Elizabeth Anscombe to her English edition. Some typesetting errors have been corrected, and the text has been repaginated.

Wolfram, S. 2002, *A New Kind of Science* (Champaign, Ill.: Wolfram Media).

Wooldridge, M. J. 2002, *An Introduction to Multiagent Systems* (Chichester: J. Wiley).

Worrall, J. 1989, 'Structural Realism: The Best of Both Worlds?', *Dialectica*, 43, 99–124.

Worrall, J. 1994, 'How to Remain (Reasonably) Optimistic: Scientific Realism and The "Luminiferous Ether"', in D. L. Hull, M. Forbes, and R. M. Burian, eds, *PSA 1994* (East Lansing, Mich.: Philosophy of Science Association), 334–342.

Worrall, J., and Zahar, E. 2001, 'Appendix IV: Ramseyfication and Structural Realism', in *Poincaré's Philosophy: From Conventionalism to Phenomenology*, Chicago and La Salle (Ill.): Open Court).

Yeung, R. W. 2008, *Information Theory and Network Coding* (New York: Springer).

Young, J. O. 2002, 'The Slingshot Argument and the Correspondence Theory of Truth', *Acta Analytica*, 17(1), 121–132.

Yus, F. 2006, 'Relevance Theory Online Bibliographic Service'. <http://www.ua.es/personal/francisco.yus/rt.html>

Zagzebski, L. 1994, 'The Inescapability of Gettier Problems', *Philosophical Quarterly*, 44(174), 65–73.

Zeigler, B. P. 1976, *Theory of Modelling and Simulation* (New York: Wiley).

Ziemke, T. 1999, 'Rethinking Grounding', in A. Riegler, M. Peschl, and A. von Stein, eds, *Understanding Representation in the Cognitive Sciences* (New York: Plenum Press), 177–190.

Ziv, Y. 1988, 'On the Rationality of "Relevance" and the Relevance of "Rationality"', *Journal of Pragmatics*, 12, 535–545.

Zuse, K. 1967, 'Rechnender Raum', *Elektronische Datenverarbeitung*, 8, 336–344.

Zuse, K. 1969, *Rechnender Raum* (Braunschweig: Vieweg). Eng. trans. with the title *Calculating Space*, MIT Technical Translation AZT-70–164-GEMIT, Massachusetts Institute of Technology (Project MAC) (Cambridge, Mass., 1970.

Zuse, K. 1993, *The Computer, My Life* (Berlin; New York: Springer).

Index

PI is a monster of a book, that undertakes the formidable task (and impossible task) of generalizing ~~and~~ information in ~~prose~~ prose.

Floridi does a great disservice to our study of information. He assumes, as there is a new term in the vicinity of epistemology that it is his task to assimilate it to German philosophy.

Locke quote (p.2) The notion that information must be blocked or defended against understands data properly, as to what it is — the overspill of concepts, but mistaken in the notion that concepts must be conserved. That he conceives the discipline as that philosophy is to say he is interested in information as another form of symmetry, like matter and energy, it is the fence against the world that is knowledge or a representation of it. Floridi assimilates the hot term, ~~but~~ but the thinking and bibliography is almost entirely caught up in the artificial intelligence model of the 80's–90's (i.e, no attempt to replicate the Cartesian subject).

If nothing else, it is important for the renewal of analytic philosophy.